GLOBAL TELEVISION FORMATS

For decades, television scholars have viewed global television through the lens of cultural imperialism, focusing primarily on programs produced by US and UK markets and exported to foreign markets. *Global Television Formats* revolutionizes television studies by de-provincializing its approach to media globalization. It re-examines dominant approaches and their legacies of global/local and center/periphery, and offers new directions for understanding television's contemporary incarnations.

The chapters in this collection take up the format phenomena from around the globe, including the Middle East, Western and Eastern Europe, South and West Africa, South and East Asia, Australia and New Zealand, North America, South America, and the Caribbean. Contributors address both little known examples and massive global hits ranging from the *Idol* franchise around the world, to telenovelas, dance competitions, sports programming, reality TV, quiz shows, sitcoms and more. Looking to global television formats as vital for various cultural meanings, relationships, and structures, this collection shows how formats can further our understanding of television and the culture of globalization at large.

Contributors: Erica Jean Bochanty-Aguero, Jérôme Bourdon, Eddie Brennan, Joost de Bruin, Chiara Ferrari, Lauhona Ganguly, Dana Heller, Michael Keane, Marwan M. Kraidy, Vinicius Navarro, Martin Nkosi Ndlela, Tasha Oren, Yeidy M. Rivero, Tony Schirato, Biswarup Sen, Sharon Shahaf, Sharon Sharp, Joseph Straubhaar, Paul Torre.

Tasha Oren is an Associate Professor of English and Media Studies, and is the Coordinator of the Media, Cinema, and Digital Studies track at the University of Wisconsin-Milwaukee.

Sharon Shahaf is an Assistant Professor in the Department of Communication at Georgia State University.

GLOBAL TELEVISION FORMATS

Understanding Television Across Borders

Edited by
Tasha Oren and
Sharon Shahaf

Routledge
Taylor & Francis Group

NEW YORK AND LONDON

First published 2012
by Routledge
711 Third Avenue, New York, NY 10017

Simultaneously published in the UK
by Routledge
2 Park Square, Milton Park, Abingdon, Oxon OX14 4RN

Routledge is an imprint of the Taylor & Francis Group, an informa business

© 2012 Taylor & Francis

Library of Congress Cataloging in Publication Data
Global television formats: understanding television across borders/
Tasha Oren and Sharon Shahaf [editors].
    p. cm.
    Includes bibliographical references and index.
    1. Television program genres.   2. Television programs—Social aspects.
    3. Television and globalization.   I. Oren, Tasha G.   II. Shahaf, Sharon.
    PN1992.55G57 2011
    791.45'09—dc22   2011013325

ISBN: 978-0-415-96544-6 (hbk)
ISBN: 978-0-415-96545-3 (pbk)
ISBN: 978-0-203-92865-3 (ebk)

Typeset in Bembo and Stone Sans
by Florence Production Ltd, Stoodleigh, Devon

CONTENTS

ILLUSTRATIONS

Figures

Tables

CONTRIBUTORS

Erica Jean Bochanty-Aguero is a Lecturer in the Department of Film and Media Studies at the University of California–Irvine. She is currently working on a book project entitled *Music That Moves: Television Music, Industrial Travel, and Consumer Agency in Contemporary Media Culture*, which examines the relationship between television and popular music in relation to the concept of media travel. She teaches classes on television theory and criticism; popular music and media; and film and television genres. She received a master's in critical studies and a Ph.D. in cinema and media studies from the University of California–Los Angeles.

Jérôme Bourdon is Professor in the Department of Communications at Tel-Aviv University and Associate Researcher with the Center for the Sociology of Innovation (CSI-CNRS) in Paris. He also collaborates with the INA (National Audiovisual Institute) in Paris, where he teaches and produces documentaries. He works on the coverage of the Israeli–Palestinian conflict in the Western media, on a transnational history of television, and on the relations between collective memory and the media. Recent publications include: "Together, Nevertheless. Television memories in mainstream Jewish Israel" (with N. Kligler Vilenchik), *European Journal of Communication*, 26(1), 2011; "Inside Television Audience Measurement. Deconstructing the Ratings Machine" (with C. Méadel), *Media, Culture and Society* 33(5), 2011.

Eddie Brennan is a media sociologist, lecturing in the School of Media, Dublin Institute of Technology. Past publications have explored institutional change in Irish broadcasting, the political role of entertainment programming and changing labor conditions in media production. Recent publications explored occupational humor as both a focus of, and a tool for media production research. Current research examines the role of media in shaping collective memory and shared visions of the anticipated future.

Joost de Bruin is a lecturer in Media Studies at Victoria University of Wellington in Aotearoa/New Zealand. He teaches in the areas of popular culture, audience studies and television studies. His research interests include global television formats, media audiences, and young people and media.

Chiara Ferrari is an Assistant Professor in the Communication Design Department at California State University, Chico. She received her Ph.D. in 2007 in cinema and media studies from UCLA–School of Theater, Film, and Television. She is the co-editor of the anthology *Beyond Monopoly: Globalization and Contemporary Italian Media* published in 2010, and her single-authored volume *Since When is Fran Drescher Jewish? Dubbing Stereotypes in* The Nanny, The Simpsons, *and* The Sopranos was published in January 2011 by the University of Texas Press. Her current research interests concern global media studies and contemporary Italian cinema, with a focus on representations of 1970s terrorism in Italian films.

Lauhona Ganguly is a Ph.D. Candidate at the School of International Service, American University, Washington DC. Her research focuses on the production of aspirations through reality TV formats and social-cultural change in India. Preliminary findings have been published in *International Cultural Policies and Power* (Palgrave Macmillan, 2010). She also teaches at the Media Studies Department at The New School, New York.

Dana Heller is Professor and Chair of English at Old Dominion University in Norfolk, Virginia. She is the author/editor of six books, including a forthcoming monograph on John Waters' film, *Hairspray*.

Michael Keane is ARC Centre Fellow at the Queensland University of Technology in Brisbane Australia. He is the author, most recently, of *Created in China: the Great New Leap Forward* (Routledge, 2007) and co-author (with Anthony Fung and Albert Moran) of *New Television, Globalization and the East Asian Cultural Imagination* (Hong Kong University Press, 2007).

Marwan M. Kraidy is Associate Professor of Global Communication at the Annenberg School for Communication at the University of Pennsylvania. His publications include *Reality Television and Arab Politics: Contention in Public Life* (Cambridge University Press, 2009), which won the 2010 Best Book Award in Global Communication and Social Change from the International Communication Association; *Arab Television Industries* (BFI/Palgrave, 2009, with J. Khalil), *Hybridity, or, The Cultural Logic of Globalization* (Temple, 2005), and the co-edited volumes *Global Media Studies: Ethnographic Perspectives* (Routledge, 2003), and *The Politics of Reality Television: Global Perspectives* (Routledge, 2010). His current book projects focus on (1) the politics and economics of Arab music videos, and on (2) identifying international theoretical foundations for global media studies, the latter with Toby Miller.

Vinicius Navarro is Assistant Professor of Film Studies at the Georgia Institute of Technology. He is the co-author (with Louise Spence) of *Crafting Truth: Documentary Form and Meaning* (Rutgers University Press, 2011).

Martin Nkosi Ndlela is Associate Professor in Media Studies and Head of the Institute for Organization and Management at Hedmark University College, Norway. Ndlela has published articles and chapters on general media studies and knowledge management. He sits in the editorial board of the *Journal of African Media Studies* and is a board member of the Norwegian Media Researchers' Association. His current research interests include media and democracy in Africa, journalism, public service broadcasting, ICT and knowledge communication.

Tasha Oren is Associate Professor of English and Media Studies and heads the Media, Cinema and Digital Studies Program at the University of Wisconsin–Milwaukee. She is the author of *Demon in the Box: Jews, Arabs, Politics and Culture in the Making of Israeli Television* (Rutgers University Press, 2004) and co-editor of *East Main Street: Asian American Popular Culture* (New York University Press, 2005) and *Global Currents: Media and Technology Now* (Rutgers University Press, 2004).

Yeidy M. Rivero is an Associate Professor in the Department of Screen Arts and Culture and the Program in American Culture at the University of Michigan–Ann Arbor. Her areas of interest are television studies, race and ethnic representation in media, and Spanish Caribbean, Latino, and African diaspora studies. Her work has been published in journals such as *Media, Culture and Society*, *Feminist Media Studies*, *Television and New Media*, *Global Media and Communication*, and *Critical Studies in Media Communication*. She is the author of *Tuning Out Blackness: Race and Nation in the History of Puerto Rican Television* (Duke University Press, 2005). Her current project focuses on Cuban commercial television, 1950–1960.

Tony Schirato is Reader in Media Studies at Victoria University of Wellington. He has recently published books on the field of sport, and on the gender theorist Judith Butler. He is currently co-authoring a book on Michel Foucault.

Biswarup Sen is Assistant Professor, School of Journalism and Communication, at the University of Oregon. His research interests include television and popular culture, new media theory, and global media studies. He is the author of *Of the People: Essays in Indian Popular Culture* (DC Publishers, 2006) and is co-editor of *50 Years of Indian Television* (Oxford University Press, forthcoming, 2011). He is currently planning a project that will look at the impact of digital technology in South Asia.

Sharon Shahaf is an Assistant Professor in Communication at Georgia State University. Her research interests include media globalization, Israeli television, and post-Zionist critique. She has published articles and monographs in *Westminster Papers in Communication and Culture*, and *Flow*. Her current book project deals with Israeli television, globalization, and Israeli national identity.

Sharon Sharp is an assistant professor at California State University–Dominguez Hills. Her research is concerned with television, genre and gender. Her essays on television have appeared in *Science Fiction Film and Television*, *Women's Studies: An Interdisciplinary Journal*, and in the anthology *Reading Desperate Housewives*.

Joe Straubhaar is the Amon G. Carter Sr., Centennial Professor of Communication in the Radio–Television–Film Department of the University of Texas at Austin. His current research concerns the globalization and transnationalization of both television and new media. He is currently working on the history of commercial television in Latin America, particularly Brazil; on media and migration issues in the U.S.A. and Portugal; on the development of the Lusophone transnational cultural linguistic media space; and on ICTs and development in Brazil and South Texas. He has an extensive history of work on globalization of television, per se, as well as the development of transnational cultural-linguistic and geo-cultural television spaces. He has worked primarily on Latin America, including being director of Brazilian Studies at UT, but also works on Asia, Europe and Africa. He is the author of *World Television: From Global to Local* (Sage, 2007).

Paul Torre is Assistant Professor in Media Industries in the College of Mass Communication and Media Arts at Southern Illinois University–Carbondale. His entertainment industry experience includes executive positions in film and television development, production, distribution and marketing; he served as VP of Programming and Production for the German media giant Kirch Media in Hollywood, overseeing co-productions and arranging global media distribution with the major studios. He has articles and chapters in the *Journal of Television and New Media* (2009), in *The Handbook of Political Economy of Communications* (Wiley-Blackwell, 20011, with E. R. Meehan), and in *Down To Earth: Satellite Industries, Technologies and Cultures* (Rutgers University Press, 2011). Current projects include work on film financing and distribution and the multi-platform gaming industry.

ACKNOWLEDGEMENTS

We would like to acknowledge and extend our heartfelt thanks to the many individuals whose help, support and generosity made this volume possible.

First, we thank our terrific contributors for their work, grace and patience. At UW– Milwaukee, we thank Patrice Petro, Anna Lemberger and Richard Meadows for their help and generous support. At UT–Austin, we thank Shanti Kumar, and Joseph Straubhaar. We thank the Communication Department at Georgia State University–Atlanta for providing a warm and stimulating environment, and Collin Coleman, Brandon Amato, and Maria Boyd for their valuable assistance at that crucial last stage.

We are also grateful to Tim Havens and Michael Kackman for co-organizing and co-chairing the two-part panel "Global TV Formats—An International Agenda for TV Studies" at the Society for Cinema and Media Studies annual meeting in Chicago, where early versions of the work in this volume were first presented. Our gratitude also goes to Matt Byrnie for his encouragement and guidance from the very start. We thank our wonderful team at Routledge and finally–and always—our own home team, our families, and especially Gil Shahaf and Stewart Ikeda.

INTRODUCTION

Television Formats—A Global Framework for TV Studies

Tasha Oren and Sharon Shahaf

With the medium now three quarters of a century old, television studies remains tethered to its historical U.S./U.K. legacy. Despite television's global reach, the radical transformations of its associated technologies and industries, and the variety in programming and audiences, mainstream television studies holds fast to its origins—both of medium and discipline. Just as the technology and broadcasting structure of television are widely regarded as having originated in Britain and the U.S., so the discipline of television studies—emerging from the meeting place of communications, film studies, literary studies, and cultural studies—maintains a U.S./U.K.-based foundation. Even today, studies of particular national television systems are examined in terms of the persistent "general" that is American and British television.

Yet, like the medium itself, its accompanying scholarly disciplines, methods and critical writings are also undergoing a process of globalization, as models of cultural imperialism, media flows, and even globalization itself are challenged by new theories and current media realities. Nevertheless, few television scholars have publicly contemplated what television studies would look like if it were to alter perspectives and address itself as a global discipline first. Such a shift is particularly challenging in light of the field's vital commitment to historicize, specify, and account for multiple local conditions.

In recent years, key television studies publications and conferences saw an increase in writing, special panels, and debates devoted to globalizing and "de-westernizing" perspectives within the mainstream of the field. Also, a maturing interchange among international scholars expanded the scope of television studies, primarily through historical accounts of various national systems. Such studies are important in broadening the field and contribute to a destabilization of core theoretical and methodological perspectives within it. Nevertheless, discrete national histories do little to fully explore the multiple contact zones of television as a global textual system. The question remains, how can television studies accommodate its demands for specificity and its investment in diversity while navigating a global shift towards television as a transnational and peripatetic medium?

Moreover, "globalization" itself poses considerable conceptual challenges for media scholars. With binary structures of core/periphery, global/local and capital/tradition still in most common circulation, emerging textual and industrial trends, as well as recent political and economic shocks, demonstrate that a more nuanced and contextualized framework is necessary for understanding the complexities of our current transnational media environment. New scholarly engagement with such shifts further illustrates the essential role that media studies can play in illuminating and theorizing the work of culture and the feel of the global.

No televisual shift has so shaken traditional scholarly models as the explosion in the first decade of the second millennium of global television format circulation. Mega-popular talent and skill competitions crown new stars in extravagant live broadcasts, drawing mass national (and sometimes regional) audiences, and triggering heated debates of cultural and identity politics; ultra-sophisticated game shows utilize (purchase, borrow, or steal) innovative "engines" (Keane and Moran 2008), offering million dollar prizes to aspiring contestants around the world; while dramatic concepts formulated both in the traditional "centers" of media production and once-"remote" cultural and geographical locales, enjoy truly global circulation through multiple international adaptations.

As a critical term within media studies, formats—when attended to at all— have been largely studied in terms of their economic and industrial use value. Albert Moran, the first scholar to consider, study and define formats as a global programming unity, defined a television format as "a set of invariable elements in a serial program out of which the variable elements of individual episodes are produced" (Moran and Malbon 2006: 20).

Accordingly, the format is generally conceived in opposition to the transnational model of program import/export trade; unlike a finished or "canned" television program, format is an easily-replicated and adaptable framework licensed through the international television market for local adaptation. In its most basic, legally sanctioned, form, it is a program concept: a list of "rules" or conventions that make up the fixed and distinct aspects of each program.

The commodity known as the format package includes not only a licensing agreement but also a wealth of documentation (known in the trade as the "Bible") of its previous local iterations, production notes and history—often including graphic design elements, character notations, musical theme and cues, staging information and other production detail—and information about ratings and target audiences. Certain packages also include audio-visual materials and on-site consultation services.

As an economic unit, then, the format can be thought of as recipe, a kit, or blueprint, yet, as Albert Moran further insists, format is not a tangible product. Rather, it is a technology of economic and cultural exchange and a service that facilitates certain televisual possibilities (Moran and Malbon 2006). This perspective, predictably, promotes an understanding of formats as a globally distributed container for locally produced content.

Television systems have always engaged in textual exchanges in the forms of influences, counter-programming, explicit business arrangements and informal circulation. Indeed, popular programming formulae were routinely adapted, franchised, bought, mimicked, and stolen for production in multiple localities worldwide. Yet the trade and circulation of formats has seen unprecedented growth in the past two decades, rising to dominance as a new industrial globalization mode. The rise to dominance of this new globalized mode of production is revolutionizing television industrial, creative and marketing strategies around the world, as players in previously hopelessly marginalized markets now successfully compete in this ever expanding market. The ability to come up with innovative broadcasting ideas on a shoestring budget—a skill every marginalized, under-financed and scrappy television industry refined for sheer survival—is now the winning asset in the new format-dominated global television industry. Players like Israel, Colombia, and the Netherlands, to name a few prominent examples, are reaping the benefits as audiences across Asia, Africa, Eastern and Western Europe, the U.S.A., and more enjoy local renditions of shows like *Ugly Betty*, *Big Brother* and *In Treatment*.

As we approach the second decade of the new millennium, formatted shows form the backbone of a multitude of broadcasting schedules across the globe. Challenging established top–bottom scenarios of media globalization as American cultural or media "imperialism," and supplementing more nuanced approaches mapping regional, transnational, and global flows of canned television products around the world (Thussu, 2007), the model offered by the global flow of television formats and their local production highlights an alternative, extremely complex and multidirectional model for television globalization. Global television formats (GTFs), more than any other model of media globalization, contain the core paradox of globalization's relation to intense "localization" and the tension between homogenization and difference involved in economic and cultural globalization processes—first identified in key writings by Roland Robertson and Stuart Hall among others (Robertson 1995, Hall 1997).

These developments in television production and programming structure complicate many long-cherished conventions of global television scholarship. Approaches that perceive contemporary media as a map of U.S. programming domination or maintain a fixed distinction between local production and import-led homogenization are radically reconfigured when faced with a maturing global industry that prioritizes both localization and standardization. Similarly, global audiences' responses to these televisual texts present new sites of investigation, offering formatted programs as cultural arenas where tensions among local, regional, national and global identities are articulated and experienced in new, inter-mediated ways. Finally, the textual and generic definitions of program types and conventions of narrative structures are here confronted with new models of content developments that are yet to be theorized.

When viewed in conjunction with technological developments, industrial strategies and textual migrations beyond the boundaries of nation, schedule, playback media, and viewing conventions, the current television environment presents substantial and creative challenges to traditional media studies. Global television formats, embedded as they are in local and global industrial, economical, textual, cultural and regulatory practices and constraints emerge as an extremely compelling focal point for the highly contextualized study of television as a global system.

Scholarly responses thus far have been primarily interested in the textual and industrial ramifications of so-called "new" media and the social logic of the equally misnamed "reality television." Fewer grappled with the globally shifting structure of television production and consumption that underlies both developments—a major focus for many of the authors in this volume. Through geographically and methodologically diverse approaches, the chapters in this collection explore the global format phenomenon and the new theoretical and analytical frameworks it makes possible. Beyond their identity as common units of economic exchange, formats here are explored as textual systems, practices of cultural exchange (formal, illicit and contentious), affective loci for audience reception activities, and both symbols and participants in the larger processes of economic and cultural globalization.

Fast, Cheap and Out of Control: The Common Biography of Global Formats

Among academics, publics and television professionals, explanatory scenarios have quickly crystallized around the emerging global "format frenzy" of the last two decades. Unified understandings of the kind of televisual texts, formulae and practices that are included, the immediate context for the emergence of global formats, and the significance of their current dominance for television globalization, are now commonplace. In these, global television formats are often described as a new phenomenon, an innovative form of televisual formal exchange which represents a break from established or traditional processes of television globalization. This notion is supported by the tendency to over-emphasize practices of official formatting and trade and to focus most attention on industrial—and attending, legal—arrangements and practices that have emerged in franchising.

This approach is common despite general acknowledgment of a broad range of both formal and unofficial exchanges, in the form of "cloning," borrowing, or influence that have all but shaped television development in virtually every case. And thus another intriguing paradox is formed in the contemporary attention to global format flows.

These collective privilegings of certain explanations and emphases in leading scenarios are themselves instructive and worthy of a brief overview here. Current attentions to global formats tend to downplay the staggering range of official and unofficial cultural and industrial practices involved in current (and historical) formal exchange. Rather than regard format as television building blocks, common scenarios focus on the relation between the sudden explosion of global formats over the last two decades and more recent trends of media globalization, namely the "communication revolution" of the 1990s.

This label is commonly used in international communication literature to describe the industrial, economic, cultural, and ideological transformations that swept the globe since the mid-1980s, in tandem with innovations in media transmission and reception technologies such as satellite, cable, and digital media. These developments facilitated the near universal application of "open skies" and "multichannelism" policies around the world, swift restructuring of broadcast systems, policy revisions, and a predominant global dissemination of a commercialized mode of broadcasting—along with a growing alarm over U.S. cultural domination and profit-driven, under-regulated media (most recently Jin 2007, Thussu 2007, Straubhaar 2007). While concerned mostly with imported products, anxiety over cultural imperialism soon included formatting practices, also associated with a relentless "Americanization" and commercialization that saw soaring demand for appealing content and plunging quality. As broadcasters turned to mass imports of cheap American "junk-TV" (Weinman 1999) they soon faced new national regulatory measures for local production quotas, designed to protect native media industries and local cultural expression. Forced to find novel ways to remain competitive while generating maximum content hours at low cost for popular appeal, programmers turned to the practiced lure of format television. As many analysts observed, producing local renditions of proven, "pre-packaged" format shows offered a convenient and lucrative loophole through the dual constraints of small production budgets and local production quotas. Formats offered tested, ratings-proven global hit formulae with locally produced credentials (Waisbord 2004, Keane and Moran 2008). Conversely, within the U.S.A., format's presence in the TV schedule went mostly unacknowledged until the massive (and unanticipated) popularity of several European-devised hits (led by *Who Wants to Be a Millionaire?* in 1999, *Survivor* and *Big Brother* in 2000 and *American Idol* in 2002), and the ensuing focus on format—and specifically unscripted—programming as counter-strategy during the Writer's Guild strike of 2007–8.

This historical focus and inflection, along with the common conflation of "format" with "reality TV"—a reduction that more often than not designates both as quintessentially low-brow—encourages an instrumental approach to formats as globalization's cynical product par excellence, as these mechanical, "cut-n-paste" global hit recipes were positioned as counters to both quality television and authentic local cultural expression.

While the historical sketch above accounts for format's lowly status—a dismissal that, for us, seemed misaligned with its impact on television development in so many markets—recent, more finely calibrated approaches to global format remain preoccupied with its West/rest axis. Format scholars Keane and Moran critiqued the global format marketplace as an arena for the centralization of global media creativity in the hands of few producers in mostly Western media hubs (Moran 1998, Keane et al. 2007), and, by contrast, Silvio Waisboard celebrated the practice as representing the resilience of the particular, the national, and the local (Waisboard 2004). As these scholars emphasized, format adaptations' distinction from the import or "finalized" media products is sourced in their preservation of local language and culture, allowing "native" producers to adjust the imported formulas to better fit their audience's cultural tastes, sensibilities, and expectations. While Moran and Keane remain the only authors of book-length projects dedicated to the analysis of format TV, scholarly attention to reality TV, while limited largely to the social and cultural implications of unscripted television, has also helped broaden the field of study and opened up interest in the format as a globally significant cultural product (Murray and Ouelette 2004, Mathijs and Jones 2005, Holmes and Jermyn 2004).

For the contributors to this volume, these commonplace scenarios, contradictory approaches, enticing paradoxes, and recent inroads are points of departure as the various chapters assembled here seek to complicate, broaden, revisit or revise understanding of format in global television studies. Looking to GTFs as vital for various cultural meanings, relationships, and structures, these chapters collectively suggest ways in which formats can further our understanding of television—as a shared and specific textual, political and popular mechanism—and the culture of globalization at large.

The chapters are assembled into four loose and interconnected categories of emphasis: theory, history, case studies and national politics. Readers may, of course, find alternative routes through the collection according to geographical areas (the Middle East, Western and Eastern Europe, South and West Africa, South and East Asia, Australia and New Zealand, North America, South America, and the Caribbean), disciplinary alignment, methodological preferences or other affinities. Several arcs cut through the various chapters in the form of leading section questions: how historical case studies inform contemporary media; how questions of national, sub-national and transnational unities compete and interact with collective cultures in the age of globalization; how textual and thematic conventions of format (both official and implicit) shape, enable and delimit meaning-making; and how conceptions of collective identity (of race, gender, sexuality, nationality, ethnicity, class, religion and politics of location) operate within global cultural economies and the changing media environment.

Part I: Theorizing Format

In the project of legitimizing the study of formats as televisual building blocks that produce meaning and cultural experience, the authors in this first section propose theoretical paradigms and analytical tools that open the format up to new as well as revised approaches. To explore the significance of formats as cultural artifacts, Vinicius Navarro turns to performance theory to help sharpen the distinction between adaptability and adaptation and to shift attention from an industry-centered promise of infinite reproduction to the culture-centered process through which the format actually circulates and establishes local identity. "More than Copycat Television: Format Adaptation as Performance" opens the volume by reassessing received approaches to format and contending that commonplace discussions of it as "translation," "negotiation," and "exchange" favor a conservative variations-on-a-theme view, which preserves the autonomy of the "original formula." Bringing the concept of performance into play, in turn, highlights related notions of action, interaction, and transaction, transferring the weight of signification from a stable "template" and its derivative renditions to particular actualizations and individual occurrences whose cultural significance cannot be confined to the merely derivative. As Navarro argues through his examination of Brazilian adaptations of dance competition formats, the notion of format production as performance allows us to grasp the "in-betweenness" characterizing local production. Through Navaro's analysis, the very process emerges as active formatting, articulating different elements together within the matrix of available cultural, national and industrial context. Adaptations thus interpret, actualize, and redefine format, rather than insert "variable elements" into an "invariable" formula.

An innovative theoretical approach to the cultural exchanges that take place when dance formats travel across borders is also the focus of the following chapter by Dana Heller. "'Calling Out Around the World': The Global Appeal of Reality Dance Formats" argues for critical dance studies' value to global television studies and demonstrates how, in the growing popularity and visibility of format dance shows and accompanying fan sites, human movement serves as "a critical marker" for the production of social and national identities. With an emphasis on the format's built-in contradictory engagement with national and cultural identity, Heller provides a nuanced counter to the claim that format television merely homogenizes, Americanizes or globalizes cosmopolitan post-national style. The popular dance format *So You Think You Can Dance* is built on the search for a popular dancer who most approximates the "national ideal" through a performance and mastery of an international array of forms and styles—often of codified and migratory styles originating primarily in African and Latin traditions—along with a local dance style as a compulsory and sentimental "heritage flavoring." Through this process, Heller argues, dance becomes an ideological allegory of difference and cultural meaning, a "discourse of the body" that paradoxically proves not the fluidity and easy transferability of movements and styles that form the show's premise, but its opposite: the ease with which ethnic, cultural and national differences (along with other markers of difference such as race, gender, class and sexuality) are essentialized at the site of the body. As Heller argues in her extended analysis of the Turkish adaptation of *So You Think You Can Dance* (*Benimle Dans Eder Misin*) and the Israeli *Nolad Lirkod*, no other format type so succinctly translates and enacts the pressures and conflicts of affiliation, identity, and difference that simmer beneath the promise of global merging, cross-fertilization, and mastery.

The intersection of format and another discourse of the body, sports, is the subject of Tony Schirato's chapter, which reconsiders the evolution of sports programming in terms of format logic. As Schirato points out, format-based structures operate across television programs that have not readily been seen as part of format television. In "Television Formats and Contemporary Sport" Schiarto reclassifies television-mediated sports as a form of format and ponders the relationship among sports, technology, and programming conventions to reveal the extent to which format imperatives have shaped the development of television sports. Treating sports television as a generic structure, the chapter argues that, like other formats, the evolving conventions of sports television (structural, technological and narratological) all work to not only "contain" the sport event but to actually shape and produce meaning within it. In this sense—and by extension—format and its historical development is here suggested as inseparable from content. Employing Pierre Bourdieu's critique of television sport as a mass spectacle, Schirato demonstrates the evolving conventions of sports television coverage, studio sports news, and even advertisements for upcoming sporting events as generic entities and as format, distinct from a simple documentation/representation of a played game, and using television technology to make the sport "more than itself." Further, with his extended example of cricket, Schirato shows the two-way interaction between the sport and television: how the game itself has changed to suit the television format (and business structure) while TV conventions evolved to capture and enhance the global pleasures of the game.

Bourdieu's classification of the cultural field also informs the chapter "A Political Economy of Formatted Pleasures," in which Eddie Brennan examines the kinds of "fun" that formats, as a particular television type, offer their viewers. Employing the framework of political economy, Brennan finds that most successful television formats are essentially similar, and offer a very limited palette of audience pleasures. Based on the pursuit of individual and materialistic goals, most television formats, he argues, are consistent with a dominant orthodoxy that regards markets as both natural and essential social structures. For Brennan, whose chapter provides a provocative counter-argument to the cultural analyses advanced by many others in the collection, format is intimately linked with wider transformations in the global media sphere as its content is determined by its profit model of low-cost, low-risk, and maximum international coherence. This, in turn, leads to programming that is seemingly isolated from local social and political concerns and aligned with the widest values and norms possible. Brennan proceeds to map a new global "media ecology" across genres such as news, documentary, current affairs, and drama that heavily favor the format structure, as entertainment, cultural technology and industry practices that are "pre-adapted" to a commercialized global media. It is these practical constraints, rather than producers' attempts to indoctrinate, which orient format pleasures towards the rules of the market, conservative values of social surveillance and conformity, and the extrinsic pleasures and rewards of the consuming individual. For Brennan, the seduction of this commercialized global media field lies in the fact that, while it enriches corporate elites, it creates popular appeal by attacking cultural hierarchies and, ostensibly, offering greater personal choice. It is through the personal acceptance of individual and utilitarian ideas that "the way of the market becomes the way of the world."

Yeidy M. Rivero's chapter, "Interpreting Cubanness, Americanness and the Sitcom: PBT-PBS' *¿Que pasa USA?* 1975–1980" bridges the theoretical and historical sections of the collection with a format-focused re-assessment of *¿Que pasa USA?*, the first bilingual situation comedy on U.S. television. Through investigating multiple readings of the show (American or Cuban, sitcom entertainment or education) Rivero also asks whether it is possible to categorize television genres as formats—when genre is defined in terms of its market considerations, programming history, and interpretive approach. Linking the program's representational strategies of the Cuban American immigrant experience with foundational conventions of the sitcom on one hand, and the process of cultural and geographical "translation" and cross-border televisual borrowing on the other, Rivero argues that such a process, in its historical specificity, is a format-transaction. The back-and-forth transfers of institutional production standards, narrative and style conventions, and professional expertise between the U.S.A. and Cuba is here recounted as a format transfer that regionalized and localized the sitcom genre. Rivera's analysis both enriches and challenges the working definition of format as it argues for the inclusion of transfers of industry, themes, and generic cultural adaptations. Format not as package but process, not only a business arrangement but a set of textual exchanges and conventions inform Rivero's reading of the show as an encounter of pre-revolutionary Cuban television with U.S. television—a stylistic reunion that also worked symbolically to emphasize the show's intended hailing of its Cuban American audience. Rivera argues that beyond theorizing what makes a format, a focus on the cultural, political and social meanings inscribed in original and adapted formats, as well as how these are read and made meaningful by their various audiences, enriches our understanding of how television functions to affirm, support or complicate cultural identity.

Part II: The Format in Historical Perspective

The act of borrowing and localizing content across media systems is a very old practice, predating not only the term's entrance into current circulation but even television itself (the practice was common in both newspapers and radio). As several studies in this section demonstrate, the basic practices of importing and circulating scripts, concepts and professionals across national TV systems predates not only current format practice but also the now-classic (and U.S. dominated) trade in "canned" program imports that proliferated in the last few decades of the twentieth century—a practice that served as a touchstone for numerous critiques about U.S. cultural imperialism that typified the era. As this group of chapters illustrates, a historical perspective on format's use internationally makes clear the extent of format's central role in shaping television history and its current textual and industrial conventions. What also emerges when we examine format in an historical perspective is the degree to which its own history is embroiled in the changing terms of national broadcasting. Format's pivotal role in that history spurred multi-layered negotiations among local/regional, national, and international interests over media policy, identity and cultural value.

In "From Discrete Adaptations to Hard Copies: The Rise of Formats in European Television," Jérôme Bourdon traces the emergence of format programming in European television, focusing on the game or quiz show, the earliest (and most maligned) format type that best embodied the strict rules and timing structures typifying its adaptability potential. Bourdon divides his account of the history of format development in Europe into three distinct eras: that of discrete, infrequent and often informal adaptation (lasting until the early 1980s), the "open replication" era that saw increased competition and new pressures forcing broadcasting systems to freely "adapt" successful American game show formulae, and the final phase, which he terms the Euro-American convergence that saw not only the normalization of the format trade but the emergence of once-public European entities as active originators and participants in the contemporary format marketplace.

As Bourdon argues, these stages in format history were not only fundamentally shaped by the changing terms of the public service model that once dominated European television but also in the changing terms of the relationship and regard for U.S. commercial programming. Format history can thus serve as a way to fully understand the degree to which these changes shaped European television industries, the evolving notions of national identity expressed through public service broadcasting, and the shifting terms of U.S./European cultural exchange. In tracing the use of the term itself, Bourdon further shows to what degree professional terminology parallels global moves towards privatization, moving from the term signifying a mere idea or content to its evolving specificity of rules, property and transferable economic value. In the latter part of his chapter, Bourdon turns to the term's scholarly use (and its relation to genre), illustrating how academic conventions about genre, format and category—and their analytical implications—could also benefit from a closer accounting of format's role in television's national history.

Euro-American cultural relations, as seen through discourses surrounding television, play out intriguingly in the Italian example, as Chiara Ferrari shows in "'National Mike': Global Host and Global Formats in Early Italian Television." This chapter explores RAI's "original adaptation" of the American game show *The $64,000 Question* in the mid-1950s as an example of early transnational content reformatting. Looking closely at the Italian show *Lascia o Raddoppia?* and at its famous Italian American host, Mike Bongiorno—"National Mike," Italy's first celebrity television personality—Ferrari counters the common "purist" thesis that sees early Italian television as exclusively and emphatically "national" in content and aesthetics. As Ferrari demonstrates, the discourse that surrounded the show's success and commentaries about it acknowledged the American origin of the format as they highlighted its distinct Italianness. Further, *Lascia o Raddoppia?* positioned its content as a perfect synthesis of global, national, and local scenarios—in a time when Italy's collective identity sought the same precarious balance.

Widely celebrated for its construction of a unified Italian national identity through its capacity to include genuine manifestations of local, regional identities (by casting idiosyncratic colorful "characters" as contestants) the program's remarkable success was simultaneously attributed to its perceived Americanness. The format's U.S. lineage was personified by its Italian American host, Mike Bongiorno, who adroitly channeled a new unified and globally aspiring Italian national identity to a largely regionally-identified audience. It is precisely in the process of format adaptation in this period of the post war "Italian miracle years" that the most salient and genuine national characteristics emerge and mark *Lascia o Raddoppia?* as a pivotal text in early Italian television. Like National Mike himself, it found its identity in a process of transformation, migration and appropriation.

Like the history of U.S.-fabricated formats in European television, the origins of the South American telenovela are steeped in shifting regional and international relations and local approaches to representations of a shared national and cultural identity within circumscribed conventions. But, as Joseph Straubhaar demonstrates in "Telenovelas in Brazil: From Traveling Scripts to a Genre and Proto-Format both National and Transnational," careful attending to the permutations of genre and format in the Latin American context—where format adaptation and localization are rich practices that pre-date television—can yield important and surprising lessons about the current and future shape of international format. The article traces the telenovela genre as it emerged from its early U.S.-based soap opera to its hybridized encounter with serial fiction in Latin America, and the complex formation of a routinized trade—a flow and standardization of scripts, licenses, packages and telenovela texts, as well as the interaction between producers, sponsors and audiences. As Straubhaar suggests, this process of hybridization and continuous exchange and specialization led to the development of a local and particular generic formation that itself became fodder for exchange and specialization, resulting in localized production of regional formats—as opposed to the continued practice of purchasing "canned" telenovelas from other producers in the region. This history helps contextualize and explain recent phenomena like *Betty La Fea* and its movement as both a "canned" product and a format property (notably across genres: as telenovela in some markets and as serial comedy, sitcom and soap in others) both within and outside Latin America. This study revises our narrative of global television exchange that holds the dominance of U.S. television and the "canned" import/export market as the norm and recent practices of format and local adaptation as a fresh departure. Instead, we may consider the canned import era a specific phase, and current format development as an ongoing practice of adaptation that is both necessary and inevitable.

The historical overview section ends by bringing us up to the recent present and another "game changer" in the development of global formats. Hollywood programming and U.S. presence in the global television marketplace remain dominant, to be sure, but in "Reversal of Fortune? Hollywood Faces New Competition in Global Media Trade," Paul Torre suggests that this hegemony is slipping away with format challenges to established business models and programming styles. Charting the recent history of Hollywood's involvement in the global TV trade, changes in regulation, technology, distribution patterns and the rapid growth of emerging global format players from China, Israel, Brazil and the Netherlands, Torre demonstrates how the media giant is struggling to adapt to new realities in content, distribution and reception of television, both around the world and within the U.S.A. Hollywood's response to these shifts and trends was developing its own formats, adapting others for local consumption, and, most significantly, "localizing" its global corporate structure to work and co-produce directly with local industries. The resulting production marketplace is a re-territorialized Hollywood, spread out and investing in local production and "technology transfer" models of content. The media trade map is increasingly less asymmetrical and more interdependent while, through a confluence of events, the shape of U.S. television has also changed in remarkable accord. Hollywood's new strategy of divesting from certain creative aspects and off-shoring content, Torre argues, may also bring about long-term consequences for its position in the global distribution of popular media content, redrawing the familiar territory largely shaped by powerhouses like U.S.-based conglomerates.

Part III: Case Study—The *Idol* Franchise

Several reality formats all but dominated discussions about GTFs in the past decade. The perceived beachheads in contemporary format success, the juggernauts that were *Survivor, Big Brother* and other "bubble" formats have currently been replaced by smaller "lifestyle" competitions and an overall muting and normalization of format content, spread out across the programming schedule. Yet, in seeking a single format show that both epitomizes format success and its long-term relationship to popular culture at large, no format program comes close to the *Idol* franchise. Introduced in Britain in 2001, this format has seen nearly 50 different international versions and has been the base format engine to hundreds of other talent competitions. As seen recently with the waning of *Idol* productions around the world—even the U.S. version, to date the most profitable format show in history, had undergone frantic restructuring and sloping ratings—the format itself has moved on. If the "bubble" format programs mark the start of the current format era, we submit the *Idol*-style, audience participation talent competition as the expanding middle—and reigning over the last decade of format evolution. As the chapters collected below suggest, the *Idol* format is particularly useful to the study of global popular culture because of its explicit investment in (and celebration of) popular market appeal and the mechanisms of cultural production. Due to its engine-dependence on local taste, popular culture, and personality (as well as its rhetorical allegiance to audience preferences), the *Idol* format is a particularly cogent example of how the "specific-within-the-universal" tension animates the global blockbuster format.

As Biswarup Sen argues in "*Idol* Worship: Ethnicity and Difference in Global Television," the format thus becomes an ideal arena for the representational production of difference. The process (both cultural and economic) by which ethnic identities within and across borders are produced within the format's shared algorithms is, in turn, emblematic of the process of globalization itself. Examining three different reality singing competitions—*Indian Idol 3*, the *Sa Re Ga Ma Pa Challenge* 2007 and the sixth season of *American Idol*—and their varied cultural and historical contexts, Sen theorizes how a format like *Idol* mobilizes versions of Indian and Indian-American identity in order to generate a politics and an aesthetic of difference. As part of the format's inherent construction, difference operates not only between *Idol* versions but also within any particular show. In this, the reality genre is, if nothing else, an "engine of difference" that enables a novel mode of subjectivity. As a stand-in for the globalization process, *Idol* highlights existing or "traditional" forms of ethnic difference. Sen demonstrates this through a case study of the cultural politics surrounding season 3 of *Indian Idol* (2007), when an Indian citizen from the "troubled" border region of Darjeeling won the competition, mobilizing the votes of Indian-Nepalese across the subcontinent, and causing ethnic riots and tensions. But *Idol* (and contemporary globalization) also produces new ethnicities that are irreducibly global and formed in opposition to an assimilationist ethic. To explore this new ethnic identity, and its manifestation within global format adaptations, Sen examines how the hyphenated Indian-American identity plays out across two different cultural-geographical locations—India's in the *Sa Re Ga Ma Pa Challenge* and the U.S.A.'s *American Idol 6* (featuring the notoriously mediocre Sanjaya Melakar, whose longevity on the show was widely perceived as suspect). As Sen argues, the insertion of a global media logic into a national frame of broadcasting (and, of course, vice versa), brings the externalities to the universal into relief as a strategic device. Moreover, Sen concludes, global formats are distinct in the circularity of their logic: They thrive on a diet of difference; what feeds them is globalization itself.

The dimensions of difference within a global logic—those of nation but also region, culture and ethnic diversity below the national scale—is also the focus of Joost De Bruin's "*NZ Idol*: Nation Building through Format Adaptation." The New Zealand adaptation of the popular commercial format is unusual because of the explicit nation-building goals attached to the publicly funded production. The chapter details the show's efforts to represent New Zealand's national identity and highlight ethnic and cultural diversity. While the program offered unprecedented visibility to a range of New Zealanders' ethnic identities that have been largely absent from New Zealand programming, De Bruin analyzes the show's representational strategies to argue that a persistent post-colonialist logic marred the program's rhetoric of diversity in nation-building. Combining interviews with key figures involved in the production of the first two seasons with extended textual analysis, De Bruin explores how ethnic and cultural diversity—articulated as explicit goals for the program—were framed and highlighted. Particularly notable are the negotiations with the format's dictates of judgment, selection, and dismissal—deemed too "brutal" in this format adaptation, and the program's self-conscious use of the signification-rich biographical vignette. These standard video location packages—background stories that provide a glimpse of the contestant's family and community life to engender sympathy, distinction, and identification in the early stages of competition—were deemed "natural" vehicles to celebrate contestants' cultural and ethnic diversity. But, as De Bruin shows, their inevitable failure to make whole the paradox of asserting cultural difference while affirming shared national identity produced these short bio-segments as the staging ground for the program's contested mission. The producer's tendency to seek "positive" representations and avoid potential favoritism prevented genuine exploration of minority contestants' lived realities or an acknowledgement of existing inequalities. Moreover, these representations reinforced a Pakeha (European descended) audience perspective on minority groups (such as the native Maori), conforming to a template of nation building that includes non-white people primarily as instrumental signs of post-colonial difference.

The question of how a global television format is "localized" in the context of contested national identity also forms the basis of the next case study, Martin Nkosi Ndlela's look at *Idol* adaptation in several African nations, "Global Television Formats in Africa: Localizing *Idol*." As Ndlela shows, African productions of the *Idol* format are a particularly useful arena for the study of the pan-national dimensions of format adaptation, the rise of alternative media distribution systems across the African continent, and the shape that media globalization takes in this context. Drawing on various public discourses from industry, audiences, and critics, this comparative analysis examines the content, style and reception of three different African *Idol* shows—*South African Idol*, *Afrikaans Idol*, and *West African Idol* —while attending to the tensions surrounding cultural, ethnic, and linguistic distinctions that accompany each program's negotiation with locality, global style, and American pop influences. The differences among the shows are as striking as they are instructive; of the three, only *Afrikaans Idol* works to maintain a local linguistic and cultural presence. Given the highly loaded legacy of the Afrikaans language in post-apartheid South Africa, Ndlela links the show's text to the aspirations of its audience, who closely identify with linguistic preservation in the changing circumstances that have transformed Afrikaans from the language of dominance to a minority dialect. By contrast, South- and West African *Idol* adaptations prefer performances and styles drawn from American pop over that of local genres and artists, and feature contestants and judges who explicitly emulate U.S. pop, rock, R&B and hip-hop stars. The dominance of English language and Western style in the two shows readily suggests the continent's colonial past and Western cultural hegemony. Yet, as Ndlela points out, audience demographics offers a complicating insight: The shows' target audiences are cable subscribers in South Africa, and the West African countries of Ghana and Nigeria, whose audiences identify as globally-minded cosmopolitan elites. For this audience, the show's attraction is not in a potential expression of their locality but in its emphasis on participation in a celebratory global.

In a counter-exploration of global TV formats from the purview of a dominant U.S. market, Erica Jean Bochanty-Aguero examines the eminently emblematic self-positioning of *American Idol* as the nexus of the global media franchise. "We Are the World: *American Idol*'s Global Self-Posturing" scrutinizes *American Idol*'s unique self-presentation on the global media stage in terms of the format's particular history, its participation in global popular culture, and its constitutive articulation of an American global. The *Idol* format's success, as many authors in this section suggest, is bound up in the program's particular agility of association between a globally linked popular and a locally defined particularity of production, audience tastes, and regional identity. Nowhere are the accompanying tensions and the cheerful posture of a globally engaged chauvinism more on display than in the *World Idol Special* that pitted an array of international format winners against each other. Bochanty-Aguero uses this occasion—an unusual instance of format logic gone "meta"—to interrogate the U.S.A.'s insistence on dominant distinction by examining how the program presents a multifaceted notion of "Americanness," as a carefully negotiated set of relations with "the world." Three other case studies of U.S.-produced departures from the format under the *Idol* brand further enhance Bochanty-Aguero's analysis. In this section she considers the conscious changes made to the U.S. *Idol* format during the outbreak of the U.S. war in Iraq, the *AI* promotional special—*World's Worst Auditions*—and the annual charity drive, *American Idol Gives Back*. Through analysis of these specials, Bochanty-Aguero illustrates how *American Idol* complicates simple notions of the national, international, and transnational while offering an ideal vantage point from which to view the U.S.A.'s articulations of its own identity, as both part of, and apart from, the global mediascape.

Part IV: Local Articulations and the Politics of Place

The chapters in this last section gather the underlying threads of politics of space and place and focus their analysis on format's direct engagement with the nation. How do global formats participate in larger processes of economic and cultural transformations? What structures of production, distribution and audience use do they introduce or change? While some in this section take on the process of format adaptation from a materialist vantage point, others rethink format's content, formal and aesthetic qualities as themselves a way into transformative global processes.

Bridging elements of *Idol*-style talent competition and audience participation with a "bubble" premise that has contestants living together and training to hone their skills, the Endemol format *Star Academy* has seen nearly 50 different iterations in Africa, Europe, the Americas, and the Middle East. *Star Academy*'s pan-Arab version, *Al-Academya*, the most popular and most controversial program in Arab satellite television history, offers Marwan Kraidy an ideal text for examining inter-Arabic politics in the era of converging multiple-media. "The Social and Political Dimensions of Global Television Formats: Reality Television in Lebanon and Saudi Arabia" demonstrates how television formats are able to impact social and political spheres by activating new communication processes among a variety of information and media technologies (what Kraidy has termed "hypermedia space"). It is in this space, within small media uses and convergence media links, that governance challenges, social shifts, and political changes have traceable, if diffused, momentum. In content, *Star Academy* has triggered controversy throughout the Arab world by raising hot-button issues such as democratization, gender relations, and Western influence. Moreover, as Kraidy argues, the format has contributed to a changing "social epistemology"—public knowledge of technical capacities—surrounding information technologies, and opened up space for changes in governance and conventions of public participation. Focusing on the show's production, reception and political impact in liberal Lebanon (where the show is produced) and conservative Saudi Arabia (the network's financier), the chapter demonstrates how various Saudi and Lebanese actors have appropriated *Star Academy* for social and political purposes in the two countries, and how public awareness of the hypermedia space engendered by the program has affected the nature of governance and mounted sustained challenges to gender norms and interpretation of Islamic rules. Thus the activities surrounding reception of reality formats serve as examples of how hypermedia space—and activists working within it—can extend the scope of agency into "real" public space.

In the following chapter, Michael Keane takes up the process of licensing, co-production and adoptions of global format in China as a primary example of cultural mediation within a (televisual) national space, demonstrating how formats are playing a central role in the transition into commercial broadcasting. "A Revolution in Television and a Great Leap Forward for Innovation? China in the Global Television Format Business" further suggests that the preponderance of formats in contemporary China is instructive to understanding the transformations in the Chinese de-networked broadcasting landscape as well as broader economic and cultural shifts in the largest television market in the world. Keane stresses the unique influence that ongoing negotiation between the production sphere and forces of bureaucratic control have over the creative product—reflecting a long-held Chinese practice of cultural borrowing and absorption as an "essentializing process" that infuses foreign elements with Chinese characteristics. Within China's complex, post-reform, fragmented television landscape, format adaptation and development is emblematic of contemporary industrial practice characterized by two opposing drives: the first (mimetic isomorphism) sees unthinking and ever-duplicating clones of existing programming that all but define creative stagnation; the second (R&D) looks outside of China for ideas and original concepts, injecting fresh creative inspiration and the opportunity for experimentation and departure from long-term, stale and politicized conventions. Keane's argument links the latter format development in China with a move toward creative content, a greater regard for audience involvement, and a developing producer–audience feedback loop—finding its most obvious example in popular audience-participation formats. The Chinese model for format adaptation serves not only as a particular case study about format localization but also an examination of how the "host" nation's particular televisual environment impacts how formats are adapted. Keane further illustrates and specifies what, for many scholars and critics, has been a vexing question of the format paradox (or what Keane calls their "dual nature") of a rapid and shallow cloning of programs with little regard for—or, in the Chinese example, sanctioned protection of—intellectual copyright on the one hand, and a creative boom in research and development across China as well as cross-cultural creative inspiration.

The focus on the linkage between the surge in format television and an overall shift to privatization within the global economy is continued in the following chapter, "Global Television Formats and the Political Economy of Cultural Adaptation: *Who Wants to Be a Millionaire?* in India." For Lauhona Ganguly, reality formats and the process of their local adaptation are important as examples of India's economic repositioning. They also promote and mediate this privatized shift by re-imagining India as a new market society, rife with opportunity. The author breaks down the dynamics and structural conditions of adaptation, translation and local reproduction by attending both to the processes that make up domestic production—along with conscious effort towards local relevance and meaning-making—and the political and economic interests that infuse this process on multiple levels. Combining cultural analysis, textual readings of the program and ancillary promotional materials, and industry and production research, Ganguly produces a multi-dimensional synthesis that associates television's work of identifying and representing what "works" in the Indian domestic context with much larger mechanisms that privilege, enable and promote specific cultural patterns, practices, and ways of life. Her analysis of the first three seasons of the *Who Wants to Be a Millionaire?* program, focusing on formal aspects of adaptation (questions, host, style, reward structure, prize money, etc.), reveals striking examples of how these texts structurally and narratively facilitate India's move to a privatized, global marketplace. Yet the process by which the show's logic comes to embody, represent and even promote global market opportunity isn't at all direct, straightforward, or natural. It is, instead, the result of a complex set of interactions between producers, the adaptation process itself, and the industrial, social and cultural shifts of which television is a part. Crucial to Ganguly's argument is the notion that no "causal mechanism" of ideological determinacy exists, and multiple and competing frames of power can produce multiple meanings. Her analysis points to a complex set of relationships through which the field of culture mediates and reshapes reality. Instead of a static analysis of ideological components, or a global/local dichotomy that ransacks format for signs of Westernization-in-replication or resistance-in-cultural-specificity, Ganguly argues for a specificity of interaction and attention to how certain interests find resonance over others both in the process of adaptation and in its varied reception.

As Ganguly and others have stressed, formats' participation in the feel of the global extend beyond their associations with economic interests to their engagement, translations, and representations of both public and private ways of life. In "Global Franchising, Gender and Genre: The Case of Domestic Reality Television," Sharon Sharp takes up the relationship between global franchising and representations of the mundane private sphere when she examines the "wife swap" format's thematic focus on housekeeping. What Sharp finds is that this most domestically-minded and family-centered format is most centrally pre-occupied with (and dependent on) representations of conflict and difference within the nation—and thus uniquely positioned to articulate national identity. This format condition makes a comparative approach of its national iterations ideal for the analysis of industrial and cultural circulation of meanings about gender, race, nation, home, class and genre. As Sharp notes, the format localizes the national audience through the specifics of social differences that are both expressed and managed by the performance of housekeeping.

In comparing the U.S., British and Chilean versions of the "wife swap" format, Sharp demonstrates the intimate connection between format rules and the kinds of domestic interaction, conflict, power relations and cultural emphasis they engender. Predictably, both the U.K. version and its official and unofficial

U.S. versions emphasized conflict over difference. The U.S. versions emphasized transformation and change and dwelled on racial difference while the U.K. version focused on gender, class and national identity. Aside from such difference, both official and unofficial adaptations remain consistently similar to the original format. Not so in Chile, where requirements of pronounced and maintained gender differences and an emphasis on monetary rewards and consumer behavior prove so powerful as to require basic changes in the show's format. Ultimately, the format offers an exceptionally flexible and affective way to address nationally inflected norms about difference, and proffers conflict resolution over changing norms as both possible and emotionally gratifying. However, as Sharp further argues, the controlled diversity of family selection, the emphasis on the nuclear family and, most importantly, the format's underlying insistence that conflict could be resolved at the site of housekeeping, all but curtail the narrative's progressive potential and fixes it to a conservative process of normalization.

In the volume's concluding chapter, "Reiterational Texts and Global Imagin-ation: Television Strikes Back," Tasha Oren argues for a reconsideration of the format's theoretical utility by asserting that TV format is uniquely instructive for both understanding the dynamics of globalization and the persistent relevance of television in a time of proliferating media and repeated predictions of television's demise. The chapter examines the theoretical trajectories of format television along three distinct lines (and tensions), arguing that formats afford fresh considerations for cultural and industrial media globalization; mediate between remote disciplinary camps within media studies, and offer new ways of under-standing contemporary television through their unique engagement with both current industry and viewing practices and long-standing televisual conventions. Oren first breaks down approaches to format in terms of textuality, structure and distribution to argue that format, far from a contemporary phenomenon or a product of globalization, must be understood as an essential component of the very logic of television.

Yet format structure, for Oren, also has poetic and metaphoric resonance with digital culture and gaming logic; its algorithmic and procedural structure and rules-in-recombination grammar promote what Oren terms a "soft protocol" for television content. Its formulaic regularity and cross-border adaptability further reinforces television format's location in the cross-current of seemingly contra-dictory temporal flows: from television's often staunchly nationalist early impulses to its push-pull engagement with globalization on the one hand, and conventional media-specific televisual content to a broad digital expansion of textual possi-bilities on the other. Formats' uniquely flexible orientation helps explain how they successfully integrate conventional staple elements with current reconfigura-tion of the relationship between global adaptability and local specificity. Through a case study of two Israeli format adaptations, the chapter points to the local programs' address and legibility as fundamentally tied to their audience's understanding of them as borderless and shared. In this, format television is one exemplary aspect of cultural production and reception where global and local are experienced not in opposition but as a union of mutually dependent states. Format is, Oren concludes, television in its purest form.

As the closing chapter reaffirms, one important aim for the collection as a whole is to argue for the importance—indeed, centrality—of format in contemporary media studies. It intends to expand the current scholarly foci on format's industrial or ideological dimensions to include its textual structure, cultural flexibility and rich theoretical possibilities in addressing television, global media and broader contemporary modes of culture.

References

Hall, S. (1997) "Old and new identities, old and new ethnicities." in A. D. King (Ed.) *Culture, Globalization and the World System*. Minneapolis: University of Minnesota Press, pp. 41–68.

Holmes, S. and Jermyn, D. (2004) *Understanding Reality Television*. London and New York: Routledge.

Jin, D. Y. (2007) "Transformation of the world television system under neoliberal globalization, 1983 to 2003." *Television and New Media*. Vol. 8. No. 3. August. pp. 179–196.

Keane, M., Fung, A. Y. H., and Moran, A. (2007) *New Television, Globalization and the East Asian Cultural Imagination*. Aberdeen, U.K. and Hong Kong: Hong Kong University Press.

Keane, M. and Moran, A. (2008) "Television's new engines". *Television and New Media*. Vol. 9. No. 2. pp. 155–169.

Mathijs, E. and Jones, J. (2005) *Big Brother International*. Brighton, U.K.: Wallflower Press.

Moran, A. (1998) *Copycat Television: Globalisation, Program Formats and Cultural Identity*. Luton, U.K.: University of Luton Press.

Moran, A. and Keane, M. (2004) *Television Across Asia: Television Industries, Programme Formats and Globalization*. London and New York: RoutledgeCurzon.

Moran, A. and Malbon, J. (2006) *Understanding the Global TV Format*. Bristol, U.K. and Portland, OR: Intellect Books.

Murray, S. and Ouelette, L. (2004) *Reality TV: Remaking Television Culture*. New York: New York University Press.

Robertson, R. (1995) "Glocalization: time-space and homogeneity-heterogeneity." In M. Featherstone, S. Lash, and R. Robertson (Eds.) *Global Modernities*. London: Sage, pp. 25–44.

Straubhaar, J. (2007) *World Television: From Global to Local*. Thousand Oaks, CA: Sage.

Thussu, D. K. (2007) "Mapping global media flow and contra-flow." In D. K. Thussu (Ed.) *Media on the Move*. London: Routledge, pp. 10–29.

Waisbord, S. (2004) "McTV: understanding the global popularity of television formats." *Television and New Media*. Vol. 5. No. 4. pp. 359–383.

Weinman, G. (1999) "The bonfire of vanities: on Israeli 'television culture.'" *Kesher*. Vol. 25. pp. 96–104.

PART I

Format Theories and Global Television

1

MORE THAN COPYCAT TELEVISION

Format Adaptation as Performance[1]

Vinicius Navarro

On December 11, 2006, a well-known Web portal in Brazil ran a story about the popularity of dance competition formats on national television. In the course of approximately 12 months, Brazilian audiences were exposed to seven dance contests, all of which recycled recognizable features from existing TV formats.[2] The first to premiere, *Dança dos Famosos* (Dance of the Famous), was in essence an indigenous version of the program known in the United States as *Dancing with the Stars* (itself an adaptation of the British TV show *Strictly Come Dancing*), although minor changes involving the number of participants and the voting rules were expected to distinguish the Brazilian show from its international counterparts.[3] First broadcast in November 2005, *Dança dos Famosos* was credited with boosting the ratings of its network, Rede Globo, and that in turn paved the way for the other shows.[4] In the subsequent months, Brazilians found themselves watching competitions that featured celebrities and non-celebrities, ballroom dancing and ice-skating, as well as unexpected combinations of seemingly unrelated formats.

As a trend that captured the imagination of Brazilian audiences, the rapid proliferation of dance competitions on network television is meaningful not simply as a domestic phenomenon but also, and particularly, as an illustration of the mechanisms that enable the global popularity of formatted programs. While the shows were locally produced and relied on local talent, they were all based on formats that originated elsewhere, "imported ideas" that were recycled by Brazilian producers. References to foreign versions of the formats were also part of the discourses through which the domestic adaptations were described. As one show followed the other, they invited comparisons not only among themselves but also with their international counterparts.[5] Yet, despite the association with foreign TV shows, the formats were easily incorporated to Brazil's television culture, a feat that could surprise neither critics nor the industry. As Silvio Waisbord notes, "[television] formats are conceived as flexible formula[e]."[6] They are templates that can be licensed to producers worldwide and turned into programs with a characteristically "local flavor." Most formats originate in Western countries but have been indigenized by television industries in different parts of the world. Even if the Brazilian shows referred back to the "original" templates, each version was expected to be culturally specific.

What distinguishes television formats from other cultural artifacts is thus not so much an essential attribute but rather the way the formula circulates, the fluidity of the format's identity. Albert Moran puts it clearly when he says that "[t]he format is a technology of exchange in the television industry," which seems to lack a "core" or "essence" and "has meaning not because of a principle but because of a function or effect." The question we should ask, according to Moran, is not what a format is but "what it permits or facilitates."[7] Moran himself answers this question by arguing that this "technology of exchange" seems destined to serve a regulatory function. There are no conventional products being traded here. Rather, formats "[help] to organize and regulate the exchange of program ideas between program producers".[8] They provide the industry with a means to package those "ideas" and control their use. As flexible formulae, formats are also expected to function as intellectual property, so that they can circulate easily but not freely.

Moran's characterization is useful because it explains the nature of the format business and underscores the significance of the format's adaptability to different contexts—the sine qua non of that business. It addresses, in other words, issues that are essential to the television industry. Lucid as it is, though, this explanation remains somewhat limited, especially when we look at the actual programs that are produced out of existing television formats. In fact, format adaptations often elude the regulatory function described by Moran, generating both "legitimate" copies and "illicit" imitations.[9] And even when the adaptation process is regulated by a licensing agreement, the resulting program may refer not only to the originating source—the "ideas" being exchanged—but also to other adaptations.[10] The dance contests produced by the Brazilian networks, for example, borrowed elements from a variety of shows and, ultimately, from each other as well. How do we account, then, for the process through which television formats circulate globally? And how do we describe a cultural phenomenon that seems to have broader ramifications than the explanation above suggests?

This chapter proposes to tackle these questions by shifting the emphasis from the adaptability of the format to the process of adaptation. I start off from the assumption that, even when they talk about the adaptation, critics often seem more interested in the flexibility of the formula than in the process through which the format is stretched, bent, and occasionally transformed. While words such as "translation," "negotiation," and "exchange" abound in existing literature on television formats, these discussions tend to favor a more conservative "variations on a theme" approach, which is expected to preserve the autonomy of the original formula.[11] As an industry executive explains, "[t]he key to most of these things is to have the kind of idea that works locally for everyone."[12] Television formats may indeed be the clearest manifestation of a cultural regime in which global reach is secured, rather than threatened, by local specificity. But if we are to understand their significance as cultural artifacts, we may need to look beyond the promise of adaptability and ask how the adaptation itself negotiates a local identity for an existing format.[13]

What I would like to do here is offer a critical alternative to the approach described above by suggesting an analogy between the format adaptation and the notion of performance. The concept of performance itself eludes simple or exact definitions, but it can inspire this discussion in very suggestive ways. Performance brings into focus the related notions of action, interaction, and transaction, all of which can help characterize the format adaptation. Furthermore, while we may say that all performances derive from a "template" defined a priori—an "iterable model," as I indicate later—it is the actualization of that model that distinguishes each individual performance. This applies equally to a live concert, a military parade, or a soccer match. By analogy, we can argue that format adaptations, too, actualize an existing model and situate it in new contexts. And we can claim that even though the adaptation may derive from an original template, its cultural significance cannot be confined to this derivative status.[14]

The most obvious benefit to be harvested from this analogy is the opportunity to reassess the status of formatted programs. As a conceptual model, performance helps differentiate adaptation from adaptability by switching the focus from the promise of circulation to the process through which the format circulates. It allows us to see the formatted shows for what they really are: instances of cultural negotiation in which a formula designed for global consumption is adapted to a local context. It is not that the promise of adaptability no longer matters, but that it cannot fully account for the relationship between the format and the adaptation. As we look at the shows, we are encouraged to think about the way the adaptation interprets, actualizes, and redefines the format, rather than consider the "variable elements" that are added to a presumably "invariable" formula, as a recent study suggests.[15] We are asked to explore the richness and complexity of the encounter between the global and the local in format adaptations.

In this chapter, I pursue this argument in two directions, both of which privilege the particularities of the format as a cultural artifact over the logic of the format business. The initial sections of the chapter examine the nature of the adaptation process and challenge the assumption that formatted programs are merely derivative renditions of a stable formula. The latter part develops the analogy between performance and format adaptation, and uses this analogy as the basis for the discussion of the cultural exchanges that take place when formats "travel" across borders. Referring to specific examples, I argue that the concept of performance helps us understand the "in-betweenness" that characterizes the process by which formats are recreated locally. I draw my illustrations from Brazilian network television but hope that this discussion will instigate questions that pertain not only to my specific examples but also to the notion of format adaptation in general.

More than Copycat TV

There is a clear paradox in standard definitions of television formats. While formats lack a "core" or "essence," they are also expected to be "original" creations. Each adaptation is presumably connected to an originating format, a reproducible formula that remains, in theory, distinct from its various renditions. For a cultural phenomenon that thrives on its capacity to generate new versions of the same show, the idea seems curious. But it is the recognition of this "original" quality that allows format owners to define the parameters within which each format can circulate, or to place various programs under the same label. The originating format appears, then, as a foundation from which all adaptations derive, the basis on which the distinction between official and unofficial copies is established. Paradoxical or not, the desire to attribute an original quality to the format does serve a purpose. It rewards the effort to regulate the production of formatted shows.

That formats also generate "illegitimate" offspring, however, suggests that what we have here is a more complicated scenario. The proliferation of unlicensed programs in different countries has granted television formats a distinctive place in the debate on intellectual property in contemporary culture. It has also shown that subjecting the circulation of formats to an original source might not be a simple task. Format "theft" is notoriously hard to punish, in part because violators tend to change the formula slightly and then claim ownership over the new version.[16] But this distance between the copy and its purported original is embedded in the concept of formatting itself, which assumes that the formula will be adapted to specific television cultures. Rather than honor the correspondence between the original scenario and its various incarnations, formatting is predicated on the notion of creative imitation. It presupposes that distance and difference are natural outcomes of the circulation of television formats.

Less obvious perhaps is the notion that format adaptation does not simply produce local variations of a pre-existing formula. It may change the formula itself, as Moran's revealing explanation of a format's "evolution" indicates:

> The process of concretization and refinement [of a format] is, potentially at least, fairly open ended. No doubt, the format for Endemol's *Big Brother* is now many times larger and more elaborate than when in 1998 the programme first went to air in The Netherlands. . . . [W]ith a programme that proves to be at least reasonably popular in its initial broadcast, the process of documentation and format assemblage is likely to continue for some time, even while the distribution of the format is taking place in different territories.[17]

What Moran describes is precisely the process through which the copies alter and recreate the original. If the format for *Big Brother* is now "many times larger" than it once was, it is as a consequence of a gesture that goes beyond the original template and, in doing so, establishes new parameters for it. A new version of the show might then include elements that did not exist before, elements that were developed in the adaptation process. Saying that the trajectory of a format is "fairly open ended" is a way of acknowledging that the programs do not simply refer to an "original blueprint"—they add to the format's design.

Moran notes later that, "under standard format licensing agreement, these variations and additions . . . become a further part of the format with ownership vested in the original licensor."[18] The idea is somewhat predictable since it attends to the interests of the format owner. But there is an underlying irony in this statement. From the licensor's standpoint, incorporating these variations to the original format represents a way of monitoring the changes that take place through the process of adaptation. It is also a means of repossessing the format once it has been transformed by its different versions. In theory the owner secures the status of the original scenario after it no longer conforms to its original design. But if licensing agreements help the licensor to take possession of "variations and additions," they are less capable of controlling the negotiations that take place as formats travel from one place to another. Nor can the regulatory mechanism restore the hierarchical distinctions that subject the formatted show to the standard formula. What Moran describes above is, in fact, a gesture that upsets these hierarchies, in which cultural exchanges that exceed the boundaries of the originating format end up altering the format itself.

There is another equally ironic implication in Moran's comments that deserves attention. The idea that the process of "format assemblage" continues over time suggests that each adaptation can potentially draw on previous adaptations, that formatted programs do not just refer to an original scenario but also borrow from one another, each version becoming then a potential source for the next one. If formats "travel by iteration," as Tasha Oren puts it, then what is iterated here is another instance of citation—another copy.[19] This complicates the notion of formatting in two related ways. First, it opens the adaptation process to different types of exchange. Instead of a unidirectional movement whereby the licensee creates a new version of an existing format—and in doing so observes the distinction between the model and its adaptation—what we have is a variety of transactions that expand the means by which formatted shows circulate. Second, since every adaptation can potentially provide referential material to subsequent versions, the status of the format ends up changing as well. In this context, the initial formula continues to play an important role, but it does not fully control the negotiations that take place in the adaptation process. Rather, it appears alongside other originating sources.

Adaptability vs. Adaptation

This argument contrasts with what I see as a more common approach to television formats, which treats the formula as a highly mobile but ultimately self-contained cultural artifact. Waisbord observes, for example, that formats "are designed to 'travel well' across national boundaries." They "eviscerate the national" so that they can be "customized to domestic cultures." And even if they are not free of cultural values (individualism, consumerism, competitiveness, and so forth), they "carry meanings that are not necessarily attached to national cultures."[20] What stands out is, of course, the adaptability of the formula, which precedes and enables the adaptation process. This line of thinking overlaps with the rationale of the format business. As another study indicates, formatted programs are "consciously created with the deliberate intention of achieving near-simultaneous international adaptation." The shows are "abstract and international in type while also being local and concrete in [their] particular manifestations."[21] While this characterization is not inaccurate, it does not say much about the adapted programs either. It implies that difference is simply added to an existing formula, rather than produced through the adaptation. It also overlooks the fact that formatted shows can travel in different directions, as I noted earlier. Although what is emphasized here is the specificity of the local version—rather than the formula itself—the local appears merely as a destination for a format that originated elsewhere, the end point in a trajectory that can only confirm the presumed autonomy of the original model.

To insist on the significance of the adaptation process is not to say that adaptability is not a key element in the formatting of television programs. That "formats are designed to 'travel well'" should be obvious in the programs' distinctively local characteristics. Formatted shows cater to the interests of specific populations and exploit the popularity of local media icons. They also solicit the participation of domestic audiences by asking people to vote for their preferred contestants. Finally, many of these shows have a strong live component, which helps create the impression that the program spills over into the quotidian of the spectators. All this seems to confirm the promise of adaptability on which the logic of the format industry is predicated. But it does not directly address the question of how formatted shows actualize and recreate the original formula. For that we might need to look at the adaptation not as the means through which the originating format congeals into an indigenized form but as a process whereby cultural relations are (re)produced. And we may choose to discuss not the purported autonomy of the formula but the way that formula is transformed through its various adaptations.

Some of my claims find resonance in studies of screen adaptations of literary texts. Adaptation critics have often questioned the authority of the literary source over its cinematic versions, arguing that faithfulness to the original, while not really irrelevant, cannot exhaust the significance of the adaptation process. Instead of focusing on fidelity, they examine the mutations that are inherent to the migration of a text from one context to another, and from one medium to another. Context tends to affect both the cultural and social meaning of a text. As Linda Hutcheon writes, "Local particularities become transplanted to new ground, and something new and hybrid results."[22] Moreover, adaptations often stand at the intersection of various texts and conjure up not only the memory of the source but also the presence of other adaptations, as Robert Stam explains: "[Adaptations] are caught up in the ongoing whirl of intertextual reference and transformation, of texts generating other texts in an endless process of recycling, transformation, and transmutation, with no clear point of origin."[23]

It is this generative quality that interests me. Bringing the source to a new context inevitably exposes the differences between the original and its adaptation, as the producer of any formatted program can easily tell. It also creates opportunity for dialogue with other texts. This multifaceted process, rather than just the promise of adaptability, is what characterizes the movement of television formats "across national boundaries."

To be sure, there are significant differences between the screen adaptation of a literary text and the creation of a formatted show. Even if we choose to overlook the nature of the format business, we will still have to account for the fact that the actualization of a successful TV formula might find no precise equivalent in other types of adaptation. Rather than apply adaptation theory to the discussion of television formats, I would thus like to propose a more specific approach, looking at format adaptations as performances, creative acts that are both context-specific and intertextually connected to other performances.[24]

Format Adaptation as Performance

Performances are context-specific because they are shaped, in part, by the circumstances in which they take place, as the somewhat redundant term "live performance" implies. On the other hand, they also exceed those same circumstances by invoking the memory of other performances, as demonstrated by the ritualized character of religious ceremonies, sports competitions, and other performance-based events. To stick with the terminology used above, individual instances of performance are dialogically related to other performances. What makes this concept particularly suggestive for us is the fact that all performances involve the actualization of an "iterable model," a "role" that is revisited every time there is a performance.[25] That the role varies according to the type of performance is less relevant than the general idea that, being different from the performance in nature, the role serves nonetheless as a reference for each individual act. Much like a format adaptation, a performance finds new contexts for an already existing model.

In some ways, the reference to performance should come as no surprise. Formatted programs have been repeatedly described as staged events, which take place in studio settings or in artificially created environments.[26] The affinity with theatrical experiences is also encouraged by the design of the programs, which may include the presence of a live audience and benefit from the attractiveness of live broadcasting.[27] Most obviously perhaps, many of these shows involve specific kinds of performance or performance-based events like games and competitions.[28] When I refer to performance, however, what I have in mind is a more general analogy with the process of adaptation, a comparison that may shed light on the way formats function as cultural artifacts. Formatted programs are performative not so much because they feature singing or dance performances but because they are themselves conceptualized as re-enactments. They presuppose the need to actualize a given set of rules, to stage a specific role.

What, then, does the analogy with the concept of performance tell us about format adaptations? And how can it offer an alternative to the notion that the adaptation is merely a local variation of a purportedly stable formula? Performance theorists have claimed that performances are both reproductive and creative gestures. They are imitations that do not simply copy an "original" but also generate new and differentiated versions of it. Richard Schechner has used the term "restored behavior" to characterize the propensity to imitate that is inherent to the notion of performance. All performances, he reminds us, are repetitions. (Is this not what allows us to recognize them as performances and, say, not as accidents?) Yet, at the same time, every performance is also unique and distinct from other performances. "Even though every 'thing' is exactly the same, each event in which the 'thing' participates is different."[29] The setting changes, and so does the act. As a result, the authority of that which is being repeated ends up being shaken by the repetition itself.[30] The "original 'truth' or 'source' of the [act]" is overshadowed by individual instances of performance, "even while that [same] truth or source is being honored."[31]

If we now extrapolate from Schechner's useful formulation, we may say that format adaptations, too, are expected to copy and imitate, but that, in doing so, they create unique instantiations of the model they are supposed to reproduce. The process by which an existing format is recontextualized does not so much confirm the invariability of the original as redefine that which may otherwise be perceived as invariable.[32] Two of the main arguments in this chapter find support in this analogy. Seen as performance, the adaptation can no longer be reduced to the inherent adaptability of the format. The emphasis now falls on the process of adaptation. Additionally, it cannot be seen merely as a derivative rendition of the original format either. Rather, it begins to appear as a productive gesture that can potentially redefine the template. Is this not what is implied in the explanation, quoted above, that the trajectory of a format is "fairly open ended," or suggested by the notion that the variations introduced by the adaptation process "become a further part of the format"?

The dance contests that mushroomed on Brazilian television starting in November 2005 offer a suggestive illustration for this argument because they draw attention to the way the adaptation process impacts both the authority and the premise of the original formulae. Trying to innovate and at the same time capitalize on each other's popularity, they utilized elements from a variety of formats and borrowed not only from foreign adaptations but also from domestic programs. The original formats were dragged into this "whirl of intertextual reference," to use Robert Stam's phrase one more time, re-emerging sometimes as hybrid programs that combined elements from different shows.

Here I would like to look more closely at two of the adaptations, both of which challenge the argument that claims to keep the copy at a safe distance from its original. The first example, *Dança dos Famosos*, was reportedly an unlicensed version of the *Dancing with the Stars/Strictly Come Dancing* format, which, despite its unofficial status, managed to appropriate the authority of the formula and influence subsequent versions. The second show, *Bailando por um Sonho* (Dancing for a Dream), stretched the premise of the dance competition format in such a way that it ended up redesigning the formula. Ironically, *Bailando por um Sonho* was allegedly the official version of the format copied by its rival.

First broadcast by Rede Globo in November 2005, *Dança dos Famosos* was a dance contest that brought together national celebrities, usually with no formal training in dance, and professional dancers. Every week, the couples—the celebrities and their instructors—faced each other on the dance floor, where they were supposed to demonstrate their skills. The elimination process, as expected, was determined both by popular and professional vote. The most conspicuous sign of innovation in *Dança dos Famosos* was probably the number of judges. The Brazilian version had two juries instead of one, and the participants were submitted to separate "artistic" and "technical" evaluations. Apart from slight changes, though, the contest remained clearly recognizable as a domestic version of the *Dancing with the Stars/Strictly Come Dancing* formula. It was hosted by a well-known Brazilian entertainer (Fausto Silva) and featured in a popular variety show (*Domingão do Faustão*), both of which added "local color" to the adaptation. That *Dança dos Famosos* was also an "illegitimate" version of a popular format, however, makes this seemingly orthodox approach to the adaptation process particularly meaningful. Here the adaptability of the formula works against the rules of the business as the copy takes the place of the official adaptation. In fact, being the first version of the format produced by Brazilian television, *Dança dos Famosos* was instrumental in defining a local identity for the formula, serving as a useful reference for the adaptations that followed.

Dança dos Famosos was a sort of trendsetter. In the wake of its success, a number of dance or dance-related competitions found their way to Brazil's TV screens. Rede Globo, the same network that produced *Dança dos Famosos*, subsequently launched a second contest called *Dança no Gelo* (Dance on Ice), a domestic version of programs like *Skating with Celebrities*. Although *Dança no Gelo* was an adaptation of a different format, much of its popular appeal was related to its successful predecessor. The new competition was in fact described as a spin-off of *Dança dos Famosos*.[33] It was slotted in the same variety show and presented by the same host. But perhaps even more revealing of *Dança dos Famosos*'s particular status was the direction taken by the licensed version of the *Dancing with the Stars/Strictly Come Dancing* format. When the new show, *Bailando por um Sonho*, finally premiered in October 2006, the formula had been significantly altered. In an apparent effort to innovate, the network (Sistema Brasileiro de Televisão—SBT) recreated the original template, incorporating features from other formats and extending the boundaries of the dance competition formula. Curiously, the official adaptation looked less like the originating format than the "bastardized" version.

Bailando por um Sonho did show unequivocal similarities to programs like *Dancing with the Stars*. But it also exceeded their premise. While professional dancers were still involved in the competition, they now stayed away from the dance floor.[34] The celebrities danced not with their instructors but with ordinary contestants, to whom they also played the supporting role. Most significantly, the emphasis shifted from the skills of the dancers to the show's philanthropic pretensions. Each one of the contestants—the real stars of *Bailando por um Sonho*—had a dream that involved financial challenges. The projects ranged from practical (starting a business) to altruistic (paying for a mother's health treatment) to eccentric (traveling abroad to meet a former coach of Brazil's national soccer team). When voting for their favorite contestants, the audience was encouraged to take into account not only the dance numbers but also the participants' dreams, the outcome of the contest being thus determined, in part, by factors unrelated to the abilities of the players.

If we are to look at format adaptations as performances, what *Bailando por um Sonho* reveals is the process by which the performance changes the role. Coming nearly one year after the premiere of *Dança dos Famosos*, the new show revisited a model that was by then familiar to Brazilian audiences. But in doing so it also exposed the "deviations" that marked it off from its predecessor. *Bailando por um Sonho* was in fact an amalgam of various programs, a concoction that capitalized on the history—both recent and distant—of different formats. It combined the formula of *Dança dos Famosos* with formats whose history can be traced back to shows like *Strike It Rich* (CBS, 1951–1958) and *Queen for a Day* (NBC, ABC, 1956–1964), both of which revolved around the financial needs of their contestants.[35] The latter was adapted in Brazil more than once with the title *Rainha por um Dia* (a literal translation of "Queen for a Day"), the last time by Rede Globo, between 1968 and 1976. A somewhat similar show called *Portas da Esperança* (Gates of Hope) was aired by SBT between 1984 and 1997. *Portas da Esperança* matched ordinary people who came to the show hoping to see their dreams come true with business owners who agreed to pay for their requests. *Bailando por um Sonho* had elements of all these programs, which were rearranged to fit the scenario of a dance contest. While the original dance formula remained recognizable throughout, the adaptation took it in a different direction and, in the process, "hijacked" the format.

Although *Bailando por um Sonho* and *Dança dos Famosos* must be viewed against the specific developments that connected different dance shows on Brazilian television in 2006, what they reveal about the process of adaptation is by no means peculiar to that history. Altering the original premise is common in format adaptations and ultimately helps extend the life of a format. Similarly, unlicensed imitations are so frequent that we cannot afford to overlook their importance. In Brazil as elsewhere, unauthorized copying is rampant.[36] Recognizing the significance of these "irregular" practices does not amount to ignoring the potential legal implications of either "tampering" with the original model or producing unofficial versions of an existing format. Neither is it to suggest that "hijacking" the formula should be construed as a form of cultural resistance. But it may be a way of broadening the debate on television formats.

"The Space in Between"

It remains to discuss what exactly the analogy between adaptation and performance can tell us about the global circulation of television formats. If the formula's adaptability does not suffice to explain the way formats circulate, how do we account for the encounter between the global and the local in formatted programs? How is the notion of performance related to the exchanges that take place when a format migrates to a different context? And how can it help us understand the way television producers negotiate a new identity for an existing format? The simplest way to answer these questions may be to say that the performance is precisely the means by which one situates an imported formula vis-à-vis the local culture. The adaptation does not simply perpetuate the original format. Nor does it merely "perform the local." Rather, it helps define the relationship between them.

Put differently, the analogy with the concept of performance honors the notion of adaptation as negotiation, translation, or exchange. It draws attention to the process through which the local identity of the format is produced out of the interplay between repetition and creativity. And it privileges neither the foreign nor the domestic but what connects them. To borrow a term from García Canclini, the adaptation–performance inhabits a sort of "interspace."[37] As García Canclini sees it, this "interspace" refers less to a physical environment than to a set of relations, the focus being not on identities defined a priori but on the way difference emerges out of conflicts and negotiations.[38] By revisiting an existing formula and submitting it to a new context, by evoking the memory of other adaptations and borrowing elements from them, formatted shows postulate this space in between as the site where the format is (re)produced locally.

At a basic level, this "in-betweenness" suggests that all formatted shows involve an interpretation of the original formula. To adapt is to make sense of a format created elsewhere, as we find out from discussions of specific formatted programs, even those analyses that privilege the status of the formula over the authority of the adaptation. In his early study of television formats, Moran argues, for example, that the Australian version of *Sale of the Century* "diminishes both the competitive and product promotion segments of the program. Instead the emphasis falls on the warm interaction, often comic, between host, hostess, models and contestants."[39] Similarly, the host of *Lar Doce Lar* (Home Sweet Home), the Brazilian version of shows like *Extreme Makeover: Home Edition*, attributes the success of the local adaptation to a culturally specific interpretation of the format. In the Brazilian adaptation, the scenario of the original formula—the renovation of a house—remains the same, but the focus is on the development of dramatic stories involving local people.[40] *Lar Doce Lar* evokes and reinforces popular sentiments about financial struggle and class difference, embodied in the drama of its "characters." In a highly inegalitarian society, it "deals with" social issues at a personal level and manages, in the end, to "solve" the problems. *Lar Doce Lar* is, in this sense, similar to shows like *Bailando por um Sonho*.

Bailando por um Sonho, however, offers a more complex example of negotiation as it demonstrates that the process of interpretation can introduce unexpected changes to the formula itself. Moreover, it expands the notion of interpretation by including references to other formatted programs. Like *Lar Doce Lar*, it situates an existing format in a culturally specific context by connecting with popular attitudes towards financial struggle. Yet, in doing so, it also submits the formula to circumstances that involve, among other things, the history of similarly oriented shows on Brazilian TV. The process through which the adaptation negotiated a new identity for the format simultaneously recalled and benefited from this history. Not only did it address the specificity of the domestic context, it also located that specificity in a certain corner of Brazil's television culture. And it complicated the idea that formatted programs must suit the interests of particular audiences because it associated those interests with other format adaptations. The design of the resulting program—a hybrid of different shows—is indicative of the complexity of these negotiations.

The emphasis on the "in-betweenness" of the negotiation can evoke an even broader spectrum of cultural relations and help avoid the risk of either claiming autonomy for the original format or treating the adaptation as a form of creative resistance. *Dança no Gelo*, the Brazilian version of *Skating with Celebrities*, for example, is noteworthy not so much because it reinvents the formula but because it explores an already existing attitude towards a specific foreign culture. In this case, the formula itself might have seemed out of place in a country without a tradition of ice-skating. The Brazilian producers presumably offset the problem by adding "local color" to the show, that is to say, by including popular TV stars in the competition and by likening *Dança no Gelo* to the well-liked *Dança dos Famosos*. It was, however, by revisiting a familiar fascination with American popular culture that the indigenous version managed to negotiate its status in relation to the originating format. In *Dança no Gelo*, this fascination became part of the very process through which local producers interpreted and recreated the foreign. The final evening of the second season (November 12, 2006), for instance, had two couples ice-skating to the sound of Broadway show tunes—and dressed for the part. Daniele Suzuki (the star of a teen soap opera) and her coach played roles from *Cats*, while Iran Malfitano (also a TV star) and his partner appeared as characters from *Phantom of the Opera*. Along with the ice-skating rink, the Broadway musicals forced the foreign back into the adapted version. Yet, ironic-ally, they seemed to refer less to the original format than to locally recognizable tastes and attitudes.

A similar example of the way existing cultural attitudes complicate the relationship between the foreign and the domestic in formatted programs can be found in *O Aprendiz*, the Brazilian version of *The Apprentice*. Produced by Rede Record, *O Aprendiz* closely followed the premise of the original format, with candidates competing for a position in a high-profile Brazilian company. The arbiter, a Brazilian advertising executive, was expected to fire one candidate in each episode and hire the winner at the end of the season. It is not only in this apparent compliance with the original scenario, however, that the exchanges between the domestic and the foreign manifest themselves in a show like *O Aprendiz*. Rather, it is the way the program mobilizes established meanings about foreign worlds and foreign cultures—in this case, the business world that inspired the original format—that characterizes these negotiations. In Brazil the term "first world" is used colloquially to designate not a geopolitical entity but a certain standard of excellence, usually more imaginary than real since many of those who use the term have not had any direct contact with the first world. Professionalism and efficiency, for example, as well as education and wealth, are all attributes described as first world qualities. By celebrating a particular ideal of social status and professional success, the Brazilian version of *The Apprentice* activated this very fantasy, invoking the presence of a foreign world that remains inaccessible to most Brazilians.

The third season of *O Aprendiz* (August–September 2006) took this fantasy one step further by including that world in the script of the show, or, more precisely, by making it coincide with the objectives of the contest. In many ways, wealth and social mobility were both the coveted prizes in the program and the underlying theme of *O Aprendiz*. In the show's third season, this promise of social status literally overlapped with the foreign contexts represented by the original program. The participants in *O Aprendiz* 3 faced each other in a competition that was expected to reward the winner not with a job in a Brazilian company but a position in an advertising agency with a Madison Avenue address.

Social mobility was now connected to the possibility of physically moving to another country.

As an example of how formatted programs negotiate their local identities, *O Aprendiz*, like the other shows, warns against collapsing the differences between adaptability and adaptation. It demonstrates that it is often by looking beyond the superficial variations recognizable in the programs that we may appreciate the relationship between global formats and their local versions. Perhaps most significantly, it encourages us to ask specific questions about the negotiations that take place when television formats begin to travel. Does the process of adaptation reproduce, distort, or reverse existing cultural hierarchies? What does the adaptation allow for, enable, or reveal? And how is the foreign interpreted, mimicked, or repossessed in formatted programs?

Conclusion

This chapter has argued that television formats are more than "programming ideas" that can be easily adapted to fit the needs and interests of television industries worldwide. They are a means through which contemporary culture circulates globally. In trying to emphasize the cultural significance of formatted programs, I proposed an analogy between the concept of performance and the format adaptation. This analogy served two purposes. It provided a way of approaching the process through which the adaptations actualize and recreate existing formats, and it brought into focus the cultural negotiations that are part of this process. Format adaptations inhabit a sort of "space between cultures," a site in which difference emerges out of imitation, where hierarchical distinctions are both upheld and upset, and from where one culture looks at and interprets another. The complexity of these exchanges suggests that it would be a mistake to equate the kind of creative copying afforded by the format adaptation with an act of cultural insubordination. But it also reminds us that it would be equally wrong to reduce the adaptation process to the promise of adaptability. Because it sheds light on the "in-betweenness" of the adaptation, the concept of performance can serve as a critical tool to explore these negotiations.

Notes

1 I would like to thank Tasha Oren and Sharon Shahaf for their insightful comments and inspiring suggestions.
2 "Programas de Competição de Dança Marcam o Ano de 2006 na TV," http://televisao.uol.com.br/ultnot/2006/12/11/ult698u11841.jhtm; accessed 12 December 2006. The seven contests were *Dança dos Famosos* (Globo), *Reality Dance* (Record), *Dança sobre Patins*, (Record), *No Ritmo da Copa* (Record), *Dançando em Hollywood* (Record), *Dança no Gelo* (Globo), and *Bailando por um Sonho* (SBT).
3 Marcelo Marthe, "Versão Brasileira: Atrações Importadas Estão Dando Novo Fôlego aos Programs de Auditório," *Veja*, May 31, 2006, 119.
4 "Programas de Competição de Dança Marcam o Ano de 2006 na TV."

5 Ibid.
6 Silvio Waisbord, "McTV: Understanding the Global Popularity of Television Formats," *Television and New Media* 5, no. 4 (November 2004): 368.
7 Albert Moran, *Copycat Television: Globalisation, Program Formats and Cultural Identity* (Luton, U.K.: University of Luton Press, 1998), 17–18.
8 Ibid., 18.
9 I use the term "adaptation" to refer both to licensed and unlicensed programs.
10 Moran himself says this much when he points out that formats are usually licensed after the production of the first program and, furthermore, when he acknowledges that the success of an adaptation tends to determine the longevity and marketability of a television format. Albert Moran, *Understanding the Global TV Format* (Bristol, U.K. and Portland, OR: Intellect, 2006), 11, 57–60. See also Moran, *Copycat Television*, 14.
11 Revealingly, the complexity of the adaptation process tends to become apparent when critics analyze specific formatted programs. See, for example, the discussion of the Chinese show *Super Girl* in Michael Keane, Anthony Fung, and Albert Moran, *New Television, Globalisation, and the East Asian Cultural Imagination* (Hong Kong: Hong Kong University Press, 2007), 131–133.
12 Peter Bazalgette, cited in Michael Collins, "Who Owns Our Lives? Copyrights and Wrongs: In the Global TV Market, Great Ideas are the Key," *Observer*, April 22, 2001, 17.
13 Some of my claims must be understood in the context of broader disciplinary differences between my approach to format adaptations and the studies mentioned in this chapter.
14 The term "performance" is used occasionally to describe the actions of the contestants in specific formatted programs. It has also appeared in phrases such as "performing the local." I am unaware, however, of other attempts to explore the analogy between the concept of performance and the adaptation process.
15 Keane et al., *New Television*, 61.
16 For a discussion of legal issues surrounding global television formats, see Justin Malbon, "The Law Regarding TV Formats" and "Can There Be Copyrights in Formats?," in Moran, *Understanding the Global TV Format*, 111–126, 127–142. For a different perspective on culture and copyright, see Laikwan Pang, *Cultural Control and Globalization in Asia: Copyright, Piracy, and Cinema* (London and New York: Routledge, 2006).
17 Moran, *Understanding the Global TV Format*, 30.
18 Ibid., 70.
19 Tasha Oren, " . . . with Just a Pinch of Local Spice: Looking Beyond 'Culture Blend' in Global Television Formats," Society for Cinema and Media Studies Conference, Chicago, March 8–11, 2007.
20 Waisbord, "McTV: Understanding the Global Popularity of Television Formats," 368.
21 Keane et al., *New Television*, 68.
22 Linda Hutcheon, *A Theory of Adaptation* (New York and London: Routledge, 2006), 150.
23 Robert Stam, "Beyond Fidelity: The Dialogics of Adaptation," in *Film Adaptation*, ed. James Naremore (New Brunswick, NJ: Rutgers University Press, 2000), 66.
24 Robert Stam points out the usefulness of performativity theory for the discussion of screen adaptations in "Introduction: The Theory and Practice of Adaptation," in *Literature and Film: A Guide to the Theory and Practice of Film Adaptation*, ed. Robert Stam and Alessandra Raengo (Malden MA, Oxford, and Victoria: Blackwell, 2005), 10–11.
25 I borrow the term "iterable model" from Derrida's critique of J. L. Austin's work. While discussing Derrida's response to Austin exceeds the scope of this chapter, his insights have been inspirational to the formulation of my arguments. Jacques Derrida, "Signature

Event Context," in *Limited Inc* (Evanston, IL: Northwestern University Press, 1988), 1–23. See also J. L. Austin, *How to Do Things with Words*, second edition, ed. J. O. Urmson and Marina Sbisà (Cambridge, MA: Harvard University Press, 1975).

26 See, for example, John Corner, "Performing the Real: Documentary Diversions," *Television and New Media* 3, no. 3 (August 2002): 255–269. See also Paddy Scannell, "*Big Brother* as a Television Event," *Television and New Media* 3, no. 3 (August 2002): 271–282.

27 For a discussion of the concept of liveness in the context of performance studies and media studies, see Philip Auslander, *Liveness: Performance in a Mediatized Culture*, second edition (London and New York: Routledge, 2008).

28 The programs in fact share several of the qualities attributed to events of this nature: a particular time frame, a set of rules, a space designated as the site where the performance takes place. See Richard Schechner, "Approaches," in *Performance Theory*, revised and expanded edition (New York and London: Routledge, 2003), 1–25.

29 Richard Schechner, *Performance Studies: An Introduction*, second edition (New York and London: Routledge, 2006), 30. For a lengthier discussion of the notion of "restored behavior," see Schechner, *Between Theater and Anthropology* (Philadelphia: University of Pennsylvania Press, 1985).

30 Interestingly, the relevance to performance studies of these interconnected concepts— repetition and creativity—has also provided the basis for conflicting arguments. Peggy Phelan, for example, has claimed that performance [art] involves "representation without reproduction," that every repetition "marks [the performance] as 'different,'" while Philip Auslander has explored the imbrications of performance and media reproduction in contemporary culture. Peggy Phelan, *Unmarked: The Politics of Performance* (London and New York: Routledge, 1993), 146; Auslander, *Liveness: Performance in a Mediatized Culture*.

31 Schechner, *Performance Studies*, 34.

32 There is here a curious overlapping between the concept of performance and poststructuralist thinking—as well as between poststructuralist thinking and the global circulation of popular culture—whose significance cannot be properly addressed in this chapter. For a discussion of the intersections between performance and various currents of thinking, see Marvin Carlson, *Performance: A Critical Introduction*, second edition (New York and London: Routledge, 2004).

33 "'Dança no Gelo' Estréia neste Domingo no 'Domingão do Faustão,'" www.folha.uol.com.br/folha/ilustrada/ult90u63275.shtml; accessed 18 November 2007.

34 In fact, the role of the professional dancer changed after the show began to air, reportedly because the audience responded negatively to the idea of a dance competition involving trios instead of couples.

35 I would like to thank Tasha Oren for pointing out the similarities between *Bailando por um Sonho* and *Queen for a Day*.

36 The most notorious case of unlicensed copying in Brazil involved an unofficial adaptation by SBT of the *Big Brother* format. See Nelito Fernandes, "Parece Igual. E é Mesmo," *Época*, 3 December 2001, 124–126.

37 Néstor García Canclini, *Diferentes, Desiguales y Desconectados: Mapas de la Interculturalidad* (Barcelona: Gedisa, 2006).

38 García Canclini's term recalls a number of discussions on culture and globalization, which share his emphasis on the negotiation of difference. See, in particular, Arjun Appadurai, *Modernity at Large: Cultural Dimensions of Globalization* (Minneapolis and London: University of Minnesota Press, 1996).

39 Moran, *Copycat Television*, 81.

40 *Lar Doce Lar* was featured in a variety show called *Caldeirão do Huck*, hosted by Luciano Huck. Marthe, "Versão Brasileira," 119.

2

"CALLING OUT AROUND THE WORLD"

The Global Appeal of Reality Dance Formats

Dana Heller

In this chapter, I would like to consider how interactive reality television contributes to the negotiation between national particulars and transnational media flows. Specifically, I want to look at the successful franchise *So You Think You Can Dance*, a dynamic global media flashpoint and a remarkably adaptable format that serves as a site of pleasurable and contradictory engagement with the sense of national culture and community that television manufactures. But what makes the show of particular interest to me is that it allows audiences, in an increasing number of television markets around the world, to collectively determine their ideal national performers through a competition that requires mastery of a virtual international smorgasbord of popular dance forms and styles, the vast majority of which originate elsewhere, or from within the national, racial, and ethnic cultures of others.

Second, in choosing to examine dance shows, I join with a growing number of scholars who have, over the past 15 years, argued for increased attention to dance as a primary site of knowledge production concerning bodies, identities, and representation.[1]

The spreading influence of critical dance studies across disciplines and interdisciplines suggests that human movement has acquired recognition as an instrumental social text that is, I contend, valuable to the development of global television studies. In general, humanities-based television studies has concerned itself principally with investigations of visual image and sound, narrative, genre, audience, historical contests, and industrial processes. Its development has tended to overlook questions of kinesthetic action and the semiotics of human movement. However, the recent surge in popularity of reality television dance shows, such as *So You Think You Can Dance* and *Dancing with the Stars*, in conjunction with the establishment of official and independent Internet fan sites, such as *Dance*

Watcher, *1000 Dance Stars*, and *Reality Dance*, suggests that the time may be ripe for opening up media and television studies to dance research. Moreover, and for the purposes of this anthology most importantly, there may be much to be gained where questions of international television marketing and format adaptation are concerned, particularly when we acknowledge that human movement serves as a critical marker for the production of social and national identities.

So You Think You Can Dance (SYTYCD) first aired in 2005 on the U.S. Fox network. It was created by the same team that developed *American Idol*, Simon Fuller and Nigel Lythgoe, and certain structural similarities apply: initially, a number of auditions are staged in various cities around the country as aspirants, including amateur hopefuls and trained professionals, compete for selection as top dancers. The narrative arc of the series is established herewith; as the abilities and personalities of auditioners—ranging from the freakishly bizarre, to the marginally skilled, to the markedly talented—are weighed by a panel of "expert" judges, the majority of whom are established choreographers and dance professionals. Their responses, in turn, when not couched in professional politesse, provide the alternating spectacles of merciless rejection ("You spin very well, but so does my wife's tumble dryer," jeers Lythgoe) and jubilant authorization to advance to the next stage of competition.[2] At last, a group of top 20 finalists are selected. The finalists then compete over a series of broadcasts wherein they are partnered and each pair assigned a dance style—quickstep, salsa, ballroom, hip-hop, lyrical jazz—through a random selection process that requires dancers trained in particular traditions to adapt quickly to unfamiliar styles. Dancers adhere to a rigorous rehearsal schedule, training as well as living together throughout the process. Each week, after all couples have performed, the weakest male and female dancers are eliminated from the competition based initially on judges' scores, and then, as the season advances, scores that combine viewers' "call-in" or "text-in" votes with judges' rankings.

At the time of this writing, the U.S. Fox network has broadcast three seasons of SYTYCD and has crowned three talented young people as "America's Favorite Dancer." At the end of Season One, on October 5, 2005, winner Nick Lazzarini was given $100,000 and free occupancy of a luxury New York City apartment for one year. At the conclusion of Season Two on August 16, 2006, Benji Schwimmer was selected to the tune of $100,000, a new hybrid automobile, and a one-year contract to dance with Celine Dion's show in Las Vegas. And on August 16, 2007, more than 11 million viewers (placing the show at number 3 for the Nielsen ratings that week) tuned in to watch the Season Three finale, as Sabra Johnson became the first female and the first African-American to win the competition, taking home $250,000 and the opportunity to join the other top nine finalists for the 2007 *So You Think You Can Dance* live nationwide tour. Indeed, with live tours, t-shirts and apparel, tote bags, coasters, pet gifts, Internet blogs, fan forums, photo galleries, and video postings on YouTube, SYTYCD has gradually become, at least in the United States, an industry in itself.

And it was during the live broadcast of the Season Two finale that host Cat Deeley officially announced that the franchise had been sold to broadcast companies around the globe and was fast becoming an international phenomenon. Following this announcement, a succession of brief video clips illustrated these developments, taking pains to highlight the cultural and national distinctiveness of adaptations clearly marked as "foreign." In what amounted to an exercise in popular exoticism, these clips suggested that the Israeli, Turkish, and Norwegian versions of SYTYCD were choreographically steeped in the quaint and colorful folk dancing traditions specific to these cultures. However, what the clips actually revealed was the manner in which dance, as a discourse of the body, is especially vulnerable to stagings and interpretations that essentialize difference in terms of fixed notions such of ethnicity, culture, and nation. And to the extent that these notions are associated with other vectors of identity, such as race, gender, class and sexuality, dance serves not only as a critical social text but one in which various discourses of difference converge and crystallize. This becomes evident not only in studying different national adaptations of contemporary reality dance formats, but when examining the historical development of dance television in discrete national contexts. For example, in the United States, popular shows such as *The Arthur Murray Party* (1950–1960), *National Bandstand* (1952–1989), *Soul Train* (1971–2006), *Dance Party USA* (1986–1992), *Club MTV* (1987–1992) register significant shifts in the status and development of embodied forms of cultural knowledge, styles of bodily presentation, and television's outreach to youth markets, which in combination have been fashioned to promote and/or subvert national attitudes toward social class, race, gender, sexuality, and modernity.[3] The disjunctures and contradictions that circulate within communicative performances of post-war American national identity are thus kinetically, albeit fleetingly, organized in these precursory forms of reality dance television.

Television in the age of the global cultural economy presents us with a vast and far-reaching array of new narratives and their counter-narratives, new points of disjuncture and their deterritorialized overlaps. However, at first glance what is most striking about the various global adaptations of SYTYCD is not how different they are, but rather how very much the same they appear. In the process of developing this essay, I have viewed clips from Denmark's *Kan du Danse*, Germany's *You Can Dance*, Greece's *So You Think You Can Dance*, Israel's *Nolad Lirkod* ("Born to Dance"), Norway's *Dansefeber* ("Dance Fever"), which began airing in 2007, and Turkey's *Benimle Dans Eder Misin* ("Will You Dance With Me"). In each instance, Albert Moran's "pie principle" of format adaptation applies, as the "crust," or generic structural container, is consistently made up of elements such as audition process, set design, signature theme music, celebrity host, jury of three or four "expert" judges (at least one of which is a popular national dance star/choreographer), and cast of anywhere from 16 to 20 youthful dancers, all with distinctive physical and personality features that make them readable as character "types."[4] Indeed, the prioritization of "character" selection over the selection of more skilled dancers, in some instances (a practice admitted to by co-creator and U.S. jurist, Lythgoe) underscores the competition's ultimate goal of determining the nation's "favorite" dancer, as opposed to its best. More significantly, it makes for good television by enhancing other widely present discursive elements, such as assiduously edited segments narrativizing the dancers' intensive training leading into performances, suggestions of conflict and/or romantic intrigue between dancers, in addition to back-story segments, struggles during rehearsals, and interviews with family members aimed at generating a sense of viewer intimacy, connection, and identification with the finalists.

Moran's "filling" (or cultural content) is where we find locally produced elements responsive to vernacular strategies of day-to-day consumption, sense-making, and television-viewing practices. In SYTYCD, these are served up neither through the championing of any dominant style of national dance nor through the ultimate selection of a representative type of national dancer, but in locally specific forms of global awareness that are manifestly reshaping the conventions of international television format adaptation in concert with the development of new media technologies, emergent political economies, and transformations of traditional notions of national identity. For example, when the rights to SYTYCD were sold to Mega Channel in Greece, producers made the decision to hold auditions in Cyprus, Melbourne, Munich, and New York.[5] The move allowed Greeks living outside of the country a chance to participate and be chosen for the show, but it just as significantly underscores the shifting ideological tensions between the state and the Greek diaspora, the conditions of which have been influenced as much by historical patterns of mass emigration as by satellite technologies that effect closure of the cultural gaps between national and expatriate television audiences.

Similarly, the positioning and performance of the host, while it may seem only marginally relevant, functions as a conveyer of meanings that are locally situated both socially and culturally. For instance, in striking contrast to Cat Deeley and Germany's Estefania Küster, whose innocuously youthful verve and likeability ensure that they will interact effectively with the dancers while not entirely overshadowing them, Turkey's adaptation of SYTYCD is hosted by 76 year old "Huysuz Virjin," a nationally famous transgender talk show host and personality. Huysuz Virjin, which translates as "Petulant Virgin," is the stage name of Seyfi Dursunoğlu, whose outrageous wit and notorious penchant for playing at the limits of cultural decorum is a regular feature of *Benimle Dans Eder Misin*'s variety show format. In a nation that is democratic, secular, sexually conservative, and predominantly Muslim, Dursunoğlu's immense popularity with television audiences points to contradictions within Turkish society and its fashioning of legibly sexed and gendered bodies. As part of her regular performance on *Benimle Dans Eider Misen*, Huysuz Virjin vies with female judge, Yonca Evsimik, for the position of top diva and exposes the fault lines of masculinity through the use of wordplay and innuendo. In the following segment from Season Two, she takes a break from the dance competition to focus on the judges, whose identities, she claims, are not quite what they seem.[6]

> *Huysuz Virjin*: I was uneasy. I felt at odds with the judges, so, kids, I went to the birth registration office and threatened the officers there so as to discover these people's [the judges'] real names, their parents' names, and their real ages. So, it turns out that Asena's [a popular singer and belly dancer] real name is Hasene and her family name is Kumatar.[7] Hasene Kumatar. Why did you change your name, huh . . . ?
>
> *Asena*: [Smiles, but does not respond.]
>
> *Huysuz Virjin*: Oh, she has no tongue in her mouth.[8] But she never stops talking backstage. And the other one [turning her attention to ballet dancer/singer Tan Sağtürk], Tan Sagmal . . . what kind of name is this? He does not have any records in Turkey. His record is French. I think he has two nationalities, two passports. So he is free to go in and out. [Sağtürk covers his face with his hand and lowers his head, appearing flustered and embarrassed.]
>
> *Huysuz Virjin*: [Turning her attention to the next judge, a Turkish pop singer] Yonca's real name is Gonca[9] and her surname is not Evcimik. What . . . wait . . . Yonca Evcimik . . . boy, I had studied this at home.
>
> *Yonca*: I don't think there is a more difficult name.
>
> *Huysuz Virjin*: I can't remember it now, I'll recall it later . . . wait, yes! Eksimik! Gonca Eksimik. [Turning her attention to the fourth judge, a Turkish fashion guru] And you all know Uğurkan Erez."[10]

While viewers familiar with the performer's comedic references and cultural status within Turkey will assuredly draw upon their own strategies for interpreting this brief segment, Huysuz Virjin's interrogation of proper naming and nationality—embodied in a performance that is itself an interrogation of proper gendering—opens a space within the narrative arc of *Benimle Dans Eider Misen* for reflection on the refashioning of subjects and their incessant migrations to and fro across geographic, national, and cultural borders. Additionally, the accusation of duplicity directed at Tag Sağtürk—that he moves freely "in and out" or back and forth across national borders—may be read as a double-entendre suggesting that he is open to sexual relations with both men and women, a shrewd reference to widespread speculation that Sağtürk is homosexual. But my point is that the multiple accents and layers of meaning contained in Huysuz Virjin's artful manipulations of language, however much they border on the risqué, ultimately make sense in the context of a global franchise that focuses on the migrations of the dancing body. For, indeed all contestants must demonstrate their abilities to move across different and contradictory bodily discourses—thus taking on and throwing off a variety of assumed social, national, and sexual postures—in order to claim the title of that country's "favorite dancer."

This is not to say that adaptations of SYTYCD are unmoored from their own imagined communities or indigenous aesthetic. Indeed, at least three adaptations that I screened included among the various compulsory dance styles at least one that ostensibly speaks to the distinctive national culture of the market in question: *Benimle Dans Eder Misin*, for example, includes the belly dance, or "oriental" category. Israeli finalists on *Nolad Lirkod* compete in the "Casablan," a reference to the popular 1964 film about Israel's struggle to integrate different nationalities and social classes into one Jewish nation. And Greek contestants who compete in that country's adaptation of SYTYCD demonstrate their mastery of the ballos. Nevertheless, these inclusions, which can be understood as a necessary part of the heritage flavoring of format adaptation, take on a nostalgic and sentimental hue in consideration of the overarching script. For in fact, the ultimate winner of any SYTYCD adaptation will be the dancer who is best able to harmonize conflicting, multiple idioms of movement—many of which are the products of an earlier cross-fertilization of ethnic dance styles, most of which have become highly stylized and codified as they've migrated to various corners of the world, and a preponderance of which originate in non-dominant Latin and Black Atlantic working class urban communities—the samba, rumba, Argentinian tango, krumping, hip-hop, break dancing, cha-cha, and jazz.

From this standpoint, SYTYCD stages "the complex effects of the commodification of cultural styles, their migration, modification, quotation, adoption, or rejection" across television systems and national markets.[11] These effects, expressed in bodily form and movement, reflect (among other things) a long history of formal conflict between postural verticality, long thought to represent the sine qua non of kinesthetic formal elegance or classical European training, and the angularity, segmentation, and percussiveness that is associated with African-based dance styles, or the pelvic rotations, wide hip gesticulation, and open-legged posturing associated with Latin dance styles. However, the long-standing and well-documented rhetorical association of non-dominant races, ethnicities, classes, and nationalities with "the body," or to low physicality as opposed to high mentality, is blurred by the complexities of global capitalism. Like Bourdieu's notion of "taste," bodily movement is socially produced and has become increasingly connected to processes of global mass culture and practices of consumption. For example, the frequently cited penetration of hip-hop culture into international youth markets around the globe, disseminated via mass-media technologies that include the movies, television, Internet, portable media players, and cellular telephones, has shifted the meaning of what was once an urban, African-American music and dance style to a consumer lifestyle, a deterritorialized marker of youth, energy, ostentation, and contained rebellion. Similarly, Latin dance styles such as the tango do not codify the Argentinian or Uruguayan social character as such, but refer to the commercial flow of global erotic economies as well as to locally manufactured fantasies of "hotness."

Wittingly or unwittingly, global television's reality dance formats allegorize the ideological work that simmers beneath conflicting forms of movement and their meanings within specific societies. In this sense, a performance on *Benimle Dans Eder Misin* that combines a demonstration of flamenco dance technique with the climactic onstage appearance of a lone female Sufi dancer, whose entrance onto the stage is set against the fusion sounds of ambient trance, evokes a highly complex network of global and local tensions, not only between different culturally prescribed ways of moving, but between local forms of secular commercialism and religious worship, and between traditional and modern Sufi Muslim beliefs concerning women's participation in public whirling rituals.[12] In this way, Turkey's adaptation of SYTYCD traffics lavishly in the sensual pleasures of global youth culture's appropriations of Black and Latin gestural and rhythmic aesthetics, while at the same time signaling and renegotiating social and national identities through movement and performance styles that enlist the body in television's own ongoing cross-fertilization of global and local markets. And although symbolic resolution of ethnic, racial, gender or religious tensions may be speciously effected through these processes, the success of the flamenco–Sufi performance in particular, like the SYTYCD franchise overall, is that it produces through juxtapositions of human movement global sentiments that are always inevitably specific to a particular history and place and cast of familiar characters, or characterizations. From this standpoint, it would be wrong to assume, as some critics of global media have, that the transnational merchandizing of "reality" television formats is tantamount to the homogenization or Americanization of global media space. Nor can we say that global media produces internationalism or cultural cosmopolitanism as the pure antithesis to national identities. As Ien Ang demonstrates, to assume such would be to ignore "the fact that what counts as part of a national identity is often a site of intense struggle between a plurality of cultural groupings and interests inside a nation, and that therefore national identity is . . . fundamentally a dynamic, conflictive, unstable and impure phenomenon.[13]

As Ang and others argue, these dynamics and instabilities are themselves the very stuff we recognize as "national identity." And as my discussion of SYTYCD is intended to show, reality dance competition formats inevitably work to allegorize and narrativize these cross-currents in ways that underscore the potential usefulness of dance studies for global television scholarship. Another format we might consider in this context is *Dancing with the Stars* (DWTS), a reality dance show that is based on Great Britain's *Strictly Come Dancing* and distributed through BBC Worldwide. The licensing rights were first sold to Australia in 2003, and since then the show has become one of BBC's top overseas exports. Under various titles, the format has been adapted in Austria, Belgium, Chile, Croatia, the Czech Republic, Denmark, Estonia, Finland, Germany, India, Israel, Italy, Japan, the Netherlands, New Zealand, Norway, Poland, Portugal, Russia, the Slovak Republic, South Africa, Sweden, Turkey, Ukraine, and the United States. These adaptations have proven to be extremely popular with television audiences in the largest markets as well as in the smallest regions, with the unexpected effect of enhancing the global visibility and popularity of ballroom dancing as a social and cultural pastime.

Unlike SYTYCD, which produces the transformation of an unknown dancer to national celebrity, DWTS relies on the established cultural capital of nationally known celebrities—actors, athletes, pop singers, talk-show hosts, models, journalists, and media "personalities"—in attracting audiences to witness their transformation from inexperienced (and often clumsy) novices into deft and graceful ballroom dancers. This is accomplished by pairing the celebrities with professional dancers for weekly "real time" performances—broadcast live, so that the camera captures every movement, every misstep, and every facial expression. The performances are scored by a panel of judges and then combined with interactive audience call-in votes. Like SYTYCD, the weekly competition culminates in a dramatic "results" show, as the lowest scoring couple is eliminated. Week by week, the group of remaining dancers is winnowed down, until the winning couple is finally determined.

In an insightful analysis of the kinds of social scripts generated by the U.S. adaptation of *Strictly Come Dancing*, Denise Davis identifies elements of the format's broad appeal that help account for its international popularity and, at the same time, its locally specific legibility. On one hand, as she aptly puts it, the show is "a grand experiment; the Petri dish on a parquet floor," as viewers in different markets tune in to watch celebrity icons who are familiar and yet remote become humanized as they attempt to master styles of movement that are wholly unfamiliar to them.[14] As their celebrity status is demystified, these contestants are often humbled before the public, which allows for a different kind of audience identification based as much in sympathy as in voyeurism—a sort of ballroom schadenfreude. For example, the question of how long Willie Thorne, the former British snooker champion, commentator, and recovered gambling addict, will last on Season Five of *Strictly Come Dancing* (alongside the question of what he's doing there in the first place) was, as the show aired a topic of considerable buzz in the U.K. blogosphere. On the other hand, all of the celebrity participants, despite differences in physical attractiveness, agility, social class, and age are confronted with the same obstacle: none of them knows how to dance. Ostensibly, this creates a level playing field among contestants whereupon anyone, through sheer determination, work ethic, and desire, can become an expert dancer. This fairy tale component of the show's arc can contain as many local particularities as discursive relations between and among celebrity contestants and viewers will produce, and is as much a part of its marketing to audiences for Танцы со звездами in Russia and locations linked to its mediascapes ("И всё-таки основная цель шоу—показать, что танцевать могут все" [And nevertheless the basic purpose of the show is to demonstrate that everyone can dance.]) as to audiences in the U.S.A. and Western Europe.[15]

However, once again it is by locating concrete flashpoints of disjuncture between official narratives of social identity (that continue to underwrite concepts of national culture and media) and counter-narratives produced by the dancing body's embrace, revision, or rejection of movement styles that we see where and how global television interacts with the local. In her reading of ABC's Season Two of *Dancing with the Stars*, Davis focuses on the "unscripted" narrative juxtaposition of the show's two African-American male contestants, rap mogul P. Miller (a.k.a. "Master P") and American football star Jerry Rice. As she demonstrates, over the course of the season an arc narrative gradually yet unmistakably emerged that established drama through the repeated contrast of the two men's movement styles, work ethic, and attitudes toward the presumed effeminacy, whiteness, and class connotations of ballroom culture. Although the story appeared "naturally" generated week to week, the resulting clash of the "gangsta" rapper vs. the "gentleman" athlete rehearsed long-held, socially constructed myths concerning race, masculinity, and black manhood in the United States. Davis shows how editing and scripted elements, in conjunction with the men's own physical and verbal negotiations of the contradictory discursive spaces that render black masculinity seemingly incompatible with the grace and social refinement of ballroom, simultaneously reinforced and challenged stereotypes of black male representation on U.S. television. Rebellious Master P, who acknowledged from the start his desire to fuse hip-hop and ballroom styles, and whose casual rehearsal schedule, non-regulation dance attire, and traipsing, graceless performances brought his professional partner to tears before the national audience following a cha-cha routine, was eliminated in the fourth round. The audience support that sustained him for the first few weeks, despite the judges' consensus that he was the worst of the dancers, reached a tipping point. The more accommodating Rice, whose dedication to the normative value of work ethic, willingness to alter his movement orientation in accordance with ballroom convention, and affirmation of the American national myth of equal mobility through hard work, was rewarded: He continued onto the finals, only to lose the competition in the last round to former boy-band singer Drew Lachey and his partner Cheryl Burke.

Research such as this offers a concrete illumination of the ways that global formats provide distinctive frames for the rearrangement of relations of national, social, and cultural authority. Analyzing and comparing these frames allows television scholars to trace the "subterranean tactics by which informal popular identities are created" within and even against static categories of national culture —the visions of which accompanied Cat Deeley's announcement of SYTYCD's explosion onto the global stage.[16] But investigations of this expansive nature require that we hold in place multiple complex systems. Indeed, from this perspective, the study of globally marketed television formats such as the reality dance format may be viewed as a contribution to translation studies or to the effort to imagine a comparativism of media cultures overall, in the sense that Michal Riffaterre understands it as an attempt "to explain what is lost and what is gained in translations between the distinct value systems of different cultures, media, disciplines, and institutions."[17]

Such translations and appropriations do not occur monolithically, of course, but in contexts that communicate the continually changing configuration of national bodies and identifications. I want to highlight this with a discussion of a segment from Israel's *Nolad Lirkod*, in which questions of bodily movement converge with questions of cultural transmission, bodily migrations, affiliation and difference, ultimately illustrating the potential responsiveness of human movement studies to some of the more well-established tools of television and cultural analysis, in particular debates about the knotty discursive imbrications of race, gender, nation, and immigration.

The segment is transcribed from an episode of the first season of *Nolad Lirkod*, which was broadcast on Keshet TV Channel 2 in 2005–6. On January 14, 2006, one of the twelve remaining finalists was Shou-ee, a female dancer who immigrated to Israel after meeting her husband, an Israeli national, in her native China. At the time of the competition, Shou-ee could neither read nor speak in Hebrew, so she communicated with the audience, with her dance partners, and with host, Zvika Hadar, in English. For Hadar, a popular television personality and comedian, Shou-ee's lack of language and knowledge of Israeli culture, compounded by her visible self-consciousness, make her an irresistible target of ridicule. "It fell down, oh god," he shrieks in a high-pitched mock-feminine voice, as Shou-ee fumbles nervously while selecting from a hat the piece of paper that will reveal the name of her partner for the dance routine. "Do you know what's written here in Hebrew," Hadar taunts. Shou-ee turns the paper upside down and back again, indicating that she cannot read it. From behind her, one of the other female dancers whispers the name in her ear. "Shai," she shouts. Her partner, Shai Fartush, then selects the second piece of paper that will reveal their dance style. "African," he reads aloud.

"No say African!" Shou-ee appears aghast and insulted. Hadar jokingly explains the dance style to her. "No rice, we eat the men now," he says in broken English.

"Oh, cannibal, ooh, big man, ah-ha, is coming. You have to run with your dancing."

The scene cuts to Shou-ee and Shai in rehearsals for the African dance routine. Shou-ee is having difficulty mastering the technique and the body movements, which their choreographer explains will be the key to success. "At the beginning, I was very embarrassing [sic] to try the movement," Shou-ee says to the camera, as she and Shai are interviewed, "because it is really against Chinese culture."

The rehearsal scene cuts to a back story segment, as viewers learn about the circumstances that brought Shou-ee to Israel. To assist with the translation, Shou-ee's sister-in-law, Shari, is introduced and the two women sit side by side and speak directly to the camera. "I met my husband in China," says Shou-ee, as romantic piano music plays gently in the background. "Love at first sight, the two of them," Shari explains. "I'm going to living [sic] here," Shou-ee continues ". . . I'm going to study Hebrew." "So I won't have to translate for her anymore," says Shari.

They are interrupted by Shari's cellphone. It's Shou-ee's husband, and his call appears completely spontaneous. "I can't believe you're calling," says Shari. Shou-ee reels with elation as she grabs the phone, "Oh my god, oh my god. I love you. I'm so happy you called to say hello to the audience." She points the phone directly toward the camera, as her husband's voice is heard saying "Shalom!"

After a warm, sentimental interview segment featuring Shai's mother, the scene cuts once again to the dancers in rehearsal. Shou-ee is bent over deeply at the waist, swinging her arms and looking for her lower point of gravity. She appears very uncomfortable. Suddenly she strands up straight and laughs. "Like a monkey, my god" she says. "Yes, like a monkey," the choreographer replies impatiently. Cut again to Shou-ee, speaking to the camera. "Slowly, slowly, I can try," she discloses. "But still it is a very embarrassing movement." Shai, sitting besides her, concludes the segment by voicing his confidence in his partner's ability to master the routine.

As the scene finally cuts to the stage and to Hadar's introduction of their performance, dramatic tension has been established, as viewers wonder whether or not Shou-ee will be able to overcome her multiple verbal and physical conflicts and her cultural resistance to the polycentrism of African dance style, which segments the body and directs movement according to different rhythmical components. However, as Shou-ee and Shai take the stage and dance to the global fusion remix of Mory Kante's 1987 "Yeke Yeke," their performance wins everyone over with its athleticism and expressivity. The studio audience responds enthusiastically (Shai has already become a popular favorite and will go on to win second place in the competition), and the judges are similarly impressed with the pair's mastery of the demanding choreography and technical components.

Ido Tadmore sums up his judgment in a word: "Bravo."

Michal Amdurski follows, addressing Shou-ee in English: "Honey, honey, honey, you don't have to be embarrassed. You did it extremely well. Unbelievably good."

After the judges deliver their remarks, Hadar announces the upcoming performers and invites viewers to stay tuned as the program breaks for a brief commercial pause. As he speaks, a boldly orchestrated musical theme strikes up in the background. In the interim preceding the commercial, a quick succession of video clips shows the dancers posturing on the urban streets and grassy hills of Tel-Aviv in tank tops, sports bras, battle fatigues, and camouflage face paint. Striking group poses that combine formal elements of fashion photography, war imagery, and hip-hop attitude, they wield an array of firearms, from small hand guns (for the women) to Kalashnikovs (for the men), thus delivering a series of tableaux that convey a mixture of national militarism and global youth culture style.

Reading these segments as a whole, we find a purposefully edited arc narrative of multiple cross-cultural, cross-social migrations and their stabilization. The hyperbolic framing of racial threat and gender exoticism (i.e. the African body as savage and "embarrassing"; the Asian female body as reticent and culture-bound) collides with an emotive rhetorical affirmation of heterosexual romantic love that is both bi-national and cross-racial. Shou-ee (whose husband is disembodied, appearing only as a voice over the wireless network) is induced repeatedly to perform her resistance to, yet desire for the national—in language, in cultural knowledge, and in love. Although she comes across as merely flighty, her body is positioned as a site of intense struggle. She is both verbally inappropriate to the Hebrew tongue and physically inappropriate to global dance styles. However, her successful adaptation to African movement, which is positively if not somewhat condescendingly evaluated in both English and Hebrew by the judges as well as by Hadar (who makes a bawdy reference in Hebrew to "key parties" following the couple's routine, only to quickly reassure Shou-ee, "don't worry"), suggests that she has found her expressive register, earned her place within a new configuration of bodily movement and social articulation. The polycentrism of African dance and its demands on the body thus stands as an allegory of the migratory demands and ideological tensions that help shape worldwide entertainments such as the reality television dance format. At the same time, the video tableaux that lead into the commercial break strikingly reveal that the bodily affects of Israeli national militarism may be reasserted and amplified within these configurations. In this locally produced narrative of self-refashioning across racial, cultural, and national boundaries, dance offers a socially sanctioned way of taming the "other" within, precisely in terms of the disciplined body's adaptability to the shifting requirements of globalization's management within distinctive imagined worlds.

We might venture further, and say that the goal of such adaptations, as Jack Z. Bratich sees the goal of Reality TV overall, "is the creation of malleable subjects adequate to new economic and social conditions."[18] From this perspective, Tom Bergeron's opening monologue from Season Two of *Dancing With the Stars*, in which he tells viewers, "What you'll see tonight, really, is the first chapter of an unfolding drama, one that will be controlled in part by you," is at once the tantalizing promise of interactive media and its signal deflection away from the fundamental technologies of Deleuze's control societies.[19] Indeed, to the extent that reality programming is above all invested in programming viewers, the ultimate goal of reality dance formats may be understood as strikingly and perhaps disconcertingly consistent with the labor demands of global capital and post-Fordist production, as the laboring subjects of globalization, like competitive dance contestants, "are trained together to work in temporary groups, to respond to tasks quickly, to assess their progress through continuous reports, and to enhance their interpersonal communicative skills."[20] The taxing physical demands, rapid adjustments to new movement styles and partners, and responsiveness to judges' criticisms while generating positive public response are tasks conducive to the development of an increasingly integrative world system that is shaping an increasingly "nomadic, self-reflexive, and flexible" body of labor.[21]

Accordingly, as Marc Andrejevic notes, interactive reality television has developed into a profitable corporate apparatus, one aimed at inducing television contestants and viewers alike to submit themselves to ubiquitous processes of surveillance. From his perspective, Foucauldian self-disclosure has increasingly become part of the labor that television viewers are induced to perform as fans. Self-disclosure, or the willing release of information to corporations about oneself and one's consumer interests, ostensibly facilitates the fashionable customization of social networks, advertising, and consumer services. At the same time, it absolves corporations of the threat that is associated with excessive electronic monitoring, totalitarian governmentality. While certain forms of aggressive commercial monitoring continue to be perceived as invasive and threatening—as in the case of unsolicited telemarketing, computer spam, and fears of identity theft—corporate strategies of inducing self-disclosure seem to positively affirm the sense that one's own interests and well-being are benefited.[22]

For participants and contestants on reality programming, dramatic self-disclosure and submission to surveillance remain the twin guarantors of authenticity and genuineness, "the promise of the real in reality TV."[23] In the U.S. version of SYTYCD, authenticity is legibly communicated through, among other things, emotional loss of control, as dancers and judges routinely shed tears or emotionally break down before the audience. Authenticity is further reinforced through the recurring theme of growth, or self-actualization, as dancers are either eliminated or advanced to the next stage of competition for exhibiting, or for failing to demonstrate, the capacity for growth and change over time. Fans similarly judge dancers and forge identifications with them based on an allegedly meritorious journey toward self-growth. A message post from "Candyce" on Realty TV Magazine.com, admits to this tendency: "omg ok, i cannot believe they left lacey there and lauren left. but oh well. i think neil should win because he's the dancer who's grown the most and deserves the title."[24] A blog by "Clark" on "Kulturblog" reiterates it: "In terms of technique Danny is by far the best. His solos have been outstanding. . . . He's always been quite good in his partnering. Further he's one of the figures who's [sic] grown the most in the show."[25]

Germany's *You Can Dance* entices audiences with a promise of reality via surveillance in a segment (that can be accessed on the show's official website) entitled "Room Check with Estefania."[26]

> [Voice Over] Imagine: In this moment a camera team forces its way into your bedroom and films every corner. What would it see? Dirty clothes or something worse? And this is exactly what the candidates from *You Can Dance* experienced. Estefania Küster went into their rooms without giving any warning . . .

Estefania's mundane discoveries—which include piles of unwashed clothing, evidence of a fruit diet, macho displays of empty beer and alcohol cans, stuffed animals, and socks drying on a heat ventilator (a trick learned from mother) —serve as innocent and unremarkable affirmations of normative gender, sexual, and Oedipal family relations. But their banality is precisely the point. "Room Check" assures viewers that they are granted unobstructed, intimate access to the most ordinary, everyday expressions of character—the inner truth— and not only to the well-rehearsed performances that constitute the staged personalities of dancers in performance. At the same time, and perhaps more importantly, "Room Check" invites viewers—ostensibly positioned as voyeurs—to enter the scene by imagining themselves similarly intruded upon and to ask themselves what, in such an instance, would be revealed. And it is precisely this mutual cannibal- ization of subject–object positions that highlights "the paradox of a surveillance economy," which on one hand acclimates viewers "to an emerging economic regime predicated on increasingly unequal access to and control over informa- tion," and on the other hand implicitly grants them control over the production of the "real," thus allowing them to forge potentially therapeutic, mobile, and transformative identifications with dancers whose very lives and fortunes are being directed by us.[27]

And yet the problem with this perspective— however rigorously theorized— is that it fails to take into account local histories, national narratives, and regional sense-making strategies that render it ultimately counterproductive for us to think of surveillance economies or their political concatenations as abstract or homogeneous. The move toward global television studies, as this collection of essays demonstrates, is a move toward understanding the work of watching and of "being watched" as rooted labor that becomes indigenized just as quickly as new global television formats are introduced into societies. And from this pers- pective, the meaning of surveillance in "Room Check with Estefania" will be grounded as much in debates concerning powers of surveillance in German history and society (as were recently reignited by the international success of the film, *Das Leben Der Anderen*), and current debates over the powers of the state to conduct counter-terrorist surveillance within Germany, as in debates over global capital- ism's powers to penetrate and produce reality in any given time and place. To put it another way, global television's "reality" is produced in the flash points where these discourses meet and compete.

Which is to say that if *Dancing with the Stars* and *So You Think You Can Dance* show us anything it is that the dancer is not always the dance. "Realities," like dance movements, are managed yet unsettled; they must be variously and continuously adapted and brokered. Movement may be softened, de-sexualized, radicalized, secularized, cross-dressed, militarized, racialized, and coutured, all of which becomes evident when we pay attention to the specific configurations of male and female partnering, the locations of the body's center(s), the closeness of the embrace, the delineation of body parts, the earth-centeredness of the feet, the power behind the "pop and lock," the aesthetics of female delicacy over male muscularity. Similarly, fantasies and anxieties concerning the national body's ability to manage contradictory discursive positions are legible in format elements that contextualize human movement and manage the ways in which bodily meanings are fashioned: costume; set design; music selection; the diverse personalities and social backgrounds of the chosen dancers; the dynamics and magnetism of their couplings; the staging, production, and editing of back-story, interview, and rehearsal segments; the evaluations of the judges; the branding and positioning of the host; the responsiveness of studio audiences; the voting patterns and "chatter" generated by viewers at home and across various media platforms, all combine to produce the one thing that television is ultimately all about: "a good story, emotionally told."[28]

Or so contends Gerhard Zeiler, chief executive of Europe's largest TV, radio, and production company, RTL Group. For Zeiler, the biggest opportunity in the age of global television formats is the "content business," by which he means story-telling, or the challenge of tailoring global stories "just enough to suit local tastes while staying true to the original idea."[29] Recognizing this industry logic and the challenge that it presents to television scholarship, this essay argues that interactive reality dance formats mobilize human movement styles and traditions to meet these new challenges. Moreover, it argues for the need to develop tools for the interpretation of dance formats as art forms that are uniquely adaptive to the discursive intertwining of global and local identities in many different parts of the world. In this, it reiterates and advances the arguments made by dance scholars such as Jane Desmond: To the extent that nationality is mapped onto bodily difference, along with other persistent categories of identity, dance represents one of the most "intensely affective" and lamentably under-valued dimensions of cultural analysis.[30] The international popularity of SYTYCD invites us to open media and television research to questions of human movement, particularly insofar as they link the mediated body to theoretical debates concerning the production of identities, subjects, and bodily materiality. Whether it be dressed for ballroom or ballos, break-dance or belly dance, the human body is a productive site of global television's industrial and textual story-telling practices. We can gain much from learning how to listen to it.

However, while global television is often thought to disrupt existing forms of national identity it also offers opportunities for new forms of "sociotechnological bonding," new ways of forging the affect of solidarity among variously situated audiences across various social channels of televisual reception and participation.[31] In such a precarious environment, the adaptability of reality dance formats may reside in the fact that they empower national versions of culture through a sort of popular cosmopolitanism that might otherwise be read as a disavowal of national-ism. The possibility, contradictory though it may seem, recalls Bruce Robbins' premise that "forms of global feeling are continuous with," rather than contrary to, "forms of national feeling."[32] Thus, kinesthetic dissonance may ultimately thicken loyalties to nation through a mass media competition that enacts an allegory of expanding transnational reach and cross-cultural mastery. And if this is the case, any critical effort to decipher what it is that gives *Benimle Dans Eder Misin* its Turkishness or *Dansefeber* its Norwegianess will need to be situated in these multiple exchanges and flows. This essay is intended as a first step toward understanding the situated and conjectural forms of nationalized internationalism in television formats that allegorize mastery over the global through a dance of difference.

Notes

1 See, for example, Jane Desmond, ed., *Meaning in Motion: New Cultural Studies of Dance*, Durham, NC and London: Duke University Press, 1997; Alexandra Carter, *The Routledge Dance Studies Reader*, London: Routledge, 1998; Ramsay Burt, *Alien Bodies: Representations of Modernity, "Race" and Nation in Early Modern Dance*, London and New York: Routledge, 1998; V. A. Briginshaw, *Dance, Space, and Subjectivity*, Basingstoke and New York: Palgrave Macmillan, 2001; Helen Thomas, *The Body, Dance, and Cultural Theory*, Basingstoke and New York: Palgrave Macmillan, 2003.

2 *So You Think You Can Dance*, Season One, July 20, 2005. Fox 43 TV, Norfolk, Virginia.

3 This process in itself has become the subject of popular legend, as evidenced in the theatrical and more recent cinematic adaptation of John Waters' *Hairspray*. Here, *The Corny Collins Show* (a fictional dance show modeled on *American Bandstand*) links a fictionalized 1960 conflict over racial integration at a local Baltimore television station to the myth of national liberal democratic progress in the struggle for racial justice and civic equality.

4 Albert Moran, *Copycat Television: Globalisation, Program Formats and Cultural Identity*. Luton, U.K.: University of Luton Press, 1998: 13.

5 www.dailyfrappe.com/Home/tabid/36/articleType/ArticleView/articleId/2358/SO-YOU-THINK-YOU-CAN-DANCE-BEGINS-ON-MEGA.aspx. Accessed: September, 25, 2007.

6 The author wishes to thank Haci Osman Gunduz, Avi Santo, Heidi Schlipphacke, for assistance with translations from Turkish, Hebrew, and German, respectively.

7 "Kumatar" literally means "someone who tosses sand."

8 An idiom is used here, which describes one who rarely speaks.

9 Translated, this means "bud."

10 YouTube. www.youtube.com/watch?v=qA1DyI9bybE. Accessed: September 25, 2007.

11 Jane Desmond, "Embodying Difference: Issues in Dance and Cultural Studies." *Cultural Critique* 26 (1993–1994): 35.

12 YouTube. www.youtube.com/watch?v=vY8IO_ilTKM. Accessed: September 25, 2007.

13 Ien Ang, "Culture and Communication: Toward an Ethnographic Critique of Media Consumption in the Transnational Media System," in *Planet TV: A Global Reader*, eds. Lisa Parks and Shanti Kumar, New York and London: New York University Press, 2003: 369.

14 Denise Davis, "More Than Just Ballroom: *Dancing with the Stars* and the Reality of Representation." Unpublished Essay. Old Dominion University. April 18, 2007.

15 http://stardance.org.ua/stardance1/. Accessed: September 25, 2007.

16 Ang, 369.

17 Michel Riffatere, "On the Complimentarity of Comparative Literature and Cultural Studies," in *Comparative Literature in the Age of Multiculturalism*, ed. C. Bernheimer, Baltimore: Johns Hopkins University Press, 1995: 67.

18 Jack Z. Bratich, "Programming Reality: Control Societies, New Subjects and the Powers of Transformation," in *Makeover Television: Realities Remodeled*, ed. Dana Heller, London: I. B. Tauris, 2007: 7.
19 *Dancing with the Stars*, 201. January 5, 2005. WVEC, Norfolk, VA.
20 Ibid., 12.
21 Ibid., 12.
22 Marc Andrejevic, *Reality TV: The Work of Being Watched*. Lanham, MD: Rowman & Littlefield, 2004: 106–8.
23 Ibid., 108.
24 "Candyce," Reality TV Magazine. "*So You Think You Can Dance* Results—Lauren Gottlieb and Pasha Kovalev Eliminated." www.realitytvmagazine.com/blog/2007/08/so-you-think—5.html. Posted: August 16, 2007. Accessed: September 26, 2007.
25 "Clark," Kulturblog, "*So You Think You Can Dance Finale*," www.kulturblog.com/2007/08/so-you-think-you-can-dance-finale/. Accessed: September 26, 2007.
26 Sat 1. *You Can Dance*. www.sat1.de/comedy_show/youcandance/. Accessed: September 26, 2007.
27 Andrejevic, 111.
28 Andrew Edgecliffe-Johnson, "Local TV Lights up Global Sets," *Financial Times*, September 13, 2007, 12.
29 Ibid.
30 Desmond, 57.
31 Bruce Robbins, *Feeling Global: Internationalism in Distress*. New York and London: New York University Press, 1999: 33.
32 Ibid., 6.

3

TELEVISION FORMATS AND CONTEMPORARY SPORT

Tony Schirato

Introduction

This chapter is concerned with the relation between television formats and developments in television-mediated sport. More specifically, it will consider how the logics, imperatives, narratives and technologies of television-as-formats transform a series of physical activities into something both other and more than itself. At a basic level and by way of exemplification, the simple division of sport into live and studio based formats (a development that has only become commonplace over the last fifty years) constitutes a significant extension of the field, producing and requiring new forms of analysis, knowledge, discourses, categories of expertise, modes of address and technologies of mediation (within both fields). For the purposes of this work the concept of the television format will be understood, following Moran, as both a "form, a formula, a style, a template in a series of different fields" and, at the same time, "a mode of procedure" (Moran 2006, 19). In other words, the concept of the format is treated here as a variation of a generic structure, with the implication being that it does more than simply contain or facilitate different contents, but actually inflects, disposes and even produces meanings, narratives, ways of seeing and modes of spectatorship. It is generic because, in John Frow's terms, it functions as:

> A set of conventional and highly organised constraints on the production and interpretation of meaning . . . its structuring effects guide, in a way that a builder's form gives shape to a pour of concrete, or a sculptor's mould shapes and gives structure to its materials. Generic structure both enables and restricts meanings, and is a basic condition for meaning to take place . . . No symbolically organised action takes place other than through the

shaping of generic codes, where "shaping" means both "shaping by" and "shaping of": acts and structures work upon and modify each other.

(Frow 2006, 10)

In keeping with Frow's notion of generic framing as a dynamic and interactive process that simultaneously shapes and is shaped, this essay will attempt to identify, explain and analyse how the content of sport has both been influenced and even transformed by, and deformed or modified, the generic formats of television. This line of inquiry is further contextualised by a consideration of what Pierre Bourdieu (Bourdieu 1991) refers to as the logics, discourses, habitus, ethos and imperatives of the relevant cultural fields – in this case sport and the television-as-business. Put simply, if we are to describe, analyse and understand the ways in which television formats and sport have influenced one another, then we need to be aware of the field-specific contexts that have provided the impetus for the development of a relationship that is both long-lived (it dates back to the 1930s) and contemporary (the contemporary sport–media nexus is really a post-1960s phenomenon).

A cultural field, in Bourdieu's sense of the term (Bourdieu 1998), can be understood as a cognate group of entities joined together by, and recognisable in terms of, certain core imperatives, values, functions, rules, categories and characteristics. Institutions, bureaucracies, titles, rules and categories are, however, only the objective manifestation of a cultural field. Fields and their objectivities are simultaneously constituted through and constitutive of a habitus, understood as an ethos and set of dispositions which are embodied by its members, animate and justify its practices, and speak (through and for) the field as a discourse-as-belief. In England (and to a lesser extent the United States) at the end of the nineteenth century the status, popularity and institutionalised nature of activities such as cricket, various forms of football and athletics testified to the transformation of a more or less random collection of games and physical activities into a recognisable and relatively autonomous cultural field, with a concomitant set of values, logics and dispositions, animated by and reproduced through a distinctive habitus. This was manifested in various ways, such as the spread and influence of the idea of the superiority of participating in games rather than simply winning them; the production of the body as a critical site of pedagogy and discipline; new forms of pleasure-as-spectatorship; the forging of a sense of communal identity through an association with sporting teams; and perhaps most significantly, the development of an entirely new relationship to the notion of play, which took on a significant cultural value despite being very much at odds with the dominant (business-driven) ethos of the time.

Sport, because of its discursive commitment to utopian principles, locates itself at what Bourdieu refers to as the autonomous pole (Bourdieu 1993), while the commercial media, which are to some extent indistinguishable from, and animated by logics and imperatives derived from, the field of business, are to be found at the opposite, heteronomous pole of the field of cultural production (Bourdieu 1993). More specifically commercial television, for Bourdieu, is dominated by the twin constraints of "time" and "effect" (Bourdieu 1998). He makes the point that even with a genre like news the very limited time available to "do" a story means that issues have to be pared back and decontextualised. The twin imperatives of time and effect make it virtually impossible for television programs to say anything that is not sensationalised or simplistic. In fact it really doesn't make sense for them to say anything much at all, which is why the news is invariably dominated by visuals. A thirty-second description of a massacre, famine, riot or war strains to have an immediate emotional effect – which is what the news is meant to accomplish. Film of a person being beaten to death, of emaciated babies, of crowds destroying buildings, or of bombs zeroing in on bridges or enemy troops takes the viewer into the story, and can provoke an immediate, and strong, response (pity, anger, fear, revulsion, elation). These field-specific logics are largely accepted, complied with and naturalised across the field and its practices, which means that commercial television formats are largely carried over and reproduced when those formats are applied, with appropriate variations, to televisual sport.

From the perspectives offered by Moran, Frow and Bourdieu, we can say that genres and formats effectively produce and delimit textual representations. Television genres and formats are derived from, and more or less commensurate with regard to, the logic/economy of time and effect. Consequently, when those genres and formats are passed onto and frame activities within other cultural fields – such as sport – there is likely to be a degree of transformation extending both ways: television formats invariably mould sport, but at the same time the disinterested, passionate and utopian dimension to sport is a potentially valuable commodity which television must accommodate.

Live Television Coverage of Sport

There has been a close relationship between the field of sport and the print media since the latter part of the nineteenth century, and prior to the Second World War radio sports coverage played a significant role in both the USA and the UK (Guttmann 1986). This changed quickly in the United States: television attracted large audiences with its telecasts of boxing and college football in the 1940s and 1950s, and generally replaced radio to the extent that while the latter had been an "essential part of daily life" in America in the 1930s, by the end of the 1940s "the average American listened to the radio for only twenty four minutes a day" (Guttmann 1986, 134). In Britain the changeover was more gradual due to the well-established status and influence of BBC radio and the relatively slow development of a national transmitter system, but whereas in the "early 1950s less than 5% of households" possessed television sets, by the 1970s "this was the proportion of those that did not" (Hill 2002, 103).

The format that most helped to sell the television–sport nexus to a wide demographic in Britain and America was the live outdoor coverage, particularly of popular events such as football games, boxing matches and horse racing meetings (see Holt 1989; Boyle and Haynes 2000; Hill 2002). Live sporting telecasts have their own particular characteristics and forms of address predicated on the imperative to simulate, as closely as possible, the "feel" of being at the game. Initially the limitations of the technology of the 1930s, 1940s and 1950s made live television sport a poor substitute for the real thing, since "cameras were fixed and were fitted with lenses that made the performers appear as tiny figures" (Cashmore 1990, 144). Referring to technical problems encountered in the BBC's televising of a rugby international between England and Scotland in 1938, and more specifically in the mismatch between the visual text and the authentic experience of live, at the ground spectators, Boyle and Haynes explain that:

> the positioning of the cameras was clearly viewed as the optimum use of the telephoto lenses to capture the play in each third of the field. The sheer bulkiness of the technology required to transmit for sport, specifically the mass of cable involved, severely restricted the mobility of the equipment. The problem of economically marshalling the technology needed on location took many years to resolve.
>
> (Haynes and Boyle 2000, 41)

However, by the 1960s techniques and technology had improved, equipment had become more mobile, and the live televisual text was now:

> able to combine documentary accuracy with a fast tension worthy of the most thrill-packed sports occasions. The high-gloss presentations had analyses of slow-motion replays and frozen moments, knowledgeable commentaries-cum-evaluations, and detailed close-ups that captured facial – and sometimes verbal – expressions that the attending fans could never pick up. Around the event, TV learned to edit events down to lean action and pad events with previews, postscripts, and all manner of factual information, all designed to make viewing from home a more enriching experience.
>
> (Cashmore 1990, 144–5)

The development of the live sport broadcast format in the United States in the 1960s (which was to bring about the transformation of sport into a more intensive televisual event, and influence approaches in Britain, Australia, Europe and Asia) was based on satisfying two imperatives that were central to the commercial television: first, appeal to the widest demographic in order to maximise revenue; and second, and by way of facilitating the first imperative, hyperbolise everything so that it becomes more dramatic, spectacular and attention-grabbing. The first significant attempt to address these imperatives came about when American television sports producer Roone Arledge introduced a number of innovations to television sport, including the aforementioned slow-motion replays, but also split screens; halftime analysis and highlights; hand-held close-up shots; situational cameras and microphones; cameras and microphones directed at the crowd to help build a sense of atmosphere; tightly edited packages that increased suspense and eliminated "slow" play; opinionated "personalities" as announcers; and Monday Night Football and the *Wide World of Sports* program. The idea was that "the marriage of sports and innovative entertainment techniques would produce higher ratings" (Roberts and Olson 1997, 418). Television had "been content to bring the viewer the game" (Roberts and Olson 1997, 418) by using a small number of static cameras. This was enough "for those who loved football, but it was not very attractive to the casual viewer" (Roberts and Olson 1997, 418) who had:

> one eye on the screen and one hand on the dial . . . Arledge wrote: "What we set out to do was to get the audience involved emotionally. If they didn't give a damn about the game, they still might enjoy the program." To do this Arledge used more cameras. He put cameras on cranes and blimps and helicopters to provide a better view of the stadium, the campus, and the town. His technicians developed hand-held cameras for close-ups. In the stadium he employed seven cameras, three just for capturing the environment. "We asked ourselves: If you were sitting in the stadium, what would you be looking at? The coach on the sideline, the substitute quarterback warming up, the pretty girl in the next section. So our camera wandered as your eyes would." Often what Arledge decided would interest his mostly male viewers were young and beautiful women . . . The game was only one part of the sporting experience.
>
> (Roberts and Olson 1997, 418)

The use of technologies and techniques that take you "to the game", along with changes to rules that are designed to make professional sport attractive to a wider demographic, has necessarily brought live sport coverage closer to the logics and characteristics of what Guy Debord calls the spectacle, a kind of hystericised and hyperbolised production of the event where "Everything that appears is good; whatever is good will appear" (Debord 2006, 15). The problem is that a sporting event rarely provides enough of the good – that is, provides enough of a distraction – to keep viewers attentive or interested for a protracted period: an NFL game may be too one-sided and therefore dead as a contest by halftime, or a soccer match may drag on towards a dull scoreless draw because neither side is prepared to risk losing. When nothing is happening in televised sport, commentators need to produce something in its place – soap-like passion, drama, scandal, rivalry, heroism, dreams, sex, celebrities, ambition, betrayal, power struggles and intrigue. These new viewers, who are often unfamiliar with rules and traditions and illiterate and/or indifferent with regard to skills, have exercised a considerable influence both over media coverage of sport and the way it's played. If this viewer is unsure whether, in Bourdieu's terms, the game "is worth the candle" (Bourdieu 2000), it's very much up to the media and sports administrators to ensure that it is – if only because being (even vaguely or ephemerally) attentive to the sports event provided television ratings and potential audiences for advertising. Consequently, televised sport is now watched by an increasing number of casual spectators who "see only violence and confusion" (Bourdieu 1991, 364). As Pierre Bourdieu writes, one only has to think of what is implied:

> in the fact that a sport like rugby (in France – but the same is true of American football in the USA) has become, through television, a mass spectacle, transmitted far beyond the circle of present or past "practitioners" ... to a public very imperfectly equipped with the specific competence needed to decipher it adequately. The "connoisseur" has schemes of perception and appreciation which enables him to see what the layman cannot see, to perceive a necessity where the outsider sees only violence and confusion, and so to find in the promptness of a movement, in the unforeseeable inevitability of a successful combination or the near-miraculous orchestration of a team strategy, a pleasure no less intense and learned than the pleasure a music-lover derives from the particularly successful rendering of a favourite work. The more superficial the perception, the less it finds its pleasure in the spectacle contemplated in itself and for itself, and the more it is drawn to the search for the "sensational".
>
> (Bourdieu 1991, 364)

This kind of bifurcation has characterised the relation between live television coverage and the sport of cricket. Commercial and television-driven imperatives have effectively led to both the live coverage and the game itself splitting into different generic formats: these are along the lines of the original version, played over five days (the test match), and the more recent one-day and twenty-twenty matches, which are concluded within eight and three hours, respectively. The live coverage of test matches reflects the pace, decorum and seriousness – the history-as-gravitas – of the game, whether it is on British, Australian, Indian, Caribbean or South African television. The technical changes and additions, such as cameras behind the bowlers at both ends, multiple cameras around the boundary, stump- and sky-cam, bowling speed readouts, and simulated ("Hawkeye") reproductions of and projections of the bowling line, length and direction, have not transformed or even impinged upon the style and pace of the coverage, or the way in which that coverage discursively and visually addresses the audience. Talking heads chat politely amongst themselves, provide a technical report on the state of the pitch, and don't become agitated or apologetic, or slip into the sensational, if there isn't a lot of immediate action. They presume that the audience is able to understand and appreciate that, because the game is spread over five days, significance and excitement will build gradually, and that there will be interest and even entertainment at the level of minutiae (a ball carefully defended, the flight achieved by a slow bowler). Live televisual test cricket is not only watched by Bourdieu's connoisseurs: the audience, regardless of their level of literacy, are interpellated as if they were connoisseurs: in other words, the commentary, visuals, information provided and forms of address – the parts that together constitute and characterise the format – are commensurate with the way in which test cricket understands the relationship between itself and its audience.

While the technical aspects of live television coverage of cricket have been refined and developed over the last forty years, the most significant changes to the approaches and imperatives of the format are to be found in coverage of one-day and twenty-twenty games. The supposed innovations that characterised the so-called "Packer revolution" of the 1970s (see Holt 1989; Cashmore 1990; Hill 2002), such as bringing in coloured clothing, stump-cameras, white balls, floodlit games, cameras at both ends of the ground and pitch-meters) were lauded for making a traditional, complex, nuanced and slow game more dramatic, interesting, relevant and involving for a generalist audience. In fact they simply brought in variations of techniques or technologies that had been in use in television coverage of American college, NFL, and NBA games for almost two decades. Even a recent development such as Skycam – used in the NFL and Australian rules to produce the effect of a soaring and swooping birds-eye view of the action – is just an extension of Ardledge's technology-driven attempt to make sport "more than itself".

International one-day matches, which date (not coincidentally) from the 1970s, are a good example of the transformation of a game in order to suit television. Unlike test cricket, one-day games are played both day and night, teams wear coloured clothing, the duration of the game is limited to approximately eight hours (and played at times that specifically fit in with the imperatives of television scheduling), and there are additional rules regarding the kind of deliveries that are legitimate, and fielding positions (which ensures that matches are livelier and more interesting to laymen). Twenty-twenty cricket, finally, is simply an ersatz and more frenetic version of the one-day game (with innovations such as "super-subs", etc.), and has only been played on a regular basis since the new millennium. It is even more designed to fit in with television schedules and requirements: games last a couple of hours, and players are wired to respond to questions from commentators – as the game is being played.

One-day and twenty-twenty cricket games are usually abhorred and avoided by traditionalists, but attract larger crowds and much higher television ratings; and the changes that have been developed in the format mirror the wider, younger, less cricket- literate demographic that make up a large part of their audience.

The most extreme and recent example of this development can be found in the Twenty-Twenty Indian Premier League (IPL) Cricket competition, which was designed primarily for live television (tickets are given away in their thousands in order to ensure a lively and visible crowd). The competition was created by the Board of Control for Cricket in India (BCCI), and television rights were secured by India's Sony Entertainment Television Network and Singapore's World Sport Group, with regional broadcasting rights being shared by networks in Australia, Britain, the Arab Gulf states, North America, South Africa, Pakistan and across Asia (see www.iplcricketforum.com/). The format is part Bollywood film, part Entertainment-Network (Indian style), with a (very quick) game of cricket sharing time with the dancing girls (and boys) and celebrities. At one game a prominent Bollywood star was refused entry to the team dugout to watch the game, so the league promptly changed the rules to allow this co-mingling of celebrities and sport – as the game is played.

Developments such as the IPL are symptomatic of the radical transformation of the live television sport coverage format, and not just with regard to cricket. Virtually all live television sport – the NFL in the United States, AFL in Australia, football in Italy, Brazil and Japan – are now tied in to servicing wider demographics – Bourdieu's laymen. Changes to the format have also changed, at what we might call a technical and generic level (format, forms of address, selection, omission and framing of shots), how games are seen and experienced. Viewers watching live television coverage of an NFL game are meant to be overwhelmed by, and caught up in, the build-up to the event. This is brought about in a number of ways. First, the upcoming game will be advertised, to saturation level, at least a week before the event takes place, usually by emphasising the significance of the game, which may be predicated on standings ("the battle for first place"), the quality of the participants ("two undefeated teams"), or the status, achievements and rivalries of some of the protagonists ("Randy Moss and Terrell Owens go head to head"; "Brett Favre is poised to break Dan Marino's touchdowns record"). The advertisement message will be accompanied by loud music and a frenetic race through clips of one team scoring, violent collisions and confrontations, superhuman bodies, players displaying extraordinary athleti-cism and skill (a spectacular quarterback pass and a diving reception), scantily clad cheer squads cavorting, and colourfully dressed and outfitted fans celebrating or in despair. The particular event is represented as both larger than life (for instance, the passion of players and spectators is beyond the ordinary and everyday) and unceasingly exciting. Players will be shown in a manner that emphasises their iconic status (a close-up of quarterback Brett Favre's grizzled, weathered and pain-ridden profile) or their imposing physicality (huge linemen shown, filmed up close and from below so that they seem to tower over the viewer). Moreover, the content, brevity and speed of the clips (in two senses: one scene quickly replaces another, and the action is often sped up) effectively work to guarantee that the game will be exciting.

Television advertisements of upcoming sporting events – a format in its own right – work to get the attention of viewers, but also dispose and create expectations: it's then up to the commentary team, and the techniques and technologies they bring to the coverage (camera angles, points of emphasis, what's shown in replays) to do everything they can to help meet these expectations, because the game itself will almost inevitably fall short of what has been promised. Even the most exciting game that goes down to the wire will have periods when nothing much is happening. Commentators can always go back to and analyse significant plays and developments, or project towards upcoming moments of excitement and drama. But for much of the time the here and now is a distraction – and a threat to the maintenance of viewer interest and attention. There are various techniques that commentators and directors use to overcome this challenge. Directors have numerous camera angles, close-ups, flying shots, blimp views and freeze frames from which to choose: there are usually enough available visuals that are sufficiently personal (the close-up of a coach's passion-filled face); sick-but-fascinating (the sight and sound of a safety flying into a vulnerable wide receiver); dramatic (the shot of a huge and imposing defensive line defending waiting to repel a running back from their one yard line); or aesthetic (the city lights at night, skaters on a nearby frozen river) to arrest and maintain viewer interest and attention for long stretches of a game, without the need for verbal hyperbole.

Verbal hyperbole, however, is always an important standby. The fact that the upcoming play in a NFL game is a relatively insignificant third (down) and seventeen (yards to get the next down) in a quiet phase of the game, perhaps just before halftime with little chance of a score, can and often needs to be transformed into a crucial moment for the quarterback, whose confidence and subsequent performance suddenly comes to depend on completing this throw; or there is a reference to the psychological blow this will deal to the defending team, who will be thrown into disarray and disorganisation if they succumb. Making too much of nothing wears thin very quickly, however. The next steps are to show replays of exciting plays that happened earlier; speculate about whether an important player is carrying an injury; show (from numerous angles) and analyse a contentious refereeing ruling that "may be crucial"; introduce a personal element by panning to a rookie running back's parents sitting proudly, or arguing animatedly, in the crowd; or if there is somebody sufficiently newsworthy, iconic or outstanding, concentrate the cameras and the commentary on that player ("Will this be the last time we'll have the privilege of watching Brett Favre on Monday Night Football?").

If a game is boring and uneventful, outdoor telecasts sometimes make use of a strategy that strongly characterises studio sport programs, where the hosts act as "personalities" who provide much of the entertainment (by arguing with each other, articulating passionate opinions and beliefs, playing the buffoon): quite simply, in the absence of a live show, commentators have to become the show. This is what often happens on Monday NFL, which promoted itself through reference to, and frequently made use of, the very recognisable, avuncular, much respected and strongly opinionated John Madden. Other telecasts have panels of commentators, usually made up of prominent ex-players, who are not particularly acute or analytical but provide a passable line of comic banter. If none of this works and all the normal avenues have been exhausted, the commentators may revert to a slightly more dangerous form of hyperbole, which is to represent and characterise the game as outstandingly boring, stupefyingly uninteresting, egregiously dull: in this way the commentators hope to turn negative capital into something above and beyond the everyday, and therefore perversely interesting.

Studio Sport

The live sport telecast offers the prospect of spontaneous excitement, passion and drama, so gaining a viewer's attention can be straightforward enough; on the other hand it's clearly a difficult proposition to maintain that attention, precisely because there's no way to control the script. The studio sport show format doesn't face that problem: while it may share the content of live sport telecasts, it has more obvious affinities with other television formats and genres such as the news, current affairs, variety and chat shows. The comparison with the news format is based on similarities with regard to how time and material is organised and structured, the function of visuals, the forms of address employed, the role and tenor of presenters, and the perceived audiences. Sport news shows are usually fronted by middle-aged men whose main role is to perform smoothness, professionalism and reliability: like mainstream news readers, they need to look, act and speak as if they're trustworthy, and know what they're talking about. In order to appeal to a wider demographic, women presenters are becoming more prevalent, but they still constitute something of an exception to the all-male rule that has dominated televised sport since its inception.

Stories are arranged, and time allocated, in terms of perceived significance and topicality, although shows on channels that telecast a particular sport are likely to focus on upcoming games; in other words, some stories simultaneously function as news reports and advertisements. The imperative to perform with reliability and professionalism means that verbal hyperbole is limited in comparison with live telecasts; and because of time constraints visuals are more modestly employed, either to show action from recently completed games (a winning touchdown, a record breaking reception), particularly spectacular action (a length-of-the-field punt return), or simply to serve as "pieces of the real" (a story about a player or team not in action recently usually features representative archival footage). This ties in with the expectation that audiences are more likely to consist of connoisseurs rather than laymen: sport news isn't directed at those with a fleeting and fashionable attachment to the field, but to long term fans who want to know and care about what is happening to their team or sport. Gaining and holding attention is much less an issue here: the fan is by definition interested and likely to hang on once the scandalous and the spectacular have given way to the minutia of team tactics and rule changes.

There are two other television sport formats that are directed at the different poles of sport connoisseurs: differentiation here is based on what Bourdieu refers to as markers of distinction (Bourdieu 1989), and in fact the audiences are likely to be split along the lines of class, profession and level of education. The first format resembles the political interview and current affairs programs; while the second shares a number of features with variety, quiz and talk shows. The first format consists of careful, informed and extended discussions and interviews: the discourse is considered and restrained rather than hyperbolic; visuals are employed as a means of furthering analysis, rather than as a spectacular end-in-themselves; and once again the audience is self-selecting, so that attention is presumed, rather than something to be continually worked on. This format is to be found predominantly but not exclusively in European countries (in a sense they are the televisual equivalent of the traditional serious sporting print press as represented by *L'Equipe*, *France Football* and *Gazetta del Sport*). The second format is best described as sport entertainment: interviews are often loud, jovial and disrespectful; comments intentionally outrageous and hyperbolic; and visuals geared towards the eccentric, weird, comic and the sexual (gratuitous clips of inadvertent collisions; egregious mistakes and embarrassing moments; scantily clad spectators and cheerleaders, and streakers). These shows, which are found extensively in the British Commonwealth (the UK, Australia and New Zealand), find their print precursors in the English "lads" magazines and tabloid press.

It's important to emphasise that the formats described here don't always manifest themselves in accordance with, or strictly adhere to, generic formulae, categories or characteristics: television formats have always found room for hybridity, and television sport is no exception. The ESPN network, for instance, runs conventional sport news and documentary formats, but it also has shows such as *Around the Horn* and *Pardon the Interruption*, which concentrate on American sport (baseball, NFL, college football) and presume an audience of connoisseurs – who want to be entertained. So discussions may start off as informed and literate, but they often degenerate into abuse, comedy and hyperbole; topics are covered in a few minutes or seconds; there is more emphasis placed on wit than there is on analysis; the participants (sportscasters and journalists) push themselves, their opinions and prejudices, to the fore; and visuals are used as the departure point for arguments rather than analysis. The issue of attention is once again central, but it's addressed and maintained by the production of an almost hysterical relation to the subject matter: comments, analysis, discussions and arguments are intense and intensive, but they always presage flight to another topic or issue.

Conclusion

Television coverage has influenced, inflected and changed the field of sport in a variety of ways: certain games, or forms of games, have arisen, come into prominence or been privileged over others; rules and playing conditions have been altered to make a sport more television-friendly; the size of television markets often determines where teams are located. Once this close relationship between television and sport developed, it fed back into and influenced the field in a number of ways. At a very basic level, television more or less picked up and tied itself to certain sports and events and ignored others. In Britain the excitement generated by live television coverage of football and the Five/Six Nations rugby competition simply reinforced their mass audiences and high media profiles. In those cases, capital simply attracted capital: demographics widened; sponsorship, advertising and broadcast rights revenue poured in; and salaries and prize-money soared. Some low-profile sports benefited from the advent of television, precisely because the pace and content of the games were highly suited either to taking spectators into the thick of the action, or because they allow for a close association between televisual images and commentary – both important components of the live coverage format. In the UK snooker and darts benefited because they are relatively static and small-space activities. Cameras can follow the action easily while also focusing intimately on the face and expressions of the players and the reactions of the crowd, and the commentators have time to presage, narrate and "build up" every shot or throw. In the USA and elsewhere poker has become a major "sport" because the scenario of a small number of players packed into a room, sitting adjacent to and continually reacting with one another, is perfect for creating and showing tension, suspense, drama and passion, and promoting larger-than-life or eccentric characters: in other words, it's well suited to live television.

Sports such as squash, table tennis, badminton, sailing and athletic field events, on the other hand, have suffered precisely because they aren't television-friendly. Squash, for instance, is both architecturally unsuitable (players could come between the ball and cameras placed behind or above the action), as well as being simply too fast for viewers to follow, or for commentators to do much more than "talk across" the action. Most tellingly, a great deal of time can be expended in a rally where the players hit the ball up and down the wall waiting for a mistake, and if the point goes against the server, then nothing has happened – and it has taken a long time to not happen. Contrast this with an NFL game, where each play can be anticipated, explained, analysed, evaluated, contextualised (by the main commentators, special comments person, sideline reporters, etc.) and broken down into multi-angled, slow-motion "slices", and where the frequency of time outs and changes of possession allows for the insertion of numerous commercial breaks. Faced with declining participation numbers and revenue, squash officials have done everything to revamp the game for television, including introducing fluorescent balls and transparent walls and changing the scoring system, but nothing has really worked. Without live television coverage the chances of squash receiving attention in studio sport are considerably reduced, which has meant that it has become a predominantly participatory, rather than a spectator, sport.

This transformation of sport by the logics and imperatives of television had another consequence: much like the newspapers of the 1890s and 1900s, television (and by extension the public relations and marketing industries) has taken on the task of widening the sports demographic, and more specifically of promoting and commoditising sport and sports consumption to groups who know little or nothing of the field and its events and activities, and traditionally have cared even less. To some extent this simply involves promoting sport globally to lucrative non-traditional sport markets (popularising men's soccer in the United States, rugby in Japan, the NFL in Europe, tennis and golf in China), as well as targeting groups based on gender (attracting women to more masculinist sports such as rugby), ethnicity (raising the profile of Australian rules football within migrant communities in Australia), class (promoting cricket and rugby to a working-class demographic in the UK) and age (making bowls, ten pin bowling and golf more appealing and relevant to younger audiences in the USA).

The contemporary field of sport initially characterised, and continues to articulate, itself as relatively autonomous, disinterested and even utopian – seemingly at odds with, and above and beyond, the more commercially driven fields of the media – entertainment and business. And yet the history of sport in the twentieth century shows that the cultural field, or amalgam of fields, that most influenced sport is media-as-business; and the textual and institutional sites that most frequently manifest and reproduce this influence are those of television. The discursive divide that separates these cultural fields is largely predicated on the fact that they (theoretically) occupy very different positions within the overarching field of cultural production (Bourdieu 1993). This is nowhere more obvious than in the relationships that are developing between live televisual formats and the sport of cricket in its three different forms (test, ODI, twenty-twenty).

An incident occurred in a match between England and New Zealand, played on June 26, 2008, on "neutral territory" – a one-day international (ODI), where the style of the television coverage is somewhere "in between" the twenty-twenty game and test cricket. A New Zealand player (Grant Elliot) was going for a run when he bumped into the English bowler Ryan Sidebottom, and was knocked to the ground and run out. The spirit of the game dictates that the fielding captain (Paul Collingwood) should withdraw the appeal – Elliot was impeded, and it would be considered the worst of bad form to maintain the appeal. Collingwood, however, refused to withdraw. This created an extraordinary furore – the New Zealand players gestured angrily from their changing rooms, the crowd jeered loudly, and journalists started writing about it in dramatic and slightly hysterical terms (would it be the end of Collingwood's career, had cricket lost its soul). In the middle of all this the television commentators (a collection of former cricket captains and other distinguished now-retired players) simply went on covering the game as if nothing much had happened; they didn't think (or were acting and speaking as if they didn't think) the incident was of sufficient importance to become the sole focus of attention. The one commentator who did try to run with and hyperbolise the incident – the ex-New Zealander wicketkeeper Ian Smith – was quickly "put in his place". In this instance, there was a refusal of the imperative to take the game too far from the values, practices and meanings of the field.

The anthropologist Arjun Appadurai has categorised cricket (Appadurai 1997) as a "hard" cultural form, by which he means that it comes "with a set links between value, meaning, and embodied practice that are difficult to break and hard to transform" (Appadurai 1997, 90). As we suggested earlier, the IPL and its television coverage have certainly moved parts of the sub-field of cricket "elsewhere" – more or less into the world of Bollywood films and the Entertainment Channel, with dancing and singing frequently punctuating the action; film and television soap stars rubbing shoulders with, and taking the spotlight from, players; and huge amounts of money becoming the focus of attention (how much will teams bid for Shane Warne, who will win the prize for the most sixes, etc.). In test and to some extent ODI cricket, on the other hand, the live format, along with its foci and modes of address, has by and large acceded to the "hard cultural form" of sport-as-ethos, without regard to, or perhaps simply disdainful of, the imperative to hystericise and hyperbolise everything. In cricket, as is the case with many other sports, their relationship with television, and specifically television formats and their forms of address, is a matter of give-and-take; an ongoing set of negotiations and struggles which neither side can afford to lose – or win.

References

Appadurai, A. 1997. *Modernity at Large*. Minneapolis: Minnesota University Press.
Bourdieu, P. 1989. *Distinction*. London: Routledge.
—— 1991. 'Sport and Social Class'. In *Rethinking Popular Culture*, ed. C. Mukerji and M. Schudson. Berkeley: University of California Press.
—— 1993. *The Field of Cultural Production*. Cambridge: Polity.
—— 1998. *On Television and Journalism*. London: Pluto Press.
—— 2000. *Pascalian Meditations*. Cambridge: Polity.
Boyle, R. and Haynes, R. 2000. *Power Play: Sport, the Media and Popular Culture*. Harlow, UK: Pearson.
Cashmore, E. 1990. *Making Sense of Sport*. London: Routledge.
Crary, J. 1998. *Techniques of the Observer*. Cambridge, MA: MIT Press.
Debord, G. 2006. *The Society of the Spectacle*. New York: Zone Books.
Frow, J. 2006. *Genre*. London: Routledge.
Guttmann, A. 1986. *Sports Spectators*. New York: Columbia University Press.

Hill, J. 2002. *Sport, Leisure and Culture in Twentieth Century Britain*. New York: Palgrave.

Holt, R. 1989. *Sport and the British*. Oxford: Clarendon Press.

Moran, A. 2006. *Understanding the Global TV Format*. Bristol, UK: Intellect Books.

Roberts, R. and Olson, J. 1997. 'The Roone Revolution'. In *Sport in America*, ed. D. Wiggins. Champaign, IL: Human Kinetics.

4

A POLITICAL ECONOMY OF FORMATTED PLEASURES

Eddie Brennan

Despite all their apparent diversity and difference, most successful television formats[1] are very similar. They offer a very limited palette of audience pleasures[2] by concentrating, for the most part, on entertainment rather than information or education. Formats are about fun. Moreover, formats promote a particular kind of fun. This chapter argues that, by promoting audience pleasures based in the pursuit of individual and materialistic goals, most television formats are consonant with a dominant orthodoxy which sees markets as the only way to organise society.[3] This elective affinity between format pleasures and free market ideology, however, does not come about through any deliberate design. Rather, it is an unintended consequence of television production's response to economic and practical necessity. In their form, content and production practices formats are pre-adapted to the demands of a globalised media market place. As we will see here, this peculiar commercial logic has given formats a peculiar signature in terms of what they can and cannot represent.

Form, Content and the Global Media Field

Before exploring these issues, it is necessary to understand format television's current prominence. Format production takes place not only at the micro level of studio operations and production decisions but also, simultaneously, as part of a complex global media environment. The rise of the format has taken place in step with the transformation of what can be called the global media field. This describes the broader system of political, economic, technological, and social processes in which television production is embedded. To gain a conceptual perspective on such a system, a model is required which transcends traditional dichotomies between macro and micro, the objective and the subjective. Bourdieu provides one such conceptual model, which allows us to understand how long-term, international processes may interact with small-scale, everyday activity in cultural production (see Wacquant 1992; Fowler 1997: 2). This merging of national and international perspectives is essential to understanding format television, which, despite its recent prevalence, is the product of long-term social transformation.

In the past thirty years, what had been largely discrete national media systems have given way to open global trade in media products. As Iosifidis et al. note, in this new "more competitive and fragmented broadcasting environment" formats make commercial sense. They "provide a cost-effective way of filling schedules with localised productions which proved more popular than imported films and series" (Iosifidis et al. 2005: 148). Since the 1970s, an austere economic climate has emerged, shaping the development and production of television programming.[4] In this transformed media environment, to be successfully produced, programmes must be cheap, reliable and popular.

Employing Bourdieu's work on cultural production, Simon Cottle has described changes in media production in terms of "media ecology". He describes how, as the "ecosystem" in which television is produced has been transformed, the form and content of programmes have changed also. Cottle elaborates on how programme form and content are shaped by this new environment. He cites the example of wildlife television, which has been transformed by "new technologies", "heightened competitiveness, industrial centralization" and "internationalizing markets" (2004: 82). Slow, in-depth programmes have been replaced by fast-paced, action-based shows (2004: 93). In-depth wildlife programmes have been replaced by shows that aim to maintain audience attention through a succession of animal predation sequences. Similar changes can be found across programmes such as news, current affairs and drama. As Siune and Hultén point out, "the important changes are not to be found at the macro level of output but within different genres: news becomes sensational, current affairs becomes infotainment and talk shows, drama becomes soap opera" (1998: 29). Within and across genres, the detailed, the slow and the serious has tended to give way to fast-paced, superficial fun. In today's austere broadcasting landscape certain genres have died out while others have become dominant. Formats, with some other popular, low-cost genres like soap opera and sport, have found their ecological niche. They have thrived in recent years because they are pre-adapted to a commercialised, global media field (see Moran 2004; 2006; Iosifidis et al. 2005; Waisbord 2004).

Format Production and Competing Visions of the Good Life

Television production, as part of general cultural production, is predominantly carried out by what Bourdieu terms the "dominated fraction of the dominant class" (1993: 38). This describes a "cultural middle class" comprised of artists, writers, teachers, television producers and so on. Bourdieu sees cultural production as the site of a class struggle between the "dominant and dominated fractions of the dominant class" (1993: 378). Or, in other words, there is a conflict between the top and bottom of the middle class. Members of the dominant fraction are, generally, producers of material wealth through commerce or industry. The dominated fraction, on the other hand, produces culture. In this conflict, cultural producers try to undermine the dominant fraction of their class by "decrying wealth, which they lack, and extolling the virtues of culture, in which they abound" (Brennan 2000: 2). Bourdieu sees this conflict as a struggle to "impose the dominant principle of domination" or ultimately "the definition of human accomplishment" (Bourdieu 1993: 41). It is a conflict between two opposing visions of happiness or the "good life". In one, happiness is synonymous with building material wealth, through money and property. In the other, the good life is built through the accumulation of cultural knowledge and associated prestige. Bourdieu describes these positions as heteronomous and autonomous principles of hierarchisation respectively (Bourdieu 1993: 40). In the first, reward is material and extrinsic to the individual.[5] Under the autonomous principles of cultural production reward is immaterial and more intrinsic.

The field of cultural production then contains two opposing sets of rules and rewards. The rules and rewards that originate in the field of cultural production see cultural producers competing to gain respect and notoriety among their peers (see Bourdieu 1985: 731). The main tools they can use to achieve this are knowledge and skills peculiar to their field (see Bourdieu 1986: 243). Contrary to these "purist" positions is a set of rules and rewards that originates in the marketplace. These are essentially the prizes of popularity and wealth. Cultural "purists" shun these rewards (see Bourdieu 1993: 38–40). Format television, however, is not for purists.

Economic and Cultural Orthodoxy

> In much the same way as the former social-democratic hegemony was maintained with different emphases and priorities by previous governments of both Left and Right, the new neo-liberal hegemony is now actively being pursued with different emphases and priorities by governments of both Right and Left.
> (O'Donnell 1999: 15)

Market-centred orthodoxy has come to dominate global politics to the extent that it now constitutes a new "common sense" (Harvey 2005: 39). In 1996, Herman and McChesney report, *Forbes* magazine "exulted" in the fact that the world's governments whether they were left or right "could no longer 'interfere' with the prerogatives of business without suffering an economic punishment that would bring them down". Governments, the magazine reported, had "effectively lost their power to govern" (1997: 32). Mass media are caught up in a corporate drive to boost the global role of markets in allocating goods and services, to diminish the role of governments and generally, to further the "commodification of everything" (Harvey 2005: 165–66).

In keeping with this general trend, the global media field has become predominantly privatised and commercial. Moran identifies an "increasing shift towards facilitating private sectoral interests in television" with "state-controlled" and "public-service television" frequently being "reallocated to private entre-preneurial interests" (Moran 2006: 3). Despite their importance to citizenship and democracy, mass media are increasingly treated like any other type of com-modity (see Corcoran 2002: 2; Herman and McChesney 1997).

It could be argued that public service broadcasters have escaped this colonisa-tion by market principles. Public broadcasters, however, have been weakened in terms of their audience numbers, their prestige and their autonomy. Most now operate according to a quasi-commercial logic. While the BBC, for example, may not deliver advertising to British audiences, it is nevertheless under political pressure to deliver low cost programmes to large audiences. It may otherwise face charges of wastefulness and a failure to deliver on a public service mandate. More significantly, persistent misdemeanours in this regard are likely to lead to budget cuts (see Buckingham 1987: 2–3; Borne 2004: 113). As a result, among both public and commercial broadcasters, "good television" is broadly synonymous with "popular television". A model of "good television" where audience and revenue figures supersede concerns with quality, prestige or critical acclaim is now in the ascendant. The rules and rewards of the market dominate. Formats have risen to prominence in a system where "purist" positions are economically untenable, culturally negligible and, increasingly, unthinkable.

The general commercialisation of cultural production has seen an attack on "purist" positions, which are cast as paternalistic, intransigent and elitist. By attack-ing cultural "élites" and thus attempting to dissolve cultural hierarchies, the dominant fraction of the dominant class moves closer to what Bourdieu sees as its goal, the creation of a single, monetary hierarchy (Bourdieu 1993: 41). Thus, the endless variety of different social games collapses into a single goal, where the only remaining model of achievement, happiness and the "good life" is one based on extrinsic validation through wealth, fame and power (see Kasser et al. 2007).

This colonisation of cultural production is consequential for producers, their occupational culture and the content of the programmes they create. In their work television producers depend in large part on instincts or hunches (Gitlin 1983: 26–27). These learned "instincts" in turn depend on a shared but often unspoken professional culture which is the product of similar conditions of employment and movement in the same social circles (see Elliott 1972: 159; Alvarado and Buscombe 1978: 251; Pekurny 1982: 136–37; Cantor and Cantor 1992: 96; Schultz 2007). As the global media system has changed so have pro-ducers' employment conditions. Most importantly in the case of format television, production work and supporting social networks have been abstracted from national contexts to become trasnsnational.

According to Moran (2006) and Waisbord (2004), the global media system now contains a transnational global media élite who share similar working conditions and professional aims. Waisbord claims that there is a "growing homogenization of the professional sensibilities among television executives worldwide" (2004: 379). This shared occupational culture is supported through trade publications, and formal and informal networks (Moran 2006; Waisbord 2004).

> Attendance at annual trade meetings, exposure to the same trade publications, and regular electronic communications have helped maintain frequent interpersonal contacts that facilitate familiarity with global trends ... These meetings are places for cultivating a similar business mindset among industry executives.
>
> (Waisbord 2004: 365)

Sharing similar concerns and working conditions, these producers develop a similar sense of what constitutes good format television. There is a loose, fuzzy but, more or less, coherent sense of what constitutes a "good" format.[6] Waisbord sees that "globalization has nurtured the formation of a cosmopolitian class of industry professionals who, from New York to New Delhi, increasingly share similar concepts and attitudes about 'what works' and 'what doesn't' in commercial television" (2004: 364). Of course, this shared sense of "what works" is equally prevalent among beleagured public service broadcasters. Formats then, in addition to being an economic necessity, have become an accepted part of producer culture. Rather than being subjectively experienced as a product of the "dull compulsion of the economic" (Abercrombie et al. 1980: 57) many producers now see formats as an obvious and common sense way of making good television.

Formats as Technologies of Reproduction

Although the term is commonly used and understood, it is actually difficult to offer a precise definition of what a format is. Moran argues, however, that to ask what a format is, is to miss the point. "Such a queston implies that a format has some core or essence" rather than being "a loose term that covers a range of items that may be included in a format licensing agreement" (Moran 2004: 6). The term is significant "not so much because of what it is but because of what it permits or facilitates". In an increasingly liberalised media system, "flows" in global media trade have extended beyond "finished televison programmes to include television-related knowledge, services and so on". There is a trade in "tangible and non-tangible elements across borders" that includes "finance, advertising, programming, scheduling practices, management outlooks and marketing strategies" (Moran 2006:

3). As an amalgam of such services and forms of knowledge, television formats are a global media product par excellence. The important function and effect of a format is that it is "an economic and cultural technology of exchange" (Moran 2004: 6). Thus, "a format is a cultural technology which governs the flow of programme ideas across time and space" (Moran 2004: 8).

Conceiving of formats as a technology allows us to see how, in their form and content, they may be related to the media "ecosystem" that has shaped them. Sterne identifies technologies as a way in which cultures and social systems may be embodied and thus perpetuated (see also Elias 1986; Latour 1991; Law 1991; Lee 1997).

Technologies are associated with habits and practices, sometimes crystallising them and sometimes promoting them. They are structured by human practices so that they may in turn structure human practices. They embody in physical form particular dispositions and tendencies – particular ways of doing things (Sterne 2003: 377).

Clearly, formats carry meanings across the globe. Yet, these meanings are necessarily divorced from national culture. For Waisbord, they are "culturally specific but nationally neutral". The "DNA" of format televison is "rooted in cultural values that transcend the national" (2004: 368). The values, which have shaped format television's "DNA" are, of course, the heteronomous principles which currently dominate the global media field. It can be posited then, following Sterne, that this system's culture, practical pressures and values have been inscribed within format television as a cultural technology.

Certain ground rules apply in the production and sale of format television. The conception of programme concepts is confined to companies, such as Endemol or Fremantle Media, who create, licence and sell formats. Outside of this, programmes are merely manufactured following these companies' instructions, which are delivered through a production "bible" and on-site consultancy. The format sales model depends on a degree of national variation without any fundamental tampering with the structure of the format. As a cultural technology format, television encourages the faithful reproduction of programme form, content and production practices. Thus, following Sterne, formats sell more than programme concepts. They export "dispositions", "tendencies" and "particular ways of doing things" that have their roots in a market orientation to cultural production (2003: 377).

Colonisation without Imperialism?

Many past studies addressing global flows in programming have seen the dominance of particular countries as a form of cultural imperialism (Tunstall 1977: Tunstall and Machin 1999). Such a model cannot hold, however, when studying television formats because, of course, they deliberately strip out most of the trappings of their culture of origin. Iwabuchi claims that "it is now untenable to single out an absolute symbolic centre that belongs to a particular country or region". The prevalence of format television "shows that the global cultural power alignment is highly dispersed and decentred" and "origins become subsumed by local transculturation processes" (Iwabuchi 2004: 33). It would appear that, in a global system of open trade in media, media imperialism is a waning concern. Many commentators have rejected the media imperialism thesis on theoretical and normative grounds (Chadha and Kavoori 2000: 416). Moreover, Chadha and Kavoori contend, the proposition that media systems in developing economies are dominated by Western media content has been undermined by a number of practical developments. While transnational media organisations play an undeniable and occasionally aggressive role, "their domination is restricted by the interplay of national gate-keeping policies, the dynamics of audience preference as well as the forces of local competiton" (Chadha and Kavoori 2000: 428).

In addition to market and regulatory checks, format television can be argued to further reduce tendencies towards media imperialism. Offering a global and, more or less, standardised business model, formats can be adjusted to the tastes and customs of local settings. Iosifidis et al. argue that "the growth in format sales and local production reinforces the notion that the most successful trade in cultural products involves the suppression of the look and feel of programming concepts which express national origins" (Iosifidis et al. 2005: 148; see also Iwabuchi 2004: 29). Formats, Waisbord argues, are "de-territorialized" without any "national home". Thus, they "represent the disconnection between culture, geography, and social spaces that characterizes globalization". Traces of national origin are deliberately removed so "domestic producers can incorporate local color". Thus, "global audiences can paradoxically feel at home when watching them" (2004: 378).

Despite such checks on unbridled cultural imperialism, Chadha and Kavoori note that there is no "room for complacency". Commenting on Asian media, they write that, while various processes have reduced the importation of foreign programming in many territories, commercialisation has become the dominant organising principle (2000: 428). As demonstrated by Cottle's model of media ecology, this almost universal move from citizen to consumer-oriented media has had traceable consequences for the nature and diversity of cultural production (see Cottle 2004) . There is an increased volume of indigenous production with more programme titles being broadcast on a growing number of channels. There is also a pronounced increase in entertainment programming. However, behind these changes, Chadha and Kavoori argue, programme diversity has actually decreased.

Even in the case of entertainment oriented programs while there is considerable plurality in numerical terms, and this is often touted as a "sign of enhanced choice", the apparent abundance is quite limited, with successful programming being based largely on the cloning of successful genres and formats – as a result there is little genuine diversity in much of the programming, except the fact that it is local rather than imported in nature (Chadha and Kavoori 2000: 429).

The media imperialism thesis may be irrelevant to understanding the politics of format pleasures. Worse yet, any concern with conflicting "national" cultures, whether positive or negative in its outlook, may actually obfuscate a political understanding of format pleasures. National markets are not being overwhelmed by cheap cultural imports. There are, however, other equally serious causes for concern. A consumer orientation in programming may be leading to an over-dependence on entertainment. A reliance on formats as a "tried and trusted" cultural technology may encourage cultural homogenisation. Ultimately, more citizen-oriented programming may be displaced leading to a public sphere that is filled with spectacle and evacuated of political content. The key point here is that these processes are not imposed from outside. Instead, they arise spontaneously from the practical pressures that prevail in a commercialised global media field.

Exemplary Formats, their Pressures and their Pleasures

To be successful, a format must be able to travel internationally, generating as many localised versions as possible. At the same time, the fundamental structure of the show must remain coherent. And, of course, there is constant pressure to deliver large audiences at the lowest possible cost. These conditions pose a number of fundamental expressive limitations on both the form and the content of a programme format. It is these practical constraints, rather than producers' attempts to indoctrinate, which orient format pleasures towards the rules and rewards of the market.[7]

Visual Medium and Extrinsic Message

Arguably, as a visual medium, television may be predisposed to representations of the "good life" that are more in sympathy with heteronomous rather than purist principles. It is more suited to displaying extrinsic rather than intrinsic rewards. As such, when displaying people and characters it is not well suited to dealing with unspoken thoughts and feelings. Iwabuchi provides a telling example in the Japanese version of *Survivor*. The show's Japanese producers decided to concentrate on contestants' inner battles rather than interpersonal rivalries. This proved disastrous. It was impossible to mediate such inner processes through the reality format. The show's Japanese producer saw that it failed because:

> The depiction of contestant emotions is much too intricate to be easily portrayed and understood . . . the emphasis on a search for the true self did not result in unexpected or exciting interpersonal relationships such as love affairs among contestants that are a significant element of international versions.

(cited in Iwabuchi 2004: 25)

Television can, of course, deal with inner life through drama productions, for example. In pared-down format productions, however, television is best suited to communicating activities that provide a level of visual spectacle. Thus, format television is more suited to portraying rewards that are tangible rather than intangible and goal orientations that are extrinsic rather than intrinsic. Beauty, fame, and the trappings of wealth and power can be readily represented through low budget television. Inner peace, knowledge and self-esteem may be laudable goals but they do not easily, or cheaply, translate into emotive, dramatic or marketable television. As low-cost, visual media, formats are already predisposed to representations of the "good life" as it is seen by the dominant fraction of the dominant class.

Time, Timeliness and Hermetically Sealed Formats

In television production, time is money. Equipment and locations must be rented by the day. More significantly, technicians, camera crews, production staff and so on must be paid by the hour. Most formats avoid the need to pay cast members or writers. Nevertheless, costs need to be controlled by working as quickly as possible. This requires a rationalised and routine approach to production. In many cases studio-based format shows such as *The Weakest Link*, *Who Wants to Be a Millionaire?* and *Are You Smarter than a Fifth Grader?* will shoot several episodes in quick succession on a single day. Thus, costs are minimised. A consequence of this, however, is that such shows are practically incapable of being timely. That is, they can make no direct reference to ongoing public events or current affairs. They are effectively self-contained and sealed off from the world around them by their production regime.

Unlike batch productions, some shows may be shot over an extended period. Programmes like *Survivor* and *Wife Swap* may be shot over several days or weeks. However, these productions face the same problem of timeliness. They tend to feature location shoots, occasionally in exotic settings. To maximise such an investment, trade will often take place in finished programmes as well as formats. Shows like *Survivor*, *Wife Swap*, and *Queer Eye for the Straight Guy* have all been exported as finished programmes as well as being traded as formats. Here timeliness is equally impossible because these programmes, in order to travel through space, must also be able to travel through time. Put simply, a programme which is intended for export as a finished product cannot make references to football games, political campaigns or social crises that will be meaningless and out of date six months after its initial transmission. Thus, while their production cycle may be longer than short-run batch productions, they are, for similarly practical reasons, equally incapable of making reference to anything outside the show's basic formula.

Many format shows are effectively live. *Big Brother* is a prominent example. While the show appears as edited highlights on a daily and weekly basis, it is also made available 24 hours a day through television and the internet. Ironically, in this example, despite the live nature of the show, external reference is impossible. *Big Brother* places its contestants under constant surveillance. The contestants, however, are isolated from all news of the outside world. Once again references within the show are confined to the bounds of the show itself.[8]

Seventeen of the twenty programmes addressed here were incapable of making external references, preventing the inclusion of political or social themes.[9] It should be noted here that the absence of timeliness is not, of course, confined to television formats. Many other genres, such as television drama, for example, are equally incapable of representing up-to-the-minute social concerns. However, beyond television's usual temporal limitations, formats are more completely isolated from the world in which their audience live. Even soap operas, with their industrialised production processes, commonly make reference to social and political issues (Livingstone 1988: 56). However, while they may travel, most soap operas are not made with a deliberate view to export. Formats, on the other hand, are. As we have seen above, the inclusion of national specificity stands in the way of the format trade. The inclusion of social and political issues from a national context risks corrupting the production and enjoyment of a reliable, low-risk format. Formats then could be compared to a computer operating system where the particular look, colour and sound can be customised. The fundamental software, however, remains sealed and cannot be tampered with. This leads to a situation where audience engagement and pleasure must be generated entirely within the confines of the show itself without reference to external concerns.

Formats' Emotional Flavours

To permit international sales, the themes at the core of any format must be as universally attractive as possible. Thus, format programmes are more likely to appeal to basic emotions rather than to stimulate questions, discussion or debate. As van Zoonen notes, shows such as *Big Brother*, and hundreds of other formats, are built on "primal experiences and emotions" or the "basic instincts" of "ordinary people" (2001: 670).

As noted, television is a visual medium. It is also an emotional medium. As Freeth argues, "television is not at heart an information medium". When television works, "it works below the belt". The medium is "best at communicating atmospheres and attitudes, personalities, motivations, hopes and fears, and the broader political and cultural significance of things" (1994: 166). The emotive nature of television does not necessarily constrain its expressive range. Television can cause emotional arousal in any number of ways. Drama, news and documentary can all be emotionally engaging while dealing with social or political themes. However, due to their hermetically sealed nature, most formats must be able to excite the emotions without reference to any broader context. Rather than creating excitement, anger or satisfaction by linking a programme to political or social issues, the emotional charge of format television must be built using the devices and people available within the programme itself.

Not only must audience engagement be created from within the confines of the format, it must also happen rapidly. In a multi-channel environment, where viewers make programme choices via remote control in a matter of seconds, it is essential to "hook" the audience as quickly as possible. There is no such thing as a slow-burning format that only becomes rewarding after persistent viewing. In a media ecology that is intolerant of risk, such an approach is practically impossible and unlikely to be considered as a programming possibility. This need to give audiences a quick return for their attention also helps to explain the individualistic nature of most formats. The formats addressed here concentrate disproportionately on the individual, rather than the family, community or broader group, as the locus of action (see Table 4.1). In this respect, they are in harmony with the individualist ethos of market orthodoxy. The individualist nature of format television, however, may again owe more to practical constraints than ideology. There is a fundamental difficulty in developing a format around collective representation and participation. Audience identification with a media character depends on recognisable social types and a viewer's ability to understand the character through the lens of their own personal experience (see Cohen 2006: 185). People can identify readily with the emotional predicaments of other individuals, typically conveyed through visual cues. However, audience identification with a heterogeneous group or team is unlikely to occur as readily. Understandably then, in the pursuit of viewing figures and economic survival, formats are more likely to gravitate towards the representation of individuals at the centre of the action.

Furthermore, the individualistic nature of format programmes may provide pleasures by serving psychological needs that arise from the individualised nature of modern societies. Many format programmes, like *Big Brother* and *Wife Swap* for example, offer pleasures of surveillance and vicarious living. Audience members can look into the lives of others for comparisons with their own lifestyle. This need to compare one's own life and habits with others is a product of the privatisation of family life (Habermas 1989: 45). This is visible in the eighteenth century in the birth of melodrama, which accompanied the separation of work and family life. Here, among the middle classes, a new isolated sense of self was created, unsupported by public life and lacking a stable, taken-for-granted world view. This persists today, creating a psychological need for reflection and validation through social comparison. There is a need to establish and reinforce visions of how life should be lived. Two hundred years ago, this was done, largely, by looking into other people's private lives through the medium of literature (see Habermas 1989: 45; van Zoonen 2001: 670). Today, manifestations of the same need for social comparison can be found in television formats.

Social comparison also underpins the way in which shows such as *Big Brother*, *The Weakest Link*, *Idol* and *Are You Smarter than a Fifth Grader* depend on schadenfreude as a key emotional ingredient (see Wong 2001). This German term refers to pleasure taken in the misfortune of others. This sentiment is commonplace in format television. A former BBC producer described to Raymond Boyle how, to attract a young audience and avoid boring them, "you need humiliation to some extent, to see people suffer" (Michelle Kurland, cited in Boyle 2008: 419). Like vicarious living, this negative form of social comparison among privatised individuals may psychologically validate one's lifestyle and sense of self (Trepte 2006: 258). Formats may project the individual as the locus of action. In this, however, they are also reflecting the lifestyles of Western audiences.

In the small sample of exemplary formats examined here, the preponderance are based on individual competition and extrinsic goal orientation. Indeed, a number of shows are based on games where the winner takes all. These include *Big Brother*, *Idol*, *I'm a Celebrity . . . Get Me Out of Here*, *Survivor* and *The Weakest Link*. Many shows are based on games that generate distrust, subterfuge and a Machiavellian approach to life. These include *Big Brother*, *The Mole*, *Survivor* and *The Weakest Link*. Such social pessimism could be interpreted as an ideological position. Curran argues that some "seemingly apolitical material" can embody "ethical codes or expressive values that lie at the heart of political creeds". He cites, for example, "egalitarianism, mutuality and a belief in human

TABLE 4.1 Programmes by goal orientation and mode of participation

	Individual participation	*Collective participation*
Extrinsic goal orientation	*Are You Smarter than a 5th Grader?* *Big Brother* *Dragon's Den* *Idol* *I'm a Celebrity Get Me Out of Here* *Next Top Model* *Thank God You're Here* *The Mole* *The Singing Bee* *The Swan* *Queer Eye for the Straight Guy* *Survivor* *The Weakest Link* *The X Factor* *Who Wants to Be a Millionaire* *Wife Swap*	*Got Talent* *The Lyrics Board*
Intrinsic goal orientation	*How to Look Good Naked*	*Test the Nation/National IQ Test*

perfectibility in the case of traditional social democracy, or possessive individuali-sm, self-reliance and social pessimism in the case of neo-liberal conservatism" (Curran 1991: 34). Again, producers do not include such ideas to indoctrinate. They are included because they are popular, easily conveyed and economically viable.[10]

Overriding themes were identifiable in the form and content of the twenty programmes addressed here. Notably, most of the shows were based on various kinds of competitions. Only three of the programmes, *Wife Swap*, *Queer Eye for the Straight Guy* and *How to Look Good Naked* could be considered to be non-competitive, self-improvement programmes. More importantly, the twenty formats analysed demonstrated a predisposition towards two central characteristics. Most were based in competition between individuals rather than teams. The main prizes on offer, and, accordingly, the predominant goal orientations, were extrinsic (see Table 4.2). That is, goals were "focused on external rewards and other people's praise", and included "striving for financial success, as well as for image and status" (Kasser et al. 2007: 7). As a cultural technology shaped by a commercialised media field, formats reproduce the extrinsic goal orientation of Bourdieu's "dominant fraction of the dominant class". In their representation of acquisitive, individual competition, formats, for the most part, are structurally predisposed to represent a single, monetary hierarchy as the dominant definition of human accomplishment.

Formats and the Fun Side of Market Orthodoxy

> The global media are the missionaries of our age, promoting the virtues of com-mercialism and the market loudly and incessantly through their profit driven and advertising-supported enterprises and programming. This missionary work is not the result of any sort of conspiracy; for the global media TNC's it developed organically from their institutional basis and commercial imperatives.
>
> (Herman and McChesney 1997: 37–38)

Herman and McChesney contend that the stability of the global corporate system as it currently exists depends "to no small extent" on the "widespread acceptance of a global corporate ideology" (1997: 34). This ideology essentially legitimates the primacy of the market, the roll-back of the state and the conflation of "freedom" with economic freedom (see Herman and McChesney 1997: 34). I am not concerned here, however, with the "ideology" of format television in the sense of a set of codified ideas about how society should be managed. My concern lies with the "pleasures" that format television may offer. I am arguing that format television offers a particular, and quite limited, set of pleasures that are rooted in the culture and practical pressures of a commercialised, global media field. Format television programmes are not, therefore, concerned with explicitly legitimating grand schemes or ideologies. Nonetheless, most format television subtly tells individuals about what is of value in the pursuit of happiness and the "good life".

As O'Donnell writes, one of the most potent aspects of the ideology of the new broadcasting environment is the fact that it is "commonsense", populist and even fun (O'Donnell 1999: 15; see also Humphreys 1996: 229). The seduction of the commercialised global media field lies in the fact that, while it enriches corporate elites, it creates popular appeal by attacking cultural hierarchies and, ostensibly, offering greater personal choice. O'Donnell identifies commercial television entertainment as a focal point for this populist strand of market orthodoxy. As a result, O'Donnell writes, proponents of a market-led society have appropriated notions of "fun" and "glamour" as their own. This, he claims, is "one of the greatest ideological steals of recent times" (1999: 15).

For clear pragmatic reasons, low-cost entertainment is an increasingly important part of the world media system. Facing harsh "economic realities", commercial broadcasters "had every reason to rely upon the kind of programming that was most likely to maximise audience and that was at the same time relatively inexpensive" (Humphreys 1996: 230). Television today is "increasingly and mainly a medium for entertainment" (De Bens and de Smaele 2001: 72). The massive increase in commercial channels in combination with "light touch" regulation has seen these new broadcasters concentrate on entertainment to the increasing exclusion of informational, educational and political programming (Brants and Siune 1998: 133). At an explicit and institutionally political level, market orthodoxy is a codified ideology. At the personal level, however, codified ideology can be left aside in favour of fun. In the case of format television, however, this is a particular flavour of fun, where the path to happiness lies in the individual pursuit of money, power and fame.

There is, of course, no intention to be a killjoy here. Entertainment is an essential part of any media system. Moreover, television entertainment can provide an essential means of conveying information and education, particularly to illiterate or less educated populations (Livingstone 1988: 73; Nariman 1993; Elkamel 1995; Singhal and Rogers 1999; Goldsmiths Media Group 2000: 44). Television entertainment can be highly political (Curran 1991: 33–34). The politics of market-led format entertainment, however, lie, in part, in the necessary absence of explicit politics. More importantly, however, they lie in the implicit celebration of liberal-individualist, utilitarian values. As Inglis notes, liberal-individualism "holds the world capitalist system together". It is "the unquestioned orthodoxy of global culture" transforming all "locals into cosmopolitans" (Inglis 2008: 257). Through the propagation of these values, under-developed countries "become the same as their Western counterparts in their immersion in the material world, their pursuit of pleasure, quest for excitement, fulfilment of desire, obsession with consuming, and obsession with self" (Inglis 2008: 190).[11] As noted above, the decline of nationalist cultural imperialism does not preclude the colonisation of national cultures by a stateless orthodoxy (see Chadha and Kavoori 2000).

TABLE 4.2 Exemplary formats

Name of format[1]	Format type	International versions	Contra flow	Industry award winner	Longevity	Subject of legal dispute
Are You Smarter than a 5th Grader?	Game show	34	No	No	No	No
Big Brother	Reality	39	No	Yes	Yes	Yes
Dragon's Den	Reality/business	8	Yes	Yes	Yes	No
Got Talent	Talent show	16	No	Yes	No	No
How to Look Good Naked	Reality/makeover	2	No	Yes	No	No
Idol	Talent show	30	No	Yes	Yes	Yes
I'm a Celebrity Get Me Out of Here	Reality/celebrity adventure	5	No	Yes	No	Yes
Next Top Model	Reality/modelling	32	No	Yes	No	No
Test the Nation/National IQ	Game show/quiz	40	No	Yes	Yes	No
Thank God You're Here Test	Acting	16	Yes	No	No	No
The Mole	Game show/adventure	14	Yes	Yes	Yes	No
The Singing Bee	Game show/music lyrics	22	No	Yes	No	No
The Swan	Reality/extreme makeover	2	No	Yes	No	No
Queer Eye for the Straight Guy	Reality/makeover	8	No	Yes	No	No
Survivor	Reality/adventure	11	No	Yes	Yes	No
The Lyrics Board	Game show/music lyrics	19	Yes	No	Yes	No
The Weakest Link	Game show/quiz	23	No	No	Yes	No
The X Factor	Talent show	40	No	Yes	No	Yes
Who Wants to Be a Millionaire	Game show/quiz	105	No	Yes	Yes	No
Wife Swap	Reality/lifestyle	2	No	Yes	No	Yes

Note: I am indebted to Anthony Quinn for his work identifying and presenting these exemplary formats.

At an institutional level the acceptance of explicit market ideology is essential to the maintenance of the currently dominant economic paradigm. At a personal level, the continuation of a tacit and unquestioned orthodoxy is equally important. As Inglis notes:

> If people become happy consuming less, there is the threat of economic depression. If people stop believing in the need to earn more to spend more, there is a danger the golden egg of world trade and globalization might become just a thin shell with no yolk to sustain it.
>
> (Inglis 2008: 190)

It is through the personal acceptance of individual and utilitarian ideas that "the way of the market becomes the way of the world" (see Inglis 2008: 162). Unlike codified ideology, which is open to discussion and debate, the ideals of today's market-led society can also be experienced, on a personal level, as a set of vague feelings, motivations and goal orientations (Kasser et al. 2007).

By their nature, television formats are visually led. To maximise returns on investment they are low-cost and low-risk. As a technology of exchange, export sales are central to what a format does. The need to attract numerous national audiences, while preserving format coherence, leads to isolation from local social and political concerns. To survive formats must appeal to values and norms that are as widespread as possible. Thus dominant formats project and reflect individualist values and extrinsic goal orientations. Format pleasures are circumscribed by the practical constraints of a commercialised media field. Ironically, the same constraints inscribe the norms and values of market orthodoxy within formats' ostensibly apolitical brand of fun.

Notes

1 It should be noted that despite the common usage of the term, format television is so varied that the term "format" itself is difficult to succinctly explain or define. (See Moran 2004: 6)
2 For a broader discussion of television pleasures see Fiske 1987: 314–15; Brown 1994: 168–69; Tulloch 2000: 61–69; Philo and Miller 2001.
3 For an account of reality television as the "secret theatre of neoliberalism" see Couldry 2006.
4 For a fuller discussion see Schiller 1971; Herman and McChesney 1997.
5 Kasser et al. describe extrinsic goals as "those focused on external rewards and other people's praise, and include striving for financial success" (2007: 7).
6 This can be described using Bourdieu's concept of habitus, which describes a lasting, general and adaptable way of thinking that shapes the way we read, understand, and react to the world around us (Bourdieu 1984: 170; see Inglis 1998: 11).
7 To explore the dominant characteristics of format television, twenty programmes that could be considered to be exemplary formats were selected (see Table 4.1). These were selected primarily on the basis of international format sales. However, the selection was also informed by other considerations. Formats were also included on the basis of:

(1) Having won recognition and notoriety through industry awards; (2) Being an example of counter-flow, selling a format from the media periphery to traditionally dominant countries; (3) Being a long running format (over five years); and (4) Having been deemed valuable enough to be the subject of legal dispute (see Table 4.2).

8 It is notable that when the British independent politician George Galloway took part in Britain's *Celebrity Big Brother* in 2006 his attempts to discuss Britain's participation in the war in Iraq were drowned out by birdsong and engine noise (see the *Guardian*, 16 January 2006). In this case, the blending of external issues and entertainment were certainly not seen to be conducive to the delivery of good format television.

9 There are, however, some notable exceptions. Shows that are shot on a weekly basis such as *Got Talent* and *Idol* may potentially include timely references to external events. Thus, unlike batch productions and expensive long shoots, they may include broader social themes that lie outside the immediate concern of the programme. Shahaf provides an extreme example of this in the case of *Kohav Nolad*, the Israeli version of the *Idol* franchise. During the 2006 Israeli–Lebanese conflict the show not only referred to ongoing events but also changed its basic form and location in response (http://flowtv.org/?p=24: accessed 12 January 2008).

10 It would be unwise to condemn all format television as being socially negative. Shows such as *How Long will You Live* or *Honey We're Killing the Kids* may disrupt viewers' sense of self around their lifestyles and consumption habits. Such shows also provide informational resources to help people change their diets, exercise regimes and so on. A small minority of television formats may provide empowerment and education. It is notable, however, that such formats have not met with great commercial success.

11 In this case, Inglis is referring to the development of liberal consumer capitalism in Ireland.

References

Abercrombie, N., Hill, S. and B. Turner. 1980. *The Dominant Ideology Thesis*. London: George Allen and Unwin.

Alvarado, M. and E. Buscombe. 1978. Hazell: *The Making of a TV Series*. London: British Film Institute in association with Latimer.

Borne, G. 2004. *Uncertain Vision: Birt, Dyke and the Reinvention of the BBC*. London: Secker & Warburg.

Bourdieu, P. 1985. "The Social Space and the Genesis of Groups". *Theory and Society*. 14(6): 723–43.

—— 1986. "The Forms of Capital", pp. 241–58 in Richardson, J. (ed.), *Handbook of Theory and Research for the Sociology of Education*. New York: Greenwood Press.

—— 1993. *The Field of Cultural Production*. Oxford: Polity Press.

Boyle, R. 2008. "From Troubleshooter to The Apprentice: The Changing Face of Business on British Television". *Media Culture Society*. 30(3): 415–24.

Brants, K. and K. Siune. 1998. "Politicization in Decline?", pp. 128–43 in McQuail, D. and K. Siune (eds), 1998. *Media Policy: Convergence, Concentration and Commerce*. London: Sage.

Brennan, E. 2000. "Cultural and Structural Change in RTÉ Television Drama". *Irish Communications Review*. Vol. 8: 1–13.

Buckingham, D. 1987. *Public Secrets: EastEnders and Itst Audience*. London: BFI Publishing.

Cantor, M. and J. M. Cantor. 1992. *Prime-Time Television: Content and Control*. Newbury Park, CA: Sage.

Chadha, K. and A. Kavoori. 2000. "Media Imperialism Revisited: Some Findings from the Asian Case". *Media, Culture and Society*. 22(4): 415–32.

Cohen, J. 2006. "Audience Identification with Media Characters", pp. 183–98 in Bryant, J. and P. Vorderer (eds), *Psychology of Entertainment*. Mahwah, NJ: Lawrence Erlbaum Associates.

Cottle, S. 2004. "Producing Nature(S): On the Changing Production of Natural History TV". *Media, Culture and Society*. 26(1): 81–101.

Curran, J. 1991. "Rethinking the Media as a Public Sphere", pp. 27–57 in Dahlgren, P. and C. Sparks (eds), *Communications and Citizenship: Journalism and the Public Sphere*. London: Routledge.

De Bens, E. and H. de Smaele. 2001. "The Inflow of American Television Fiction on European Broadcasting Channels Revisited". *European Journal of Communication*. 16(1): 51–76.

Elias, N. 1986. "Technization and Civilization", pp. 212–29 in Goudsblom, J. and S. Mennell (eds), *The Norbert Elias Reader*. Oxford: Blackwell.

Elkamel, F. 1995. "The Use of Television Series in Health Education". *Health Education Research*. 10(2): 225–32.

Elliott, P. 1972. *The Making of a Television Series: A Case Study in the Ssociology of Culture*. London: Sage.

Fowler, B. 1997. *Pierre Bourdieu and Cultural Theory: Critical Investigations*. London: Sage.

Freeth, M. 1994. Television's Dangerous Liaisons', pp. 165–74 in Haslam, C. and A. Bryman (eds), *Social Scientists Meet the Media*. London: Routledge.

Gitlin, T. 1983. *Inside Prime Time*. New York: Pantheon Books.

Goldsmiths Media Group. 2000. "Media Organisation in Society: Central Issues", pp. 19–68 in Curran, J. (ed.), *Media Organisations in Society*. London: Arnold.

Habermas, J. 1989. *The Structural Transformation of the Public Sphere*. Cambridge: Polity Press.

Harvey, D. 2005. *A Brief History of Neoliberalism*. Oxford: Oxford University Press.

Herman, E. and R. McChesney. 1997. *The Global Media: The New Missionaries of Corporate Capitalism*. Washington, DC: Cassell.

Humphreys, P. 1996. *Mass Media and Media Policy in Western Europe*. Manchester: Manchester University Press.

Inglis, T. 1998. *Lessons in Irish Sexuality*. Dublin: University College Dublin Press.

—— 2008. *Global Ireland: Same Difference*. New York: Routledge.

Iosifidis, P., Steemers, J. and M. Wheeler. 2005. *European Television Industries*. London: BFI Publishing.

Iwabuchi, K. 2004. "Feeling Glocal: Japan in the Global Television Format Business", pp. 21–35 in Moran, A. and M. Keane (eds), *Television Across Asia: Television Industries, Programme Formats and Globalization*. Abingdon, UK: RoutledgeCurzon.

Kasser, T., Cohn, S., Kanner, A. D. and R. M. Ryan. 2007. "Some Costs of American Corporate Capitalism: A Psychological Exploration of Value and Goal Conflicts". *Psychological Inquiry*. 18(1): 1–22.

Latour, B. 1991. "Technology is Society Made Durable", pp. 103–31 in Law, J. (ed.), *A Sociology of Monsters: Essays on Power, Technology and Domination*. London: Routledge.

Law, J. 1991. "Monsters, Machines and Sociotechnical Relations", pp. 1–23 in Law, J. (ed.), *A Sociology of Monsters: Essays on Power, Technology and Domination*. London: Routledge.

Lee, M. 1997. "Relocating Location: Cultural Geography, the Specificity of Place and the City Habitus", pp. 126–41 in McGuigan, J. (ed.), *Cultural Methodologies*. London: Sage.

Livingstone, S. 1988. "Why People Watch Soap Opera: An Analysis of the Explanations of British Viewers". *European Journal of Communication*. 3(1): 55–80.

Moran, A. 2004. "Television Formats in the World/the World of Television Formats", pp. 1–8 in Moran, A. and M. Keane (eds), *Television Across Asia: Television Industries, Programme Formats and Globalization*. Abingdon, UK: RoutledgeCurzon.

Nariman, H. N. 1993. *Soap Operas for Social Change: Toward A Methodology For Entertainment-Education Television*. London: Praeger.

O'Donnell, H. 1999. *Good Times, Bad Times: Soap Operas and Society in Western Europe*. Leicester, UK: Leicester University Press.

Pekurny, R. 1982. "Coping with Television Production", pp. 131–43 in Ettema, J. and C. D. Whitney (eds.), *Individuals in Mass Media Organizations*: Beverly Hills, CA: Sage.

Schultz, I. 2007. "The Journalistic Gut Feeling: Journalistic Doxa, News Habitus and Orthodox News Values". *Journalism Practice*. 1(2): 190–207.

Singhal, A. and E. M. Rogers. 1999. *Entertainment-Education: A Communication Strategy for Social Change*. Mahwah, NJ: Lawrence Erlbaum Associates.

Siune, K. and O. Hultén. 1998. "Does Public Broadcasting Have a Future?", pp. 23–37 in McQuail, D. and K. Siune (eds), *Media Policy, Convergence, Concentration and Commerce*. London: Sage.

Sterne, J. 2003. "Bourdieu, Technique and Technology". *Cultural Studies*. 17(3/4): 367–89.

Trepte, S. 2005. "Social Identity Theory", pp. 255–72 in Bryant, J. and P. Vorderer (eds), *Psychology of Entertainment*. New Jersey: Lawrence Erlbaum Associates.

Tulloch, J. 2000. *Watching Television Audiences*. London: Arnold.

Tunstall, J. 1977. *The Media Are American*. London: Constable.

Tunstall, J. and D. Machin. 1999. *The Anglo-American Media Connection*. Oxford: Oxford University Press.

Wacquant, L. 1992. "Toward a Social Praxeology: The Structure of Logic of Bourdieu's Sociology", pp. 2–59 in Bourdieu, P. and L. Wacquant, *An Invitation to Reflexive Sociology*. Cambridge: Polity Press.

Waisbord, S. 2004. "McTV: Understanding the Global Popularity of Television Formats". *Television and New Media*. 5(4): 359–83.

Wong, James. 2001. "Here Looking at You: Reality TV, Big Brother and Foucault". *Canadian Journal of Communication*. Vol. 26: 33–45.

Van Zoonen, L. 2001. "Desire and Resistance: Big Brother and the Recognition of Everyday Life". *Media, Culture and Society*. Vol. 23: 669–77.

Other Sources

Corcoran, F. 2002. "The Co-habitation of Public and Private Broadcasting". Submission to the Ministerial Forum on Broadcasting, May 2002. Retrieved 10 July 2002 from www.forumonbroadcasting.ie.

Couldry, N. 2006. "Reality TV, or the Secret Theatre of Neoliberalism". www.goldsmiths. ac.uk/media-communications/staff/realitytv.pdf. Accessed 2 October 2008.

Moran, A. 2006. "The Significance of Format Programming for PSB". Keynote Speech. RIPE Conference, Amsterdam.

Shahaf, S. 2006. "Israeli *Idol* Goes to War: The Globalization of Television Studies". http://flowtv.org/?p=24. Accessed 12 January 2008.

5

INTERPRETING CUBANNESS, AMERICANNESS, AND THE SITCOM

WPBT-PBS's ¿Qué pasa U.S.A.? (1975–1980)

Yeidy M. Rivero

I was about 10 or 11 years old when I, together with my parents, religiously tuned in weekly to the situation comedy *¿Qué pasa U.S.A.?* While I do not recall the specific year the show aired in Puerto Rico, I do remember that it was broadcast on WIPR-Channel 6, the island's public television station. Watching one of my favorite sitcoms on what I then considered the boring channel was rather odd. However, I never thought it strange that the Peñas, *¿Qué pasa U.S.A.?*'s working-class three-generation Cuban/Cuban-American family, resided in Miami or that some of the characters communicated bilingually in English and Spanish. For me, *¿Qué pasa U.S.A.?* was a show that resembled other locally produced situation comedies broadcast on commercial television, with the difference that the Peña family were Cuban immigrants who, instead of residing in Puerto Rico (like some of my childhood friends), lived in Miami (like many of my friends' relatives). Probably as a result of the principal characters' cultural references and their accents in Spanish, I decoded *¿Qué pasa U.S.A.?* as a Cuban sitcom.

Fast-forward to 2004. I was invited to write a 500-word encyclopedia entry on *¿Qué pasa U.S.A.?* Without having any information on the show at hand, I immediately accepted. This was an opportunity to revisit a program I loved. After conducting the research I realized the uniqueness of *¿Qué pasa U.S.A.?* Sponsored by the U.S. Office of Education Emergency School Assistance Act–Television Program (ESAA-TV), *¿Qué pasa U.S.A.?*—considered the first bilingual situation comedy broadcast on U.S. television—addressed the cultural-generational misunderstandings and the socio-cultural adjustments endured by the Peñas, a 1960 Cuban exile family. An ESAA-TV grant of $250,000–$300,000 per year provided the only financial support for the show's production on

WPBT, the Miami–South Florida Public Broadcasting Service (PBS) station. While initially *¿Qué pasa U.S.A.?* aired only in Florida, after the 1977 season the program was carried on PBS nationally, calling the attention of regional and national television critics, all of whom praised the show's production values. Even though *¿Qué pasa U.S.A.?* was considered one of ESAA-TV's most successful programs, the show ended in 1980 after WPBT decided not to reapply for an ESAA-TV grant.

Besides learning about *¿Qué pasa U.S.A.?*'s production, one of the most intriguing aspects of my research was discovering the ways in which ESAA-TV, the production team, and regional and national newspaper reviewers construed the sitcom. For instance, for the ESAA-TV office, the show was a well-executed bilingual educational program. For the *¿Qué pasa U.S.A.?* producers, on the other hand, the sitcom was an avenue to help Cuban-American adolescents to navigate through their Cubanness and Americanness. And, for U.S. television reviewers, *¿Qué pasa U.S.A.?* was a high quality show that resembled other situation comedies produced by Hollywood. Each group conveyed very specific and distinct cultural, political, social, and television meanings. Nonetheless, with the exception of the production team, U.S. commercial television and the U.S. cultural landscape served as the primary arenas for comparison. While as a child I classified *Qué pasa U.S.A.?* as a Cuban sitcom based on the characters' ethnicity and cultural references, ESAA-TV and television reviewers understood the show as distinctly American, anchored in the U.S. sitcom genre.

The decoding dissonance I encountered between *Qué pasa U.S.A.?*'s production and reception motivated me to reexamine the show. In this essay I therefore analyze the sitcom, paying particular attention to how ESAA-TV, the production team, and regional and national newspaper reviewers assessed the show in terms of genre, culture, politics, audiences, and television. In other words, what factors made *¿Qué pasa U.S.A.?* an original or unoriginal, a Cuban or American sitcom? Also, by analyzing *¿Qué pasa U.S.A.?*'s production and reception, a secondary query guiding this project relates to the possibility of categorizing television genres as formats. Simply put, how do our selection of sources and our knowledge of a particular television market, programming history, and culture infuse our interpretation of what can be classified as a format?

My interest in issues of categorization and interpretation has been sparked by recent scholarly discussions regarding what constitutes a format. In "Television's New Engine," Michael Keane and Albert Moran call for a clear-cut distinction between formats and genres, arguing that television formats are "'ready-made' products for the insertion of local content," artifacts of contemporary television's industrial-based processes and transformations.[1] Genres, on the other hand, relate to narrative form and structure. For Keane and Moran, formats' "new engines" (i.e., programming innovations) have invigorated television's "finished genres," thus diversifying television's programming offerings. "In the past," they observe, when "finished" genres such as sitcoms or soaps were in need of some refreshing it was more often done by creating a spike—by introducing cameo guest appearances into sitcoms or manufacturing soap opera must-see events such as a character wedding or murders.[2]

Based on Keane and Moran's argument, prior to today's format exporting trend, television genres experienced modest creative renovations.

Also crafting a clear distinction of format and genre but exclusively focusing on one television market, Omar Rincón contends that in Colombia, what are generally known as television genres (i.e., situation comedies, variety shows, telenovelas, etc.) are considered formats.

> For us, formats are the industrial packaging of information. Genres are the tone of the narrative. There are different ways to resolve the narrative conflict and these tones determine the genre. For example, *Betty's* [*Yo soy Betty la fea*] format is the telenovela and the genres are melodrama and comedy.[3]

Using the Colombian telenovela as his main example, Rincón asserts that as an industrial product the telenovela has "devoured" all other formats. Consequently, in Colombia, local industrial conditions, the creative input of the people involved in production, the audience, and, more recently, the buying and adaptation of foreign formats (all of which have been transformed into telenovelas) have influenced programming innovations. What Rincón brings to the discussion of formats is the interconnection of television programming to industrial, economic, and cultural changes that are not necessarily a product of today's global format trafficking. In addition, the Colombian case illustrates the importance of examining multiple factors to comprehend programming transformations at the local, national, and global levels.

Taking into consideration the aforementioned discussion and using *¿Qué pasa U.S.A.?* as a case study, in this essay I suggest that in particular markets and historical moments, television genres have operated as formats. To be sure, the purpose of this essay is not to define format and genre. Rather, the objective is to expand the categorization of format to be inclusive of the travels and the industrial, thematic, and cultural adaptations of television genres. Hence, borrowing Silvio Waisbord's definition of formats as "programming ideas that are adapted and produced domestically" and Jason Mittell's conceptualization of television genres as "historically situated cultural products constituted by media practices and subject to ongoing change and redefinition," I argue that as a situation comedy format, *¿Qué pasa U.S.A.?* translated (moved) elements of Cuban and U.S. commercial television to the realm of U.S. public television.[4] Additionally, the show culturally, linguistically, and performatively translated (decoded) aspects of Cuban and American culture and the Cuban exile condition. Through its production, textual representation, and intended audience (Cuban-American adolescents and the Miami Cuban exile community), *¿Qué pasa U.S.A.?* altered the geographical, thematic, and cultural traits that had been part of the U.S. sitcom genre.

Equally important, in terms of politics, the sitcom challenged the discourse of a singularized upper-middle class and Cuba-centric Cuban Miami community. Linked to right-wing conservative politics (particularly regarding U.S.–Cuba relations), uninvolved in the Civil Rights struggles, and coming from a upper-middle class economic background, the wave generally known as the "golden migration" fostered class, ethnic, and racial distinctions between Cubans and other Latino groups. Whereas many members of the 1959–1962 exile group were indeed part of Cuba's elite, those who migrated through the 1965–1973 "Camarioca boatlift" and the "freedom flights" came from a lower middle-class background.[5] Accordingly, by depicting the 1960 émigré Peñas as a six-member, two-income family, living in the lower middle-class neighborhood known as Little Havana and uninterested in Cuban politics, *¿Qué pasa U.S.A.?* attempted to transform the notion of a homogeneous ultra-right and economically solvent Cuban exile identity.

As I explain below, this representation, as well as the utilization of the situation comedy genre for educational purposes, was directly and indirectly influenced by both the institutional parameters of the ESAA-TV program and by the media professionals involved in the production. The somewhat unrestrictive creative nature of ESAA-TV and the mandate to hire minority media professionals and attract particular regional and national minority audiences created a space for a sitcom produced by and targeted at Cuban/Cuban-American Miamians. Politically speaking then, the show discursively intertwined Cubanness and Cuban-Americanness with the ethnic, class, and cultural marginalization experienced by 'Other' Hispanic/Latino communities and immigrant groups. Televisually speaking, *¿Qué pasa U.S.A.?* (re)connected pre-revolutionary Cuban television and U.S. television in a new geographical and temporal place (Miami in the 1970s) while introducing a singular cultural and immigrant experience into the U.S. sitcom genre.

ESAA-TV: Television Produced by and for Minority Communities

The 1972 Emergency School Aid Act (ESAA) bill was a governmental intervention to address the legacy of school segregation from the pre-1954 *Brown vs. Board of Education* era, by eliminating the sustained ethnic, economic, and educational inequalities present in the post-Civil Rights era. The bill had three primary objectives: (1) "to assist school districts to meet special problems incident to desegregation"; (2) "to encourage the voluntary elimination, reduction, or prevention of minority group isolation in elementary and secondary schools"; and (3) "to aid school children in overcoming the educational disadvantages of minority group isolation."[6] Through federal monetary assistance, local school districts with a sizeable minority student population obtained funds to develop educational programs with the purpose of obliterating segregation and discrimination. Besides taking into account race, ethnicity, and class, the bill also considered language and culture as aspects that might affect children's learning environment and their possible feelings of isolation. Thus, ESAA was designed for ethnic minority children as well as for non-English speaking children (some of whom, of course, corresponded to both categories). A "minority group," according to ESAA, referred to "persons who are Negro, American Indian, Spanish-surnamed American, Portuguese, Oriental, Alaskan natives, and Hawaiian natives" and "persons who are from environments in which a dominant language is other than English."[7] School districts requesting funds could focus on educational issues regarding biculturalism and bilingualism or racially informed problems affecting their elementary or secondary schools.

A minimum of 3 percent of the ESAA funds was allocated for the development of what was known as ESAA-TV, educational television programming to promote "positive racial attitudes in children."[8] The scientifically measured educational success of *Sesame Street* served as the primary model for ESAA-TV shows.[9] Still, besides its function as a supplementary teaching tool à la *Sesame Street*, ESAA-TV was also envisioned as on-the-job training for minority media professionals. All the awarded proposals required minority personnel in important positions such as administrators, writers, talent, producers, and project managers. Consequently, ESAA-TV's secondary purpose was to train a group of minority media professionals who, through working on ESAA-TV, would obtain experience and increase their future job opportunities in the television industry.

ESAA-TV shows were additionally conceptualized as "purposing programming," and as such they were designed to attract particular minority groups in either regional and/or national contexts.[10] For example, ESAA-TV target audiences included Chinese-Americans in San Francisco, Puerto Ricans in New York and Connecticut, Mexican-Americans in Texas and Los Angeles, Hispanics across the country, Japanese-Americans and Vietnamese-Americans in Los Angeles, Native-Americans in Menominee County, Wisconsin, and African-Americans in Washington, D.C. and Florida. Both regional and national shows (differentiated by funding levels) had the option of focusing on one or more of the following categories: expression skills, reading skills, cultural programming, bilingualism and biculturalism, and interracial and interethnic tension and conflict resolution.[11]

Reaching the minority target audience was one of the primary objectives of ESAA-TV programming and a major concern for ESAA-TV television producers. As noted in a study sponsored by the U.S. Office of Education,

> ESAA-TV series must compete with the high budget, high production value commercial series which do much to condition viewers' taste. The necessity

of appealing to the target audience in a competitive market is clearly an important consideration in producers' formatting decisions.[12]

Whereas the phrase "condition viewers' taste" suggested a patronizing perspective regarding commercial television's allegedly faulty citizens/viewers in general and minority audiences in particular, the issue of market appeal opened the doors for a situation comedy about a Cuban/Cuban-American family on WPBT-PBS.[13] It is worth mentioning that after independent producers were granted contracts they had administrative and creative freedom in terms of genres, content, and talent. Still, even though all 30 non-profit organizations that obtained contracts from 1973 to 1979 were able to select any genre, the Community Action and Research, Inc. (CAR, the Cuban-American organization that spearheaded *¿Qué pasa U.S.A.?*'s proposal)/WPBT team was the only group who utilized the situation comedy, a genre that has been historically linked to U.S. commercial television.[14]

According to a *¿Qué pasa U.S.A.?* production member, preliminary research conducted in the Miami–South Florida area established that the primary target audience—Cuban-American adolescents—preferred the situation comedy genre. Additionally, this research showed that the general Cuban exile population (the secondary target audience), favored situation comedies over dramatic series.[15] The Cuban-American adolescents' choice might have been the result of the popularity of programs such as *All in the Family*, *The Mary Tyler Moore Show*, and *Sanford and Son* (among others), which established a new style of sitcom that addressed social issues prevalent in the 1970s and explored what many considered risqué subjects. The older (monolingual) segment of the Cuban exile population, on the other hand, might have preferred sitcoms based on their familiarity with this type of programming from Cuban commercial television.

Introduced in Cuba in 1953, the first Cuban sitcom, *Mi esposo favorito* (My Favorite Husband), was an unauthorized translation and adaptation of *I Love Lucy*'s scripts. Although the illegal acquisition of the *I Love Lucy* scripts created a heated debate between Desi Arnaz and the author of the Cuban version, the show's success prompted the production of other sitcoms.[16] It was precisely in this period of the early 1950s that, in the Cuban–U.S. television context, U.S. television genres operated as formats.

Following the commercial tradition initiated in the 1940s radio era, U.S. companies such as Proctor and Gamble and Colgate-Palmolive continued their business alliances with Havana-based advertising agencies (for example, Sabatés, Crusellas, and Obelleiro-Carvajal) and introduced U.S. television genres/formats to Cuban television. The general industrial packaging and selling of these genres/formats included the concept, the sponsor, and, in the case of some fiction shows, the scripts.[17] These industrially and culturally adapted genres/formats, which ranged from variety shows, panel shows, game shows, political commentary shows, and sitcoms (as well as the already indigenized telenovelas), dominated prime-time entertainment programming in pre-revolutionary Cuban television and in the early years of Fidel Castro's revolution. Hence, the Cuban exiles who resided in 1970s Miami were already quite familiar with the sitcom as well as with other television genres adapted from U.S. television.

But producing a sitcom not only had the potential to attract the bicultural and bilingual Cuban-American adolescents and their Cuban exile parents and grandparents; it also provided an opportunity to hire some of the highly experienced Cuban television professionals who settled in Miami. Therefore, the CAR/WPBT team selected a genre that audiences were familiar with and equally important, that Cuban émigré media professionals had already mastered. For example, while other ESAA-TV producers were struggling to find trained actors, the *¿Qué pasa U.S.A.?* production had a vast pool from which to select. Four of the six members of the Peña family were performed by respected actors who had established careers in Cuba. Likewise, when ESAA-TV producers had to rely on non-minority scriptwriters, the *¿Qué pasa U.S.A.?* production first hired the renowned Cuban scriptwriter Alvaro de Villa, and then Luis Santeiro, who at that time was an inexperienced yet film school-trained writer.[18] Although unnoticed by the ESAA-TV office and the television reviewers, the *¿Qué pasa U.S.A.?* television professionals' expertise, university training, and cultural capital were instrumental in the sitcom's high quality production values.

The preliminary audience survey validated the selection of the sitcom genre for educational purposes, yet, the CAR/WPBT team also needed to justify an educational program targeted at Cuban-American adolescents. The pedagogical rationalization was clearly laid out in the proposal submitted to the Department of Health, Education, and Welfare (HEW). *¿Qué pasa U.S.A.?*'s educational objective was to "improve inter-ethnic and intra-ethnic relations in general and help Cuban-American adolescents in particular to become bicultural, well-adjusted, [and] self-fulfilled individuals."[19] Citing multiple social scientific studies and newspaper articles, the proposal foregrounds the Cuban-American adolescent's bicultural identity crisis, the narrow knowledge of "Anglo teachers" about Cuban culture, Dade County's limited bilingual education programs, and the mainstream media exclusion of Cuban themes.[20] In addition to the aforementioned educational objectives, the CAR/WPBT document also focused on what was characterized as the ethnocentrism of the Cuban exile community. This Cuban ethnocentrism included the Miami Cuban community's self-containment, Cuban émigrés' resistance to becoming U.S. citizens, and the Cuba-centered curriculum of the private schools own by Cuban exiles. Furthermore, the proposal devoted several paragraphs to the Cuban elderly population and their cultural isolation, their lack of interest in learning English, and their fixed longing for a return to Cuba.[21] Hence, even though *¿Qué pasa U.S.A.?*'s main purpose was to help Cuban-American adolescents to comfortably embrace their Cubanness and Americanness, the veiled message was for their parents and extended family members: Cuba is the remembered, loved, and nostalgically imagined homeland;

the U.S.A. is the present and, for better or for worse, it is ours and our children's and grandchildren's new home.[22] By attempting to de-mythologize the hopes of a future return to Cuba (and circuitously, the fall of Fidel Castro and socialism on the island), *¿Qué pasa U.S.A.?* was intended to transform the Cuban exile community into Cuban-Americans and, as a result, into U.S. Latinos/Hispanics.[23]

Employing approximately a 60 percent English-language, 40 percent Spanish-language dialogue, enough for a monolingual viewer to understand, the sitcom had the potential to attract various generations within Miami's Cuban community and the general Miami audience. In this way, *¿Qué pasa U.S.A.?*'s primary end of demonstrating "the inter-ethnic and intra-ethnic pressures experienced by Cuban adolescents" and its secondary intent of showing "the self-containment of the Cuban subculture" could reach the sitcom's audiences.[24] These educational and political goals merged through the use of bilingualism, which was constructed in the proposal as a pivotal tool to "break down cultural isolation."[25] Directly and indirectly, *¿Qué pasa U.S.A.?* was an ideological push towards assimilation.

Considering *¿Qué pasa U.S.A.?*'s genre, the combination of Cuban and Cuban-American professionals, the target audience, and the proposal's objectives, the translation (movement) of aspects associated with Cuban television to U.S. television, the process of translating (decoding) elements of the Cuban exile condition, and the adaptation of the U.S. sitcom genre began at the pre-production stage. The utilization of the sitcom functioned as a re-encounter between pre-revolutionary Cuban television and U.S. television. This re-encounter symbolically brought to light the long established U.S. capitalistic interests in Cuba, Cuba's appropriation of the U.S. broadcasting model, and Cuban television's indigenization of U.S. genres and program concepts. As a radio, television, and advertising hub, Havana was one of the most important Latin American media centers during the 1940s and 1950s, positioning Cubans as regional authorities on commercial radio and television production. In the context of *¿Qué pasa U.S.A.?* this expertise was present in the people behind the production of the show and in the casting of Cuban performers who carried with them their television knowledge—and for one actress, star status—from pre-revolutionary Cuban television.[26] Although some of the media professionals and the Cuban actors bridged *¿Qué pasa U.S.A.?* with 1950s Cuban television, the inclusion of Cuban-American performers and head scriptwriter, the show's objectives, and the location of production, re-inscribed the show as a product by, for, and about those in the diaspora.

The particularities of the Cuban diasporic community were also present at the pre-production stage. According to an ESAA-TV official, the proposal's reviewers "were astounded that a proposal of this quality came in under the small-funding category."[27] (Based on this comment and the available ESAA-TV documents, it seems that neither the reviewers nor the ESAA-TV office were aware of the demographic characteristics of the early 1960s immigrants and the television expertise of those behind *¿Qué pasa U.S.A.?*'s production.) The hiring of college-educated Cuban-American television professionals, the Cuban actors, and the description of the audience included in the proposal, allegorically conveyed the class, educational, and professional background of those who migrated in the early 1960s. In addition, the proposal's reference to the Cuban exile population's refusal to become U.S. citizens hinted at their status as political exiles, which provided the Cuban émigrés with federal monetary assistance to start their life in the U.S.A. and with the option, if desired, to apply for U.S. citizenship.[28] Nevertheless, while behind the scenes *¿Qué pasa U.S.A.?* mirrored the Cuban exiles' economic and political privileges (particularly in comparison to other Spanish Caribbean and Latin American immigrants), the CAR/WPBT proposal redefined the general Cuban Miamian community's class spectrum by conceptualizing a sitcom about "a typical working-class extended Cuban family."[29] By describing the family as "typical" and "working-class" the proposal linked the Cuban exiles' condition to the struggles undergone by other immigrant groups. As a result, the CAR/WPBT representation of the Peñas as a "typical" Cuban family in fact created an atypical image of the Cuban community from the one that dominated the U.S. mainstream media.

The Peña family's class, their exile status, and the diegesis and production's geographic and temporal stage—1970s Miami— bring us back to the U.S. sitcom genre. In the 1970s U.S. television landscape, *All in the Family* reintroduced the working-class family that inhabited the fictional world of most of the early 1950s domestic sitcoms.[30] In a similar vein, *¿Qué pasa U.S.A.?* followed in the working-class path re-established in *All in the Family* while also conveying the immigrant experience of the 1950s ethnic working-class sitcoms. As several scholars have argued, those 1950s ethnic working-class sitcoms negotiated issues of immigrants' homeland traditions and assimilation.[31] Likewise, *¿Qué pasa U.S.A.?*'s proposal and, as I will soon discuss, the text, addressed the difficulties of assimilation and the conflicts between the Cuban and American ways of life. Nonetheless, by representing a Cuban/Cuban-American family who openly argued about financial difficulties, cultural differences, and racial prejudice, *¿Qué pasa U.S.A.?* disrupted the general conformity of the 1950s ethnic-working class sitcoms and their exclusively European immigrant experience, as well as challenging the binary European-American and African-American ethnic spectrum that characterized 1970s domestic sitcom families (i.e., *All in the Family*, *Sanford and Son*, *Good Times*, and *The Jeffersons*). In short, *¿Qué pasa U.S.A.?* linked the 1950s ethnic sitcom, the 1950s Cuban adaptation of the U.S. sitcom genre, and the 1970s socially engaged U.S. sitcom, while at the same time introducing the particularities of the post-1959 Cuban migrations.

Last, and interrelated, *¿Qué pasa U.S.A.?* moved the immigrant life portrayed in U.S. sitcoms and the site of television production to Miami. This movement removed New York City's reputation as the unique location for U.S. immigrants (as presented in *The Goldbergs*) as well as the status of New York City, Chicago, and Burbank as the only sites of sitcom production. Taped before a live studio audience (a production practice associated with the genre), *¿Qué pasa U.S.A.?* followed the sitcom's narrative conventions of order, confusion, and restoration of order. Yet the episodes were performed in Spanish and English, allowing those with cultural and linguistic competence in the studio and at home to comprehend the humor, the culture, the history, and the stories specifically related to the Cuban exile and Cuban-American population. Those viewers, such as the critics, who were unfamiliar with the language and culture or the particularities of the production got only part of the story and thus created diverse interpretations framed by their understanding of the Cuban exile community, the sitcom, and television.

Translating and Interpreting the Peñas

The Peña family included the adolescents Joe (born in Cuba, raised in Miami) and Carmen (born and raised in the U.S.A.), the parents Pepe and Juana (born and raised in Guanabacoa, Cuba), and the grandparents Adela and Antonio, both of whom, like their daughter Juana and their son in-law, spent all of their life in Cuba before migrating to the U.S.A. The extended family lived in a three-bedroom, one-bathroom house decorated with simple furniture and house items. The modest living room, dining room, and kitchen (where most of the episodes' action takes place) represented a departure from Antonio's, Adela's, and Juana's life in Cuba. Coming from a middle-class background, Antonio and Adela had a comfortable life in Guanabacoa, a financial solvency that allowed Juana to devote herself to study voice lessons without ever having to work. Even after marrying Pepe, a hard-working, conservative, and somewhat rough and short-tempered working-class man, Juana had a cozy lifestyle. Whereas Pepe only had a high-school diploma, he was able to establish his own business in Havana, which provided financial stability for his family. This middle-class status and, more broadly, the family's world, changed in the U.S.A.

With less than perfect English—learned after migrating—Pepe worked as a construction worker in Miami. Despite the fact that Pepe firmly believed that men should be the breadwinners and that women should stay at home, his salary and the hours of overtime could not sustain a six-person household or pay for the private Catholic school where he enrolled Carmen. To Pepe's distress, Juana had to find a job as a seamstress in a dress factory. Having Juana as an income provider not only altered the traditional gender roles Pepe believed in but it also transformed Juana's exile perspective. Contrary to Pepe, who hoped to return to Cuba ("This is not home. This is temporary. Here, we are just dropping by!" ["Citizenship," 1977]), Juana opened herself to the possibilities of a new beginning in the U.S.A. Juana's hard work, dedication, and commitment to learn English (like Pepe, she learned the language in exile), earned her a promotion to "floor lady" (the seamstresses' supervisor) and provided her with the opportunity to enroll in bookkeeping classes paid for by the factory. Even though Pepe went ballistic when Juana "did not ask for permission" to sign up for bookkeeping courses ("Juana Gets Smart," 1977), Juana, while still believing in Cuban traditions, recognized that some U.S. 1970s societal changes offered her and her family an array of diverse possibilities. To a certain extent, Juana's receptiveness facilitated her understanding of who Pepe, Adela, and Antonio classified as the "American-ized children"—Joe and Carmen.

Joe and Carmen were two generally well-behaved adolescents who were trying to cope with the clashes between Cuban and American ways of life. Of the two, the 15 year old Carmen was the one who underwent a more restrictive Cuban upbringing. From having to take a chaperone to the school prom ("Super Chaperone," 1976) to being forced to date a "nice Cuban boy" as a way to dissuade her from going to college which, according to the family, would "condemn her to spinsterhood" ("Los novios," 1976), the Peñas tried to reproduce the old country's gender roles. As expected, this culturally constructed gender dichotomy provided a less strict environment for the 17-year-old Joe. As a young man, Joe was applauded by his family for his multiple love conquests ("Los novios") and Pepe also suggested that as a "red-blooded Cuban American boy" he was supposed to sleep around ("Virginity," 1977). Certainly, similar to Carmen, the relationship between Joe and his family was thorny. For example, he tried to convince his parents and grandparents that they were too strict with his sister and, like Carmen, he was bothered by his family's over-protectiveness ("Growing Pains," 1977; "Joe Goes to the Hospital," 1977). In fact, of the two adolescents, he was the more antagonistic one. However, the conflicts between Joe and his family related to general cultural practices and not the particularities of traditional gender roles. Having to go to a funeral of an elderly woman he did not know ("The Farewell Party," 1978) or arguing with his grandmother because she thought that Jewish people lived in sin and thus needed to be converted to Catholicism ("Patria and Company," 1978), were some of the instances in which Joe struggled with his family's mores. And for Joe, the family members who represented what he deemed as recalcitrant Cuban traditions were Adela and Antonio, his grandparents.

Adela and Antonio survived the exile by dreaming of a future return to Cuba. Actually, on several occasions, Adela stepped out of the house saying that she was going back to Guanabacoa right then ("Ay Abuela," 1977). For them, living in exile was painfully difficult. Neither Adela nor Antonio understood a word of English and they were not interested in learning the language. They were certain that they would soon be returning to Cuba thus, why learn the language or become U.S. citizens? As the concerned Antonio asked Patria, a New Jersey relative who was engaged to a Jewish-American man, "no Spanish? But Patria, what is he going to do when we go back to Cuba?" ("Patria and Company").

Antonio and Adela lived immersed in their memories of Cuba, recollections that, as literary scholar Gustavo Pérez Firmat writes regarding the Cuban exile Miami community, produce a temporally static and historically untouched Cuba, a fantasy created in the exiles' minds.[32] In the case of Antonio, he replicated his Cuba by playing dominoes with other elderly Cuban men. Adela, on the other hand, went to church, talked to other friends from Guanabacoa, watched Spanish-language TV, and anxiously waited for a funeral so she could learn what had happened to other exiles ("The Farewell Party," 1978). Nonetheless, Antonio's and Adela's replications of Cuba and their perceptions of Cubanness were shattered by the American/foreign surroundings and, more importantly, by their grandchildren and their school friends. Carmen and Joe were daily reminders of how (in their views) American culture can corrupt Cuban morals and traditions. In response, Adela and Antonio became cultural soldiers combating what they understood as the obliteration of Cuban culture. They involved themselves in Joe's and Carmen's affairs even though no one asked them for their help or opinions. Thus, the well-intentioned but sometimes misguided actions of Antonio and especially Adela, along with their lack of English-language skills, caused numerous misunderstandings for the nuclear family and for those Cuban-Americans and Americans who visited the Peñas' home.

The secondary characters incorporated into almost every episode were Carmen's best friends from Catholic school, Violeta (Cuban-American) and Sharon (Irish-American). Additionally, some episodes included Mrs. Allen, a white American neighbor who disliked the Peñas and Cubans in general, and Marta, a Cuban neighbor who spent most of her time gossiping about other Cubans. Violeta was a witty and outgoing young woman who was utilized in the narrative to satirize Cuban and American cultures ("Honey, these Americans resolve everything by going to the psychiatrist . . . my mother resolves things by a little trip to my uncle's botánica," ["The Confession," 1979]) and to present a slightly more lenient Cuban upbringing. Sharon was an intelligent and open-minded adolescent who was eager to learn about Cuban culture. Nonetheless, as a feminist, Sharon could not understand why, for example, the Peñas were so strict with Carmen and behaved differently towards Joe or why Pepe was outraged at the possibility of Juana going to school. Sharon was used as a conduit to discuss some aspects related to 1970s social transformations particularly regarding feminism. As well, by asking questions about particular Cuban practices (for example, the Santeria religion was the topic of the 1976 episode "Spring Cleaning"), Sharon was employed in the narrative to explain Cuban cultural traditions that were generally foreign to most Americans.

In other instances, Sharon together with Mrs. Allen brought to the forefront signs of prejudice against Cuban exiles and Latinos/as by the mainstream culture. Hiring practices that "discriminated" against whites and seeing Cubans as a menace to a peaceful (white) community, were some of the themes discussed in ¿Qué pasa U.S.A.? ("Se nececita ser bilingüe," 1977; "One Saturday Afternoon," 1978;

and "The Encounter," 1978). Consequently, while most of the narrative focused on the Cuban community's struggles to accept their new life in the U.S.A. and their difficulties with the biculturalism and bilingualism of the young Cuban-American population, the sitcom also considered the mainstream culture's intolerance toward minority groups.

In its five years of production, *¿Qué pasa U.S.A.?* explored a variety of socially, culturally, and politically significant themes that included and also transcended the Cuban/Cuban-American Miami community. The Cuban diaspora in Venezuela, New Jersey, and New York, some Cuban exiles' obsession with material assets, the community's racial and ethnic prejudices against other groups, the gay movement and issues of homophobia, the feminist movement, and the emergence of equal opportunity programs, were some of the issues that the Peñas and friends encountered in the program's 39 episodes. That said, although diasporic Cubanness was the center of *¿Qué pasa U.S.A.?*, the subjects of Fidel Castro and the Cuban Revolution were never discussed in the narrative. Hence, even though members of the Cuban-American community in Miami, the Carter administration, and Fidel Castro promoted dialogues during the late 1970s, the Peñas, their friends, and their neighbors were totally isolated from these conversations and debates.[33] The Peñas lived in a 1970s Miami that was at the forefront of U.S. socio-cultural changes but that concomitantly coexisted in an imagined Cuba framed in a temporal stasis, a place where the post-revolutionary nation-state and its citizens were absent.

This thematic avoidance of Fidel Castro's Cuba called the attention of one particular reviewer who, in his "Chronicle of Higher Education" piece, criticized the sitcom for its lack of engagement with issues pertinent to exile-island politics and the exiles' motivations for migrating. As he stated,

> Millions of us—and millions more of our ancestors—have undergone such an experience [becoming American], but are the Peñas like the rest of us? Why did they leave Cuba? Are they in touch with family and friends who remained? Are they permanently Americans, or do they dream of going back? The programs provide no clues.[34]

Whereas, as this reviewer indicated, none of the episodes dealt with the reasons why the Peñas migrated to the U.S.A., the "dream of going back" was present throughout the entire series via the grandparents' characters. What seems to be the reviewer's limited (or non-existent) Spanish proficiency and his political take on the Cuban Miamian community framed his assessment of the show. Nonetheless, despite his criticism of *¿Qué pasa U.S.A.?*'s dismissal of Cuban exile politics he, similar to other columnists, praised the sitcom in terms of its production values. As he noted, "I don't know the amount of the federal grant for the series, but it appears to have been generous, for the program is as professional in its design and production as anything that comes out of Hollywood."[35]

As I mentioned in the introduction, the *¿Qué pasa U.S.A.?* team produced the show with the financial constraints of a budget of $250,000–300,000 per year. Still, more than the production's financial limitations, what is interesting about the aforementioned comment (as well as other reviewers' assessments) is the ways in which U.S. commercial television and production practices served as the only parameter for comparison. In other words, based on the reviews, *¿Qué pasa U.S.A.?* was a high quality show probably as a result of its Hollywood-style financial backing or perhaps because of creative input from Hollywood. The Cuban-trained media professionals, their experiences in pre-revolutionary Cuban commercial television, and 1950s Cuban television in general were not considered as possible factors in the sitcom's success. Instead, the television critics attempted to make sense of its bilingual narrative, genre, and high quality production by comparing *¿Qué pasa U.S.A.?* to other Hollywood products.

Across the board, the critics applauded *¿Qué pasa U.S.A.?*'s artistic and production qualities. A *New York Times* television reviewer remarked, "Indeed, it [*¿Qué pasa U.S.A.?*] puts many commercial productions in the genre to shame."[36] Echoing the *New York Times'* comments, the television critic for Cleveland's *Plain Dealer* wrote, "It may be that my sense of humor is not what it should be, but the funniest show that I've seen since arriving here some weeks back was a situation comedy—on Public Television yet," while the *San Antonio Express* reviewer began their column with "Move over, Archie and Dingbat, Chico and The Man, et. al. Make room for the Peñas . . . "[37] For the television critics, *¿Qué pasa U.S.A.?* was one the best sitcoms of 1978, a program that with its bilingual and accented English-language voices, and through what were described as innovative plots, revamped the situation comedy genre as well as altering public television's programming.

The use of bilingual dialogues captured the attention of all the reviewers. Prefacing *¿Qué pasa U.S.A.?* as "TV's first and only bilingual situation comedy," most critics were surprised by their ability to comprehend the narrative's main themes and to find the show humorous, even if they missed what they categorized as the "funniest parts"—the dialogue in Spanish. Although measuring comedy is almost an impossible task, it is important to note that the majority of the Spanish-language dialogue utilized in *¿Qué pasa U.S.A.?* was delivered by the most experienced performers in the sitcom—the actors who played the grandparents. Consequently, these performers' know-how and talent, together with the Cuban studio audience's familiarity with the actors, might have accounted for the reviewers' perception that the best comedic lines were delivered in Spanish. Albeit one reviewer confessed her annoyance with not understanding half of the episodes ("The bilingual interaction proves somewhat exasperating at times, when high school Spanish leaves one left out in the cold on some of the best jokes coming from the grandparents"), most reviewers welcomed the linguistic uniqueness of *¿Qué pasa U.S.A.?*[38] As the *New York Times'* reviewer observed, "The use of two languages may be bothersome to viewers at first—especially when the laughter of the studio audience is triggered by the Spanish dialogue—but it soon enough becomes natural, as indeed it is in a bilingual household."[39] For this reviewer, the bilingualism present in *¿Qué pasa U.S.A.?* mirrored the linguistic quotidianity many American families experience, even if this everyday reality was rarely portrayed on commercial or public television.

The theme of bilingualism took another turn in the review published in *Newsday*. In his piece, the columnist employed *¿Qué pasa U.S.A.?*'s dialogue in Spanish as way to criticize PBS's preference for high-culture and British-made programming. As the reviewer noted,

> Listening to the first episode of a sitcom that I only half understood was an epiphany. At first hearing the live, Spanish-speaking audience laughing at the jokes is a culture shock. You get angry. You bunch of elitist snobs on public TV. You're already speaking British English that I don't understand. What will you do next to keep me out of it—Molière, in the original French?[40]

In a foreshadow of Laurie Ouellette's research on U.S. public television, the *Newsday* critic incisively attacked both the network and its well-educated middle/upper-class audiences, calling attention to the high-culture discourse that plagued PBS since its inception.[41] Indirectly, this critic also brought to light the network's marginalization of the ethnically and economically diverse U.S. publics.

But the enthusiastic reviews were not enough to keep *¿Qué pasa U.S.A.?* on national television. The ESAA-TV legislation did not require PBS to feed ESAA-TV shows, therefore, only 30 percent of ESAA-TV programming was broadcast on PBS. Yet, even those shows such as *¿Qué pasa U.S.A.?* that were picked up by the network were at a disadvantage by being scheduled during what Dave Berkman, the director of ESAA-TV, described as "toilet time." As he observed,

> Our very best series was a bilingual sitcom, *¿Qué pasa U.S.A.?* In reviewing the series, both Les Brown of the New York Times and Marvin Kitman of Newsday said it was the best sitcom, commercial or otherwise, they'd seen that year. Each went on to wonder why WNET scheduled it in a 4:00 p.m. Saturday slot? An embarrassed Channel 13 immediately rescheduled it for Sunday evening at 7:00 p.m.[42]

Scheduling problems, lack of promotion, some of the actors' opportunities in Hollywood (Rocky Echevarría, also known as Stephen Bauer, and Andy García began their careers in *¿Qué pasa U.S.A.?*), and the departure of the head scriptwriter, probably accounted for WPBT/CAR not reapplying for an ESAA-TV grant. *¿Qué pasa U.S.A.?* ended production in 1980 and, a couple of years later, President Ronald Reagan's administration dismantled ESAA-TV.

¿Qué pasa U.S.A.? and the Situation Comedy as a Format

¿Qué pasa U.S.A.?'s institutional, geographic, and cultural place of production illustrates how, in the U.S.-Cuban diaspora television context, the situation comedy genre traveled as a format. By adapting Hollywood and Cuban commercial television production styles to the WPBT/PBS/ESAA-TV institutional structure, by transforming U.S. sitcom immigrant themes to the temporal and geographical locality of 1970s Miami, and by targeting the Cuban exile/Cuban-American community, *¿Qué pasa U.S.A.?* regionalized/localized the situation comedy format. In other words, as a "ready-made" set of institutionally designed production parameters and narrative style conventions, the situation comedy format was regionalized/localized to accommodate the WPBT/ESAA-TV Miami production site and audiences. Through this adaptation, *¿Qué pasa U.S.A.?* culturally, politically, linguistically, and ethnically innovated the U.S. and pre-1960s Cuban situation comedy genre.

¿Qué pasa U.S.A.? should be regarded as an American, Cuban, and Cuban-American sitcom classic, a product that exemplified the socio-cultural, economic, and television particularities related to the Cuban diaspora. As a diasporic cultural product, *¿Qué pasa U.S.A.?* carried with it the migratory movement of certain sectors of the Cuban community while also symbolically transporting elements of pre-revolutionary Cuban television. These foreign ingredients were combined with the emergence of a post-1959 Cuban-American identity and a new style of situation comedy in the U.S.A. The sitcom genre then became the television place where 1950s U.S. and Cuban television and 1970s U.S. television merged. The short-lived ESAA-TV legislation provided the impetus to create this temporally, culturally, and linguistically mixed television place on public television.

As a diasporic cultural artifact, *¿Qué pasa U.S.A.?* also challenged the mainstream media constructions of a singular, economically solvent, right-wing, and anti-Castro, Cuban exile community. As Myria Georgiou and Roger Silverstone write, "diasporic media are involved in the development of ideologies and representations outside the major global and national media and the mainstream national and international political arenas . . ."[43] Even though *¿Qué pasa U.S.A.?*'s silence on issues of Cuban exile and Cuba-related politics could be perceived as problematic, one should recognize the political relevance of the show. *¿Qué pasa U.S.A.?*'s primary political objective was to transform the Cuban exiles into U.S. immigrants.

The *¿Qué pasa U.S.A.?* case study illustrates how, in particular instances, television genres have functioned as formats. Furthermore, the analysis presented here also reveals the ways in which our selection of sources and familiarity with a program history and television market might shape our interpretation and categorization of formats. Certainly, no one can deny that today's proliferation of format development and exportation has revolutionized the global television industry. However, more than focusing on what constitutes a format, it might be more productive to examine the cultural, political, and social meanings inscribed in original and adapted formats and the ways in which these products are decoded by audiences. This type of analysis could expand our understanding of the multiple factors that shape local, national, and diasporic television.

Acknowledgments

Special thanks to the *¿Qué pasa U.S.A.?* and ESAA-TV television professionals who provided valuable information about the sitcom and the federal program. *Mil gracias* to the librarians at the University of Miami's Cuban Heritage Collection for their extraordinary help, ongoing assistance, and support.

Notes

1 Michael Keane and Albert Moran, "Television's New Engine," *Television and New Media* 9, no. 2 (2008), 164. Also see Albert Moran, *Copycat TV: Globalisation, Program Formats and Cultural Identity* (Luton, U.K.: University of Luton Press, 1998).
2 Keane and Moran, "Television's New Engine," 158.
3 Personal interview, May 25, 2008, Bogotá, Colombia. Also see Omar Rincón, *Narrativas mediáticas: O cómo se cuenta la sociedad del entretenimiento* (Barcelona, Spain: Gedisa, 2005).
4 Jason Mittel, *Genre and Television: From Cop Shows to Cartoons in American Culture.* (London: Routledge, 2004), xiv, 3; Silvio Waisbord, "McTV: Understanding the Global Popularity of Television Formats," *Television and New Media* 5, no. 4 (2004), 359.
5 María de los Angeles Torres, *In the Land of Mirrors: Cuban Exile Politics in the United States* (Ann Arbor: University of Michigan Press, 1999); and Alejandro Portes, and Robert L. Back, *Latin Journey: Cuban and Mexican Immigrants in the United States* (Berkeley: University of California Press, 1985), 86.
6 Education Amendments of 1972, "Title VII—Emergency School Aid," P.L. 92–318, 421-442.
7 Ibid.
8 Bernadette Nelson, Daniel Sullivan, Joseph Zelan, and Susan Brighton, *Assessment of the ESAA-TV Program: An Examination of its Production, Distribution and Financing* (Cambridge, MA: ABT Associates Inc., 1980), 2.
9 For analysis of the categorization of "high quality" children's television shows, see Heather Hendershot, *Saturday Morning Censors: Television Regulation before the V-Chip* (Durham, NC: Duke University Press, 1998).
10 Nelson, et al., *Assessment of the ESAA-TV Program*, 12.
11 Ibid., 41. The national series received up to $3 and $4 million per year. ESAA-TV official, e-mail communication, April 2005.
12 Nelson, et al., *Assessment of the ESAA-TV Program*, 96.
13 A very similar approach regarding commercial television programming and ethnic minority audiences defined U.S. public television since its inception. See Laurie Ouellette, *Viewers like You?: How Public TV Failed the People* (New York: Columbia University Press, 2002).
14 ESAA-TV official, e-mail communication, April 2005.
15 *¿Qué pasa U.S.A.?* production member, e-mail communication, April 2005.

16 H. Espinet Borges, "'Mi Esposo Favorito' 'I Love Lucy,'" *Carteles*, August 16, 1953;
    H. Espinet Borges, "'I Love Lucy'? . . . 'No!'—dice Condall,' *Carteles*, August 23, 1953.
17 Oscar Luis López, *La Radio en Cuba* (Havana: Editorial Letras Cubanas, 1998).
18 de Villa resigned during the show's early production stages.
19 Writer's package for *¿Qué Pasa U.S.A.?*, 1976, 11. Luis Santeiro's papers, Cuban
    Heritage Collection, University of Miami, Florida.
20 Writer's package for *¿Qué Pasa U.S.A.?*, 1–9.
21 Ibid., 5.
22 For information on Cuban-American culture and the processes of assimilation, see
    Gustavo Pérez Firmat, *Life on the Hyphen: The Cuban-American Way* (Austin: University
    of Texas Press, 1994), 4–20.
23 According to María de los Angeles Torres, whereas by the mid-1970s there were still
    "exile oriented" and "immigrant oriented" organizations," the majority of the Cuban
    exile community concentrated their efforts on attaining political power in the U.S.A.
    Torres, *In the Land of Mirrors*, 84–104.
24 Writer's package for *¿Qué Pasa U.S.A.?*, 12.
25 Ibid.
26 Velia Matínez, the actress who played the grandmother in *¿Qué Pasa U.S.A.?*, was a
    widely known and respected actress in Cuba.
27 ESAA-TV official, e-mail communication, April 2005.
28 Torres, *In the Land of Mirrors*, 75.
29 Writer's package for *¿Qué Pasa U.S.A.?*, 16.
30 Ella Taylor, *Prime-Time Families: Television Culture in Postwar America* (Berkeley:
    University of California Press, 1989).
31 George Lipsitz, "The Meaning of Memory: Family, Class, and Ethnicity in Early
    Network Television Programs," in Lynn Spigel and Denise Mann (eds.), *Private
    Screenings: Television and the Female Consumer* (Minneapolis: University of Minnesota
    Press, 1992), 70–108; and Vincent Brook, *Something Ain't Kosher Here: The Rise of the
    "Jewish" Sitcom* (New Brunswick, N J: Rutgers University Press, 2003).
32 Pérez Firmat, *Life on the Hyphen*, 7–8.
33 Torres, *In the Land of Mirrors*, 94–100.
34 Robert Sklar, "PBS 'Americanizes' a Cuban Family," *The Chronicle of Higher Education*,
    April 30, 1979.
35 Ibid.
36 Les Brown, "TV Weekend," *New York Times*, June 16, 1978.
37 William Hickey, "Reflections in a Busman's Eye," Cleveland *Plain Dealer*, January 25,
    1978, 8-D; "*Que pasa U.S.A.?*" *San Antonio Express*, January 8, 1978.
38 Diane Wright, "Que pasa U.S.A.? In New Bilingual Show, Grandma Gets All the
    Jokes," January 18, 1979. Luis Santeiro's papers, CHC.
39 Brown, "TV Weekend."
40 Marvin Kitman, "Que pasa? Something funny," *Newsday*, January 19, 1978.
41 Ouellette, *Viewers like You?*
42 Dave Berkman, "Confessions of an Ex-Bureaucrat," *Public Telecommunications Review*
    8, no. 6 (1980), 18.
43 Myria Georgiou and Roger Silverstone, "Diasporas and Contra-Flows Beyond Nation-
    Centrism," in Daya Kishan Thussu (ed.), *Media on the Move: Global Flow and Contra-
    Flow* (London: Routledge, 2007), 34.

PART II
Transnational Formats

Historical Perspectives

6

FROM DISCRETE ADAPTATIONS TO HARD COPIES

The Rise of Formats in European Television

Jérôme Bourdon

To understand what is a format, this chapter suggests it is best to start with history, and to ask "When was the format?" When did the notion receive its modern meaning of standard, replicable, internationally marketable, and potentially successful formula? I will investigate this while focusing on specific actors, television professionals who started using the term and believing in the thing, and on a certain region, Western Europe.

Why professionals? Media theories should not ignore the pragmatic knowledge of social actors. Before it started being researched, "format" had long been a term of broadcasting parlance, first in the U.S.A., then in England, and later moving from English to other languages. Why Western Europe? We are not in search of a hypothetical European television culture, or of specific "European formats." Western European public service television systems will be used to exemplify the rise of the notion in an initially indifferent or hostile context. The notion slowly emerged from a system of discrete adaptations. This is a symptom of deep changes in global television history. More precisely, it helps explain why we can now write about television programs, once considered as deeply national, particular creations, as standardized products, which can be translated easily from one culture to the next, or, even better, conceived from the start as global.

The History of Format Adaptation in Europe: Three Stages

How did this transformation take place? We will propose a periodization of the history of European television based on two parameters: its conflicting relation with the U.S.A., and the evolution of its notion of public service. The first of the three periods here is that of discrete adaptations; until the early 1980s, while British broadcasting borrowed the use of "format" from American English, other languages had their own terms for referring to "ideas" or "formulas" for programs. Such formulas were borrowed and adapted from country to country, primarily from the U.S.A. to Europe, especially in the game show genre, and often without monetary transaction. It is difficult to trace the flow of adaptations as the process did not sit well with public service supporters whose main missions were to provide national information and culture as opposed to global entertainment. The second period is that of open replications of mostly American formats, starting from the 1980s, when the term "format" and its derivatives entered professional parlance. At this stage, commercial and sometimes public television, in search of successful formulas at a time of brutally increased competition, acquired and faithfully adapted American game-show formulas. The third period, that of Euro-American convergence, started in the late 1990s with the rapid success of new formats, which now came partly from Europe and added a new genre, that of reality television—whose emergence, in many respects, is highly symptomatic of the dramatic change taking place in European television history.

Preliminary: The Thing and the Word[1]

Before moving to history, some clarification about the word "format" is needed in order to avoid anachronism. "Format" moved from French to English in the mid-nineteenth century, as a term from printing, referring to the size of the page. In English, it received the meaning of technical standard, notably in computers but also in television. The word, along with this connotation, was then adopted from English into many languages.

It is also in English that the word was first related to media content. According to Camporesi (Camporesi, 2000), at the time the BBC adapted wining American formulas to its radio (and later television) needs, the word "format" was rarely used, and writers referred instead to formula, idea, invention, etc. When the word was used, it did not have exactly the same industrial connotations as today, it meant something more related to "idea" or "formula." One example from the U.S.A.: "It is very important for the TV art educator to know what he believes and why he wants to use TV. His aims determine program format and content. Producers find educators unsure of their goals . . ." (Wilson, 1955). In such a case, "form" could have been used. It is not sure whether the author is actually referring to some rigid formula, or rather, simply, to some "envelope" for the content. Obviously, looking back from our age of "global formats," we might project the industrial and commercial connotation on a term which was probably used in a more flexible manner.

When did "format" become a detailed formula, explained in various documents, and with commercial value and legal implications (Challis and Coad, 2004)? Within Europe, it is certainly in the U.K. that this took place, with the rise of the commercial network ITV, the first European network to massively and faithfully adapt American "formats," giving a decisive push to this semantic and professional change. In the rest of Europe, the word (or in French, German or Spanish, *formato*—the new meaning of an old word) entered television parlance in the age of privatization, becoming a key term in the late 1980s or 1990s. This new lexicon was connected to a change in values across the continent. The main terms of reference for discussing television were no longer esthetics (as they had been, although briefly and not with much success, in the 1950s), or politics (as in the 1960s and 1970s), but economics. In a nutshell, discussions over the efficiency of formats became central, as those on the objectivity of news receded, and as debates about television's esthetic potential became a thing of the past.

Before "Formats": The Age of Adaptations and Borrowings

A history of formats has to start with the search for similar practices of copying and reproducing ideas for shows, even without the term. Long before professionals started talking about "formats," formulas for programs, as well as newspapers and other kinds of media content, were either bought and faithfully copied, or at least borrowed, adapted and domesticated. Television format, in this sense, is the most recent stage of a very old history. The problem of both the historian and the theorist is to identify exactly what was borrowed. Often it does not belong to the quantifiable—as in the original meaning of the word "format" or page size. The question is not related only to media or television history; one can easily claim that the whole history of ideas and arts is rife with imitation. However, "one must distinguish between the normal imitativeness of art and the industrialized excess that is television's sincerest form of fawning on itself" (Gitlin, 1983, p. 71). Systematic imitation for industrial purposes ("industrial excess"), however, had started before television; it is tied to the history of both capitalism and modern media. To seduce consumers, capitalism has to face a paradox: both to produce the same, faithfully reproduced, and the new, unexpected, born from nowhere. Gitlin has brilliantly analyzed this paradox for American television series, but the thirst for imitations was, very early on, an international phenomenon, not least because global borrowing went, and remains to a certain extent, largely unnoticed—bringing much to the borrower, without having to remunerate owners of original ideas who tended to focus on national markets. The history of the press is replete with loose borrowing and adaptations of ideas from its inception. Maybe the first example of systematic international "format" borrowing took place at the end of the nineteenth century. This was the age of a first globalization of media forms (if not format), in two related domains, the print press and advertising. Three cities, New York, London and Paris, invented the mass circulation popular press, and in both London and Paris newspaper editors got their inspiration from American formulas (Pope, 1978; Wiener, 1996).

In European radio or television, early international format adaptation is difficult to trace. The main reason for this is related to the public service ideology which dominated its early history. Public service broadcasting's (PSB) main aims were to inform and educate. Public service supporters such as Tracey (1998) would later insist that entertainment mattered, and should be made with "style" or "élan" and not simply with efficiency, but this assertion was difficult to translate into concrete practices. With or without "style," popular entertainment never sat well with influential television critics through the late 1960s (Bourdon and Frondon, 2002, for examples in France, Germany, Italy and Spain). Further, producers and directors of drama (not to mention documentaries), the most prestigious among television professionals, expressed open contempt for producers and hosts (often the same persons) of game and variety shows.

Format adaptation started with entertainment programs, particularly with the genre based on strict rules and timing, the game show—or more precisely, the quiz. But this very precision is more easily done in English as the distinction between game and quiz has never been well established in Europe, where in most cases the same word is still used for both, e.g. *jeux (télévisés)* in French, or *concursos* in Spanish. For European professionals, adapted game shows were not perceived as a specific sub-genre within the game show spectrum.

Apart from the emphasis on culture, there is an aspect of PSB which most of its academic theoreticians and supporters are less keen to emphasize: public service was a very national ideology, and, in the case of at least two countries, France and the U.K., an imperial ideology. Public service had to "serve the nation" and to help consolidate, build and transmit a national culture where some genres such as literary adaptations and historical programs (drama and documentary) played a key part. Finally, public service was "national" in another, but related, sense: in-house production was dominant, and this was proudly emphasized. The "non-national" was both the foreign and the private. Format adaptation often started within the nascent and private production sector as adaptations of foreign (mostly U.S.-originated) ideas, where entertainers looking for ways to connect quickly to a wide audience found the best resources. In short, format adaptation contradicted almost everything public service broadcasting stood for.

Entertainment producers who adapted programs felt they were a minority within public service broadcasting. They also shared a specific form of "American-ophilia." Following a long tradition of professional "pilgrimages" starting with advertising and the press in the nineteenth century, many of these producers traveled to the U.S.A. for both business and pleasure, and often picked up ideas there. Most borrowing did not take place on a commercial basis, in days when "plagiarism was rife." When it happened at all, "early payments for the use of program ideas were ad hoc and more in the nature of a courtesy to the original producer or owner" (Moran, 1998, p. 18). A license fee system emerged only in the 1970s and was systematized in the 1980s.

Cultural nationalism was so strong that even entertainers insisted on the national character of their activity, and this from the very start, in the country which was the first major adaptor of American formulas. The first European adaptors, British radio producers (Camporesi, 1994; Hilmes, 2007) insisted on the necessity to twist and adapt the format to their special needs—transforming, as they explained at length, these U.S. ideas to suit British mentality, taste, tradition. In other countries, entertainment professionals did the same, boasting of their ability to domesticate American formats, to give them some "national" flavor, which was often defined negatively. Since U.S. television culture was criticized as too fast, too flashy, too coarse, and too expensive, Europeans slowed down the pace of quizzes, incorporated them into longer shows (a process an Italian critic would later call "theatrical dilatation"), and reduced the value of prizes. In quizzes, they introduced some "serious" knowledge and an academic flavor, if not academic judges, to help contestants. Further, adaptations were scheduled on a less frequent basis than in the U.S.A., and for shorter stretches of time— not for a whole season, rarely for years (or with frequent breaks). The public was not to be "chained" to television with regular viewing habits, but, to the contrary, stimulated, if not disrupted. It was also a way for television to show its creativity and ability to renew itself.

The European adaptations of *Candid Camera*, for example (original U.S. version on CBS, 1960–67) all tried to incorporate the sketches into longer programs and sometimes spectacular shows. Starting in Italy as *Specchio Segreto* ("Secret Mirror"—RAI1, 1965, eight programs of 1 hour) and in Spanish as *Objectivo Indiscreto* later that same year, there was an emphasis on the moral conclusion. In Spain, the program was controversial because it supposedly exploited "innocent" victims by ridiculing them. In France, *Candid Camera* started in 1966 under the title *La camera invisible* after a television director had seen the program in the course of a pleasure trip to the U.S.A. and picked up the idea. It was presented as a purely national invention, and became a huge success, again with some moral claims about its content.

In such ideological settings, and with such reluctance, why resort to adaptations at all? In the late 1950s and the early 1960s, television had barely started in Europe. It was present in the majority of households only in the U.K., where it benefited from the early start of BBC television in 1936. French television really started only after the war, was inaugurated in Italy and Germany in 1954, and came to Spain in 1956. Television quickly turned out to be a greedy machine, consuming show after show, expanding its broadcasting hours in a "natural" manner which few people questioned, like a "horseless carriage" (Katz, 1973). And to feed the machine, one had to produce. In most countries, entertainment and hosts turned out to be a good resource, popular, reproducible from one week to the next, even if they were not highly regarded. From the start, the relation of public television with the popular (in the double sense of the successful and that of reaching a wide audience) was highly ambivalent (Bourdon, 2004), and entertainment adaptations played a key part in this complicated relation.

There were some cases of adaptations within Europe, and, even less frequently, from Europe to the U.S.A. German television occasionally borrowed formulas from other countries like Italy (*Der Grosse Preiss*, 1974–93, is the German version of the Italian *Risciatutto*), and later exported its own formats, like *Wetten Dass* (ZDF, 1981) to the U.K., Italy and, a rare feat before the age of reality shows, the U.S.A. Created in the 1950s, the French game show *La Tête et les Jambes* which involved teams of two partners with physical and intellectual abilities, was exported to Spain—and also, in the 1970s, to the U.S.A. The game show spectacular known in the U.K. as *It's a Knock-Out*, which started as *Campanile Sera* ("Evening Churchtowers") on RAI in 1960, became one of France's television "classics" as *Intervilles* ("Between Cities"). It was used as a political tool to foster European unity—as *Jeux sans frontières* ("Games without Borders"), created in the wake of a meeting between French president De Gaulle and German chancellor Adenauer.

Overall, however, the traffic of ideas long took place on a "one-way street," to quote the document which would, in the 1970s, draw worldwide attention to the phenomenon (Nordenstreng and Varis, 1974). Besides the U.K., the other country where borrowings of U.S. ideas took place on a "major" (quantifying the phenomenon is difficult) scale was probably Spain, showing that the question of American imports is not connected mostly to pre-existing cultural affinities, but instead to television structures. Both a "Latin" and an Anglo-Saxon country were early and heavy importers of American fare, and in both cases, the explanation lies in the early and massive introduction of commercial financing. ITV, created in 1955 in the U.K., and public television in Spain which started one year later, were financed mostly from advertising revenues from the very start—although in Spain television was a department of the office of broadcasting attached to the Ministry of Information until the 1970s.

It is not the place here to go into historical details (see Bourdon, 2008a, for more national examples) but each country had its own relation with American culture and its own import structures. In Italy, the relation was more open, heir to a long tradition and fed by the Italian-American diasporas. It has even been said that in those early years, "when television aspired to a faraway American dream, it most clearly found its originality" (Buttafava, 1980). France probably adapted fewer programs, which could be linked to "Gallic pride," but I would again prefer the structural explanation to the cultural one; France had a strong group of private producers in radio, even before the war, which moved to television where they imposed their formulas and dominated broadcasting entertainment until the early 1980s.

The 1980s: American Copies

While it is hard to know exactly when this policy of discrete adaptations ended, it is clear that European television entered the age of formats in the 1980s and 1990s, with the rise of powerful commercial stations—and, in two cases, the actual privatization of a public channel—in almost all European countries. The change went beyond television; it was connected to "deregulation," an ill-chosen but widespread term, meaning the withdrawal of the state from major sectors of economic life. Television was not completely "deregulated," but submitted to regulation other than the direct public management that had prevailed in the past. The state released its grip on economic life by creating public "independent author-ities" (again, independent deserves quotation marks), in charge of supervising but not directly managing, sectors of social life, including communication (broadcast and telecommunications). Overall, the term "commercialization" is much more apt than "deregulation" to describe the overall process.

The new actor, which mattered most, was not the "independent authorities" but new commercial stations who quickly dominated the whole field of tele-vision. Public service television often had no choice but to imitate many of the strategies and practices of these commercial broadcasters. This process had a decisive impact on European format circulation. It would be wrong to state that formats were "imposed" on European television culture, since to a large extent this was "self-inflicted imperialism." European television professionals were eager to feed the beast, to find ways of filling schedules, and filling them with some guarantee of success. However, it should not be forgotten that U.S. exporters had long been waiting for European television stations to open up, deploring their poor understanding of programming and their lack of interest in American fare that did so well in many parts of the world. Their wishes were fulfilled in the course of a few years. The once reluctant European markets became greedy importers. For U.S. program exporters, Europe became the new "promised land" (Segrave, 1998, p. 174). The trend started with new, relatively poor commercial stations who bought old series and provided the staples for Berlusconi's or Murdoch's new channels.

Attention soon switched to formats, and often to old formats which had been previously ignored. In the 1980s and 1990s, format trade become a systematic policy, as new commercial stations born from deregulation started systematically exploiting U.S. catalogues. Not only were old formats imported, but the delay between a U.S. invention and its export became much shorter. Although the nationalistic rhetoric did not entirely disappear, new television professionals boasted the opposite of their predecessors, not the ability to transform "foreign" models according to national needs, but, rather, the ability to be as "professional" and as "effective" as the Americans (Bourdon, 2008a). On the whole, and way beyond television, European public discourse (despite appearances to the contrary sometimes) started giving much more credit to American culture, especially in the field of economics and commerce. America has been partly rehabilitated by politicians; neoliberalism has become the model for policy at large, even when the official discourse continued to defend public services and the welfare state.

On European screens, the symbol of this transformation was the arrival of *The Price is Right*, created in 1956 by Goodson-Todman for NBC. It embodied everything public service television had once reproved: emphasis on money and commerce, pure spectacle without any form of cultural knowledge. Most European commercial stations bought the rights for the game, starting with

Berlusconi's Italia Uno in 1983 (*OK il prezzo e giusto*), and continuing with ITV in 1984, TF1 in 1988 (*Le Juste Prix*), RTL (*Der Preiss ist heiss*), among many others. In a different style, *Wheel of Fortune* (created in 1975 by Merv Griffin; it became a success on U.S. local stations in 1983), was another European hit in the late 1980s and the 1990s. In Italy, it was first broadcast on the now defunct commercial station Odeon TV, until Berlusconi bought it in 1989. *Wheel of Fortune* was first broadcast as a long weekly show on Canale 5 on Sunday evenings, becoming a daily program in 1991.

European–American Convergence and the Age of Reality Games

Before moving to our third period, the age of reality shows, one should remember that despite the hype around "reality," adaptations of game shows they have been continually successful worldwide and remain so till this day; the genre keeps on circulating, no less than reality television, and with new major providers such as Australia. In Europe, a producer who plays a key part in the history of reality television, Endemol (Delmas and Richebois, 2006) is also a major provider of game shows. For the historian of formats, it is difficult to evaluate the significance of reality television, because of the hype (including the academic hype) surrounding the genre. Many commentators talk about "reality television" as a new genre which has emerged in the last 10 years or so. However, the label "reality television" has a long history, and, to complicate matters further, many would-be historians of the label reframe documentaries or magazines as "forerunners" of reality shows. The label "reality television" (or "reality shows") started being used in the late 1980s, with programs like *Unsolved Mysteries* (NBC, 1987) *Rescue 911* (CBS, 1989) or *America's Most Wanted* (Fox, 1988–), a show actually adapted from a German program (see below). In the late 1980s, some sort of reality television (and some labeling) was present in most European, and many Latin American countries. In Italy, the third public channel, RAI3, long a minor player in the highly competitive (including within public service) Italian television landscape, raised its share and drew huge attention in the late 1980s by introducing new formats which were theorized as *televisione verita*. Although many of those formats were original, they had much in common with U.S. reality television.

The attempts at definition started at that time. Let us note that the search for the perfect definition of the content of a genre is in vain. A genre is basically what a society feels exists as a genre a complex relation between social context and some discursive traits which can be quite unstable, especially at the time of emergence when qualification is part of a complex negotiation between industry (which did not initiate the label), critics, and audiences. In the case of "reality television," all attempts have to wrap up different categories together. Thus, the first "reality" programs were of two kinds at least, which both borrowed from old trends in the documentary tradition: emergency workers, to use Dovey's qualification (Dovey, 2000; see also Hill, 2000), and emotional programs (showing ordinary people in real-life situations). The "emergency workers" programs followed social workers, policemen, doctors in their work. The emotional programs had "ordinary" people, talking about real-life problems in emotional terms, confessing crimes, or asking for missing people to come back.

What was the relation with the notion of "format"? Most of those reality experiments did not become long lasting formats, and most didn't cross borders. *C'eravamo tanto amati* ("We All Loved Each Other so Much," originally the name of a famous 1974 Italian movie), an Italian format which showed partners of several couples fighting on the set (supposedly in attempts at reconciliation), was adapted to American television, but did not last long. The most successful format actually was an old format later rebranded as "reality": *Crimewatch UK* (started 1984 on BBC1). The show was based on *Aktenzeichen XY: ungelöst* ("File XY: Unsolved"), an old and very successful German magazine program (as a term, "reality TV" was unknown in 1967, when the show was introduced on the second German channel, ZDF). This monthly program called on audience members to solve criminal cases, and used live phone conversation and re-enactments and immediately caused a debate due to its "graphic" and "unethical" character. Besides the U.K., the program was adapted to France, Israel, and finally the U.S.A. as *America's Most Wanted*. The idea of asking the audience to help solve criminal cases or trace missing persons had some ancestry in the press and radio, but the German program was the first to work this concept into a long, emotionally involving program.

Another characteristic of this first chapter in the history of reality programming is their "public service" ambitions (or claims). They were supposed to help restore law and order, or solve personal problems, and emphasized the direct collaboration of public professionals, the police, the judiciary, or psychologists. The public service rhetoric is to be found in Germany, Italy, and France. It was not accepted everywhere, however. In France, the most famous host for the new reality program, journalist Jacques Pradel, was mockingly mourned as the "former journalist" Jacques Pradel by some colleagues. In Germany, *Aktenzeichen* had been very controversial from the start, and questioned for its sensationalism, for its inflated record of solved cases (exactly like its successors would be 20 or 30 years later) (Bourdon, 2008b).

Why this early stage of reality television did not generate many successful programs remains to be researched. Some characteristics of the programs may provide part of the explanation. The public service claims were difficult to manage: many programs involved some sort of collaboration with public service institutions or professions, such as the medical profession, the judiciary and the police. In many countries, it created controversies within those institutions, which were not used to so much media exposure, while television was accused of encroaching on the role of the police (in Italy), psychologists (in France), etc. In addition, the management of emotions on the set could be difficult, resting on a complex chemistry between a star host (a key ingredient) and guests.

The new wave of 1980s reality television succeeded because it crossed highly emotional programs with the genre which had lent itself most successfully, so far, to formatting and globalization: the game show. The new "reality games," as they would come to be called, had much in common with the "confessional" or "emotional" strand of the previous reality programs which centered on the extraordinary emotional experiences of ordinary people. But they were also games, in the most traditional sense of the term; carefully selected candidates competed in different arenas, and the winner pocketed a hefty prize. Based on a precise set of rules, forsaking most of their public service claims, they could easily be codified and commoditized as formats. What was new, then? The answer is not simple, as the hype about novelty is part of the discursive context which has helped give a social basis to the genre. Some maintained that the novelty lay in their "real life" (as opposed to studio) settings. But the "real life" settings, be they deserted islands or large apartments, were carefully selected (sometimes created from scratch), charted and packed with cameras. The "real" (or the pseudo-real) here was not used as a studio, but turned into (or conceived as) a television studio from the start, although a new kind of studio, one which fitted perfectly the industrial logic of formatting. The main criterion is less that of location than the nature of the competition. Mostly, people do not compete verbally for knowledge (as in most game shows), or physically in some sort of a sport-derived game. They expose themselves; they become highly involved emotionally, over long periods of time, in front of huge audiences.

The new reality games are also programmed in specific editions consisting of a series of episodes (10–20) with a careful build-up towards the finale. Participants are not only called upon to answer questions, but to perform feats of strength, and demonstrate their powers of seduction and manipulation: they fight, scream laugh, or more often, cry. Close-ups of faces loaded with emotions (again, an old staple of television), are central to the genre. Reality games also include confessional interviews where participants report on their feelings: this reflexivity belongs to a larger cultural transformation where vulgarized psychology plays a central part (Illouz, 2007). The shows exploit or encourage hostile feelings between participants (e.g. teams have to vote to eliminate members one by one). The host can be harsh on candidates. A trend which had appeared in early game shows is now systematically exploited: participants do not come on the show for money only, but in order to achieve celebrity status. This status, in turn, is used by the channels to expose their successful participants (or their families and friends) in other shows. The programs are sometimes called "reality-based," but they are based on a reality which television itself has produced: "TV-based reality TV" could be a better name for the genre.

The story of successful formats has been told often. The first reality game to succeed internationally was the Swedish *Expedition Robinson* (later known as

Survivor), started in 1997 by private producer Strix for the first public channel, SVT1. Presented in carefully edited weekly episodes, *Survivor* is based on a contest between two teams of eight candidates placed for some 40 days on an "exotic," remote island packed with cameras. For embattled public broadcaster SVT, *Survivor* was a highly successful program. The suicide of one of the participants in the first edition in July 1997 (after the broadcast) was no real obstacle to success—indeed, the chronicle of scandals or incidents (about exposure, or violence) was quickly integrated into the marketing of the genre.

The outstanding performance of the program in the U.S.A. made *Survivor* a global, or at least, a Western phenomenon. As Endemol Holland head John de Mol (Schlosser, 2000) has noted, the U.S. detour is necessary to gain true access to a global market—like Jacques Derrida, a television format needs the American seal of approval to become a global product. In the U.S.A., reality television helped revive network TV, which had been continuously declining in an increasingly diversified television environment. In August 2000, the *Survivor* finale on CBS posted the highest ratings of the television season after the Super Bowl. In Europe, though successful, *Survivor* was never the social phenomenon that *Big Brother* would become.

By far the most successful European reality format continent wide and worldwide, *Big Brother*'s first edition was broadcast on Dutch television in September 1999–January 2000. *Big Brother* is also, in its short life-span, one of the most researched programs in television history. *Big Brother* quickly became the most watched program of the year. It was adapted, with the same outstanding success (the press used metaphors like earthquake, revolution, etc.), in some 60 countries (Lochard and Soulez, 2003), with many variations, and also multinational editions (e.g. in English-speaking Africa and the Arab world). Even more than game shows, which had once generated very similar indignation but had become a staple of television since, reality television had the power to provoke controversy and to fuel "media panic" (Biltereyst, 2004).

If *Big Brother* was the mold for many other similar shows, where "ordinary people" live together for some time and have to perform challenging tasks with an amount of self-exposure until only one wins the big prize, another major trend of so-called reality programming brought viewers back to an old formula, the talent show, which had a long career worldwide on radio and television. Again, with a difference: the systematic personal exposure of participants through interviews and special reports. More carefully formatted than earlier talent shows, and involving careful and systematic merchandising of everything related to the show (music, stars, stories), these programs were less controversial than *Big Brother* or *Survivor*, and more readily adapted and routinized into schedules. Among the winning formats: *Star Academy* (created by Endemol Spain, started in France and Spain in 2001 and today broadcast in some 50 countries), *Pop Idol* (U.K., Fremantle Media—formerly Pearson television, created on ITV in 2001, adapted by more than 20 countries), and *Popstars* (created in New Zealand in 1999, adapted by more than 50 countries).

One characteristic of this new age should be emphasized: the international adaptation of formats became highly visible. The first period was one either of discretion, or of emphasis on the originality of the new version. In the 1980s, format adaptation became public first in the professional world as new, young media professionals wanted to demonstrate they were good at getting high audiences. Knowing which format to copy became something to be proud of, not to hide. In the last 10 years, publicity around format circulation has become part of a new reflexive interest in the globalization of culture. Format circulation became a topic for public discussions among media professionals, among academics (as the ones writing in this book) and also a topic for the mainstream media. Television audiences became aware that the show which would have been said to be "typically French" was actually a copy of a foreign program—although we do not know to what extent. This international character was sometimes used as a marketing ploy (in some countries a special program was devoted to other editions of *Big Brother*, and in several cases, candidates of different national editions of *Big Brother* were swapped for a short period, usually a week). Although, as "the export of discursive practices is much less visible than the export of actual movies and television series" (Chalaby, 1996, p. 323), this visibility depends much on the willingness of social actors to hide or to publicize the process. We have entered an age where publicity about the success of a format has become part of the format, which shows to what extent formatting is an economic process: everything can be put to task to make a show successful.

Format is about successful formulas, replication, commoditization, and cultural hype both as moral panic and marketing strategy. In addition, it is part of a growing body of legal texts trying to define, and, more importantly, protect formats. The word also entered the legal domain where it quickly caused many headaches. For the legal definition of a format is far from clear. It is now a major preoccupation in the industry as format licensing is "a massive industry worth tens of millions of dollars" (Challis and Coad, 2004)—still much less than the money generated by drama sales worldwide. Besides the sale of format, there is also a massive "copycat industry." But what legal protection can formats receive? In various legal systems, there is no protection at all for "ideas" per se, only for the way they are packaged, but this is to be "sufficiently" specific, and no judge, in any country, has risked explaining what is "sufficient" to protect a format. This takes us back to old legal debates about the difference between the protection of "ideas" per se, which does not exist, and of the "expression" of ideas (which is possible). As a United States judge pointed out in 1930, "Nobody has ever been able to fix that boundary, and nobody ever can." In the world of television, the topic started receiving much legal attention in the 1990s. More and more legal decisions, in different countries, tend to protect the "expression" of the "ideas" attached to a format. In 2003, Endemol successfully sued a Brazilian company for a blatant copy of *Big Brother* (Challis and Coad, 2004). Despite the intricacies, it seems safe to assume that, as elsewhere, the holy principles of law will be adapted to the new requirements of social and economic life, and that this kind of jurisprudence is bound to develop.

Discussion: Format, Genre and Globalization

This short history of the rise of formats can help us define the notion more precisely. It is too simple to define format as a replicable formula for a program. A format is not only a formula which can be copied easily. It is a formula which fits into the needs of a new market: the market transforms formula into formats and also stimulates the creation of formats. In the later stages, format has become something which can be publicized as such, adding a new dimension to the notion.

The notion of format has become so prevalent in debates about television that it sometimes competes with "genre" as a way of categorizing programs. Both notions entertain a complex relation. So far, I have used the notion of genre unquestioningly, referring to some formats as pertaining to genres as species belonging to a category. However, genre is no more a "natural" category than format. It is even more complex, in many ways, because of its long history in poetics and literature, from which it moved to the media, and also because it moves between everyday and "scientific" language.

I would like to suggest here that we should avoid going too far on this path where we organize television programs in wide categories ("genres"), which could be easily subdivided in sub-categories ("formats"), with each genre including a list of formats. Television historians and theorists would then follow ancestral traditions of poetics by trying to draw charts of genres and sub-genres. But "genre" and "format" do not belong to the same intellectual traditions, and it is misleading to mix them in such a way. Genre is part of what we called earlier, after Gitlin, the "normal imitativeness of art," while format belongs to the "industrial excess of culture." Thus, format is not in relation to genre as the sub-category to the category. In the new global industrial age, television professionals (and professionals of commercial culture) constantly try to turn genres, formulas, ideas, into successful formats, and to turn a major successful format (like *Big Brother*) into a matrix for other formats. This is what has led Jeremy Tunstall to coin the phrase "genre-format" about new Hollywood cinema genres (Tunstall and Machin, 1999, p. 22). The dialectical relation between genre and format, now a global phenomenon, started in American television and cinema. One could read the history of prime time fiction as a series of attempts at transforming each new successful format into a genre; let us say, turn *Charlie's Angels* into the "feminine yet hyper-professional female agents managed by an invisible male boss" (there were such attempts, mostly unsuccessful). Gitlin (1994) has identified three strategies to exploit the success of series: spin-offs (putting one successful character of an old show into a new storyline), copies (reproducing the basic elements of a successful storyline—but first, deciding what is "basic"), and recombinants (of elements taken from different successful series). The new success of "format television" could be analyzed as a transfer of those strategies to "factual" TV. The straightforward copy is the main strategy, but reality television is also very much made of spin-offs and recombinants (rural drama background + celebrity + *Big Brother* = *The Farm*).

Although historians loathe predictions, it might be safe to suggest that some genres which have not been subject to transformation into formats will certainly undergo the process, as the "horseless carriage" is endlessly raking the cultural present and past, without respect for certain hierarchies and areas which have long resisted commoditization. Take the example of news. Everyone looking at the main TV news, in any given country, finds the same "format": for 30 minutes or so, a single presenter-journalist (the anchor)—more rarely a couple of anchors—faces the camera, tells the viewers what happened during the day, interviews guests in studio and reporters on locations, proposes reports from different places with commentary via the reporter's voiceover, while the same reporters, "on location," address the viewers and add their own narratives to the main narrative of the anchor. This apparently "natural" formula is the product of a long history of convergence around a U.S. model (Bourdon, 2000). Once, there was no anchor, only a voiceover; the anchor was not a journalist; there were several presenters during the same edition; or presenters changed from one day to the next—and other differences regarding the role of correspondents, of experts in studio, etc. News has been discreetly, but very effectively, formatted from a variety of formulas into a single, rigid pattern. Beyond news, current affairs and the information genre also have a rich history of magazines which were copied, again, starting mostly from America. Thus, in 1965, French TV adapted the already old U.S. format known as *Meet the Press*.

Yet, news and current affairs have not been labeled formats, and rights for those formats have not been commercialized (although talk shows have been, but only in the last 20 years). News and current affairs were too serious, close to the hardcore (public service) mission of information to be commercialized in such a way. Only news reports have been commercialized, but even this is far from a general process; some specific images are just given over, and many others are part of a wide international system of exchanges like the EVN (EuroVision News). Format circulation has been widespread in entertainment not only because the genre (especially game shows) can easily be "formatted," but because it has been considered as outside the core of public service, or only as a marketing ploy to serve cultural and informational aims. However, with the rise of commercial television, and commercialism at large, the range of the commodifiable and the formatable is expanding (as it is in other areas of social life). This is increasingly occurring with drama, and what was once mostly an American process is turning into a global one. Some telenovelas are now being formatted. The Colombian telenovela *Betty la fea* (RCN, 1999–2001) ("Ugly Betty") is an excellent example of this "formatting" of fiction. The show itself, dubbed, has been successfully sold to some 30 countries including most of Latin America, but the format has been just as successful, and achieved high ratings, especially in Germany—and the German version has been sold to France, dubbed. Some countries have developed the series further and proposed original episodes, "based on *Betty, la Fea*" as the credits put it.

Finally, the history of formats might shed some light on the development of cultural globalization, or, more aptly, glocalization, to quote Robertson's (1995) classic article. Formats are often described as part of a way to introduce the foreign into the national, to make cultures similar. But the process of format adaptation also forces producers to adapt the global to the national, rethinking—and reconceptualizing—their own national culture. Remember the first age of "format" (or formula) circulation, which caused British producers to underline their Britishness by contrast with the "aggressive, fast," American culture. At the same time, they were defining "Britishness" in a homogeneous and distinct way. As elsewhere, globalization and nationalization (that is, the endless (re)construction of national cultures) go hand-in-hand. It is true that format production is standardized, but "production standardization is (also) a feature of each production context rather than a universal" (Ellis, 2004, p. 277). Even if producers in the age of formats do not hesitate to underline the foreign origin of formats, they have their own national rhetoric, different from that of their public service minded predecessors. Without reference to high culture or education, they all note that their local version of, say, *Big Brother*, is typically French, or Canadian, or Argentinian, because of the local setting, the ways men and women relate to each other, the transgressions they will not allow (as opposed to the more violent/erotic/commercial/macho Other). How much of this is national self-righteousness, self-fulfilling prophecy, or the nation reinventing itself, remains to be analyzed in each case. Global formats thus might be a new way to continue the old process of national integration and of the "invention of tradition" (Hobsbawm and Ranger, 1983).

Note

1   I owe this section to my colleagues at the European Television History Network: Valeria Camporesi, Alexander Dhoest, John Ellis, Eggo Mueller and Mari Pajala.

References

Belmas, D. and Richebois, V. (2006) *L'Histoire secrète d'Endemol*. Paris: Flammarion.

Biltereyst, D. (2004). Reality TV, troublesome pictures and panics: reappraising the public controversy around reality TV in Europe. In S. Holmes and D. Jermyn (Eds.), *Understanding Reality Television*. London: Routledge, pp. 91–110.

Bourdon, J. (2000). A history of European television news: from television to journalism, and back. *Communication, the European Journal of Communication Research*, 25(1): 61–84.

—— (2004). Old and new ghosts: public service television and the popular. A history. *European Journal of Communication*, 7(3): 283–304.

—— (2008a). Self-inflicted imperialism? On the early Americanization of European televisions, in W. Urrichio (Ed.), *We Europeans: Media, Representations, Identities*. London: Intellect, pp. 93–109.

—— (2008b). Searching for an identity for television: programmes, genres (with J. C. Ibáñez, C. Johnson and E. Müller), in J. Bignell and A. Fickers (Eds.), *A European Television History*. London: Blackwell, pp. 101–126.

Bourdon, J. and Frondon, J. M. (Eds.) (2002) *L'œil critique. Le journaliste critique de television*. Paris, Brussels: De Boecke and INA.

Buttafava, G. (1980) Un sogno americano. Quiz e riviste TV negli anni 1950, in G. Buttafava, A. Grasso, M. Lombezzi and T. Sanguineti, *American Way of Television: Le origini della TV in Italia*. Florence, Italy: Sansoni, pp. 59–82.

Camporesi, V. (1994). The BBC and American broadcasting, 1922–55. *Media, Culture and Society*, 16(4): 625–39.

—— (2000). *Mass Culture and National Traditions. The BBC and American Broadcasting 1922–1954*. Florence, Italy: European Press Academic Publishing.

Chalaby, J. K. (1996) Journalism as an Anglo-American invention: a comparison of the development of French and Anglo-American journalism, 1830s–1920s. *European Journal of Communication*, 11(3): 303–26.

Challis, B. and Coad, J. (2004) Format fortunes: is there now a copyright for the television format? (consulted 24.01.08 at www.spr-consilio.com/artip19.htm).

Dovey, J. (2000) *Freak Show. First Person Media and Factual Television*. London: Pluto Press.

Ellis, J. (2004) Television production. In A. Hill and R. Allen (Eds.) *The Television Studies Reader*. London: Routledge, pp. 267–74.

Erlinger, H. D. and Foltin, H. F. (Eds.) (1994) *Geschichte des Fernsehens in der Bundesrepublik Deutschland, Band 4. Unterhaltung, Werbung und Zielgruppenprogramm*. Munich, Germany: Wilhem Fink Verlag.

Gitlin, T. (1994 [1983]) *Inside Prime Time*. New York: Pantheon Books.

Grasso, A. (1992) *Storia della televisione italiana*. Milan, Italy: Garzanti.

Hill, A. (2000) Crime and crisis: British reality TV in action. In E. Buscombe (Ed.) *British Television: A Reader* (pp. 219–34). Oxford: Clarendon Press, pp. 219–34.

Hilmes, M. (2007) Front line family: "women's culture" comes to the BBC. *Media, Culture and Society*, 20(5): 5–29.

Hobsbawm, E. and Ranger, T. (Eds.) (1983) *The Invention of Tradition*. Cambridge: Cambridge University Press.

Illouz, E. (2007) *Cold Intimacies: The Making of Emotional Capitalism*. Oxford: Polity.

Katz, E. (1973) Television as a horseless carriage. In G. Gerbner, L. P. Gross and W. H. Melody (Eds.), *Communications Technology and Social Policy: Understanding the New Cultural Revolution*. New York: John Wiley, pp. 381–92.

Lochard, G. and Soulez, G. (2003) La télé-réalité : un débat mondial. *MédiaMorphoses*, special issue. Unnumbered.

Moran, A. (1998) *Copycat TV: Globalisation, Program Formats and Cultural Identity*. Luton, U.K.: University of Luton Press.

Nordenstreng, K., and Varis, T. (1974) *Television Traffic—A One-Way Street*. Paris: UNESCO.

Pope, D. (1978) French advertising men and the American promised land, *Historical Reflections*, V: 117–39.

Robertson, R. (1995) Glocalization: time–space and homogeneity–heterogeneity, in M. Featherstone, S. Lash and R. Robertson (Eds.), *Global Modernities*. London: Sage, pp. 25–69.

Schlosser, J. (2000) The man behind the camera. *Brodcasting and Cable,* July 3, p. 16.

Segrave, K. (1998) *American Television Abroad: Hollywood's Attempt to Dominate World Television*. Jefferson, NC and London: McFarland.

Tracey, M. (1998) *The Decline and Fall of Public Service Broadcasting*. Oxford: Oxford University Press.

Tunstall, J. and Machin, D. (1999) *The Anglo-American Media Connection*. London: Sage.

Wiener, J. (1996) The Americanization of the British press, 1830–1914. In M. Harris and T. O'Malley (Eds.), *Studies in Newspaper and PeriodicalHistory*. Westport, CT: Greenwood Press, , pp. 61–74.

Wilson, F. (1955). Letter in *College Art Journal*, 14(2): 164. Reporting on a seminar at Cornell in 1954.

7

"NATIONAL MIKE"

Global Host and Global Formats in Early Italian Television

Chiara Ferrari

Ten years after its foundation in 1944, the Italian public broadcaster RAI aired its first official show on January 3, 1954. The program, *Arrivi e Partenze* ("Arrivals and Departures"), was broadcast from Rome International Airport (and a few other major airports and ports throughout the peninsula) and featured a series of interviews with contemporary celebrities—both Italian and foreign—who were either arriving in or leaving Italy. Mike Bongiorno, a young Italian American journalist who had previously worked from the U.S.A. as a correspondent for EIAR (the radio broadcaster from which RAI developed), hosted the show.

Considering the cinematic legacy of neorealism—an emblematic example of national visual style based on modesty and lack of glamour in the aftermath of World War II—RAI's rather frivolous debut in broadcasting seemed to contradict the most genuine aspects of Italian identity at a time where the whole nation was still in ruins. Less than nine years after the official ending of the war (April 1945), however, Italy presented many characteristics that shared little with the visual and narrative ideals of Neorealism. After the harsh times of World War II and the immediate post-war years, in fact, Italians were eager to embrace a more modern kind of society based on regained wealth and finally being part of a more global sphere. RAI understood the changes in Italian society and exploited them to create a kind of programming that—while still considering national and regional aspects of the country and the audience—could provide some new perspectives, including some international views. It is not a coincidence, then, that *Arrivi e Partenze* showed several foreign celebrities in major Italian cities, as if to testify to Italy's legitimate place in the international arena. The very beginning of television in Italy, therefore, was marked by the necessity to find a balance between national and international concepts of identity and culture, but also between local and global ideas of entertainment.

In this dynamic environment, Mike Bongiorno found fertile ground to establish himself as the first true personality in Italian television, supported by RAI executives who saw in him the perfect vehicle to introduce American TV formats, with which he was familiar, into Italian broadcasting. Mike (as all Italians address him to this day) was born Michael Nicholas Salvatore Bongiorno in New York in 1924, but emigrated as a child to Turin with his mother, following his parents' separation. After finishing school in Italy, Mike began writing for *La Stampa*, one of the best-selling Italian newspapers, published in Turin, but he soon got involved with the Italian Resistance movement in World War II, after the fall of Mussolini on September 8, 1943. Once the war was over, Mike returned to New York in 1946 to continue his career as a journalist, but remained involved with Italian radio and collaborated with EIAR shows *La Voce dell'America* ("The Voice of America") and *Voci dal Mondo* ("Voices from the World").[1] It was the creator of these shows, Vittorio Veltroni, who convinced Mike to return to Italy and, given his success on the radio, to start his career as a television host for RAI.[2]

Veltroni understood Mike's potential to become Italians' new favourite star, because of his heroic involvement in the Italian resistance during the war, but also due to his knowledge of and familiarity with the American model of TV entertainment and its formats. Veltroni could not have been more right and farsighted. After *Arrivi e Partenze* and a few other programs, Mike's popularity exploded thanks to what is almost unanimously considered the most legendary and successful program in Italian television history: the quiz show *Lascia o Raddoppia?* (literally, "Leave or Double?"), broadcast by RAI from 1955 to 1959 as an "original adaptation" of the famous American game show *The $64,000 Question*. While it sounds contradictory and paradoxical, the term "original adaptation" describes quite precisely the way *Lascia o Raddoppia?* was conceived by RAI writers and executives and discussed by viewers and critics alike. It is hard to find precise industrial and legal information about how exactly the formula for *Lascia o Raddoppia?* was imported to Italy, but the discourses that surround its success on Italian television and the popularity it achieved among its audience seem to provide a more interesting point of view for the analysis of the TV show as an example of early content reformatting. Contemporary reviews and commentaries of the program, in fact, developed two parallel narratives: on the one hand, they acknowledged the American origin of the format to increase its prestige (among the viewers) and its cultural capital (among the sponsors) as a successful program imported from overseas. On the other hand, however, those same critics and commentators made sure to highlight how the show was not a mere copy of its American equivalent, but was instead a "most Italian edition with very distinct characteristics," a program that could finally allow regular citizens to express their genuine local identity on national television.[3] What seems particularly interesting about *Lascia o Raddoppia?* and its cultural significance in Italy, then, are the discourses that defined the program as a perfect synthesis of global, national, and local scenarios in a time when the country was reconstructing its own identity based on this precarious balance.

Endless pages have been written in Italy both about *Lascia o Raddoppia?* and about "Il Mike Nazionale" ("National Mike") to celebrate and analyze the role of early Italian television as the most unique—and perhaps significant—factor responsible for the formation of Italian national identity in the aftermath of World War II. Mike Bongiorno and *Lascia o Raddoppia?* have often been championed as the leading causes of the cultural, linguistic, and "psychological" unification of Italy at a time when Italians still strongly identified along regional and provincial—as opposed to national—lines. The reasons for such a fundamental role, as will be examined in detail in the following pages, lie in a combination of factors that include, among others: the specific post-World War II historical time in which early television in Italy came about; the economic boom that Italy underwent in the late 1950s and early 1960s (the so called "miracolo italiano," the "Italian miracle"); the technological advancements that increased mobility while decreasing geographical distances; the sociological implications of early television's "collective viewing," since TV sets in the 1950s were often purchased and displayed in bars or movie theaters where people gathered precisely to watch television; and, perhaps more significantly for this study, the increasing influence of the "American dream" and ideals fostered by Hollywood and the Marshall Plan.

While considering the significant changes in Italian society in the aftermath of World War II and the noticeable increase of products and ideals imported from America, many television scholars in Italy have claimed that the American television model has significantly influenced Italian television only after the deregulation of the late 1970s, and the consequent rise of private commercial networks, especially the Berlusconi Group. Such scholars, the so-called "purists," tend to describe early Italian television as fundamentally "national" in terms of content and style, and argue that RAI, although borrowing commercial formats from the U.S.A., provided, at first, educational programs and Italian-style entertainment for the family. This position argues that those pioneering TV executives adopted a strategy of programming whose goal was to educate the population and, through television, spread a type of "high culture" to which most Italians had not been previously exposed.[4]

The perspective explored in this chapter, contrary to the common "purist" thesis that early Italian television is exclusively and exquisitely "national" in content and aesthetics, depicts the origin of television in Italy as an arena for multi-layered negotiations between regional, national, and international dynamics, and between local and global players. At the center of this arena was "National Mike," the "King of Quiz," the "Father of Italian Television"—as he has been affectionately re-baptized throughout the years—who synthesized, mediated, and ultimately sold these apparently separate worlds to his adoring viewers.

Despite the many analyses of Italian television and its early protagonists, in fact, not enough has been said about the highly paradoxical characteristics of Mike and *Lascia o Raddoppia?* as distinctive unifying factors for Italian national identity. After all, Mike Bongiorno is an American who later emigrated to Italy, and *Lascia o Raddoppia?* is not an original RAI production, but the adaptation of a successful and well-tested American format. It is precisely in the process of format adaptation, however, that the most salient and genuine national characteristics emerge. As TV critic Aldo Grasso contends: "The difference with the American version mainly lay in the search for 'characters,' in the dramatic dilatation, and in all those additions that Mike called 'the entertaining side dish.'"[5] Before the deregulation of the late 1970s, then—when Italian television was flooded with foreign products that would fill in the increased programming schedule—*Lascia o Raddoppia?* became the most significant example of how early television in Italy developed and found its identity in these processes of transformation, adaptation, and appropriation of American texts, models, and formats. As mentioned earlier, it is hard to mark the legal trajectory of *Lascia o Raddoppia?* and to establish if the program was officially licensed as a format and sold to RAI. As Albert Moran discusses, prior to the Copyright Act of 1976—which established more clear regulations about TV content reformatting—it was difficult to hold single national media industries accountable for importing and adapting formats and formulas without paying the proper licensing fees to the original producers.[6] For this analysis in particular, I would argue that establishing whether *Lascia o Raddoppia?* was imported as a licensed format or not does not provide essential information about the "American-ness" of the show as opposed to its more genuine "Italian-ness." The audience, in fact, knew perfectly well that the formula of the program was imported from America, but did not consider it any less Italian for this reason.

This chapter discusses various contestants and episodes of the Italian show, and explores the socio-cultural environment of early Italian television understood in the broader historical context of the "miracle years." The chapter re-contextualizes the role of *Lascia o Raddoppia?* and Mike Bongiorno within the landscape and discourse of early Italian television, and examines the global factors—together with the more genuine national elements—that allowed Mike's show to become an unparalleled cultural phenomenon in Italian broadcasting. In particular, the chapter explores *Lascia o Raddoppia?* and the complex layers of its "unifying mission," and examines Mike's persona as the living synthesis of global and local identities in early Italian television.

Italian Identity . . . or Lack Thereof: Early Television and the Miracle Years

In discussing identity, one must inevitably consider the complexities that the concept entails, as every identity is shaped by many different constituents that touch upon the most diverse and profound aspects of human being—both as an individual and as part of a community. When it comes to a nation's identity, the task is not any easier when one considers the multi-layered factors involved in the cultural, historical, geographical, and political development of nations. Italian communication scholar Giovanni Bechelloni identifies territory as an essential aspect of the very existence of a nation and its identity, together with a common language shared by its citizens and a sense of belonging to a collective historical and cultural heritage. Territory, language, and memory, as Bechelloni contends, are without a doubt the main factors that allowed Italians to be "nationalized" through the development of a collective Italian national identity. However, such a sense of national identity in Italy was constructed fairly late and in somewhat unconventional ways, when compared to other European countries.

In Italy, in fact, it has been particularly difficult to create and establish a unified sense of national identity over the centuries, one major reason being what Antonio Gramsci has defined as the lack of a "national-popular." Referring to romantic literature and history, Gramsci identified the national-popular (in Europe) as a truly indigenous cultural form of expression able to address the needs and concerns of the subaltern classes, and cited the French Revolution as the most significant inspirational event for such a concept. In Italy, however, a genuine form of national-popular was never developed for two major reasons. On the one hand, Italian intellectuals were never able to merge with and write about the subaltern class in truly realist terms. On the other hand, even when such discourses were successfully developed, they were always based on European experiences, and did not address the specific indigenous nature of the Italian subaltern class. These conditions have contributed to the absence of a unified idea of "Italian culture," able to create a popular sense of belonging to the nation. Elaborating on Gramsci's ideas, David Forgacs finds the lack of the national-popular has had important consequences for Italian culture in general:

> As a cultural space . . . Italy has not been strong and effectively homogenized by a powerful Italian national culture over the last century . . . There has been an unusually high openness to non-national cultural goods, such as to throw into doubt the existence of cohesive "national" culture from the consumer's point of view.[7]

In consumerist terms, then, if compared to other European countries with "stronger" (or at least "earlier") national identities, Italy has been particularly exposed to and influenced by foreign products, specifically American—a tendency that most clearly manifested itself during the "miracle years" (1958–63), when the American lifestyle and glamour became the cultural models to imitate. Such openness to foreign products and the lack of a genuine sense of belonging to the nation have traditionally been supported and increased by the strong identification Italians feel with their regional environment, more so than with the nation as a whole. During fascism, Mussolini had tried, and to some extent succeeded, to build a stronger sense of national identity based on the mythical idea of a reborn Roman Empire in contrast with the strong regionalism of the country, and certainly found some consent among Italians. Such an idea of "heroic" national identity, however, was ultimately imposed through a dictatorial regime, and therefore enthusiasm for a possible "ideological unification" faded with the fall of fascism.

As opposed (or in addition) to the efforts made towards unification during the fascist years by Mussolini (and even earlier by the revolutionary movements of the Risorgimento that brought the geographical unification of the country), it seems that a stronger feeling of belonging to the Italian nation was developed in the aftermath of World War II—a feeling more related to popular culture than to the political and ideological struggles of the nineteenth century and early twentieth century.

Many critics and scholars in Italy, in fact, have argued that one of the ways in which Italian identity has been constructed is through early Italian television in the 1950s. One of the reasons for such a claim is that early TV finally showed Italians their national territory, beyond municipal or regional lines. As mentioned, Italians tend to identify more easily and strongly with their native city or region, than with the nation as a whole. But early television—through the news and neorealist documentaries made specifically for the small screen—provided Italians with a tangible image of their national territory and its people. In addition, since broadcasting was happening simultaneously throughout the entire peninsula and the islands, Italians also felt that the whole territory was embracing and enjoying this new and revolutionary means of communication, thus overcoming geographical as well as class divisions.

Early television, however, did more than show Italians visible evidence of their country in its totality. Given that most TV hosts were invited to speak "proper" Italian, as opposed to regional dialects, the country was also unified linguistically at a time when the preferred method of expression was the dialect. Italy is divided into 20 regions, each of which presents different linguistic characteristics. Such differences in diverse dialects are often incomprehensible for Italians who do not come from the same region; also, marked accents, even when official Italian is spoken, still identify a person as from a specific city or region. Even linguistically, then, Italy was strongly based on regionalism, and television offered an opportunity to smooth out such divisions.

Finally, and most important, television offered Italians the "idea" of Italy—a sense of belonging to a common heritage and sharing historical memory, but also sharing a tradition of popular cultural manifestations. Such an idea of Italy was especially achieved through the broadcasting of game shows such as *Lascia o Raddoppia?* (1955–59), because the most popular questions in the show were often based on topics such as the opera, soccer, and Italian history or literature, themes that all Italians could relate to.

The dynamics just described assume even greater importance when considering the popularity the quiz show quickly achieved, which caused the proliferation of "collective viewing settings," a factor that increased the sense of "national aggregation" among Italians. In 1955, in fact, television sets were still not as widely spread among Italian families as they would be after the economic boom. Most fans of the program, therefore, had to rely on the benevolence of a few better-off neighbors who opened their houses for friends and relatives to watch the quiz show on TV. Even more significant, however, is the involvement of public spaces such as cinemas, theaters, and bars in *Lascia o Raddoppia?*'s viewing ritual. Bar owners understood the potential of the quiz show to attract customers who did not own a TV set, and public viewing in bars became a popular form of congregation for the show's cheering fans. Movie theater owners also played a significant role in the creation of the *Lascia o Raddoppia?* phenomenon. When RAI began broadcasting the quiz show on Saturday nights, suddenly movie theaters emptied, despite the fact that Saturday night had traditionally been the most profitable time slot for theater owners in Italy. This situation moved movie exhibitors to ask RAI for a switch in the show's programming from Saturday night to Thursday night. Such a change had two major consequences, the first being the association of Thursday with the "quiz genre," since after that time and for a few decades following, all quizzes on prime-time would air on that day of the week, especially those hosted by Mike Bongiorno. The second consequence relates once more to the idea of collective viewing, since after the change in programming, movie theaters would still be empty on Thursdays, forcing theater owners to change their tactics. Once again understanding the popularity of the medium, and in particular of *Lascia o Raddoppia?*, owners decided to install TV sets in their theaters, and agreed to interrupt the projection of the movies at half time on Thursday nights in order for the audience to catch their favorite TV show and then finish watching the movie at the end of the program's airing.

These highly significant sociological events not only testify to the immense popularity of the quiz, but also explain the changing dynamics of Italy in the miracle years. Italians were finally going out and merging with other Italians— a situation that forced them to speak the national language instead of the dialects, which were still, at the time, the preferred method of communication among family members. In this scenario, *Lascia o Raddoppia?* although—or, perhaps, precisely because—imported as a formula from the U.S.A., soon achieved the unique trademark of cult program and distinctive symbol of the new consumerist Italy in the post-war "economic miracle." In the second half of the 1950s, in fact, the escapism and entertainment of Mike's quiz show, more than the raw style of neorealist documentary filmmaking, were able to represent and offer evidence of the sociological, cultural, and economic changes that were happening in Italy. Part of these changes involved the embrace of new "dreams of wealth"— dreams traditionally associated with America—and *Lascia o Raddoppia?* with its opulent gold coins made those dreams come true for the lucky contestants who managed to win on the show, but also made the audience feel that it was acceptable to have those dreams in the first place.

Lascia o Raddoppia?: Italian Phenomenon with Global Flavor

Considering these premises, *Lascia o Raddoppia?* undoubtedly represented, at the time, an example of American entertaininment and commercialized television, by feeding the Italian viewers' desire for fame and wealth in the miracle years. The quiz show, however, also exemplifies quite well the model proposed by Bechelloni, by which territory, memory, and language are fundamental elements in the creation of a country's national identity, in particular in the creation of the Italian identity. Mike's use of the Italian language, analyzed, among others, by renowned linguist Tullio De Mauro and by semanticists such as Umberto Eco, deserves to be closely examined together with other aspects of Mike's star persona in the following section. The focus, therefore, lies here on territory and memory— two particularly significant factors in the analysis of the unifying function of *Lascia o Raddoppia?* for the formation of Italian national identity.

As far as providing Italians with the idea of a shared territory, *Lascia o Raddoppia?* presents at least two characteristics that are worth examining. First, the quiz show, while not offering actual images of the country, still provided picturesque stories of different Italian cities and regions thanks to the anecdotes of the contestants, who were eager to share the peculiar characteristics of their hometowns with Mike and his viewers. Mike Bongiorno, who had the peculiar ability to understand which contestants had the potential to become real characters on TV, supervised the choice of the participants. Their stories and personalities, which often seemed the incarnation of certain "types" and protagonists of Italian literary classics, encouraged comic actors all over Italy to reproduce hilarious parodies, and inspired Italian film directors to create equally classic movie characters based on those early game show contestants.

Second, and perhaps more important, by offering a Seicento (the first rear-engine car produced by Italian automaker Fiat) as a consolation prize, *Lascia o Raddoppia?* had a revolutionary impact on the imagination of the Italian people. At a time when most people still used public transportation, the Seicento symbolized newly gained mobility and the freedom to visit a still unknown country for most Italians. Discussing the cinema of the miracle years in Italy, Angelo Restivo examines mobility as one of the most distinctive traits of that period and of the profound changes the country underwent after the war. He provides evidence about the geographical as well as the mental remapping of Italy and examines, beyond the filmic texts, several advertisement campaigns from the popular news magazine *L'Espresso* during the economic boom. Restivo claims that the advertising in the weekly magazine of the early 1960s was "dominated by travel and movement, and it attempted to inscribe mobility within the traditional images of the nation."[8] One such ad promoted the completion of l'Autostrada del Sole, the "Highway of the Sun," which "was of great symbolic importance to the new Italy, as it not only linked the North to the South in a kind of transportational 'backbone,' but also was the visible sign of government's progressive alliance with the new economy."[9] Cinematic signs of the new mobility could also be found in films such as *La Dolce Vita* (Fellini, 1959) and *Il Sorpasso* (Risi, 1964) in which both protagonists, Marcello and Bruno (played respectively by Italian icons Marcello Mastroianni and Vittorio Gassman), drive sports cars that implicitly elevate their narrative role (and social status as well) when compared with the other characters in both films, who either ride scooters or take the bus.

While *Lascia o Raddoppia?* did not give away expensive sports cars (or Cadillacs like the original U.S. version did) but the less glamorous Seicento, the program was still fundamental in filling the Italian people's imagination with the idea that mobility was possible. And the popularity of *Lascia o Raddoppia?* lay precisely in the idea that what the show offered was within the economic reach of an increasing number of Italians—the new consumers of the new Italy—as opposed to the unrealistic mirage of Marcello's and Bruno's sports cars.

As far as providing Italians with a sense of collective memory, the role of *Lascia o Raddoppia?* was no less significant. In order to understand its fundamental function in shaping a sense of shared heritage among Italians, it is imperative to clarify the distinction between game show and quiz show. Often the two terms are used interchangeably to indicate a television program in which the contestants participate in a game and must answer certain questions in order to remain on the show and ultimately win the final prize. Although there have been various formats belonging to both categories, the major difference between game and quiz show lies in the structural function and in the difficulty of the Q&A process. In game shows the contestants usually answer one or a few simple questions, trying to guess, for example, the object that corresponds to the highest monetary prize (*Deal or no Deal*), the correct price of certain goods, which they can later win (*The Price is Right*), or the right letter that completes mysterious words and sentences (*Wheel of Fortune*). These programs illustrate the basic mechanism of the game show, a mechanism in which asking questions is only an entertaining excuse for the participants' choices of usually random objects, prices, or letters, as in the examples described. In these cases, in fact, answering a question correctly depends more on luck than on real knowledge about a certain subject matter.

Quiz shows, on the contrary, and especially those like *The $64,000 Question* or *Jeopardy!*, require the contestants to answer more complex questions and to give answers on the basis of their expertise on often specific subject matters. Thus, questions and answers are the very structuring elements of these programs and the rivalry among contestants is palpable, as concentration is key to performing at one's best. *Lascia o Raddoppia?* is to be included in this second category, since all the participants had to pick an area of expertise in advance, a specialty on which all questions would be based. After strict selection aimed at testing the effective knowledge of the chosen subject matter—as well as the participants' screen presence—the contestants were invited to the RAI studios to participate in the game. The rules of the program, which mirrored quite closely those of *The $64,000 Question*, provided that each contestant would be asked eight questions during the first night, for a total possible preliminary victory of 320,000 lire. After getting through the first round of questions successfully, the contestants were invited to come back the following week to answer only one question. At the beginning of each new episode after the first night, Mike would ask the participants whether they wanted to leave the show with the money gained the preceding week (*Lascia*) or if they wanted to try a new question and possibly double their money (*Raddoppia*)—in case of correct answer—and retain the right to go back for another week. The highest sum that the contestants could win, after five weeks on the show, was 5,120,000 lire (approximately $200,000 nowadays).[10]

Initially, as part of the official rules established by the Italian producers, the contestants were obliged to choose their area of expertise from a list of subjects provided by RAI. The list consisted of: numismatics and philately, fashion, gastronomy, athletics, physical and natural sciences, theater (drama or variety show), fine arts, Italian literature, Italian history, cycling, opera, chamber and symphonic music, pop music and jazz, cinema, and soccer. While not always as directly "Italian" as was the case with literature and history, this list included many subjects that certainly created among the Italian people the sense of sharing a common heritage and common passions. Cycling and soccer were, at the time, the most popular sports in Italy and were the favorite topics of discussion in bars, piazzas, grocery stores, and schools. The opera has always been associated with the musical tradition of Italy—the cradle of *il bel canto*—and it is something that Italians display with pride. Similarly, fashion and style are also very distinctive aspects of Italian culture, the symbols of the so-called "made in Italy" exported worldwide. Finally, in terms of fine arts, Italians feel particular gratification in remembering that their country is the birthplace of geniuses such as Leonardo Da Vinci and Michelangelo.

Lascia o Raddoppia? certainly did not "create" the passion for soccer and cycling or the pride for the opera or the Mona Lisa. What the quiz did, however, was to remind Italians that those passions and proud feelings for a past perhaps gone could cross regional boundaries and were the quintessential elements of a common heritage they undoubtedly shared. While cheering for their favorite contestants on the show, Italians discussed their passions and opinions, their personal knowledge and preferences, and Italy quickly became united in the name of *Lascia o Raddoppia?*

The topics chosen by the contestants on the show, however, reveal much more about the characteristics of the show beyond its function as a cementing factor for national identity. Barbara Scaramucci and Claudio Ferretti report how, from a contemporary study carried out after 15 episodes of *Lascia o Raddoppia?*, the most popular subjects among the contestants were those related to music (without specification as to which category), cinema, and soccer.[11] While music can be seen as a less significant factor in this discussion because the preferences spanned genres and styles (with no particular attachment to any national or international environment), cinema and soccer can be interpreted as the quintessential difference between *Lascia o Raddoppia?*'s global and local appeal. After all, cinema is usually and symbolically associated with Hollywood, and soccer is, to this day, the Italian national sport par excellence. And it was precisely in the question category of soccer that *Lascia o Raddoppia?* produced one of the first and most popular contestant-celebrities in the history of the Italian TV quiz: the curvy blonde Paola Bolognani. Nicknamed "the lioness from Pordenone," the city in Northern Italy where she came from, Paola looked a lot like Ginger Rogers and reminded the viewers of such Hollywood glamour. Her marked Friulan accent, however, reminded Italians of the elite mountain warfare of the Italian Army—the Alpini— and her encyclopedic knowledge of soccer, which enabled her to win the maximum prize on the show, transformed Paola into an "all Italian-style" idol.[12]

The dynamic between global and local factors become even more visible when the rules of *Lascia o Raddoppia?* were modified, and contestants could now choose any area of expertise without being limited to the categories originally imposed by RAI. A particularly interesting subject that emerged under the game's new regulations was the history of the United States, a specialty in which another woman, Giovanna Ferrara, won *Lascia o Raddoppia?*'s biggest prize. Even more interesting, given the peculiarity of the occasion, was the invitation that Giovanna Ferrara received, thanks to her impressive knowledge of U.S. history, to travel to the U.S.A. and participate in an episode of the original format *The $64,000 Question*—an invitation which she accepted.[13] In this respect, then, *Lascia o Raddoppia?* became a true vehicle for America, not only symbolically but in very practical terms, as Giovanna Ferrara's U.S. trip exemplified.

This dynamic balance between the regional, national, and American charac- teristics embedded in the show not only intrigued the quiz's fans, but inspired, just one year after *Lascia o Raddoppia*'s debut on RAI, Italian cinema and one of its most renowned protagonists: comic genius and one of the most beloved Italian actors, Antonio De Curtis, "Totò." In 1956, Athena Cinematografica-Titanus released *Totò, Lascia o Raddoppia?*, a story of gambling and gangsters that parodied the popular quiz show. Totò plays Duke Gagliardo della Forcoletta, an aristocrat now living in complete poverty, who has an obsession with horse racing and gambling. Gagliardo discovers in the beginning of the film that he has a daughter whom he has never met, and that she is soon going to get married. Upset for not being able to provide her with any economic security, and sure of his knowledge of the equestrian sport, he decides to participate as a contestant in *Lascia o Raddoppia?* to win the final prize of 5,120,000 lire. This simple plot triggers the action for a hilarious comedy in which the duke must face the threats of two gangsters (one Sicilian and the other an Italian-American from Chicago) who bet each week on whether he will leave the show or double his money.

One of the most interesting aspects of the film is the theme song, titled after the popular quiz and sung by one of the gangsters' mistress, a nightclub singer. The song's lyrics were particularly significant at the time, as they describe viewers' craze for the show, and most important, they acknowledge *Lascia o Raddoppia?* as a format imported from the United States:

> *é un' altra importazione che ci viene di laggiù*
> it's another importation from "that place far away"
> *é come un pacco dono che ci dona la TV*
> it's like a wrapped gift that TV offers us

There was no real need to specify where or what "that place far away" was, which testifies to the accepted belief, in the miracle years, that America was the only model to imitate, the wrapped gift Italians were eager to receive, especially through television. In this parody and self-referential celebration of *Lascia o Raddoppia?*, Totò was masterly in mocking the contemporary enthusiasm for America and American ideals. By constructing his character in particularly "national" and "regional" terms (he represented the old Italian aristocracy while speaking with a marked Neapolitan accent) he created a comic opposition to the Italian-American gangster, who constantly reminded the viewers of the criminal customs of Chicago, but also to Mike Bongiorno, who starred in the film as himself and was clearly overwhelmed by the duke's picturesque presence on the show (much as he was often overwhelmed and embarrassed by the actual contestants during the real TV show).

Totò accurately reproduced the idiosyncrasies and the anxieties, but also the odd local peculiarities of the most famous contestants on the show who have been analyzed through the years in stark contrast with Mike's mediocrity. Thus, Totò managed to re-create those bizarre moments of the show where Mike, with his naïve, innocent blue eyes and shy smile, was always able to restore order and bring his American professionalism to bear on the situation. The following section analyzes Mike Bongiorno's star persona and his capacity to be completely "out of place" and yet so perfectly in charge of *Lascia o Raddoppia?* by embodying that global flavor Italians eagerly searched for while at the same time caring deeply for the contestants' manifestations of local identity.

Il Mike Nazionale: King of Quiz, Champion of Mediocrity

Without a doubt, the most renowned critical discussion of Mike Bongiorno has been that of Umberto Eco who, in 1963, published a seminal piece on the TV host titled "Fenomenologia di Mike Bongiorno" ("Mike Bongiorno's Pheno-menology"). Eco found in Mike's mediocrity the secret of his success and defined Bongiorno as the emblem of TV stardom. Eco, in fact, identified a new tendency related to the coming of television, different from the characteristics of film: the fact that television offered, as an ideal to imitate, "not a superman anymore, but the everyman."[14] Within this tendency, Eco championed Mike Bongiorno as its most genuine personification:

> We have in Italy the gaudiest case of reduction from the superman to the everyman in the figure of Mike Bongiorno and the history of his fortune. Idolized by millions, this man owes his success to the fact that in every act and with every word of the character he creates in front of the cameras, he appears to be an absolute mediocrity (this is the only virtue that he possesses in excess); this is accompanied by an immediate and spontaneous charm explicable through the idea that, in him, one cannot perceive any fictional construction: it almost seems that he sells himself as he is, and what he is does not place any spectator in a state of inferiority, not even the most inexperienced. Every spectator sees the portrayal of his own limits glorified and officially rewarded with national authority.[15]

Similarly to the Seicento awarded as consolation prize, to which Italians could legitimately and realistically aspire, so Mike represented a "model" that offered values and characteristics everyone could identify with. What Eco calls "mediocrity," however, translates, in reality, to a series of "personal skills" that allowed Mike to enchant his audience: certain gentle ways in hosting his shows with enthusiasm, and yet without any screaming or over-the-top dramatization (famous was—and still is—Mike's recurring line "Allegria, amici ascoltatori!"—"Cheers, viewers my friends!"); the capacity to genuinely care about and respect the show's contestants and to be moved by their stories, victories, and defeats (legendary were Mike's real tears on TV after the ultimate victory on the show of Felice Mannarelli, an extremely poor young man who had learned about international history reading books under the only street lamp in his small town, almost losing his sight doing so)[16]; and finally, Mike's extraordinary talent in choosing the contestants for *Lascia o Raddoppia?* according to certain peculiarities and odd characteristics that, once brought to screen, transformed the participants into true celebrities, opposite whom Mike accepted the role of mere foil. And the weirder the contestants, the better *Lascia o Raddoppia?* worked.

It was precisely in the stark contrast between Mike's mediocrity and the contestants' strangeness, in fact, that the "Mike myth" was created, in his capacity to bring order to what seemed a Fellini-esque circus of types and stereotypes, members of the aristocracy, dandies, and voluptuous *maggiorate* (buxom women). In this last "category," beyond the already mentioned Paola Bolognani, was the celebrated presence on the show of Maria Luisa Garoppo, whose energy and sensual charisma often embarrassed Mike. Maria Luisa, a tobacconist from Piedmont, was probably the most famous among *Lascia o Raddoppia*'s *maggiorate*, and reminded Italians of Sophia Loren and Silvana Mangano (and some might argue that she would later inspire Fellini in his creation of *Amarcord*'s legendary tobacconist). Maria Luisa was an expert on classical mythology and gained, after a few weeks on the show, an ironic nickname from the audience—a nickname which reflected once again the global and national characteristics of Italy and *Lascia o Raddoppia?* in the miracle years. In reference to the size of her breasts, Italians renamed her "Petto Atlantico"—literally, "Atlantic Breast"—a linguistic joke that parodied the more famous "Patto Atlantico," the Italian term for the North Atlantic Treaty Organization, NATO.[17]

Perhaps even more significant for our discussion of the show's global and local dynamics, however, was the participation of Nigerian contestant Olabisi Ajala, a sophisticated world traveler and secretary to his country's prime minister. Olabisi was an attractive and charismatic black man who held a degree in psychology from Columbia University and was an expert in ethnology, the subject he chose for *Lascia o Raddoppia?*. Olabisi recurrently appeared on TV wearing traditional Nigerian clothes, and he managed to transform every night on the show into a celebration of his ethnic and cultural heritage.[18] The final night, however, Olabisi entered the TV studio wearing an impeccable tuxedo, while Mike wore the traditional Nigerian costume, demonstrating once more his ability to interact with his contestants' most genuine aspects of identity, be it regional Italian or foreign and "Other."[19]

What stood out in this parade of caricatures and contestants was the "all-American" and "boy next door" innocence Mike exuded: a complete lack of malice, which led him to make several embarrassing blunders, became his trademark over the years. One notorious gaffe happened during an episode of *Lascia o Raddoppia?* in which Mike, asking a question about Pope Paul VI, referred to "Paul Vi" instead of "Paul the Sixth," without completely realizing his mistake until the contestant asked for clarification.[20] The audience, however, has always forgiven Mike, and loves him precisely because he makes worse mistakes than the viewers could make. Together with his evident ignorance of the questions asked in the show, Mike's use of the Italian language has always been a particularly rich source of his blunders. As Eco writes:

> Mike Bongiorno speaks a basic Italian. His speech carries the maximum possible simplicity. He abolishes subjunctive forms, subordinate clauses, and he almost manages to make syntax invisible. He avoids pronouns . . . he does not deal in parenthetical sentences, or elliptical expressions. He does not hint, and only uses metaphors that are well established in the common lexicon. His language is rigorously referential . . . no effort is necessary to understand him. Any spectator feels they could be more eloquent than him.[21]

In terms of language, as much as in terms of personality, Mike has never intimidated his viewers. He spoke a simple kind of properly pronounced Italian, which did not contain any American accent, but lacked any sophisticated vocabulary. During *Lascia o Raddoppia?*, Mike's linguistic deficiencies were made even more visible by contrast with another "contestant made celebrity"—fashion expert Gianluigi Marianini—a dandy from Turin who spoke an extremely baroque and artificially ornate Italian. In complete opposition to Marianini's overly sophisticated expressions, linguist Tullio De Mauro reminds us how Mike's Italian has been ironically described by critics as consisting of "fifteen words," and cited as the most exemplary case of the new "informal standard Italian" of television.[22] Simpler and more direct than the formal Italian of theater, literature, and politics, "television Italian" has provided viewers with a unified national form of expression, which, unlike local dialects, is able to overcome regional borders.

Linguistically, in fact, early Italian television and *Lascia o Raddoppia?* offer yet another multilayered scenario for local and global discussions. At a time when most Italian TV hosts—mainly from Rome, the seat of RAI headquarters—were asked to abandon their regional inflection and speak "proper Italian" to their viewers, Mike had to abandon his own accent, which was not regional, but foreign. Early television in Italy, then, took on this unifying role and invited its early protagonists to smooth out any linguistic characteristics that were either too local (regional) or too global (American), for the sake of an imagined—but still non-existent—homogeneous nation and national language.[23] Referring to *Lascia o Raddoppia?*, Aldo Grasso claims Italians have learned their language thanks to Mike's Italian rather than Dante's Italian, and that early television has had, perhaps, a more "egalitarian" role than the *Divina Commedia* in unifying the country linguistically, because television is a medium for the masses, while the *Commedia* is a literary work accessible exclusively to intellectuals.[24] As an additional paradox, then, even linguistically Mike managed to unify a country, one which did not speak his own native language, but perhaps needed the external influence of a TV host who did not bring with him his regional background, but a wave of "global" fresh air.

Lascia o Raddoppia?: A Few Theoretical Considerations

Grasso's argument about *Lascia o Raddoppia?* and Mike's essential function in the linguistic and cultural unification of Italy is supported by the role the quiz show had in education policy making during the miracle years. In 1962, in fact, the Italian government launched a reform of the junior high school system upon realizing that most Italians were unable to answer the questions asked on the TV show, even if the subjects were part of the schools' curricula.[25] Although *Lascia o Raddoppia?* has shaped Italian identity in various and complex ways, this institutional reform was undoubtedly the most evident and indicative sign of the quiz show's capacity to transcend its entertaining role and to influence the most genuine and fundamental aspects of Italian culture and society.

Lascia o Raddoppia? is one of the first examples on Italian television of how adaptations of foreign formats can recreate texts that possess genuine and specific characteristics of "the nation." In the postcolonial era it is certainly problematic to discuss the idea of a unified nation without taking into consideration the multiple layers of diversity every country now includes within its borders. When considering Italy, in particular, it is imperative to discuss the idea of the nation as shaped by many regional factors, which have traditionally provided Italians with stronger elements of identification than those provided by the nation as a whole. Part of the popularity and the success of *Lascia o Raddoppia?* consisted precisely in its capacity to address the country's identity through local (and regional) manifestations of identity—represented by the show's contestants—and to merge them with more global factors (Mike, American ideals, mobility) to create a new image of Italy that matched the characteristics of the country in the post-war era. Similarly, the vital role of *Lascia o Raddoppia?* as an essential factor for the linguistic and cultural unification of Italy depended on the balance between local and global factors. It appeared evident to the Italian people in the miracle years that they needed a mediating (and mediated) national—and not only regional—language and culture to negotiate and legitimize Italy's status in the new international arena.

Lascia o Raddoppia?, however, not only had a fundamental role in shaping a new Italian identity in the miracle years, but it also had important consequences for the history of Italian television more specifically. By establishing certain generic tendencies together with certain expectations in the audience, the quiz show set standards that would characterize Italian broadcasting later on through the coming of commercial television in the early 1980s, and all the way into the contemporary era.

One of these consequences matches the paradoxical global–local characteristics of Mike's quiz show. The success of *Lascia o Raddoppia?*, in fact, on the one hand opened the door to increasing importation of foreign program formats, especially game and quiz shows (strongly present in contemporary Italian television), but on the other it favored the creation of several original Italian quiz show formats, which exploited those elements that had been particularly successful for the Italian audience. Even more strongly than *Lascia o Raddoppia?*, *Campanile Sera* ("Evening Bell-tower"), hosted again by Mike Bongiorno, reiterated the importance of representing regional and municipal identities to address the new national face of Italy. *Campanile Sera*, an RAI original format on the air from 1959 to 1962, substituted the unique participation of single contestants in studio with the collective participation of entire towns across Italy who would challenge a rival town. While one specific contestant was still chosen to answer the questions in the TV studio, the rest of the town's population would participate from "home" through various competitive activities, and the final victory depended on the combined performances. It is with *Campanile Sera* that Italians finally saw images of their country within a quiz show. Before the beginning of the actual game, the contestants' hometowns were shown on television together with a cheering crowd gathered in the main *piazza* to celebrate the event and to try to be seen on television. Italians, therefore, were offered visible evidence of their own country, many locations of which were still generally unknown, but could nonetheless be seen on their screen. Writing about the major programs that have shaped and changed Italian history, former mayor of Rome Walter Veltroni (son of that Vittorio mentioned in the introductory paragraphs) contends about *Campanile Sera*: "those few images [shown at the beginning of the TV program] used to generate, in terms of fame and tourism, much more than a thousand commercial tourism campaigns could do today."[26]

Also, with *Campanile Sera* Mike dived even more deeply into Italian national and televisual culture. His name and persona came to be associated—a unique case in Italian television—not only with specific successful programs, but also with the very concept of the TV quiz as a genre, something Mike had "learned" in the U.S.A. but managed to make uniquely Italian for RAI. After "accompanying" the Italian audience through the miracle years with *Lascia o Raddoppia?* and *Campanile Sera*, in fact, despite a temporary decline in the second half of the 1960s, Mike was once again the protagonist of Italian television in the early 1970s thanks to yet another quiz show: *Rischiatutto* ("Risk It All," 1970–74). *Rischiatutto* would be Mike's vehicle for accompanying his audience through other important years and events in Italian history. After the dreams of mobility and regained wealth of the 1950s, many of the illusions of the miracle years disappeared, giving way to the political terrorism of the 1970s, the so-called *anni di piombo* ("lead years").

The late 1970s, however, are of particular interest in the history of Italian television, since after the deregulation of broadcasting systems all over Europe, RAI's monopoly came to an end, and Italian television welcomed the beginning of the *neotelevisione*, characterized by privately owned networks. The most famous among the new owners was Silvio Berlusconi who, in the early 1980s, looked for a sensational way (i.e. a TV personality) to launch his chief channel, Canale 5. Berlusconi found such a personality in Mike Bongiorno, who transferred from RAI to the Fininvest Group in 1982, to host the new quiz show, *Superflash*. The groundbreaking novelty of *Superflash* was that of including advertising within an Italian quiz show for the first time, officially shaping Italian private broadcasting after the model of American commercial television. In the newly glamorous Italy of the 1980s, Silvio Berlusconi soon became the champion of such a model, quickly understanding the importance of the equation viewer = consumer, and exploiting Mike's power in promoting and selling any product to such viewers. Commercial television, which has been the foundation of American broadcasting since its origins, became the most distinctive trait of Italian *neotelevisione*, and is the final confirmation that "National Mike" has indeed shaped the face of Italian television like no other Italian has done.

Conclusion

This chapter has explored an early case of program reformatting on Italian television to problematize the notion that globalization exclusively represents a threat to local manifestations of identity in the media. *Lascia o Raddoppia?*, imported from America as an adaptation of *The $64,000 Question*, has achieved an unparalleled significance in the cultural landscape of Italian television for its capacity to include genuine manifestations of local identity within a foreign formula. Part of the merit of its success both as a television text and as a phenomenon of popular culture is to be found in its host, Mike Bongiorno, who embodied the dichotomy between global and local forces at play in post-war Italy. While it cannot be established with certainty whether RAI paid official licensing fees to the American network to import and broadcast the format on Italian television, the discourses that marked the debut of the show and accompanied its increasing success made no secret of the origins of the program's formula. Its American-ness was exploited and represented a form of prestige which added to the show's characteristics, which remained, nonetheless, deeply rooted in the contestants' regionalism. For this reason, *Lascia o Raddoppia?* challenges the purist thesis that early Italian television, even when importing foreign formats, was exclusively national in both content and style, and invites us to reconsider early broadcasting in Italy as a complex and multi-faceted arena for global and international discussions.

Notes

1 Scaramucci, Barbara and Claudio Ferretti. *La Vita È Tutta un Quiz*. (Rome, Italy: REI-ERI, 2005): 25–26.
2 Scaramucci and Ferretti. *La Vita È Tutta un Quiz*: 26.
3 Luigi Scotti, "Pioggia di Milioni anche alla Television italiana."
4 An example, among others, of such a tendency was the decision to produce and broadcast theater dramas (by Beckett, Goldoni, Chekhov, Ibsen, Ronconi, Fo, Strelher, etc.) as *tele-dramas*, so that Italians could become familiar with classical texts while watching television. In short, the goal was that of combining "mass education" with high production values. What reinforces such an argument is the widely accepted idea that early television in Italy strongly contributed to the unification of the country as an "imagined community" sharing geographical, economic, and linguistic characteristics (see, among others, Aldo Grasso's *Storia della Televisione Italiana*).
5 Aldo Grasso, *Storia della Televisione Italiana*. (Milano: Garzanti, 2004): xiv.
6 Albert Moran, "The Pie and the Crust." In *The Television Studies Reader*, ed. Robert Clyde Allen and Annette Hill (London and New York: Routledge, 2004): 260.
7 David Forgacs, *Italian Culture in the Industrial Era. 1880–1980*. (Manchester and New York: Manchester University Press, 1990): 28.
8 Angelo Restivo. *The Cinema of Economic Miracles*. (Durham, NC: Duke University Press, 2002): 72.
9 Ibid., 73.
10 As mentioned earlier on in the chapter, the contestants were awarded a Seicento as a consolation prize if they could get through the second night successfully, winning at

least 640,000 lire. Another automobile by Fiat, the 1400 model, was awarded to those contestants who could answer all the questions correctly but fell on the final night. While both cars were awarded as consolation prizes and only the most expert contestants would get the 1400 by proceeding successfully until the final night, the Seicento seems to have a much more powerful role in the Italians' imagination, to the point that it is the only consolation prize that people remember from *Lascia o Raddoppia?* (see Scaramucci and Ferretti, *La Vita È Tutta un Quiz*: 17).

11 Scaramucci and Ferretti. *La Vita È Tutta un Quiz*: 16.
12 Ibid., 53.
13 Ibid., 61.
14 Umberto Eco, "Fenomenologia di Mike Bongiorno," In *Diario Minimo* (14th ed.) (Milan: Bompiani, 2005): 29 (my translation).
15 Ibid., 30 and 67.
16 Scaramucci and Ferretti, *La Vita È Tutta un Quiz*: 31.
17 Ibid., 55.
18 With the participation of Olabisi Ajala, *Lascia o Raddoppia?* offered for the first time a dignified representation of immigrants on Italian television. This tendency, however, was soon lost in the general whitening of Italian television, whose programming usually lacked, and lacks to this day, any realistic representation of immigrants. Minister for Internal Affairs Giuliano Amato highlighted this negligence at the latest conference on immigration issues held in Genoa in September 2006. Amato denounced the problematic and almost non-existent representation of immigrants on Italian television and invited networks executives and producers to create TV fiction that could better and more realistically represent the role of immigrants in contemporary Italy. Significantly, Amato complained that, although audiences can see black characters portrayed as doctors or other highly respected professions on American television, on Italian television "we are stuck to representations such as that of Mammy from *Gone with the Wind*" (Pieracci, Alessandra. "Datemi un medico nero in tv," *La Stampa*, September 19, 2006.). In this light, then, the role of *Lascia o Raddoppia?* as a revolutionary program that introduced global elements in a newly rising Italy, assumes even greater significance.
19 Scaramucci and Ferretti, *La Vita È Tutta un Quiz*, 66.
20 Ibid., 33.
21 Eco, "Fenomenologia di Mike Bongiorno," 32.
22 Tullio de Mauro, "Il Linguaggio Televisivo e la Sua Influenza," in *I Linguaggi Settoriali in Italia*, ed. Gian Luigi Beccaria (Milan: Bompiani, 1973): 111.
23 A notable exception to this is Mario Riva, the most popular host of early Italian television along with Mike Bongiorno. Riva hosted *Il Musichiere* ("The Music Box"), a musical quiz show broadcast from 1957 to 1960 (the year of his premature death), and also based on an American format, *Name That Tune*. Riva used on TV a particularly strong Roman accent, but his inflection was so caricatured that it was ultimately used to mock the use of regional accents as stereotypical and old-fashioned, as opposed to proper Italian.
24 Grasso, xv.
25 Ibid.
26 Walter Veltroni, *I Programmi Che Hanno Cambiato l'Italia*. (Milan: Feltrinelli, 1992): 37.

References

Bechelloni, Giovanni. "Televisione e Nazionalizzazione degli Italiani," in *La Chioma della Vittoria: Scritti sull'Identità degli Italiani dall'Unità alla Seconda Repubblica*, ed. Sergio Bertelli. Florence, Italy: Ponte alle Grazie, 1997: 415–42.

De Mauro, Tullio. "Il Linguaggio Televisivo e la Sua Influenza," in *I Linguaggi Settoriali in Italia*, ed. Gian Luigi Beccaria. Milan: Bompiani, 1973: 107–17.

Eco, Umberto. "Fenomenologia di Mike Bongiorno," in *Diario Minimo* (14th ed.). Milan: Bompiani, 2005: 29–34.

Emanuelli, Massimo. *50 Anni di Storia della Televisione Attraverso la Stampa Settimanale*. Milan: Greco & Greco Editori, 2004.

Forgacs, David. "The Mass Media and the Question of a National Community in Italy," in *The Politics of Italian National Identity: A Multidisciplinary Perspective*, ed. Gino Bedani and Bruce Haddock. Cardiff: University of Wales Press, 2000: 142–62.

Grasso, Aldo. *Storia della Televisione Italiana*. Milan: Garzanti, 2004.

Moran, Albert. "The Pie and the Crust," in *The Television Studies Reader*, ed. Robert Clyde Allen and Annette Hill. London and New York: Routledge, 2004: 258–66.

—— *Copycat TV: Globalisation, Program Formats, and Cultural Identity*. Luton, U.K.: University of Luton Press, 1998.

Moran, Albert and Justin Malbon. *Understanding the Global TV Format*. Bristol and Portland, OR: Intellect Books, 2006.

Moss, Howard. "Language and Italian National Identity," in *The Politics of Italian National Identity: A Multidisciplinary Perspective*, ed. Gino Bedani and Bruce Haddock. Cardiff: University of Wales Press, 2000: 98–123.

Neri, Vito. "Si Chiamerà 'Venti Più Uno' il quiz che sostituirà Lascia o Raddoppia," *Sorrisi e Canzoni* 38, September 22, 1957: 4–5.

Negus, Keith and Patria Román-Velázquez, "Globalization and Cultural Identities," in *Mass Media and Society* (3rd ed.), ed. James Curran and Michael Gurevitch. London: Arnold, 2000: 329–45.

Piano, Giuseppina. "Mike: Ora Sono un Italiano Vero," *Repubblica*, February 8, 2003.

Pieracci, Alessandra. "Datemi un Medico Nero in TV," *La Stampa*, September 19, 2006.

Restivo, Angelo. *The Cinema of Economic Miracles*. Durham, NC: Duke University Press, 2002: 72–73.

Scaramucci, Barbara and Claudio Ferretti. *La Vita È Tutta un Quiz*. Rome, Italy: REI-ERI, 2005.

Scotti, Luigi. "Pioggia di Milioni anche alla Television Italiana," *Sorrisi e Canzoni* 48, November 27, 1955.

Veltroni, Walter. *I Programmi che Hanno Cambiato l'Italia*. Milan: Feltrinelli, 1992.

8

TELENOVELAS IN BRAZIL

From Traveling Scripts to a Genre and Proto-Format both National and Transnational

Joseph Straubhaar

The global creation and flow of television genres and formats should be thought of as a complexly articulated, fluid process of hybridity whose integrative effects do not necessarily eliminate cultural difference and diversity but rather provide the context and boundaries for the production of new cultural forms marked by local specificity. In this respect, Ang (1996) observed,

> What becomes increasingly "globalized" is not so much concrete cultural contents, but, more importantly and more structurally, the parameters and infrastructure which determine the conditions of existence for local cultures. It can be understood, for example, as the dissemination of a limited set of economic, political, ideological and pragmatic conventions and principles which govern and mould the accepted ways in which media production, circulation and consumption are organized throughout the modern world.
>
> (153–154)

Genre and Format

In this chapter, we argue that there are several layers of genre, proto-format commercialization of program elements, and current commercially licensed formats. Some genre traditions, like melodrama, tend to be large, over-arching categories that already have a long history before television (Martín-Barbero 1993). Specific genres of television production, like the U.S. soap opera or the Latin American telenovela can develop within that larger tradition. Even more specific genres, like the Brazilian socially engaged or historical telenovelas, versus the romantic Mexican Cinderella story telenovela (Hernandez 2001), develop or emerge over time within those genre traditions.

Television formats are now often distinguished as a parallel category which looks at forms of television that are packaged for licensing, transfer across cultures, and localized adaptation or implementation by regional, national or local networks. Specific formats are often imported and adopted. They can feed into genre development, grafted on to older traditions.

In this study, I will tend to define a format very narrowly as a specific production package that is transferred from one television production entity to another to be adapted into a local version. This narrow definition is designed to make it easier to distinguish formats and genres. The arrangement is most often commercial, sold or licensed for specific fees or a share of profits (Moran 2004). However, non-commercial stations or networks can also share formats, as when Nordic national public networks obtain formats from the BBC.

Reality TV formats or game formats are among the most prevalent current and widely traded examples of formats. Some authors, like Shahaf, see specific implementations of formats into certain kinds of genres, such as the music competition genre within reality shows, like *Pop Stars* or *American Idol*. So specific formats can arise, like reality television competitions, which form specific genres within it, like the song contest or the dance contest (Shahaf 2007). These genres retain characteristics common to major formats, like the song contest genre, that eliminates contestants in successive rounds, like other genres typical of the reality show.

Genres represent long-term development, the national or cross-cultural, hybrid development of well-understood, widely accepted categories over time. Schatz (1988) made a distinction about film that we can apply to television. He compared the deep structure of a film genre, as a sort of social contract between industry and audience, and a genre film, a specific enactment or production of the genre. Analogous might be the deep structure of melodrama as a sort of global meta-genre, the soap opera as a twentieth-century adaptation of that tradition, the telenovela as a region-specific deep structure of television genre, and ABC's *Ugly Betty* as a particularly popular licensed format adaptation to the U.S.A. of the Latin American genre based on a specific production, *Yo soy Betty, la fea*, produced in Colombia, exported widely (Mato 2005), and remade in the United States (Bielby and Harrington 2005).

Moran (2004) argued that there is a widespread push toward local production that can use locally originated concepts, program ideas from co-production, and imported program format adaptation. Moran (2004) observed that producers have been informally borrowing formats for a while, increasing co-production, and particularly increasing the formal licensing of formats. The first two of these, along with substantial trade in telenovela scripts, have been true of the telenovela industry in Latin America since the early 1950s but formal trade in complete program packages is much more recent.

In Moran's (2004) terms, the telenovela was introduced as a sort of genre localization or co-production between the outside sponsor, usually one of the multinational soap companies, like Colgate-Palmolive, which had sponsored or even co-produced soap operas in the U.S.A. or elsewhere, who brought in considerable genre and production knowledge, and local producers, who adapted or localized it to their circumstances and culture, also building on other serial or melodramatic traditions that came to Latin America from a variety of sources (Mazziotti 1993). The original genre pattern of radio soap opera passed indirectly from the United States to Brazil via prior cultural adaptations to more reconfigured and culturally proximate forms in Cuba, Argentina, and elsewhere in Latin America.

Some new genres have become the focus for a global form of flow and adaptation, the licensed format trade. Format, in this sense, is a more specific framework for production than genre. According to Moran (1998), "a television format is that set of invariable elements in a program out of which the variable elements of an individual episode are produced" (p. 13). So a melodrama or prime-time serial is a genre. The concept, script, and production guidelines of *Desperate Housewives* constitute a specific format. This is so even if it is subtly transformed from the U.S. style of prime-time serial to, say, the distinctive Latin American telenovela, which most would argue is now a different genre (La Pastina et al. 2003). Moran (1998; 2004) observed that the two main kinds of formats are (1) drama, situation comedy, or scripted entertainment, and (2) reality shows, including game shows, talk shows, and live dramatic situations, such as MTV's *Real World*. Those represent several different genres.

This paper argues that one part of what became the telenovela genre originally came from the localization in Cuba of a distinctly American genre, the soap opera, pushed by the agency of Colgate-Palmolive and other American advertisers. However, what eventually took place in Cuba and elsewhere in Latin America was the hybridization of that localization effort together with other traditions of serial fiction, under the agency and efforts of producers and entrepreneurs like Goar-Mestre. Even more profound was a diaspora of the new telenovela genre and further glocalization of it across Latin America, as it was further adapted by local cultural industries. This was visible in two particularly important ways: the dispersion of telenovela writers, directors and entrepreneurs across Latin America, and a strong regional traffic in telenovela scripts that began in the 1950s. This traffic of scripts and professionals is an important precedent for the current global trade in television formats, based on scripts, licensed production books or packages, and consultants. This chapter concentrates on the impacts of that diaspora of genre, scripts and professionals and adaptation of those genre traditions in Brazil.

Genres

Mittell (2004) argued that genres should account for the particularities of the medium (TV versus film), negotiate between specificity and generality, develop from discursive genealogies (such as the examination of telenovelas below), be understood in cultural practice, and be situated within larger systems of cultural hierarchies and power relations. Different groups, such as critics, producers, advertisers, distributors, programmers, and audiences, very often structure genre categories quite differently (Feuer 1987). For example, critics are usually aiming for theoretical understanding, either of cultural/textual forms in themselves (Mittell 2004) or of the complex practices between industry and audiences. Feuer (1987) called the first focus aesthetic and sees the second as focusing on cultural ritual, producing common understandings between audiences and producers. Being trained more as a social scientist than a literary scholar, I tend to lean toward the second definition. In contrast to either of these academic goals, producers use genre categories to try to figure out what institutional structures, such as network managers and advertisers, will let them produce the programs that interest them, while also generally trying to please audiences. Some recent work by Havens (2006) and Bielby and Harrington (2005) seeks to examine more of the role of producers and programmers as industrial middlemen in genre and program development and flow. Exploring the growth of these common understandings between audiences and producers, while finding larger genre and format patterns in them, is the overall goal here.

In particular, here we want to look at the way a new television genre, the telenovela, was developed in an interplay between a base genre, the America soap opera; a first round of hybrid genre development in Cuba and elsewhere in Latin America; and the national particularization of the new regional genre in places like Brazil. We want to look at the interplay between sponsors, television industry producers, the evolving genre texts or scripts, and the evolving regional and national audiences.

Precedents of the Format Trade in the Latin American Telenovela Industry

The primary question of this essay is whether the practices of telenovela industry that built up in Latin America can be seen as a precedent for the emergence of the format trade as it is currently being theorized and understood. In general, this examination of the case of telenovelas will help establish the general importance of several needs that also drive practices of the format trade. First, perhaps, is that audiences prefer local faces on screen (Straubhaar 1991) to the extent that a local version of a game or reality show that might be more cheaply imported whole will actually make more money despite its higher local production costs (Moran 2004). Second, television producers can lower the risks of expanding into new genres by adapting programs that have worked well elsewhere, as telenovela producers do when they produce their version of a show or script that has been a hit elsewhere in Latin America. Third, television producers, particularly working in a genre that is new to them, will often be lacking forms of expertise, like scriptwriting in the early days of the telenovela, which can be imported and adapted. Fourth, all of these things also make it cheaper to produce a new program by importing a script, if not a whole format, despite the cost of acquiring it. Fifth, all of these things may over time permit development of a new "local" genre and a supporting cultural industry to emerge from these kinds of glocalization or hybridization processes. So in the long run, we might see more fully localized cultural industries in nations and regions, producing variations on what might then be a distinctive Latin American form of the soap opera (Straubhaar 1982) or a new Arabic form of the song contest reality show (see Kraidy 2007).

It will help to understand some of the specific practices that emerged early in the 1950s, like the sale and licensing of telenovela scripts between writers and companies across Latin American borders, or the flow of business and production personnel between countries, or the borrowing and adaptation of commercial television practices related to telenovela production and programming. Taken together, these and more recent practices show how a transnational but culturally and linguistically specific set of conventions and practices spread and were adapted in a way that anticipates some of the current spread and adaptation of formats for game or reality shows.

We see the enactment and adaptation of a general genre, melodrama, into a more specific commercial form that is transnational across the Latin American region. The commercial nature of the spread and adaptation is one of the interesting precedents for how cultural industries can perceive a commercial advantage in acquiring program elements to produce their own versions or adaptation. The creation of a routine trade in those elements also anticipates the current format trade. The cultural-linguistic specificity of this trade in Latin America may also anticipate some of the regional specificities I think we are beginning to see in the format trade, as certain kinds of formats find pathways or barriers created by cultural practices in some markets and regions, even as some seem to find almost global forms of adaptation.

This study focuses first on the emergence of what we call here the meta-genre of melodrama. Then it examines the various cultural influences and inputs into the specific Latin American genres of the radionovela and the telenovela. One of the important inputs was sale of scripts between countries for both radio and television, as well as the migration of key writers, entrepreneurs, etc. between countries. We examine that briefly as a precedent for the current format trade. We then examine genre development in Brazil within the larger Latin American telenovela tradition and the interplay it has with old and new forms of commercialization, that anticipate the format trade.

The Melodrama Tradition

Telenovelas in Brazil and elsewhere in Latin America most clearly evolved from earlier, similar programs on radio. However, they did not develop only from the radio matrix. Other traditions in serialized fiction affected the development of the telenovela genre in the Latin American region as well. From the serial fiction *fueilettons* in France and the centuries-old *cordel* (chapbook) literature in Brazil, the genre evolved in each country within Latin America with certain peculiarities (Martín-Barbero 1993; Ortiz and Borelli 1988), again reflecting the complexity of both telenovela origins and adaptations.

Martín-Barbero (1993) shows that telenovelas are based on what this study calls a meta-genre of melodrama that came to Latin America from long-term roots in a number of earlier forms in print, circuses and traveling shows, folk poetry performed orally, folk and professional drama, and radio theater and novelas. Different forms of these are found in various parts of Latin America, but Martín-Barbero and others like Nora Mazziotti (1993) find the gradual evolution of a set of melodramatic roots for the subsequent development of first radionovelas and then telenovelas.

The *fueilleton*, *foletin*, or *folhetim* tradition was central, according to many scholars (Hernandez 2001; Martín-Barbero 1988; Rowe and Schelling 1991). Authors like Balzac and Dickens published widely read, very popular works as serials in periodicals in the 1800s. Many of the famous serious novels and stories of the era had a sense of melodrama in their genre appeal. They helped begin to build a mass audience for the melodrama genre that laid both bases and boundaries for the telenovela genre (Straubhaar 2007). Some argue that print serials helped create a mass audience for newspapers, radio and television in turn (Hernandez 2001). This shows how one side of the genre development equation (Feuer 1987), audience expectations, was being developed or prepared by earlier forms of melodrama in ways that telenovelas could draw on.

Serial melodramas in print also contributed key specific, dramatic, genre-related tropes and narrative forms, like the cliff hanger ending at the end of an episode that brings the reader, listener or viewer back for the next episode to see what happened. Serial novels and serial stories in newspapers, like the popular French stories of Eugène Sue, also opened a key current characteristic, the systematic absorption of reader feedback in the writing process, which Martín-Barbero calls the telenovela's "permeability to the transformations of modern life" (cited in Hernandez 2001: 56).

Martín-Barbero also emphasizes the local roots of melodrama in Latin American folk poetry and drama, although those roots are also hybridized between European literary and dramatic traditions, such as the popular theater of the French Revolution, and indigenous and African roots from their early beginnings (1987). In Brazil, these were very visible in the *literatura de cordel*, literally stories on a string, chapbooks or cheaply printed pamphlets strung over strings for sale in marketplaces (Slater 1982). These cheap, popular booklets frequently told classic melodramatic stories, which were both read directly by audiences and chanted or performed by singers or story-tellers, which provided a tradition of oral performance of stories that fed into radionovelas in Brazil, Cuba and other places (Hernandez 2001).

Melodrama in film circulated widely in the region, particularly in films from the golden age of Mexican cinema in the 1940s and 1950s (Martín-Barbero 1995). These melodramas helped create an urban culture that saw the genre as normal, as one of the first grand narratives of modern life and development that they had been exposed to. They helped create a region-wide appreciation of the genre and its narrative forms.

Radionovelas

As radio developed in Latin America in the 1920s, the fueilletons, or folhetins in Brazil and folletines in Spanish-speaking Latin America, were having a period of great popularity among readers. In Cuba, for example, books and folletines were read out loud to tobacco rollers in factories, which developed styles of reading that influenced radio theater and radio novelas (Hernandez 2001). The popularity of that tended to carry the serial genre into radio as a form of radio theater. Indeed, in Argentina and elsewhere, radionovelas were simply called radio theater for quite a while until the radionovela name became attached to a more specific genre of radio melodrama.

Radionovelas were developed in a number of countries, drawing on both national and regional Latin American ideas. National radio dramas in Argentina and Cuba are seen as particularly important sources of ideas by Hernandez (2001), but many countries, including Brazil, had important local drama traditions and industries that provided ideas, writers, actors, etc. to radio drama and radionovelas.

However, Cuba was a particularly important source of the radionovela scripts that circulated throughout the region. C.M.Q., the leading Havana commercial radio station of the 1940s and 1950s, "flooded" Latin America with exported scripts (Sinclair 1999), influencing the radio productions of Azcárraga, who started and owned Televisa, which created the dominant telenovelas of Mexico (Fernández and Paxman 2001). In Brazil, the first radionovela of 1941 was an adaptation of a Cuban script (Morreira 1991).

Many of the major Latin American common ideas about radio and telenovelas that were imported from Cuba into other Latin American countries also represented an indirect American influence on the Latin American genre. The specific commercial form of radionovelas was first developed in pre-Castro Cuba at the behest of Colgate-Palmolive, an American corporation that wanted to sell soap. Seeing how soap operas reached the targeted U.S. female consumer market for their products, these corporations then introduced the genre first in Cuba, then later in the rest of Latin America. Audience response was strong and ensured that advertisers would supply the economic resources for continued and expanded production of telenovelas in an increasing number of countries.

Colgate and the Sidney Ross Co. helped invent the radionovela and later the telenovela in a pioneering operation in pre-Castro Cuba, where "the American soap opera" was "translated and exported" (Katz 1977: 117).

> Some say that the telenovela is merely the U.S. radio soap-opera transposed. But not only had Latin American radio long used the serial story format, so also had Latin American newspapers. Any search for cheap programming to build audience loyalty could scarcely fail to arrive at the formula of a serial drama with a tiny cast and minimal studio set. The key point about the telenovela is that it originates from a need to fill time (including daytime) cheaply . . .
>
> (Tunstall 1977: 176)

The commercial form clearly built on other narrative traditions and oral drama traditions, but the package of the specific radio genre that we think of as the Latin American regional radionovela was clearly shaped by the interaction of advertiser desires expressed by Colgate-Palmolive, the emerging business model of Cuban radio station entrepreneurs which also built closely on U.S. models (Schwoch 1990), and the narrative genre shaped by Cuban writers and actors, working within the larger tradition of Latin American melodrama (Mazziotti 1993).

In Moran's (2004) terms, the radionovela and, later, the telenovela, were introduced as a sort of genre localization or co-production between the outside sponsor, who brought in considerable genre and production knowledge, and local producers, who adapted or localized it to their circumstances and culture. The original genre pattern of radio soap opera passed indirectly from the United States to Brazil via prior cultural adaptations to more reconfigured and culturally proximate (Straubhaar 1991) forms in Cuba, Argentina, and elsewhere in Latin America.

Foreign influences on the telenovela were pronounced at first. American soap operas on radio and television provided models for the radionovelas and later telenovelas which developed throughout Latin America. American advertisers often encouraged Latin American broadcasters to produce these programs because they were effective in reaching mass audiences.

The original American influences were diluted as the basic novela form spread throughout Latin America. Cuban and Mexican writers and producers who had worked for the Cuban stations moved on to Brazil and Argentina after Castro's takeover (Sanchez, interview, 1978). Brazilian television stations imported scripts and even finished telenovelas (to be dubbed into Portuguese) from Argentina and Mexico up through 1964.

American corporate advertisers also did continue to have some direct influence on the Brazilian telenovela programs, funding their development and training writers, producers, and technicians. Florisbal (interview, 1979) observed that advertisers sometimes paid technicians and actors when television stations could not or did not.

For example, in the early 1960s Colgate-Palmolive hired Brazilian writers to adapt Argentinian telenovela scripts as well as writing their own (Walter Durst, *Jornal da Tarde*, October 14, 1970). This illustrates the degree to which continuing American influences on the telenovela were mixed with other Latin American influences and indigenous Brazilian creations.

Florisbal estimated that the influence of American advertisers continued until the late 1960s. After that, TV Globo and, later, TV Tupi acquired sufficient market strength and financial stability to be independent of advertisers' "suggestions" (interview, 1979).

The Common Genre Roots of Latin American Telenovelas

The economic and commercial structure of Latin American television, including Brazil, was strongly affected by the models and direct actions of U.S. companies (Fox 1997). However, the development of programming, including the telenovelas, was more complexly hybrid. It developed in a Latin American cultural matrix that emphasized certain themes, which then began to vary considerably as national telenovela genre variations developed.

> The telenovela exploits personalization—the individualization of the social world—as an epistemology. It ceaselessly offers the audience dramas of recognition and re-cognition by locating social and political issues in personal and familial terms and thus making sense of an increasingly complex world.
>
> (López 1995: 258)

The Latin American telenovela, in almost all its variations, focuses on several central themes that were not central to American soap opera (Straubhaar 2007), so it represents considerable adaptation (Moran 2004). These new themes include class roles and conflicts—for example, maids versus housewives—as well as social mobility out of poverty. They also include themes that were once more prevalent in film and early U.S. television, such as the hardships faced by people moving from the countryside to the city to take industrial jobs, but are much more common and relevant now in Latin America.

Audience feedback shaped the productions away from elite-focused dramas toward a mass culture form that resonated more with a variety of traditions and plot devices and that could involve both men and women, peasants, urban workers, and the middle classes (Martín-Barbero 1993). This cultural formation spread all over Latin America, with distinct adaptations, so that Brazilian telenovelas are quite different from those of Mexico (Hernandez 2001).

National Variations on the Telenovela

Across Latin America, the telenovela as a genre has a common history, as noted above. However, different countries' television networks and producers have employed quite varied themes, narrative styles, and production values that have become more differentiated or nationalized over time.

According to López (1995), for example, Mexican telenovelas, particularly those from Televisa, tend to be more openly emotional, very dramatic weepers, and most often are ahistorical telenovelas with no social context provided, although some recent productions have begun to show very generalized differences between rich and poor neighborhoods. Hernandez calls these "blandas," or bland telenovelas (2001), compared with Brazilian or Colombian novelas, which are more hard-edged and social, which he calls "dura" or tough (2001).

Colombian telenovelas tend to have more comedy and irony along with a greater concern for context. Venezuelan productions are more emotional but do not have the "baroqueness" of Mexican sets. Brazilian telenovelas are the most realistic, with historically based narratives that have a clear temporal and spatial contextualization (López 1995). However, as Hernandez (2001) notes, the number two stations or networks in several countries have started to compete with dominant national networks by borrowing tricks from the networks of other countries. So when TV Azteca wants to contrast its programming in Mexico with that of Televisa, it could borrow more social and issue-oriented telenovela genre conventions from Brazil. These variations show how the common history, from European melodrama to Colgate-Palmolive soaps, has been adapted and reconfigured by producers interacting with distinct national cultures and audiences, as well as by national competitors who try to both imitate and distinguish themselves within national cultural market frameworks. These telenovela genres reflect considerable national adaptation of the regional genre, but all are faithful to the melodramatic roots of the genre.

Brazilian Radionovelas and Telenovelas

The radionovela reached Brazil in 1941. Radionovelas were first imported into Brazil in the 1940s in the form of scripts from Mexico, Argentina and Cuba, translated into Portuguese from Spanish (Sanchez, interview, 1978). The success of the genre on Brazilian radio stations led to an increasing amount of time and resources devoted to it.

The leap from radio to television in Brazil took only a decade, 1941–51. Brazilian producers initially mostly adapted foreign literary works, following the melodramatic genre formula established by the Cuban radionovelas of rather bland, not particularly culture-specific stories. They were in fact often based on imported scripts. One of the first major Brazilian telenovelas, for example, was *Eu compro esta mulher* (I will buy this woman), based on a Cuban script. This pattern of Brazilian reliance on internationalized scripts, either directly imported or written in the pattern common across Latin America of bland, deterritorialized romances, persisted into the 1960s.

Radionovelas and early serialized TV shows had a fundamental role as a breeding ground for the genre, creating a Brazilian television adaptation of melodrama that is hybrid but which gradually became distinctive. Scriptwriters were trained in the melodramatic conventions and gradually adapted them to fit Brazil, reconfiguring both the U.S. and Latin American genres.

Brazilian radio produced also copied, reworked and "Brazilianized" American variety shows, comedies, and radio theater and drama shows (Raoul Silveira 1975; Porto e Silva, interview, 1979). These program formats changed even more as they were adapted for use on television. Raoul Silveira (1975: 16) also observed that the television industry in the U.S.A. could draw on experience from the film industry, whereas Brazil could not do so to the same degree. Therefore, Brazilian television leaned particularly heavily on the experience of commercial radio in both programming and financing. It also leaned on traditions of national theater, film, circus and a national version of cabaret theater, like vaudeville (Sodré 1972).

While emphasizing radio's program content in his own analysis, Milanesi (1979: 79) observed that, "before television existed or while it was still restricted to a few urban centers, radio was, above all else, the principal vehicle for advertising and selling, or if you will, the principal stimulus to the growth of the internal market." The commercial structures of radio, such as hiring artists, producing programs and advertisements, buying recorded programming, selling advertising time, and campaigning for listenership, were applied directly to television. The men who started commercial television broadcasting in Brazil had been successful with a commercial approach in radio and applied it directly to television.

The Economics of the Rise of Brazilian Telenovelas in the 1950s–1960s

The radionovelas were also adapted for television, beginning in 1951. They were not initially dominant, as television was a much more elite medium in the 1950s, with an audience that was more interested in musical variety and original dramas. Telenovelas were (and are) more oriented toward mass audiences, which began to direct programming choices as television and sets became more widely distributed in the 1960s (Mattos 2000).

Furthermore, industrial factors favored a move away from original one-off dramas toward serials. Porto e Silva observed that costs of producing original television dramas in Brazil grew excessive (interview, 1979). In contrast, a 1950s telenovela would have 15–20 episodes using the same actors, story line and props, so it offered producers a considerable financial advantage over individual television dramas, for which producers had to do and re-do sets, scripts, etc. The economic attraction of imported, "canned" U.S. programs also began to increase for the same reasons. Porto e Silva also noted their role in replacing live dramatic and musical productions (interview, 1979).

The combination of telenovelas, imported films and series, and *shows de auditório* emerged as the television broadcasters' response to the changes in audience demand in the 1950s. The change in demand was, itself, due to changes in the supply of sets and the increase in demand for them. Those increased dramatically after 1964, when the military government decided to install telecommunications infrastructure to carry signals further across Brazil, and subsidized credit to enable TV set purchases, since the military saw improved communications with the Brazilian population as a matter of national security (Mattos 2000). These changed factors of supply and demand also shaped the actions of the advertisers and advertising agencies, the other major components of the television industry.

These commercial media structures, indeed the entire market economy of Brazil, were reinforced by foreign commercial interests. Besides such enduring systemic influences, there were many specific American influences on the pre-television Brazilian radio and press empires. They included advertising sales of equipment and technology, financing, sales of recorded music, and the supply of news items by AP and UPI. When television developed in the 1960s, it suffered the additional influences of direct American investment and the borrowing of American network management ideas, particularly at TV Globo, which was started in a joint venture in 1964 with Time-Life, Inc. (Hertz 1987).

Beyond American influence on the general Brazilian commercial system and on specific techniques of the advertising industry, I also found examples of influence on individual television programs by American advertisers and advertising agencies, particularly in the 1950s and 1960s:

> In the past, between 1950 and 1967, before the TV Globo Network became so powerful, programming was decided half by directors and half by the wishes of advertisers. For example, Gessy-Lever bought the U.S. series *Bonanza* and brought it to TV Tupi in São Paulo to sponsor in 1956. It was the first foreign series to be imported. In domestic productions such as telenovelas, the role of advertisers was strong also. For example, the [British] advertising agency Lintas, representing the [U.S.] Unilever group, wanted to reach housewives through telenovelas, which are a more economical vehicle than theater [the major program form at the time] and

have greater mass appeal. Up until 1965, Lintas was involved in all aspects of the telenovelas: selecting cast and script, paying the actors when the station was low on money, etc. Various advertisers would say to stations that they wanted this or that and get their way.

(Florisbal, interview, 1979)

The telenovela itself presents an interesting example of American influence. Although the telenovela, as noted above, was originally created by Latin American producers for an American corporation, the program form has developed far beyond the circumstances in which it was begun, i.e. as a gambit to sell soap. The telenovela is a program form that captivates the Brazilian audience more thoroughly than any comparable medium or art form. It is a commercial product of a cultural industry but it now is a medium for Brazilian, not foreign, popular culture.

The telenovela was embraced early by advertisers who became more interested in television as a means of promoting mass consumption items like soap, food products, soft drinks, beer, household items, etc. This shift in advertising was, nevertheless, restrained by the still limited purchasing power of lower-class incomes.

Paradoxically, this limited capacity for non-essential spending by the population works to create a larger television audience by restricting the leisure possibilities available to Brazilians. To a certain extent, this made television advertising and programming decisions problematic. The broad mass of the audience had limited purchasing power, so programmers had to decide if they wanted to aim their material at them or at a more restricted audience with higher purchasing power. The decision was not virtually automatic, as it was in the U.S.A., where the broad audience had purchasing power. A few broadcasters in São Paulo have, in fact, enjoyed reasonable success in deliberately programming to selected higher-class audiences in the 1970s. Most broadcasters chose to program to the mass audience and rely on advertising that sold mass interest products, particularly during the rapid expansion years of the 1960s.

In 1971, 70 percent of the audience in Rio was made up of classes C and D,[1] so programming had to respond to the popular culture, the symbols and interests of the new audience classes. These tended to be folklore and entertainment from the interior of the country, not the high culture favored by the elites of Rio and São Paulo . . . But the new programming was not planned and imposed by experts, either Brazilian or American. It came from the market forces. The logic of the market was to grab the advertising money that was being offered by providing the programming which would draw in the mass audience.

(Muniz Sodré, interview, 1978)

Brazilian Telenovelas in the 1960s

The same programming formats that emerged in the 1950s, telenovelas and *shows de auditório*, remained popular in the 1960s. By the end of the 1960s, the systems of production for these programs constituted thriving, autonomous "cultural industries" within the Brazilian television industry. In his study of the "massification" of television programming by the Brazilian cultural industry, Sodré (interview, 1978) emphasized the importance of these nationally produced formats, the telenovela and *show de auditório*. He noted that the *auditório* show, *Chacrinha*, the most famous of the genre, "was financed by a Brazilian supermarket chain, Casas da Banha, which wanted to sell common products like fish and soap to classes C and D. These 'grotesque'[2] popular shows were financed by advertisements for common products."

Two Brazilian program forms not only held their own against American and other imported programs, but grew quickly and steadily in their shares of audience hours throughout the 1960s. Those were telenovelas and *shows de auditório*, or live variety shows. Musical programming did not increase its audience hour share but it held a strong third place among Brazilian program forms and also received strong critical support.

Telenovelas and *shows de auditório* have been singled out by academic and newspaper critics (Sodré 1972: 36; Artur da Távola, *O Globo*, March 26, 1974) as the most important popular culture entertainment forms in recent Brazilian history. They rose in popularity because they were good vehicles for Brazilian popular culture. They were widely produced because they were both popular and economical. Tunstall (1977: 176) noted that these two basic formats, the telenovela and the marathon variety show, were the "authentic local programming" which developed throughout Latin America "before the flood of U.S. television imports began," around 1960.

The telenovela and the *show de auditório* both evolved considerably during the 1960s. Their elaboration as program forms and the growth of their popularity reflected an essentially "Brazilian" vision of the mass audience and the mass culture that audience wanted for entertainment.

Telenovelas grew particularly rapidly in importance in the 1960s. By the end of the decade, they were the paramount Brazilian television programming form, in terms of the representativeness of their cultural content, their economic importance within the television industry and their probable impact upon the audience.

Here is an example of how Brazilian TV programmers were thinking about the role of the telenovela. *Mercado Global* (January 1976) quoted José Bonifácio, TV Globo production director, who at that time worked for TV Rio:

> TV Rio did not think that its comedy shows were competitive so Walter
> Clark, then Director of the station, and I decided to try telenovelas to reach

the public. We launched *Renúncia*, which had been a success in radio. It was fairly successful but I was already looking at *O Direito de Nascer*. [This novela was an adaptation of a classic Cuban telenovela called *El Derecho de Nascer*—"The Right to Know Who Your Parents Were"] It was an interesting episode. No one wanted the idea, except Clark and me . . . In transmitting the finished work, it was the same fight: TV Record was the leader of the group that TV Rio belonged to and Record did not want to produce it because they were afraid of the production costs and afraid it might fail . . . TV Rio and TV Tupi joined to broadcast it.

In the 1960s, all of the major stations had contributed something to the growth of the mass-appeal program formats. TV Excelsior, TV Tupi and TV Globo produced telenovelas. For the stations that could afford to produce them, the telenovela became the dominant Brazilian television entertainment form and probably the most important product of Brazilian mass culture and the Brazilian cultural industry. TV Tupi produced telenovelas throughout the decade and TV Bandeirantes began to do so in 1979, when it had begun to become a network. Nevertheless, as Rohter (1978: 57) observed, "the emergence, growth and continued success of the telenovela is inextricably linked with the rise of TV Globo." *Veja* (October 6, 1976) noted that,

> Globo did not invent the novela but from its studios came the decisive contribution in the novela's transformation into an almost cinematic genre of Hollywood dimensions and yet [a genre] most typically Brazilian in its language, plots and rhythm of production.

Another demonstration of the development of telenovelas' popularity can be seen by listing the most popular program in Rio de Janeiro of each year in the 1960s:

1960	(variety show) *Noite de Gala*, TV Rio
1961	(variety show) *Noites Cariocas*, TV Rio
1962	(comedy) *O Riso e o Limite*, TV Rio
1963	(variety show) *Noites Cariocas*, TV Rio
1964	(imported series) *Peter Gunn*, TV Rio
1965	(telenovela) *O Direito de Nascer*, TV Rio
1966	(*show de auditório*) *Discoteca de Chacrinha*, TV Excelsior
1967	(game show) *Telecatch*, TV Globo
1968	(telenovela) *O Homen Proibido*, TV Globo
1969	(telenovela) *A Rosa Rebelde*, TV Globo
1970	(telenovela) *Irmãos Coragem*, TV Globo.

(Artur da Távola, *O Globo*, April 9, 1977)

The highpoint of influence on Brazilian telenovelas by other Latin American programs came with *O Direito de Nascer*, a romantic, even melodramatic story about a young lawyer trying to find out who his parents were. One of the major Cuban radionovelas, it was adapted in Brazil as a radionovela in 1959. While it had good success on radio, the same plot was a smash success on television in 1964–65, pulling together the romantic plot elements, visual and mass culture appeal that "consecrated the popular success of the telenovela" (Porto e Silva, interview, 1979).

In 1964, Brazilian television producers at TV Excelsior examined the success of the regular, nightly telenovelas in Argentina and decided to increase their production to that level. (For the first few years of the 1960s, telenovelas were broadcast, like their radionovela predecessors, on non-daily schedules.)

The telenovela increased its share of total audience hours in São Paulo rapidly from 2 percent in 1963 to 12 percent in 1965, 13 percent in 1967 and 18 percent in 1969. After a plateau at 17 percent in 1971, the telenovela climbed into complete domination over all other program forms, domestic and imported, in the 1970s.

Brazilian television producers also began to increase the length of a typical telenovela's duration from 4–6 weeks to 9–10 months, enabling them to build up considerable audiences but preserving the necessity to have a plot which builds to a climax. This stands in sharp contrast to American soap operas, where a given show and basic plot line, such as *As the World Turns*, can continue for 20 plus years.[3]

By the late 1960s, at least, the telenovela was fast becoming a very distinctive national program format in Brazil. The telenovelas seemed to suffer remarkably little American influence in their content or substance. And no critic that I am aware of has noted lasting Argentinian, Cuban or Mexican influence, either, at least after the 1960s.

Comments by telenovela writers indicate that they feel the essential elements of their plots have remained fairly constant throughout the years: the likeable young hero, the repressed woman wanting to break out of her societal bonds, the young lovers, the search for the protagonist's true identity, the guilty secret, the villain, tragedies, suspense and the final happy ending (Bráulio Predroso and Walter Durst, *Jornal da Tarde*, October 14, 1970; Plinio Marcos, *Isto É*, February 28, 1979). This is the stuff of romantic fiction all over the Western world.

The details of the story line or manifest content of some telenovela plots were usually borrowed from foreign works of fiction in the 1950s and early 1960s, and occasionally after that in the 1970s. But these plots were nearly always adapted for the medium by Brazilian authors. Borrowed foreign plots were increasingly displaced[4] by purely Brazilian themes: current life in both lower and middle classes, historical and regional themes, and some current issues, such as ecology or Indian acculturation to outside life.

One telenovela in particular marked a shift away from the melodramatic telenovela tradition which Brazil had shared with other Latin American countries, exemplified by the imported *O Direito de Nascer* (*Isto É*, February 28, 1979). The 1968 telenovela by Brazilian writer Bráulio Pedroso, *Beto Rockefeller*, came out of a strain of mass culture that was very distinctly Brazilian, despite the protagonist's last name.

> *Beto Rockefeller* was a classic Rio "rounder" (*boa vida*), a "classic Brazilian." The show was popular because it was very satirical and treated real national issues directly. It crystalized a moment of transition, raising our consciousness about treating our own national reality . . . After *Beto Rockefeller*, the system of adapting foreign material diminished and the amount of national content in themes, plots and characterizations grew steadily.
>
> (Porto e Silva, interview, 1979)

This telenovela started the redefinition of the genre in Brazil and was aired by Rede Tupi in 1968 and 1969 (Mattelart and Mattelart 1990; Ortiz and Borelli 1988; Straubhaar 1982). *Beto Rockfeller* escaped the traditional Latin American artificial dramatic attitudes and speech patterns. It used colloquial dialogue typical of Rio de Janeiro. The dramatic structure, narrative strategies, and production values were also modified. *Beto Rockfeller* was the story of a middle-class young man who worked for a shoe store but, with charm and wit, got himself mixed up with the upper class, passing himself off as a millionaire. The telenovela got very high audience ratings, leading the network to stretch it to almost 13 months, much longer than the usual 6–8 months (Fernandes 1987).

TV Globo, which up to that point had followed a traditional style of telenovelas with exotic settings and plots, saw the audience interest in *Beto Rockfeller* and championed the style. In this process, the genre was reshaped, distancing the Brazilian telenovela from the Latin America model.

Gradually, certain Brazilian authors, such as Daniel Filho, Janete Clair and Dias Gomes, became nationally famous for writing original telenovela scripts. Together with other writers who adapted Brazilian historical and fictional works for telenovelas, these Brazilian writers slowly pushed out the Argentinian and Mexican scripts and writers, steadily "Brazilianizing" the medium (Sanchez, interview, 1978).

Some critics, like Miceli (1972: 162–167), argued that, despite the popularity and mass appeal of a Brazilian production like *Beto Rockefeller*, none of the products of Brazil's cultural industry really represented a Brazilian mass culture. He felt that cultural expressions or symbols on Brazilian television reflected only fragmented societal segments, such an elite ideology very much penetrated by foreign ideas, a middle-class ideology of self-contradictory elements dominated by reflected upper-class ideas, and folk or "rustic" expressions, which, when articulated, were typically repressed by the other groups. He saw no room for a mass culture in Brazil that was even relatively coherent or indigenous.

Miceli's analysis was intended to be polemic, to raise questions. It succeeds well at that, but with it, I find that he and like-minded critics miss a crucial point. That is that there are, in fact, Brazilian television productions like telenovelas and *shows de auditório* which are distinctly not high culture, which appeal to a mass audience of both the middle and lower classes (as defined by education and consumption habits) and which were consistently produced in industrial scale by Brazilian broadcasters, even though their basic forms as commercial entertainment reflect some residual foreign sources and influences.

Another analyst of Brazilian mass culture, Muniz Sodré, felt that telenovelas were a genuine, even valuable expression of Brazilian mass culture.

> I include the telenovela in the genre of mass literature. I don't agree with those who complain that the telenovela is "low level." I think it is the *folhetim* ["chap book" style mass literature of the nineteenth century] of today . . . Janete Clair (one of the most popular telenovela authors) has the flair for mass culture [*talento folhetinesco*]. She does not complicate language; she acts within the limits of the *folhetim* of today. She "familiarizes" the language, since the telenovela is aimed at the family group.
>
> (*Folha de São Paulo*, July 8, 1978)

Although *Beto Rockefeller* was produced by TV Tupi, and several other outstanding telenovelas were produced by TV Excelsior and TV Tupi in the mid-1960s, the consolidation of the telenovela as a successful (in audience popularity) expression of Brazilian mass culture took place at TV Globo. According to *Veja* (October 6, 1976), TV Globo made "the decisive contribution in the telenovela's transformation into an almost cinematic genre of Hollywood dimensions, and yet one most typically Brazilian in its language, plots and rhythm of production."

TV Globo paid well enough in the late 1960s to attract the best actors, writers and directors in Brazilian cinema and theater to work in telenovelas instead (Rohter 1978: 57). It was common practice for Brazilian actors and playwrights to work in telenovelas, movies, and the theater all in any given year. This led to a remarkably high level of telenovela quality, which was financially rewarding to the artists and writers as well to TV Globo, since it drew in fairly overwhelming audience and advertiser interest.

By the end of the 1960s, the production of telenovelas by TV Globo and TV Tupi, which maintained a small but respectable audience, was becoming a very stable, self-contained cultural industry. It no longer needed the kind of infrastructural support that American advertisers had given to telenovela production in the early and mid-1960s (Florisbal, interview, 1979) or the kind of guidance about audience tastes and interests that advertising agency research departments had provided to them (Dualibi, interview, 1979).

The telenovela industry was only beginning to set up a consistent set of values and symbols to guide and characterize the content of its products by the end of the 1960s. But telenovelas were criticized several times in 1964–68 for showing too much violence at times when children were watching (*O Estado de São Paulo*, August 22, 1964; September 9, 1964; August 15, 1967). Telenovelas were also seen as promoting materialism and consumer values (Artur da Távola, *O Globo*, September 3, 1974). Interestingly, these were not seen as foreign or foreign-influenced values, but as Brazilian values deserving question.

Brazilianization of the Telenovela in the 1970s

By 1969, all the major Brazilian television broadcasters of the time, the national networks TV Globo and TV Tupi and the independent São Paulo stations TV Record, TV Excelsior and TV Bandeirantes, perceived that telenovelas were the program form most preferred by the Brazilian mass audience. In 1969, all of them produced at least four telenovelas each.

There were not enough viewers or advertisers in the market to support this level of production. By 1970, TV Excelsior had been dissolved and TV Bandeirantes stopped making telenovelas. By 1974, TV Record also stopped making them, leaving only the networks, TV Tupi and TV Globo, which had national economic bases to support them. In light of this, they went for the "easy solution" of substituting imported programs for their attempts to create their own telenovelas.

Since the late 1960s and early 1970s, the Brazilian telenovela has slowly evolved away from the general Latin American model. Straubhaar (1982; 1984) described a "Brazilianization" of the genre in two senses: a significant amount of national production, as the telenovela came to fill 3 hours of prime time 6 nights a week, and an equally significant adaptation of the genre to reflect national culture. The TV Globo network, in particular, invested heavily in production values, such as the use of external shots that had previously been avoided due to production costs. Globo also promoted a modernization of the telenovela's themes to include current issues, and appropriated texts produced by Brazilian writers, novelists, and playwrights.

In this process, Globo created what it termed, in its own publicity, the "Padrão Globo de Qualidade" [The Globo Pattern of Quality] (Herold 1986; López 1995; Straubhaar 1982). This high level of production quality began to differentiate Brazilian telenovelas, particularly those of TV Globo, from others in the region and even more from the American soap opera. This shows a reconfiguration of the Brazilian telenovela in not only genre form but production quality as well.

In a major stylistic departure from some other forms of telenovela, Brazilian telenovelas are "open works" or an "open genre" (Mattelart and Mattelart 1990: 41). During production, creators receive direct and indirect input from viewers and fans, theatrical productions, commercials, elite and popular press, institutional networks, audience and marketing research organizations, and other social forces in society, such as the Catholic Church, the government, and activist groups

(Hamburger 1999). This responsiveness to audience input is stronger in Latin American telenovelas than in many other global forms of melodrama, and it is particularly notable in Brazil, where TV Globo has extensively developed its methods of researching, anticipating, and tracking audience preferences and reactions (Straubhaar 1984).

This mode of production was influenced by the military regime's censorship practices, which slowly forced many writers to leave the theater and the feature film industry and find refuge in television. Television became a space in which, even if censored, writers managed to stretch the limits of what was acceptable in the repressive atmosphere of the 1970s. Telenovelas did not break completely with their melodramatic roots, but rather incorporated a national voice. They introduced a popular language, using colloquialisms and characters rooted in the daily life of the Brazilian metropolis. But this process was limited by what was perceived to be the target audience's expectations. Klagsbrunn (1993) felt the incorporation of reality into Brazilian telenovelas was but a superficial image of the actual problems affecting the nation:

> The telenovela reflects social aspects and problems faced by Brazilian society superficially, not conclusively, as usually occurs in genres adopted to entertain the masses. Since social criticism and suggestions regarding the path to be taken are not the main target of telenovelas, as this would alienate a significant number of viewers, social and political problems are merely included in a secondary role.
>
> (p. 19, my translation)

In the 1970s, the telenovela overtook the *show de auditório* as the archetypal "Brazilian" television entertainment but the *shows de auditório* did not disappear. Through most of the 1970s, Sunday afternoons and evenings were dominated by a pre-recorded, slickly produced variation of the *show de auditório* produced by a veteran of the genre, Silvio Santos, and called *Fantastico*. *Fantastico* was very illustrative of how TV Globo approached programming. First, it was well organized and handsomely produced. Second, it featured a wide variety of expensive talent and a diversity of subjects. Third, although it contained news and even public affairs-type documentary, it was very apolitical. Fourth, it was nationally oriented, not parochially centered on either Rio de Janeiro or São Paulo.

The networks were increasingly able to reach a national mass audience and to supply it with a larger percentage of nationally produced programming, if that was what it wanted. As far as demand was concerned, the audience wanted Brazilian popular or mass culture (telenovelas, *shows de auditório*, comedies, soccer and music) and they increasingly constituted a mass of consumers who could support advertisers who paid for the programming the audience preferred.

The fact that a typical telenovela lasted 8–9 months also permitted their authors to incorporate audience feedback into the writing and production process after the initial planning of the program. Some feared that this would increase the influence of marketing considerations in adjusting programs to audience tastes. But some Brazilian critics saw this as a positive development and noted that this particular quality set the telenovela apart from other dramatic forms, allowing a more genuine interchange between writer and public (Artur da Távola, *O Globo*, September 2, 1974).

By the mid-1970s, Globo had differential profiles of the audiences for its various telenovelas at 6, 7, 8 and 10 p.m. (Rohter 1978: 58). The telenovelas were definitely crafted to appeal to the particular audience of the various evening prime-time hours. Writers were guided by research departments of the broadcasters and advertising agencies in selecting themes and characters of greatest appeal. This integration of research into production was greatest at TV Globo (Sanchez, interview, 1978; *Veja*, October 6, 1976). This helped TV Globo keep its high relative independence in programming judgment.

Rohter (1978: 5g) quotes TV Globo research director Homero Sanchez:

> The average viewer of novelas in Brazil is a woman under forty. She is married, Catholic, has two children and is a member of the lower middle class . . . We start off at 6 p.m. with something that will make a woman think of the time of her grandparents, something that is pure and full of romanticism. Then at seven we come with something a bit lighter and more juvenile [to also appeal to the large numbers of children watching then]. We break for a bit of action at nine . . . by then the man has eaten, read the paper and relaxed a bit so we hit him with *Kojak* or *S.W.A.T.* and then at ten switch to something very adult so we can attract both man and wife. That is when we get a chance to experiment with our novelas a bit.

Competing with Imported Programs: Brazilian Telenovelas

Although the basic form of the Brazilian telenovela was set in the 1960s, the decade of the 1970s was the period when the telenovela really flowered as Brazil's paramount mass culture entertainment form. Outside influence on them dwindled and they became, as Sodré (*Folha de São Paulo*, July 8, 1978) declared, the "mass literature" of Brazil. The most popular telenovelas were those of TV Globo. TV Globo consolidated telenovela production on an industrial scale, usually giving viewers four different, well-produced programs each night except Sunday.

The percentage of São Paulo audience hours drawn by telenovelas was more than double the percentage of any other Brazilian program form and almost equal in 1975–77 to the audience hours drawn by imported series and feature films combined. Telenovelas had 17 percent in 1971, 22 percent in 1973, 20 percent in 1975 and 22 percent again in 1977.

Although TV Globo definitely dominated telenovelas in the 1970s, all these various telenovela experiments were important. Both Moya (interview, 1979) and Porto e Silva (interview, 1979) observed that TV Globo had copied many of its techniques from earlier producers, particularly TV Excelsior. TV Globo successfully synthesized many elements of style and put a firm production line under them. As Porto e Silva noted, the difference in quality between a TV Globo telenovela and one on TV Tupi was obvious.

In 1979, TV Tupi was crippled by economic problems but it still produced three or four nightly telenovelas, some of them introducing controversial themes such as Indian problems or environmental concerns and drawing a certain audience. After a decade of building up its economic base and production capacity, TV Bandeirantes re-entered the telenovela competition in 1979 with two nightly programs, which met with fair audience success.

By the mid-1970s, a number of Brazilian critics began to praise the telenovela for its representation of Brazilian culture and its relatively high quality in comparison to other television program forms. In 1974, Artur da Távola (*O Globo*, March 25, 1974) wrote:

> In the future, telenovelas such as "Beto Rockefeller," "As Bruxas," "Nino, o Italianinho," "Selva da Pedra," "Bandeira 2," 'Vitória Bonelli," "O Bem Amado" and "Os Ossos do Barão," will be analysed as the consolidation of television theater in Brazil, as a cultural and artistic expression mixed with popular level diversion. The telenovela is a totally new genre in the history of dramaturgy.

Non-Brazilian communications researchers were inclined to agree. Katz (1977: 196) noted that TV Globo's late evening telenovela "is now a serious affair, relating to real-life people and contemporary social issues." Read (1976: 91) and Tunstall (1977: 176) also noted that telenovela or "serial" programs are among the most popular and representative of non-American productions.

The creativity of telenovela authors, directors and actors did suffer serious outside influences. But these seemed to relate more to the industrial pattern of the Brazilian television system than to any observable foreign influence. This was a change from the 1960s, when American advertisers and Argentinian scripts had detectable influence.

It seems to me that Brazilian telenovelas are the products of a unique, distinctively Brazilian cultural industry. They seem to have become, in the view of credible Brazilian critics such as Artur da Távola and Muniz Sodré (see his comments on telenovelas, 1997: 270), a unique Brazilian form of mass drama or mass "literature." While telenovelas do suffer commercial influences from the industry that makes them, the processes of that industry also seem to be essentially "Brazilian."

More Political Telenovelas in the 1980s

Beginning in the late 1980s, as a result of the political *abertura* (opening) that started with the transition from military to civilian government (Straubhaar 1989), and continuing now, telenovela writers have increased the visibility of their social agendas and included national political debates in their narratives (Porto 2005). The commercial nature of telenovelas also evolved; these texts were used to sell not only products targeting housewives, but sports cars, services, and many other products targeted at different audience segments. Although they still have some room for creativity in plot lines, telenovela writers must now also bow to commercial imperatives and write such product placements into their scripts, in cooperation with network commercial departments. Even the commercial form of the soap opera has been reconfigured to exploit Brazilian culture and rules.

Intentionally or not, Globo transformed the Brazilian telenovela into a forum for the discussion of Brazilian reality. Globo has brought into the majority of Brazilian households current issues in the social and political arena. In a historical analysis of the development of telenovelas in Brazil, Hamburger (1999) argued that these texts have created a space in which to discuss the nation. They have become the way the nation is currently imagined (Anderson 1983).

These changes in style led Brazilian telenovelas to become more dynamic and more closely associated with current events in the life of the nation (e.g., thematic inclusion of elections, strikes, and scandals that were happening in "real" life). Attention to social events and issues, such as the 1995 telenovela about landless people, *O Rei do Gado*, ("The Cattle King") is one major development that differentiates Brazilian telenovelas from others in Latin America.

The "melodramatic glue" maintaining these texts' popularity with audiences has been modernized. Still, these melodramas have remained loyal to traditional topics such as romantic desire and conflict, social mobility, and the expected happy ending. The genre structure of the telenovela constrains writers within the commercial and genre conventions, but also gives them resources with which to reach the audience with a message. This is reminiscent of Giddens's (1984) theories of how structure provides both constraints or limits and resources to social actors. One of the more socially minded telenovela authors, Benedito Rui Barbosa, who wrote *O Rei do Gado* in 1994–95, maximized that space and resources to discuss land reform. One of the latest Globo telenovelas in 2008, *Duas Caras* ("Two Faces") highlights the story of a young man's corrupt and "two-faced" ascendancy to wealth and credibility, for which he ultimately pays through a three-year prison sentence. Intertwined with the main story line are subplots featuring a powerful *favela* or slum leader and his god-like reign, a local politician's turbulent campaign, and a drama-ridden university administration headed by a powerful woman.

The New Regional Marketplace for Telenovelas, and Beyond?

The increasingly political and social commentary oriented direction of many of the TV Globo telenovelas marked a new wave of differentiation of the Brazilian form of the telenovela from directions in the genre taken elsewhere in Latin America. Hernandez (2001) observed the development of what he saw as two forms of the telenovela genre, the *duro* (strong, more political o social-commentary oriented) and the *blanda* (milder, more romantic, less political). He noted that among the top Latin American producers, Mexico and Venezuela tend to make blander, more romantic telenovelas, while Brazil and Colombia tend to make more openly political or social ones. He further noted, however, that with the development of new competing networks in the 1980s and 1990s, if the dominant network, like Globo in Brazil, made strong novelas, then a competing network might either import or make blander ones, as did SBT (Sistema Brasileira de Televisão). Conversely, when Azteca wished to challenge Televisa in Mexico, it initially hired a production company, Argos, to make stronger, more political or social telenovelas (Hernandez 2001).

This added a new layer to an already rapidly evolving market. By the 1990s, the Latin American market had stratified and grown. Roncagliolo (1995) described it as having three layers. At top were net exporters, particularly of tele-novelas, but also variety shows, comedies, music and sports, like Mexico and Brazil. Next were new exporters, like Argentina, Chile, Colombia and Venezuela, which both imported and exported, but were increasingly self-sufficient in key genres like telenovelas. Last were a number of smaller, poorer countries, like the Dominican Republic, which imported most of their programming from larger Latin American producers. More recently, there are new forms of operation based in Mexico that focus on exports to the Hispanic market in the U.S.A. (Piñón López 2007) or in Miami, which aim to be more transnational, creating material largely for export (Mato 2005).

It is becoming harder to characterize Latin American television by country, although countries have often tended to be branded together with key export genres; Mexico and Brazil, for example, are branded in global marketplaces as primary producers of telenovelas (Havens 2006). According to Bielby and Harrington (2005: 911),

> In the context of global TV trade fairs, the two main strategies for con-structing brand identities are programming genre and national identity. "Programming genres and subgenres form the primary product in international television, around which many distributors build their cor-porate identities" ... So Brazil gets a reputation for its telenovelas, Scandinavian countries for reality shows, Japan for its anime, and Germany for its action shows. National images are used by some distributors as a marketing tool; we say some and not all because building a nation-based

brand is expensive and not all sellers can afford to do so. . . . National images can also be used by buyers as another piece of (albeit unreliable) data on which to make purchasing decisions . . . as well as by local schedulers in promoting imported programming.

However, seen at a less global, more nuanced level, within the region, Brazil has aspiring networks creating more romantic telenovelas, and Mexico has Azteca creating, at least initially, more social ones. To do this, they can use direct program imports, but increasingly turn to importing less tangible genre and format resources.

For example, SBT in Brazil began to compete with TV Globo in the early 1990s in telenovelas by importing them from Mexico and dubbing them. Since the imported Mexican programs were notably different from the dominant form on TV Globo, they found an audience that wanted lighter, more romantic telenovelas (La Pastina 1999). SBT did relatively well, holding onto the second place in the Brazilian market, with simply importing and dubbing Mexican telenovelas at relatively low cost for a decade. However, they began to get more competition from a third network, TV Record, and found that to maintain their audience for Mexican-style telenovelas, they had to import the scripts and adapt them to the expectations of Brazilian audiences, using Brazilian actors, starting in 2001. So in theoretical terms, a demand by the audience, forced by increased competition, led to a need for greater localization of the Mexican-style telenovelas in Brazil.

Other Latin American networks also began to find it more advantageous in national market competitions to import scripts and produce localized versions of regionally successful programs than to simply import canned programs, a logic that Moran (2000) has observed in Asia and elsewhere with game shows and reality TV shows. Hit telenovelas, like *Betty la fea* ("Ugly Betty") also can drive both imports and format-style adaptations.

The Colombian hit *Betty la fea* ("Ugly Betty") was simply imported into a number of countries, including almost all of Latin America and the Hispanic U.S. market, and was dubbed into other languages for several other markets (Rivero 2003). It was also exported as a script or format to a number of other markets and remade or adapted into local versions. Perhaps the two most notable adaptations for our purposes were an adaptation in Mexico as a localized telenovela called *La Fea Más Bella* (The "Most Beautiful Ugly Girl") in 2006–07 by Televisa, and an adaptation not as a telenovela but as a serial comedy in the U.S.A. as *Ugly Betty* by ABC, 2006 to 2010. The Televisa production adapted it to their style with a well known popular cast. They kept some of the main original plot elements, like Betty's support from her group of friends, the Uglies, but discarded others. The American producers originally intended it to look more like a tele- novela with a daily serial approach, but ended up making it look much more like a conventional sitcom, with weekly episodes that do build somewhat in a serial fashion, but also work as stand-alone episodes. They also dropped more of the original plot elements, such as the group of friends, and centered it more on her own nuclear family.

Conclusion

So to conclude, we note several things about genre and format in telenovelas. First and foremost, the flow of telenovela scripts in Latin America, dating from the 1950s, shows that to some degree the idea of exporting key format elements, such as scripts, as well as writers, entrepreneurs and consultations has been around a long time, predating the export explosion of canned American television programs in the 1960s. This shows that the idea of borrowing, buying and adapting key elements of production, but then doing national versions, is a key form of culturally hybrid production (Kraidy 2005) that again predates, to some degree, the predominance of U.S. cultural product exports noted by studies starting with Nordenstreng and Varis (1974). So localization and adaptation of imported television format elements has been part of the hybridity of transnational television, at least in Latin America, since the 1950s.

Second, perhaps most interesting, is the historical evolution of the telenovela genre in Latin America as a dialogue between regional and national cultural traditions. Almost all countries, including the current dominant producers in Brazil and Mexico, imported format elements, scripts, and writers from Cuba or elsewhere in crucial initial stages. However, almost all those countries in Latin America that were large enough or rich enough to eventually produce telenovelas (Straubhaar 2007) ingrained those imported elements into their own cultural matrices, adapting genre and even formatted scripts to their own specific cultural histories (Rowe and Schelling 1991), as we see in the example of SBT in Brazil eventually deciding that to be more audience-competitive it had to import scripts rather than programs from Mexico. This shows that imported genres and formats can be very important in guiding the development of a cultural industry and its genre forms, but that in the medium to long run, seeing the history of globalization as hybridity, cultural adaptation of imported forms is necessary, maybe inevitable.

Third, telenovelas still have large global circulation as exported programs, primarily in Latin America, but also dubbed into a variety of other languages. This export circulation can be large, particularly with a hit like *Ugly Betty*, but as some of the counter-flow literature, such as Biltereyst and Meers (2000), notes, the volume of their actual exports peaked in the 1990s and still pales compared to the export flow of U.S. programs.

Fourth, in line with point two about the long run tendency toward adaptation of outside television genres and formats as part of the long-run flow of hybrid cultural development (Kraidy 2005; Pieterse 2004), telenovelas are now increasingly exported as formats and scripts, not just as cheap, canned programs.

That may be a new form of counter-flow (Thussu 2007), perhaps a more far-reaching one, since the U.S.A. has consistently shown itself resistant to the inflow of canned programs, but open to the import of genre ideas and formats. That has been most visible with non-scripted programs like reality shows, which are heavily imported everywhere, including the U.S.A. But it seems to be increasing with scripted formats like *Ugly Betty* as well.

The U.S. appetite for scripted format imports increased considerably in 2008, following its long-held appetite for imported reality formats. That is a current example of how far up the spectrum of producers the flow of scripted formats may go. But perhaps it is even more interesting to look back at almost 60 years of the flow and adaptation of scripts for the telenovela genre in Latin America for a sense of how deeply the transnational flow of scripted genres might work itself into national and regional televison, as well as how those flows will be localized and hybridized.

Notes

1   In the categories of Brazilian market research, Class C is the lower middle class and Class D comprises the working class and working poor.
2   Sodré (1972) defined his concept of "grotesque" as a deliberately outrageous combination of traditional, even archaic popular culture with mass media such as magazines and television, the cultural industry, in an exploitative mix of traditional folk culture and modern mass culture.
3   Rohter (1978: 58) quoted Brazilian telenovela author Daniel Filho about the difference between telenovelas and American soap operas. "They're not the same . . . If I am in competition with anything on American television, it's the dramatic series and the kind of things that Paddy Chayefsky and Rod Serling used to do . . . I could continue [my plots] indefinitely [like U.S. soaps] but . . . when you do that . . . the quality falls."
4   According to the archives available, the following foreign plots were used during the 1960s. 1960: *Anna Karenina*, *The Prince and the Pauper*; 1962: *Cleopatra*; 1963: *Scrooge*, *Snow White*, *The Prince and the Pauper*, *Treasure Island*; *Toulouse Lautrec*; 1964: Oscar Wilde stories, *The Maltese Falcon*, *The Count of Suffolk*; 1966: *Corsican Brothers*, *Anna Karenina*; 1967: *The Trapp Family*, *Les Misèrables*; 1968: *The Prince and the Pauper*; 1969: *Heidi*; *Uncle Tom's Cabin*; 1970: *Simplesmente Maria* (Mexican, about an upwardly mobile maid) (Archives of TV Cultura, São Paulo, 1979). After a 1963–64 peak, the number of foreign plots declined to one or two per year out of ten to twelve total telenovelas.

References

Anderson, B. (1983). *Imagined Communities: Reflections on the Origin and Spread of Nationalism.* New York: Verso.
Ang, I. (1996). *Living Room Wars: Rethinking Media Audiences for a Post-Modern World.* New York: Routledge.
Bielby, D. D. and C. L. Harrington (2005). "Opening America? The telenovela-ization of U.S. soap operas." *Television and New Media* 6(4): 383–399.
Biltereyst, D. and P. Meers (2000). "The international telenovela debate and the contra-flow argument." *Media, Culture and Society* 22: 393–413.

Dualibi, Roberto (1979). Interview with author, at DPZ Propaganda, Ltd., São Paulo, March 6.

Fernandes, I. (1987). *Memoria da telenovelabrasileira*. São Paulo: Brasiliense.

Fernández, C. and A. Paxman (2001). *El Tigre: Emilio Azcárraga y su imperio Televisa*. Mexico City: Grijalbo Mondadori.

Feuer, J. (1987). "Genre study and television." In R. C. Allen (Ed.) *Channels of Discourse*, pp. 138–145. Chapel Hill: University of North Carolina Press.

Florisbal, Octavio (1979). Interview with author, at AgenciaLintas/SSC&B, São Paulo, March 8.

Fox, E. (1997). *Latin American Broadcasting*. Luton, U.K.: University of Luton Press.

Hamburger, E. (1999). "Politics and intimacy in Brazilian telenovelas." Unpublished Ph.D. dissertation, Department of Anthropology, University of Chicago.

Giddens, A. (1984). *The Constitution of Society: Outline of a Theory of Structuration*. Berkeley: University of California Press.

Harrington, C. L. and D. D. Bielby (2005). "Global television distribution: implications of TV 'traveling' for viewers, fans, and texts." *American Behavioral Scientist* 48(7): 902–920.

Havens, T. (2006). *Global Television Marketplace*. London: British Film Institute.

Hernandez, O. D. (2001). "A case of global love: telenovelas in transnational times." Unpublished Ph.D. dissertation, University of Texas–Austin.

Herold, C. (1986). "Brazilian television in the 1980s: the making of 'Brazilianized' culture." Unpublished paper. Austin, TX: University of Texas at Austin.

Hertz, D. (1987). *A Historia Secreta da Rede Globo*. Porto Alegre, Brazil: Tche.

Katz, E. (1977). "Can authentic cultures survive new media?" *Journal of Communication* 27(2): 113–121.

Klagsbrunn, M. (1993). "The Brazilian telenovela: a genre in development." In A. Fadul (Ed.) *Serial Fiction in TV: The Latin American Telenovelas*, p. 251. São Paulo: Robert M. Videira.

Kraidy, M. M. (2005). *Hybridity, or the Cultural Logic of Globalization*. Philadelphia, PA: Temple University Press.

—— (2007). "Reality television, politics, and democratization in the Arab world." In I. A. Blankson and P. D. Murphy (Eds.) *Negotiating Democracy: Media Tranformations in Emerging Democracies*, pp. 253–278. New York: SUNY Press.

La Pastina, A. (1999). "The telenovela way of knowledge." Unpublished Ph.D. dissertation, University of Texas–Austin.

López, A. M. (1995). "Our welcomed guests: telenovelas in Latin America." In R. C. Allen (Ed.) *To Be Continued . . . Soap Operas Around the World*, pp. 256–275. London and New York: Routledge.

Martín-Barbero, J. (1987). *De los medios a las mediaciones: Comunicacion, cultura y hegemonia*. Barcelona: G. Gili.

—— (1988). "Communication from culture: the crisis of the national and the emergence of the popular." *Media, Culture and Society* 10(4): 447–466.

—— (1993). *Communication, Culture and Hegemony: From the Media to the Mediations*. Newbury Park, CA: Sage.

—— (1995). "Memory and form in the Latin American soap opera." In R. C. Allen (Ed.) *To Be Continued . . . Soap Operas Around The World*, pp. 276–284. London and New York: Routledge.

Mato, D. (2005). "The transnationalization of the telenovela industry: territorial references, and the production of markets and representations of transnational identities." *Television and New Media* 6(4): 423–444.

Mattelart, M. and Mattelart, A. (1990). *The Carnival of Images: Brazilian Television Fiction.* New York: Bergin & Garvey.

Mattos, S. (2000). *A televisão no Brasil : 50 anos de história (1950–2000).* Salvador: Pás.

Mazziotti, N. (1993). *Acercamientos a las telenovelas latinoamericanas.* In A. Fadul (Ed.) *Serial Fiction in TV: the Latin American Telenovelas,* p. 251. São Paulo: Robert M. Videira.

Miceli, S. (1972). *A Noite da Madrinha.* São Paulo: Editora Perspectiva.

Milanesi, L. A. (1978). *O Paraíso via EMBRATEL.* Rio de Janeiro:, Editora Paz e Terra.

Mittell, J. (2004). *Genre and Television.* New York: Routledge.

Moran, A. (1998). *Copycat Television: Globalisation, Program Formats and Cultural Identity.* Luton, U.K.: University of Luton Press.

—— (2000). "Copycat TV in the Asian/Pacific region?: Australian pilot research." Political Economy Section at 22nd General Assembly and Scientific Meeting of the International Association for Mass Communication Research, Singapore.

—— (2004). "Television formats in the world/the world of television formats." In A. Moran and M. Keene (Eds.) *Television Across Asia: Television Industries, Programme Formats and Globalization,* pp. 1–8. London: RoutledgeCurzon.

Morreira, S. V. (1991). *Radio no Brasil.* Rio de Janeiro: Rio Funda Editora.

Moya, Alvaro de (1979). Interview with author, at Universidade de São Paulo, March 7.

Nordenstreng, K. and T. Varis (1974). *Television Traffic: A One-Way Street.* Paris: UNESCO.

Ortiz, R., Borelli, S .H. S., and Ortiz, J. M. (1988). *Telenovela: história e produção.* São Paulo: Brasiliense.

Pieterse, J. N. (2004). *Globalization and Culture: Global Mélange.* New York: Rowman and Littlefield.

Piñón López, J. d. D. (2007). "The incursion of Azteca America into the U.S. Latino media." Unpublished Ph.D. dissertation, University of Texas–Austin.

Porto, M. P. (2005). "Political controversies in Brazilian television fiction: viewers' interpretations of the Telenova Terra Nostra." *Television and New Media* 6(4): 342–359.

Porto e Silva, Flavio. (1979). Interview with author, at Informacões da Area de Comunicação de Massa do Centro de Arte Brasileira do Departamento de Informação e DocumentaçãoArtistica (IDART) da Secretariade Cultura da Prefeitura de São Paulo, March 8.

Raoul Silveira, J. (1975). "O desenvolvimento da televisão no Brasil." *O Estado de São Paulo,* October 4. São Paulo: Suplemento do Centenário.

Read, W. H. (1976). *America's Mass Media Merchants.* Baltimore, MD: Johns Hopkins University Press.

Rivero, Y. M. (2003). "The performance and reception of televisual 'ugliness' in *Yo soy Betty la fea.*" *Feminist Media Studies* 3(1): 65–81.

Rohter, L. (1978). "The noble hours of Brazilian television." *American Film Institute Bulletin* no. 4 (February): 56–59.

Roncagliolo, R. (1995). "Trade integration and communication networks in Latin America." *Canadian Journal of Communications* 20(3): 335–342. Available online at www.cjc-online.ca/index.php/journal/article/viewArticle/882/788

Rowe, W. and V. Schelling (1991). *Memory and Modernity: Popular Culture in Latin America.* London: Verso.

Sanchez, HomeroIcaza. (1978). Interview with author, at RedeGlobo de Televisão, Rio de Janeiro, August 22.

Schatz, T. (1988). "The genius of the system : Hollywood filmmaking in the studio era." New York: Pantheon.

Schwoch, J. (1990). *The American Radio Industry and Its Latin American Activities, 1939–1990.* Chicago: University of Illinois Press.

Shahaf, S. (2007). "A globalized outlook for television genre theory: negotiating nationalism and commercialism through global formats in Israeli television." Paper presented at the Society for Cinema and Media Studies Conference,Chicago, March 8–11.

Sinclair, J. (1999). *Latin American Television : A Global View.* New York: Oxford University Press.

Slater, C. (1982). *Stories on a String: The Brazilian Literatura de Cordel.* Berkeley: University of California Press.

Sodré, M. (1972). *A comunicação do grotesco.* Rio de Janeiro: Editora Vozes.

—— (1977). *O Monopólio da Fala.* Petropolis: Editora Vozes.

Straubhaar, J. (1982). "The development of the telenovela as the paramount form of popular culture in Brazil." *Studies in Latin American Popular Culture* 1: 138–50.

—— (1984). "The decline of American influence on Brazilian television." *Communication Research* 11(2): 221–240.

—— (1989). "Television and video in the transition from military to civilian rule in Brazil." *Latin American Research Review* 24(1): 140–154.

—— (1991). "Beyond media imperialism: asymmetrical interdependence and cultural proximity." *Critical Studies in Mass Communication* 8: 39–59.

—— (2007). *World Television: From Global to Local,* Thousand Oaks, CA: Sage.

Thussu, D. K. (Ed.) (2007). *Media on the Move: Global Flow and Contra-Flow.* New York: Routledge.

Tunstall, J. (1977). *The Media Are American.* New York: Columbia University Press.

9

REVERSAL OF FORTUNE?

Hollywood Faces New Competition in Global Media Trade

Paul Torre

"Poor Hollywood" and a Media Market in Flux

> Television networks, still recovering from the writers' strike held their Upfronts last week, and the news is not so great. The networks are looking for a combined total of nearly $9 billion from marketers, but with recession either looming or already here depending on your mood, nobody seems to be willing to buy.
>
> (Swearingen 2008)

> Hollywood might be facing a crimp in its $6 billion international TV export business. Big-studio series are way too popular to fall out of favor with viewers around the world anytime soon, but the cost of producing them is spinning out of control stateside—and the asking prices for them on the international market are beginning to be balked at.
>
> (Brennan and Turner 2008)

The major studios in Hollywood, those who produce television for the world market, are apparently in trouble. Stories about their "tough times" seem ubiquitous. Consumers are watching less and less traditional TV, or perhaps the audience is "fragmented," or at least television advertising revenue is falling under pressure from newer and more exciting media, and Hollywood is the poorer for it (Schneider 2008). These same dynamics appear to be afflicting traditional television outlets around the world, and multiple reports in recent years indicate that "finished" television programming from Hollywood (sitcoms, dramas, MOWs) is pressed to find consistent audiences and revenues in the overseas market as well (Brennan and M. Turner 2007; Keane et al. 2007: 159; Sinclair and G. Turner 2004: 44).

In this chapter, I will discuss recent developments in the global media market, along with special attention to the economic impact of the explosion of the global television format trade. My point of reference in this exploration will be to examine how Hollywood has responded to these changing dynamics in the business of global television programming sales. I will examine how Hollywood's traditional (and traditionally dominant) media businesses are adjusting to changing economies, and how media producers from around the world, in their exploitation of television formats, have been able to directly compete, and also better monetize niche markets, affecting Hollywood's bottom line and future prospects (Keane and Moran 2008: 158). In short, I concur with Michael Curtin's estimation that, "Hollywood hegemony is far more tenuous than it might appear" (2007: 10).

The broader business of global television distribution has been dominated by the major studios in Hollywood, and by their glossy and expensive product. Disney/ABC's *Lost* and *Desperate Housewives* are sold around the world; News Corporation/Fox's *24* and *The Simpsons* are sold around the world; Viacom/CBS sells the *CSI* franchise around the world (Horan 2007; Munoz 2007). Today, the three most widely watched television programs are still from the United States, but as I will discuss, Hollywood is losing its grip on the global television market (Mediametrie 2008; Arango 2008). After all, even if Hollywood's product continues to be highly desirable, this does not mean that Hollywood will be able to exploit its product efficiently—the loss of revenue to the global piracy industry, for instance, is one of several inescapable realities presented by new technologies in our media marketplace. The sharp increase in television trade of global television formats, where a series concept is adapted in numerous other contexts by multiple media producers, is another reality, another complexity that is challenging longstanding dynamics in the business of media trade. These fluctuations and their impact demonstrate an "asymmetrical interdependence" within the global media economy, where Hollywood is primary, but dependent upon revenue flows from overseas (Straubhaar 2007).

A "golden age" for U.S. television's international distribution began in the 1970s, with programs such as the worldwide hit *Dallas*, and continued into the late 1990s, when Hollywood saw a downturn in bulk package television sales (Torre 2009). Local language productions, or homegrown television series, began to exhibit increasingly higher production values and become more and more popular (Kapner 2003). Current patterns in increased television format distribution are easily linked to a decline in the international appetite for U.S. product that began in the mid-1990s, especially product destined for network prime time across Europe, Asia, and South America (Tunstall 2008: 102).

The trading of global television formats has become a complex area of analysis for media scholars, blurring the sharp distinctions between homegrown and imported product, and between the local and the global, creating so-called *glocal* product. Such study involves a shifting terminology for analyzing permutations and contested contexts of contemporary media trade, encompassing dynamics of power and cultural exchange. Comparing the pragmatics of *volume of media trade* vs. the economic *value of media trade* is another piece of the puzzle, as these reflect the broader concerns of *flow*, *counter-flow*, *contra-flow*, and *multi-directional flow*, which refer to the abstract balance of media trade, and a continuum, perhaps, from benign *cultural exchange* to malignant *cultural imperialism* (Thussu 2007: 11).

The worldwide reach and impact of Hollywood entertainment product reveals a concomitant reliance upon revenue from media outlets abroad. In the last few decades, the costs of production and distribution have gradually eaten away at profit margins, underscoring the system's dependency upon foreign revenue. Hollywood's dramatic expansion into the international television market can be traced to the gradual relaxation of Federal Communications Commission (FCC) regulations concerning both financial interest and syndication (FIN-SYN), and ownership and conglomeration, leading up to the deregulatory provisions of the 1996 Telecommunications Act. Subsequently, major studios worked with their newly acquired networks to package television series, TV movies, and feature films into large television programming packages for international distribution, called "output deals." These bulk packages were intended to provide a large slate of programming for a newly privatized international broadcasting system, with its explosion of new channels, each in dire need of product, which maximized the revenue flow back into the United States (Torre 2009). Growing competencies in local production, however, along with a desire for culturally familiar product, led national media industries around the world to seek out other arrangements, including international co-productions, localized co-productions, and acquisition and production of television formats of one kind or another (Moran and Malbon 2006; Straubhaar 2007: 24–25).

The list of popular and perennial television series produced by Hollywood is a long one, especially beginning in the 1990s. Many of these domestic hits were translated into profitable runs internationally, as well—successes include long-running series such as *Friends*, *ER*, *Star Trek Voyager*, and *J.A.G.*, that have provided hundreds of episodes of programming. In addition to any long list of Hollywood television hits, however, there is a much longer list of Hollywood's television flops. The business of producing successful U.S. network and cable series has always been tricky—hopes are high as a series launches in the fall, but not a few American series are cancelled within weeks of launch, many are cancelled before the end of the calendar year, and most are cancelled by the end of the season. From the studio's perspective, early cancellation may be a way to cut losses, but the already sunk costs of (multiple) pilot development and series production are the much greater loss.

In the past decade, a steady, and often substantial rise in production costs, coupled with this high failure rate, led the major studios and their affiliated networks to explore the world of reality television and to look beyond ideas developed in-house, to imported formats from overseas (Keane et al. 2007: 85).

Who Wants to Be a Millionaire? came to America from Britain's Celador Productions; The Netherlands' Endemol provided U.S. networks with *Big Brother* and *Fear Factor*; (American) *Idol* is exported to the United States by Fremantle Media, another British media company. And yet there were financial risks involved in this turn to these global television formats. Homegrown sitcoms and dramas could be replayed during the off-season, and then syndicated later on, but networks found that there was little audience interest in seeing reruns of a reality series like *Big Brother*. In addition, ABC's over-reliance on *Who Wants to Be a Millionaire?*, in their airing of four hour-long episodes per week, led to a ratings downturn for several seasons after *Millionaire's* cancellation, as ABC had not devoted their creativity and resources to developing a strong slate of original programming. (This was several seasons before ABC launched hits like *Lost* and *Desperate Housewives*, and an imported telenovela format, *Ugly Betty*). I will return to this increasingly common practice of importing formats by U.S. networks and cable outlets later on.

In light of these developments in the global media market of today, the interlocking relationships between content creation, distribution patterns, and delivery technologies are shifting significantly. The recent surge in the worldwide production and distribution of television formats has made the calculus of media exploitation more complicated. Powerful media companies that have enjoyed a longstanding dominance, including and especially those in Hollywood, are facing new competitors; distribution is becoming increasingly decentralized. Ancillary revenues are providing sufficient income allowing for lower-cost television productions that, once formatted, can easily circulate regionally, if not globally. The expanding, more accessible world of tradable television formats is breathing new life into a broader, more inclusive business of global media (Keane et al. 2007; Moran 2008: 467). There are numerous new production entities—in some cases from beyond the central global economic and cultural circuits—and their influence is magnified as their formats move from one territory to the next, gaining audiences, and generating revenues as they travel.

In response to these transformations in the global media landscape Hollywood has chosen to respond in two particular ways, both of which involve a turn toward global television formats, and both of which indicate a pronounced lack of long-term planning, that threatens to further destabilize the traditional Hollywood business model. On the one hand, *Hollywood has adapted*, by formatting its domestic television programming abroad. On the other hand, *Hollywood has adopted*, by importing a new wave of television formats into the home market, adopting foreign programming for its domestic audience.

I will begin by examining some new and stronger competitors of the Hollywood model of distribution within the global television marketplace.

Hollywood Faces New Competition

> To be successful in the international distribution business today, it takes a lot more than a catalogue chock full of programming that buyers want. It's necessary to come up with creative financing formulas, appreciate the challenges faced by independent producers, gather up-to-date knowledge of markets around the world and, of course, have a keen understanding of broadcasters' needs. During the last ten years, a group of distribution companies in Europe have developed all these attributes and have become "mini-majors." They have the breadth of contacts and programming that allows them to sell around the world and become significant competitors for the Hollywood studios.
>
> (Jenkins 2007)

A number of media companies are reconfiguring themselves, developing their production and distribution capabilities, and expanding their resources and reach. As part of this industry-wide effort to retool, smaller television companies and their executives are seeking training in the business of developing and producing television formats for local consumption and global export.

The launch of the Format Academy for Entertainment Television, with its Entertainment Master Class, was announced on October 8, 2007 at MIPCOM, the international media trade festival held each fall in Cannes, France. The Format Academy was positioned as a unique opportunity for international television programming executives to study under leading experts in the field of global television format production and distribution.

As advertised in early 2008, only 40 participants would be accepted for the training program, and they would "learn the craft and business of formatting from leading figures in international entertainment television—from idea to screen and beyond" (Entertainment Master Class). Topics for the program included how to design one of several different television formats, including sketch comedies, game shows, variety and event shows, etc. Next on the agenda: how to pitch, budget, cast, produce, schedule and market that format for the local, and perhaps global market. The training program would take place over five weekends in five locations: Berlin, Copenhagen, Lucerne, Toronto, and London. A unique educational experience, in such exotic locales, has its price, of course: Format Academy participants would pay €15,000 for the privilege (transportation not included). Seminars and sessions were to be led by master trainers: including executives from Fremantle Media (United Kingdom), ProSiebenSAT.1 (Germany), and from Endemol (the Netherlands). The business of global television format development, production, and distribution is perceived as the wave of the future, and such educational opportunities, primarily targeted at independent media executives from European markets, are meant to empower those who understand the potential of global television formats, or aid those who are struggling to adapt to a television business in flux.

Many of the Format Academy's teachers represent the expertise of a middle tier of media companies. The proliferation of global television formats has elevated innovative and creative companies from relatively minor, to relatively significant players within the world of global media trade (Guider 2008; Keane et al. 2007: 41). A number of production companies in Europe have attained this status and achieved remarkable success. The United Kingdom has several key producers and exporters of television programming and formats, including the private media companies, Fremantle Media Enterprises and ITV Plc., and the publicly supported ventures, BBC Worldwide and Channel 4 International. An important factor in the UK format business is new media ownership regulations, approved by Britain's 2003 Communications Act that, in a manner not unlike FYN-SYN, has assigned intellectual property rights to the production company, rather than the network. This provides producers with an added incentive to develop programming concepts for worldwide franchising (Garside 2007). Formatted programming from the UK accounts for roughly 40 percent of the total global flow, with annual revenues of more than €1 billion (Esposito 2008). The Netherland's Endemol, long known for successful franchising of reality and game formats, is currently following the strategy of other mid-level media companies by broadening out to include distribution of telenovela and other fiction formats as market demand shifts (Havens 2006: 57).

Germany's SevenOne International, the distribution division of the network family, ProSiebenSAT.1, has emerged from the wreckage of the 2002 bankruptcy of the Kirch Group to produce numerous event mini-series, television movies, and a variety of formats. In some cases they acquire the rights to a format and distribute throughout Europe and beyond (Waller 2007). One of the most important media markets is the DISCOP convention held annually in Budapest, where SevenOne has sold format rights to networks in Hungary, Bulgaria, and Latvia. Representing Germany's second major public broadcaster is ZDF Enterprises, which has been selling formats of their decade-long variety show phenomenon *Wetten Das . . . ?* ("Wanna Bet . . . ?"), finding customers in China and recently in the United States (Burns 2004). These and other German format rights traders service Europe primarily, but with a growing business in Eastern Europe, South America, and Asia.

In a *Hollywood Reporter* article entitled "TV with Foreign Accent puts Pressure on U.S.," Elizabeth Guider (2008) points to "a more level playing field in content creation and greater professionalism in the execution of small-screen content everywhere around the globe," where "ideas now come from every nook and cranny of the world—from Scandinavia, from Israel, and from Brazil." The article refers to the current crop of format producers exhibiting creativity and sophistication, mentioning a new level of professionalism and production expertise, and expressing pleasant, if condescending, surprise that these qualities would be found in production executives from Brazil, Israel, or China. This is the new reality in the global television media market; there are more and better competitors within the television business, exhibiting a growing facility with production techniques and distribution savvy. They sell to or represent networks that want to acquire imported media selectively, on their own terms, incorporating local input.

Colombia's Radio Cadena Nacional (RCN) began producing *Yo Soy Betty la Fea* in 2000. Since that time, versions of *Ugly Betty* have been adopted by more than 70 countries, where multiple less-than-attractive Bettys speak more than a dozen languages. In several countries, *Betty* airs in two versions, with both a local adaptation and a regional or global import vying for the hearts of audiences. This is another distinctive characteristic of the global television format trade; there is room for multiple competitors in a market. Multiple versions can coexist, since re-versioning adds to the broader, transmedia story, often with little cannibalization of revenues.

It is no surprise that ABC's English-language *Betty* has traveled directly to the UK and Australia, but Germany's *Betty*, *Verliebt in Berlin*, has been sold as a format to Hungary, Bulgaria, France, and Canada. Mexico's Televisa has licensed their format of *Betty*, *La Fea mas Bella*, to China's Hunan Satellite Television, where it is entitled *Chou Nu Wu Di* ("The Ugly Girl with no Rival"). In these instances of *post-formatted distribution*, added revenues flow back to Colombia and RCN (Chavez 2007). In addition, in an intellectual property twist, characters and plotlines that are developed on top of the original *Betty* concept by the adaptor are repackaged by RCN, with these new characters and story arcs offered as permutations of the product for sale to other networks in other contexts (Winslow 2004). The *Betty* phenomenon has energized the Colombian television industry, producing $50 million in export revenue for RCN, and generating hundreds of new jobs in the first five years (Kraul 2006; de la Fuente 2006) (see Figure 9.1).

Media companies from Israel have also found success in the global format trade, with the Dori Media Group generating telenovela and format-related sales of more than $18 million for 2007 (60 percent of overall revenue, and an annual increase of 71 percent). A few years ago, Dori's dealings with a mere 11 countries and a catalog of only 1,500 hours of programming may have seemed paltry compared with a pan-European powerhouse like Fremantle Media, but Dori has carved out a profitable and growing niche. They offer a comprehensive "novela package" for their broadcaster clients, many of who are new to the formatting business. Dori Media is a leader in telenovela adaptations for new media, offering their soapy thriller, *Amanda O*, as a cross-platform production that can be presented as 26 episodes in hour-long television slots, or alternatively, as 130 9-minute Internet episodes, or 500 2-minute mobisodes for cell phones (Carugati 2008a; dorimedia.com). Much of Dori Media's product is produced in South America, especially Argentina, where they produce *Lalola*, a gender-switching drama where a womanizer suddenly turns into a woman, and gains a new perspective. *Lalola* was first broadcast in Argentina in the fall of 2007 and by the middle of 2008, Dori had sold format rights to more than 52 countries including France, Italy,

FIGURE 9.1 *Ugly Betty* around the world. Clockwise from upper left: India, Mexico, Russia, Spain, with the Colombian original in the middle, and the U.S. version in the background. Arranged by the author.

Germany, Russia, Mexico, Chile and Vietnam. And add the United States to that list, as Sony Pictures Television and the Fox Network acquired the franchise rights to develop a pilot for the fall of 2009.

These new competitors in the business of global media trade present a unique and sustained challenge to Hollywood as they create innovative products, build out their client base, and occasionally ally themselves with one another in joint ventures of production and distribution. Media executives from Israel, China, Argentina, Bulgaria, or Italy can avail themselves of new educational opportunities, such as those offered by the Format Academy. More and more small and mid-sized media companies are exchanging the creative, technical, and financial information necessary to television format production and distribution. Rejecting top-down political economy models, Keane et al. point to the innovation found in small and mid-size media companies that operate according to a "new global model of integration," where "digital technologies have reduced production costs," and allowed for "accelerated catch-up . . . facilitated by a proliferation of global and regional production networks that have acted as conduits for knowledge diffusion" (2007: 41, 51).

These new competitors within the world media market are able to tailor their offerings, in a manner which often undercuts the attraction of "over-produced"

Hollywood product, and with their client-networks, *jointly create* a development, production, promotion and exploitation process that stands in contrast to the Hollywood studio's not infrequent obsession with overseeing and tightly controlling their intellectual property. These new players, new markets, and new dynamics are combining to reformat global media economics.

Reformatting Global Media Economics

> The bottom line of the television industry—the financing of its programs—is under siege from the threat of diminishing audiences . . . the role played by formats as a kind of circuit-breaker in the trend towards low-cost programming illustrates the profound institutional shifts confronting the medium of broadcast television.
>
> (Keane et al. 2007: 159)

> The connection that telenovelas create with the audience is so strong that viewers want to extend the TV experience into other aspects of their lives: whether it's catching a mobisode on a cell phone while commuting to work, reliving the excitement of an episode on DVD, listening to the CD soundtrack while driving in the car, reading a magazine dedicated to a favorite novella, or wearing a T-shirt with a novela's logo.
>
> (Alvarado 2007)

Viewers love global television formats. Audiences flock to the event programming of reality and game shows. People connect with the serialized drama in season after season of telenovelas. As a result, global television formats make good business sense for the producer, the distributor, the broadcaster, and associated promoters and merchandisers. In his article entitled, "Makeover on the Move: Global Television and Programme Formats," Albert Moran underscores the multiple benefits of format adaptation for skittish television programmers in the midst of a media system in continuous turmoil and, beginning in 2008, a global economy in sustained recession. Beyond the concrete elements provided in the format package (the series bible, scripts, and additional production details), a purveyor of formats often functions as a long-term executive producer, working side-by-side with the in-country production company. The most compelling reason, however, for turning to proven formats is that they provide one of the best guarantees of commercial success, and they serve to mitigate the risks of developing and producing new television programming (Moran 2008: 462). Furthermore, global television formats can be exceedingly efficient in delivering substantial (or at least sufficient) profits, with lower barriers to entry (i.e. lower production costs).

The ancillary revenues generated by global television formats can be formidable, and *Pop Idol* offers one example of a format phenomenon. Over the course of its multi-season run in the United States, *American Idol* generated hundreds of millions per year, and when including the overall value of third party deals, the total may reach a billion dollars, (James and Fernandez 2008; Iosifidis et al. 2005). *Who Wants to be a Millionaire?* also created this order of impact and generated this level of revenue (Cooper-Chen 2005). Most of the business of global television formats, however, is significantly smaller in scale, but similarly expansive in the scope of the exploitation mechanisms. There are three key factors in the efficiencies of format exploitation, and these are central to their appeal to small to mid-size producers, distributors, and broadcasters. First, formats offer comparatively lower costs of production. In many cases this is attributable to fewer industrial overheads, and follows from the fact that most production elements have been pre-tested. Second, formats are designed to take advantage of multiple delivery platforms. The series, and associated content, can be delivered to television, the Internet, and to cellular. Third, formats are ready-made to be exploited via dozens, if not hundreds, of related products, tie-ins, and cross-promotions.

Israel's Dori Media Group produces telenovelas at home, and in Latin and South America. Dori Media originally developed a program called *Rebelde Way* in Argentina, but the series was franchised in dozens of other countries, including by Televisa in Mexico. The Dori/Televisa version of *Rebelde* ("Rebels") is set at an exclusive private high school near Mexico City, where a group of sexy and rebellious teens forms a band (named "RBD"). Per the quotation at the top of this section, *Rebelde's* promotional and merchandising plan included the usual T-shirts, comic books, jewelry, shoes, the show's distinctive school uniforms, and a personal fragrance line for each character, along with hundreds of millions of dolls representing the characters of *Rebelde* and the actual RBD band. The real life band RBD has sold more than 11 million albums and toured North and South America. It is not surprising that ancillary revenues can comprise a significant portion of overall revenues (DMG Annual Report 2008).

Many formats, especially of the telenovela variety, are targeted at youth audiences around the world (and at their discretionary spending). In Germany, *Verliebt in Berlin* (their *Betty*) aired on SAT.1, the older-skewing, stolid and traditional German channel. The broadcaster discovered, however, that the series attracted a young, highly educated, and progressive demographic, and subsequently launched numerous brand extensions with youth appeal (Alvarado 2007). In addition to monetizing content within the usual media of magazines, DVD sets, and music CD compilations, the producers created Internet and mobile media channels around *Verliebt in Berlin*, and promoted cell phone based contests, and other cross-platform initiatives that utilized audience interactivity to build audience share. This German version of *Betty* was subsequently reformatted in France, where it attracted a similar audience of young professional women, and the identical transmedia, multi-platform brand extension strategies were employed there (Alvarado 2007).

In the business of global television formats, alliances may be necessary to reach a new market or solidify a presence in a new sector, and in 2005, German distributor SevenOne International partnered with Israeli broadcaster Keshet, to distribute Keshet's popular game shows, including *On the Level, What's Going On*, and *Mind Games*. In addition, as part of this agreement, the two companies collaborated on short-form 3D animated material and other mobile applications, designed for distribution beyond television, demonstrating their convergence strategy of "holding the market niches of the future," and claiming that, "with the worldwide distribution network and experience of SevenOne International and the unique material of Keshet Formats, together we can achieve a strong market position" (SevenOne International 2005).

Nimble media companies, producing innovative content, employing new delivery technologies across platforms, and penetrating developing markets—when these elements are combined they amount to a (partially) reformatted global media economics. As Keane et al. note, the function of the *distribution* of formatted programming is transformed,

> whereby each broadcast of a format adaptation in another territory or another time becomes part of a snowballing package that is the continuing object of distribution . . . adaptation and rebroadcast add markedly to its industrial and cultural richness, as well as to its complexity.
>
> (2007: 199)

In my examples, I am drawing attention to select developments and specific alliances that indicate new models in the development, production, distribution and exploitation of media. Joseph Straubhaar draws valid distinctions between truly global television systems and, "phenomena that are more precisely transnational, geocultural, or cultural-linguistic" (2007: 105). It is important to delineate the scope of change in the media economic systems operating globally and/or transnationally; whether these new systems and operations indicate thoroughgoing revision or substantial evolution remains to be seen. I will return to these broader issues momentarily; my concern at this stage is to analyze how Hollywood has responded or reacted when confronting these new players and patterns over the last few years. How has Hollywood adapted to this new market for global television formats?

Hollywood Adapts Around the World

> It's no secret that international markets have become more sophisticated about craving homegrown hits, as opposed to the days when the U.S. provided the vast majority of the world's TV content, and simply dubbing "Bonanza" and "The Beverly Hillbillies" passed for entertainment. Sony keeps slogging along in the format game with scripted fare, mining its vast library to transform series— as opposed to just translating them—for consumption abroad. Some of those shows were clear-cut winners originally, but others well off the beaten track have found new life through this particular makeover process.
>
> (Lowry 2004)

In the face of sliding overall international demand for American television programming, Hollywood has contemplated new production and distribution strategies. To counteract new developments in global media distribution, the Hollywood studios have formatted their own product for sale, co-produced local content, and even "localized" their global corporate structures by working directly with producers in foreign markets, and effectively assisting and supporting local industries.

Warner Bros., and their International Television division, has converted their latest television series in a number of deals in the last few years, shopping format rights for *Without a Trace* and *Cold Case* within Asia, and selling the format for *The Bachelor* to both Slovakia and the Czech Republic. Warner Bros. has also recycled material from their past library, franchising rights to several different Russian broadcasters for *Perfect Strangers*, *Step By Step*, and *Full House* (TimeWarner Press Releases 2006; 2007).

In 2005, Disney attempted to sell format rights to two of their successful reality shows (*The Amazing Race* and *Extreme Makeover*) directly to broadcasters in India. After they were unsuccessful, Disney offered the format rights to Sony's AXN Asia channel and to Sony Entertainment Television (SET), a Hindi language entertainment channel (Indiantelevision.com 2005). Sony is one of the most experienced and established of the studios in local productions and local/regional distribution, and the best example of Hollywood adapting (both literally and figuratively) around the world.

Sony, and their Sony Pictures Television International division, develop and produce local language television series in multiple markets in Europe, Asia, and South America (Brennan 2004). As the quote at the beginning of this section indicates, Sony has been working in the format business for more than a decade, and has seen some success.[1] *The Jeffersons* is reformatted in Turkey as *Tatli Hayat* ("The Sweet Life"), a version of *Bewitched* plays in Japan, a reformatted *Mad About You* airs in Chile, and a version of *Married with Children* charms audiences in Russia . In the case of *The Nanny*, after the original U.S. version aired successfully in nearly 100 countries in the 1990s, the series was reformatted in Argentina, Russia, and a number of other countries. The actual series ended production in the U.S.A. in 1999, but after running out of episodes for format sales abroad, Sony commissioned the original writers to create dozens of additional scripts solely for the purposes of reworking them around the world (Brennan 2004; Levy 2007).

The overall *formatting process* includes a variety of negotiated elements, representing a continuum of potential working relationships, with the rights holder and purchaser agreeing to the roles that each will play. One production company acquiring the rights may simply want quick delivery of the format package (the bible, scripts, etc.), another company may request a great deal more assistance, and over the course of the production process. Sony offers a suite of services, extending to what could be considered *format co-productions*, with studio executives and producers in-country and on-set, supporting and supervising production of versions of Sony library product. In many of these cases, Sony initiates the formatting process by providing a "flying producer," who will consult both remotely and then by flying into town to work with local writers and oversee the initial shoot. As an example, Sony has utilized seasoned writer-producer Dean Hargrove, who has an extensive list of credits, including *The Man from U.N.C.L.E.*, *Columbo*, *Perry Mason*, *Matlock*, and *Diagnosis Murder*. Hargrove has flown to many production sites to shape story and character arcs with the local writing team, and has subsequently worked with the production crews as they shoot and post their first few episodes (Brennan 2001; Dunlap 2008).

In another format production, Sony adapted a dog-and-detective tale called *Tequila and Bonetti* that had a short run on CBS in 1992. Sony relocated the American series to Italy, beginning production in 2000. The studio retained the original American actor, Jack Scalia, as an Italian-American cop, who in the Italian version moves to Italy to connect with his roots. The series was shot in both Italian for the local network and English for resale in other territories in the region (Brennan 2001; Lowry 2004).

In this manner, Sony's supervised formatting activities are closer to a typical co-production, and as a result, Sony expects a healthy portion of the revenues generated, perhaps collecting format fees, co-production fees, distribution fees, and a share of product placement and other ancillary revenue. In some cases then, particularly when partnering with a major distributor like Sony, formatting can become less profitable than anticipated, with associated formatting fees eating into the profits for the local producer. Production budgets for the format compared to the original U.S. production may be ten or twenty times *less*, which means profits are easier to reach, but lower budgets, with lower production values, can also mean less resale and ancillary opportunities (Brennan 2004; Winslow 2004).

Additionally, Sony Pictures Television Germany, with Sony-owned production studios outside Cologne, has produced a number of original comedy series that have performed quite well in prime time on the RTL Network, one of Germany's strongest private television stations. *Ritas Welt* ("Rita's World") is about a grocery store clerk and her friends and family, and *Alles Atze* ("Always Atze") is about a German storeowner and his Turkish sidekick. These Sony local language productions, launched in 2000, have garnered high ratings and won German broadcasting awards.

Facing competition from format purveyors from every side, Sony and the other Hollywood studios have adjusted to this contemporary media business reality by adapting their programming and their corporate structures, partnering with producers and broadcasters around the world. In their examination of global television trade, Keane et al. point to a concept of *technology transfer*, involving the dissemination of styles of management and production, and the positive effect of:

introducing best practices, training, and efficiencies in domains where these were absent. Joint ventures, co-productions, and franchises are vehicles for technology transfer [and] the transfer of "international" production and marketing techniques has in many cases empowered television producers long accustomed to operating according to routines bounded by national imaginations and constrained by national policies.

The very process of co-production of media, regardless of the precise nature of the arrangement, initiates this "transfer of techniques across systems," with the delivery of format materials and the interactions with studio production executives introducing, "a range of ideas, innovations, management styles, and social relations" (2007: 87–88). Facing an increasingly competitive media market, the Hollywood studios have been forced to employ all of the clichés of customer-oriented business-speak: when partnering with clients, they must speak their language and meet them on their own terms and on their own turf. Beyond the simple distribution of media product, therefore, joint ventures of format development, production and exploitation necessarily include exchange of creative personnel and the transfer of business practices and technologies.

Local producers and broadcaster may find that their latest format acquisition fails in their market, or that they are compelled to share revenues, but in the end they will be getting more for their money. Hollywood is *adapting* around the world by reallocating a portion of its development, production and promotion resources overseas. The perceived necessity of transferring these resources to its partners abroad, ultimately leads to growing competencies of local television producers and in local media industries. The subsequent regional circulation of formats, and the further transfer of technologies, generates media trade dynamics that are increasingly *less asymmetrical, and more interdependent.*

Hollywood Adopts: A Devil's Bargain?

> If you thought the Academy Awards were dominated by foreigners, wait until you see this year's TV pilot season. With networks' appetite for scripted imports growing, format acquisition and packaging has become big business. All major talent agencies are dispatching agents to territories around the globe with marching orders to snatch anything that looks promising for the U.S. As a result, there are often multiple U.S. producers vying for the rights to some shows.
>
> (Andreeva 2008)

I have discussed the challenge presented by new competitors in the business of global media distribution, and how the Hollywood studios have extended their operations abroad to address them. I want to return now to the U.S.A. and examine developments on the home front, exploring another example of Hollywood adapting to the growing market for global television formats.

In the past decade, there has been a marked increase in formats imported into the U.S.A. for both network and cable outlets, and that trend has accelerated in the last few years. Hollywood has adopted formats from every category, including game shows, variety shows, reality shows, and adventure contests, and there has been a resurgence in scripted formats of comedies and dramas (Smith 2006). Format scholars struggle to qualify or categorize the multiple variations of formats, especially since formats often utilize juxtapositions of various generic and practical elements as part and parcel of their marketable value and appeal (see Keane et al. 2007: 60f).

A number of the pilots ordered for the fall launch of the 2008/9 U.S. television season originated from overseas, as shown in Table 9.1.

In addition, in the fall of 2008, for the first time in more than a decade, a Canadian series (*Flashpoint*) was "reverse simulcast" from CTV in Canada to CBS in the U.S.A. (Stelter 2008). The sudden proliferation of foreign formats and programming on U.S. television was connected to a variety of economic factors and developments, not least of which was the 2007–8 Writers Guild of America strike.

When the Hollywood writers went on strike beginning on November 5, 2007, and for 100 days, the development and production process for the networks' fall television launch ritual was severely disrupted (Carter 2008b). In the midst of the strike, however, the U.S. networks enjoyed healthy ratings from their imported—and unscripted—global television formats. Franchised programs such as *The Biggest Loser*, *The Apprentice*, *Wife Swap*, *Dancing with the Stars*, and especially *American Idol*, performed impressively, even when facing off against the final pre-strike episodes of the American-made hits, *Grey's Anatomy* and *C.S.I.* NBC substituted a revamped *American Gladiators* for the drama *Chuck*, and found that the combat format was getting 60 percent higher ratings (Carter 2008a). ABC signed a deal to format the legendary German variety show *Wetten Das . . .?* ("Wanna Bet . . .?") (ZDF Press Release 2008). Facing a labor revolt

TABLE 9.1 Global television formats imported into the U.S.A. (2008/9 season)

Title	Format origin	Studio/producer	U.S. outlet
Eleventh Hour	U.K./ITV	Disney/Jerry Bruckheimer	ABC
The Ex-List	Israel/Keshet	CBS/Paramount	CBS
Kath and Kim	Australia/ABC	NBC-Universal	NBC
Life on Mars	U.K./BBC	Fox/David Kelley	ABC
Ny-Lon	U.K./Channel 4	CBS/Paramount	CBS
Secret Diary of a Call Girl	U.K./ITV	Showtime/Paramount	Showtime
The Philanthropist	U.K./Channel 4	Fox	Fox
Worst Week	U.K./BBC	CBS	CBS

Source: Compiled from information in Carter 2008c; Elliot 2008; Spence 2008.

of indeterminate length, American programmers cast about for solutions and imported formats looked more and more appealing. At the January 2008 NATPE programming convention, NBC Universal CEO Jeff Zucker proclaimed that the TV industry needed to be "re-engineered and re-imagined" (Guider 2008).

Zucker and NBC had already been contemplating a wholesale re-evaluation of the expensive pilot production process prior to the strike, but another indicator of Zucker's broad vision of a "re-engineered and re-imagined" TV industry was demonstrated in a simple *personnel* matter—the hiring of a television executive the previous spring—that was symbolic of Hollywood's reaction to the new realities, presented by an evolving global media trade.

The elevation of format television *wunderkind* Ben Silverman to chairman of the NBC network in May of 2007 was testament to the power and perceived longevity of the worldwide trend toward global television formats. In a *Fortune Magazine* profile entitled "The Player: NBC Hired Ben Silverman to Shake up Hollywood and Reinvent Television," the decision to hire Silverman was attributed to "his knack for developing foreign concepts for the U.S. market, including *The Office* and *Ugly Betty*, and for coming up with reality-TV schlock, laden with product placements, like NBC's *The Biggest Loser*" (Siklos 2008). NBC latched onto Silverman's familiarity and facility in global television formats as the necessary and sufficient qualification to run their network. That one U.S. network would take this significant step of entrusting its broader business to a relatively inexperienced and unproven executive indicates the rising instabilities (and rising panic) in the traditional television network model. It also points to Hollywood's strenuous efforts to maintain a leading position in global media trade. While Silverman was considered to be a competent, and lucky packager of talent, his abilities as a network programmer and major network manager were untested (Carter 2007).

As he was being hired, Silverman talked up the fact that he would be bringing a new era of quality television to NBC, along the lines of legendary and respected producer-executives Brandon Tartikoff and Norman Lear. His first move, however, was to acquire the format rights to another Colombian telenovela with the eye-catching title *Sin Tetas No Hay Paraiso* ("Without Breasts, There Is No Paradise"). Media critic Kim Masters described the colorful project: "the original format tells the story of a young woman determined to escape poverty through big *kaboombas*. She becomes a prostitute and finds herself entangled with a drug dealer. *Caliente!*" Silverman planned for corporate synergies by producing an English-language version for NBC, and a Spanish language version for NBC's Telemundo (Masters 2007). Silverman's talents were assessed to lie in the area of *packaging* and understanding multiple media elements: according to one writer, he "*gets* the whole media enchilada," and was adept at integrating the creative development, the advertising, the technology, and the global distribution (Siklos 2008). These are certainly the skills needed for proficiency in exploiting the global television format economic model.

In Hollywood, a revolving door keeps studio heads and network executives circulating—it is difficult to hold a position for any length of time. The media business is notoriously fickle, and boards and shareholders are often clamoring for new blood. As with many businesses today, quarterly profits and attempts to game the financial system by manipulating a company's stock price, lead media executives to make decisions for the short term, without regard for long-term, and possibly negative, consequences. In an interview with the *Los Angeles Times* entitled "Television's Foreign Affair," Silverman laid out his broader global strategy, and demonstrated a muddled, if not shortsighted perspective:

> We're opening doors to the entire world and we're not just looking to one place for those ideas. I want to bring an entrepreneurial energy to our broadcast channel and work with our foreign partners, because the foreign marketplace is incredibly rich right now, and if we can come up with ideas that sell globally from the beginning, like "Heroes," it benefits how you finance them. These partnerships also make sense because our foreign partners will put money into a show, which gives us big, big production values.
>
> (Fernandez 2008)

Silverman speaks of "opening doors" to the "ideas" and "entrepreneurial energy" of the world, plainly referring to importing formats from Europe, South America, and elsewhere. And yet, when he talks about coming up with "ideas that sell globally," he neglects to distinguish between homegrown properties, where NBC-Universal would control all rights, and acquired projects, or those co-produced, where NBC is controlling limited rights. In the acquisition of formats, NBC is not actually coming up with original ideas. Instead, the U.S. networks are purchasing format concepts, and trading on the creativity of others. Silverman also refers to "foreign partners putting money into a show," and the resulting "big, big production values." Aside from the surprising admission that Hollywood now needs foreign money to be able to afford high production values, this comment reveals Hollywood's cautious, risk-aversion. Instead of shouldering the risks in order to secure the rewards, the strategy proposed by Silverman and NBC was to take on foreign investors, and to hedge their bets. In July of 2009, after two years of falling ratings and profits, Ben Silverman was ushered out the door. And in December of 2010, Jeff Zucker agreed to resign from NBC-Universal as cable giant Comcast acquired and restructured the film and television conglomerate (Carter 2010).

While global television formats "stimulate consumption, promote producer-consumer interactivity, and transfer technology," the choice to devote resources in this direction can have, "negative effects, such as an increasing network dependency on formats to the detriment of investment in new local content" (Keane et al. 2007: 87). Hollywood's decision to embrace global television formats, therefore appears to be a devil's bargain, an undercutting of the traditional economic system of exploitation that Hollywood has employed to great effect for many years. In their attempts to lower production costs and find something different, Hollywood executives are revealing a pessimistic view of their television programming, as having limited shelf life, and a shortened life cycle. When Hollywood studios import global television formats they are declining to support their own development and distribution divisions; they are acquiring concepts from elsewhere, off-shoring their creative industries, and choosing to produce less content for international distribution. This focus on imported content raises the question of "whether big-time Hollywood has run out of creative steam, or if its cautious and cumbersome system has made it too difficult and expensive for fresh ideas to break through" (Smith 2006). The decisions to rely on creative and financial infusions from imported formats, and to recycle library product as formats abroad, point to a weakening Hollywood television business; an industry that is struggling to maintain dominance, but from a defensive crouch.

Global Television Formats and the Future of Global Media Trade

> More and more non-U.S. producers and content creators are taking advantage of low-cost technologies, ever-proliferating formats, and a perception that America might be, at least momentarily, stumbling to keep its place in the global biz.
>
> (Guider 2008)

> The format is a stage of development in the evolution of television, anticipating and responding to the media post-broadcasting environment of increased market uncertainty . . . the television industry worldwide has been forced to reexamine what it does, how its audience has drifted, and how it can generate income.
>
> (Keane and Moran 2008: 158)

The explosion of the television format trade—locally, regionally and globally—has had a significant impact on the overall economics of the media business, and the television industry will continue to evolve as new competitors and program formats proliferate. The scale, scope, and cumulative impact of this evolution is difficult to quantify, but I believe that it is appropriate to characterize recent developments as *threshold events*, as Hollywood and the global media market as a whole reacts and adapts.

Multi-directional media flows have accelerated dramatically, along a commercial and cultural continuum, and are gradually decentering global media trade. These dynamics are allowing Hollywood's competitors to chip away at entrenched media interests, perhaps allying themselves with other regional players in setting up a bulwark against a lessening flood of Hollywood product. Format purveyors in media centers in Europe, Asia, and South America have developed new techniques and technologies, expanding their reach, directly contesting U.S. control over television exports, and acting as counterweights to Hollywood's influence (Straubhaar 2007: 110; Curtin 2007: 23).

Hollywood's new competitors are acquiring clients through a commitment to more tailored customer service. These companies, like the formats they develop, are masters at adapting to the needs of their clients. An interview with ITV's Peter Iacono (formerly of Sony Pictures Television International) featured a question about how UK companies like ITV are able to compete with a Hollywood studio like Sony. Iacono responded: "I believe that ours is much more of a nurturing business in terms of the shows we have, the production partners we work with, and the clients we sell to . . . I do believe we can deliver even better client service" (Carugati 2008b). This is the strength of companies that orient their business models around format production and distribution: they employ new and innovative media practices, and are continuously refining their development, production, distribution, promotion and merchandising strategies as they interact with the marketplace (Chalaby 2005: 30). Moreover, global television formats offer a more favorable risk/reward calculation and, going forward, buyers are likely to forgo more expensive product from the Hollywood studios.

Though the studios may excel in the exploitation of their film properties, Hollywood has not managed to employ equivalent efficiencies in their global television distribution operations. On the homefront, Hollywood has reduced its production of original television programming, and is obtaining product for its domestic outlets from foreign producers and distributors of television formats. The economic barriers surrounding and protecting Hollywood's domestic market have been breached. Even if the U.S. media empire is on balance the world leader, it is looking more and more like a follower.

In this chapter, I have explored how Hollywood is losing money and losing its grip on the global market, and for a variety of reasons. No collapse is imminent, and Hollywood is struggling mightily. As I have discussed, however, the studios have been reactive and short-sighted in their response to new competition from global television formats and, as Straubhaar pragmatically observes, "not all conglomerate growth represents a lasting or sustainable accumulation of economic power" (2007: 100). In the market for global television formats, regional trade is increasing, and local and regional media industries are gaining strength as a result, thus generating a more balanced, symmetrical, and interdependent global media system.

Note

1   Sony is a Japanese-owned media company and electronics manufacturer, but Sony's media interests find their clearest base in Hollywood, where the company has feature film and television production facilities, along with many of the executives who control Sony's global media operations. It is important to note that Sony's extension into the

world wide business of formats is partly due to their being precluded, by FCC ownership regulations, from owning a television network in the U.S.A., and so they have devoted a significant portion of their television sales and production efforts to other countries around the world.

References

Alvarado, M. T. 2007. Spreading the love. *WorldScreen*. June 2007. www.worldscreen. com/print.php?filename=merch0607.htm (accessed October 14, 2007).

Andreeva, N. 2008. TV's efficiency exports. *Hollywood Reporter*. March 5, 2008. www. hollywoodreporter.com/hr/content_display/news/e3ic8069f8098734cd4fe7a5ea8e0615 765 (accessed March 7, 2008).

Arango, T. 2008. World falls for American media, even as it sours on America. *New York Times*. December 1. www.nytimes.com/2008/12/01/business/media/01soft.html

Brennan, S. 2001. Abroad jump. *Hollywood Reporter*. March 27, 2001. www.hollywood reporter.com/hr/search/article_display.jsp?vnu_content_id=812634 (accessed August 8, 2007).

——— 2004. SPTI reviving old TV faves in Latin America. *Hollywood Reporter*. www. hollywoodreporter.com/hr/search/article_display.jsp?vnu_content_id=1000518336.

Brennan, S. and M. Turner. 2007. Are overseas buyers cooling on U.S. hits? *Hollywood Reporter*. October 5, 2007. www.hollywoodreporter.com (accessed March 12, 2008).

——— 2008. International buyers rethink pricey U.S. shows. *Hollywood Reporter*. April 3, 2008. www.hollywoodreporter.com/hr/content_display/features/international/e3i1 773b9d1d4828bb0f5efb9c65f9cbf49?pn=2 (accessed May 28, 2008).

Burns, R. 2004. German television. In *Contemporary world television*, ed. John Sinclair and Graham Turner, 70–74. London: British Film Institute.

Carter, B. 2007. NBC's turnaround artist, relying on insider tips. *New York Times*. July 9, 2007. www.nytimes.com/2007/07/09/business/media/09silverman.html?scp=1&sq =NBC percentE2 percent80 percent99s percent20turnaround percent20artist&st=cse (accessed July 9, 2007).

——— 2008a. Reality TV is no lightweight in the battle to outlast strikers. *New York Times*. January 14, 2008. www.nytimes.com/2008/01/14/business/media/14ratings.html?scp =1&sq=reality+tv+is+no+lightweight&st=nyt (accessed January 14, 2008).

——— 2008b. Networks ponder poststrike landscape. *New York Times*. January 26, 2008. www.nytimes.com/2008/01/26/arts/television/26seas.html?scp=1&sq=networks+ ponder++&st=nyt (accessed January 27, 2008).

——— 2008c. A world of imports. *New York Times*. August 26, 2008. www.nytimes. com/2008/08/26/arts/television/26form.html?scp=2&sq=world+of+imports&st=nyt (accessed August 27, 2008).

——— 2010. Zucker announces departure from NBC. *New York Times*. September 24. http://mediadecoder.blogs.nytimes.com/2010/09/24/zucker-announces-departure-from-nbc/

Carugati, A. 2008a. Dori Media's Nadav Palti. *WorldScreen*. June 2008. www.worldscreen. com/interviewscurrent.php?filename=palti0608.htm (accessed June 17, 2008).

——— 2008b. ITV's Peter Iacono. *WorldScreen*. October 2008. www.worldscreen.com/ interviewscurrent.php?filename=iacono1008.htm (accessed December 23, 2008).

Chalaby, J. 2005. From internationalization to transnationalism. *Global Media and Communication* 1(1): 28–33.

Chavez, G. 2007. Passion travels. *WorldScreen*. April 2007. www.worldscreen.com/featuresarchive.php?filename=novelas0407.htm (accessed June 24, 2008).

Cooper-Chen, A. 2005. A world of "Millionaires": global, local and "glocal" TV game shows. In *Global entertainment media: content, audiences, issues*, ed. Anna Cooper-Chen, 237–251. Mahwah, NJ: Lawrence Erlbaum Associates.

Curtin, Michael. 2007. *Playing to the world's biggest audience: The globalization of Chinese film and TV*. Berkeley: University of California Press.

de la Fuente, A. 2006. "Ugly Betty" grows into swan around globe: telenovela takes off in many territories. *Variety*. February 5, 2006. www.variety.com/article/VR11 17937365.html?categoryid=14&cs=1 (accessed June 3, 2008).

Dehnart, A. 2008. American Idol made $63 million for 19 Entertainment in 2007. *Reality Blurred*. www.realityblurred.com/realitytv/archives/american_idol_6/2008_Mar_06_19_entertainment_earnings (accessed March 10, 2008).

Dori Media Group Annual Report 2007. 2008. Dori Media Group. www.dorimedia.com/content.asp?page=financialresults (accessed December 22, 2008)

Dunlap, B. 2008. Making ideas travel: wanted: flying producer. *WorldScreen*. April 2008. www.worldscreen.com/featurescurrent.php?filename=flyingproducer.htm (accessed April 23, 2008).

Elliot, S. 2008. U.S. television taps more imported series. *New York Times*. May 19, 2008. www.nytimes.com/2008/05/19/business/media/19adcol.thml (accessed May 29, 2008).

Entertainment Master Class. 2008. *The Format Academy for Entertainment Television*. www.entertainment-masterclass.tv/home_en.html (accessed January 20, 2008).

Esposito, M. 2008. UK rides high as exporter of television formats. *Campaign*. April 4, 2008. www.brandrepublic.com/Campaign/Features/Analysis/800196/ (accessed May 2, 2008).

Fernandez, M. E. 2008. Television's foreign affair. *Los Angeles Times*. April 20, 2008. www.latimes.com/entertainment/la-ca-international20apr20,0,133721 (accessed April 21, 2008).

Garside, J. 2007. Think global, act local: why formats are TV's new lingua franca. *The Sunday Telegraph* (London). www.telegraph.co.uk/money/main.jhtml?xml=/money/2007/04/15/cctv15.xml (accessed April 21, 2008).

Guider, E. 2008. TV with foreign accent puts pressure on U.S. *Hollywood Reporter*. February 1, 2008. www.hollywoodreporter.com/hr/content_display/news/e3i2b58004ff7cfb 2628ccafdb8a9a8c176 (accessed April 12, 2008).

Havens, Timothy. 2006. *Global television marketplace*. London: British Film Institute.

Horan, N. 2007. Quality U.S. TV: a buyer's perspective. In *Quality TV: Contemporary American television and beyond*, ed. J. McCabe and K. Akass. New York: I. B. Tauris.

Indiantelevision.com. 2005. Sony Entertainment Television (SET) acquires *Extreme Makeover*, AXN *The Amazing Race* from BVIT. October 17, 2005. (accessed December 9, 2008).

Iosifidis, Petros, Jeanette Steemers and Mark Wheeler. 2005. *European television industries*. London: British Film Institute.

James, M. and Fernandez, M. E. 2008. Ad buyers hooked on "Idol" too. *Los Angeles Times*. January 13, 2008. www.latimes.com/entertainment/news/story?coll=la-headlines-entnews (accessed January 14, 2008).

Jenkins, B. 2007. The big guns. *World Screen*. http://worldscreen.com/print.php?filename= distributors1007.htm (accessed March 23, 2008).

Kapner, S. 2003. U.S. shows losing potency around the world. *New York Times.* http://query.nytimes.com/gst/fullpage.html?res=980CE5DB103FF931A35752C0A965 9C8B63&sec=&spon=&emc=eta1 (accessed December 7, 2008).

Keane, Michael, Anthony Y. H. Fung and Albert Moran. 2007. *New television, globalisation, and the East Asian cultural imagination.* Hong Kong: Hong Kong University Press.

Keane, M. and A. Moran. 2008. Television's new engines. *Television and New Media.* 9(2): 155–169.

Kraul, C. 2006. Ugly never looked so good. *Los Angeles Times.* September 16, 2008. www.latimes.com/entertainment/news/la-fi-betty16sep16,1,3651902.story?coll=la-headlines-entnews (accessed September 18, 2006).

Kun, J. 2006. We are a band, and we play one on TV. *New York Times.* July 9, 2006. www.nytimes.com/2006/07/09/arts/music/09kun.html (accessed December 24, 2008).

Levine, S. and D. Schreiber. 2008. Sony pictures entertainment completes acquisition of 2waytraffic. *Variety.* www.sonypictures.com/corp/press_releases/2008/06_08/0604 2008_SPE_Acquires_2WayTraffic.html (accessed June 7, 2008).

Levy, C. 2007. Still married, with children, but in Russian. *New York Times.* September 10, 2007. www.nytimes.com/2007/09/10/world/europe/10sitcom.html (accessed September 10, 2007).

Lowry, B. 2004. For Sony, it's a small world, after all. *Variety.* March 14, 2004. www.variety.com/article/VR1117901624.html (accessed September 6, 2007).

Masters, K. 2007. Without breasts there is no paradise: Ben Silverman buys his first show for NBC. *Slate.* June 15, 2007. www.slate.com/2167727 (accessed September 6, 2007).

Mediametrie. 2008. The Monte-Carlo TV Festival and Eurodata TV worldwide announce the winners of the 3rd International TV Audience Awards. Press Release, June 13, 2008. www.tvfestival.mc/2008/modules/PHOTOS_NEW/eurodataUK.pdf (accessed July 19, 2008).

Moran, A. 2008. Makeover on the move: global television and programme formats. *Continuum.* 22(4): 459–469.

Moran, Albert and Justin Malbon. 2006. *Understanding the global TV format.* Bristol, UK: Intellect.

Munoz, L. 2007. "Simpsons" show global appeal. *Los Angeles Times.* July 31, 2007. http://articles.latimes.com/2007/jul/31/business/fi-homerabroad31 (accessed July 31, 2007).

Schneider, M. 2008. Needed: network bailout? Bad economy slows ad sales. *Variety.* November 23, 2008. www.variety.com/VR1117996347.html (accessed November 25, 2008).

"SevenOne International enters into cooperation with Keshet Formats." 2005. ProSieben SAT1. September 23, 2005. http://en.prosiebensat1.com/pressezentrum/prosiebensat1 mediaag/2005/09/x00790/ (accessed November 25, 2007).

Siklos, R. 2008. The player: NBC hired Ben Silverman to shake up Hollywood and reinvent television. *Fortune Magazine.* October 27, 2008. http://money.cnn.com/2008/10/27/magazines/fortune/Silverman_Siklos.fortune/ (accessed December 16, 2008).

Sinclair, John and Grahme Turner. Eds. 2004. *Contemporary world television.* London: British Film Institute.

Smith, L. 2006. Taking hits from the Brits. *Los Angeles Times.* November 7, 2006. www.latimes.com/entertainment/news/cl-et-british7nov07,1,500518.story?coll=la-headlines-entnews (accessed November 8, 2006).

Spence, R. 2008. Hollywood execs tune in to Isreali television. *Forward.com* March 13, 2008. www.forward.com/articles/12942/ (accessed June 19, 2008).

Stelter, B. 2008. Canadians sneak across border, hide on CBS. *New York Times*. July 11, 2008. http://tvdecoder.blogs.nytimes.com/2008/07/11/canadians-sneak-across-border-hide-on-cbs/?scp=1&sq=canadians percent20sneak percent20across&st=cse (accessed September 9, 2008)

Straubhaar, Joseph. D. 2007. *World television: from global to local*. Los Angeles: Sage Publications.

Swearingen, J. 2008. Television upfronts see media budgets down. *Business Network Industries*. http://industry.bnet.com/advertising/2008/05/19/television-upfronts-see-media-budgets-down/ (accessed June 12, 2008).

Thussu, Daya Kishan. Ed. 2007. *Media on the move: global flow and contra-flow*. London: Routledge.

TimeWarner. 2006. Warner Bros. International Television makes new format deals with Russian broadcasters for productions of *Suddenly Susan*, *Perfect Strangers*, *Step By Step*, and *Full House*. timewarner.com. October 30, 2006. (accessed 12/9/08).

—— 2007. Warner Bros. International Television to license format rights to hit drama series *Without a Trace* and *Cold Case*, from Jerry Bruckheimer Television. timewarner.com. March 13, 2007. (accessed 12/9/08).

Torre, Paul. 2009. Block booking migrates to television: the rise and fall of the international output deal. *Television and New Media*. 10(6): 501–520.

Tunstall, Jeremy. 2008. *The media were American: U.S. mass media in decline*. New York: Oxford University Press.

Waller, E. 2007. Geller conjures up German format deal. *C21Media.net*. www.uri-geller.com/2007-General-Pics/c21/C21Media.htm (accessed November 25, 2007).

Winslow, G. 2004. Scripted for success. *WorldScreen*. April 2004. www.worldscreen.com/featurescurrent.php?filename=0404scripted.htm (accessed May 1, 2005).

ZDF Enterprises. 2007. Hit format "Wanna Bet . . . ?" now also in U.S. Press Release. March 19, 2007. www.zdf-enterprises.de/en/hit_format_wanna_bet_now_also_in_the_u_s.14046.htm (accessed December 22, 2008)

PART III

Case Study

The *Idol* Franchise

10

IDOL WORSHIP

Ethnicity and Difference in Global Television

Biswarup Sen

The worldwide success of the *Idol* format[1] may not require any explanation. We live under the ubiquitous sign of globalization; and hence it should come as no surprise that mass media—which together constitute an ecumenical vehicle of culture with an insatiable appetite for profit—would generate forms (or formats) of art that travel with ease and are translatable into every context. The reception of these formats is, at one level, as unproblematic as its dissemination. To be global (and who isn't?) is to be eagerly accepting of certain languages, technologies, discourses and styles.[2] The craze surrounding competitive singing can then be explained as one more instance of borders proving permeable to the formulas of international popular culture. It is my argument that in order to understand the unique valence and significance of global formats, we need to go beyond issues of production, distribution and reception, and focus instead on the phenomena that arise from their *instantiation*. This is so because implementing a format in a specific context has consequences that are neither written into the "program" nor purely derivable from local conditions. Let me provide an illustration. The call-in talk show has recently become a staple on Indian television. The format and content of these shows would be familiar to most Western viewers—a regular host, one or more "experts" discussing politics and culture, and a final segment devoted to phone calls from the public. A consideration of the Bengali talk show *Matamat with Kabir Suman*[3] disturbs the natural assumption that television formats translate seamlessly into other cultural contexts. On almost every episode of *Matamat*, standard practice seems to break down: viewers call in but cannot be heard, hosts refuse to hang up on inaudible callers pleading and cajoling them to speak up, callers hang up just as they are connected. For those accustomed to the swift termination of botched calls on shows like *Larry King*, Bengali call-in shows may appear comically ineffective. Another reading, however, suggests that is not only ineptness at play here, but the traces of an anterior culture that reveal themselves as old-fashioned courtesy and perseverance. These abortive calls are more than mere miscommunication, they also alert us to the gap that exists between universalizing global technologies of the self and intransigent instances of the local. The constitutive logic of the global contemporary demands that the social be subjected to ceaseless televisual representation—hence the proliferation of channels, the advent of 24/7 broadcasting, and the hysterical announcements of presence (channels repeatedly advertising their own content) that characterize Bengali television today. There is a "too-muchness" to this apparatus that far exceeds what cultural production in the relatively underdeveloped context of Bengal can hope to keep pace with. The result is not just thinness of content, but a radical disjuncture between the imperative of instant communication and an anachronistic code of speech and manners. The failed show thus imparts an important lesson: Even as things tend towards uniformity at the dictate of global forces, the local emerges as points of unmediated singularity in unexpected places and in unforeseen ways.

Matamat with Kabir Suman works as a powerful heuristic because the entire phenomenon of contemporary Indian television may be analyzed as an outcome of inserting global media logic into a national frame. The medium was introduced in 1959 as an educational tool, and for the next three decades all television programming in the country was conducted under the auspices of the Ministry of Information and Broadcasting.[4] In keeping with this tutelage the governing aesthetic was "socialist realist," consisting of endless coverage of ministers and bureaucrats cutting ribbons and attending official functions and ceremonies, news reporting that flirted with propaganda, rhapsodic accounts of progress in agriculture and heavy industry, and large doses of high culture and folk art deemed beneficial for the citizenry. Broadcasting style mimicked content: announcers were middle-aged, conservative in dress and demeanor, resolutely free of emotion and prone to the deliberate and grandiloquent tone characteristic of so much nationalist rhetoric. This stern governmental monopoly over broadcasting was surprisingly broken when permission was granted for CNN's coverage of the Gulf War to be shown via satellite transmission. The immense popularity of this broadcast amongst the urban elite spelled the end for media autarky: global television erupted onto the Indian screen in 1991 with the setting up of a five-channel satellite service provided by the Hong-Kong based Star TV (now part of Rupert Murdoch's News Corporation). The next year saw the establishment of Subhash Chandra's ZEE-TV, India's first privately owned network.[5] These institutional changes caused a revolution in television content: Star introduced Channel V (an Indian version of MTV) as well as StarMovies, India's first pay channel. And Zee-TV "broke television taboos by broadcasting programmes about such topics as sex, relationships and horoscopes."[6] The last 15 years can be characterized as ones of frenetic growth. Major companies like Star, Zee and Sony are complemented by myriad smaller cable networks; and most consumers can access over 100 channels of programming in English, Hindi and several other regional languages.

This new broadcasting climate has led to the adoption of the entire range of global television formats: 24-hour news channels, investigative journalism, true crime, game, talk, quiz and fashion shows, music videos, and a variety of singing contests. *Indian Idol* first aired in 2004 but was neither the first or only show of its kind. The Indian audience's appetite for singing-based reality programs is very large and has accommodated several other shows with essentially the same format—*Sa Re Ga Ma Pa Challenge, Star Voice of India, Fame Gurukul, Music Masti Aur Dhoom, Samsung Singer* and a planned *Bathroom Singer!*[7] Given that such shows exemplify the successful implementation of global formats in the Indian marketplace, those interested in issues of global flows must then ask: what are the externalities that come into play when a "universal" format like *Idol* is inserted into specific cultural contexts? I address this question by looking at three specific shows—*Indian Idol 3*, the *Sa Re Ga Ma Pa Challenge 2007* and the sixth season of *American Idol* that presented the unforgettable Sanjaya.[8] Taken together, these texts—featuring native and diasporic South Asians—illustrate how a format like *Idol* mobilizes versions of Indian and Indian-American identity in order to generate a politics and an aesthetic of difference. In what follows I propose to do the following: analyze the notion of global format to show how it constitutes a new and powerful aesthetic category; examine the nature of reality programming to understand why the most successful global formats are reality shows; and finally look at how a reality format like *Idol* functions so successfully at a global level by routing difference through ethnicity.

Global Formats

As is well known, processes of transnational integration and convergence have led to the globalization of every aspect of media.[9] This is true at the level of ownership and production—the advent of mega corporations like Time Warner, News Corporation, Disney and Bertelsmann; of distribution—Hollywood today earns more from exports than from domestic sales; and consumption—computer games created mostly in Japan and the United States find their most avid fans in places like Korea or Finland.[10] Finally, globalization also impacts media at the level of creativity and aesthetics through the emergence of global formats. The import of all these changes has been the occasion for heated debate. As one commentator puts it, the theorist of cultural globalization can adopt "either a negative or positive perspective on the brave new world they see as coming into being."[11] Thus, some critics have charged that globalization represents a new stage in the evolving world capitalist system in that it fosters the creation of a transnational capitalist class and state.[12] Its effect then is to initiate a second wave of cultural imperialism that utilizes neo-colonial dependencies in order to maximize profits for transnational entertainment industries and to threaten the

very existence of national and local media systems. Those viewing the phenomenon from a more "positive perspective" argue that globalization has in
fact been beneficial for the global South. For example, it has enabled a reversal
of commodity flows—Bollywood films now have huge markets in North America
and the United Kingdom,[13] while Mexican and Latin American *telenovelas* find
audiences in the West and many other parts of the world. As Arjun Appadurai
argues, the global cultural economy cannot any longer be read in terms of the
existing center–periphery model, nor does it necessarily imply homogenization
or Americanization. In fact, he writes, "globalization is itself a deeply historical,
uneven, and even *localizing* process."[14]

The study of global formats, I would like to suggest, is especially helpful in
trying to deduce the cultural consequences of globalization. To understand why
this is so, we must begin by clarifying the very notion of a format. In one sense,
formats are the very shows they inhabit—thus *American Idol*, *Big Brother*, or *Survivor*
can all be considered to exemplify a particular type of format. But as Albert Moran
has perceptively pointed out:

> In a real sense, to ask the question "What is a format?" is to ask the wrong
> kind of question. Such a question implies that a format has some core or
> essence. As our discussion suggested "format" is a loose term that covers a
> range of items that may be included in a format licensing agreement. The
> term has meaning not so much of because of what it is, but because of
> what it permits or facilitates. The format is a technology of exchange in
> the television industry which has meaning not because of a principle but
> because of a function or effect.[15]

In other words, formats are relatively content-free; they are "forms" plus a set
of economic parameters that enable them to be easily franchised. This structure
can be seen as yet another instance of the devaluation suffered by works of art
in a commercial age; I would, however, like to suggest that the format's skeletal
constitution comes with considerable advantage. It is precisely because formats
have so little "essence" or meaning that they acquire the potential to be the most
global of all cultural productions. As an industry professional puts it,

> [It] is a recipe which allows television concepts and ideas to travel without
> being stopped by either geographical or linguistic boundaries. To achieve
> this, the recipe comes with a whole range of ingredients making it
> possible for producers throughout the world, to locally produce a television
> programme based on a foreign format, and to present it as a local television
> show perfectly adapted to their respective countries and cultures.[16]

In other words reality shows consist of a few simple rules and operations that
are implemented in a range of settings in order to produce a series of outputs;

the format then, is a variable that is initially empty and gets a value only when plugged into specific game situations. Thus the *Big Brother* format yields *Big Brother Africa* in one instance and *Bigg Boss* (India) in another. There is a constitutive logic of difference at play here: the format can in one sense be described as the sum of all possible variations of a single concept or algorithm. That difference is purely a function of local conditions: culture, ethnicity, nationhood, religion and so on. The study of formats, far from being a meditation on a universal form, amounts then to an investigation of multiple differences between a series of contexts. Difference operates not only between versions of the same format (the many instantiations of *Big Brother*) but *within* a particular show as well. A consideration of a single season, or even a particular episode, of any reality show alerts us to the fact that every reality show generates meaningful difference between individuals over the course of its run. Contestants in a reality show are strangers to each other at the beginning of the season-opener; they develop temporary relations over the course of the episodes, these relations are violently terminated as the show progresses in search of a winner. This is in marked contrast to the way standard literary texts function: every novel or film begins with a set of inter-connected characters—those who happen to be strangers usually don't remain so (they fall in love for example). Such tales typically close with union—"and they lived happily ever after"—or occasionally with division and discord. In either case though, the end-state is relational.[17] In reality shows however, there is a disavowal of relation, a gesture made possible by the centrality of elimination in all reality formats. Elimination is a dizzying exercise that removes the individual from a temporary society and hurls him outside of all relations—a violent "thrownness" into oneself as it were.[18] A reality show is that adventure in which every player is a survivor, and every man and woman an island. The return to self is illustrated by the practice of having the fallen contestant deliver an upbeat monologue (turning away from the game and looking straight at the camera) about self-worth and empowerment. This is the show's radical moment: it depicts the individual as one who bears no relation to the field of the other, who is, in short, utterly different. In enabling this novel mode of subjectivity, reality television functions as a *difference engine* that processes the ephemera of games and contests in order to produce the individual as both separated and sovereign.

Certain facets of social being—race, religion, ethnicity, and sexuality—serve especially well as raw materials for this project of differentiation. Consider the strategy employed by the producers of *Survivor* in two successive seasons when they feared that ratings were on the decline: in *Survivor: Panama* (Season 12) contestants were divided into "tribes" based on age and gender; in *Survivor: Cook Island* (Season 13) the four competing teams were comprised of African-Americans, Caucasians, Hispanics and Asians respectively. Reality television's appetite for difference helps make it the global format *par excellence*, because globalization itself is fundamentally based on the category of difference. The original fear regarding the process[19]—that it would turn the world into one vast homogeneous whole—has proved to be quite unfounded. On the contrary, it seems that we give far more credence to particularistic descriptions of identity, hence the emergence of terms like local and marginal, minority and ethnicity.

A recent text on the topic defies ethnicity in the following manner:

> *Ethnic group* refers to descent and culture communities with three specific additions:
>
> 1   that the group is a kind of sub-set within a nation-state
> 2   that the point of reference of difference is typically culture rather than physical appearance, and
> 3   often that the group referred to as "other" (foreign, exotic, minority) to some majority who are presumed not to be "ethnic."[20]

It is possible to quibble with the specifics of this definition, but Eaton's basic thrust—that ethnicity is coeval with modernity—is quite incontrovertible. Indeed the term refers to a phenomenon as thoroughly contemporary as religious fundamentalism, the "ethnic" cannot be thought without first acknowledging the capitalist nation-state. Indeed, one could go even further and claim that ethnicity is postmodern and doubly so: postmodern as concept because it foregrounds difference for difference's sake, and post-modern as historical phenomenon because it comes in the wake of globalization. Given ethnicity's congruence with postmodernity there is much to be gained therefore from an analysis of the role it plays within global television. Such an inquiry will help us to appreciate reality TV's great appeal as well as provide important insights into the general nature of transnational programming. In what follows I look at three instantiations of the *Idol* format in order to determine how ethnicity functions as a strategic device within a specific global format. I begin the section by discussing the context within which ethnicity operates in modern India. I then look at *Indian Idol 3* (2007) to see how ethnicity highlights regional and local differences and how the cultural politics of a "troubled" region gets represented within a reality format. Next, I examine how a particular version of ethnicity—that of the hyphenated Indian-American—plays out in the *Sa Re Ga Ma Pa Challenge*. Finally I analyze the celebrated figure of Sanjaya (*American Idol 6*) to show how ethnicity can function as a backdrop for the very idea of difference.

Globalization and Ethnicity

The modern history of the Indian subcontinent is deeply marked by issues surrounding ethnicity. Given the bewildering mix of languages, religions, kingdoms and castes that have made up the cultural landscape it has been a matter of some debate whether an entity termed "India" existed before the colonial period. Whatever the merits of this perspective it is undoubtedly true that the post-independence history of the country (1947 onwards) has seen constant struggles that have risen from the claims and demands of a multitude of ethnic groups. The governmental slogan which rapidly attained the status of a hoary cliché—"Unity in Diversity"—was an acknowledgement of the fact that the nation-state was a tenuous coalition between a vast number of political and cultural fractions which had distinct identities of their own. I would like to draw attention to four major instances that illustrate how the Indian state's attempt at building a homogeneous nation came up against strong ethnicity-based roadblocks. The first two cases center on linguistic issues that cropped up immediately after independence. Even after the departure of the British the Indian government persisted with the colonial system under which "states" were conceived of purely administrative categories whose geography subsumed a heterogeneous mix of linguistic groups. Thus, the province of Madras included both Tamil- and Telegu-speaking people; similarly Bombay was comprised of Gujaratis and Marathis. Telegus launched an agitation for a separate state in the early 1950s, and unable to contain this demand the government reorganized the old Madras province into two states: a Telegu-speaking Andhra Pradesh and a Tamil-speaking Madras. The claims of ethnicity were formally recognized with the passing of the States Reorganization Act of 1956. Soon afterwards the state of Bombay was divided into Gujarat and Maharashtra, similarly the erstwhile Punjab would become Haryana and Punjab.[21] Language was also at the center of yet another conflict between ethnicity and nationalism. The Indian government—dominated by Hindi-speaking North Indians—decided that English would be replaced by Hindi as the sole "national language" after a brief transition period. This decision led to violent protests in those parts of the country where the population spoke one of four Dravidian languages quite unrelated to Hindi. These "language riots" convinced the central government that its language policies needed to be put on hold. This retreat would prove to be permanent: decades later English continues to function as one of two national languages.

The other two encounters between state and ethnicity centered on the traditional issues of religion and caste. In tune with the practice in modern capitalist democracies, the Indian state sought to establish a uniform code of laws for all its citizens. Thus the Hindu Succession Act (1955) gave women equal rights with men in the matter of succession to and the holding of property while the Hindu Marriage Act (1956) made monogamy the only legal form of union while providing for divorce with alimony and maintenance.[22] However, this attempt to universalize the legal system had to be aborted in the case of the Muslim minority. Much against the wishes of a number of secular leaders, the government decided to maintain a separate set of laws—known as the Muslim Personal Law—which would govern India's large Muslim minority. The logical inconsistency behind this move was not unnoticed by critics of the new code. N. C. Chatterjee, a lawyer arguing to retain the old Hindu laws, pointed out that if monogamy was a blessing and polygamy is a curse, then why not rescue our Muslim sisters from that curse and from that plight?[23] This was a sort of "separate but equal" policy; Muslims would be equal to other citizens when it came civil and criminal law but separate when it came to domestic matters. And finally, the state's designation of low caste and tribal populations as Scheduled Castes and Scheduled Tribes was yet another concession to the powerful presence of ethnicity. "Scheduled Castes" referred to the Untouchables—that is members of the very lowest castes who had traditionally suffered severe discrimination and oppression based on their position in the caste hierarchy. The Indian government's decision to reserve them a percentage of all government jobs, spots in educational institutions and seats in Parliament and local assemblies, was an attempt to compensate for historical injustices that had been prevalent for thousands of years. The same logic was at play in designating the hill people of northeastern India as Scheduled Tribes. These laws may have been enacted but the changes they aimed at were much harder to achieve: caste conflicts still plague the nation, and the northeast remains an unassimilated region.

Ethnicity was present as a strongly differentiating force in Indian society even before the era of globalization. As is well documented, globalization encourages particularistic, fissiparous movements: Yugoslavia, Kosovo, Quebec, Scotland, the Basques, Eritrea, Kurds in Iraq, Sudan and most recently South Ossetia and Georgia are all cases in point. While there may be no one explanation as to why this is the case, most analysts agree that globalization exacerbates extant ethnic identities and differences. Post-globalization India too continues to witness numerous conflicts based on ethnicity: Three new states—Chattisgarh, Jharkhand and Uttaranchal—have been created in the last decade in response to ethnic movements, and according to a recent survey, post-independence India has had to contend with at least four major secessionist movements—in Kashmir (1989 to the present), Nagaland (1947 to the present), Mizoram (1965–85), and amongst the Sikhs in Punjab (1980–84).[24]

This complicated history of ethnic relations would inevitably find its way into television. The third season of *Indian Idol* was a perfect illustration of the manner in which such forces get mobilized as a category of difference within the frame of reality programming. As noted earlier, song contest shows are very popular with Indian audiences. While it is true that almost all contestants on *Idol*-type shows gain massive exposure, the fanfare that surrounded *Idol 3* was of a different magnitude. When Prashant Tamang, an Indian citizen of Nepalese origin, made it to the finals, the entire Nepalese diasporic community in his hometown of Darjeeling celebrated the rise of this "ethnic hero":

> The hills of Darjeeling are burning again. But this time with mobile phones and landlines instead of guns and kukris. And all because of one boy, Prashant Tamang, a resident of Darjeeling and the finalist on the third *Indian Idol* contest on Sony Entertainment Television. The other finalist is Amit Paul from Shillong.

Prashant seems to have succeeded where the politicians have failed—and that is to successfully unite the Nepalis, not only in Darjeeling but across the country. Just recently, a ban on liquor was enforced in Darjeeling to curb trouble during voting. Talk about star power![25]

And when Tamang was selected as the winner of *Idol 3*, the impact went beyond the local and the cultural:

> Nepal and the Nepali-speaking diaspora worldwide erupted in joy after their newest icon, Indian policeman Prashant Tamang, vanquished his closest competitor Amit Paul to lift the third Indian Idol title in Sony Television channel's hugely popular reality show.
> The rallies were reminiscent of another national celebration last year, when similar late night demonstrations erupted following King Gyanendra's decision to surrender the power he had seized through a coup and restore democracy.[26]

It was inevitable that an event of such large scope would at some point be inserted into the realm of political discord:

> Several people were injured after fans of newly-crowned Indian Idol Prashant Tamang clashed with locals in India's eastern state of West Bengal on Friday, media reports said. An estimated 2,000 ethnic Nepalese were marching to the district administration office in the Siliguri town to protest a radio jockey's comment against Tamang, a Nepalese-born star of the TV show which is India's version of American Idol.

According to local news outlets, a radio jockey of Red FM, a Delhi-based private FM channel, recently referred to Tamang as "Bahadur"—a term often used by people to hail security guards in India. Fans said it was a derogatory way to refer to Tamang or the ethnic Nepalese living in India.[27]

Fortunately the story has a happy ending: the ethnic furor subsided without causing too much violence, while Tamang himself was able to obtain extended leave from his job as a policeman and embark on a multi-city tour to the United States!

Indian Idol 3 exemplifies how global formats function as conduits for the politics of difference. What the show enabled in this instance was the expression of local pride and regional identity; more significantly, it brought to public notice the complicated and fraught politics that characterizes India's northeastern provinces. Prashant Tamang's victory was celebrated so fervently in Darjeeling because he was local, and because he was Gurkha. For many years now the Gurkhas—Nepalese immigrants living in India—have been agitating for a separate homeland. Tamang's victory quickly turned into a symbol for this cause.

Coincidentally, his fellow finalist Amit Paul hailed from Mehgalaya, another of the country's "troubled" spots. It is perhaps fitting that both finalists represented a "tribal" population[28] that has traditionally been described as simple, happy and *musical*. The reaction to *Idol 3* went beyond this benign stereotyping: Tamang and Paul, it was alleged, became finalists only because the minority communities they came from were better able to mobilize phone voters. We can begin to see how global formats acquire relevance and ratings by incorporating ethnic differences into game logic. While the contestant-to-contestant relation in any reality program is formally antagonistic—there exists an imperative to vanquish one's opponent—a show acquires far more significance when that contradiction gets imbued with a set of social and historical parameters. In the case of *Idol 3* the empty antagonism between crooners gets filled with the specific history of ethnic conflict in modern India and thus creates a countrywide controversy.

Global formats thrive on a diet of difference; what feeds them is globalization itself. It does so, I argue, in two different ways. First, as we have just seen, globalization makes existing ethnic differences more visible and pronounced. It also, I want to claim, actually produces *new ethnicities*. The history of globalization has always been one of movement: of goods, of capital, of ideas, and of human populations. The period immediately after the Second World War is especially significant because it witnessed a massive movement of a labor force from the "underdeveloped" periphery to the developed West. This movement of peoples changed the demographic composition of the center and led to the creation of a host of hyphenated ethnicities—Black-British, Turkish-German, Algerian-French, Chinese-American and many others. These immigrant groups differ from their predecessors in one crucial respect: they have not melded into the "melting pot" and continue instead to straddle multiple worlds and traditions. In other words, these new ethnicities are irreducibly global.

The story of Indian immigration to America perfectly exemplifies this new model of ethnicity.[29] Previous to the 1960s there were very few Indians living in the United States—in 1940, for example, the U.S. census counted only 2,405. Quite astonishingly this number had not changed in 40 years, the 1900 census having recorded as many as 2,050 Indians! What this demographic inertia points to is the complicated history of racism and exclusion that characterized American immigration policy over this entire period. By the latter half of the nineteenth century, America was in the grip of an anti-immigration fever; this movement culminated in the Immigration Act of 1882 that made it unlawful for Chinese laborers to enter the United States. Indians were not subject to this Act and between 1904 and 1910 more than 5,000 of them, mainly peasants from the Punjab, had settled in the lumber towns of Washington state and the agricultural fields of California. It wasn't long however before these new immigrants, a majority of who were Sikhs, came to be seen as a threat to white labor. Anti-"Hindu" riots broke out all along the West Coast—in Bellingham, Washington in 1907 and in Live Oak, California in 1908 for instance—while the Asiatic Exclusion

League issued warnings about a new "menace" from India and observed that "From every part of the Coast complaints are made of the undesirability of the Hindoos, their lack of cleanliness, disregard of sanitary laws, petty pilfering, especially of chickens, and insolence to women."[30] The U.S. Congress reacted quickly, and in 1917 passed a law placing India, along with other Asian countries, in a "barred zone." This law prohibited the entry of Indian laborers into the United States, but still left undecided the status of those Indians already residing in the country. The matter lay under the jurisdiction of an old law passed in 1790 that declared that only "white persons" could be considered eligible for citizenship. Indians, in the judgment of contemporary historians and anthropologists, were thought of as "Caucasian." Did this mean that they were also "white" and therefore eligible for citizenship? Public opinion did not think so. The Asiatic Exclusion League, in a document published in 1910, held that the Caucasian "forefathers of the Hindu went east and became enslaved, effeminate, caste-ridden and degraded" and that Americans should not be asked to receive this "horde of fanatics" into their midst. The issue then went to the courts. Two decisions—the 1910 *U.S. v. Balsara* and the 1913 *U.S. vs. Ajoy Kumar Mazumdar*—held that Asian Indians were Caucasian and therefore eligible for citizenship. This victory was, however, short-lived, for in the deciding 1923 decision in *U.S. v. Bhagat Singh Thind* the Supreme Court ruled that Asian Indians could not be naturalized because "white" and "Caucasian" were not synonymous. "It may be true" the Court declared "that the blond Scandinavian and the brown Hindu have a common ancestor in the dim reaches of antiquity, but the average man knows perfectly well that there are unmistakable and profound differences between them today."[31] The Thind decision shut the door on any future immigration from India, and was the reason why there was no net gain in America's Indian population between 1900 and 1940. The small Punjabi community that had stayed on was unable to reproduce itself. Most of them were males and were unable to bring back brides for fear of being denied re-entry. Many ended up marrying immigrant Mexican women, and merged into the larger Hispanic population. Today, little trace of them remains. The saga of the first Indians in America was doomed to end in utter anonymity.

The greatest impact on contemporary Indian immigration came with the changes in American laws in 1965. While the old 1790 law restricting immigration only to whites had been repealed in 1952, immigration policy continued to be discriminatory—countries in South and East Asia were allowed only 100 immigrants per year, while those from Europe were permitted much larger numbers. Under the new Act, Asians and Africans gained equal status with Europeans. Indians took full advantage of this latitude, and starting from the early 1970s the average number of Indian entrants was over 20,000 each year. According to INS figures, a total of 469,000 Indians were admitted into the United States between 1961 and 1990.[32] Predominantly Gujarati (60 percent) and Punjabi (30 percent), this group was composed largely of professionals, skilled white-collar workers and small business owners—thus 83 percent of Indians who entered the U.S.A. between 1966 and 1977 came under the category of "professional and technical" workers, and included 20,000 scientists, 25,000 doctors and 40,000 engineers.[33] Given this background, it is not surprising that as of the 2000 U.S. Census, 57 percent of Indians held a Bachelor's or higher degree, compared to 20 percent nationally; 30 percent were employed in professional specialty occupations compared to a national average of 13 percent, and median household income was $60,000 compared to $41, 000 nationally.[34]

This recent immigration has engendered a specific version of hyphenated ethnicity—*Indian-Americans*.[35] I have already pointed out how such a form of ethnicity is mediated by the forces of globalization. There is little doubt that current technologies and practices—cheaper travel, internet-based communication, the growth of multinationals, outsourcing and body shopping—prolong and perhaps even infinitely defer the standard process of assimilation. If in the traditional scenario the prefix (the "Italian" in Italian-American) was destined to wither away, globalization makes possible its constant renewal. New ethnicity is therefore constituted by a double dialectic of difference: between *Indian*-American and American on the one hand and between Indian-*American* and Indian on the other. Consequently the immigrant subject is claimed by both her lands: Jhumpa Lahiri is awarded a Pulitzer for being an American writer who delicately chronicles the lives of immigrant South Asians; in Calcutta, however, she is claimed as a Bengali littérateur who has succeeded on the world stage. New ethnicity in the age of globalization is two-directional, tracing a perpetual pendulum motion between two cultures and lands.

New ethnicity is a natural fit for the global reality format. Take the example of *Sa Re Ga Ma Challenge*—one of the many versions of *Idol* that is wildly popular with Indian audiences. The show's structure adheres to the standard formula: contestants perform live, are judged by "eminent" personalities, each episode ends with one or more eliminations, and after several rounds the show produces a winner. What made the 2007 version of the show of special significance was the participation of one particular contestant. While all other contestants were of local origin, Mauli Dave—raised in Texas by Gujarati parents—was the first Indian-American to be featured so prominently in a national television program. Dave's resume reflected the imprint of hyphenation: as an American teenager she became Indian-American Teen Queen in Houston; as an Indian daughter she underwent a rigorous training in Indian classical music that would serve her well during the competition. Dave exemplifies the *new ethnic*: a triangulated outcome of American, Indian, and Indian-American. Such a figure has proved enormously appealing to contemporary Indian cultural production. Bollywood, for example, has been radically transformed by the emergence of the "NRI film"[36] featuring characters of Indian parentage that have grown up in either Britain or the United States.[37] The same concept has also been exploited by English-language filmmakers like Meera Nair (*Monsoon Wedding, The Namesake*) and Gurinder Chadha (*Bhaji on the Beach, Bend it like Beckham*) as well as by fiction writers like Jhumpa Lahiri and Bharati Mukherjee.

Fully aware of the drawing power of the new ethnic, the Indian entertainment industry is strongly proactive in its quest for globalized versions of "Indianness." Thus auditions for *Sa Re Ga Ma Pa* are held not only in Indian cities but also in London, Johannesburg, and Dubai, as well as several venues in the United States. Dave was discovered during one of these contests, and it is not entirely coincidental that she was first spotted by the noted Bollywood music director Bappi Lahiri—the man who fused Western disco and Hindi pop.[38] Not surprisingly, Dave's performances on the show reflected her dual legacy: she sang some numbers that were restrained and largely classical in inspiration as if to emphasize her fealty to her roots; for other rounds she belted out songs ("Mast, Mast") which overlaid Americanisms over racy Bollywood songs. Dave's appeal lay in the matrix of ethnic possibilities she invoked and inhabited, and as these postings from fans on a Dave website demonstrate, her difference from the average Indian led to curious modes of identification:

> Mauli, Keep it up. We will with you and your singing is very strong. We all USA, UK. And Gujarat with you. I pray God You will be a Winner.

> HiMauli, hw r U? this is Haren Gandhi from Indian Air Force. im a big fan of YOU. I love to c u preform. and i love it wen Bhappi Da has told u dat U r Indian SHAKIRA!!!!!

> Hi, Mauli
>   you are living in Houston, Texas, USA but you sing the hindi songs very well. i know it u belongs Gujurat. i pray the god he must make you the winer of the Saregama chalange -2007. [sic][39]

In spite of a wide fan base, Dave would not make it to the finals. Her fans had feared the worst "I don't understand why people want to eliminate Mauli Dave because she is from US" and when she was finally eliminated one of them wrote "mauli..i cannot believe u got out..i creid hella much..i live in california usa and i watched u ever since ur mayi mayi preformance.[sic]"[40]

Indian Idol and *Sa Re Ga Ma Pa* exemplify the intricate ways in which globalization, ethnicity and television formatting are intertwined in contemporary global culture. Whereas *Indian Idol* illustrates how already existing ethnic differences get called on and exacerbated within the framework of reality television, *Sa Re Ga Ma Pa* bears witness to the emergence of new forms of ethnicity which then inflect cultural production around the world. In both cases, the reality format functions as an ideal space for the interplay of these factors and thus proves to be a most effective instrument for the dissemination of global culture. I want to end this chapter by briefly reflecting on the meteoric career of Sanjaya Malakar, a contestant in the sixth series of *American Idol*.[41] For the duration of the contest Sanjaya was America's most famous celebrity—discussed on every talk show, featured and parodied on numerous YouTube videos, and generating thousands of postings on various blogs and websites. He was simultaneously loved and despised: the 13-year old Ashley Ferl became a minor celebrity for crying copiously at his concert, while the MySpace blogger identified as "J" went on a hunger strike to protest his participation; Diana Ross pronounced that "Sanjaya is love" while Simon Cowell threatened not to return to *Idol* if Sanjaya won the entire contest.[42] Although Sanjaya would only make it to the top 7 before being eliminated, he subsequently became a sort of permanent celebrity. He appeared on numerous talk shows, was featured in several magazines including *US Weekly*, *People*, *Time*, and *Teen*, and was ranked third in *Time*'s 2007 online poll "The Most Influential People of the Year." In the same year he was named "Best TV Reality Star" at the 2007 Teen Choice Awards and also won the title of "Favorite Reality Game Loser" at Fox's 2007 Golden Reality Awards. Most recently, he has been commissioned by Nationwide for a series of commercials, demonstrating that he is now set for a post-*Idol* career.[43]

The phenomenon that is Sanjaya begs easy explanation. A first response would be to take recourse to the notion of "celebrity culture" and argue that the entertainment industry requires constant replenishment and thus invents a succession of figures like him to function as the fuel for the culture machine. These manufactured celebrities require little or no talent—a point that faux supporters like Howard Stern and votefortheworst.com were presumably trying to make in the case of Sanjaya. As the website puts it:

> Votefortheworst.com was started in 2004 to support voting for the entertaining contestants who the producers would hate to see win on American Idol. . . . It's simple a show like American Idol is not about singing at all, it's about making good Reality TV and enjoying a guilty pleasure . . . We think that the less-loved contestants are more entertaining than the producer favorite, and we want to acknowledge this fact by encouraging people to help vote for the amusing antagonists that annoy the judges.[44]

However patronizing this stance, there is an intuition embedded here—there is more to entertainment than mere talent, and more to the "worst" than sheer mediocrity—that goes beyond condescension. Sanjaya's lack of talent may have facilitated his appropriation as postmodern kitsch but the Sanjaya phenomenon contained a surplus not reducible to a mere spectacle of ineptitude.[45] What then accounts for the legion of "Fanjayas" as his supporters came to be known? The answer, to be a little provocative, lies in his hair and his skin.

Sanjaya Malakar was born of an Indian father and an Italian-American mother in the town of Federal Way, Washington. Though bi-racial, his brownness and his name determine him as Indian-American.[46] What implications does such a marking have for television audiences? Numbering close to 2,000,000,

FIGURE 10.1
Mauli as all-American
teen queen

FIGURE 10.2
Mauli marching in the Indian-
American parade in New Jersey

FIGURE 10.3 The Wavy Wallop

FIGURE 10.4 Mo-hawk

FIGURE 10.5 Bandana Badness

Indian-Americans are scarcely visible in the national landscape: barring a few personalities like Dr. Sanjay Gupta, M. Night Shyamalan, Jhumpa Lahiri, Kal Penn and Bobby Jindal,[47] they are not part of the general culture and can therefore be said to constitute a "silent minority." This sociological truth has a crucial semiotic implication: bearing an ethnicity that mainstream America is unacquainted with, Sanjaya qua body is equivalent to a sign without a referent, he is an "other"—that is, inscrutable. In other words Sanjaya assumes a privileged position within the text of *Idol* as the signifier of radical alterity. Reality shows work, I have argued earlier, by producing meaningful differences between individuals. In Sanjaya's case this process of differentiation was applied to the self. He reinvented himself every week, thus generating enormous suspense about the "next Sanjaya." This constant transformation was achieved partly through the agency of hair. Sanjaya understood that hair—the most modifiable part of our body—is an implement by means of which the self secedes from its earlier image and re-posits its look. He skillfully employed a marvelous repertory of hairstyles in order to stage a striking theater of the self. A web feature entitled "Sanjaya: The Hair Chronicles" traced the drama over eight acts: The Wavy Wallop (young David Cassidy), MJ Marvel (low rent Michael Jackson impersonator), Straight and Simple (using a flat iron), Shirley Temple Surprise (curly locks), Farah Fawcett Flip (70s winged swoops), Mohawk/Faux-Hawk/Pony Hawk (seven strategically placed ponytails—his piece de resistance), Greased Lightning (jazz sophistication) and Bandana Badness (the country look he sported on the night of his elimination).[48]

The sequence of Sanjaya's hairdos chronicles a journey which consists of a series of self-expressive iterations—each at variance with its predecessor, each a different avatar of the individual self. This multiplicity of form makes Sanjaya the ideal symbol of an age characterized by a profuse proliferation of differences. The traces of ethnicity that he bears enable his figure to play the perfect part in a format that is outward bound and always for export. The Idol that we worship as we watch this entrancing duet between ethnicity and difference is the Idea of the global itself.

Notes

1 The format debuted as *Pop Idol* on British television in October 2002. The American version began its first season on June 11, 2001. The format now has spin-offs in over 40 countries. (http://en.wikipedia.org/w/index.php?title=Pop_Idol (Accessed February 12, 2008).

2 To give just four examples: the phenomenon of "Crazy English" in China, the use of mobile phones in Africa, the spread of NGO-driven human rights discourse in Bangladesh and the adoption of rap by French-Algerian youth living in the suburbs of Paris.

3 The show aired on Tara Newz, a 24-hour news channel; it was cancelled in 2007.

4 Initially television broadcasting was overseen by the government agency responsible for radio (All India Radio). In 1976 the government set up a second agency—

Doordarshan—which would be responsible only for television. The other landmark developments in this period—the introduction of color television and cable broadcasting—both occurred in 1982. See P. C. Chatterjee, *Broadcasting in India* (New Delhi: Sage Publications, 1991), 51–57.

5 It is of course not a coincidence that these developments took place exactly when the Indian state renounced the socialist model and "liberalized" the economy by removing restrictions on market forces.

6 Daya Kishan Thussu, "Localizing the Global: Zee TV in India," in *Electronic Empires: Global Media and Local Resistance*, ed. Daya Kishan Thussu (London: Arnold, 1998), 278.

7 One ought to beware of reading this phenomenon as an *Idol* effect. Not only did Indian television feature singing contests well before the debut of *Pop Idol*—*Sa Re Ga Ma* started in 1995—it could be argued that participatory singing (to play with Henry Jenkins' notion) has been integral to Indian culture for a very long time.

8 The *Hero Honda—Sa Re Ga Ma Pa Challenge 2007* aired on Zee TV. It premiered May 4, 2007 and ran until October 2007. Sanjaya Malakar appeared on the sixth season of *American Idol* (Fox TV). It premiered January 16, 2007 and its final episode aired May 23, 2007.

9 The term globalization is both fuzzy and contested. I am using the term in a purely descriptive sense here and would go along with John Dunning's assertion that globalization means "the connectivity of individuals and institutions across the globe, or at least, over most of it." *Making Globalization Good: The Moral Challenges of Global Capitalism*, ed. John Dunning (New York: Oxford University Press, 2003), 12; and Albert Moran's claim that "The notion of globalization is the assertion that a worldwide system of economic, cultural and political interdependence has come into being or is in the process of formation." *Copycat TV* (Luton, U.K.: University of Luton Press, 1998), 2.

10 As Allen Scott points out, rental fees generated by exports of film and tape amounted to $8.85 billion in 2000 as compared to $1.68 billion in 1986—an increase of 426 percent. In the year 2000, the gross domestic box office receipts for motion pictures in the United States was $7.66 billion. Thus not only have exports grown much more rapidly than domestic markets over the last 15 years or so, but they now also exceed domestic box-office receipts by a considerable margin. Though most exports are to other industrialized nations, exports to what Scott terms "The Rest of the World" also increased fourfold between 1995 and 2000. Allen J. Scott "Hollywood in the Era of Globalization: Opportunities and Predicaments" *YaleGlobal*, November 29, 2002, http://yaleglobal.yale.edu/display.article?id=479 (accessed April 20, 2008). In the case of television, Hollywood accounts for about 75 percent of worldwide television revenues, and between 1984 and 2005 television syndication revenues for U.S. distributors rose from $500 million to $6.5 billion. See Timothy Havens, *Global Television Marketplace* (London: BFI, 2006), 28–29. And, according to one projection, worldwide game industry revenues (revenues from hardware, software and peripherals) was to rise from $25.4 billion in 2004 to $54.6 billion in 2009. Feldman, Curt, "Analyst: $26 billion game industry in 2008" Gamespot, June 29, 2005, www.gamespot.com/news/2005/06/29/news_6128342.html (accessed April 21, 2008).

11 Albert Moran, *Copycat TV* (Luton, U.K.: University of Luton Press, 1998), 3.

12 See William Robinson, *A Theory of Global Capitalism: Production, Class and State in a Transnational World* (Baltimore, MD and London: Johns Hopkins University Press, 2004) for a cogent exposition of this perspective.

13 Thus *Om Shanti Om* featuring the Bollywood superstar Shah Rukh Khan had earned $35 million worldwide (as of December 13, 2007) and had made it to the Top Ten box office list in Australia, New Zealand and the United Kingdom. www.boxoffice mojo.com/movies/?id=omshantiom.htm (Accessed March 20, 2008).

14 Arjun Appadurai, *Modernity at Large: Cultural Dimensions of Globalization* (Minneapolis: University of Minnesota Press, 1996), 17.

15 Moran, *Copycat TV*, 17–18.

16 Quoted in Albert Moran, *Understanding the Global TV Format* (Bristol, U.K. and Portland, OR: Intellect Books, 2006), 27.

17 The notable exceptions are to be found in certain genres like westerns or detective stories where the hero rides off into the sunset after the final shootout or retreats into asociality after the dénouement. I would argue that it is precisely the most formulaic texts that are capable of producing a hyper-individual like the characters played by John Wayne or the classic Sherlock-Holmes type detective.

18 I am playing with Heidegger's notion here. In the Heideggerian schema Dasein (being) is thrown into a world (history that is). In the ontology posited by Reality TV Dasein is hurled from the world into itself.

19 A fear captured by the term "cultural imperialism."

20 Steve Eaton, *Ethnicity* (Cambridge: Polity Press, 2003), 27.

21 These divisions were also based purely on language—Gujarat was comprised of Gujarati speakers, Maharashtra of Marathi speakers, Haryana on Hindi and Punjab on Punjabi.

22 Percival Spear, *A History of India. Volume II.* (New Delhi: Penguin Books, 1978), 251.

23 Ramachandra Guha, *India After Gandhi: The History of the World's Largest Democracy* (Basingstoke, U.K.: Macmillan, 2007), 237.

24 *Ibid.*

25 http://specials.rediff.com/movies/2007/sep/20sld1.htm (Accessed August 28, 2008).

26 http://www.earthtimes.org/articles/show/112720.html (Accessed August 28, 2008).

27 http://www.earthtimes.org/articles/show/115512.html (August 28, 2008).

28 I am referring here to India's northeast, a region inhabited by Nagas, Mizos, Khasis, Garos and other ethnic groups.

29 A lot of the material in this section is drawn from Ronald Takaki, *Strangers from a Different Shore: A History of Asian Americans* (New York: Penguin Books, 1989).

30 *Ibid.*

31 Ibid, 298–299.

32 Padma Rangaswamy, *Namaste America* (University Park: Pennsylvania State University Press, 2000), 3.

33 Vijay Prashad, *The Karma of Brown Folk* (Minneapolis: University of Minnesota Press, 2000), 75.

34 www.iexpressusa.com (Accessed June 24, 2005).

35 I have italicized the term because there is no agreed upon nomenclature to refer to Americans who are of Indian origins. First generation immigrants (those born in India) usually think of themselves as Indians, while those of the second generation often refer to themselves as "desis" (a term that literally means "of the country" but is actually closer to "homeboy" in sense). To add to the confusion, immigrants from India, Pakistan, Bangladesh and Nepal are collectively referred to as South-Asians.

36 NRI is the acronym for Non-Resident Indian, a bureaucratic category that refers to Indians living abroad as well as people of Indian origin (those who have at least one parent or grandparent who was Indian).

37 The trend was established by *Dilwale Dulhania Le Jayange* (1994), one of the biggest blockbusters of the 1990s. There have been many successful NRI films since then, a lot of them featuring Shah Rukh Khan, India's pre-eminent male movie star.

38 See Biswarup Sen, *Of the People: Essays on Indian Popular Culture* (New Delhi: Chronicle Books, 2006), 103–107.

39 www.maulidave.com (Accessed February 20, 2008). Grammar and spelling in all the above quotations (and the ones that follow) are as in the original.

40 www.maulidave.com (accessed February 20, 2008).

41 The season ran from January 16 to May 23 of 2007. Sanjaya was eliminated on April 23 after making it to the top seven.

42 For Ferl see http://en.wikipedia.org/wiki/American_Idol_(season_6)#.22The_crying_girl.22; for J see http://news.sawf.org/Gossip/35418.aspx; for Cowell see http://www.starmometer.com/2007/03/27/if-sanjaya-wins-i-quit-simon-cowell/ (Accessed September 1, 2008).

43 http://en.wikipedia.org/wiki/Sanjaya_Malakar (Accessed August 28, 2008).

44 www.votefortheworst.com/about_us Accessed 9/1/08

45 He is very different from someone like William Hung who was notorious for his off-key performance of Ricky Martin's "She Bangs" in the third season of *American Idol*.

46 The same logic ensures that Barack Obama is thought of by everyone, including himself, as African-American.

47 Dr. Sanjay Gupta is a medical correspondent for CNN, M. Night Shyamalan directed *The Sixth Sense*, Jhumpa Lahiri has won the Pulitzer Prize for fiction, Kal Penn acted in *Harold and Kumar go to White Castle*, and Bobby Jindal is the current governor of Louisiana. This list deliberately omits spiritual gurus like Deepak Chopra, Rajneesh and the Maharishi Mahesh Yogi because they are Indian and not Indian-American.

48 http://television.aol.com/show/american-idol/65307/tv-show-features/sanjaya-malakar-hair (Accessed September 2, 2008).

11

NZ IDOL

Nation Building Through Format Adaptation

Joost de Bruin

Introduction

Three seasons of *NZ Idol*, the New Zealand adaptation of the global *Idols* format, were aired on public broadcaster TVNZ's channel TV2 in 2004, 2005 and 2006. The final episode of the first season was the most-watched television programme in New Zealand in 2004, with 1.4 million people, a third of the New Zealand population, tuning in (South Pacific Pictures, 2004). In terms of ratings *NZ Idol* has been one of the most successful locally made television programmes of the last decade. At first glance, *NZ Idol* has also been very successful in representing ethnic and cultural diversity. In the auditions phase of the show young New Zealanders of 16 years plus from a range of backgrounds are featured, and in the subsequent phases the audience gets to know a selection of them intimately. The winners of all three seasons (Ben Lummis in season 1, Rosita Vai in season 2, and Matt Sounoa in season 3) have Pacific Island roots, and as a result three young "brown" people were crowned "New Zealand Idols." This is remarkable, since according to a previous study by Misha Kavka (2004: 231) non-white people have largely been absent from New Zealand reality TV programmes. A closer look suggests, however, that featuring contestants from different cultural back-grounds in *NZ Idol* generally serves a particular nation building agenda that New Zealand is heavily involved in as a postcolonial society, in which ethnic minorities are subjected to representations that favour the interests of dominant cultural groups. The aim of this nation building agenda is to establish a new and distinct sense of national identity which will set New Zealand apart from Britain, the former colonial power, and other English-speaking nations.

The New Zealand television landscape is characterised by an abundance of American and British material and a dearth of local New Zealand programming. Due to the relatively small size of the population, 4.2 million people, and the availability of relatively cheap English-language programmes from other countries, locally made programmes are relatively expensive and therefore rely on public funding (Horrocks, 2004). The agency responsible for the largest part of public funding is NZ On Air. It funds "programmes and broadcasts, not otherwise provided in a commercial market, which are widely accessible, reflect New Zealand's diversity, are rich in information and—across the range of programming—are entertaining for all New Zealanders" (NZ On Air, 2008). Through its dependence on public funding, New Zealand-made television is generally expected to represent the nation and its citizens in a way that appeals to all. There is a continuing demand of New Zealand television to "give us our country" (Turner, 2004: 90).

According to the most recent census, New Zealand is becoming increasingly ethnically diverse. In 2006, the New Zealand population was made up of 68 per cent from European backgrounds (also referred to as Pakeha), 15 per cent Maori (the indigenous people of New Zealand), 9 per cent from different countries in Asia (but mainly China and India), and 7 per cent from Pacific Island states such as Samoa, Tonga and the Cook Islands (Statistics New Zealand, 2006). There has been considerable debate about how ethnic diversity has been represented on New Zealand television screens. Until the launch of Maori Television (which is a free-to-air television service aimed at revitalising Maori language and culture) in 2004, mainstream media have portrayed Maori largely through a Pakeha worldview, resulting in concerns about both under-representation and misrepresentation (see Te Kawa a Maui Media Research Team, 2005). Asian and Pacific Island New Zealanders have mainly been featured through special interest programmes broadcast in "the margins of the 'mainstream' television schedule" (Kothari et al., 2004: 136).

Claudia Bell (1996: 128) has argued that television in Aotearoa/New Zealand (Aotearoa is the Maori name for New Zealand) has always aimed to foster a sense of togetherness and national belonging. Her account is sceptical of these representations: "Television likes to give the impression that as a nation we are homogeneous and egalitarian. It is in their interests to do so. Yet how can any country of many diverse groups seem to have a national identity in common?" (Bell, 1996: 132). Other authors have pointed out that national identity is inevitably a construction, and that it is vital to question what lies behind particular constructions. Richard White states in his book *Inventing Australia*: "When we look at ideas about national identity, we need to ask, not whether they are true or false, but what their function is, whose creation they are, and whose interests they serve" (White, 1981: viii). Accordingly, Bell's main concern with New Zealand television is that while it claims to address all citizens equally, its images and stories in fact primarily serve the interests of Pakeha New Zealanders by foregrounding a worldview that they can comfortably relate to. In this way, television in New Zealand perpetuates historical inequalities, as argued by Jo Smith:

Given its history of European colonisation, what gets counted as "common" to Aotearoa/New Zealand is often a homogeneous and Eurocentric expression of cultural belonging, a homogeneity that extends itself through the very technological, social and economic processes of society. Television is key to the dissemination of these narratives of a "common" national imaginary.

(Smith, 2006: 27)

This mode of address is arguably echoed in NZ On Air imperatives, which stress rather unproblematically that funded programmes should "promote and foster the development of New Zealand's culture" (NZ On Air, 2008) and should aim to appeal to "all New Zealanders."

The first season of *NZ Idol* received cultural subsidy from NZ On Air (the agency agreed to fund NZ$450,000, which was about 10 per cent of the proposed budget). In return, the producers committed themselves to making a television programme which would promote several aspects important to NZ On Air: ethnic and cultural diversity; positive representations of young people; and attention for New Zealand popular music. Based on interviews with key figures involved in the production of the first two seasons of *NZ Idol* and textual analysis of examples the interviewees talked about, this article explores how ethnic and cultural diversity—in itself a significant accomplishment of the show—was framed within *NZ Idol*, as well as the broader question of how the *Idols* format was translated into a local television programme. The six people who were interviewed are: Andrew Shaw (executive producer season 1); Mandy Toogood (producer season 1); Adrian Brant (executive producer season 2); Nicola van der Meijden (producer season 2); Victoria Spackman (legal and business affairs manager of South Pacific Pictures, the company that produced the show); and Chris Caradus (general manager commercial business affairs TVNZ).

The *Idols* Format

The *Idols* format has been sold to over 40 territories worldwide (Fremantle Media, 2007). All local adaptations of the *Idols* format essentially have the same goal: to address the entire nation in a quest for the one "idol" that can be admired by all. The search for this idol is split into four stages: (1) regional auditions (which in the case of *NZ Idol* were held in Auckland, Wellington and Christchurch), (2) a "theatre round" in which contestants engage in several workshops and start performing on stage, (3) individual studio performances by a selected number of contestants, and (4) the live shows, in which the remaining 10 contestants sing on stage in front of a large and enthusiastic crowd. In the final phases viewers can vote for contestants by phoning in or sending text messages (Holmes, 2004: 153–154). The television programme in which this process is covered has, in the case of *NZ Idol*, a duration of 17 weeks.

The *Idols* format is owned by two transnational entertainment corporations: Fremantle Media and 19 Entertainment. It has been adapted in New Zealand by local independent producer South Pacific Pictures (SPP). SPP has signed a joint venture agreement with Grundy, the Australian branch of Fremantle, which gives them first access to Fremantle formats. *Idols* was the first format that was adapted under this agreement. SPP pitched *NZ Idol* to public broadcaster TVNZ, and the two parties decided to jointly approach national funding agency NZ On Air for cultural subsidy.

Even though all adaptations of the *Idols* format are structured in similar ways, there is room for the incorporation of local meanings. Research suggests that this applies to global formats more generally. Albert Moran (1998) was one of the first academic scholars to point out that the global format trade does not necessary lead to standardisation and cultural imperialism, but can offer possibilities for localised articulations. Silvio Waisbord claims that "[f]ormat television shows (. . .) organize experiences of the national" (2004: 372). Formats may be culturally specific, but are nationally neutral; they can be made national by including local narratives, events and characters. The local adaptation of global formats can therefore create opportunities for audiences to recognise themselves as members of national communities.

Feeling involved and part of a national community seems especially pertinent regarding the *Idols* format. Henry Jenkins (2006: 70) discusses how *American Idol* aims to forge an intimate connection with the audience by, on the one hand, building up a file of stories about the contestants, their motives, backgrounds and families; and, on the other hand, offering possibilities for audience participation through voting. Due to the serialised nature of the show viewers are able to develop a relationship with the contestants. Over the course of the show contestants are transformed from competitive individuals (in the auditions phase) to people with a rich social network (especially during the live shows). Through clips of the contestants interacting with each other and going home to their respective hometowns to introduce their families and friends to the audience, viewers are invited to be a part of these social networks (Reijnders et al., 2007: 283).

According to Matthew Stahl (2004: 214) *Idols* differs from other TV talent shows in its focus on the subjectivities of the contestants. The biographical vignettes included in the live show phase create "narratives of authentication." Stahl argues that in these vignettes in *American Idol* the social identities of class, race and gender are overshadowed by individual character traits such as musical talent or a strong work ethic, which makes it easier for a range of audience members to relate to contestants (ibid.: 221). Henk Huijser states more or less the opposite regarding *Australian Idol*: "What has come across strongly during the last three seasons is that there appears to be very little 'silencing' or 'erasing' of ethnic, class and gender identities; instead, there seems to be a confident foregrounding of these differences" (2007: 135). The *Australian Idol* contestants had considerable agency in performing complex cultural identities in the vignettes. The way in which

NZ Idol has used biographical vignettes to represent diversity is explored in the second half of this article. First I address the more general question of how the *Idols* format was translated into *NZ Idol*.

Adaptation

The executive producers of the first and second seasons respectively had different views of what issues are involved in translating a global television format. The executive producer of the second season, an experienced Australian television producer who was hired by SPP just before the start of the second season, emphasised that the *Idols* format works the same way in different countries because of the universal appeal of music:

> Formats, I mean here's another phenomenon which really I don't think many people are aware of, most formats do not travel internationally. Probably (. . .) *Idol* is one of the only formats that has travelled internationally because of music being a common denominator in all countries. It doesn't matter about the language, music is music. And people like music, it is a way of life and every country, it doesn't matter what religion, what language, there is always a pop star, an image, an icon that is held up there as a performer whom basically younger people look up to and they adore this character. So it lends itself very nicely to going into any country. (. . .) Every country has its own local music and local musicians, so giving the opportunity to New Zealanders to become a pop star is no different than to any other country, it just lends itself to it and that's why it is successful.
>
> (Adrian Brant, executive producer season 2)

The executive producer of the first season was the Chief Operating Officer of SPP at the time. The reason such a high-ranked SPP employee took on the role of executive producer was that *NZ Idol* was the first big entertainment production for a company specialised in drama production, and the first format adapted under the joint venture agreement with Grundy. This producer was involved with the making of the show at an early stage and also took part in negotiating the contract with the format holders. He explained that there were specific cultural issues pertinent to adapting the format to the New Zealand context:

> You scale it up or you scale it down depending on the size of your market, what you can afford to make in terms of a production. And then you add the culturally positive and subtract the culturally negative. (. . .) The culturally positive is that there is no shortage of musical talent (. . .). *NZ Idol* would be a new young face of New Zealand, it wouldn't just be a bunch of kids who'd been through classical training, these would be kids

from South Auckland and Porirua and small town New Zealand who could just *sing* and who really like to sing. (. . .) The thing to promote was this is New Zealand where anyone can be Prime Minister if you know what I mean. If you've got it, you can get out there and you can do it, you might win it. And that's the kind of New Zealand thing, the fearlessness of it. The culturally negative: we had to soften the brutality of the show, in order to make it acceptable to the way New Zealanders feel about fairness to one another. Everyone knows almost everyone in this country. The six degrees of separation exist for all of us. So, I knew that it couldn't be as ferocious as *American Idol*, or even *Australian Idol*. (. . .) New Zealanders wouldn't tolerate too much of that kind of cruelty. They want harsh and fair, but that sense of fairness is very important to the New Zealand self identity.

(Andrew Shaw, executive producer season 1)

Contrary to his successor in the second season, the executive producer of the first season thus emphasised that the *Idols* format had to be adapted to the New Zealand market and New Zealand sensibilities. His account is more in line with academic theory about format adaptation, which stresses that there is room for the incorporation of local meanings. Local meanings, in this case, are local music scenes, a sense of "fearlessness," and New Zealand ideas about fairness. Another factor to take into account is budget. When comparing *NZ Idol* with other adaptations of the *Idols* format, the producers of both the first and the second seasons highlighted implications of the small budget that New Zealand television makers have to work with:

Budget, absolutely budget. Our budget, I mean overseas people that make *Idol* can't believe that it is possible for us to make it with the budget that we have here. It's such a drop in the bucket and it's because of our population. We can't justify a bigger budget because we don't have the bigger population who is going to watch it to be able to generate the advertising revenue to put back into the programme so it's just, that's just the reality of it. In Australia, Guy Sebastian when he won, which was just before our first series, their budget for the final was just over half of our entire budget for the whole series.

(Mandy Toogood, producer season 1)

Budget and population. Very hard making the poor cousin show. The second series in Australia went "right we're going to do a new set, we're going to do bang, bang, bang" and we're just going, "well we can repaint it, we could put some more lights up . . . " I mean, we had some money, it's just we can't turn it into the extravaganza that they can.

(Nicola van der Meijden, producer season 2)

Both producers compared *NZ Idol* to *Australian Idol*, which functions as benchmark for what an *Idols* show could look like. Working with small budgets is something that New Zealand producers are generally coping with and almost all local productions rely on NZ On Air funding (Horrocks, 2004). In the case of *NZ Idol*, producer SPP and broadcaster TVNZ approached the funding agency for cultural subsidy for the first season. They perceived that the show would match with NZ On Air's objectives:

> NZ On Air primarily support non-commercial ventures so one of the rationales was that it was a very expensive show and commercially it was touch and go whether we would make it or not. So it would be very helpful if they would fund some. And also it did fit in, it was promoting music, promoting youth, (. . .) auditions for example weren't just held in Auckland, there was one in Auckland, one in Wellington and one in Christchurch. They were all around the country. I think that everyone pretty much understood that a disproportionate number of Maori and Pacific Island people would be involved.
>
> (Chris Caradus, general manager commercial business affairs TVNZ)

The opportunities for representing Maori and Pacific Island performers in *NZ Idol* was used as one of the major selling points in the proposal submitted to NZ On Air:

> In New Zealand, we have a multiculturalism that sets us apart from other territories that have successfully screened the "Idol" format. You only have to look at the music charts to see the mix of young Pakeha, Maori and Polynesian performers who are succeeding in the entertainment industry. The new emergence of Maori and Pacific Islanders who embrace their own sound has encouraged a new generation of kids with talent to believe that they too may make it one day. *NZ Idol* will be the platform from which this new talent can make a break. With these performers comes a greater cultural mix of audience members. *NZ Idol* presents an opportunity to grab this cultural mix and give them primetime entertainment that has greater relevance to them than ever before.
>
> (South Pacific Pictures, 2003: 6)

The *Idols* format was thus regarded as a unique opportunity to involve and capitalise on the talent pool of young performers in Aotearoa/New Zealand, particularly those from Maori and Pacific Island (or Polynesian) descent. The producers assumed that a multicultural mix of contestants on the show would result in a multicultural audience.

Applying for public funding forced the producers of the first season to reflect on ways in which *NZ Idol* would be distinctively "New Zealand." Through the funding application the *Idols* format was effectively localised before the show itself had been made. One element that needed to be changed in comparison with adaptations such as *American Idol* and *Australian Idol* was the "brutality" of the show, specifically the way contestants are treated by the judges in the auditions phase. On the other hand, regional and cultural diversity were seen as logically flowing from the *Idols* format:

> *NZ Idol* was different, as opposed to overseas versions, because it had NZ On Air money. And it's probably the only show in the world of that format that had cultural subsidy. And the funding agency was very, very sensitive to a positive reflection of the cultural diversity. They need not have worried. And they were also concerned about the harshness. It was a happy coincidence of perspectives that we were never going to have a problem with cultural diversity and we also knew it couldn't possibly be as hard as *Australian* or *American Idol*. (. . .) The show was absolutely built on a stick for regional and cultural diversity. Kids come from everywhere, and they're all walks and make up.
>
> (Andrew Shaw, executive producer season 1)

Cultural Diversity

The producers of the first season were convinced that the group of contestants on *NZ Idol* would be culturally diverse. Apart from the possibilities that the *Idols* format offers, this belief was attributed to the make-up of the New Zealand music scene:

> Look, you won't find this written anywhere, except when you write it, but this was going to be brown *Idol*. Because the music industry and music in this country are dominated by Maori and Polynesian rhythms. I mean there are great European or Pakeha performers, but this was going to have a very contemporary urban-Maori, urban-Polynesian feel.
>
> (Andrew Shaw, executive producer season 1)

> From series one through our belief was that 80 to 90 per cent of our talent was going to come from our Polynesian and Maori community, because that is where our singing base is. And it was actually very interesting to find out that in reality there was a far more even split than that in terms of both the auditions for *Idol* and who was getting through, it was a far more even split between Polynesian, Maori and Pakeha. (. . .) Probably in Auckland the balance was slightly more skewed a little bit browner. But still in Auckland we thought it was going to be just a brown wash really. We just thought this is where all our talent is. Just look at South Auckland,

the music that is coming out of South Auckland, I mean it is extraordinary and we just thought no whitey is going to get in here, they won't deserve to, but we were really pleasantly surprised. It was probably more like (. . .) a 65/35 or 60/40 split maybe in Auckland. But it wasn't the 90/10 or 95/5 which we thought it was going be.

(Mandy Toogood, producer season 1)

Auckland is the largest New Zealand city with a population of 1.3 million people. As stated by the 2006 census, Auckland is, moreover, the most ethnically diverse region in New Zealand (Statistics New Zealand, 2006). Two-thirds of all Pacific Islanders in New Zealand live in Auckland, and South Auckland especially has a high density of people from Pacific Island and Maori backgrounds. South Auckland is known for its vibrant hip hop culture which draws on American hip hop but mixes this with Pacific and Maori influences (see Zemke-White, 2004).

When talking about the accomplishments of the South Auckland music scene Mandy Toogood, producer of the first season of *NZ Idol*, reflected on her belief or perhaps even anxiety that the programme would be "taken over" by successful Pacific and Maori performers. This did indeed eventuate in the sense that the winner of the first season, Ben Lummis, is from South Auckland and from Maori and Pacific Island descent, yet the contestants who made it through the auditions and to the top 10 were from a range of ethnic backgrounds. Toogood was pleasantly surprised with a more even split between "brown" and "white" people because this makes better television:

It just wouldn't be good for television if going in front of the judges out of 100 people 90 of them were Polynesian males aged 20, it just doesn't make good telly. And they might all be brilliant but they'll all have something very much the same about them, and likewise if you've got 90 white blonde pretty girls, it would be equally boring.

(Mandy Toogood, producer season 1)

While the producers of the first season expressed a belief that the programme would be dominated by Maori and Pacific talent, their successors in the second emphasised that the *Idols* format allows equal opportunities for everyone and that race, ethnicity or cultural background did not play a role in the selection of contestants for *NZ Idol*:

It was absolutely first in first served, based on the applications. It was never based on age, well it was based on age because you had to be in the bracket [between 16 and 29 years old], but within the bracket it was totally random. Basically it was what we processed by the time we had enough to stop it. It was not race or age or anything based whatsoever. But there was a large range, from Indian people right through to Polynesian, English, European, American. Quite a vast range of people.

(Nicola van der Meijden, producer season 2)

And that's the great thing about it, it doesn't matter what race you come from or how rich or how poor you are, everyone has got an equal chance because it is judged on performance. You could come from the poorest background but if you've got a beautiful voice and you can sing you'll get selected. It doesn't matter how rich you are. In a show like this it is purely on your performance. We don't care, as I say, "I don't care if you're black, white, if you're Chinese or you know, Asian, or anything. It's got nothing to do with it, it is not going to get you selected. All that is going to get you selected is your voice, and your attitude as well, your performance, it is all about performance."

(Adrian Brant, executive producer season 2)

The differences in the ways in which the producers of the first and second seasons talked about cultural diversity in relation to *NZ Idol* are striking. Whereas the former stressed the success of local music scenes, even to the point of implying that "brown" people predominantly have musical talent, the latter emphasised absolute equality in selection of candidates, resulting in an attitude of ignorance of cultural differences. These differences can be explained by the dissimilar contexts in which the producers made the programme. The producers of the first season were involved in tailoring the *Idols* format to specific "New Zealand" cultural issues, and applying for funding from NZ On Air forced them to reflect on how the programme would be culturally diverse. The producers of the second season, which did not receive NZ On Air funding, were working on an existing show and could use the first season of *NZ Idol* as a blueprint.

Regardless of the dissimilarities in ways of talking about cultural diversity, the producers of both seasons agreed that a multicultural group of contestants presented opportunities to localise the show and make New Zealand viewers feel involved:

People cared about the show because they cared about the kid from Dannevirke [a small town in the south of the North Island] and they knew his story because we said, hypothetically one of five kids, part Maori, etcetera. And that's what you do, you build up a file so the audience becomes interested in the fate of their favourite. When you get down to the twenty four, through the research process that these kids go through you find out an awful lot about them. (. . .) Once we know all that about them and once we've spent time with them you look for stories that suit them. People have a story to tell, whether it's interesting family background, or they've overcome some adversity or they've got a unique perspective on life and you start to look for ways that you can expose that personality profile and then do back stories on them. You go back to the little home town where the whole community is in the hall on a Sunday night just to watch him or her. And it's about them, where they've come from and the people that support them.

(Andrew Shaw, executive producer season 1)

The biographical vignettes especially, in which contestants travel home to meet their friends and family and thereby show the *NZ Idol* viewers where they are from, are instrumental in forging a connection with the audience, as also pointed out by Stahl (2004: 14) and Jenkins (2006: 70) with regards to *American Idol*. *NZ Idol* producers emphasised the importance of creating different characters through these vignettes:

You're trying to find different things for each of them. So you don't want to end up going to everybody's workplace and school because that's just boring. So you try to find out different, not only different things to do with them, but different ways of doing it. (. . .), trying to find interesting and creative ways of seeing another side of these people that isn't the traditional "let's go home and talk to mum and dad and see you at school."

(Mandy Toogood, producer season 1)

Regarding these vignettes in *Australian Idol*, Huijser (2007: 135) argues that stories about contestants in which distinctive class, ethnic or gender identities are brought to the fore can contest dominant notions of national identity. In *NZ Idol*, on the contrary, it seems that cultural differences between contestants can be explored, as long as they serve a sense of national belonging in which all New Zealanders are involved:

Like Rongo in series two was from down on the east coast. Very New Zealand story. They'd go out and get all their seafood from the beach and just a very New Zealand story. (. . .) He lived in this little caravan out the back. Not just because he is a Maori boy living in a small town, it was Kiwi, but this little caravan out the back and just the way they lived and what they ate and it was very sort of old school Kiwi I suppose.

(Nicola van der Meijden, producer season 2)

Nicola van der Meijden, the producer of the second season, thus emphasised that the vignettes need to have a "Kiwi" feel. "Kiwi" is a colloquial term used to describe New Zealanders, although it is not necessarily a term Maori feel involved with (Turner, 2007: 97). Representations of New Zealanders as "Kiwis" generally reinforce the project of nation building in which predominantly Pakeha New Zealanders aim to carve out a new and distinct national identity for themselves. Van der Meijden talked about how New Zealand television producers are usually expected to make programmes that are about "New Zealand":

> So much of the time our direction is to make it about New Zealand. (. . .) It is always the directive we are given, we are spending all this money to make this big show, New Zealanders want to see themselves and they want to see New Zealand and we need to make sure we translate it so it is a true home grown show.
>
> (Nicola van der Meijden, producer season 2)

The vignettes thus revolve around a paradox: on the one hand, contestants have to be different from one another, on the other, they all have to represent New Zealand. It is in these vignettes that the tension between cultural and ethnic diversity versus nation building processes becomes the most pronounced.

Vignettes

The *NZ Idol* vignettes were generally 2.5 minutes long and were shot in documentary style. To a New Zealand audience the vignettes would have been reminiscent of the documentary series *Heartland*, aired in the mid-1990s, in which local communities in New Zealand were portrayed in a romanticising manner. In the vignettes, which were aired during the live show phase of the programme, we follow the contestant to their home town. As a result, vignettes were shot in several locations all over New Zealand. Generally, we first see footage of a main street or scenery typical for the region, after which the contestant's parents are interviewed. They talk about what their child was like growing up (invariably parents talk about a musical talent that was always there) and we see photos or home video footage of the contestant in different phases of their lives. Contestants emphasise how important their family is to them and how hard it is being away from their loved ones. We see them interacting with family members and friends, which in most cases culminates in people making music and singing together.

Michael is the runner-up of the first season of *NZ Idol* and his vignette was included in the Top 7 episode. We follow Michael back to his family's farm in Taupo, a small city in the centre of New Zealand's North Island. All the elements described above are present, but it is striking how Michael and his family are positioned within the clean, green and beautiful New Zealand landscape. They are interviewed sitting outside on the lawn with green scenery in the background, we see a photo of Michael as a child in an empty green landscape, the family plays cricket in the garden behind the farm, and Michael is riding on a motorbike through the paddock. The beautiful New Zealand landscape is a powerful element of the way Pakeha New Zealanders like to see themselves. In the absence of clear common historical roots, nature can offer an alternative marker for a distinct national identity (Bell, 1996: 29). Therefore, the focus on nature in this vignette works particularly well for this Pakeha contestant.

Luke is also a contestant from the first season of *NZ Idol*, yet his vignette is very different from Michael's. Luke's vignette was aired in the Top 10 episode. Luke is from mixed Pakeha/Maori descent and in the vignette his mother talks about her son teaching kapa haka, Maori performing arts, to young people. We see Luke at his marae (Maori meeting area) with his kapa haka youth group. He explains what kapa haka is about: "Kapa haka is the performing arts of Maori, telling them the old ways and the ways that Maori have gone through life." It is striking that Luke has to define kapa haka for the audience. The presumption is, arguably, that the viewers of *NZ Idol* do not know this. This representation of Maori life is therefore characterised by what Barry Barclay has called "talking out": "to convey to others something of what Maori life is like" (1990: 76). The vignette focuses on Maori aspects of Luke's life in a way that is comprehensible for a non-Maori audience.

Rosita is the eventual winner of the second season of *NZ Idol*. Her vignette was included in the Top 3 episode. We visit Rosita's parents and she is interviewed sitting between them on the couch. Referring to her parents she talks about how hard it was growing up with these "tough cookies to crack." Other family members turn up for a family dinner and Rosita greets them in Samoan. Rosita explains that she always wanted to be a singer but that her parents did not approve. Her mother says she did not think singing was the right thing for her: "typical Samoan mother, I would like her to do something different." This is a different picture of New Zealand society again: a large family from Samoan descent in South Auckland. References to the strictness of Samoan parents are another example of "talking out" to a majority audience, who may not have an in-depth understanding of Samoan New Zealand culture.

Rongo is a Maori contestant from the second season and his vignette was aired in the Top 6 episode (this is the vignette producer Nicola van der Meijden talked about when explaining vignettes need to have a "Kiwi" feel). Standing on a hill overlooking his hometown, Rongo says "Kia ora New Zealand and welcome to Mohaka!" (kia ora is an informal Maori greeting). While Rongo explains that Mohaka has a population of only 200 people, we see people fishing and collecting shell food on the beach. Next we see footage of a powhiri (Maori welcoming ceremony) and Rongo and some other family members are welcomed onto the marae. His parents continue to talk about his *NZ Idol* experience in voice over. Rongo introduces us to his little cousin Mohaka, who is named after the town. She sings a song, which is interrupted by the voiceover of his mother talking about the positive responses from people regarding Rongo's *NZ Idol* journey. In this vignette the use of voiceovers is particularly noteworthy. On two occasions, a representation of Maori culture (a Maori welcoming ceremony, a child singing a Maori song) is laid over with a voiceover of Rongo's parents talking about their son's performance in *NZ Idol*. This seems crude, and can be read as a suggestion that a mainstream audience will not be very interested in listening to the Maori voices in the vignette, which are thereby effectively silenced.

These four vignettes each portray New Zealand society in a different way. By representing young people from Maori, Pakeha and Pacific Island backgrounds a more diverse picture of people living in New Zealand is presented than in previous New Zealand reality TV shows. Similar to what Huijser (2007: 135) has argued in relation to *Australian Idol*, contestants are given space to perform different ethnic identities, but these performances are all framed in a way that pleases a mainstream, or, more specifically, a Pakeha audience. Michael's story depicts a lifestyle that many Pakeha New Zealanders can relate and aspire to, while the other three vignettes each in their own way showcase a non-Pakeha culture to *NZ Idol* viewers. In addition, the limits of these vignettes become evident in reflecting on what is *not* shown. Mandy Toogood talked about the lived realities of the top 10 contestants of the first season:

> With some of these kids the reality is that there is not a lot going on in their lives. They come from very underprivileged backgrounds and there is not a lot to see. [Joost: Do you show that?] No, no we don't. Well I wouldn't. I mean, there were cases when we did, there was one particular contestant I recall who said "I'm happy for you to talk about"—she was a solo Mum—"happy for you to talk about my child, but I don't want you coming to my house because I don't want people to see how I live." Absolutely of course, no way in the world would we think of crossing that boundary. Because the other thing is, with the *Idol* branding, it is to no one's benefit to make them look bad. And there is also another element that has to be carefully looked after and that is the perception of fairness. I'm talking mainly now about when we get to top ten, when you're in the top ten there has to be the perception that everyone of those kids is treated fairly. As far as the amount of on air time they have in their story, the sorts of things that we do have to be seen as evenly distributed amongst the ten. You can't be seen to have a favourite. It is absolutely crucial to the *Idol* branding, well in my belief it is.
>
> (Mandy Toogood, producer season 1)

The *Idols* format favours positive and neutral vignettes. Each story has to carry the same weight and dwelling on social problems that contestants face in their daily lives would create favouritism. The resulting representation of cultural diversity creates a rosy picture of the nation which does not acknowledge existing inequalities between people. This resonates with what Claudia Bell writes about the aforementioned New Zealand documentary series *Heartland*:

The myth-making overlooks accounts of small-town alcoholism, unemployment or domestic violence, or any expression of dissatisfaction. All is
well. And fun. Togetherness, friendship, hard work and an assumed sense
of unity subsume any differences which may be present. The makers are
quite sure that viewers do not want a sociology lecture; they want entertainment.

(Bell, 1996: 142)

The same applies to *NZ Idol* vignettes, in which New Zealand is portrayed as a
multicultural society in which everything is alright. A contrived sense of togetherness is evidently more important than unpleasant realities.

Another perspective that is useful for analysing the biographical vignettes
is cultural appropriation. This is especially relevant in relation to the Maori
contestants. There is a long history of incorporating Maori in representations of
the New Zealand national imaginary. For example, Maori people and Maori
culture have been used in tourist brochures which promote the country since
the 1870s (O'Connor, 2004: 167). The question is who benefits from these
appropriations:

Much has been written about the appropriation of symbols of indigenous
people by colonisers and settlers. It has been suggested (. . .) that this is
done in an effort to create for the settlers a distinctive new identity, one
that correlates with their new surroundings.

(O'Connor, 2004: 166)

In this way, featuring Maori cultural elements such as kapa haka and a powhiri
in *NZ Idol* contributes to a sense of a colourful New Zealand identity, rather
than serving purposes which may be important for Maori. The fact that Luke
has to explain to the *NZ Idol* audience what kapa haka is about and the inter-
ruptions of Maori customs by voiceovers in Rongo's vignette illustrate that the
target audience of *NZ Idol* is not (just) Maori New Zealanders.

Additional to vignettes in which contestants show the viewers where they
are originally from, *NZ Idol* also used vignettes which allowed the audience a
glimpse of contestants' daily life during their time on the show. There was a marked
difference between the first and second seasons in how these vignettes were
deployed by the producers. In the second season, in line with the claim by
executive producer Adrian Brant that *NZ Idol* was "all about performance," they
zoomed in on the contestants' journey of becoming pop stars. For example, there
was an autograph session in a mall, a visit to a radio station, and a dinner with
the *NZ Idol* judges which was presented as an opportunity to ask them advice
about how to be successful in the music industry. Other vignettes looked at how
contestants had progressed through the competition over the course of the

season. In short, the second season's vignettes emphasised acquiring the necessary skills to become a pop star and competing with others in the process, which gave the show an underlying logic of individualistic competition.

In the first season these vignettes were used for different purposes, namely to show to the audience how the contestants bonded as a group. They were filmed while participating in a range of outdoor activities such as go-karting, visiting a theme park and the zoo and bungee jumping from the Auckland Sky Tower. The contestants were also shown partaking in initiatives which benefited other people, for example buying a birthday present for one of the contestants, visiting children in hospital and helping out at the local animal shelter. Producer Mandy Toogood considered these vignettes one of the main attractions of the first season of *NZ Idol*:

> What that did for the home audience was to create the sense of them being a team, how they got on and how they related with each other, and I think that was part of the magic and charm of what worked for series one. And I really think series two didn't do that. (. . .) I think there was a dinner once at the beginning of the series but other than that it was all separate. It was all just their individual weekly interviews and going home and you never got a sense of them bonding as people, just being together and doing fun things together.
>
> (Mandy Toogood, producer season 1)

The first season correspondingly contained representations of a unique multi-cultural community of young people. The top 10 contestant group of both seasons was ethnically and culturally diverse, but while in the second season young people from different cultural backgrounds were mainly shown competing with one another, in the first season they were portrayed while establishing their own sense of community. This process of establishing a community can be elucidated with the Maori concept of *whanaungatanga*, which signifies a sense of family connection established through shared experiences, which provides a sense of belonging (Maori Dictionary, 2008). The importance of taking care of other people, which is captured in the concept of *whanaungatanga*, was visible in the vignettes. An example is the vignette included in the Top 7 episode of the first season, in which contestant Dave receives a birthday gift from the *NZ Idol* community. In this vignette we see people, not just the contestants but also members of the crew including the vocal coach, the dancing coach and the producers, contributing money towards the gift. Dave receives his gift at a surprise party which has been organised by *NZ Idol* and his family, and the vignette ends when he expresses his gratitude and his love for the *NZ Idol* contestants.

In contrast to the biographical vignettes of contestants going home, in which tensions between cultural diversity and nation building purposes in the end advanced a rosy picture of New Zealand as a multicultural society, the first season's additional vignettes established a unique sense of multicultural community between contestants from different backgrounds. This representation can be seen as a counterpoint to the representations of cultural diversity which cater for the interests of dominant groups.

Conclusion

The three seasons of *NZ Idol* have unquestionably been a success in terms of audience ratings. Whether the show has been successful in representing the ethnic and cultural diversity of contemporary New Zealand society is a more difficult question to answer. *NZ Idol* has offered something that its New Zealand predecessors in the reality TV genre have not, by featuring young performers from Maori, Pacific Island and Pakeha backgrounds. Nevertheless, ethnic and cultural diversity on the show is framed by the imminent prerequisite to address the wishes and aspirations of a mainstream audience. *NZ Idol* seems therefore caught up in processes of nation building that New Zealand television programmes in general have to respond to.

The core of the nation building agenda is a quest for a new sense of identity for New Zealand as a postcolonial society. Television in New Zealand has been one of the purveyors in this quest by providing "common narratives" that all citizens are supposed to relate to. Stephen Turner has labelled the dominant posture of national identity in New Zealand "passive-aggressive" (Turner, 2007: 88). He also argues that "local image-making is overdetermined, charged by a colonial history, and somewhat obsessively predisposed to self-representation" (Turner, 2004: 96). National funding agency NZ On Air's decree that funded television shows should "promote and foster the development of New Zealand's culture" seems to illustrate this.

It seems ironic that the *NZ Idol* producers have used the global *Idols* format to create a very New Zealand television programme. In spite of fears of standardisation and cultural imperialism that global television formats may elicit, *NZ Idol* reproduced existing ways of representing New Zealand localities in the biographical vignettes, for instance. This reinforces Waisboard's assertion that "[f]ormat television shows (. . .) organize experiences of the national" (2004: 372). The *Idols* format evidently left the local producers enough room to resort to tried and tested techniques of representation.

Applying for NZ On Air funding stimulated the initial producers to articulate how *NZ Idol* would provide audiences with opportunities to recognise themselves as belonging to a national community. Cultural diversity within the programme as well as the attraction of a multicultural youth audience were used as unique selling points in the funding proposal that was submitted to NZ On Air. Yet diverse representations were also seen as logically flowing from the *Idols* format, resulting in, according to the executive producer of the first season, "a happy coincidence of perspectives." The format prescribed equal treatment of all contestants, leading to biographical vignettes that all carried similar "weight." In terms of representation this means that contestants could perform a range of identities, as long as vignettes appeared positive and neutral. This in turn led to a range of "safe" multicultural representations, which worked well for the purposes of constructing a harmonious New Zealand identity.

The differences between the first and the second season of *NZ Idol*, both in terms of representations within the programme and the discourses producers used to talk about *NZ Idol*, reflect diverging approaches to ethnic and cultural diversity. While the producers of the second season did not think cultural background played a role in the programme at all and seemed to favour an individualistic competitive logic, the producers of the first season anticipated and capitalised on a culturally diverse group of contestants. The vignettes in which they were depicted as establishing their own unique sense of (multicultural) community disappeared in the second season. This seems regrettable, since these vignettes counterbalanced the framing of the going home stories, which either showcased a non-Pakeha culture to a general audience or featured lifestyles Pakeha New Zealanders can relate and aspire to. These additional vignettes also resonated with Maori views of life, which is refreshing in a context in which Maori culture is generally appropriated to create a colourful national identity and is therefore superseded by the bigger New Zealand nation building project.

References

Barclay, Barry (1990). *Our Own Image*. Auckland: Longman Paul.

Bell, Claudia (1996). *Inventing New Zealand: Everyday Myths of Pakeha Identity*. Auckland: Penguin Books.

Fremantle Media (2007). "*Idols*." www.fremantlemedia.com/our-programmes/view/Global+Hit+Formats/viewprogramme/Idols (accessed 26/11/2007).

Holmes, Su (2004). "'Reality Goes Pop!': Reality TV, Popular Music, and Narratives of Stardom in *Pop Idol*," *Television and New Media*, 5(2): 147–172.

Horrocks, Roger (2004). "Construction Site: Local Content on Television." In Roger Horrocks and Nick Perry (Eds), *Television in New Zealand: Programming the Nation* (pp. 272–285). Melbourne: Oxford University Press.

Huijser, Henk (2007). "*Australian Idol* versus Cronulla: Whither the Postcolonising Nation?" *New Zealand Journal of Media Studies*, 10(2): 131–143.

Jenkins, Henry (2006). *Convergence Culture: Where Old and New Media Collide*. New York: New York University Press.

Kavka, Misha (2004). "Reality Estate: Locating New Zealand Reality Television." In Roger Horrocks and Nick Perry (Eds), *Television in New Zealand: Programming the Nation* (pp. 222–239). Melbourne: Oxford University Press.

Kothari, Shuchi, Sarina Pearson and Nabeel Zuberi (2004). "Television and Multiculturalism in Aotearoa New Zealand." In Roger Horrocks and Nick Perry (Eds), *Television in New Zealand: Programming the Nation* (pp. 135–151). Melbourne: Oxford University Press.

Maori Dictionary (2008). "Whanaungatanga." www.maoridictionary.co.nz/index.cfm?dictionaryKeywords=whanaungatanga&n=1&idiom=&phrase=&proverb=&loan=&search.x=21&search.y=14 (accessed 08/10/2008).

Moran, Albert (1998). *Copycat Television: Globalisation, Program Formats and Cultural Identity.* Luton, UK: University of Luton Press.

NZ On Air (2008). "About Us." www.nzonair.govt.nz/about_us.php (accessed 18/09/2008).

O'Connor, Briar (2004). "The Dilemma of Souvenirs." In Claudia Bell and Steve Matthewman (Eds), *Cultural Studies in Aotearoa/New Zealand: Identity, Space and Place.* Melbourne: Oxford University Press (pp. 161–174).

Reijnders, Stijn, Gerard Rooijakkers and Liesbet van Zoonen (2007). "Community Spirit and Competition in *Idols*: Ritual Meanings of a TV Talent Quest." *European Journal of Communication*, 22(3): 275–292.

Smith, Jo (2006). "Parallel Quotidian Flows: Maori Television On Air." *New Zealand Journal of Media Studies*, 9(2): 27–35.

South Pacific Pictures (2003). *NZ Idol Is? NZ On Air Funding Proposal.* Auckland: South Pacific Pictures.

—— (2004). "18 Million Watch *NZ Idol*'. www.southpacificpictures.com/default,346.spp (accessed 10/01/07).

Stahl, Matthew Wheelock (2004). "A Moment Like This: *American Idol* and Narratives of Meritocracy." In Chris Washburne and Maiken Derno (Eds), *Bad Music: The Music We Love to Hate.* New York: Routledge (pp. 212–232).

Statistics New Zealand (2006). "QuickStats About Culture and Identity." www.stats.govt.nz/census/2006-census-data/quickstats-about-culture-identity/quickstats-about-culture-and-identity.htm (accessed 09/06/08).

Te Kawa a Maui Media Research Team (2005). *The Portrayal of Maori and Te Ao Maori in Broadcasting: The Foreshore and Seabed Issue.* Wellington: Broadcasting Standards Authority.

Turner, Stephen (2004). "Representing the Country: Adidas Aotearoa." In Roger Horrocks and Nick Perry (Eds), *Television in New Zealand: Programming the Nation* (pp. 90–102). Melbourne: Oxford University Press.

Turner, Stephen (2007). "Inclusive Exclusion: Managing Identity for the Nation's Sake in Aotearoa/New Zealand." *ARENA Journal*, 28: 87–106.

Waisbord, Silvio (2004). "McTV: Understanding the Global Popularity of Television Formats." *Television and New Media*, 5(4): 359–383.

White, Richard (1981). *Inventing Australia: Images and Identity 1688–1980.* Sydney: George Allen & Unwin.

Zemke-White, Kirsten (2004). "Keeping it Real (Indigenous): Hip Hop in Aotearoa as Community, Culture and Consciousness." In Claudia Bell and Steve Matthewman (Eds), *Cultural Studies in Aotearoa New Zealand: Identity, Space and Place* (pp. 205–228). Melbourne: Oxford University Press.

12

GLOBAL TELEVISION FORMATS IN AFRICA

Localizing *Idol*

Martin Nkosi Ndlela

Introduction

During the last decade, popular television formats have been replicated across the globe for local or regional consumption as program imports, adaptations, clones or imitations, raising questions on the possible ramifications of such cultural inflows. For Africa the international program flow and the influence of Western media content has been a contentious issue for decades, underlying the cultural imperialism thesis of the 1970s and 1980s, and the centre–periphery paradigms which conceptualized the series of dependency relationships. In African media research concepts like cultural colonialism, media imperialism, neocolonialism, Americanization, homogenization, have been used to denote the unequal flow and influence of Western media products in Africa. Within the framework of media globalization some scholars have even propounded a scenario of the emergency of a global culture mediated by the dominant Western media. The central issues in African media discussions have mainly revolved around the flow of finished media programs and their perceived detriment to local cultures and identities. What is missing in the African research literature is the attention to television formats, a phenomenon described by Keane et al. (2002) as a vehicle for localization, since what is imported is not the content itself, but a recipe for creating a local version. Global reality format shows thus create a new picture. As Hartley describes the new situation;

> the novelty of "reality" format shows from the business point of view is that a single (global) concept or format can be reproduced or "reversioned" in different (local) markets. The production company can profit from global distribution while the local audience actually sees a show that is to all intents and purposes their own.
>
> (Hartley 2006: 15)

Drawing on the contemporary scholarship on media globalization, this chapter analyses the adaptation of the global television reality format, *Pop Idol* in Africa. It looks at how a foreign format originating from the West is indigenized to suit local audiences and the challenges encountered in this adaptation. The chapter focuses on the cultural dimensions of format adaptation, seeking to unravel the extent to which the adaptation represents the local cultural context and claims to local ownership. It also discusses the relationship between global format and its localization, as represented by the nature of style, production patterns, content and presentation. Three show variants analyzed in this chapter are the *South African Idol* (Seasons 1, 2, 3, 4), the *Afrikaans Idol*, and the *West African Idol*. For analytical purposes four seasons of the national *South African Idol* are grouped together as one case, while the intra-national *Afrikaans Idol* and *West African Idol* are analyzed separately. The pan-African *African Idol* which covered southern and eastern Africa is not included in the case studies as it only premiered in April 2008 when the research was already under way. The analysis searches for global regularities and local specificities in the shows.

Global Television Format

The multifaceted globalization processes have had profound influences on the broadcasting landscapes in Africa. The intensification and effects of neoliberal globalization have dramatically changed the television system in Africa and greatly increased the interconnectivity of African television industries with the global television business. This interconnectivity happens through structural and institutional linkages which in turn enable the distribution of reality television formats. The core driving forces for reality television and format transfers in Africa are the political and economic changes since the late 1980s and developments in new information and communication technologies.

Perhaps the fundamental factor behind the intensified interconnectedness, which has seen the growth of global media-related markets in Africa, is the wave of political and economic liberalization that swept across the continent in the late 1980s and early 1990s. The rapid transformation of the broadcasting industry in Africa can be attributed to the fact that many governments underwent a dramatic democratization process during this period, thus paving way for a liberal, multi-party political framework. They also adopted neoliberal economic policies such as market deregulation, decentralization, and relaxation of foreign-ownership regulations. The deregulation policies opened way for the expansion of commercial television companies. Economic liberalization also facilitated the entry of transnational corporations seeking to enhance profits in the untapped African market. The radical political and economic reforms affected the broadcasting systems by transforming them from monopolies of centralized and government controlled institutions to plural and diversified landscapes with independent and market-oriented players. The underlying philosophy behind these changes is that media freedom and diversity are essential to social and economic development, as well as to the development of democracy.[1] A major, visible structural change in the broadcasting landscape in Africa is the shift from government monopolies to a three-tier broadcasting system comprising of public service broadcasting, commercial broadcasting and community broadcasting. A listing of television stations across Africa is indicative of the steady growth in broadcasting liberalization, with several countries boasting more than five television stations.[2] There are, however, still a number of barriers constraining the development of broadcasting in Africa. The size of the country, its political framework and level of economic development are determinant factors on the number of television stations available in the country. As Opoku-Mensah (1998) has observed, political and economic barriers continue to impede the development and implementation of sound broadcasting policies, policies which promote both the independence and diversity of broadcasters.

Another fundamental force behind the transformation of television industries in Africa is the developments in new information and communication technologies. New technologies have reinvigorated African television, enabling national broadcasters to increase accessibility, commercialize and expand their programming services, as well as spurring commercial sector innovations. Satellite television has been relatively more successful than cable television, which is hampered mainly by poor infrastructures. While satellite technology has increased the number of channels and services available in Africa, it is mainly accessible to the wealthy in urban areas. Nevertheless, several satellite television initiatives are being explored across the African continent. The South African-based multinational media conglomerate, Naspers, is the main provider of pay television in Sub-Saharan Africa. Its subsidiary, Multichoice-owned Digital Satellite Television (DStv) is the largest satellite television provider in Sub-Saharan Africa. French-owned Canal+ is the main provider of satellite television in French-speaking Africa through its subsidiary Canal Horizons. Other providers include MyTVAfrica, which is owned by Dubai-based Strong Technologies, the British-based Gateway Communications's GTV and the Nigerian-based High Television (HiTv). The entrance of new players into the broadcasting system in Africa has created a multi-channel landscape.

The emergence of a multi-channel landscape has created demand for new content and audiences with enough capital to constitute niche media markets. As Baltruschat (2002) has noted, new program format and genre hybridization are linked to an increasingly fragmented and competitive film and television market. Format transfers thus fill the gaps as alternative to expensive program acquisitions. Format transfers invariably address the problem of content, which has dodged the television industry in Africa since inception. As noted by Tedros (1962: 189) "the problem of programming and financing is extremely acute in Africa, . . . since there are no established professional cinema, drama or theatre industries in the continent." He further argued that until such program-producing industries were created, broadcasters in Africa will be obliged to make extensive use of foreign "canned" programs which may appeal to Western viewers but are often of little or no interest to Africans. However, there has been a notable change in the consumption of "canned" programs, because Africa is today producing and consuming its own programs, albeit formatted programming. The neoliberal reforms in Africa and developments in new technologies have opened up opportunities for African television industries to operate within the global television format business framework.

A global format business model is slowly transforming the content of television in Africa, which in the past relied mainly on imported programs from other parts of the world, often reflecting the postcolonial linkages. French Africa has relied heavily on French language productions or adaptations, while Portuguese Africa has found solace in Portuguese language productions and adaptations, and finally the English speaking countries have been avid consumers of English language programs mainly from U.S.A., U.K. and Australia. Common to all these consumption goods is their origins in the Western world. New developments within have witnessed a steady increase of inter-African program exchanges, with Nigerians and South Africans attaining more influence in English speaking Africa, partly due to their global corporate communication linkages.

While initially consumption patterns followed what Tedros (1962) called importation of "canned" programs, the situation on the ground has fundamentally changed to format transfer, adaptations, cloning and imitations. Formats are now used as templates for local production. As Moran (1998) has noted, formats are traded around the world, with the expectation (or assumption) that the local buyer has merely to add local talent to a predetermined structure. This creates a scenario whereby "a dozen media companies are able to do business worldwide by selling the same idea, and audiences seem to be watching national variations of the same show" (Waisbord 2004: 359). Formats, as Moran and Keane (2004: 13) has noted, have become "the key to understanding the changing relationship between peripheral media systems and the distribution dominance of U.S.A. (Hollywood)." Referring to the Asian growth areas, Keane has observed that television formats have emerged over the past years as an exemplary mode of flexible production within television systems outside of the Western hemisphere, traveling along routes set by new global media missionaries. Adoption of television formats is increasingly becoming a strategy for television networks with regional or global expansion ambitions. This strategy is deeply embedded in the market and is driven by a desire to capture audience categories at the top echelons of the Living Standard Measurements (LSM).

M-NET and Reality TV Formats

A South African pay-TV channel, M-Net (Electronic Media Network), a subsidiary of Naspers, has established itself as a major player in the adaptation of international formats. M–Net's role in the global television franchise business can be understood in light of South Africa's outward looking media industries. Broadcasting reforms in post-apartheid South Africa have closely followed international trends and reflect an embracement of neoliberal communication policies. Anchored in a relatively stable neoliberal environment, South African media conglomerates like Naspers have exploited their advantaged position by expanding into the less tapped African market spanning areas in Internet, pay TV, print and technology. Motivated by capitalist expansionist agendas, South African-based pay-TV services providers like M–Net have penetrated television markets across Sub-Saharan Africa. With this base M–Net is in a much more advantageous position to acquire national and international television format franchises. Another advantage is that South Africa boasts one of the largest economies in Africa, is home to multinational companies, and has one of the best developed infrastructures in Sub-Saharan Africa. Thus South Africa is itself a market. M–Net has been able to broadcast to 1.23 million subscribers in 41 African countries, bringing to its subscribers a number of original international reality program adaptations as well as world-renowned formats such as *Big Brother*, *Idol*, and *Deal or No Deal*.

Idol has undoubtedly been one of the most successful format adaptions by M–Net. Originating from the London-based Fremantle Media, which is itself a unit of German-based giant Bertelsmann, the interactive reality television show *Pop Idol* has grown to stand as one of the clearest manifestations of globalized television formats. The music talent search program *Idol* has through national and international franchises acquired a global reach, making it one of the most popular television format franchises in the world. According to the CKx[3] website, local adaptations of *Idol* collectively air in more than 100 countries around the world. In Africa M–Net holds franchise rights for the program format and has since 2002 produced a number of series: *South African Idol 1* (2002), *South African Idol 2* (2003), *South African Idol 3* (2005), *South African Idol 4* (2007), *South African Afrikaans Idol* (2006), *West African Idol* (2007), and *African Idol* (2008).

South African Idol: Songs, Repertoire and Audiences

Focusing on both production and consumption processes in the adaptation of *South African Idol*, paradoxes and inherent contradictions of the global and local emerge. *Idol* is produced locally for local audiences but within the global television format confines. As an adaptation of a global format *South African Idol* still has to contend with local realities such as linguistic and cultural diversity in South Africa. It also has to contend with contestants' and audience perceptions of "idols," pop genre, choice of songs, repertoire and presentation styles.

South African Idol attracted thousands of pop idol hopefuls from different cultural and economic backgrounds. The unifying factor is the pop music genre and the quest for fame and stardom amongst youthful contestants. Youth across South

Africa share an overriding aspiration for fame and an insatiable need to idolize film and pop stars. The globalized nature of media content distribution leads to a situation where certain pop stars are idolized across the globe. The understanding of pop music in the South African context is aptly described by *Idol* judge Randall Abrahams as

> Popular music that is most often sung in English and broadcast on commercial radio stations throughout the country. A number of contestants do enter the competition and perform songs in local languages but these tunes are usually well known and melodic therefore not straying too far from the broad sound of pop music.
>
> (Interview, 02/07/2008).

The logic of commercial radio stations' music choices therefore provides a guide to what would be regarded as pop music. The English language medium through which most of the commercial radio stations in South Africa are based becomes the natural language for contestants. For South Africa this linguistic choice seems natural given the extensive use of English in the media, business, education and government. Even though the country has 11 official languages, English and Afrikaans are still the dominant official languages. Afrikaans' influence is to a certain extent waning. African languages like Zulu and Xhosa are widely used by Africans but as noted by Spencer (1985), South Africa's African languages apparently have little symbolic value to either their speakers or to those with whom their speakers come into contact. One contention as noted by Thobeka Mda (1997) is whether, with the advent of Black majority rule in South Africa, African languages deserve their newly elevated status as official languages. African languages seem to lack the perceived advantages associated with English. For media critics, the hegemony of English is a manifestation of cultural imperialism, given that English is today regarded as one of the vehicles through which American or Western values are spread throughout the world.

While during the audition phases, entrants could sing from a wide spectrum of music in both English and local languages, it is apparent what kind of pop idols the producers and judges were looking for, what kind of idols entrants wanted to be and what kind of idols audiences were looking for. Thus there was also a confluence of understanding between the contestants, producers and audiences. Song selection in all four *South African Idol* seasons represents a who's-who of the Western pop charts and the choices are biased towards English. A quick scan of the songs sung by the contestants in, for example, *Idol 4* reveals this tendency. Popular choices include well known pop icons like Van Morrison, U2, Seal, The Beatles, Luther Vandross, The Pretenders, Beyoncé, Christina Aguilera, Shania Twain, Mary Mary, George Michael, Bon Jovi, Stevie Wonder, Riahanna, Whitney Houston, Abba, Chris Isaac, Bryan Adams, Toni Braxton, Craig David, Jesse McCartney, All 4 One, Gloria Estefan, and Frank Sinatra.

In *Idol 4*'s thematic session "Divas and Crooners" for the Top 9 contestants, where contestants were allowed to select the smoothest, swingiest, and most romantic songs of the modern repertoire, the list produced was predominantly American. Perhaps the nearest *Idol* came to the local or national was when Top 7 contestants performed under the thematic session, "The Best of South Africa" which featured groups and singers like Mango Groove, Jamali, Brenda Fassie, Prime Circle, Vicky Sampson, Just Jinjer and Ringo Madlingozi. In Top 6, the contestants riveted to Western pop icons like John Mayer, Maroon 5, Bryan Adams, Pussycat Dolls, Sean Kingston, Lemar, Pink, Rihanna and Beyoncé. The trend continues in the choices of the Top 5 finalists.[4] In the stage where the Top 4 contestants were asked to choose two songs from their own music idols, pop stars like Celine Dion, Christina Aguilera, Creedence Clearwater Revival, Anastacia and Chaka Khan were chosen.[5] The American pop charts also dominated the Top 3 phase where contestants had to perform three songs: one chosen by the judges, one chosen by the producers and an unplugged song of their choice. This song selection, either done by judges or by contestants themselves shows the influence of Western pop music, more particularly American pop music, on the youth in Africa. These choices are indicative of the notions of celebrity produced in national contexts like South Africa. The judges' own intention is to produce young stars who are accepted in the "pop" marketplace (*Idol* judge Abrahams, interview 02/07/2008), and at the same time not to produce copycats (*Idol* judge Penny Lebyane, News24 interview, 06/06/2002). However, by choosing these songs *Idol* aspirants show signs of copycatting, or emulation of *American Idol* and the British *Pop Idol*.

The type of song chosen, the dress, and the prizes are all symbolic of Western consumerist culture. As described on the M-Net website, the *Idol 4* winner, Jody Williams

> sang her new single, *Love is All Around* clutching her glamorous strapless dress against her body. She has also performed Luther Vandross'[6] *Dance With my Father*, and her songs were recorded and distributed by one of the world's largest recording companies, SonyBMG.

The package of prizes awarded to the *South African Idol* 2007 winner and runners up illustrates the Western orientation of the program too: a recording contract with SonyBMG; a brand new customized Citroen "*Idol* Edition" C2 1.6VTS; a PSK-915 Docking Station; a portable DVD player; a laptop with internet connectivity; an MP3 player; a car navigation system; an Xbox 360; vouchers from popular magazines; a wireless handheld microphone; and free hair care and skin care. All these gadgets are symbols of global popular culture. The winner also got a personal videotaped message from global pop music icon Celine Dion, and not from a South African star.

To some South Africans therefore, the song selection, style and performance in the *Idol* competition obscured the South Africanness of the show. The shows were more a celebration of the global than the local. A comment by a viewer in a discussion forum in the SA Rocks blog aptly describes how *Idol* was perceived in certain segments;

> "I watched *Idols* last night. I wish I could say it was the local one, but I truly feel like it isn't local at all.
>
> I watched one of the young Black female singers belt out an awesome rendition of a Mary J. Blige song. There was nothing individual, local or fantastic about this song or the *Idols* rendition. It was American, it was generic, it was boring, bland and unoriginal.
>
> South Africa has so many amazing artists, songs and personalities. I saw none of this in Tender's performance last night. What I saw were contestants trying to be as American as possible. I wanted South African, I wanted new, fresh, contemporary artists and instead I got old, out dated, American rubbish.
>
> Is this what the producers are asking for? Is this what the make-up artists are after? Who is defining what the look of the contestants should be? What is wrong with these people trying to create the newest South African copycat of an American idiot?"[7]

The issues raised by this commentator are striking. He/she questions how would-be-stars have no local musicians as idols, but rather have an inclination towards American music icons. He/she sees nothing local in the costumes donned by the *Idol* contestants. On a similar note, *Idol* judge Penny Lebyane has argued that, "the public needs to realize that we're not looking for copycats here. Many South African artists don't make it in New York or London. They come back because they are unoriginal, they are copycats."[8]

The issues discussed above typify the complexities involved in the adaptation of international television formats like *Pop Idol* into a local phenomenon. To what extent was *Idol* a representation of South African culture and identity? Issues of identity in South Africa invariably feature ethnic tensions that have bedeviled the country for many decades. Therefore when it comes to the audience, a crucial element of *Idol*'s format, the adaptation of *Idol* in South Africa requires an analysis of the socio-political context. According to mid-2007 estimates from Statistics South Africa,[9] the country has a diverse population of approximately 47 million, of which Africans constitute 38 million (79.6 percent), Whites 4.3 million (9.1 percent), Coloreds (mixed race) 4.2 million (8.9 percent) and Asians 1.2 million (2.5 percent). The African population is culturally and linguistically diverse. South Africa has just emerged from decades of racial segregation, prejudice and oppression. The economic consequences of apartheid are still manifested in the living standards, with Whites occupying the top levels in the Living Standard Measurements, and thus forming approximately 80 percent of M-Net's subscriber base in a country with an 80 percent Black population. It is primarily due to this imbalance in audience ratio that adopted formats like *Idol*, *Big Brother*, and *Who Wants to Be a Millionaire?* have been beleaguered by controversies. Pitout (2005), in the case of *Big Brother South Africa*, has noted how the producers attempted to customize the location to give it a South African flavor, only to emerge with a setting whose major signifiers were that of a typical White lifestyle.

In a contest like *Idol* where the winner is selected on the basis of audience telephone calls and Short Message Services (SMS), the voting population is crucial for contestants. In relation to *South African Idol 1*,[10] Gladwin (2002) noted that the demographic of the voting public was influencing the results. According to News24, the audience "kept voting off the most talented contestants—who just happened to be Black."[11] The situation became more acute when towards the final the audience had to choose between a White and a Black contestant. The contest was won by a White contestant, Heinz Winckler, and expectedly drew criticism from social commentators. As reported by the BBC, some commentators argued that race was a determining factor, and as aptly put by *The Star* journalist, Gaynor Kast, "some sections of our society still think in Black and White and *Idol* proved once again that there are people who see colour."[12] The *Sowetan* newspaper described the show as a "racial fiasco."[13] The issue of racism dogged most of the *South African Idol* seasons.

Accusations of racism were also leveled against *Idol* judges. In *Idol 1* (2002), judges like Penny Lebyane and Randall Abrahams were accused of being racist when they criticized White contestants.[14] As Lebyane puts it herself, "people are saying that I haven't been consistent with my comments about the White contestants and that because I'm Black, I'm making negative comments about the White contestants."[15] Another Black judge, Mara Louw-Thomson, was accused of favoring Blacks by viewers in the M-Net message and bulletin boards. Mara, who had judged in the 2003, 2005 and 2007 seasons, argued that, "in the previous series Black people accused me of favoring White children. Now the Whites are accusing me of favoring the Blacks. It's a battle that I can't win."[16] The accusations of bias and racism from the audience are a reflection of the nature of the audience watching them. As noted by Carl Fischer, M-Net's head of local production, "reality programs like this actually say more about the community that watches them."[17]

The problems arising from the South African version of *Idol* highlights the importance of context in the adaptation of formats. Adapting the formats entails much more than simple adding local talent to prescribed structures. It manifests the audience's relation to the global and to the local and their expectation of what a "pop idol" should be like. To some sections of the population the question was to what extent did the adaptation of the *Idol* format meet with the local, while to others the question was the extent to which it resembled the original format. The South African *Idol* show can be construed as a clear demonstration of the uneasy relationship between the local and global.

Afrikaans Idol—Emphasizing Localness

Afrikaans Idol invokes a new dimension in the contradictions between the local and the global. Unlike the outward looking *South African Idol*, *Afrikaans Idol* was more inward looking, more ingrained in the local Afrikaner culture. This *Idol* variant represents a fundamental departure from the South African *Idol*. While it keeps the same format as the international version of *Idol*, it is named after a linguistic group in South Africa, the Afrikaans, instead of national or regional variants common with *Idol* franchises. It was designed for Afrikaans speakers in South Africa, Namibia and small populations across Southern Africa. It was hosted in Afrikaans, thus replacing English, the lingua franca of *Idol* variants in Africa. *Afrikaans Idol* is also unique because it replaced all the *South African Idol* judges and program hosts in the production processes. Furthermore it was distributed through M-Net's sister company KykNet—a solely Afrikaans television network.

Afrikaans Idol has thus been celebrated by its audiences as a true representation of Afrikaans language and culture. For those concerned with the preservation of Afrikaans language and Afrikaans music, *Afrikaans Idol* is a clear manifestation of sustained efforts to reject domination and marginalization of Afrikaans in the new South Africa. From a cultural imperialism perspective this resistance can be conceived as rejection of cultural imperialism exerted through the medium of English language, and Western pop music. It is not surprising therefore that the headline sponsor of KykNet's *Afrikaans Idol* was the Afrikaans Language and Cultural Organization (ATKV), an organization that has since 1930 played a crucial role in protecting and promoting Afrikaans language and culture.

Afrikaans Idol should be analyzed within the South African language policies which have lately seen the fall of Afrikaans as a privileged language, although it remains one of the official languages. Historically, Afrikaans is an Indo-European language derived mainly from Dutch, but nominally bred in South Africa. It has over time emphasized its uniqueness and difference from Dutch and has undergone a major lexical development to fully achieve official language status in 1925, thereby relegating Dutch to foreign language status (Mda 1997). Under the Afrikaner-dominated governments, Afrikaans was promoted as one of the major languages of instruction (alongside English) at schools for English, Afrikaners, Coloreds and Indians. The Afrikaner-dominated governments also had a conceited policy to impose Afrikaans on Africans. Such a policy was, however, bound to fail because to the Black population (who preferred English), Afrikaans was considered the language of the oppressor due to its association with apartheid. Attempts by the apartheid government to impose Afrikaans on the Black population through a decree—the Afrikaans Medium Education Decree of 1974 —led to the infamous Soweto Uprising of 1976, where protesting Black school-children were brutally killed by the police. Afrikaans has thus been a source of contention in the language politics of South Africa.

The fall of apartheid also saw the fall of Afrikaans' dominance, although it remains one of the country's 11 official languages. In practice English is the main official language, while Afrikaans and the African languages have a restricted usage. Afrikaans speakers resent the dominance of English. From a superior status, Afrikaans has shrunk to a category whose survival depends on the constitutional protection and enforcement of "minority rights."[18] As noted in an open letter sent to President Mbeki in 1999 by a prominent group of Afrikaans-speaking South Africans, there is a growing perception of the progressive marginalization of the language, alienation of Afrikaans universities, and affirmative actions which impact negatively on Afrikaans-speaking people. As noted by Mda (1997):

> Afrikaners argue that Afrikaans and Afrikaners were born and bred in South Africa and thus have a claim to indigenous status. Although the Afrikaans language was privileged along with English during apartheid era, Afrikaans speakers in the present era have demanded protection of the rights of their language as an indigenous language and have protested against the English language, which they deem a "foreign" European language, being accorded a superior status and thereby dominating the local languages, including Afrikaans.

This *Idol* variant should thus be understood within the post-apartheid linguistic discourses centered upon the preservation of Afrikaans language and hence Afrikaaner cultural identity. It reflects concerted attempts to localize a global format by asserting the cultural identity claims of Afrikaans speakers.

While academics like Giliomee (2004) have predicted the demise of Afrikaans in public life, Afrikaners still represent a niche cosmopolitan audience. The majority of Afrikaners occupy top levels in Living Standard Measurements (LSM), thus making them economically attractive for subscription-based television like Multichoice. Afrikaners still enjoy enormous economic power, which in turn has ensured the survival of Afrikaans media.

In terms of songs and repertoire, *Afrikaans Idol* differs remarkably from other *Idol* variants in Africa. While in audition, entrants could sing in any language; after reaching the Top 100, they had to sing in Afrikaans only, which also implied that they also sang Afrikaans songs.[19] The show thus featured top Afrikaans songs like *Kaapse Draai* by Nadine, *In Die Middel* by Irene van Wyk, *Keer og Keer* by Georgia, *Agter Elke man* by Steve Hofmeyr and *Blouberg se strand* by Laurika Rauch. The show also had a thematic section for "alternative Afrikaans hits." Alternative Afrikaans music has its roots in the late 1980s where youth started an underground music movement to express their dissent against Afrikaner culture. As noted by Jury (1996) their music expressed a radical non-acceptance of Afrikaner nationalist ideology and offered a critical re-appraisal of hegemonic Afrikaner culture. *Afrikaans Idol* can thus be conceived as a celebration of Afrikaans history and culture. Nevertheless global regularities are present in *Afrikaans Idol*, first being the customized format itself, notions of celebrity and global media production. But within this global media are strong local specificities as reflected in language, songs, repertoire and reception. *Afrikaans Idol* was hugely successful in terms of ratings, interactive use of communication tools and audience appeal.

In the post-apartheid racial categorizations, there has been a concerted effort by White Afrikaners to incorporate previously excluded people of mixed race (coloureds), who mainly have Afrikaans as their first language. In *Afrikaans Idol* the identity constructions centered mainly on linguistic affinity rather than race. Nevertheless the race issue surfaced in forum discussions and in the media coverage of the *Afrikaans Idol*, its judges and contestants. Conversations about race issues are inescapable in post-apartheid South Africa.

West African Idol: Adaptation or Emulation

West African Idol is yet another strategy by M-Net to adapt the international format. Aired in M-Net Africa in 2007, *West African Idol* sought to incorporate diverse countries throughout the West African region. With judges Abrewa Nana Dorcas (Ghanaian), Dede Mabiakwu (Nigerian) and Dan Foster (American), *West African Idol* ambitiously sought to find the best pop talent in the region. In the West African context, what should localization of *Idol* entail? Some would argue that it should entail the use of African languages in the show, given that language is a vital element of music, as well as cultural identity. However, West African languages are vast and diverse, and are either underdeveloped or simply marginalized in the mainstream media where European languages compete against each other for domination. European languages thus offer compromise lingua francas as official languages in most countries. European languages, however, also have their variations across the regions of Africa. For example, English has its variations such as the *pidgin* English spoken widely across West Africa. The use of European languages, especially English, can therefore be a hindrance to talented non-English speakers or second language speakers. Due to this language restriction, and despite its name, the *West African Idol* turned out to be more or less a Ghanaian and Nigerian *Idol*, and consequently an Anglophone West African show. Auditions took place in the Anglophone cities of Lagos (Nigeria), Calabar (Nigeria), Abuja (Nigeria) and Accra (Ghana). This may also be attributed to the fact that Ghana and Nigeria have the most M-Net subscribers in West Africa. They are also economic powerhouses of West Africa.

In terms of songs, styles and language, the show did not differ much from *South African Idol*. Contestants sang most of the songs in English, and chose songs popularized by American singers like Celine Dion and Michael Jackson. Contestants also chose American pop icons as their favorite artists. As noted in one forum discussion:

> I observe that ALL the contestants were singing songs in English. I think something is terribly skewed here . . . aren't there beautiful African songs that can showcase a singer's talent???. And every single contestant on the website cited NOT one African Artist as their "Favorite Artistes."[20]

Lack of localization in the production has been cited as a compromising factor in *West African Idol*. Judges were accused by some sections of the audience of emulating their *American Idol* counterparts, thus digressing from the local context. The judges dismissed some contestants because of heavy African accents. As one blogger noted in the discussion forums:

> Was it just me or is "International Standard," American. Some of those guys could sing but the Nigerian or Ghanaian accent stood out, was that bad? My people, even Americans have accents, what is this? Are we all not speaking this one English?:
>
> (posted April 4, 2007)[21]

The paradox is that the judges who were dismissing contestants on the basis of African accents shared the same accents. One commentator in the discussion forums noted that Abrewa Nana (a Ghanaian musician) had the audacity to dismiss contestants on the basis of accent. "She was heavily accented and yet had the guts to disqualify people for not having the American accent."[22]

The issue of language, as already discussed in the context of South African versions of *Idol*, alienates *West African Idol* from its context, seeking instead to mask the African personality, culture and music while preferring Americanized Africans with a global linguistic appeal. The search for the *West African Idol* could thus be construed as a search for the most Americanized aspirant. Use of English can arguably be perceived as a perpetuation of cultural hegemony, given that English is the bearer of Western culture and cultural imperialism in Africa. Nevertheless English is the language of business, education and administration in Ghana and Nigeria, and most M-Net subscribers are English speakers. As Osborn (2007)[23] has argued in the case of Nigeria, English is a status symbol, "the better you speak, the more you uphold your social-economic status in the society."

Pertaining to the issue of race, which manifested itself in *South African Idol*, the West African version experienced no such problem. This is primarily because Ghana and Nigeria do not have a politically and socially constructed racialization as is the case with South Africa. Racialization in South Africa was for decades aided by the elaborate ideological framework of apartheid. Race relations and race consciousness are much more acute in South Africa than in the West African case. Identity politics in countries like Nigeria is manifested more through ethnic, religious, communal and regional constructions. Therefore participants, audiences and judges in *West African Idol* were likely to be more conscious of other identity constructions than race.

Emerging Issues: Globalization or Localization

In adapting *Idol* to the African context several issues emerge, and amongst these is the phenomenon of globalization versus localization. Put in other words, "how can the global be local?" (Eriksen 2005: 25). Localizing a television format would entail a certain degree of adaptation, to meet the requirements of a specific linguistic or cultural context. Localization of a television format is, however, substantially complex, as it may entail drastic rethinking of the format design, which in turn might result in a format substantially different from the originating culture. Moran (2004) observes that there is a recognition that the original set of ingredients and their organization may have to be varied in relation to aspects of the new television setting such as production resources, channel image, and buyer preferences. Three *Idol* variants, *South African Idol*, *Afrikaans Idol*, and *West African Idol*, illustrate the complexity and magnitude of adaptation that Moran describes.

The adaptation of *Idol* in Africa had to confront a number of problems. The demographic of the audience is so complex and heterogeneous that finding common ground was a mammoth task. For example, given that audience voting is crucial in the selection of winners, issues of multiculturalism, tribalism, and favoritism posed questions of fairness, especially in racially or tribally divided societies. What criteria should be applied to defining the musical content? What standards should be used to judge the best talent? There are many differences between African and Western music (format origin) when it comes to basic elements of music like rhythm, melody, harmony and texture—elements which are essential aspects of a musical performance.

Another issue that arises in the adaptation of the *Idol* format is the genre. *Idol* is based on pop music, an imprecise category of modern music not based on any genre. It is a type of music defined by market considerations, the number of sales or performances in a given period. Given the diversity in Africa there is no distinctly African pop music. At any given time there is a wide range of music which can be called African pop due to its popularity and commercial success. Kwaito music in South Africa, urban groove in Zimbabwe and highlife in Ghana are good examples representing a wide range of hybrid urban forms which blend elements of Western pop and disco with local features. The *Idol* adaptations, with the exception of *Afrikaans Idol*, do not seem to be associated with this kind of "African pop music." Rather, *Idol* defines pop music by the degree of inclination towards Western pop music—"basically that of rock and its variants including disco, heavy metal, punk rock and rap which spread throughout the world and became the standard musical idiom for young people in many countries."[24] This is the same music that dominates the playlists of commercial radio and television stations.

Conclusion

It is evident from the *Idol* variants presented above that in the case of television formats, globalization processes have played a big role in format transfers. However, it is not just the format that gets transferred, as content might to a certain extent reflect the Western culture. As Lee (2004) argues, the global circulation of Western-centered, or more specifically, American-centered cultural products, contributes to the formation and dissemination of a global shared culture. The emerging global culture, as Berger (2003) notes, is a Western and indeed American provenance, penetrating the rest of the world at both elite and popular levels. Television formats like *Idol*, and their expansion into Africa, look for the existence of niche-media markets and a cosmopolitan audience with a truly global outlook. They represent a global cultural production that can be enjoyed and appropriated by young people in diverse cultural contexts. It is yet to be seen whether the attempts to localize formats will translate to an expansion of the creativity within the local production industries.

In the context of globalization, how would these format-driven initiatives draw leverage from the global templates for the benefit of not only the niche markets but also the general television market? Television broadcasters in Africa would have to tap into the cultural registers of their sophisticated and fragmented audiences. It is a challenging task, given that certain sections of the audiences have an inclination towards an American-like *Idol*, while some view this adaption as cultural imperialism. Against this evident fragmentation of audience, the global television format model is clearly a site of contestation between the countervailing discourses of the local and the global, of cultural heterogenization and homo-genization. To those occupied with the cultural imperialism thesis, the *Idol* adaptions, with the exception of *Afrikaans Idols*, were nothing more than the idolization of American pop culture, and did not do much for the promotion of African idols and African music. The choice of styles, songs and language are all ingredients which set the *Idol* adaptations apart from their context. *Afrikaans Idols* stands out as an exception, in that it promoted Afrikaner idols and music. It deliberately detached itself from English-dominated pop music. *South African Idol* illustrated what Bernstein has described as South Africa's "long standing, close connections with Western countries" and a country which therefore "has long been subject to globalizing forces emanating from Britain, the United States, and elsewhere" (Bernstein 2000: 185). Adaptation of television formats like *Idol* show a country that is open to many kinds of globalization forces and that is keen to establish itself as a strong international trading link to the rest of Africa. The *Idol* adaptations in Africa demonstrated the South African media industry's affinity with the economic alliances within the global media industries. In contrast to program importations, the format adaptations, despite encounters with certain issues of the national, ethnic, regional or global, have the capacity for hybridization, thereby circumventing questions of cultural imperialism.

Notes

1 Windhoek Declaration on Promoting an Independent and Pluralistic African Press.
2 These countries include Nigeria, South Africa, Cameroon, DRC, Ivory Coast, Ghana, Kenya, Senegal.
3 http://ir.ckx.com/
4 "Songs, Style & the Jet Set," M-net news 16/11/ 2007 at www.mnet.co.za/idols/news/news_article.asp?Id=350 (accessed 30/06/2008).
5 "Idols Take on their Idols—Vote Now!" www.mnet.co.za/idols/news/news_article.asp?Id=357 (accessed 30/07/2008).
6 Luther Vandross , an American musician.
7 http://sarocks.co.za/2007/10/22/lets-discuss-idols-south-africa/
8 www.news24.com/News24/Archive/0,,2-1659_1204906,00.html (Has racism marred SA idols? (accessed 30/01/2008).
9 www.statssa.gov.za/
10 www.realitynewsonline.com/cgi-bin/ae.pl?mode=1&article=article1964.art&page=1 (accessed 1 February 2008).
11 www.news24.com/News24/Archive/0,,2-1659_1204906,00.html ("Has Racism Marred SA Idols?") (accessed 30/01/2008).
12 http://news.bbc.co.uk/1/hi/entertainment/tv_and_radio/2065167.stm (accessed 30/01/ 2008).
13 www.buzzle.com/editorials/6-16-2002-20565.asp (accessed 14/07/08).
14 *Guardian Unlimited* (Guardian Newspapers, 2008) Published: 6/16/2002 (accessed 30/01/2008), see also www.news24.com/News24/Archive/0,,2-1659_1204906,00.html ("Has Racism Marred SA Idols") (accessed 30/01/2008).
15 www.news24.com/News24/Archive/0,,2-1659_1195831,00.html ("What Makes a Racist?") (accessed 30/01/2008).
16 www.news24.com/City_Press/News/0,7515,186-187_1809741,00.html ("Idols Fans Accuse Mara Louw of Bias") (accessed 30/01/2008).
17 Ibid.
18 See for example the UNESCO World Languages Report at www.salanguages.com/unesco/afrikaans.htm
19 www.tonight.co.za/index.php?fSectionId=360&fArticleId=3178051 ("KykNet Hosts Search for an Afrikaans Idol").
20 www.nigeriavillagesquare.com/board/blog-feeds/36782-idols-west-africa.html
21 www.africanpath.com/p_blogEntry.cfm?blogEntryID=505
22 www.africanpath.com/p_blogEntry.cfm?blogEntryID=505
23 Don Osborn, "African Languages: How English Threatens Indigenous Languages (Nigeria)," Monday July 9, 2007. (www.mail-archive.com/africanlanguages@yahoogroups.com/msg00544.html (Retrieved 15.04.2009).
24 *Britannica Concise Encyclopedia.*

References

Baltruschat, Doris. 2002. "Globalization and International TV and Film Co-productions: In Search of New Narratives." Paper presented at the conference Media in Transition 2: Globalization and Convergence, May 10–12, at MIT, Cambridge, Massachusetts, U.S.A.

Berger, Peter L. 2003. "The Cultural Dynamics of Globalization," in *Many Globalizations: Cultural Diversity in the Contemporary World*, ed. Peter L. Berger and Samuel P. Huntington. Oxford: Oxford University Press.

Berger, Peter L., and Huntington, Samuel P. 2003. *Many Globalizations: Cultural Diversity in the Contemporary World*. Oxford: Oxford University Press.

Bernstein, A. 2000. "Globalization, Culture, and Development. Can South Africa be More than an Offshoot of the West?" in *Many Globalizations: Cultural Diversity in the Contemporary World*, ed. Peter L. Berger and Samuel P. Huntington. Oxford: Oxford University Press.

Eriksen, Thomas H. 2005. "How Can the Global Be Local? Islam, the West and the Globalisastion of Identity Politics," in *Media and Glocal Change. Rethinking Communication for Development*, ed. Oscar Hemer and Thomas Tufte. Göteberg, Sweden: Nordicom.

Featherstone, Mike (ed.) 1990. *Global Culture. Nationalism, Globalization and Modernity*. London: Sage Publications.

Giliomee, Hermann. 2004. "The Rise and Possible Demise of Afrikaans as Public Language," *Nationalism and Ethnic Politics* 10(1): 25–58.

Gladwin, Andrew. 2002. "South African *Idols*—mired in controversy," www.realitynewsonline.com/cgi-bin/ae.pl?mode=1&article=article1964.art&page=1 October 7, 2002 (accessed 1 February 2008).

Hartley, John. 2006. "Television and Globalisation," in *Tele-Visions: Concepts and Methods in Television Studies*, ed. Glen Creeber. London: British Film Institute.

Jin, Dal Yong. 2007. "Transformation of the World Television System under Neoliberal Globalization, 1983 to 2003," *Television and New Media* 8: 179.

Jury, Brendan. 1996. "Boys to Men: Afrikaans Alternative Popular Music 1986–1990," *African Languages and Culture* 9(2): 99–109.

Keane, M., Fung, A. and Moran, M. 2007. *New Television, Globalisation, and the East Asian Cultural Imagination*. Hong Kong: Hong Kong University Press.

Lee, Dong-hoo. 2004. "A Local Mode of Programme Adaptation. South Korea in the Global Television Format Business," in *Television Across Asia. Television Industries, Programme Formats and Globalization*, ed. Albert Moran and Michael Keane. London: Routledge.

Mda, Thobeka V. 1997. "Issues in the Making of South Africa's Language in Education Policy," *Journal of Negro Education* 66(4): 366–375.

Moran, Albert. 1998. *Copycat TV: Globalization, Program Format and Cultural Identity*. Luton, U.K.: University of Luton Press.

—— 2004. "Television Formats in the World/The World of Television Formats," in *Television Across Asia. Television Industries, Programme Formats and Globalization*, ed. Albert Moran and Michael Keane. London: Routledge.

Moran, A. and Keane, M. 2004. *Television Across Asia: Television Industries, Programme Formats and Globalization*. London and New York: RoutledgeCurzon.

Moran, Albert and Malbon, Justin. 2006. *Understanding the Global TV Format*. Bristol, U.K.: Intellect Publishers.

Opoku-Mensah, Aida. 1998. *Up in the Air? The State of Broadcasting in Southern Africa.* Zambia: Panos Institute.

Pitout, Magriet. 2005. "Big Brother South Africa: A Popular Form of Expression," in *Big Brother International: Formats, Critics and Publics,* ed. Ernest Mathijs and Janet Jones. London: Wallflower Press.

Spencer, John. 1985. "Language and Development in Africa: The Unequal Equation," in *Language of Inequality,* ed. Nessa Wolfson and Joan Manes, 387–397. Berlin: Mouton.

Tedros, G. 1962. "Television in Africa," *International Communication Gazette* 8: 189.

Varis, Tapio. 1986. "Trends in International Television Flow," *International Political Science Review* 7(3): 235–249.

Waisbord, Silvio. 2004. "McTV: Understanding the Global Popularity of Television Formats," *Television and New Media* 5: 359.

13

WE ARE THE WORLD

American Idol's Global Self-Posturing

Erica Jean Bochanty-Aguero

On March 11, 2008, *American Idol* revealed its new look for Season 7. Introducing the episode, Ryan Seacrest addressed the audience, "We promised *you* the best talent yet, and *they* delivered. We promised *them* a whole new look, and *we* delivered. *This* is *American Idol*." Following Seacrest's opening remarks, a computerized *American Idol* logo fills the screen, spinning in gyroscopic circles. Cut to computer simulated female and male Idols walking to center stage as they *breath in* the scent of fame and *peer out* at thousands of fans who fill a grand stadium; a silhouette of Los Angeles's urban skyline appears in the distance. At center stage the female Idol victoriously raises her microphone, pointing to the sky, and the image rapidly travels upwards. As the image continues to zoom out, the *Idol* stage becomes more distant and is replaced by the *American Idol* logo. Like a symbol on a map, the logo becomes planet earth's core. The image continues to pull back, until we are given a space-eye-view of earth with "American Idol" written across the screen, bifurcating the globe (see Figure 13.1). In contrast to *American Idol*'s original opening sequence, which showed computer generated Idols ascending to the *Idol* stage, Season 7's new opening sequence, with its subtle yet significant inclusion of global imagery, articulates how *American Idol* centrally positions itself in relation to *Idol*'s global media franchise and the transnational entertainment community.[1]

Since launching in 2001 as *Pop Idol* in the U.K., Fremantle Media and 19 Entertainment's *Idol* format has been licensed to over 40 media territories, all of which produce local versions (e.g. Armenia, Latin America, Pan-Arab countries, Canada, Australia, Poland, Norway, Indonesia, North/South Africa, etc.). As posted on Fremantle Media's website, the *Idol* format "has gone on to take numerous nations by storm, dominating television ratings around the world, and creating major new recording artists wherever it goes." Within the *Idol* franchise,

American Idol's success has become a crucial component of the *Idol* brand and an important marketing point to sell the format to other media territories.[2] *American Idol*'s status as a global TV format and its relation to the international entertainment industry is a crucial part of *American Idol*'s televisual identity. *American Idol* is not just an "American" singing competition, but a television show that articulates its place within regional, national, and global space by positioning itself in relation to "other" international *Idol* adaptations. Furthermore, *American Idol*'s presence extends beyond U.S. borders—it's internationally distributed in 130 countries, and often competes with local adaptations from other countries. *American Idol*, therefore, postures itself for "American" as well as "other" global television audiences.

Unlike the opening title sequence that situates *AI* at the earth's center, this chapter seeks to place *American Idol* within a more critical context. Although *Idol* is one of the most widely distributed global TV formats and *AI* is the most profitable and pervasive adaptation within the franchise, scholarly discussions of *American Idol* tend to focus primarily on its national significance.[3] This chapter de-centers perceptions of *American Idol* as purely "American" by examining the show from both national and global perspectives, arguing that *American Idol* is "simultaneously global and local" due to its "interconnectivity" with international media industries and audiences.[4] In doing so, I examine how *American Idol* presents a multifaceted notion of "Americanness" as the show negotiates its local and global status by positioning itself in relation to the "world." *American Idol*'s global self-posturing can be read as a self-conscious attempt by the program to locate, place and "re-center" itself within a non-U.S. global TV franchise and a complex global mediascape.

American Idol, Global Television, and Industrial Practice

By examining *American Idol*'s global self-posturings, this chapter draws upon the tenets of global television studies and adds to emerging debates on media globalization by illustrating how nationally specific programs can in fact have internationally specific functions. Global television studies have highlighted the complex interrelations and configurations of the "national" and the "global" in relation to television production, distribution, and consumption worldwide. As Lisa Parks and Shanti Kumar astutely point out, instead of studying television as a *distinctly* national phenomena, global television studies underscores how

> global television should not be conceptualized as something "out there" to be explored and studied, something Other that is separate from us. Rather, it is part of the very social fabric that gives shape to us as individual subjects and imagined communities . . . If we see ourselves as *part* of global television rather than *distinct from it,* perhaps we will become more active in struggling over the uses of the medium and its global futures.[5]

In conceptualizing television as a shared global phenomenon, global television studies has sought to question, problematize, and *struggle with* simple configurations of media globalization, cultural imperialism, national television, audience reception, indigenous production, televisual flow, and industrial practices in relation to the worldwide circulation of televisual content. Following the tenets of global television studies, this essay hopes to illuminate how *American Idol* is *part* of global television rather than *distinct from it*. In doing so, I will show how an examination of *American Idol* articulates and complicates simple notions of the national, international, transnational, and global in our contemporary mediascape.

Moreover, a study of *AI*'s global self-posturing adds to the burgeoning area of global TV format scholarship. The circulation and adaptation of global TV formats, such as *Idol*, in different national locations is central to contemporary debates on media globalization.[6] As Silvio Waisbord notes, the massive changes in the structure of television systems in the 1980s and 1990s led to the increased interconnectivity and globalization of the television industry and the increased popularity of television formats.[7] Waisbord argues how the increased circulation of global TV formats reveals "two developments in contemporary television: the globalization of the business model of television and the effects of international and domestic companies' attempts to deal with the resilience of national cultures."[8] The popularity of global TV formats therefore "reflects where economics and culture meet in the global market."[9] In contrast to homogenized "global" entertainment, Waisbord argues how the

> international flows of standardized, delocalized formats prove that audiences cling to local and national consciousness . . . this may seem ironic only if we assume that globalization inevitably eliminates cultural diversity and breeds homogenization . . . global media and the national are not antithetical but, actually, are integrated in complex ways . . . the popularity of television formats is at the crossroads of global and local dynamics of the cultural economy of television.[10]

And it is this precise cultural and economic crossroads between the local and the global enabled by TV formats that I wish to explore through an analysis of *American Idol*'s self-posturing.

Lastly, my examination of *American Idol*'s global self-posturing not only links *American Idol* to its larger global franchise, but also links global TV format scholarship to studies of "industrial reflexivity and critical practice" within the entertainment industry. In *Production Culture*, John Caldwell examines how "industry self-analysis and self-representation now serve as primary on-screen entertainment forms across a vast multimedia landscape. Stylish on-screen metacommentaries now pervade the world of both viewer and producer."[11] Caldwell highlights the important cultural meanings and industrial implications of the entertainment industry's "new industrial narcissus" that is self-consciously displayed and exhibited on "the screen, outside, and in the public."[12] Following Caldwell's lead, this essay will examine *American Idol*'s global self-posturings as self-conscious on-screen performances enacted by the franchise. These reflexive presentations articulate the ways the *American Idol* franchise negotiates contemporary political, cultural, economic, and industrial conditions through the adaptation of the *Idol* format. *American Idol* self-consciously positions itself in relation to the global television industry by claiming national, international, transnational and global identities, thereby presenting a rich discourse on media globalization. By framing *AI* in "global" terms, these self-posturings can be viewed as an attempt by the franchise to manage our complex and "unruly" contemporary mediascape[13]—a mediascape shaped by transnational media conglomerates, satellite technology, media convergence, and characterized by postnetwork, multichannel, global media flows.[14] *American Idol* defines and "re-centers" itself in relation to our contemporary mediascape as a means to rhetorically reassert "American" dominance of the global television market despite the threatening presence of non-U.S. global TV format franchises.

God Bless American Idol

American Idol's second season illustrates how the show adapted the *Idol* format by positioning itself in relation to other nations—particularly, in relation to Iraq. Aired from January to May, Season 2 coincided with the U.S. invasion of Iraq on March 19, 2003. In response to the war, *American Idol* adapted the *Idol* format in order to highlight patriotic discourse and the show's democratic voting process. In their article on *Popstars*, a precursor to *Idol*, L. S. Kim and Gilberto Blasini correlate reality TV to "the style and rhetoric of documentary" arguing that reality TV "primarily communicates not a story but an argument" about the historical world.[15] In view of Kim and Blasini's assertion, the following examination of *American Idol*'s second season reveals how the *Idol* singing competition becomes *less* a story about young adults wanting to become the next *American Idol* and *more* a symbolic argument about the "reality" and possibility of democratic practice in the U.S.A. during wartime.[16]

American Idol's celebration of patriotic values and democratic practice via televisual means had political implications that sharply contrasted with representations of non-democratic ideals associated with Iraq and propagated by the media at the time. For example, the disparity between *Idol*'s idyllic stage and images of war torn Iraq—framed by the media as the consequence of Saddam Hussein's oppressive power—was reinforced nightly by Fox news teasers that played during commercial breaks promoting the 10 o'clock news that followed *AI*'s broadcast. Despite the horrors of war, the Bush-Cheney administration dubiously sold the war to the American public by justifying the U.S. invasion of Iraq as a means to seek justice for 9/11, protect democracy at home, promote democracy abroad, and extinguish terrorist groups (e.g. Al-Qaeda) and dictators (e.g. Saddam Hussein) who threatened American ideals, values, and prosperity. Within this context, *American Idol* became symbolic of democracy's real-time preservation in the U.S.A. while the U.S. military were fighting to convert "Oriental" values abroad and safeguard "American" ideals at home.[17] Much like television's response to 9/11, *American Idol*'s explicit adaptation of the *Idol* format illustrates how global TV formats, like fictional programming, can respond to national and international issues.[18] Through the show's performed patriotism and democratic process, *American Idol* positioned itself as "public service" television that worked to unite the nation in a time of crisis. As Lynn Spigel points out with regards to post-9/11 programming, "entertainment and commercialism were rearticulated as television's 'public service.'"[19] The following analysis will show the various ways *American Idol* adapted the *Idol* format in order to posture itself as commercial entertainment that also acted as "public servant"—a television program that reinforced national support for the war as well as the nationalist myth of democracy by repurposing musical performance and the *Idol* format.

One of the most explicit changes to the program once the war began was the show's integration of patriotic symbols within its text: audience members waved American flags and patriotic signs; lighting design of the performance stage reflected the colors of the American flag (red, white, and blue); U.S. military dressed in formal regalia became regular audience members; the show positioned *Idol* contestant Lance-Corporal (LCpl) Joshua Gracin, a Marine, as the contestant who could be called to duty at any second; and Lee Greenwood's "God Bless the U.S.A.," a patriotic country song, became Season 2's musical anthem. A week after the war began, the song was introduced as a group number and was performed multiple times throughout the season. Each performance celebrated the U.S. military by either highlighting Josh Gracin's voice in solo, images of uniformed servicemen in the audience, or images of civilian audience members waving red-white-and-blue signs stating "Josh Gracin/Bush 2004," "Josh Gracin is our American Idol," or "God Bless Joshua Gracin." In one performance the contestants wore fashionable fatigues; most notably, Ruben Studdard wore a "502" area code fatigue print jersey that signified Studdard and Birmingham Alabama's patriotic support for the troops abroad. Viewers' enthusiastic response to the performances "motivated the immediate recording and release of the song on a CD single, which entered the Billboard Hot 100 list in first place. Fifty cents from every sale of the recording were donated to the Red Cross."[20] The inclusion of patriotic symbolism and discourse within the *Idol* format not only illustrates how *AI* took on political meaning, but also how music became a means to legitimize *AI* as a commercial institution. For example, as Katherine Meizel argues "the 2003 Red Cross single" shows

> how elements of civil religion may serve to legitimize commercial institu-
> tions, tempering the profit-making with charity . . . as indicated in the case

of *American Idol*'s performance and recording of "God Bless the U.S.A," the combination of civil-religious and political symbolism can also motivate people to act economically, capitalistically.[21]

Throughout Season 2, *American Idol* combined this patriotic discourse with democracy promotion. First, *American Idol* employed democratic formal strategies (via "liveness," camera movement, editing, and direct address) that worked to symbolically unite the American viewing public, celebrity judges, and *Idol* contestants as a national collective with host Ryan Seacrest constantly addressing viewers as "Americans"—equal citizens of the United States of America. Second, not only did the show promote the American Dream (by representing cultural and social mobility as audience members became celebrities and celebrities became audience members), but also it centralized the American audience by acknowledging their crucial role in exacting change through the democratic process of selecting an *American Idol*. Third, *American Idol*'s declaration of democratic ideals and celebration of patriotism intensified in Season 2's finale.

Promoted as the media event of the year, not only did the finale change its taping location from a mid-size studio to the Universal Amphitheater (which Ryan Seacrest and the contestants directly acknowledge in "awe"), but also the show mimicked the broadcast of a presidential convention/election: Clay and Ruben (the finalists) became candidates, not contestants; "live" reporters in both Ruben and Clay's hometowns conducted grand political rallies with enthusiastic fans; audience members held customary campaign signs stating quasi-political slogans such as "Clay for President," "Clay makes me tingle," "America loves Ruuuuben [sic]," "Ruben is my velvet teddy bear;" and throughout the show Ryan Seacrest announced the states won by each candidate (e.g. "Clay has just won the state of Florida" or "Ruben has won the state of Alabama"), even though *American Idol*'s voting system is technically based on the popular vote and viewers can vote multiple times. Furthermore, when Ryan Seacrest announced that 24 million votes were received for the final countdown he made a humorous aside that the number of votes were "even more than a presidential election."

However, according to *American Idol*, patriotism and democracy is only achieved through performance and consumption. For example, as Ryan Seacrest states to the audience,

> Things are going well, we just got off the phone with Neilson sound scan and they confirmed that the contestants have the number one single with "God Bless the U.S.A.," Kelly Clarkson will have the number one album. This thing works! Plus, we're the most watched TV show in America!

This statement demonstrates a variety of claims the show is making: the success and mobility of "average" Americans to stardom, the American public's role in making *American Idol* product number one, and Ryan Seacrest's statement that "this thing works" illustrates how these achievements are a result of *American Idol*'s format—*American Idol* unites the nation through the consumption of musical entertainment—the singing competition. Through patriotic imagery, musical repurposing, and electoral parody the franchise self-consciously reinforced the capitalist ideal of "commercialism as patriotism" by reducing the international conflict between the U.S.A. and Iraq to musical entertainment that promoted a one-sided nationalist view of reality thereby excluding a Middle-Eastern or international perspective.[22]

Ultimately, Season 2's heightened patriotic and democratic discourse exploits the war in Iraq to symbolically represent how democracy is alive and well on *American Idol*. The "war on terror" will not only continue to spread democracy to the Middle East, but will also preserve democracy at home as symbolized by *American Idol*. By equating *American Idol* with democratic and patriotic values the *Idol* format legitimizes itself as a television format that can bring together *one* nation through the collective, democratic, and patriotic practice of consumption. Furthermore, as Katherine Meizel argues, the civil–religious values inherent in *American Idol* (e.g. patriotism and democracy leads to citizenship through consumption) become global product, thereby making American *Idol*'s "nationally" specific values part of a global market—a market that reconstitutes the nation-state as both global and local—a "glocal" enterprise. [23] However, the type of glocalization circulated by *American Idol* (especially during Season 2) is based on an imbalance of power, which privileges an "American" nationalist perspective.[24] During Season 2, *AI* postured itself in order to relocate itself within *Idol*'s global media franchise as a national program, to promote its role as "public servant" that unifies over 30 million American viewers nightly, to endorse "American" values thereby containing the "unruly" and "messy" realities of international conflict, and to reassure its viewers of the United States' political strength and resiliency after 9/11. During Season 2, *AI* presented the American public with a media spectacle where entertainment and politics converge on the *Idol* stage. However, as noted, the program presented a highly mediated simulation of democracy (via televisual form and style versus systematic practice) and thus resides in the imaginary. Like Baudrillard suggests regarding Disneyland, *American Idol* self-consciously promotes an imaginary democracy that, in turn, allows us to feel (if only for the moment) that democracy "really" exists beyond the *Idol* stage in the United States.[25]

The United Nations of Pop

Whereas *American Idol*'s second season demonstrates how the *Idol* format adapts in relation to U.S. national and international issues, the *World Idol* competition illustrates *American Idol*'s place in relation to the *Idol* transnational franchise. Aired on Christmas day in 2003, *World Idol* functioned as a thinly veiled attempt to promote the upcoming *Idol* seasons in 2004; to gain revenue through telecommunication voting (e.g. phone calls and text messaging); to capitalize on advertising revenue—the show had an excessive amount of commercial breaks (which in the U.S. version consisted of after-Christmas sale ads); and to re-stoke interest in past *Idol* winners signed to BMG records—owned by Freemantle Media's parent conglomerate Bertlesmann AG.

World Idol consisted of original *Idol* winners and judges from eleven different countries spanning five continents: Europe, North America, Africa, Australia, and the Western portion of Asia (the Pan-Arab Nations). Fans from each country voted for their favorite *Idol* via telephone and text messages. Produced in the U.K., the show comically referred to itself as "The United Nations of Pop" with British host, Ant, joking "I feel like Kofi Annan." The episode's introductory montage furthers the show's global self-posturing as images of *Idol* winners from around the world are shown arriving and touring London—the apex of *Idol's* international summit. In voice-over, hosts Ant and Dec narrate,

> The winning *Idols* from 11 nations have flown over 40,000 miles to come here to London . . . They are competing for the votes of a massive worldwide audience to win the coveted title of *World Idol* . . . It's the biggest show on the planet . . . It's *World Idol*.

As these remarks attest, the show clearly positions itself as a vehicle to foster a transnational global television community united by the mutual selection of an international pop star. However, a closer look at the program illustrates how *World Idol* actually reinstates and then erases national borders in the name of "global" television.

World Idol embodies rich and complex discourse about the contradictions and power relations associated with global TV formats. For instance, *World Idol* can be viewed as an attempt by Fremantle Media to promote itself as the sole creator of the *Idol* format—a worldwide television phenomena. In doing so, the show "others" the U.S.A. as well as other participating countries. However, the show's explicit method of "othering" is carried out in a distinctly self-aware manner. The hosts perform a parody of chauvinism that works to frame this act of national superiority within a comedic context. By doing so, the franchise participates in a critical industrial practice that self-consciously pokes fun at the potential cultural politics and power relations that an international media event, like *World Idol*, can evoke. The franchise actually acknowledges the power dynamics within the *Idol* franchise, but then contains and naturalizes the potential "unruly" or "messy" reality of these cultural, economic, and national tensions by framing such power relations within parody. However, instead of using parody to critique and dismantle chauvinistic beliefs by providing an intellectual and satirical critique of such power structures, the program actually neutralizes such beliefs by couching these tensions within simplistic configurations of parody that "poke fun at" cultural, economic, and national difference. For example, the American version of *World*

Idol directly confronts the at-home audience by exposing their American-centric ideologies. Ant and Dec explain to the American public the program's voting rules, emphasizing how U.S. viewers must cast votes for "other" participating countries (since Kelly Clarkson automatically gets maximum points from the U.S.A.—as do all Idols from their home nation). As Dec condescendingly remarks, "Now, we'll spell this out 'cause it may come as a bit of a shock, but there is an entire world out there . . . outside of America." Ant responds, "Even though you guys have a world series with the only nation competing, you're gonna have to face the facts and vote for another country!" Jokingly Dec adds, "Seriously, try it—you might like it."

Ironically, while the British hosts expose American tunnel vision, *World Idol* itself illustrates a British-centric self-posturing. For example, Britain's Will Young is introduced in relation to an *Idol* origin story and the hosts call him "The very first *Pop Idol* . . . born here on this very stage." In contrast, throughout the broadcast, contestants from different nations are introduced in relation to national stereotypes. For example, before introducing Germany's Alexander Klaws, the hosts characterized the Germans as people who have brought the world "efficiency, David Hasselhoff fans, and blunt mullets." Similarly, the hosts characterized Belgium as "home of waffles, chocolate, and that's about it really." These seemingly commonplace achievements are mirrored in the unremarkable critiques the German and Belgium *Idol* performances received. Additionally, France was lambasted for not participating in the competition at all, as the hosts proclaim: Dec: "Welcome back to *World Idol*. We are battling it out for world supremacy." Ant: "So it is no surprise to learn that France gave up early, threw in the towel, and decided not to take part. Not many French here tonight." Later in the show, the hosts call the French "quitters." These comments expose the deep-rooted and continuing Francophobia—the hostility toward and beratement of French government, culture, society, and people—propagated within both British and American culture.

Moreover, the Polish were characterized as backward and confused. In a montage sequence that recaps the *Polish Idol* season, images of eccentric old-world Polish men auditioning for *Idol* are paired with the hosts in voice-over stating,

> There seemed to be some confusion regarding what *Polish Idol* is all about. Some people were too old. Some seemed to think they were on the antiques road show. Some, well, we have no idea. Thankfully, one girl had the right idea. Baby-faced 16-year-old Alex. Glammed-up, she sailed through to the final . . . Will the baby of the bunch have the maturity to win over the world?

Once stripped of her "Polishness" and glammed-up as a pop star, *Polish Idol* fit within the Westernized parameters of the *Idol* format. Lastly, the *Canadian Idol* was introduced with these opening remarks "What has Canada ever given us, ice hockey, enormous moose, and Celine Dion . . .But it's not all bad. They also produced a fantastic Idol, Ryan Malcolm." These comments poke fun at Canadian pop culture tastes, while at the same time illustrating how, despite Canada's entertainment shortcomings, thanks to the *Idol* format a fantastic recording artist was created.

This notion of "othering" carried over to the *World Idol* performances and the debates that ensued regarding what constitutes a "World Idol." On the one hand, *World Idol*'s parodic tone, signified by the hosts' banter and the introduction segments, comically softened the politics of difference espoused by the show. On the other hand, the singing performances and judging segments took on a much more serious tone that reflects the overall logic of the franchise and program—the *Idol* franchise's business motivations that privilege Western musical styles and that value bottom-line economic practices over cultural diversity.

General consensus among the judges seemed to appoint Britain's Will Young, Australia's Guy Sebastian, the U.S.A.'s Kelly Clarkson, and Norway's Kurt Nilson as title contenders who fit most easily within the *World Idol* mold in relation to song choice, physical appearance, voice quality, charisma, and star factor. However, contentious debate arose in relation to many of the performances. For example, Belgium's Peter Evrard, who performed Nirvana's "Lithium," was celebrated by the Belgian judge for being unique and breaking the *Idol* mold by bringing rock to the competition. The Lebanese judge complimented Peter on his look and voice, but thought there was room for improvement. The German judge thought *Idol* "isn't the place" for Peter, as he would be better suited in a rock band versus as a solo artist. In response, Simon Cowell, representing the United States, gave an uncanny response:

> *Simon Cowell* (U.S.A.): This is the weirdest show I have ever been on in my life. The show is called *World Idol*. We have the Lebanese music advisor telling somebody doing a Kurt Cobain impersonation whether he is any good. I am not being rude, but I mean it's just so weird. This would be Kurt Cobain's biggest nightmare because you are conforming, and rock-and-roll is about not conforming . . . so therefore you are a sheep in wolves clothing.
>
> *Peter Evrard* (Belgian Idol): So a rock band doesn't make any CD's because that's selling out?
>
> *Pete Waterman* (U.K.): If you were serious, you wouldn't be on this show.
>
> *Peter Evrard*: I'm very serious about my music, but you guys made it this way. The industry made it this way that young artists cannot find a contract anymore . . . where I'm from.
>
> *Pete Waterman*: If that's true, how did we get Kurt Cobain?
>
> *Simon Cowell*: He did it through being real.

This exchange between judges and contestant, most notably Simon Cowell[26] and Peter Evrard, not only illustrates the parameters of what constitutes a *World Idol* according to the *Idol* franchise (a pop star constructed for mass consumption), but also Peter's retort illustrates the *Idol* franchise's media power and gate keeping function that contradicts the openness and hopeful possibilities the show often tries to convey. Furthermore, Cowell's critique of the judges—in particular, the Lebanese judge—exposes *Idol*'s privileging of Western values as the standard to judge the competition. Whereas the locally produced versions of *Idol* can reflect national or generic flexibility, the "world" stage permits only one *Idol* mold dictated by those who have financial interests in the show (Simon Cowell and the U.K.'s Fremantle Media). In short, global homogenized pop becomes the standard the *Idol* executives and the companies with financial stakes in the show promote. Furthermore, four of the eleven judges were of British origin,[27] and the words used by the judges (most notably, Simon Cowell) and hosts (Ant and Dec) clearly placed "the United Kingdom in a position of cultural superiority," thereby undermining the show's pretense of being "The United Nations of Pop."[28] National Idols come to the "world" stage, a stage ruled by a British cultural imaginary, instead of a more international forum where local specificities are valued.

Diana Karazon's performance is another example that illustrates problems of translation between locally produced *Idols* and the "world" stage. Karazon, from Jordan, was the only contestant who sang in her native Arabic language, mirroring her performances on the *Pan-Arab Idol* competition. While many of the judges congratulated her courage to do so, their comments reflect how her actions compromised her chances of winning. For example:

> Nina De Man (Belgium): I am sure Diana you are well aware of the fact that your language imposes restrictions on the votes. I am going to be very honest with you here. I think the spot of *World Idol* is going to be a very tough one for you. But I did find your performance absolutely enchanting, inspiring even, and I am sure people all over the world will feel the strength in your voice and enjoy it thoroughly.
>
> *Simon Cowell* (U.S.A.): I actually wouldn't have a clue whether that was any good or not.
>
> *Pete Waterman* (U.K.): Did you like it?
>
> *Simon Cowell*: No, but I do think she has a good voice.
>
> *Elias Rahbani* (Pan-Arabia): I want to tell you one thing. We are not judging the lyrics or the music. We are judging the voice. OK? You sung the way that you have sung before and thank you.
>
> *Ian "Dicko" Dickson* (Australia): Diana, the true beauty of music is that it translates language barriers and that's what I saw today. I saw a beauty. I didn't understand your language. I am too, very proud that you came

here and represented a huge part of the world frankly. And I feel very proud to be part of a program that can embrace a culture like yours. Thank you.

This debate illustrates the importance of language within the *Idol* franchise, in particular, and global television formats, in general. On the one hand, the success of global TV formats, like *Idol,* depend on the localization of the format—producing international adaptations locally and using the host country's national language. On the other hand, *World Idol's* privileging of the English language exposes how the franchise actually exploits this process of localization through language in order to sell the show to worldwide media territories and increase global revenue. While this act of localization could produce progressive outcomes by increasing locally produced shows and decreasing the dominance and importation of English-language Hollywood product, through the *World Idol* competition, the *Idol* franchise articulates how English-language entertainment is economically superior because it can transcend national boundaries. Although the Australian judge believes the "true beauty of music is that it translates language barriers," the *Idol* franchise, as evidenced by Simon Cowell's remarks, only seems to embrace national difference when it financially benefits the franchise. Ironically, the contradictions expressed by the judges—congratulating Diana for her performance, yet penalizing her for doing so—demonstrate how nationally specific entertainment can actually be more authentic, unique, and culturally valuable than nationally non-specific entertainment that depends on conforming to a "global" homogenized standard. According to *Idol*, in order to be marketed and sold globally, the *World Idol* must erase national markers and transform into a Westernized pop star.

Despite Cowell's intervention, or because of it, the winner of *World Idol* was Norway's Kurt Nilsen, who was labeled by the Australian judge as "a hell of a marketing challenge" because he had a "voice of an angel" but "looks like a hobbit." However, in contrast to Diana Karazon's song choice, Kurt sang U2's global pop song "A Beautiful Day." So ultimately, the contest *was* about the best voice, but only if that voice sings English-language pop while looking hip and "global," not local. Although *American Idol's* Kelly Clarkson came in second place, the show positioned her as a viable international star while at the same time reminding American audiences that *American Idol* is part of a much larger U.K. based media franchise.

Ultimately, through the *World Idol* competition, the *Idol* franchise oscillates between parody and serious debate in order to self-consciously frame the cultural, political, and economic stakes of the show. On the one hand, the hosts' parody of chauvinism attempts to neutralize the show's cultural politics. On the other hand, the judging segments reinstate the chauvinism espoused by the franchise. *World Idol* therefore becomes a rich example of the power dynamics within *Idol's* global TV format franchise incited by the convergence of different international *Idols* onto one "world" stage. Through the *World Idol* competition, the *Idol* franchise's "global" self-posturing contains the diversity of *Idol*'s various international iterations, in order to privilege a simplified Westernize "global" standard.

The World's Worst Auditions

Whereas *World Idol* promotes the erasure of nation in exchange for finding international pop stars, *American Idol Presents: The World's Worst Auditions* illustrates how *American Idol* performs a similar process of "othering." Before crowning Carrie Underwood as *American Idol*'s Season 4 winner (May 24, 2005), Fox aired an "all-new" special episode entitled *American Idol Presents: The World's Worst Auditions* (May 19, 2005). Featuring re-purposed *Idol* auditions from around the globe, talking-head interviews with *Idol* executives, and Ryan Seacrest's voice-over narration, the pseudo-documentary clip-show promotes *Idol* as a global phenomena and positions *American Idol* in relation to *Idol*'s international adaptations. However, instead of celebrating the individual successes of other *Idol* programs*, American Idol Presents: The World's Worst Auditions* attempts to foster community between *American Idol* and "other" licensed versions through a shared *schadenfreude*[29]—in other words, through a shared viewing pleasure derived from experiencing the misfortune and humiliation of desperate international contestants. However, as the opening sequence of the episode illustrates, the comparison between *AI* and "other" licensed versions function *less* as a way to foster global communion and *more* as a way for *American Idol* to assert its cultural superiority within the franchise.

The episode begins with clearly marked "ethnic" footage of *Idol* auditions from around the globe with Ryan Seacrest in voice-over stating:

> We all know just how successful *American Idol* has become. The judges are famous. And the stars, talented and not-so-talented, have become household names . . . but it doesn't stop there. The format has been copied by 31 different countries which means there are 31 different Simon Cowells. Unlucky for us, they have copied us in other ways: for every Keith, there's a Claus; America has a genie in a bottle, and the U.K. has a woman with a wand; and in Australia they have their own William Hung.
>
> We've estimated that over 1 million people have auditioned to be their country's Idol. And to all the competitions, they bring their cultures, their languages, and their hairstyles, but there is one thing they all have in common—They Suck, Big Time!

As the opening sequence illustrates *American Idol Presents: The World's Worst Auditions* produces *schadenfreude* not only by depicting the bad music produced in the auditions, but also through the cultural differences these performances represent (whether it be Claus's clog dance, Australia's William Hung double, or songs sung in foreign languages). Furthermore, Ryan Seacrest positions the international auditions as mere copies of the original—*American Idol*. In short, *American Idol* is the franchise with "American" aura and the other international adaptations are sub-par "ethnic" replications.[30]

However, despite these differences, Seacrest continues, "If it's one thing that unites us, it's the auditioners . . ." He then poses the question, "Are we really all that different?" The pseudo-documentary clip-show superficially answers this question by highlighting elements of the auditions that cross cultures therefore bridging the gap between *American Idol* and the international adaptations. However, in making these comparisons, the international Idols are repeatedly characterized as ethnic Other. For example, in the segment on how Idol wannabes shamelessly use gifts as bribes, the episode compares an *American Idol* contestant who sweetens each judge with a personalized glitzy top hat to a Polish contestant who brings the judges a prehistoric jawbone. Later in the episode, Paula, Randy, and Simon are visually compared to their Polish judging doubles. In particular, an image in split screen comically juxtaposes Paula Abdul (glammed-up for the cameras) next to her Polish double (an older woman with thick bottle cap glasses). Both comparisons characterize *Polish Idol* (contestants and judges) as backwards and primitive in contrast to *American Idol* (contestants and judges), who have a more developed and sophisticated sense of style and entertainment. Although *American Idol* wannabes lack talent, they have the cultural capital to survive within and understand the *Idol* franchise whereas other cultures, such as the Polish, do not.

Another example that highlights difference over community occurs in a segment depicting international *Idol* contestants performing Elvis songs. The montage sequence travels around the world depicting Elvis-styled performances from nine different countries (the U.S.A., New Zealand, Germany, Scandinavia, Kazakhstan, Portugal, Australia, Poland, and the U.K.). From Kazakhstan's female/Asian Elvis to the U.K.'s British spoken word rendition, the various performances not only reinforce each country's inability to authentically impersonate Elvis, but also highlight the ethnic and cultural differences between the "international" others and the "real" Elvis—an Anglo-American rock-n-roll star. Furthermore, in addition to the montage sequence's articulation of U.S. cultural superiority, the choice to include various Elvis-themed auditions functioned as a way to publicize Elvis's music catalogue, which is owned by Bertelsmann Music Group (BMG)—as already noted, Bertelsmann also owns Fremantle Media, the licensee of the *Idol* franchise.[31] This dissonance between the U.S. original and the ethnic/international copy is further reinforced throughout the episode when contestants cover Western pop songs with foreign accents. For example, *schadenfreude* humor based on ethnic difference is evoked through a distinctly Dutch rendition of Frank Sinatra's "My Way," a German cover of Bryan Adam's "Summer of '69," and the Polish Elvis's "Love Me Tender." The use of language as the means to evoke an ethnically based *schadenfreude* is also reinforced when contestants sing poorly in their native language. The humor in these performances depends on the audiences' inability to understand the language and their perception of foreign languages as uncanny, funny, and otherworldly (again reinforcing the superiority and universality of the English-language).

The episode ends with the graphic of a spinning planet earth. In voice over, Ryan Seacrest states, "Well, that about wraps up the tour around the world of bad singers, but remember there is talent on our planet . . .we'll see you at the final on Tuesday . . ." Cut to a medium shot of Carrie Underwood and Bo Bice, *American Idol*'s Season 4 finalists waving to the at-home audience. This ending clearly marks *American Idol* as *the* franchise with talent and reinforces the argument *American Idol Presents: World's Worst Auditions* makes throughout the episode. While the episode attempts to foster community with international *Idol* adaptations via a shared experience of bad auditions and *schadenfreude*, a closer look at the episode illustrates how *American Idol*'s televisual identity is predicated *less* on creating global kinship and *more* on "othering" the global *Idol* community. Furthermore, the episode positions *American Idol* as the geographic location within the international franchise where true talent exists—the United States of America. Whereas all *Idol* auditions are based on a process of "othering" (good versus bad talent), *American Idol*'s conscious comparison of international *Idol* wannabes in relation to itself makes this difference a cultural one, illustrating how *American Idol* contains the threat of the international "other" by self-consciously positioning itself at the apex of the *Idol* franchise.

American Idol Gives Back?

The final example I would like to discuss illustrates how *American Idol* positions itself as both local and global philanthropist through the special television charity event *Idol Gives Back*. This star studded two-night TV "extravaganza" aired during Season 6, on April 24 and 25, 2007.[32] The first night consisted of *Idol* contestants singing "life anthem" songs of compassion and hope, in keeping with the *Idol Gives Back* theme (e.g. Eric Clapton's "If I Could Change the World," Faith Hill's "There Will Come a Day," and John Lennon's "Imagine").[33] Ryan Seacrest introduced the show stating, "Tonight we are celebrating a very special show. We have the same judges and the same contestants but one huge difference. The calls you make will not only save your favorite contestants, they will also save lives." Each vote saves lives by Newscorp (Fox's parent conglomerate) donating 10 cents per vote to the Charity Projects Entertainment Fund, a fund created for the event that consists of nine charitable organizations that help children locally, in the U.S.A. and globally, in Africa. In addition to Newscorp and *AI*'s regular sponsors (Ford, AT&T, and Coca-Cola), *Idol Gives Back* also partnered with Exxon, ConAgra Foods, MySpace and Allstate Insurance. The second night of the event, the results show, was modeled after a telethon. Throughout the show viewers "gave back" by making phone donations or by downloading musical performances on iTunes from both evenings. In total, 75 million dollars were raised and the monies were equally distributed amongst the nine participating charities. While I commend *American Idol* for integrating giving into the program, the show was saturated with commercialism, illustrating how consumption and charity go hand-in-hand in an *Idol* world. Viewers "give" by consuming the show, voting, and purchasing *Idol* product on the internet. In return, *Idol* (and its corporate sponsors) "give back" to the community in order to gain publicity and reap tax benefits.

In doing so, *Idol Gives Back* clearly functions as a branding and marketing campaign. First, the results show not only brands' corporate sponsors as socially responsible citizens, but also brands *American Idol* as a socially and globally aware television program. The two-hour results show mixed live inspirational musical performances (that doubled as publicity stunts for past *Idol* winners and other Sony BMG artists) with documentary-styled mini-films that showed *American Idol* judges in Africa, Louisiana, and inner city Los Angeles. Each vignette not only highlights the sharp contrast between the *Idol* stage and "real" life, but also depicts how the judges negotiate these adverse environments. The depiction of Africa in these vignettes is particularly problematic. Instead of focusing on the African experience, these vignettes highlight and enhance narratives within *American Idol*'s existing story world. An illuminating example is Simon Cowell and Ryan Seacrest's trip to Africa. Throughout the season Simon and Ryan have an antagonistic relationship, but through their shared experience of extreme poverty in Africa their relationship develops. In short, they make peace and bond. Furthermore, Simon's reaction to the living conditions and death of women and children mirrors his judgments of bad performances on the show. After seeing Emma, an impoverished African woman dying from AIDS, Simon leaves the room emotionally distraught and states, "this is just intolerable . . . it's just unbelievable." Simon's normally apolitical judgments become politicized and create awareness regarding AIDS in Africa. However, scenes like these also exploit dire situations in order to reinforce *American Idol*'s philanthropic image. For example, these scenes emphasize *less* the problems of Africa and *more* the discovery of the "real" Simon, a man, not a persona, with compassion and feeling.

Another example of the way *Idol Gives Back* exploits images of Africa, occurs in Carrie Underwood's music video of "I'll Stand By You." Sponsored by Ford Motor Company, the video aired during the results show and was available for download on iTunes. The video depicts the crisis of orphaned children in Africa due to the AIDS epidemic. As Underwood sings "I'll Stand By You," images of children in pain, tombstones of fallen village members, and dying parents comforted by Underwood are mixed with images of happy children as they listen to Underwood sing, learn to play the guitar, and make Carrie Underwood paper mache dolls in school. Shot during Underwood's trip to Africa, this sequence not only acts as a promotional vehicle for the single "I'll Stand By You," but the imagery of Underwood as savior and mother alludes to iconic images of global celebrities in Africa (Madonna, Princess Diana, Katherine Hepburn, or Angelina Jolie). In a sense, the video places Underwood, the previous year's *Idol* winner, on par with global celebrities. Furthermore, the video places Underwood and *Idol Gives Back* as *the* agent for change, whereas the children are passive recipients. The music video promotes global change through Underwood's role as "*Idol* ambassador" who reassures African youth that she will stand by them, teach them how to sing her songs, and make Carrie Underwood dolls. While the video's depiction of African youth in both joy and pain is clearly moving and expresses compassion for global communities in need, the video illustrates an imbalance of power that promotes Western celebrities and organizations as the solution to Africa's problems. However, photo-ops, money and large organizations are not the agents that will change the infrastructural problems in Africa. In fact, many critics believe, certain African societies and countries have grown more dependent on these organizations in contrast to those which help communities rebuild from within.

Idol Gives Back is an extremely rich text that functions on a variety of levels, and while the show raises awareness of the problems children face both locally and globally, ultimately, it does so to give back to itself and the *Idol* franchise. AI self-consciously postures itself as global and local philanthropist in order to mask and contain the huge financial stakes of the franchise and other transnational corporations in the name of charity.

American Idol Goes Global?

Through the process of "de-centering" *American Idol*, this chapter has begun to highlight the important ways *American Idol* defines and "re-centers" itself in relation to the *Idol* global TV format franchise: first, by adjusting its format to adapt to international conflicts involving the U.S.A. —such as the Iraq War; second, by aligning itself with the Westernized values of its U.K.-based parent franchise— exemplified by the *World Idol* competition; third, by "othering" international *Idol* adaptations in order to position itself as the "true" original—as illustrated by *AI Presents: The World's Worst Auditions*; and last, by posing as local and global philanthropist in order to market its products and brand itself as charitable not commercial—through the *Idol Gives Back* televised event. More so, from a cultural perspective, the examination of *American Idol*'s proliferation as a television music format that claims both national and international identity illustrates not only how notions of nationhood, globalization, television, and popular music intersect, but also how audio-visual artifacts and "global" ideologies circulate within a mediascape characterized by industry conglomeration, media convergence, and fluid borders. Therefore, it is important to de-center global TV formats from their national origins in order to further understand how global TV formats, like *American Idol*, circulate and function.

Fig. 1a

Fig. 1b

Fig. 1c

Fig. 1d

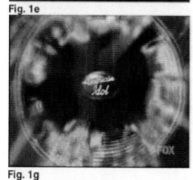

Fig. 1e

Fig. 1f

Fig. 1g

Fig. 1h

FIGURE 13.1 *American Idol* Season 7 Opening Sequence

1a: *American Idol* logo
1c: Idol breathing in the scent of fame
1e: Idol victoriously raises the microphone
1g: *American Idol* logo as Earth's core

1b: Digitized Idols walk to center stage
1d: Idol peering out at thousands of fans
1f: Zoom out from centre stage
1h: *American Idol* logo bifurcating the globe

278 Erica Jean Bochanty-Aguero

This chapter has also attempted to highlight the ways *AI*'s self-posturing can be viewed as self-conscious rhetorical iterations by the franchise that work to contain the "unruly" and "messy" realities of international conflict, transnational media corporations, imperialist beliefs, and "glocal" issues such as poverty. These posturing techniques performed by the franchise can be viewed as "on-screen metacommentaries" that illustrate how the *Idol* franchise self-consciously negotiates the politics of global TV formats through the process of format adaptation and self-representation. Ultimately, understanding the way global TV format franchises posture themselves or present themselves to the public will enable us to become more critically aware of the cultural, economic, and industrial politics posed by global TV formats.

Notes

1 Similar global self-posturings occur throughout the series. For example, Ryan Seacrest often frames *American Idol* as the agent for historical change—constantly reminding the audience how *AI* votes received, viewer ratings, and downloaded songs continually break records within music and television history as well as within the "global" franchise. In the season finale, Seacrest made sure to emphasize how the finale—"a historic event"—will be seen by millions of people throughout the world, thereby illustrating how the U.S. audience is part of a larger segment of viewers throughout the "world."

2 For example, Fremantle Media uses *American Idol* in its marketing campaign. As Fremantle Media's website describes, the *Idol* format is

> One of the most successful formats in the world, local versions of *Idols* have now aired in over 40 territories. In the USA, *Idols* is the No.1 series with an audience of 37 million viewers. The global number of votes for *Idols* has now exceeded three billion!
>
> Retrieved on 6/26/08 from www.fremantlemedia.com/our-programmes/view/Global+Hit+Formats/viewprogramme/Idols

3 For an interesting analysis of *American Idol* in relation to narratives of meritocracy, see Matthew Stahl "A Moment Like This: American Idol and Narratives of Meritocracy" in Chris Washbourne and Maiken Derno (eds.), *Bad Music: The Music We Love to Hate* (New York: Routledge, 2004). For an interesting analysis of *American Idol* in relation to affective advertising techniques, see Henry Jenkins "Buying into *American Idol*: How We Are Being Sold on Reality TV," in *Convergence Culture: Where Old and New Media Collide* (New York: NYU Press, 2006).

4 My examination of *American Idol* from both a local and global perspective due to the format's "interconnectivity" with international media industries and audiences draws from Silvio Waisbord's (2004) examination of global TV formats in the article "McTV—Understanding the Global Popularity of television Formats." Katherine Meizel's (2007) work also looks at global implications of the *Idol* format in her dissertation "America Singing: The Mediation of Identity Politics in 'American Idol.'"

5 Lisa Parks and Shanti Kumar. *Planet TV* (New York: NYU Press, 2003), p. 3.

6 See Moran 1998; Waisbord 2004; Moran and Malbon 2006; Keane et al. 2007. For more general studies about the global TV marketplace, see Havens 2006 and Steemers 2004.

7 Some of the changes Waisbord (2004) points to include: the domination of a privatized model for television; the increased commercialization and standardization of the global television industry; the emergence of satellite transmission and multi-channel television;

the rise of non–U.S. producers and exporters of programming; and rising concerns about copyright infringement.

8 Waisbord 2004: 360.

9 Waisbord 2004: 367.

10 Waisbord 2004: 367.

11 John Caldwell. *Production Culture: Industrial Reflexivity and Critical Practice in Film and Television* (Durham, NC: Duke University Press, 2008), 1.

12 Caldwell, *Production Culture*, 1.

13 For more on the "unruly" nature of the contemporary mediascape and the production industry see Caldwell, *Production Culture* in general and in particular the book's conclusion "Shoot-Outs, Bake-Offs, and Speed Dating," 325–331.

14 My use of the term "mediascape" draws upon Arjun Appadurai's conceptualization of the term in the essay, "Disjuncture and Difference in the Global Culture Economy." As Appadurai (2006: 590) states,

> Mediascapes' refer both to the distribution of the electronic capabilities to produce and disseminate information (newspapers, magazines, television stations, film production studios, etc.), which are now available to a growing number of private and public interests throughout the world; and to the images of the world created by these media. These images of the world involve many complicated inflections, depending on their mode (documentary or entertainment), their hardware (electronic or pre-electronic), their audience (local, national or transnational) and the interests of those who own and control them.

15 Kim and Blasini 2001: 294–295.

16 Kim and Blasini (2001) discuss a singing competition similar to *American Idol* entitled *Popstars*. However, whereas Kim and Blasini's study focuses on notions of multicultural identity in relation to the American Dream with regards to *Popstars*, this study on *American Idol*, focuses on another aspect of the American Dream—how the show promotes democracy as the means to achieve the American Dream. Kim and Blasini's correlation of reality TV and documentary form provides a useful framework from which to conceptualize reality TV programs and differentiate their function from fiction programming.

17 My use of the word "Oriental" draws from Edward Said's concept of "Orientalism" which outlines the Western tradition's inaccurate understanding of the East. Lynn Spigel in her (2007) article also examines how "Orientalism" is present in post-9/11 programming, such as NBC's *The West Wing*.

18 Lynn Spigel examines the changes in television programming after 9/11 in relation to entertainment genres versus news coverage in Spigel 2007.

19 Lynn Spigel's study argues how post-9/11 changes in television programming reflected a return to telelvision's role as "public servant." Building upon Spigel's study, I argue how *American Idol*, a reality show, also participated in promoting television as a "public servant." See Spigel 2007: 627.

20 Meizel. 2006a: 500.

21 Ibid.: 501.

22 Lynn Spigel discusses the concept of "commercialism as patriotism" in relation to post-9/11 programming (2007: 627).

23 Meizel further argues,

> with its electoral procedure and its American Dream narrative, American Idol works as a vehicle for democratic symbolism . . . American Idol and its nationally specific civil-religious implications become part of the global market. . . serving what William I. Robinson has called the transnational state.
>
> (Meizel 2006: 501)

24 For example, politically (the show's patriotic discourse privileges U.S. policy versus international law); industrially (transnational media corporations benefit most from the *Idol* formats worldwide distribution versus localized production companies); and culturally (the show promotes Western-centric values where citizenship is based on consumption versus other more diverse cultural value systems).

25 Baudrillard states, "Disneyland is presented as imaginary in order to make us believe that the rest is real, when in fact all of Los Angeles and the America surrounding it are no longer real, but of the order of hyperreal and of simulation." (2001: 172). While I would not go as far to say that everything outside of *American Idol* is a hyperreal simulation, I do believe that in the U.S.A. ideas, information, and public dialogue (that ensure a vital democracy) are increasingly being mediated through television and electronic media. Television programs, such as *American Idol*, parody and simulate the democratic process in order to reassure the public that democracy continues to exist in the United States (even in a corporate media society). However, if we look at the history of our nation, the U.S.A. has consistently promoted a democratic image while compromising the realization of democracy in practice.

26 Throughout the show, Simon Cowell and Pete Waterman create a U.S.A./U.K. union and both seek to ensure the financial interests of the U.K.-based *Idol* franchise by promoting *Idol* as a format that creates pop stars for mass global consumption.

27 The Australian, German, British, and U.S. judges were all of U.K. origin. Whereas the South African, Pan-Arabian, Belgium, Norwegian, Netherlands, Canadian, and Polish judges were from their own nation. However, all judges were part of the larger *Idol* franchise.

28 Meizel (2006b: 3) discusses the political implications of the British/U.S. alliance on the show in the article "'The United Nations of Pop': Geopolitics and Genre in World Idol.".

29 *Schadenfreude* is the sentiment of enjoying the misfortunes of others. Derived from German, the word literal translates to *schaden* meaning "harm/damage" and *freude* meaning "joy."

30 Here I am evoking Walter Benjamin's use of "aura" in his watershed essay "The Work of Art in the Age of Mechanical Reproduction, in *Illuminations*, ed. Hannah Arendt, trans. Harry Zohn (New York: Harcourt, Brace & World, 1968).

31 *American Idol*'s "Idol Gives Back" episode on April 27, 2007 also highlighted Elvis through the broadcast of a live televisual duet of Elvis and Celine Dion singing "If I Could Dream." Celine's label, Columbia, is also owned by BMG. The revival of Elvis was made possible by impressive CGI technology that altered the image, reminiscent of Nat "King" Cole and his daughter's duet of "Unforgettable."

32 Due to the success of the broadcast, *Idol Gives Back* returned during Season 7.

33 For more information see www.americanidol.com/idolgivesback/

References

Appadurai, Arjun. 2006. "Disjuncture and Difference in the Global Culture Economy." In *Media and Cultural Studies: Key Works*. Ed. Meenakshi Gigi Durham and Douglas Kellner. Malden, MA: Blackwell Publishing.

Baudrillard, Jean. 2001. "The Precession of Simulacra." In *Media and Cultural Studies: Keyworks*. Ed. Douglas Kellner and Meenakshi Gigi Durham. Malden, MA: Blackwell Publishing.

Benjamin, Walter. 1968. "The Work of Art in the Age of Mechanical Reproduction." In *Illuminations*. Ed. Hannah Arendt; trans. Harry Zohn. New York: Harcourt, Brace & World.

Havens, Timothy. 2006. *Global Television Marketplace*. London: BFI.

Jenkins, Henry. 2006. "Buying into *American Idol*: How We Are Being Sold on Reality TV." In *Convergence Culture: Where Old and New Media Collide*. New York: NYU Press.

Keane, Michael, Anthony Fung, and Albert Moran. 2007. *New Television, Globalisation, and the East Asian Cultural Imagination*. Hong Kong : Hong Kong University Press.

Kim, L. S. and Gilberto Blasini. 2001. "The Performance of Multicultural Identity in US Network Television: Shiny, Happy Popstars (Holding Hands)." *Emergences* (11)2: 287–308.

Meizel, Katherine. 2007. "America Singing: The Mediation of Identity Politics in *American Idol*." Ph.D. dissertation, Dept. of Ethnomusicology, University of California–Santa Barbara.

———— 2006a. "A Singing Citizenry: Popular Music and Civil Religion in America." *Journal of the Scientific Study of Religion* 45(4): 497–503.

———— 2006b. "'The United Nations of Pop': Geopolitics and Genre in World Idol." Unpublished Paper.

Moran, Albert. 1998. *Copycat Television: Globalisation, Program Formats and Cultural Identity*. Luton, Bedfordshire, U.K.: University of Luton Press.

Moran, Albert and Justin Malbon. 2006. *Understanding the Global TV Format*. Portland, OR: Intellect Books.

Parks, Lisa and Shanti Kumar. 2003. *Planet TV*. New York: NYU Press.

Pinker, Beth. 2007. "Behind the Music: The Execs Behind 'Idol.'" *Hollywood Reporter*, March 20.

Spigel, Lynn. 2007. "Entertainment Wars: Television After 9/11." In *Television: The Critical View*. 7th Edition. Ed. Horace Newcomb. New York: Oxford University Press.

Stahl, Matthew. 2004. "A Moment Like This: American Idol and Narratives of Meritocracy." In *Bad Music: The Music We Love to Hate*. Ed. Chris Washbourne and Maiken Derno. New York: Routledge.

Steemers, Jeanette. 2004. *Selling Television: British Television in the Global Marketplace*. London: BFI.

Turner, Mimi. 2007. "Idol Worship: Television's Force of Nature Teaches the World to Sing." *Hollywood Reporter*, March 20.

Waisbord, Silvio. 2004. "McTV—Understanding the Global Popularity of Television Formats." *Television and New Media* 5(4): 359–383.

PART IV

Trans-Formats

Local Articulations and the Politics
of Place and Nation

14

THE SOCIAL AND POLITICAL DIMENSIONS OF GLOBAL TELEVISION FORMATS

Reality Television in Lebanon and Saudi Arabia

Marwan M. Kraidy

When scholars and policy makers contemplate the Arab "media revolution," they mostly think of Al-Jazeera and its news competitors. They are guided by the assumption that all-news satellite television networks are the predominant, even the single, shaper of the Arab public sphere, a perspective exacerbated by the September 11, 2001 attacks. Drawing on a larger work (Kraidy, 2009, forth-coming), this chapter presents an alternative view, emphasizing instead the combined impact of Arab entertainment television and small media such as mobile phones on Arab governance. It explores how entertainment television is an active contributor to shaping what Arab publics discuss and do in both the social and political realms. As local (in this case regional/pan-Arab, reaching two dozen Arabic-speaking countries) adaptations of global television formats, Arab reality television shows exhibit a combination of signs and practices from several worldviews. As such, this chapter will show how Arab reality shows are open to multiple processes of appropriation and redeployment. Though numerous scholars have for years studied the differentiated "reception" of television texts in various contexts, this chapter focuses specifically on television formats in a context of growing media convergence and protracted political instability and social upheaval. Specifically, it focuses on reality television's social and political impact, which stems primarily from its activation of new communication processes between a variety of information and media technologies creating what I call "hypermedia space." In the new Arab information order, reality television activates hypermedia space because it promotes participatory practices like voting, campaigning and alliance building, via mobile telephones and related devices.[1]

Hypermedia space is a broadly defined symbolic field created by interactions between multiple media, from micro text messaging to region-wide satellite broadcasting. The term "hypermedia" captures the technological convergence and media saturation that characterize many contemporary societies, while emphasizing the speed and convergence of communication processes. The "interoperatibility of once-discrete media . . . linked *together* into a single seamless web of digital-electronic-telecommunications" (Deibert, 1997, pp. 114–115) creates a space with many "points of access" that are personalized, mobile, non-conspicuous and networked, and therefore not easily subjected to overt social or political control. Even as technological convergence in the Arab world is still in its infancy, Arab hypermedia space is constituted by various types of communicators (citizens, consumers, activists, etc.) using email, mobile telephony, text messaging, digital cameras, electronic newspapers, and satellite television. This space's non-hierarchical nature invites a rethinking of Arab information dynamics.

Hypermedia space is changing Arab governance, i.e. the management of social relations between citizens and of political relations between citizens and the state. The convergence of small media like mobile phones and digital cameras, with big media like television and newspapers, has already changed how information is accessed and controlled. The fluid political situation prevailing in most Arab countries, attributed by many in the region to the neo-conservative theory of creative chaos that is widely believed to guide U.S. Middle East policy, has emboldened activists to use information technologies for social and political gain. Whether governments respond with repression, as in Egypt during the 2005 presidential elections, with a mix of repression and accommodation, as in Saudi Arabia over the past decade, or dissolution, as in Lebanon during the so-called 2005 "Cedar Revolution," their relations with their citizens have changed drastically in the new communication environment.

How does hypermedia space contribute to changing the ways in which Arab citizens and regimes access, use, create and control information? How do the new information dynamics affect the way citizens and governments relate to each other? To address these questions, this paper focuses on Saudi Arabia and Lebanon, where recent social and political developments constitute propitious opportunities to explore the impact of hypermedia space on Arab governance. These two countries play an instrumental role in shaping the Arab information revolution and occupy the poles of the Arab socio-cultural spectrum. Saudi Arabia is the Arab world's most socially conservative nation, where public life is ruled by the strictest interpretations of Islamic texts. Lebanon is the Arab world's most socially liberal society where Christians assume an influential, albeit receding, public role. Whereas Saudi entrepreneurs with royal connections finance Arab media, Lebanese journalists, producers and managers populate the industry's ranks. For a quarter century, the convergence of Saudi capital and Lebanese talent has driven major Arab media developments that cannot be captured by simply a comparative study of the two countries, since it would gloss over the complexity of the connection between Saudi Arabia and Lebanon. Rather, Saudi Arabia and Lebanon are better understood as a dynamic pair whose multifaceted interactions shape a hypermedia space that "covers" the entire Arab region.

Understanding the impact of hypermedia space on Arab governance requires a triple analysis of socio-political context, technical developments, and major events that act as catalysts. It requires addressing questions like: What are the social and political contexts in which lead actors—activists, citizens, viewers, callers, consumers, etc.—actively use information and media technologies to challenge prevailing (social, political, economic, etc.) arrangements? Do "new" media increase the power of citizens and governments to communicate and act? What catalyst-events trigger uses of technology for social and political change? In a regional Arab situation of crisis and amidst intense global geo-political interest in the Middle East, Saudi Arabia and Lebanon are experiencing political tensions that are different but related. Both countries are awash with media and information technologies that operate within weak or inexistent regulatory frameworks and policy regimes subservient to executive fiat. In this context, reality television acts as a catalyst (among others) because its commercial and dramatic logics promote participation in public events through the interactive use of information technologies, in activities like voting, mobilization, and alliance building. In this chapter I seek to demonstrate how popular reality television programs help establish dynamic links between socio-political contexts ripe for change and the technical capacities of new media, thus activating hypermedia space.

Hypermedia space blurs boundaries between producers and consumers of information, between popular culture and politics, and between various nationally based cultural spheres brought into contact by the transnational scope of hypermedia space. This blurring of boundaries is aided by the protean nature of television formats, which leaves gaps in cultural translation that local actors can exploit as they publicize their causes. This article examines how one reality television program in particular has contributed to changing the "social epistemology"—the public knowledge of technical capacities—surrounding information technologies in Lebanon and Saudi Arabia. This program, *Star Academy*, has triggered controversy throughout the Arab world and articulated hot-button issues in Arab public discourse, such as democratization, gender relations, and Western influence. This article will endeavor to explain how various Saudi and Lebanese actors have appropriated *Star Academy* for social and political purposes in the two countries, and how the public awareness of the hypermedia space engendered by the program has affected the nature of governance in both countries. This chapter—part of a larger ongoing book manuscript on the social and political impact of Arabic-language reality television—concludes with a discussion of how hypermedia space contributes to shifts in the nature and boundaries of social and political agency.

The Saudi-Lebanese Connection: The Context of Arab Reality Formats

The military conflicts that have destabilized the Middle East since the end of World War II have been the main impetus for the development and growth of Arab media. War was either the *raison d'être* or an opportunity to thrive for both Nasser's Voice of the Arabs radio in the 1950s, and Al-Jazeera TV in the 1990s. Most analysts refer to the 1991 Gulf War as a momentous event that triggered the growth of Arab satellite television. At that time, the Saudi government, which kept its citizens uninformed of Iraq's invasion of Kuwait for three days, found that Saudis and viewers throughout the Arab world had turned to CNN for information. Saudi rulers realized that they needed an Arabic-language counterbalance to CNN to expand their regional influence, and Saudi businessmen close to the royal family saw a lucrative business opportunity. The Saudi strategy of internationalizing Saudi media ownership, hitherto restricted to newspapers, entered a crucial phase (see Boyd, 2001) with the 1991 launch of Middle East Broadcasting Center (MBC) in London by the then Saudi king's brother-in-law. At the same time, the Egyptian government launched the Egyptian Satellite Channel (ESC) to pre-empt the effect of Saddam Hussein's propaganda on Egyptian soldiers deployed in the U.S.-led Operation Desert Storm. These developments, followed by the launch in 1996 of Al-Jazeera from Qatar and the satellite channels LBC and Future TV from Lebanon (see Kraidy, 2002), and of Saudi-owned, Dubai-based Al-Arabiya in 2003, are milestones in the history of Arab satellite television.

Before the onset of the Arab satellite revolution, the proliferation of unlicensed radio and television stations during the 1975–1990 Lebanese civil war had developed a large pool of creative and managerial talent. Political parties and warring factions launched several dozen unlicensed television stations that functioned as mouthpieces. One of these stations is particularly relevant. The Lebanese Broadcasting Corporation went on the air in 1985 as a platform for the Christian-nationalist Lebanese Forces militia, and rapidly became the most watched station in Lebanon. As the longest running privately owned Arab television channel, LBC reflects the rise of American-style broadcasting over the older, European-inspired, system. This is evidenced by the station's choice of a three-letter acronym name, its focus on entertainment programs, and its reliance on advertisements. Even as a partisan voice in the war, LBC from its early days was run as a business, for example broadcasting special Ramadan programs for Muslim audiences during the civil war. The 1989 "Document of National Understanding" signed in the Saudi resort city of Ta'ef, put an end to military conflict in Lebanon and called for the reorganization of the Lebanese media within a "modern" regulatory framework. The resulting 1994 Audio-Visual Media Law was hailed as the first broadcasting law in the Arab world, but its implementation favored media institutions owned by leading politicians, cut down the number of television stations to five (Kraidy, 1998) and sent hundreds of media professionals into unemployment.

Saudi entrepreneurs with plans to launch satellite television channels found a large pool of qualified and available Lebanese media professionals lured by steady employment and big salaries. Their hiring in the early 1990s followed a long history of Lebanese journalists and advertising executives working in Saudi Arabia and other Gulf countries. MBC hired many Lebanese before the 1994 Audio-Visual Media Law and its 1996 implementation, but the hiring of Lebanese intensified after 1996. Another lure was the promise of editorial independence, since MBC studios were initially located in London. Dubai TV, Al-Arabiya and others also have a high number of Lebanese on their staff. In 1996, when LBC and Future TV initiated satellite broadcasting of entertainment programs, they compelled MBC, in operation on satellite since 1991, to enhance its entertainment offerings and change the proportions of news, current affairs and entertainment in its format. In the early 2000s, MBC and other channels moved to Dubai's Media City, a free-trade zone dedicated to media and information technology in the United Arab Emirates, and now host to approximately 200 satellite channels. In 2003, the launch of Al-Arabiya, a 24-hour news network, to counter Al-Jazeera, continued the "alliance" of Saudi money and Lebanese skills: Al-Arabiya is currently headed by a Saudi general manager, Abdel Rahman al-Rashed, and a Lebanese director of programs, Nakhlé al-Hage.[2] (See chapter 3 in Kraidy, 2009, forthcoming, for a detailed analysis of the Saudi-Lebanese connection.)

Adapting global formats has been central to the growth of the Pan-Arab television industry. In the Arab world—as in many other regions of the world —"adaptation" can mean a variety of things, ranging from "inspiration" to contractually sanctioned format adaptations. While there are many instances of inspiration, poaching and imitation in the pre-satellite era (see Khalil, 2004), the race to develop exciting programs that appeal to a broad, transnational audience exacerbated format adaptation. The most famous shows on Arab television today are adapted from Western programs. This applies to political talk-shows like Al-Jazeera's *al-Ittijah al-Mu'akis* ["The Opposite Opinion"] a copycat of CNN's *Crossfire*, and to daytime women's programs like MBC's *Kalam Nawa'em* ["Sweet/Women's Talk"] inspired by ABC's *The View*. It was, however, the reality television wave that arrived in the early 2000s that made officially adapted formats a dominant feature of Arab programming grids. Reality television shows were the most popular and most controversial format adaptations, chief among them the Endemol-owned format adapted by the Lebanese Broadcasting Corporation as *Star Academy*.

Star Academy and the Saudi-Lebanese Connection

The multiple entanglements of the Saudi-Lebanese connection and its decisive role in shaping Arab hypermedia space are represented in the production and reception of LBC's *Star Academy*, the most popular and most controversial program in Arab satellite television history. The terrestrial station, LBC International (LBCI) is registered in Lebanon and subject to Lebanese law. Its satellite channel Al-Fada'iyya Al-Lubnaniyya (The Lebanese Satellite Channel, known as LBC-Sat) on the other hand, is a multinational corporation registered in the Cayman Islands, primarily to circumvent Lebanese media ownership laws. Since its founding in 1996, Saudis have owned nearly half of LBC-Sat. Saudi mogul Saleh Kamel initially owned 49 percent of the shares and was known to brag in public of his ability to influence programming content, especially in curbing material of a sexual nature that he deemed inappropriate to Saudi sensibilities (see Habib, 2003). For his own business reasons and also because LBC management probably resisted his meddling, Kamel sold his shares to another Saudi mogul, prince Al-Walid Bin Talal, Saudi royal and investor extraordinaire with interests in media companies. Bin Talal bought Kamel's shares for US$100 million in 2000, at which time the company was worth around US$200 million. With this massive influx of equity, LBC gained the resources to compete regionally, in addition to a degree of political protection since Bin Talal is close to Lebanese president Emile Lahoud. Most importantly, LBC was in position to "retaliate" to the challenge posed by MBC's launch of *Man Sa Yarbah Al-Malyun*, the Arabic version of *Who Wants To Be A Millionnaire?*, the first Arabic television format-adaptation and the most popular Arab satellite television program in the pre-*Star Academy* era. This Saudi-funded program featured Lebanese host George Qordahi and Lebanese executive producer Salwa Suwayd, another product of the Saudi-Lebanese connection.

Launched by LBC in December 2003, *Star Academy*, now with three seasons completed (this analysis refers to the first season unless indicated otherwise), is a watershed Arab media event. Adapted from a format owned by the Dutch format house Endemol after successful French and British adaptations, *Star Academy* has a large staff by regional standards. It began with a pan-Arab casting campaign that selected 16 young Arabs, including two Lebanese and one Saudi, from a pool of 3,000 applicants (personal interviews: Alavanthian, 2004; Al-Daher, 2004 and 2005; Saad, 2004). Both LBCI and LBC-Sat broadcast the show from "The Academy," a four-story building near LBC headquarters, where contestants are sequestered for the four months of the program. They are watched by viewers throughout the Arab world every night during a half-hour show reporting on the day's events and called "Access," in addition to a two-hour weekly show airing on Friday called "Prime." A dedicated satellite channel called "LBC Reality" broadcasts live scenes from the Academy, 24 hours a day for four months. Contestants spend their time attending classes and rehearsals with teachers who each Monday nominate two contestants for possible termination for non-satisfactory performance. The nomination kicks off five days of voting and campaigning during which viewers build coalitions with friends, schoolmates, neighbors or family members and send text messages to be aired on music television channels, all in support of the nominee they want to stay in the program. These "democracy-like" activities conclude with the end of the Friday Prime when voting results are announced and the losing nominee exits the show.

Star Academy was instantly popular. Market researchers found massive audiences in most Arab countries, breaking records in some. The show's demographics included young and old, women and men, urban and rural. Empty streets during daily "Access" shows prompted some restaurant owners to complain that *Star Academy* was bad for business while other restaurateurs increased their profits by setting up large screens. The excitement reached its peak during the Friday "Prime" when the weekly round of voting ended and the results were released. Discussion boards, fan sites and blogs in Arabic, English and French animated the internet. Text messages sent by viewers extolling favorite contestants were played on moving screen tickers by music television channels and talk-shows and newscasts on Al-Jazeera and others reported the gossip, developments, and voting results. *Star Academy* was a media event, or, more specifically, a "hypermedia event."

As a production, *Star Academy* is a result of Saudi capital and Lebanese talent. As a hypermedia event, it reflects the clash between the economic imperatives of the Saudi–Lebanese connection on the one hand and the cultural differences between Saudi Arabia and Lebanon on the other. The program was immensely popular in both Lebanon and Saudi Arabia. According to IPSOS-STAT, an international polling firm with a strong presence in the Middle East, *Star Academy* grabbed 80 percent of the 15–25 audience in Lebanon, and after a few weeks, according to market researchers I spoke with between May and July 2004, had captured a large proportion of the audience in Saudi Arabia. In Lebanon, the program's popularity made it subject to daily editorial commentary and news reports, street conversations and communal viewing. A Sunni Muslim cleric and a couple of journalists criticized the show, but with little effect. In Saudi Arabia, however, as will be elaborated shortly, *Star Academy* was extremely controversial.

Star Academy articulated the central governance challenge in both Lebanon and Saudi Arabia. In Lebanon, the challenge is political, and entails finding equilibrium between confessional identities and national unity. In that context, this article will show how *Star Academy* was appropriated by anti-Syrian demonstrators in the wake of the assassination of Rafiq al-Hariri, its immense popularity making it an effective political tool. In Saudi Arabia, the central challenge is social, and requires striking a balance between strict interpretations of Islamic texts and what Saudi rulers regard as the imperatives of modernization. As the next section illustrates, hypermedia space has made this ever-moving equilibrium extremely precarious.

Governance, Hypermedia and Social Reality in Saudi Arabia

Saudi Arabia has a fragile political system whose backbone consists of the several thousand members of the royal Al-Saud family (see Salameh, 1980, for a historical analysis). The continuing protection of the United States and the agreement between the Al-Saud and Al-Shaykh families whereby the former gives political protection to the latter while the latter endows the former with religious legitimacy, are two pillars of the Saudi order. The alliance between Al-Saud royals and Al-Shaykh clerics has contained tensions between the enshrinement of Islamic values and the modernization drive espoused by Saudi kings since the 1960s. Since the 1980s the royal family has positioned itself as an arbiter, albeit authoritarian, between religious activists, liberal reformers, and business interests in the kingdom. In the aftermath of terrorist attacks within their territory in the last few years, Saudi authorities have launched their own campaign against radical violence in the kingdom and continue to cooperate with the United States in its Middle East policy.

Media and information technologies have historically been at the center of debates and struggles between various Saudi groups. Media issues are related to salient topics, such as Western influences on a society that prides itself to be the cradle of Islam, and expose the Saudi paradox of a capitalistic economy dependent on trade with foreigners in a conservative society with influential elements who are hostile to foreign influences. Radio in the 1930s, television in the 1960s, satellite dishes and the internet in the 1990s, and mobile phones in the 2000s have triggered contentious debates about the Islamic common good, gender relations, and Western influence. For example, the impending introduction in the early 1960s of television to Saudi Arabia was vehemently opposed by religious clerics and activists, who argued that television pictures violated the Islamic prohibition on reproducing human faces and figures. King Faysal Ibn Sa'ud, however, was convinced that media and information technology were central to his modernization drive. To garner support, he convened a meeting of critics and clerics and presented his case:

> Painting and sculpture are idolatry, but is light good or bad? The judges pondered and replied that light is good; Allah put the sun in the heavens to light man's path. Then asked the King, is a shadow good or bad? There was nothing in the Qur'an about this, but the judges deduced and ruled that shadows are good, because they are inherent in light, and even a holy man casts a shadow. Very well then, said the King, photography is good because it is nothing but a combination of light and shade, depicting Allah's creatures but leaving them unchanged.
>
> (quoted in Eddy, 1963, p. 258)

Compromise through persuasion is a hallmark of Saudi governance and has historically prevented tensions between contending forces in the kingdom from escalating. The decision to allow television into the country came with strict censorship guidelines which among other things prohibited women who are not fully clothed, who are dancing, participating in sports, or engaged in "overt acts of love"; in addition to references (not exclusively to women) to betting, gambling, alcoholic beverages, Zionism, depictions of violent or sexually arousing scenes, and denigration of the royal family, other countries, or any of the "heavenly religions" (Shobaili, 1971). These guidelines were easy to enforce in the pre-satellite era, when Saudi officials censored production, programming and transmission. The erosion of control initiated by satellite broadcasting in the early 1990s increased with the development of hypermedia space in the 2000s, as the internet, then mobile telephones with digital cameras became ubiquitous.

The internet was greeted with ambivalence in Saudi Arabia, with the government seeing its potential for both modernization and subversion, while Islamist activists embraced it as a tool to "spread good and combat evil." The internet was introduced in 1999, and by April 2003, there were 21 functioning internet service providers and around 1.6 million users ("Analysis: Saudi rulers," 2004). A February 12, 2001 ministerial resolution banning content critical of the Saudi state, advocating violence, or slanderous, sets the censorship parameters enforced at the King 'Abdul 'Aziz City for Science and Technology (KACST), the centralized internet node for the entire country. According to *Saudi Gazette*, 25,000 new sites are blocked every month ("Saudi Internet," 2001).

Mobile phones were initially uncontroversial because they were considered culturally neutral. A 2003 report estimated the number of Saudi mobile lines to be double the number of landlines (respectively 7.2 to 3.5 million) ("Saudi Arabia," 2004). This relaxed attitude changed with the introduction of text messaging, digital cameras, and especially bluetooth wireless technology (see for example "Bluetooth in," 2005). Bluetooth gives a new twist to a well-established flirting ritual in Saudi Arabia in which an interested youth surreptitiously throws a piece of paper with their phone number on it in front of their object of attraction as their paths cross in a mall or other public space. Bluetooth updates this ritual by enabling users to know whether the person they are interested in is amenable to conversation. The most important element of bluetooth is that its activation signals a readiness to socialize. "Using bluetooth is much better than trying to throw the number to the girls through car windows, or in the shopping center," said a Saudi teenager, "through bluetooth I guarantee that the other party chose to accept my number or the file I sent. In other words, I don't impose myself on anyone" (Aboud, 2005). The Commission for Commanding the Good and Forbidding the Evil, a body with police powers operating from the Ministry of Religious Affairs, thought otherwise, and many schools and gyms banned camera-equipped phones on their premises (Akeel, 2005). An April 2005 law stipulates 1,000 lashes, 12 years in jail, and a fine of 100,000 Saudi riyals, or around US$26,670 for anyone caught engaging in "phone pornography" ("New Saudi," 2005). The popularity of *Star Academy* in Saudi Arabia intensified debate surrounding interactive features of mobile phones such as bluetooth and text-messaging.

Star Academy and Gender Relations in Saudi Arabia

Star Academy triggered a firestorm of controversy in Saudi Arabia. A columnist called it "a whorehouse" and clerics distributed cassette tapes of sermons titled

"Satan Academy," reflecting a hostile segment of the social and religious elite (see Al-Dakhil, 2005). On the other hand, the program was very popular and lucrative for telecommunications companies who profited from the voting process, since viewers had to pay the equivalent of US$2 or 3 each time they voted via text-messaging. Saudi viewers experienced tension between their attraction to the program and religious injunctions against it. As is customary in Muslim societies, viewers sought religious opinions, known as *fatwas*, to resolve the conflict. The numbers of *fatwas* about *Star Academy* requested by viewers was so great that the "Permanent Committee for Scientific Research and the Issuing of Fatwas," which is one of the highest religious authorities in the nation, issued a detailed *fatwa* which prohibited financing, watching, discussing, voting, or participating in *Star Academy* ("Fatwa Concerning," 2004) As custom dictates, the *fatwa* was replete with *isnad*, references that grounded and found support for it in the *Qur'an*, Islam's holy book, and *Hadith*, the collected speeches of the Prophet Muhammad. It began with a preamble that included the committee's finding that:

> After studying the matter, the Committee thinks that these shows should be banned and it is *haram to watch them, finance them, take part in them, call them to vote or to express admiration of them*, because of what these shows include of allowing forbidden things concerning which there is consensus that they are forbidden, and doing so brazenly ... What brazenness in committing haram and immoral actions can be worse than these shows which include a number of serious evils?

The evils include "free mixing of the sexes," "blatant promotion of immorality," and "the call to remove modesty and pride from the hearts of Muslims." After explaining these points, the clerics conclude with the injunction to Saudi viewers that:

> It is not sufficient for you to abstain from watching these shows; you should also advise and remind those whom you know watch them or take part in them in any way, because that comes under the heading of cooperating in righteousness and piety, and forbidding one another to engage in sin and transgression.

The central source of anger and objection in Saudi Arabia was *Star Academy*'s portrayal of gender relations. The prevention of *ikhtilat*, or gender mixing, is the pillar of Saudi social organization. Wahhabi doctrine considers *hudud*, or the boundaries between public and private space, divinely decreed in the *Qur'an* and therefore sacred. Men and women are only allowed to interact once sanctioned by marriage and only in private space.

Star Academy violates the key rule restricting male–female interaction to private family space, since males and female participants in the show share living space for 4 months. Although bedrooms and bathrooms are separate, male and female contestants interact closely, touch each other's bodies often, and dance on stage together. Some "Access" shows even featured pillow fights and occasional incursions of members of one gender into the sleeping quarters of the other. There were also rampant rumors of sexual affairs, the most persistent of which involved Bashar the Kuwaiti and Sophia the Moroccan. The *fatwa* of the Standing Committee for Academic Research and Issuing Fatwas makes it very clear that the central concern was the role of women in society and their relations with men, lingering on the "immorality" of indecently dressed women, and mentioning explicitly women who look directly into men's eyes and women who dance in "seductive" ways.

According to Fatima Mernissi (1987), a leading feminist sociologist from Morocco, Islamic theology believes that female sexuality is active while male sexuality is passive. As a result, she argues, controlling women's sexuality is essential for social order because giving free reign to women's sexual desires brings *fitna*, or discord, upon Muslim societies. In addition to religion, history makes the status of women a particularly sensitive issue in the Arab world because of past attempts by French and British colonial powers to change indigenous laws related to women. As a result, the status of women historically evolved into a symbol of cultural and religious authenticity, and of resistance to colonial and imperial power. By featuring active and attractive women who interact closely and compete with men, *Star Academy* violates rules of male–female interaction that prevail in Saudi Arabia.

While on the screen every episode of *Star Academy* displays multiple violations of *hudud*, the interactions the show activates in hypermedia space call for the active violation of sacred boundaries by Muslim viewers. The internet is awash with pictures of *Star Academy* participants and video segments of the show. Bloggers scrutinize individual performances and evaluate voting results. Perhaps more importantly, by repeatedly inviting people to vote by text messaging using their mobile phone, *Star Academy* helps develop public awareness of the technical capacities of information technologies. Because its dramatic structure and financial performance depends on viewers' votes, *Star Academy* helped disseminate the idea of information technology as a lifestyle device. Once only a business tool, mobile phones have now become a social industry of their own, including personalized accessories, and ringtones. The best example is perhaps the so-called "Islamic phone," a mobile phone with a lunar calendar, special rings at prayer times, and even a compass pointing to the holy city of Mecca. Interactive television shows like *Star Academy* at the same time promote and depend on the new "electronic" lifestyle. Turn on an Arab music video channel at any hour of the day or night, and tickers moving at the bottom of the screen display love messages between young Arabs who usually reveal only their first name while small multimedia colored flags sometimes declare the text-messager's nationality. There are even digital love scales, with groups of friends voting on the compatibility of two people they know. Arab hypermedia space hosts social relations that are frowned upon in Saudi public space.

Media and Governance in Lebanon

While *Star Academy* posed a social challenge to Saudi governance, in Lebanon it articulated a political struggle, in line with that country's history of political and media fragmentation. Lebanon's experience with the mass media is unique in the Arab world and influential beyond the country's small territory. Since the nineteenth century, Lebanese journalists have founded major Arab newspapers, including Egypt's *Al-Ahram* and Saudi Arabia's *Al-Sharq Al-Awsat*. In the television era, Lebanon was the only Arab country not to have a fully state-owned national television station. Launched at the initiative of private business interests who approached the government for a broadcasting license in the 1950s, Télé-Liban was, from its founding in 1959 until the early 2000s, a hybrid, half-private, half state-owned entity. In wartime, several unlicensed competitors outperformed Télé-Liban, and in the early postwar years the station's private shares functioned as a "spare tire" for politicians who were uncertain about getting a license. When licenses were awarded in 1996 according to the 1994 Audio-Visual Media Law, Télé-Liban fell into a protracted decline (see Kraidy, 2005).

Just as Télé-Liban was symptomatic of a weak state, its unlicensed competitors symbolized the strength of civil society and confessional politics. The war precipitated the creation of a media landscape as diverse and fractured as Lebanon: conservative and radical, Christian and Muslim, secular and religious, capitalist and communist. The postwar regulatory challenge consisted in finding a formula that restored the authority of the state while preserving a politically representative media system. The licensing process was nakedly political, distributing licenses to leading politicians according to the Lebanese confessional power-sharing formula, which distributes resources and positions according to sectarian affiliation. Thus there was a Maronite station (LBC), a Sunni station (Future TV), a Shiia station (National Broadcasting Network, or NBN) and a Greek Orthodox station with Druze influence (Murr Television, or MTV). Additional licenses were later given to Hizbullah's Al-Manar, to a Christian station operated by the Maronite clergy, Télé-Lumière, and to New TV, formerly owned by the Lebanese communist party (Kraidy, 1998). The equilibrium achieved by licensing stations according to confessional criteria, periodically shaken by inflammatory broadcasts or state harassment (Kraidy, 1999)—and with the notable exception of the shutdown of MTV in September 2003—lasted until the tumultuous events of 2005.

Television assumed a central political role on February 14, 2005, when a massive car bomb killed the former prime minister Rafiq al-Hariri, on a major Beirut seaside thoroughfare. Future TV reacted immediately to the late morning bombing that killed its founder, and morphed into a full-time anti-Syrian screen clamoring for Lebanese independence. A diagonal black band on Future TV's logo signaled mourning and an on-screen digital calendar marked the days since Hariri's assassination. The channel became a full-time propaganda machine, celebrating Hariri's legacy, attacking the Syrian regime widely perceived to be behind the assassination, and keeping a focus on the UN investigation initially headed by German judge Detlev Mehlis. Future TV talk-shows featured a parade of anti-Syrian speakers while special music videos and promotional clips asking for "the truth" flooded the program grid. This situation prevailed until December 2005, when a new general manager was asked to bring Future TV back to a semblance of normalcy to stop the gaping financial losses of the previous 11 months (personal interview: Ayntrazi, 2005). LBC, whose political bosses were allies of Hariri's bloc in parliament, focused exclusively on the assassination only for a few days before going back to regular programming, thus avoiding the crippling financial repercussions of "opening the air" completely to the Hariri story. Both Future TV and LBC's editorial lines were highly critical of the Syrians and favorable to U.S. and European intervention against Syria.

On the opposite side, New TV, owned by Hariri foe Tahssin Khayyat, and Hizbullah's Al-Manar expressed a different narrative, opposed to Western interference in Lebanon and concerned about "U.S.–Israeli plans" for the region. While they did not explicitly support Syrian interference in Lebanon, both stations refrained from criticizing the Syrian regime and both were critical of the UN Mehlis investigation. New Television, which in the past had been critical of the Syrian–Lebanese security apparatus, propounded the secular version while Al-Manar put forth a religiously colored rendition of the situation. Both channels questioned the version of events given by the other side, oftentimes in a tit-for-tat direct questioning of facts. For instance, both stations raised suspicions about the number of demonstrators on March 14, 2005, which was over 1 million according to LBC and Future Television. When Future Television showed footage of demonstrators and claimed they were not Lebanese, Al-Manar retaliated by inviting some of the persons shown to demonstrate, on live television, that they were, in fact, Lebanese.

Reality Television and Hypermedia in the Cedar Revolution

If initial responses to Hariri's assassination confirmed that television stations in Lebanon remained primarily political instruments, the demonstrations that ensued, known as the "Cedar Revolution," indicate that the participatory activities called for by a program like *Star Academy*, like voting by mobile phone and using text messaging to build alliances and promote contestants, can in some cases have concrete political applications. The ways in which demonstrators used mobile phones, television and vocabulary from *Star Academy* and other reality television programs suggests that the combination of hypermedia space and popular culture can have a powerful impact on public life in the Arab world.

Several signs using the language of reality television could be seen among protesting crowds during the "Cedar Revolution." This was evident in the massive March 14, 2005, "opposition" demonstration against the Syro–Lebanese security apparatus, whose main demands were the withdrawal of Syrian troops from Lebanon and the resignation of Lebanon's leading politicians and security officers. Consider a hand-made, English-language sign carried by a demonstrator: the words "Lahoud Nominee" (referring to Lebanese president Emile Lahoud, whose term was illegitimately extended by Syrian fiat) sit atop the exhortation "call 1559" (in reference to the United Nations resolution calling for the withdrawal from Lebanon of Syrian troops and intelligence operatives). The sign is effective because it replicates weekly reality television rituals like nomination, mobilization, and voting, with which a vast number of Arab viewers are familiar.

When this ritual is transposed onto a sign carried by a Beirut demonstrator and captured by the cameras of myriad Arab satellite television channels and individual mobile phones equipped with digital cameras, it articulates a political agenda concisely and effectively. It uses a vocabulary that most Arabs, familiar with *Star Academy*, recognize and understand. The message on the sign, consisting of a few words and four digits, is eminently media-savvy in an age of image and sound bites. Expressing a complex political issue in a snapshot rich with meaning, it is perfect material for the frantic and repetitive news cycle of channels such as Al-Arabiya and Al-Jazeera in addition to CNN and other Western networks. Since nominations and Short Messaging Service voting are part of reality television rituals worldwide, the message has a potentially global audience. Satellite television financed by Saudi Arabian tycoons brought Lebanese politics to pan-Arab audiences, and popular culture made it widely palpable.

Reality television responded directly to Hariri's death in a way that one expects from news but not from entertainment media. Lebanese channels are pan-Arab leaders in entertainment programming and have produced and broadcast the most highly rated Arab reality television programs. *Superstar,* the Arabic version of *American Idol,* has completed three successful seasons on Future TV (Kraidy, 2006a, 2006b). *Star Academy* is aired by LBC, a channel that has historically opposed Syrian intervention in Lebanon. Immediately after Hariri's assassination, Future TV suspended regular programming, unified its hitherto separate terrestrial and satellite broadcasts, and postponed indefinitely the third installment of *Superstar.* However, previous *Superstar* contestants were summoned to record patriotic songs and shoot music videos that were incessantly played for months.

On *Star Academy*, a rehearsal was interrupted live on the air to announce Hariri's death. Then LBC went into a week of mourning. Unlike Future TV, LBC did not suspend its regular programs, but dedicated current affairs news and talk-shows to the issue. The *Star Academy* Prime that followed the mourning period turned into a patriotic fest where contestants hailing from throughout the Arab world sang patriotic Lebanese songs against the backdrop of a huge Lebanese flag.

The *dénouement*, presumably called in by millions of Arab voters (but, as the rumor mill suggested, possibly staged by LBC officials), was pure political spectacle: The Syrian contestant was voted out, and an eerie silence wrapped her humiliating exit from the stage.

The unceremonious on-stage dismissal of the Syrian candidate symbolically echoed the forced resignation of Omar Karameh, who was Lebanon's prime minister. In a rare moment in Arab politics, popular demonstrations had compelled a leader to resign. The importance of this event should not be underestimated. With thousands of Syrian troops still on Lebanese land and their colleagues in the *mukhabarat* (secret police) still haunting Lebanese streets and psyches, hundreds of thousands of demonstrators nonetheless called for and obtained the resignation of a sitting prime minister who was backed by Syria. Of course, without the support of the United States and France, who found a shared national interest in the Lebanese issue, and the tacit approval of Saudi Arabia, the Beirut demonstrations may have been quelled. Nonetheless the television cameras of Arab (Saudi funded) and Western channels, feeding live pictures to a worldwide audience, played a crucial role in sustaining the demonstrations. The demonstrators did not take US–French–Saudi support for granted, but courted and nurtured it, putting on an attractive visual spectacle for television cameras that took scenes and pictures that were then sent back and forth in an activated hypermedia space.

The demonstrators on Beirut's Martyrs Square were media savvy. Their main message was "national unity." Early on, leaders of the opposition agreed to instruct their followers to wave nothing but Lebanese flags. This strategy pre-empted state repression under the guise of banning sectarian demonstrations and preserving national unity. The demonstrations against Syria's policies towards Lebanon were organized by the "March 14 Opposition," a heterogeneous coalition of political forces that cut across Lebanon's various religious communities, and included a variety of student, professional, and civil society groups and unions. Media and public relations professionals put together a human Lebanese flag made of 10,000 people holding cardboard squares painted white, green or red. Young women painted small Lebanese flags on their cheeks like English soccer fans, and the less inhibited among them painted the flag on other body parts certain to attract the cameras. The absence of the usual multi-colored range of flags representing sectarian or partisan loyalties, and the proliferation of Lebanese flags had a symbolic impact on swaths of public opinion in a country ordinarily marred by multiple political, religious and social cleavages. The "other" demonstration, organized by Hizbullah and its allies, also featured a proliferation of Lebanese flags. (It is important to note that the Free Patriotic Movement, headed by retired army general Michel Aoun, was a major participant in the March 14 demonstrations, but later broke with the Hariri-dominated coalition that organized these demonstrations and concluded a memorandum of understanding with Hizbullah.)

The Beirut demonstrators exploited hypermedia space to their full political advantage, using mobile phones, digital cameras and the internet, in addition to courting television news cameras. Demonstrators took pictures using their mobile phones equipped with digital cameras, which they promptly transmitted to news organizations or to friends who uploaded them on websites dedicated to their cause. These "citizen-correspondents," as a columnist in the Lebanese daily newspaper *Assafir* called them, ensured that their cause would be seen across the world. Unlike the conspicuous CNN and Al-Jazeera cameras, the invisible cameras of thousands of demonstrators acted as non-obtrusive surveillance system that went a long way in pre-empting repression by the security apparatus. The proliferation of cameras is likely to have contributed to preventing clashes between demonstrators and counter-demonstrators, no easy feat when one considers that between 1.5 and 2 million Lebanese, or between a third of or half of the total population of the country, descended on the streets of Beirut in the span of a week in March 2005.

When the Lebanese army established checkpoints around central Beirut to prevent demonstrators from reaching demonstration sites, soldiers at some checkpoints whispered to the demonstrators that they supported them, a nugget of information that was immediately "blasted" via text messages, allowing demonstrators to converge on checkpoints where soldiers or commanding officers appeared sympathetic to their cause. At other checkpoints, young women put red roses in soldiers' hands and rifles, thus "disarming" them and helping flows of men and women alerted via text messaging "blasts" to reach designated protest areas. Mobile phones helped demonstrators mobilize and organize; cameras and reality television vocabulary helped them propagate their message.

Hypermedia Space, Reality Television and the Future of Arab Governance

The hypermedia space resulting from multiple configurations between various media can be said to be an alternative space for Arab social and political relations. Shaped primarily by the Saudi–Lebanese connection, Arab hypermedia space is taken up in different ways in Saudi Arabia and Lebanon. How hypermedia space is used is therefore dependent on political context, availability of technology, and most importantly the willingness of people to use hypermedia space for specific purposes. The commercial and dramatic logics of reality television help to activate these hypermedia flows. Viewers of *Star Academy* consume and produce information about contestants on the internet, mobilize and create voting coalitions using mobile phones, read and write about them in the papers, and create blogs or fan sites. They respond to "expert" opinions by journalists and talk-show guests who comment on reality television. Reality television, in other words, brings knowledge of hypermedia space to the everyday, mundane level.

As a result, whether posing a social challenge in Saudi Arabia or articulating a political struggle in Lebanon, hypermedia space is contributing to changes in Arab governance. Viewers participating in reality television rituals learn that sending a flow of text messages in favor of a *Star Academy* contestant to music television channels that post them on moving tickers, helps generate chatter about the contestant in question and thereby increases their visibility and ultimately their chances of outlasting the competition. This knowledge can be tapped by political activists who "plug into" networks of friends and acquaintances engaged or familiar with reality television, converting them partially into instruments of political mobilization. The resulting large numbers of demonstrators, once on television news, become a potent tool of political pressure in the context of Arab politics, where leaders are increasingly concerned with their legitimacy. Arab leaders also know that in a media-saturated world where Arab regimes are under the microscope of the U.S. administration and international public opinion, in addition to internal pressures of various kinds, clamping down on demonstrators can be counter-productive.

The flags, cameras and mobile phones did not, on their own, prevent the Syrian–Lebanese security apparatus from repressing the demonstrators, but their combination with pressure from the United States, France and Saudi Arabia did. Saudi Arabia, whose billionaires finance Arab media, was on the side of the "Cedar Revolution," so Saudi officials did not attempt to limit coverage of the demonstrations. In addition, LBC and Future TV, two powerful outlets, were supportive of the "March 14" demonstrators. The alignment of the political-economic structure of Arab media with the interest of the Lebanese demonstrators and against the Syrian regime made the "Cedar Revolution" a more important event than it would have otherwise been. The potency of hypermedia space depends on the ability of activists to use media and information technologies, but also on the political decisions of "big" media owners, a dependence that is nonetheless not complete since Al-Jazeera, opposed to the Saudi regime and to United States policies in the Middle East, gave sustained and overall positive coverage to the Beirut demonstrations.

In Saudi Arabia, hypermedia space is radically different from the heavily policed public space where interaction between non-married males and females is strictly prohibited. The interactivity and mobility inherent in hypermedia space subverts a principle that is at the heart of Saudi social organization. The popularity of reality television, coupled with the wide availability of information technology, in a socially restrictive context, activates new information permutations that undermine the social order. The most important challenge probably resides in the "alternative" male–female relations portrayed on *Star Academy*, with women interacting and competing with men. Similarly, hypermedia space empowers Saudi women who are disempowered in Saudi public space. (Interestingly, the February 12, 2006 resolution about the internet does not explicitly mention women or sexual issues.) It is no coincidence that women make up two thirds of Saudi internet users ("Country Profile," 2006). When people purposely use deterritorialized, interactive and mobile technologies such as the internet and mobile telephones, they can undermine social and political boundaries from within, and therefore they are much more difficult to control. Under propitious politico-economic conditions, hypermedia space acts potentially as an incubator of social change.

In Lebanon, hypermedia space contributed to the momentum of a political coalition that went from being the opposition in March 2005 to taking the majority of seats in the parliament by June of the same year. For more than a decade, Lebanese security forces in coordination with Syrian intelligence, had quelled demonstrations, jailed activists, and harassed anyone suspected of political opposition. While a changing geopolitical climate and U.S.–French support were instrumental to the initial success of the "Cedar Revolution," the judicious use of small and big media connections by the demonstrators was an important factor in sustaining the movement. Besides mobilization and coordination, hyper-media space was a crucial tool in conveying an image of national unity—albeit contrived, temporary and fragile— that prevented security forces from justifying a clampdown on activists with the claim of controlling sectarian demonstrations. Thus demonstrators made the Lebanese flag, as a putative symbol of national unity, ubiquitous, painted on signs and bodies, posted on websites, and most importantly saturating television footage.

By making the capacities of hypermedia space visible to Arab viewers, inter-active, multimedia-using reality television shows like *Star Academy* pose a social challenge in Saudi Arabia and articulate a political struggle in Lebanon. In these two countries and elsewhere in the Arab world, activists struggling to grab social and political agency, that is, the ability to not follow a predetermined course of action, find hypermedia space useful because agency resides partly in hypermedia space. Bolter and Grusin argue that

> [M]edia do have agency, but that agency . . . is constrained and hybrid . . . the agency of cultural change is located on the interaction of formal, material, and economic logics that slip into and out of the grasp of individuals and social groups.
>
> (Bolter and Grusin, 1999, p. 78).

When individuals and communities "connect" and activate information configura-tions towards achieving social or political objectives, they fulfill the agency potential of hypermedia space (albeit tactically and temporarily, as it turned out in the case of Lebanon). Most importantly, as examples discussed previously demonstrate, hypermedia space operates as a tool to extend the scope of agency into "real" public space.

The social and political significance of hypermedia space will probably outlast the current craze of reality television. When individuals engaging in contentious politics become producers of information, old understandings about the political impact of mass media and the formation of public opinion no longer make sense. The most significant development in the Arab public sphere is the ease and speed with which information circulates between myriad information technologies with varying size, scope and uses. Information therefore originates from new groups, circulates in new ways and reaches new publics. In these convoluted processes, format adaptations are particularly susceptible to manifold uses and receptions because they provide a social and political canvas on which various groups can latch their claims and counter-claims. Notably, because they articulate "foreign" values, global televison formats are likely to stir controversy, leading to contentious politics in which information circulates between various interconnected technologies.

These new information dynamics in the Arab world are already having profound political consequences. Arab publics know that "big" media outlets are bound by their funders' agendas. Al-Jazeera's editorial line will not violate the principles of Qatari foreign policy, and Al-Arabiya is an instrument of Saudi policy. Similarly, al-Hurra is unable to shed the stigma of being a tool of the U.S. government, and mainstream Western news outlets rarely oppose their governments' foreign policies. The use of "small" media, on the other hand, depends on the work of interconnected small groups of activists who know and trust each other. This trust endows the information circulated between them with a level of believability that governments and big media newsmakers can only dream about. Increasingly media-savvy, technology-proficient and politically emboldened, aided by the converging interests of telecommunications and media corporations, these groups are poised to continue stirring the Arab political soup. Even as the reality television craze appears to be losing steam, it has unleashed new information configurations that will outlast it.

While talk of reality television directly bringing democracy to the Arab world is based on incomplete analyses and an overly optimistic outlook, Arab activists have drawn lessons from the reality television phenomenon that they are now using more or less successfully in political action. In this environment, top-down communication strategies may lose "hearts-and-minds" battles to small groups of mobile, motivated and networked activists. Arab governments and U.S. "public diplomacy" strategists appear to be late in learning the same lesson. Centralized broadcasting facilities, in Cairo or Springfield (headquarters of the unsuccessful U.S. government Arabic-language television channel al-Hurra), increasingly look like massive artillery cannons shooting blanks, while activist groups have shown they are capable of scoring political points with the tools of the digital age with laser beam precision. The constantly shifting communication order—or disorder— they are creating is poised to influence Arab governance as governments and large-scale mass media organizations could be reduced to watching and commenting, or, more ominously, co-opting hypermedia space and its nascent publics.

Notes

1   This chapter draws on my recent work (Kraidy, 2009, forthcoming) on the social and political impact of Arab reality television and is based on 16 months of non-continuous fieldwork in Beirut, Dubai, Kuwait, Paris and London, including 100 interviews with media producers, directors, and commentators. Fieldwork was partly funded by the United States Institute of Peace and American University's Research Competition Award. Writing began at the Woodrow Wilson International Center for Scholars in Washington, DC, from September 2005 to May 2006, continued under the auspices of the Scholars Program in Culture and Communication at the Annenberg School for Communication (Spring 2007), and completed at ASC in the following year. The section about Saudi Arabia draws heavily on Kraidy, Marwan M. (2006c, September 4), Hypermedia and Governance in Saudi Arabia, *First Monday*, www.firstmonday.org, which benefited from considerable feedback from Sandra Braman and Thomas Malaby.
2   Dawud-Al-Sharyan, a Dubai-based journalist, was appointed in October 2006 as deputy general manager of Al-Arabiya, reflecting a trend to employ more Saudis and Gulf Arabs in Saudi-owned companies.

References

'Abbud, Ghada (2005, February 10). Teenagers Sinking Their Teeth Into New Technology, *Arab News*.

'Akeel, Maha (2005, January 10). Camera Phones Legal but Individual Restrictions Apply, *Arab News*.

Alavanthian, Sebouh, Director of Programming, Lebanese Broadcasting Corporation, personal interview, LBC headquarters, Adma, Lebanon, July 5, 2004.

Al-Daher, Pierre, General Manager, Lebanese Broadcasting Corporation, personal interview, LBC headquarters, Adma, Lebanon, July 5, 2004.

Al-Daher, Pierre, General Manager, Lebanese Broadcasting Corporation, personal interview, LBC headquarters, Adma, Lebanon, August 21, 2005.

Al-Dakhil, Munira Muhammad (2005, February 27). Destructive Academy is Harmful to the Family, *al-Riyadh*.

Analysis: Saudi Rulers Ease Their Grip on the Media, BBC Monitoring Media Services, May 28, 2004. London: British Broadcasting Corporation.

Ayntrazi, Tariq (2005, December 18). General Manager, Future Television (Beirut), Dubai, United Arab Emirates.

Bluetooth in Saudi Arabia Prospers in Lost Time (2005, February 10). *Al-Hayat* [in Arabic].

Bolter, Jay and Grusin, David (1999). *Remediation: Understanding New Media*. Cambridge, MA: MIT Press.

Boyd, Douglas (2001) Saudi Arabia's International Media Strategy: Influence Through Multinational Ownership, in K. Hafez (Ed.), *Mass Media, Politics and Society in the Middle East* (pp. 43–60), Cresskill, NJ: Hampton Press.

Country profile: Saudi Arabia (2006, July 28). Available http://news.bbc.co.uk/1/hi/world/middle_east/country_profiles/791936.stm. London: British Broadcasting Corporation.

Deibert, Ronald J. (1997). *Parchment, Printing, and Hypermedia: Communication in World Order Transformation*. New York: Columbia University Press.

Eddy, W. (1963). King Ibn Sa'ud: Our Faith and Our Iron. *Middle East Journal*, 17(3), 257–263.

Fatwa Concerning the Program *Star Academy* (2004). Standing Committee for Academic Research and Issuing Fatwas [In Arabic].

Habib, Osama (2003, December 3). Alwaleed Buys Large Stake in LBC SAT, *Daily Star*.

Khalil, J. F. (2004). Blending in: Arab Television and the Search for Programming Ideas, *Transnational Broadcasting Studies*, 13, Available www.tbsjournal.com

Kraidy, Marwan M. (1998). Broadcasting Regulation and Civil Society in Postwar Lebanon, *Journal of Broadcasting and Electronic Media*, *42*(3), 387–400.

—— (1999). State Control of Television News in 1990s Lebanon, *Journalism and Mass Communication Quarterly*, *76*(3), 485–498.

—— (2002). Arab Satellite Television between Regionalization and Globalization, *Global Media Journal*, *1*(1), available http://lass.calumet.purdue. edu/cca/gmj/new_page_1.htm

—— (2005). *Hybridity, or the Cultural Logic of Globalization*. Philadelphia, PA: Temple University Press.

—— (2006a). Reality Television and Politics in the Arab World (Preliminary Observations), *Transnational Broadcasting Studies*, *2*(1), 7–28, also available http://www.tbsjournal. com

—— (2006b). Popular Culture as a Political Barometer: Lebanese–Syrian Relations on *Superstar*, *Transnational Broadcasting Studies*, June, available www.tbsjournal.com.

—— (2006c, September 4). Hypermedia and Governance in Saudi Arabia, *First Monday*, *11*(9), available www.firstmonday.org/issues/special11_9

—— (2009). *Reality Television and Arab Politics: Contention in Public Life*. New York and London: Cambridge University Press.

Mernissi, Fatima (1987). *Beyond the Veil: Male-Female Dynamics in Modern Muslim Society*. Bloomington: Indiana University Press.

New Saudi Law to Jail, Lash Cellphone Porn Users (2005, April 16). Riyadh, Saudi Arabia: Reuters.

Sa'd, Roula, director of promotion and marketing, Lebanese Broadcasting Corporation, personal interview, LBC headquarters, Adma, Lebanon, July 5, 2004.

Salameh, Ghassan (1980). Political Power and the Saudi State, *MERIP Reports*, no. 91.

"Saudi Arabia," *CIA Factbook* (2004).

Saudi Internet Rules (2006). Available www.al-bab.com/media/docs/Saudi.htm

Shobaili, A. S. (1971). A Historical and Analytical Study of Broadcasting and Press in Saudi Arabia. Unpublished doctoral dissertation, Ohio State University, Columbus, Ohio, U.S.A.

15

A REVOLUTION IN TELEVISION AND A GREAT LEAP FORWARD FOR INNOVATION?

China in the Global Television Format Business[1]

Michael Keane

The People's Republic of China has never really countenanced a scarcity of domestic television content. Supply has been constant, indicating both the importance and the sheer size of the sector. The nationalized broadcast media has for several decades churned out cheaply produced films, documentaries, dramas, and news programmes. During the last two decades of the twentieth century, however, audience demand for domestic content began to wane as more international programmes found their way into schedules, particularly in southern China. China's accession to the World Trade Organization in December 2001 seemed to herald soul-searching among its media mandarins. What would happen? Would China be inundated by foreign content (the worst case scenario) or would China, as it has done over time, absorb and regulate foreign influences?

The reasoning behind the latter proposition is important to acknowledge, as it indicates a belief that size does matter, and that culture, like water, seeks its own level. The essence of the argument goes something like this: China is "characteristically different" from any other nation such that "foreign" cultural influences are absorbed and transformed by (dominant) Chinese cultural genes. Many examples can be found in history. There was Genghis Khan, who invaded China in the thirteenth century; the subsequent short-lived Yuan Dynasty failed to have any lasting cultural impact upon China. There were the Manchus—Jürchen tribesman who invaded from across China's northern frontiers in the seventeenth century—who agreed to uphold China's traditional beliefs and structures in order to gain social cooperation (Spence 1990: 3). In the modern era there was Deng Xiaoping's version of capitalism, which came to be cleverly recoded as "a commodity economy with socialist characteristics." In speaking of the tradition of cultural borrowing and indigenization, the business analyst Li Conghua notes,

"In the longer term China accommodates what it can, transforms what it can't accept to its own needs, and that which is extreme, extraneous, or atypical, is ejected" (Li 1998: 18).

This historical legacy of localization supports the belief within China that cultural borrowing is an essentializing process. By virtue of this fact issues of intellectual property are often obscured. The stock phrase "with Chinese characteristics" (*you Zhongguo tese*) is more often than not associated with China's embrace of things foreign. However, this cliché obfuscates rather than explains the nature of Chinese society and its "characteristic" relationship with the global community. While China is certainly different, and while it maintains a long cultural tradition, it is by no means exceptional. Many of the changes occurring in Chinese society are predictable, rational, and in accord with global transformations. This is certainly the case in point when considering China's uptake of television formats.

The licensing, co-production, and adaptation of television formats provides a potent illustration of how cultural exchange is mediated across national televisual spaces. A qualification that needs to be stated at the outset, however, is that China is a transitional state where the creative element that one normally takes for granted when talking about film and television production has been stymied over time by the need to appease officialdom. Nevertheless, this is precisely where television formats provide a mechanism to move forward. Chinese television stations are actively pursuing viewers as they move towards self-reliance; as they evolve into commercial enterprises programmes are now viewed as intermediate products used to produce audiences rather than as the raison d'être of their existence.

In describing the state of play of television formats in China in this chapter I will therefore look at how formats have assumed an important development role. To illustrate the changing television environment in the context of formatting I use the concepts of *mimetic isomorphism* and *R&D*. These two ideas capture two sides of format activity in China today. Isomorphism refers to the tendency of producers to mimic and even clone without due consideration of market flooding, while R&D describes how the format process contributes to "know-how" and ideas, which are developed either internally within the organization or transferred from outside the system. As might be expected, the sheer scale and rapid expansion of China's format activity makes any pretence of comprehensive mapping futile. What I will endeavour to do in this chapter, however, is to present a snapshot of format activity through several genres that have been amenable to licensing or cloning. They include game shows, children's television, soap operas, and reality television.

Background

In early 1999 I began to be interested in how international television formats were being replicated within the rapidly commercializing Chinese television industry. This interest was stimulated by my earlier research on television drama (Keane 2002b), which had led me to conclude that structural factors and organizational dictates predisposed Chinese producers towards wide-scale content mimicking. By the mid-1990s television delivery platforms were ample but programme genres and formats were mostly prosaic, determined by decree rather than demand. Instead of a smorgasbord of choice, Chinese television viewers were being fed a limited buffet of cheap programming garnished with occasional delicacies from Taiwan, Hong Kong, or overflows from Western (usually American) schedules. In providing for potential abundance, cable channel platforms had inadvertently exposed a deficit of quality domestic fare and in doing so had challenged the supply-side logic of a programme distribution system founded on barter. The inefficiencies of this model, combined with the commercial aspirations of a number of prominent media organizations, led many to search for new ways of delivering entertaining yet inexpensive programmes.

Formats have undoubtedly changed the television environment in China. Television formats, particularly soft genres such as variety, games, and quiz shows, are prevalent among Chinese television schedules—but such profusion is relatively recent. In 1999 the topic of "television programme formats" (*dianshi jiemu xingshi*) did not feature in scholarly journals or television tabloids. Programming at China Central Television (hereafter CCTV), the pre-eminent national broadcaster, was still being largely developed from within. Provincial, city, and cable stations selectively scheduled finished imported programmes, with minimal incidence of foreign format replication.

The following year saw formats emerge as a programme development strategy in China. To understand this transformation we need to factor in changes in the international television landscape as well as note the increasing maturity of Chinese television. As Albert Moran (1998) has demonstrated, international television networks had for some time recognized the economies of scale that formats offered, leading to substantial format franchising across national networks. The talking point in television trade journals and the popular press during much of 2002 was the popularity of reality formats such as *Survivor* and *Big Brother*. This hyping of reality television was also picked up in China. About the same time a disparaging expression "cloning" (*kelong*) began to be used to describe opportunistic copycatting of programmes among Chinese broadcasters. To further underline this trend, there was talk of a great leap forward made in programme innovation in Hunan—the very birthplace of Mao Zedong, the great icon of the Chinese Communist revolution. Here were developments worth following. Hunan Satellite Television had staked a position as China's most commercially savvy broadcaster and was cleverly localizing programmes from Taiwan and Hong Kong.

During the period 2001–2, I witnessed a growing awareness of the transferability of formats within China, both from producers and academics. The former group were relatively pragmatic about the business ethics of using of other stations' (and other nations') ideas, while the latter condemned format cloning as a sure sign of the inevitable dumbing-down of Chinese culture and the onset of cultural globalization. In addition to academic critique, popular recognition of the format phenomenon was steadily growing. During a focus group discussion I conducted at Beijing's Qinghua University in July 2000, participants nominated Taiwanese and Hong Kong entertainment programmes as the source of many new ideas in Chinese television. Some were able to indicate Chinese programmes that were derivative of foreign programmes, but were unable to actually identify the names of the original.

In the space of a few years the television format went from being unsighted to being acknowledged, for better or for worse, as an important development in the Chinese television industry. The term "reality television" (*zhenren xiu*) also entered into the Chinese industry lexicon in 2002 with the broadcast of Sichuan Television's *Into Shangrila* (*Zouru xianggelila*), and Guangzhou Television's *The Great Survival Challenge* (*Shengcun da tiaozhan*). The similarities went deeper than just titles. In June of that year I was tracking the origins of CCTV Channel 2's *The Dictionary of Happiness* (*Kaixin cidian*). *The Dictionary of Happiness* was an enormously successful local quiz show that had cleverly refashioned the key elements of Celador's global format *Who Wants To Be A Millionaire?*—including the "life-lines" of "phone a friend" and "ask the audience"—into a domestic quiz format. During a conversation I had with the producer, the term "format" (*xingshi*) was used a number of times and the point was made that formats were playing an important role in programme development. In response to the obvious question about origins, the response was almost predictable: the process of making *The Dictionary of Happiness* had begun with a provisional search of international programming for ideas that might be appropriate (*heshi*) for China. A CCTV research team had subsequently spent several months devising the appropriate format and carefully piloting before launching it on the national broadcaster (Zheng 2002, personal interview).[2] Despite the producer's claims that the Chinese version was unique, CCTV's format was obviously a direct copy of the international version. In taking this example as a barometer of the format environment it is also obvious that many producers realize they are culpable but understand that there is no legal recourse available to the format rights holder if the copier makes minimal changes.

China Within the Format: Isomorphism

Television formats are undoubtedly a key element of television programming in China. But are television formats in some way indicative of social relations in contemporary China? Can their recent profusion be seen as a metaphor for China's transition from a command to a commodity economy? Or conversely, to use a Marxist approach, does the nature of contemporary China *reflect* the high incidence of format cloning? These are two positions that are worth exploring. Let us take the latter first.

Today in China residual elements of bureaucratic control co-exist uneasily with sporadic outbreaks of entrepreneurial activity. A combination of a legacy of state control and the influence of a great cultural tradition have led many writers and pundits to claim that China is the great localizer of foreign ideas, thus the description "Chinese characteristics" referred to earlier. Rather ironically, as we shall discover, the presumption that foreign ideas are indigenized or filtered devalues the role of local ingenuity. In actual fact, it is not so much the hybridization of foreign ideas that is at play, but the copying of foreign ideas already localized within China.

To explain what is in actual fact a domino phenomenon, I will use the term *isomorphism*. As used by institutional theorists, isomorphism describes how organizations come to resemble one another in the marketplace (Guthrie 1999). Three kinds of isomorphism can be identified in the Chinese economy: coercive, mimetic, and normative. *Coercive* relates to pressures to conform, particularly from policy directives; *mimetic* implies "follow the leader" practices, especially in conditions of risk and uncertainty; while *normative* explains the process of businesses taking on institutional norms that have become "best practice" within industries. While all three models help explain various aspects of the development of China's media industries, mimetic isomorphism is the key to understanding the nature of formatting.

The isomorphic nature of China's media is reflected in the development of television. This "new" media technology began in China on 1 May 1958 with the first broadcast from Beijing Television, which was renamed China Central Television (CCTV) in 1976. Television was controlled and administered by officials in Beijing, with the Chinese Propaganda Department acting as the sole arbiter of taste. It was not until the 1980s that the medium was liberated and allowed to consider its audience. This coincided with the deregulation of administration and the expansion of four tiers of broadcasting: central, provincial, city, and county. During the period from 1984 to 1990 the number of terrestrial stations increased from 93 to 509 (Huang 1994: 223). By 1995 there were reportedly 2,740 television channels including educational channels and cable stations. Television programmes were being beamed off 96,530 ground relay stations to China's remote regions (Tu 1997: 4).

Cable networks had begun earlier during the 1970s. Initially established to provide wired loudspeaker networks during the 1950s, the cabled signal transmission system was later applied to television signal distribution with master access television (MATV) distributing free-to-air signal transmissions (Harrison 2002; Shoesmith and Wang 2002). The first cable system was set up in 1974 in the Beijing Grand Hotel, and in 1982 the government decided that all new residential blocks would be equipped with ducts for cable television. By 1998 China's rollout of cable exceeded 1,340,000 kilometres and by 1999 there were 80 million subscribers to cable television (Tu 1997: 4).

The deregulation of television and the rush to set up stations led to a supply-driven media environment in which cooperation between stations was a means of ensuring distribution. Of course, the legacy of state planning and the "iron rice bowl" practice of lifetime employment also contributed to the lack of competitiveness. Television stations, in particular the big urban stations, employed many people; those who worked in such occupations were inclined towards conservatism such that keeping officials happy was as much a priority as satisfying the imagined viewer. To underscore this, the guiding principle underpinning state television—as espoused by the Minister of Radio, Film and Television (MRFT)—was that television served the "nation and the people'.

Prior to 2001, and in contrast to privately owned and operated media systems in capitalist mixed economies, China's nationalized broadcasters were not consolidated into competitive networks, but rather operated according to geographically determined logistics premised on the ideal of ensuring that information and propaganda reached all segments of society. This logic has created a system that rewards non-competitive behaviour. Under the planned economy, and particularly in the Chinese media, organizations were subject to *coercive isomorphism*: they were similar in terms of structure and administration, and content production followed a pattern decreed by political mandate rather than popular demand. The role of propaganda department officials at the station level served to ensure that programming decisions were politically correct, while the in-house integration of production and broadcasting meant that there was no possibility for the development of independent production houses pitching ideas or formats to the marketplace. From the early years of China's television industry to the mid-1990s, aesthetic boundaries were drawn by Ministry of Culture dictums with more than a little "guidance" from Propaganda Department mandarins.

In order to appease the requirement that television was in fact "serving the people and the nation," the majority of television dramas produced were "mainstream melody works" (*zhuxuanlü*), a term that by 1987 had been officially inscribed as broadcasting's equivalent of socialist realism (Keane 1999: 254; Zhang 1994: 2). This genre paraded role models with progressive sensibilities acting out narratives of social change that were in effect redolent endorsements of the government's reform policies. By 1998, following the success of CCTV's costume epic *Romance of the Three Kingdoms* (*Sanguo yanyi*), Chinese television schedules witnessed a noticeable swing towards Royal Court costume dramas: this was a genre that China's television producers have generally believed they understand better than their compatriots in Taiwan or Hong Kong (see Yin 2002; Keane 2002b). The most notable of these were *Prime Minister Liu Luoguo* (*Zaixiang Liu Luoguo*) (1996), *Yongzheng Dynasty* (*Yongzheng wangchao*) (1998) and *The Eloquent Ji Shaolan* (*Tongzui tieya Ji Shaolan*) (2001). In 1999 the hegemony of Royal Court dramas was usurped temporarily by historical recreations and celebrations of events surrounding the birth of the People's Republic of China in 1949.

In effect, these trends underscore the structural dynamics underpinning Chinese economic reforms. Endowed with a massive but not necessarily affluent domestic market, China's development has been a story of many small empires rather than national champions devouring all competitors. Reform, which began in 1978, has led to a commercial environment typified by miniaturization and duplicate construction (Gore 2000: 136). Miniaturization refers to the practice of multiple small-scale commercial enterprises unable to grow to become champions in their own right because of limited access to capital. "Duplicate construction,"on the other hand, describes the process by which enterprises replicate each other's activities, even including infrastructure, resulting in a fragmented marketplace typified by a great deal of parasitic localization and little real innovation. Here the emphasis is on growing local industries rather than national or international networks. While essentially a neo-classical model of growth, this kind of duplication encourages "capital-less capitalists" (Gore 2000: 136) who do not bear the whole risk of failure. This phenomenon can be observed in the Chinese television industry as it morphed from a centralized propaganda monolith under the great helmsman Mao Zedong to a thousand-headed flotilla of quasi-commercial stations under the decentralizing reforms of Deng Xiaoping and his successor Jiang Zemin.

Although business logic drives the thinking of many of the new breed of broadcasters such as Hunan Electronic Broadcasting (the commercial arm of Hunan Television in South China), the competitive ethic has not magically transformed China's media into centres of innovation. Despite the consolidation in 2001–2 of a number of larger provincial media operations into vertically integrated media centres such as the China Film, Broadcasting and Television Group (CRFT), the Beijing Radio, Film and Television Group (BRFT), and the Shanghai Media and Entertainment Group (SMEG), the flotilla effect of "un-networked" broadcasters, particularly cable stations, had already created the foundation of *mimetic isomorphism*. The difference with coercive isomorphism is that television stations, rather than taking their lead from policy, follow the lead of other stations: if a station is successful in a form of programming, its success will be quickly replicated by its neighbours, even to the extent of copying what is in essence intellectual property. One station's research is appropriated by other stations with the result that the marketplace is flooded by programmes that do not just look alike, but are similar in name, design, and duration. This strategy is evident in both large and small stations. The key point to be made here is that isomorphism and cloning do not necessarily lead to a more innovative media environment. The format, as a readymade template for success, reduces the need for risk, but promotes a "follow the leader" mentality.

The Format Within China: A Great Leap Forward

While format appropriation follows the logic of isomorphism that typifies the Chinese economy as a whole, formats do offer strategies for Chinese producers seeking to break away from stereotyped traditional genres. As the political bound-aries that have insulated China become increasingly more porous, and foreign programmes make inroads into schedules, producers are receptive to ideas that have had proven resonance in culturally proximate locations.

In applying these ideas the format becomes a vehicle for experimentation with producers taking the "crust" and inserting local ingredients. Of course, there are the ethical issues associated with copying. The tactic of deliberately taking ingredients from programmes with established market success is now rife in China. This is not to suggest that Chinese television formats are in breach of intellectual property regimes. Despite well-documented incidences of piracy on the audio-visual black market in China, television formats represent a different order of complexity. As indicated elsewhere in this collection, no legal mechanism currently exists to prosecute format content predators.

Moreover, while the conventional wisdom about copyright is that it protects the innovation commons by ascribing value to original ideas (in turn developing a strong industrial ethos), in China the process of cultural borrowing arguably breaks down the rigor mortis of state control of ideas. For a long time programming had been commissioned on the basis of a public service model of broadcasting, a one-to-many model that served the interests of propagandists, stifled the creative intent of China's television professionals, and ultimately delivered audiences a bland serving of politicized fare.

The emergence of formats can therefore be linked to the growing liberalization and interactivity of content, and the genesis in China of creative content. The use of the term "creative content" in this context refers to a greater appreciation of the feedback loops existing between producer and audience, the most obvious manifestations of which are the involvement of the audience in the "show" itself or the provision of a vehicle for audiences to interact with production through cross-media platforms. Without doubt, in-studio live broadcasts are the earliest forms of interactive television and they have also been the most amenable formats for localization in China. They vary from genres such as variety arts shows and talk shows to more structured formats such as quiz and game shows.

The growing influence of studio audience formats during the past decade has been described as the democratization of Chinese television, providing an increased role for ordinary people to participate, relegating the parade of politically approved celebrities to special event genres. According to the producer of *The Dictionary of Happiness*, the democratization of taste has occurred because the "Chinese audience's assessment of celebrities now varies greatly": a sea-change induced by the tendency for celebrities to dominate, leaving little space for participation by audiences (Zheng 2002: 9). This is as much an indication of the increasing exposure of celebrities as an indictment of the envy directed towards "success stories" in a society long accustomed to social equalization.

Another commentator has referred to the evolution of the participant (*jiabin*— literally "honoured guest') as indicating a general shift from television's elevated status to a true medium of mass consumption. In this account those who were formerly "designated" to grace the small screen were the bright shining national emblems: "politicians, heroic figures, models and stereotypes, the socialist van-guard, performers, expert scholars, and celebrities" (Yang 2000: 16). The common person could not imagine a role except as a cipher in a live audience whose capture by the camera highlighted delight in the performance. In celebrating this demo-cratization of taste, Yang writes, "the Chinese word *jiabin* had been formerly associated with activities and contact among people, but today it has become the favourite salutation in television programmes" (Yang 2000: 4).

Variety, Games, and Quizzes: The Road Ahead?

> Just like master Lu Xun said: at first, there was no road in the world but when more and more people walk the same way, there is a road. . . . It is because there is the phenomenon of "follow the leader" and "cloning" that we see an early stage of diversification of television styles and genres of programming.
>
> (Yang 2000: 13)

When Lu Xun, the great Chinese writer and revolutionary thinker, penned his famous reference to trail-blazing in the face of considerable social pressure during the 1930s he could never have imagined his words might be later used to describe the evolution of electronic game shows in China. Everyday life in China prior to the Communist revolution of the following decade was simple, with the local teahouse or opera providing the medium for social intercourse.

Despite the obvious banality of comparing traditional culture to mass variety television, we can locate a common ingredient: live audiences. The first genre of television programming to make use of live audiences, albeit in a passive role of amused spectators, was the "evening party" (*wanhui*), itself a sub-genre of the arts variety programme (*zongyi jiemu*). These kinds of programmes are heavily format-driven in the sense that a standard structure exists into which new content and performances are added. While incorporating elements common to variety shows across Asia, the Chinese variants have been overtly politicized. The first variety show in China was Guangdong Television's *A Kaleidoscope of Colours* (*Wanzi qianhong*). In 1984 CCTV introduced *Weekend Arts* (*Zhoumo wenyi*), followed by *Variety Kaleidoscope* (*Zongyi daguan*) and the *Zhengda Variety Show* (*Zhengda zongyi*) in 1990.

While most of these shows can be classified as original formats drawing on traditional genres of performance, the *Zhengda Variety Show* can be considered as China's first authentic variety–game show format. The show was a joint venture between a Thai–Chinese company (the Zhengda Consortium) and CCTV. Its success and longevity can be primarily attributed to an audience fascination with the world outside China and the rising prominence of celebrities at the time of its inception in 1990. Special guests engaged in a quiz format where content was drawn from footage of nature and foreign customs. Audience members, drawn from industrial work units and decked out respectively in different colours, engaged with the panel. By 1997 the *Zhengda Variety Show* format was beginning to suffer the fate of most successful programmes in China: it was being heavily imitated throughout ther country. In July 2002 the original quiz format was dispensed with and the programme took on all the visible manifestations of the global quiz challenge format *Dog Eat Dog*, distributed by ECM. In this refashioning there was no license deal with ECM, just a very expedient replication of the format "with Chinese characteristics" added.

However, the mutation and cannibalization of variety, game, and quiz shows occurs on a regular basis. There is often a sense of desperation at stake here. Hunan Satellite Television thought it was on to a winner in 1996 when it produced *The Citadel of Happiness* (*Kuaile da ben ying*), a musical variety show targeted at the youth audience. The format consisted primarily of apolitical entertainment content, based around social issues, youth lifestyle, and popular music. The station outlaid a great deal of money promoting the show, bringing in celebrities from Hong Kong and Taiwan. The pay-off was that advertising rates exceeded expectations, but within a short space of time its own format had been cloned into more than 100 local variants within China itself. None of its imitations attained the heights of the original—a fact attributed to its youthful hosts Li Xiang and He Ling and the producers' savvy in keeping one step ahead of its imitators. However, the show's executives soon attracted the displeasure of CCTV stalwarts who attempted to wreak collateral damage on the programme by asserting that it was a rip-off of Taiwanese formats. Called to defend the integrity of *The Citadel of Happiness*, the producer refuted claims that the programme was appropriated from Taiwan, citing a long pedigree of similar variety formats in the USA and Japan (Wang 1999).

During the period 2001–2 licensed game shows began to feature heavily on the schedules of China's provincial broadcasters, if not on CCTV. In 2002 the Japanese network Tokyo Broadcasting System's (TBS) format *Happy Family Plan* (*Shiawase Kazoku Keikaku*) was sold to Beijing Television and presented to Chinese viewers as *Dreams Become Reality* (*Mengxiang chengzhen*). This is a game format in which a family member is given a difficult task to perform within a limited time on television and 7 days to prepare. The camera tracks the preparation and the ultimate performance of challenges, such as memorizing all the stops along a dozen bus routes, or balancing a coin on one's nose and allowing it to fall into a small receptacle held between the lips. In contrast to Japan, these challenges are shared among all the family members, not just father. *Happy Family Plan* has been one of Japan's most successful exports, so much so that TBS unsuccessfully sought a dispensation from China's Ministry of Culture to prevent local "knock-offs" of the format. The Chinese version offered individuals the chance to win prizes of up to 5,000 renminbi (US$600), while the successful family could take home as much as 20,000 renminbi (US$2,400).

In 2002 the BBC format, *The Weakest Link*, distributed by ECM Asia, introduced its "walk of shame" to Chinese audiences. China's version, entitled *The Wise Rule* (*Zhizhe wei wang*), was produced by Nanjing Television, with the provincial station gaining the franchise following reports that negotiations with Shanghai Television for a local production of *Who Wants To Be A Millionaire?* had broken down due to haggling over how the industry bible was to be interpreted. Meanwhile CCTV, in the context of media commercialization now a direct competitor of Shanghai Television, was busy localizing its own *The Dictionary of Happiness*, which effectively became the "take the market" brand-name quiz show in China. As mentioned earlier, *The Dictionary of Happiness* producers were less concerned with the niceties of who owned the format rights and who devised the ideas for "ask the audience" and "phone a friend." In February 2003, the quiz format entered a new era of viewer participation with *Everybody Wins* (*Jintian shei hui ying*), produced by the Singaporean entrepreneur Robert Chua, the founder of China Entertainment Television (CETV). This was launched on Shanghai's second network, Shanghai Oriental Television, on New Year's Day (18 February 2003). The key principle of this show is participatory greed, with everyone having a chance to grab a share of prize money if their personal home phone numbers, ID numbers, or car license plates match with a seven-digit "lucky number" formed from the final digit of each player's score.

One of Taiwan's contributions to the format traffic between Taiwan and the Chinese Mainland was the television dating show, which achieved wide exposure throughout the Chinese speaking world with *Special Man and Woman* (*Feichang nannü*) and *I Love The Matchmaker* (*Wo ai hongniang*). Although the "perfect match" concept of strangers meeting across a floodlit studio was standard television fare in almost every country by the 1990s, the Taiwanese format, which entailed a question exchange allowing a number of couples to form a love-match, took participation to a new level with added moral support and barracking by a live studio audience. Phoenix Television (Hong Kong) began distributing the former to Chinese cable stations in July 1997. With the concept capturing the imagination of audiences desperately seeking release from pedagogic sermonizing, Hunan Satellite Television quickly produced a Mainland version, *Romantic Meeting* (*Meigui zhi yue*).[3] The success of the group date format soon spawned a rash of clones (Luo 2000; Yang 2000).

Exchanging Children's Worlds: *Sesame Street*

> We used adult programme formats and applied these mechanically to children's content with the result that adults felt it was all infantile and children felt it was dreary. The reason for this is obvious: those who create children's shows are adults and they are used to using adult thought processes to observe and regulate the world of children.
>
> (China Cue Online 2000)

Shanghai Television's *Sesame Street* (*Zhima jie*) illustrates the R&D contribution that the licensing of television formats can make to the development of television industries. Produced under license to Children's Television Workshop

(CTW), *Sesame Street* premiered on the small screen on Shanghai TV Channel 14 on 14 February 1998. The Chinese version is one of many adaptations currently circulating. *Sesame Street* has been shown in over 140 countries, in some cases broadcast in the original English, at other times being dubbed into the vernacular, and in many cases being completely re-versioned. In 1996 the *Sesame Street* idiom of "fun education" was introduced to a production team at Shanghai Television. The actual re-formatting of the CTW "model" was a complicated procedure, requiring extensive workshopping both on a technical and political level. The Chinese team comprised eighteen child education specialists, headed by the renowned physicist and head of Fudan University, Professor Xie Xide. New characters such as Xiao Meizi (Little Berry) and Huhu Zhu (Puff Pig) were added to accommodate local idioms. Part of the R&D meant sending the Shanghai Television producers to New York to work with their American counterparts. This exchange was funded by the US giant General Electric, which no doubt had its own commercial agenda. The outcome of the pre-production workshop and training was a reference volume outlining in detail the minutiae of production. The programme is now syndicated throughout China, as are *Sesame Street* products and the CTW website.

According to one enthusiastic report, the sinicization of *Sesame Street* was in the same order of technology transfer as the Sangtana motor vehicle, which borrowed German technology, workmanship and standards and applied Chinese materials and labour (China Cue Online 2000). The report further opines that Shanghai Television's reputation, and Chinese pedagogic practice in general, benefited from the collaboration.

Soapy Formats: *Joy Luck Street*

> Another problem was the form and content itself. Chinese audiences now demand distinctive tastes in their entertainment. English and Chinese tastes in entertainment are not the same. For instance, European people like to watch the subtleties in people's relationships, the rich, psychological and emotional conflicts that occur. Chinese audiences appreciate more traditional narratives.
>
> (Han 2000, personal interview)[4]

The case of *Joy Luck Street* (*Xingfu jie*), a co-production based on the long-running English melodrama *Coronation Street*, provides a salutary example of an ambitious attempt to replicate the Western "never-ending" serial soap drama in Chinese soil. In this case Granada Media, the English copyright owner of *Coronation Street*, provided production capital through a venture with the Hong Kong-based Beijing Yahuan Audio and Video Production, with production support also supplied by the Beijing Broadcasting Institute. Granada have invested heavily in this production over 5 years, hoping that the series, screened on ninety cable channels in a special syndicated timeslot called *6.30 Theatre*, will capture the hearts and minds of Chinese housewives (Saywell 2000).

The localization of *Joy Luck Street* provides another example of how format licenses, particularly those that travel from afar—in this case from northern England to a modern Chinese city—require substantial reworking to embed them in the local cultural milieu. In order to make this production the Chinese team had to restructure many of their work practices to incorporate continuous script-writing and shooting, working in rotating teams. Eugene Ferguson, the Granada link person who was responsible for the liaison between the Chinese teams and the English teams, commented that the Chinese team was introduced to techniques such as simultaneous plot lines (Ferguson 2002, personal interview).[5] This was confirmed by one of the lead actors, who said there were a number of technological breakthroughs in comparison with Chinese soap operas such as Ying Da's *I Love My Family* (Han 2000, personal interview). In the Chinese tradition the script was reworked and revised into its final form before finally going into production. With *Joy Luck Street*, however, the script was prepared while shooting, and then adjusted according to the popular response. The process was extremely complicated and created problems for many of the participants, particularly the requirement of writing the script, translating it into English, and sending it to Granada for confirmation and revisions.

The Chinese *Joy Luck Street* experience has been far from a seamless transfer of the original *Coronation Street* format into the Chinese environment. Difficulties were encountered in transferring the nuances of the English working-class milieu into the Beijing streetscape. The original Hong Kong director had to be replaced after eighteen episodes and the narrative of dysfunctional families had to be reworked to accommodate Mainland Chinese values. By the time the series had achieved fifty episodes, however, the Chinese team felt that the series had overcome its Western deficiencies and acquired a distinctive local feel (Han 2000, personal interview).

Extreme Reality: *Into Shangrila*

> So we don't think it is *just* about formats when we think of reality television programming. From a format perspective it is a very strategically commercialized television programme and a media commodity. It is in fact a particular format that is operationalized by media in a digital era. We have been the first in the Chinese television industry. We have used high technology and we have used the idea of new formats.
>
> (Chen 2002, personal interview)[6]

Reality television (*Zhenren xiu*) is arguably a genre tailor-made for Chinese audiences. Recent Chinese attempts to exploit the genre draw on a tradition of socialist realism, socialist "mock" documentary, and myths of collective struggle.

Without doubt the most innovative and ambitious reality programme to hit Chinese screens in recent years is *Into Shangrila* (*Zouru Xianggelila*), produced by the Beijing Weihan Cultural Company in association with Sichuan Television, with the indirect contribution of more than 100 websites, 160 newspapers, 4 mobile phone networks, and 29 television stations nationwide. Drawing on the *Survivor* (*Shengcunzhe*) narrative of photogenic, healthy people left to fend for themselves in the wilderness, *Into Shangrila* brings together eighteen young Chinese from different provinces, all preselected by participating stations to battle against the elements and nature in the Himalayan foothills at altitudes of 5,000 metres. Divided into two teams, "Sun" and "Moon," participants cooperate to win the ultimate glory of success rather than merely seeking to outdo each other.

Into Shangrila, while unlicensed, draws on many of the technical breakthroughs of international versions of *Survivor*. It was shot using DV format, itself an innovation in Chinese television production, allowing cameras to track the young adventurers as they struggled against the elements, their own failings, and their comrades. Unlike licensed international formats such as *Joy Luck Street*, *Sesame Street*, *Dreams Become Reality*, and *The Wise Rule*, which have been allowed entry via joint ventures with Chinese production companies, the producers of China's ultimate reality format decided to go it alone based upon their experience in "cast of thousands" documentaries. In 1992 *Into Shangrila*'s director Chen Qiang was a producer of an epic documentary series *Ferrying the Yellow River* (*Duguo huanghe*) that proselytized national unity through thirty-two short films each representing aspects of Chinese society along 5,646 kilometres of the legendary Yellow River. The making of the documentary was itself tracked by more than eighty newspapers and twenty television channels. In 1996 Chen was again at it with another epic multimedia production called *Ardently Loving 2000* (*Kuai 2000*) that was broadcast on 127 channels including CCTV and Phoenix Television.

Chen, who graduated with a media and public relations degree from New York University in the late 1980s, had learnt the lessons of Western marketing, even if his strategies contradicted the value chain of Chinese programming, where product is routinely exchanged on the basis of demand for a particular type or genre to fill schedules rather than on programme innovation. *Into Shangrila* was subsequently constructed as a media event. According to publicity reports approximately 230,000 people applied to be participants on the programmes, among whom 70 per cent were male and 30 per cent female. Also interesting was the reported publicity that 14,000 of the applicants had either a master's or a Ph.D. The actual process of choosing the people was conducted via the Internet with a 24-hour live coverage of the participant's backgrounds. Finally, there was a pilot in February 2002, followed by the actual broadcast in August 2002.

This promotional strategy is unsurprisingly analogous to the hype that has accompanied the *Survivor* and other reality formats in Western television industries. Chen maintained that "the selling of the event has implications for the advertising revenue. It is a public relations project" (Chen 2002, personal interview). To get the programme up and running was a considerable achievement in China, where media innovation is not for the faint hearted. Part of the public relations strategy was enlisting the support of China's cultural watchdogs, who had to be convinced of its social and pedagogical benefits. Moreover, to ensure that the programme was differentiated from the Western *Survivor* formats, a special symposium was arranged in collaboration with CCTV in which the specificity of Chinese reality television was debated (CCTV 2002).

In contrast to media systems in the West, media distribution infrastructure and its administration is monopolized by state-linked organizations. The commercial considerations that apply to mounting an interactive reality format rely heavily on government being engaged in the operation. Chen managed to convince Chinese Communist Party officials that the format was a great leap forward into the digital revolution, enlisting the government's support in using the Qianlong web portal to link 123 websites. Chen maintains that the initial rationale for this programme was a technological revolution in communication that the innovation offered, not the aping of a particular Western format. He says that he only became aware of the "original" *Survivor* late in the programme's development stage (Chen 2002, personal interview).

What Do Formats Mean for Chinese Television Production?

I have argued that formatting in China, as elsewhere in this study, is a means of replicating programmes that are successful in attracting audiences. The format is a recipe, a package, or even a combination of technologies. Formats impact upon television environments in terms of how they are produced, distributed, and bundled together with other services. However, host television environments (and local cultural sensitivities) also impact upon the manner in which formats are localized. China presents an example of the dual nature of formats.

The tendency towards isomorphism illustrates many of the negative responses of the format turn. In short, the rapid cloning of other people's intellectual endeavour in order to achieve instant ratings without the need for programme development (R&D) is indicative of a tendency within China to view copyright as something that can be overlooked, except of course when one's own programme is cannibalized. For foreign companies pitching their wares into the Chinese market the issue of protection is a significant one, and in many instances it is expedient to make a programme sale, and aggregate value from associated advertising packages, ignoring domestic copycats. The problem of a deficit of hard currency in the Chinese market also poses problems for international companies seeking to sell formats. Advertiser-funded packages, a familiar mode of programme financing in China in which advertising time is bundled into the deal, provide an alternative strategy. For format owners prepared to go the distance in legal disputes, however, the pay-off is less certain as legal processes are convoluted and time consuming with no guarantee of success. The British distributor ECM was one of the more successful companies to pursue legal action. In October 2002 it forced Shenzhen Cable TV to pay costs over the pilfering of the "know-how" of its *Go Bingo* format, elsewhere licensed in China as *Lucky 52* (*Xingyun52*)

(Stein 2002: 20). ECM, however, has been less successful at the time of writing in its pursuit of costs from other media institutions, including CCTV, which has "liberally borrowed" from its *Dog Eat Dog* format.

The process of research and development can be observed in a number of successful licensed formats. China's adaptation of the children's show *Sesame Street*, the Granada/Beijing Yahuan production *Joy Luck Street*, and Nanjing Television's *The Wise Rule* represent a degree of success, although the real pay-off for the franchiser is not so much the sale of programme rights as having a presence in the biggest television market in the world. As I have pointed out, many programme formats have dispensed with the compromises and costs required to license overseas productions. These include CCTV2's *Dictionary of Happiness*, *Zhengda Variety Show*, and China's ultimate reality show *Into Shangrila*. The decision here to bypass the formalities and costs of buying format rights is not unique within the context of Asian production. What it does mean, however, is that there are now precedents established for local companies to draw attention to if they are adjudicated to have wilfully exploited the creative ideas of others. But as I have also explained, by far the great bulk of format cloning occurs within Chinese networks. This is a direct consequence of the fragmented nature of television production and a distribution system based on programme barter. As China moves to tighten up its intellectual property regime, and as the principle broadcasters begin to realize the value of copyright in the media marketplace, we may see a greater formalization of format exchange within China and between Chinese television stations and international format distributors.

Notes

1 I would like to acknowledge the help with obtaining sources given to me by RanRuxue and Yin Hong of Qinghua University in China.
2 Interview conducted on 21 June 2002 with Zheng Wei, producer of *The Dictionary of Happiness*, CCTV.
3 The word *meigui* literally means "rose'.
4 Interview conducted on 25 September 2000 with Han Xiaolei, actor in *Joy Luck Street*.
5 Interview conducted on 15 October 2002 with Eugene Ferguson, Granada producer for *Joy Luck Street*.
6 Interview conducted on 25 June 2002 with Chen Qiang, producer of *Into Shangrila*.

References

China Cue Online (2000) "How children's television shows are borrowing from overseas" (Ertong dianshi jiemu ruhe jiechuan chuhai). Online. Available HTTP: www.chinacue.com.cn/cue/topic/zmj.htm (accessed 11 May 2000).

Gore, L. (2000) "A meltdown with 'Chinese characteristics'?" In R. Robison, M. Beeson, K. Jayasuriya and H-R. Kim (eds.) *Politics and Markets in the Wake of the East Asian Crisis*, London: Routledge.

Guthrie, D. (1999) *Dragon in a Three-Piece Suit: the emergence of capitalism in China*, Princeton, NJ: Princeton University Press.

Harrison, M. (2002) "Satellite and cable platforms: development and content," in S. H. Donald, M. Keane and H. Yin (eds.) *Media in China: consumption, content and crisis*, London: RoutledgeCurzon.

Huang, Y. (1994) "Peaceful evolution: the case of television reform in post-Mao China," *Media, Culture and Society*, 16 (2): 217–41.

Keane, M. (1999) "Television and civilization: the unity of opposites?" *International Journal of Cultural Studies*, 2 (2): 246–59.

—— (2002) "Television drama in China: engineering souls for the market," in T. Craig and R. King (eds.) *Global Goes Local: popular culture in Asia*, Vancouver: UBC Press.

Li, C. (1998) *China: the consumer revolution*, Singapore: John Wiley and Sons.

Luo, M. (2000) "Under Cupid's Altar" (*Zou xia shentan de qiupide*), unpublished master's dissertation, Beijing Normal University Research Institute.

Moran, A. (1998) *Copycat Television: globalisation, program formats and cultural identity*, Luton, U.K.: University of Luton Press.

Saywell, T. (2000) "Will soaps wash in China?" *Far Eastern Economic Review*. Online. Available HTTP: www.chinatopnews.com/BBS/Square/messages/904.html (accessed 9 December 2000).

Shoesmith, B. and Wang, H. (2002) "Networks and industrial community television in China: precursors to a revolution," in S. H. Donald, M. Keane and H. Yin (eds.) *Media in China: consumption, content and crisis*, London: RoutledgeCurzon.

Spence, J. D. (1990) *The Search for Modern China*, New York: W. W. Norton & Co.

Stein, J. (2002) "Dollar values," *Television Asia*, October: 20–2.

Tu, C. (1997) "The development and legal policies of China's broadcasting network" (*Woguo guangbo dianshiwang de fazhan jiqi falu zhengce*), *Dianshi Yanjiu* (*Television Research*), 6: 4–7.

Wang, B. (1999) "A report on the TV programme *The Citadel of Happiness*" (Guanyu *Kuaile da benying* de qingkuang huibao), Internal document.

Yang, B. (2000) *Feeling the Pulse of the Contestant* (*Bamai jiabin*), Beijing: China International Broadcasting Publishing.

Yin, H. (2002) "Meaning, production, consumption: the history and reality of television drama in China," in S. H. Donald, M. Keane and H. Yin (eds.) *Media in China: consumption, content and crisis*, London: RoutledgeCurzon.

Zhang, J. (1994) "Strike up the music of the times: on the mainstream melody and television drama," *Chinese Television* (*Zhongguo dianshi*), 9: 2–5.

Zheng, W. (2002) "Rang mengsui *Kaixin cidian* yiqi feixiang" (Let your dreams and *The Dictionary of Happiness* fly away together), in W. Zheng (ed.) *Kaixin cidian Quizshow*, Wuhan: Chenjiang wenyi Publishing.

16

GLOBAL TELEVISION FORMATS AND THE POLITICAL ECONOMY OF CULTURAL ADAPTATION

Who Wants to be a Millionaire? in India

Lauhona Ganguly

Rama Krishna Guggila is 35 years old and lives in the Khammam district of the southern state of Andhra Pradesh in India. He holds a medical degree from a university in Hyderabad and hopes to emigrate to the United States someday. Mohit Mahipal, on the other hand, lives in the northwestern state of Haryana in a small town called Hissar. He is 27 years old, married, and sells photographic goods. Mahipal and Guggila do not have much in common in India's socio-culturally and linguistically diverse society. But they are motivated by a shared impulse: to participate on "reality television" shows and earn extraordinary amounts of prize money—10 million Indian rupees, to be precise, as promised on the Indian adaptation of the global format of *Who Wants to Be a Millionaire?* on which they both appear.

Adaptations of global television formats have been at the center of India's booming private television industry. In particular, adaptations of "reality shows," as an entertainment genre, have been very popular with audiences. As a result, today each major network—both domestic and transnational—broadcasts adaptations of global "reality TV" formats. This phenomenon played out on television screens is simultaneous with a larger but not unrelated development: India's gradual shift towards privatization and liberalization as the operating logic of joining a global economy. State controlled developmental models of economy are being replaced by private enterprise and global competitive market relations.

The following discussion draws correspondences between the ongoing political-economic changes in India and the socio-cultural work of adapting a global format for domestic audiences. The chapter argues that adaptations of global formats of "reality TV" have entered Indian homes, night after night on private entertainment television networks, to offer a new market driven social milieu. The narrative and discursive appeal of "reality shows" suggest a re-imagining of

India: where "common people" can take a chance, seize opportunities, unleash entrepreneurial spirit, be competitive and possibly "win." Adaptations of global formats of reality game shows provide new cultural practices to mediate everyday life in a fast changing India. The television experience is located in the social context of political, economic change to understand the social and cultural implications of India's encounter with the world.

This chapter focuses on the first global format of a "reality–game" show to reach India—*Kaun Banega Crorepati* (KBC), the Hindi version of *Who Wants to be a Millionaire?* KBC's "reach" among the Hindi speaking general entertainment population has been the highest of any program in its day part, registering a high 15 percent in 2000 for KBC I followed by a higher 24 percent for KBC II in 2005 (*Hindu Business Line*, 2005). The third season in 2007 continued the trend. The immense popularity of the show forced other networks to include reality game shows as a necessary strategy of programming schedules. The appeal of reality shows as promoted by the television networks in general, and KBC in particular, is centered on the idea of "ordinary people"—providing a platform for the masses to be visible (even if for fleeting television moments); to participate (even if within the confines of studio reality); and to compete for extraordinary sums of money. India's cable and satellite (C&S) homes have increased from 25 million in 2000 to 71 million in 2007 (the third largest total after the U.S.A. and China) (*Hindustan Times*, 2007). This growing universe of people who regularly tune in to watch the adaptations of global formats of reality shows makes it imperative to ask what are the limits and range of possibilities that identify the "ordinary" and its extraordinary promise. Analysis of KBC, between its launch in 2000 and its latest season in 2007, focuses on the discursive claims of "reality," "representation" and the articulation of narratives of "change" that enable new ways of living and making sense of the social transformations in India.

Research focuses on the discursive practices used to "adapt" from the format "production bible." Textual analysis will look at the specific meanings, ideas and frameworks of comprehension that are built into the show (and its promotion) as selective organization of cultural material. Interviews with producers and network executives, along with press releases and media coverage of the show, will situate the creative practices within the institutional and industrial context and enable understanding of the structural limits within which the global format is adapted for Indian audiences. Critical discourse analysis links the "text" and the "con-text" to understand how adaptations of global formats, such as KBC, mediate the changing national realities—in both material and ideational forms.

Global Media, Cultural Practices and Fields of Power

Borrowing from Bourdieu's formulations, the following analysis of KBC is organized in terms of cultural practices—conceptualized in a dialectical relationship connecting culture, structure and power. Cultural "practices" occur when class-based socializations, traditions, expectations, aspirations and knowledge intersect with new structural limits. Analysis of cultural practices reveals the embedded social rationality at work as structural demands are filtered through traditional dispositions and actors adapt to the new constraints and opportunities. The conceptual framework emphasizes practices as plural and often tactical, so that social power is understood in terms of a constant struggle—domination in the cultural domain. Strategies, such as cultural adaptation of global formats; of participating on the reality—game shows; of viewing habits, etc., as discussed in the analysis of KBC, are informed practically—as whatever motivates action toward consequences that matter to localized understanding.

KBC as an enactment of locally significant cultural practices refers to adaptation of a global format, and hence a global media system of format production—distribution—adaptation—consumption. In order to understand the range of meanings generated by the adapted format we must account for the moments of cultural translation that mark the moments of adaptation, within the circuitry of media practices. Stuart Hall has provided us with a model that situates the different moments of production—distribution—consumption—reproduction in social contexts of meaning making. Producers or professionals "encode" meaning within determining conditions of structural power while audiences "decode" in the context of lived experiences. Hall's model shares a sense of the practical with Bourdieu's emphasis on the dialectical dynamics of cultural practices and structural power, but faces specific challenges in a global media market.

Identifying strictly bounded notions of communities or localities of audiences within specific political-economic contexts has become untenable due to the emergence of a transnational public sphere. Advances in telecommunication networks and global media systems allow cultural forms to travel from one social context to another. But Hall's model does not account for questions of cultural translation. When programs are translated or reproduced using local idioms, what are the dynamics of meaning-making and structural conditions of content production? The treatment of encoding—decoding as discrete acts does not account for the interactions that produce hybridized program content. For instance, the "production bible" that comes with the purchase of license to reproduce *Millionaire* is "decoded" by producers in the domestic context and "(re)encoded" into a new avatar. How do we then account for the punctuated process of "encoding"—"decoding-(re)encoding"—"decoding" in format adaptations? Media ethnographers investigating mass media in its local forms have resisted derivative arguments that view cultural acts as structured renditions of social power, and often looked at the constitution of meaning as subversive acts by producers and audiences who (re)interpret texts (for a detailed discussion on the developments in the field, refer to Kraidy, 2005). Others have problematized the exclusive focus on textual-discursive readings (Morley, 1995) or called for alternative frameworks that take localized but relational and processual approaches to hybrid discursive formations (Kraidy, 2005).

Cultural translation and adaptation of global formats for domestic audiences as analyzed here is not understood in terms of a "global–local" encounter, where the "local" becomes bracketed as a descriptive category in global schemes—ready, available and stagnant in time and space. It is therefore important to clarify that in examining KBC we do not look for replication of the format as a measure of increasing cultural connection to its Western origins, and "Westernization" of "Indian" society. Nor do we look for lingering and resistant cultural differences that distinguish KBC from the global and "Western" format as a uniquely "Indian" show. Ideological impact, or the generation of meaning frameworks that enable "knowing" and "being" in the social world are not captured in culturally static responses or global–local binary frameworks that remain outside the historically constituted, intersected and interconnected cultural contexts.

The advantage of an approach that reframes social power in terms of practices and fields is that it emphasizes how responses (of producers and viewers alike) can be multiple and diverse across competing fields of power. We may therefore delimit cultural practices from derivative arguments that view cultural acts as structurally determined results of social power and in its stead focus our analysis on the specificity of the social interaction and how certain interests find resonance over others. The analytical framework employed in this chapter situates the transformations in the television experience (as an instance of socio-cultural activity) within the ongoing structural adjustments in the country. The interconnectedness of different fields of power is mapped to understand how social power—in economic, cultural, social and symbolic fields—intersects to render specific social realities. Analysis of KBC therefore establishes the productive relationship between the material and ideational forces and teases out the discourses emerging from that "inter-animation" (Rajagopal, 2001). As the mediating form, KBC refers to the social organization of power. As such, it is argued here that culture is where political realities are, and will increasingly, be shaped.

Formats and the Logic of Cultural Adaptations: Why, or "Why Not?"

On July 3, 2000, *Who Wants to Be a Millionaire?* debuted on Star TV as *Kaun Banega Crorepati* (KBC). The Indian reproduction of the show format, franchised from Celador Production, U.K., broke the worldwide record in viewership for the format. In only four weeks after launch, nine out of every ten Indian cable and satellite (C&S) viewers were exposed to KBC (Nair, 2008). The format's arrival in India is, however, connected to a global media network of places, professionals and practices, and refers to socio-cultural and industrial-economic considerations that frame the work of format adaptation.

When the show was launched in 2000, Star TV was making a pitch to establish itself in the Hindi language general entertainment market on its own. Star TV, which is part of Rupert Murdoch's media conglomeration News Corporation, had entered India in a business tie-up with a domestic enterprise called Zee TV. Under the terms of the partnership Zee TV had successfully limited Star's Indian presence to the marginal English language market while capturing the coveted Hindi language market for itself. When Subhas Chandra, owner of Zee TV, bought out Murdoch from the tie-up, he emerged as a national hero who had restored pride in India's competitiveness to withstand foreign interests. Star on the other hand was left with an urgent need to establish its credentials as a "national" broadcaster in the revenue-rich Hindi speaking market.

KBC was at the center of Star TV's programming strategy to bring audiences to its network. Sameer Nair, who was the network executive in charge of programming and the brain behind adapting the *Millionaire* format for India, contextualized the introduction of KBC in terms of specific programming needs: (1) a different and unforeseen program concept to distinguish Star TV from its competitors; (2) a high cost, high scale, high quality program to establish Star's premium branding; and (3) igniting familiarity and enabling easy association for families to establish Star as a national broadcaster. KBC fit the requirements. According to a TAM study in 2000, Star TV's channel share went up from 2 percent to 25 percent for the 9–10 p.m. day part when KBC was broadcast. In the second season (2005), the channel share was 10 percent four weeks prior to telecast and increased to 38 percent with KBC's telecast (*Business Today*, 2006). When KBC III was launched in 2007 it took the channel's share from 12.4 percent to 24.36 percent (Krishna, 2007).

The decision, by Nair, to project the Indian version of the format as the flagship show for Star's entry into the general entertainment market emerged from the business ideas and "functionalities" favored by a global network of media executives. Colleagues at News Corporation's Hong Kong office sent a tape of the *Millionaire* format to Mumbai for Nair's consideration as a potential import for the Indian market. Formats are provided for consideration with detailed empirical data on ratings and revenue generation to prove their validity as a "working format." Nair explained his decision to adapt the format thus:

> You know its like saying when you make cars or you make refrigerators, what you invariably do is . . . it is known as "technology transfer." So you get the technology and you reproduce it in India to suit your conditions and you move on. I mean *why not?*
>
> (Nair, 2008)

Not all "working formats" sell (or are "received') equally with audiences though —which makes the task of producing a cultural product (even a "franchised" and "formatted" show) fundamentally distinct from that of selling the functionality of cars or refrigerators. Television, as a medium of transmission, works in an inherently contradictory way. On one hand, it links together different spatial and temporal realities under one circuit of production and consumption. Viewers enjoy a privileged onlook at other's lives, without participating, and at the same time (and space) find a sense of closeness and reciprocity. On the other hand, there are gaps—both spatial and temporal—between production and consumption. The absence of any necessary relationship between the moments of production and consumption poses a specific challenge for producers: how to capture the associative–imaginative processes that viewers use to fill the gaps? In other words, producers must create content that appeals to both collective sensibility (that underlies our social associations) and individual identification (that often fuels our imaginations).

This need to pitch at two distinct levels of the social and the individual is particularly significant in the adaptation of formats for domestic consumption. Adaptations are accompanied by self-conscious "cultural" claims. Producers must necessarily identify what "works" for an "Indian" sensibility and what does not; what allows easy associations in "India" and what does not; what is familiar to an "Indian" and what is not? Simultaneously, producers must disentangle an "individual" appeal: what motivates or engages the individual and allows for new ideas to be accepted. While this is arguably true of domestically conceptualized programming as well, in the case of format adaptation producers (and network executives) actively mediate and define the terms of cultural translation while staying true to the format rules. Nair, for instance, suggests creative glee at the way he and his team toyed with the "format" regulations to shape it for Indian audiences and make it an "Indian" show. He notes (Nair, 2008) that producers were sent from London to the studios in Mumbai "to check whether we were meddling with their, you know [laughs], precious format . . . But you couldn't pin anything on us because it was still within the format. And it was totally different, and they knew it was totally different."

This creative "difference" that defines format adaptation is, however, a dynamic process. The "Indian" sensibility that reshapes the *Millionaire* format to, arguably, make it a "different" show refers to a range of social connections, associations and imaginations that are at play as India is integrated into a neoliberal global economy. In adapting a format, television producers and network executives work as cultural mediators. But the business of television producers and network executives, though creative and symbolic in nature, is identified in terms of ratings and revenue generation. The economic motives of the producers are therefore fundamentally tied to their role as social-cultural mediators. It is therefore important to ask the following questions. How do political and economic interests enter the work of culturally translating a format into its domestic (and "Indian") version? How does it impact the work of identifying and representing what "works" in the Indian domestic context? And indeed, how are certain cultural patterns, practices and representations privileged that enable certain realities, or ways of life?

Reality Formats and Representational Spaces

In India, KBC is often considered a "quiz show." Elsewhere, the *Millionaire* format is often called a "game show." What remains central to the format, and qualifies it as a "reality format," however, is the idea that "real" people can be on the show and earn "real" money. "Reality television" often accommodates hybridized versions of different sub-genres (for example, game shows, dramatic narratives, talent searches, etc.). Murray reminds us that extra-textual factors can sometimes supersede the textual characteristics because of the material ways "genres" are culturally defined, interpreted and evaluated to suggest a program's social weight and cultural value. The same format can be a quiz show or a game show and still be a "reality show." The hyphenated set of generic characteristics allow "in-between" spaces that are easily adapted to cultural specificities. It is therefore important to consider the notions of "reality" offered through the "in-between" spaces of a reality format and its adaptations in specific contexts.

In reality formats, representational frameworks are made accessible through the depiction of the ordinary (ambition, determination, greed, jealousy, etc.) while extraordinary circumstances or challenges sustain curiosity because they may subvert the ordinary. A new transformational reality is made possible even as it draws from the world of the familiar and mundane. Viewers are encouraged to test out their own notions of the real, ordinary and the intimate against the representations before them (Corner, cited in Murray and Ouellette, 2004). A new space is created between the distinctive relationship of truth telling (as representation of authentic experiences) and mediation (as popular entertainment). Reality formats are thus able to claim to represent reality with inherently open-ended textual characteristics. What matters then is not what is real or not, but how certain elements are depicted as real and how such depictions interact with participant–viewer agency to render new political and economic imaginaries meaningful.

Focusing our analysis on these in-between spaces of adaptations and reality representations highlights how the cultural practices can be unpredictable in nature, even when they serve specific power structures. The new market driven social milieu, that an analytical investigation of KBC reveals, is not an automatic result of structural reforms towards a liberal market economy. Instead, as a cultural form, it allows us to consider how the ordinary, mundane, everyday world is rearticulated within the new commercial, industrial and structural relations of power, so that on-going social transformations become familiar, meaningful and perhaps even accepted. Cultural practices that "adapt" the global format into its Indian iteration take place within intersecting social, political, economic and cultural fields of power. As global media systems expand into emerging markets, analysis of KBC enables understanding of how meaning can be both culturally specific and globally shared.

Between Reel and Real: *Kaun Banega Crorepati* in India

The *Millionaire–KBC* format arrived in India in an increasingly global and competitive television market. But unlike Europe or the United States, the entry of reality shows in India did not take place in the context of cost cutting and creative labor strikes. In contrast, investments associated with the high scale of production, licensing fee and telephony infrastructure needed to accommodate viewer participation were considerably high. But the high "price point" was meant to be understood as the promise of a premium media product, and perhaps more significantly, as Star TV's (the broadcasting network's) commitment to the Indian market made in the name of a national narrative of change.

Star TV's then chief of programming suggests particular disdain for the way business was conducted on Indian television at the time of KBC's launch: "The price point in Indian television at that time used to be very low. You know, they used to pay peanuts for shows and if you pay peanuts you get monkeys kind of thing" (Nair, 2008). Peter Mukerjea, CEO of Star TV at the time, declared to the press:

> To me this is not about money. Ratings and revenue are a by product. The moot point is that Star TV gets elevated to a position of leadership . . . Indian TV has to rise out of the Rs.7–8 *lakh* (Hindi term for 100,000) bracket . . . look at the licensing and merchandising that accompanies *Baywatch* or *Ally McBeal*. This can happen here also. I passionately believe Indians are a global community. We have to adopt a global approach.
>
> (Aiyar and Chopra, 2000)

The almost paternal tone of Star TV's network executives was not without reason. Over night KBC's success had changed the rules of the game. For the first time in the Indian industry it became possible to command highest advertising rates without national reach. Those outside the C&S universe—and without the purchasing power that drives advertiser interest—were left out of the count of "national" broadcasting. The C&S subscription fee averaging Rs.100 to Rs.150 per month remains much higher than the majority of Indians can afford when poverty, malnutrition, and infant mortality levels are increasing at alarming rates (Global Hunger Index, 2006). But KBC's popularity within the C&S population creates new aspirations to acquire new competencies that allow entry into the premium world of Star TV's reality shows. Not surprisingly then, the majority of the 25,000,000 calls per episode come from non-metropolitan and small towns (India TV News, 2006). Bourdieu conceptualizes "practice" as acquired competencies. Individuals learn practices by way of being integrated and shaped in particular social environments, which in turn allows for negotiating skills with others in the social domains. The practice of calling into reality shows becomes a point of entry into certain competencies and aspirations.

At the network end, KBC's popularity prompted a series of cloned shows and competing offers for prize monies. The question, according to rival Zee TV's CEO, R. K. Singh, was "should we trigger a runaway expectation of money? Or should we temper it? We felt it was not a desirable tendency for a responsible TV channel given the social situation. But we will not shy away from competition" (*India Today*, 2000). While Star TV entered the field of cultural production with its own repertoire of resources and competencies associated with global media conglomerations, the struggle to dominate and establish leadership over the field is expressed in terms of defining what counts as "capital" or valuable resources and strategies in the field. Therefore even Murdoch's Star TV needed to acquire "national" capital by appealing to a national narrative of value addition: high quality programming on a par with international standards; high scale of production that includes mass participation; and a new reality format that invokes ordinary lives. But as Bourdieu has argued, the dominant group in the field defines what may be considered "resources" to serve their own interests; while groups seeking to acquire resources inevitably reinforce the definitions that structure the field. Executives at Zee TV, though loath to imitate its rival's strategies and arguably, morally alarmed at the rising monetarism, must necessarily engage with the newly established rules of the game. What emerged was a range of reality shows, lures of prize money and promises of life altering experiences in this ratings and revenue war on television screens. As a social phenomenon this meant new practices introduced to the cultural realm that translated the logic of a market economy, profit seeking orientations and individual ambitions. As reported in a leading magazine, the "quiz show has replaced the (comatose) stock market as the middle class' favorite 'get-rich-quick' scheme" (Malik et al., 2000).

Correspondences between the political-economic settings in which KBC is adapted for the Indian audiences do not suggest a causal mechanism between what transpires on television screens and its social impact. Social transformation is impacted by more than the television experience. But a media-centric analysis that examines the circuitry of communication, tracing its open-ended gaps, paths, sites and social relations, offers a unique everyday context to understand how cultural forms mediate and reshape realities. The discussion here is organized in terms of components that characterize the KBC format and key aspects of its adaptation in the Indian context. The components are: (1) the promotional material, and how it identifies the show for Indian audiences; (2) the game structure of the format, and how it facilitates new associations, meanings and ways of life; (3) the questions, and what is the logic of inclusion and exclusion that links the show to market needs; (4) the reward structure of the format, and how it rationalizes new notions of choice; (5) the hosts of the show, and the role they play in branding the show's appeal; and finally (6) the language used in the show, and how shifting usage reflects changing social needs.

Promotions and Possibilities

The promotional film announcing KBC III to its viewers declares: "some questions can change lives." The host looks into the camera to remind his viewers that we go through life constantly searching for a magic answer to our daily troubles. What we do not realize, he tells us, is that the one right answer can come only if we have the one right question. So, we can keep searching and travel the world looking for the right question—or, we can try our luck at the show and win the prize money as the perfect solution to all our troubles. The world of the show offers a new reality to those who have the will to alter the course of their life.

Another promotional film traces the story of a little boy with a penchant for asking questions. Children tend to ask questions and we often find that trait endearing. In the course of time they are either distracted or disciplined. But some don't. Some children persist, as does the child in the film. The viewer is taken on the boy's life journey: his success in school as a teenager; his insatiable curiosity; constant questioning as to where life is taking him; and his struggles as he leaves home to go to a new city (Mumbai) and find his place in the world. The voiceover reminds us that what goes around eventually comes around, and if we persist we may find destiny (*takdeer*) places us where that child finds himself now: the superstar film actor who hosts KBC III. Consistent with Indian moral philosophy the voiceover in the film does not slight destiny or fate, but there is a distinct suggestion of an awakening of the human "will" that aspires—is indeed necessary—to chart the course of life.

The promotional film for the first season of KBC spent more time initiating viewers into a new world of reality television, but the central message of the show has been consistent through its three seasons: life is unpredictable and those who take risks and do not shy away from trying their luck at the game of life can succeed. The structural and social conditions that define the scope of individual action fade away. Instead, what is emphasized is the private space of the individual's talent and agency towards lifestyle aspirations, maximizing happiness and optimizing success. In a narrative centered around personal responsibility, self-discipline, free choice and self-sufficiency, the individual achievement or failure is placed against "the order of the self" (Murray and Ouellette, 2004).

Such a narrative resonates with the historical transformations taking place in India as the state is integrated into a neoliberal global economy. Bourdieu argues that neoclassical economics (which is the foundation of the theory of the social in neoliberal thought) only recognizes the individual, whether it is dealing with companies, trade unions or families. Central to neoliberal thought is the idea of rational, individual self interest as the basis of all economic activity. The individual is prioritized while the "collective" is seen only in its inhibitory role. This allows neoliberal discourse to "embark on a program of methodical destruction of *collectives*" (Bourdieu, 1998: 95–96, original emphasis). In the 2001 budget, for instance, the then finance minister proposed de-protecting organized labor. Companies could then be sold or liquidated with greater ease; companies with less than 1,000 workers (versus the existing cap of less than 100) could sack employees without government consent; and labor could be hired on a contractual basis without any obligation to offer permanent jobs. The arguments supporting such positions claimed that dismantling the trade unions' "clamoring for rights" would free private enterprise and create more growth opportunities (Barman, 2001). As the public sector shrinks, state services are privatized, corporations cut jobs to stay competitive and new jobs offer limited or no pension plans, a growing anxiety at being unhinged from the securities of life must be rearticulated into a new system. Reality game shows offer new imaginations in terms of opportunities (the focus on ultimate prize money), codes ("the end justifies the means" rules of the game), actors (individual players) and models (competitive game formats) for success. A new market driven social milieu emerges in which the state's role in regulating socio-economic activities is considered to inhibit individual ambition.

The Game Structure and Disembedded Individuals

In each show, 10 participants compete for the "Fastest Finger First" round. The winner is invited to walk across to the main stage to be on the "Hotseat" and field a series of 15 increasingly difficult questions leading to the prize money. A participant can choose one of four possible answers provided to her for each question. If unsure, she may access four "Lifeline" options called "Audience poll" (that is, take the studio audience's opinion), "Phone a friend" (who may provide the correct answer), "50–50" (that is, limit answer options to two) and "Flip the question" (that is, change the question). Each "Lifeline" can be used only once.

The game structure of the show prioritizes the individual as the only legitimate actor in the intimacy of close-up camera shots. All that matters is the decisiveness, confidence and agency of the individual player. Like in the original *Millionaire* format, the studio stage is circular and is a small globe of its own, where traveling disco spotlights create intimacy among the audience, possible players, contestants and the host. The close-ups of the men and women cut randomly as the logo is superimposed on it and the long shot of the host walking onto the set, entering the world of the *Millionaire/KBC*, tracks in to a mid-shot as he welcomes and introduces the show. In KBC I and II, as the contestants are chosen, they follow him on to the "hot seat" and the lights fall on them in multiple beams. The background goes dark and the audience is merely an aural presence to heighten the tension along with the music that reaches a crescendo. The traveling beams of light provide movement in the frames as the participants sit with faces stiff with anxiety. The host Amitabh Bachchan (in KBC I and II) looks at them with a steady gaze and responds to their answers with "Are you confident?" "Is this your final answer?" "*Lock kiya jaye?*" ("Should I lock your answer as final?"). Right or wrong answers decide destinies for its participants.

According to Sidhartha Basu, the producer and director of KBC, it is "not just another quiz game . . . [but] human drama . . . about hope and disappointment" (Basu, 2008) that is central to the show's appeal.

> The central drama of the *Millionaire* format anywhere in the world is the ordinary man grappling with his sense of certainty and grasp of facts, on the horns of a dilemma heightened by an extraordinary, life-changing stake . . . That's its universal appeal, whether it's in a broke former Soviet state of Georgia or in long capitalist Japan.
>
> (Basu, 2008)

But certain competencies are important in this dramatic contest, as evident in Nair's refutation of any claims that equate the "human drama–risk taking–destiny deciding" game to notions of gambling or greed. Nair explains, "We do not say greed is good. We say intelligence is useful" (Nair, 2008). Answering questions on the show—or playing the game—is therefore more than a question of knowing the right answer or not. "Intelligence" in Nair's open-ended use suggests good judgment about knowing the limits of one's competencies and resources; deciding what is in the realm of possible and what is outside; which resources are more useful than others; and how various resources and capabilities can be combined to bear upon reality to produce favorable outcomes. "Intelligence" refers to a broad and complex combination of what in Bourdieu's formulation may be identified as "capital" and "practices" at work. It is therefore imperative to also examine the "questions" at play in terms of what invokes, informs and mobilizes "intelligence" and the practical–tactical contexts in which it acquires significance.

Questions for the *Aam Aadmi* (Common Man) and *Aurat* (Woman)

The *Millionaire*/KBC format reserves relatively easier and "populist" questions especially for entry calls that allow callers to compete for participation on the show. Easier questions allow for early success and entice both the participants and the viewers into the game. Entry questions can be based on elementary science such as, naming a nonrenewable source of energy or the degree of heat at which water usually boils. The questions can become more difficult at subsequent levels. For example *If you planted the seeds of Quercus Robur, what would you grow?*; *Where was Chanakya* (a political thinker and administrator of ancient India) *educated?*; or *What was Nutan's* (a famous Hindi actress) *first film?* A wide range of "populist" topics are covered, including Hindu mythology, cricket and Hindi films. The assumption of median education while designing the question pool for KBC is basic schooling and the "knowledge" base involves a daily newspaper or television news (Basu, 2008). But a closer look reveals that the show prioritizes certain notions of knowledge, education and cultural capital. Editorial decisions respond to market conditions, concerns and considerations—in order to support the format's claims of invoking "ordinary people."

Nair recalls his interest in the *Millionaire* format was partly based on the fact that Indians are known to place a premium on knowledge, education and quizzing. Education is historically connected with social hierarchy, whether as the reserve of high castes in feudal social conditions or that of high class in a more modern India. The quiz game shows on television in the 1980s reflected this social bias in the type of questions and the formal disciplinary education it warranted. In the earlier state-driven bureaucratic setup of the Indian economy, coveted professions like the civil services required in-depth and wide-ranging knowledge. Elite education was consistent with the idea of a professional commitment and social mobility.

In a post-liberalized India the market replaces the state in defining the operative principles for social spaces. As a result, more skills-based and improvised perceptions of whatever works for immediate goals is also gaining precedence. For example, short-term courses in computer training and speaking English with an Americanized accent provides a job in a customer service call center with relatively decent pay even if it does not offer job security or career growth. Meanwhile, an undergraduate degree in physics or history is becoming largely useless on the job market. As a network executive accountable to ratings and revenue generation, Nair's perception of India's interest in "knowledge" and "education" is also defined in terms of mass accessibility and popular entertainment. In (re)defining what "works" as "knowledge" or "education" in today's market driven India, the producers of KBC allow new resources, associations, dispositions and competencies to be introduced as cultural and economic capital. Roadside stalls sell "guide books," such as *Bano Crorepati* and *The Next Crorepati*, while sales of more established publications, such as the *Bournvita Quiz Book* or *Manorama Year Book*, have increased significantly (Sinha, 2000). The show promises a fortune for those who can apply their random general knowledge in televised guesses. More than the questions themselves, what matters is the ability to "guess" the right answer, selecting one of the four choices presented to the participant and moving closer to the ultimate prize. In this process—which seemingly transcends social differences—access to the prized sum of money is given to whoever uses the "rules" of the game successfully. The show thus creates an abstracted world of longing and earning, that an "individual" can relate to, irrespective of class, ethnic, linguistic, communal or gender differences.

These developments are, however, not limited to the realm of theoretical speculations. Media reports point at the growing phenomenon of quizzes, scratch card freebies, online punting, lottery schemes, casinos and gambling proposals that have emerged in a "luck-and-buck" "craze" never seen before (Ray, 2000).

Consumer markets too offer a variety of quizzing schemes that involve free gifts or reduced prices with the purchase of products. An article in a leading national magazine credits KBC for providing the "first spark" which

> though did not involve gambling, immediately had millions of Indians who possibly did not know how many zeros a crore [Hindi term for ten million] has wearing their fingers out dialing in from dawn to dusk in search of easy riches.

The article goes on to cite a psychiatrist explaining the phenomenon as:

> This is a change which Indians are experiencing over the last decade or so. Unlike the previous socialist-driven environment wherein giving up was considered a thing of style, the current system encourages acquisition as the call of the day. You need almost anything and everything to remain in control of your situation.
>
> (Ray, 2000)

Garcia-Canclini argues for an analytical relationship between consumption and citizenship so that consumption, as a selection of goods and appropriation of goods, is defined by what we consider valuable and how we want to integrate and distinguish ourselves in society. What emerges then is a new form of citizenship that is answered through the consumption patterns and answered in the private realm of commodity consumption and the mass media, more than in the abstract rules of democracy or collective participation in public spaces (Garcia-Canclini, 2001). Television in India is a "one television per home" market, that is, family viewing is the dominant context of television experience. But families in most Indian households include parents (averaging 35 years or above), children (including young adults) and grandparents. The prime time 9–10 p.m. day part when KBC is screened therefore has a very wide pool of audience-participant profiles. It is also very complex, given India's heterogeneous social make-up in terms of religious, caste, class, educational, regional, cultural, linguistic, gender or other social markers. The challenge as explained by Basu, the producer and director of KBC, is to "be really diverse, yet tap the popular pulse" (Basu, 2008). In other words, the market requires opening up of the "knowledge" base to "homemakers" and "others" (who may not have access to formal education and disciplinary knowledge). In order to justify prime time scheduling the show must necessarily address its appeal to everybody in the family. The male "head of the family" is no longer the only earning member or decision maker. Women, as well as children, participate in the consuming choices of the family. What we find happening in the show KBC is a spiraling movement—where the market pushes social change which in turn is reinforced, validated and further pushed along by prime time television experience. Questions of identity, popularity or community—whether social, cultural or political—are thus accommodated within market relations.

Rewards Structure and Risk Taking as Choice

The KBC format offers a reward structure to its participants and viewers. Strategic use of individual agency and competency (or "intelligence') can earn a maximum of *crore* or 10 million rupees. The end goal of winning the ultimate amount provides a clear sense of the high stakes involved in the game. But it is also possible to play, and gain, smaller amounts of money. The increasingly difficult levels of questions are matched by increases in prize money. The sum of money is approximately doubled at each subsequent question. The prize money is, however, not cumulative, leaving the participant free to choose if she is going to gamble losing the sum she may have already earned by attempting the next question or not. Playing the game requires risk taking. But the converse is also held true: taking risks is itself an indication of participation. Risk taking is necessary if one is to move forward and win; refusal to risk is equated with denial of opportunities to advance.

KBC II features Surinder Mittal (name changed), who is a software engineer from Mumbai. He has successfully answered questions worth 50,000 rupees. He now has a choice to either go home with what he has earned so far or go on to the next stage of the game—play to double the amount or possibly lose it. His sister waits in the audience, breathlessly praying for her brother. The music stops. The camera too stops its dizzy swirl around the crowd and rests on a close-up of Surinder. He decides to take a chance. As he later explains in a dialogue with the host, "one has to take a risk—otherwise one cannot move ahead in life."

Outside the reel and in his "real" social life, Surinder faces increasing inflation, a high cost of living, and receding job or social securities. The information technology (IT) sector where Surinder works is believed to be driving India's growth as an economic power on the world stage. The practice of outsourcing business processes and IT functions from the corporations based in the West to cheaper labor in India is believed to have created over a million jobs by 2008 (Dutta, 2002). However, the Planning Commission's Special Group on Job Creation reports that the number of jobs created in the post-liberalization decade of the 1990s was less than a third of the corresponding number in the decade before liberalization. According to the report, the number of unemployed people is expected to increase sharply to reach a stunning 45 million people (Kang, 2002). Surinder, like others, has no choice but to take "risks"—of migrating to the metropolis to escape unemployment in his hometown, of taking a job without a contract, of taking loans to build a social life without an assured income. Risk taking is a compulsion, not a choice. However, how is it that the accompanying gloom of the word "compulsion" is replaced—or at least presented as such—by a much more cheerful word, "choice," without having to address the difference between the two? The show accommodates the world view of taking risks without having to address the embedded compulsions of the political and economic order. The world view is thus de-problematized and the culture of "risk taking" is delinked from the political and economic conditions which shape it. This is consistent with what Bourdieu calls neoliberalism's tendency—and political need—to de-historicize and de-socialize visions of the social world.

Host to Dost (Friend): Shifting Narratives of Self

The *Millionaire* format calls for a host who facilitates the quiz game. But KBC distinguishes itself in how the hosts are creatively used to provide a subtext on the changing narratives of self in India. When Nair first began thinking about producing KBC as Star's prime time line up, his primary concern was to establish brand recognition for Star TV. By his own analysis the "easiest" thing to do was to take a photograph of India's iconic film star Amitabh Bachchan and paste Star TV and KBC logos next to his face. In a study on Egypytian television as a cultural form that molds social life, Abu-Lughod argues that stars, as a crucial extra-textual element of shows, often give names, faces and personalities to television's construction of a "nation" (Abu-Lughod, 2005). As discussed above, KBC's promotional films also indicate a similar process at work. Over its three seasons, KBC has featured two of India's biggest film stars as the show's host—using their celebrity status for brand-name recognition and their personal journeys in the film industry for the show's narrative on opportunities, possibilities and individual ambition.

The film industry in India produces the highest number of films in the world. But the industry's resilience and success is best understood in terms of its competitive edge over Hollywood productions both in the domestic and South Asian market as well as in sections of the global market. Indian audiences— a complex social composition of caste, class, religious and regional orientations —have created their own heroes. Faced with the need to make the show distinctly "Indian" when it was first launched in 2000, Star TV programming executives exhibited their commitment to the domestic market by commissioning Amitabh Bachchan, as the host. The third season was launched with Shah Rukh Khan, who is another iconic, and significantly younger, movie star. The connection to the popular film industry has no doubt helped bring viewers to KBC. But perhaps more importantly for the purposes of our analysis here, the skillful and creative crafting of their personalities onto KBC's narrative enabled a discourse of change.

Bachchan's personal career reflects India's national trajectory in many ways. He started his career in the 1970s as the "angry young man" — a one-man-army fighting the corrupt political systems to give voice to the disenfranchised Indian working class. He was the hero of the masses. Yet off screen he is known for his suave, sophisticated manners; his private school education; his flawless Hindi and English diction that comes with elite upbringing; his connections to India's political and industrial leaders; and an aura of refined mystique inherited from his father who was one of India's leading Hindi poets. As a result, Bachchan has miraculously straddled India's many constituencies and emerged as a "pan-Indian" hero. As KBC's host, he came a long way away from being the anti-establishment young man, to explaining the rules of the game and "locking" the "right" answer for instant, personal fortunes. From the honest, family oriented, frugal hero, he turned into one who celebrates money—traditionally seen as a crass and shallow craving. The changing social agenda where the rhetoric of social development has been abandoned in favor of an individual entrepreneurial spirit in a global economy is poignantly captured by Bachchan's transformation. He himself comments,

> It is the state of the nation and the circumstances, which will guide what you are like, what you wear, what you do, etcetera. In the 70s, when you talk of the Angry Young Man—it was not something I had designed, but it was perhaps a feeling that the nation and the circumstances at the time needed to be told—that the system was not performing. . . . Today, things are different. The system works—or supposedly works. It is economic progress that is the new benchmark. Those issues are non-existent, the rebel of those years is now 64 and it is commercial success that counts. So roles are designed accordingly and they are appreciated because they reflect the times.
>
> (*Times of India*, 2007, p. 14)

In contrast to Bachchan's personal trajectory, Khan, who hosts KBC III, is known as the middle-class boy from Delhi, with his unshakable ambition, hard work, talent and charisma. Promotional material and interviews with Khan before he took over as the new host reiterate his "ordinary" beginnings, his singular passion for films, his secular orientation (he is a Muslim married to a Hindu woman) and his sincere desire to retain his connection to the humble reality of middle-class life in India, despite his celebrity status and obvious financial well being that puts him in another class. He flaunts his success and enjoys it with the self-righteousness of someone who has earned his stardom with sincerity. As a younger celebrity with a cosmopolitan flair and a fan following that matches Bachchan's stardom, Khan offers a new direction to the show that is more in cue with the "Gen Next," that is the two thirds of India's population that is below 35 years (Star TV press release, 11/26/06).

In KBC III, Khan introduces himself as the *dost* (friend) and not a "host." The show's hosting style respectfully distinguishes itself from the previous two seasons: Khan's youthful accessibility and irreverence versus Bachchan's paternalistic formality and refinement. Bachchan's presence on KBC I and II helped anchor KBC in a national narrative and allowed instant recognition in terms of a pan-Indian identity and national ancestry. For instance, KBC often opened with "A.B.'s *gyan*," which is a poetic and philosophical monologue by Amitabh

Bachchan (A.B.) on life, values and wisdom. Formulaic notions of the host's role in the format are rejected in favor of reframing the host within a paternal Indian-ness. Khan's presence on the other hand suggests the forward strides and tales of change. An article on popular culture's impact on branding in the "Consumer Life" section of the business newspaper *Economic Times* argues that an "unconfident India" in 2000 found Bachchan "compelling" in KBC because

> his demeanor of royalty and leadership was accepted as the necessary gospel that the laity must adopt to come up in life . . . If KBC 1 set the stage for the competitive Indian, KBC 3 has set the stage for the Indian who is comfortable in his own skin and wants the world to know it.
>
> (Kaushik, 2007)

The sense of "comfort" is directly correlated with "self esteem" and "nationalistic pride" based on "economic success and the rise in the GDP." The article goes on to argue that "India in the 2000's is an emerging power which the West is being forced to recognize and fraternize with" (Kaushik, 2007). The hosts on KBC therefore do more than facilitate the game structure or provide entertaining interactions with the participants. The personal narratives of the star hosts are incorporated into KBC's branding to resonate with India's skewed, under-35 demography—as a quality format that is globally connected but uniquely pan-Indian in sensibility; respectful of traditional heritage but one that is eager for change and global interactions.

A new discursive space is thus created around the hosts (and the show) by producers and social commentators that allows new cultural practices (such as participating in a reality game show) to become meaningful acts in the economic, cultural and national fields. In the process a new historically shaped view emerges that allows political-economic shifts towards neoliberalism to appear disembodied and interest-neutral. "KBC is the face of a new Indian who is willing to break the rules, be himself, enjoy the game, and lose no sleep over losing if the reward at the end of it is a positive experience" (Kaushik, 2007). Nobody questions the rules of the game, or who benefits from the regulative-functioning principle. Most participants on the show who do not win any money report to the media that the experience was still worthwhile because they got to meet the star host of the show. While, on one hand, their rueful comments reiterate the prize money as the real attraction, they also indicate a new opportunistic compromise with what life doles out. A new way of dealing with life is made available to viewers through a new game show—the prize money is indeed a bonus.

Language and Narratives of Change

The embedded discourse on KBC suggests a narrative of India's forward move-ment. If the change of hosts for the show implies shedding the past and embracing a brave new world, the shifts in the treatment of language used on the show also suggest similar trajectories. KBC began, in the year 2000, with a need to establish its national credentials. Adaptation of the *Millionaire* format, according to Star TV executives (and as discussed above), elevated the Indian television experience to a new standard of international quality and enabled Indians to participate in a "global community." But in contrast to its "global" associations, the language used on KBC I and II was a particularly formalized, stylized and refined Hindi. KBC appeared unique among other television fare and consistent with the host's sophisticated persona. A contextualized look, however, reveals issues of traditionalism, modernity and nationality embedded in the show's use of language.

In KBC I and II, the *shudh* (pure) Hindi used on the show appealed to national identity in terms of antiquity—rendered with dignity and authority in Bachchan's paternal, baritone voice. The Western program format, re-versioned in *shudh* Hindi by an "international" media company, is thus made acceptable, indeed "national" in its purist claim. Traditional modes are creatively invoked and self-consciously posed against the changing ways of life. The questions on the show are asked in Hindi but the textual graphic on the bottom of the screen appears in English. Nair recalls the production team deliberating over this inconsistency but choosing English text because the Hindi "did not look good" (Nair, 2008). On one hand, the use of Hindi evokes Indian roots and access to the masses; on the other hand English texts refer to standards of quality, elite-based aspirations and a global outlook. When Bachchan asks the computer for the correct answer, he refers to it as "computer-*ji*." In Hindi, the suffix *ji* is added to suggest respect for seniors, or even contemporaries. The computer is personalized in the language, and the process is almost akin to asking for one's future to be read by an astrologer blessed with powers of knowing the future. The computer in this case holds the answer to the participant's fate. The local meaning-making process is therefore carefully embedded in the show in a precarious balance between tradition and modernity, technology and astrology, family "values" and individual ambition, all the while pushing towards a brave new world that offers riches for those willing to compete.

KBC III abandons the formal and pure Hindi used by Bachchan in favor of an informal, colloquial Hindi sprinkled with English and regional Indian languages (depending on participants' home towns). The titles KBC *Pratham* (first) and *Dwitiya* (second) lose their Sanskrit-ized flair and acquire numerical simplicity as KBC III. A more functional approach frames the world view as traditional modes and cultural habits fall by the side. In the opening sequence of KBC III the new host performs a lengthy monologue in purist Hindi. He pauses to look at the camera (and at India) to ask if anybody understood anything. He replies to his own rhetorical question that, since nobody speaks in that stylized version anymore, it is not necessary on television either. There is no need to prove cultural moorings and KBC III, with its attention on more advertiser-friendly younger viewers, claims to represent contemporary social realities. "Computer-*ji*" too changes to computer "*dada/bhau/garu*," etc., which translates into "elder brother." The suave host of the show has explained that nowhere in the world has the format of the show been adapted to include a new term for the computer. Instead, the computer, as he puts it, "is just there, just a thing." He exhibits a personal ease with objects of modernity. But in India, participants want to show "respect" for the computer and so he felt he should refer to it as an "elder brother." While there is a distinct slide from a strictly formal "computer-*ji*" to a more familiar "computer-*bhau*," the computer as a source of knowledge is still a modern entry into traditional social spaces. Familiarity with computers suggests socially privileged access to higher education, training and global ties. The introduction of the computer as a capital or everyday resource of economic life must first be accommodated through a process of cultural translation and negotiation. Social transformation is accommodated within the market's need to render new realities; and ordinary lives on reality television screens perform to commercial ends. Cultural practices are articulated within consumption patterns which simultaneously provide new national narratives.

Conclusion

The unprecedented popularity of reality–game shows in India is significant in terms of its articulation of certain discourses of reality, representation and change at a moment of national transition. This chapter has explored the social situatedness of the television experience and adaptation of global formats of reality television shows to understand how cultural processes may mediate and shape social change. Discursive analysis looks at the creative logics and how they are implicated in social relations of power that support particular ideological constructions. Analysis of the show and discussions on the public sphere (identified in terms of news reports, opinion pieces, talk shows), suggest correspondences between the discourses of social change on KBC and political-economic shifts in India. Analytical attention is not intended to categorize or catalogue the global aspects of a format and the local aspects of its adaptation. Rather, an examination of the cultural practices that inform the adaptation of a format, on the cultural domain, maps the fields of power that intersect and interconnect across social, cultural, political and economic realms. Analysis of the show KBC provides a point of entry into understanding India's social transformations towards a market-oriented global political economy.

India's rising power on the world stage has been accompanied by a central paradox that raises fundamental questions about the nation's potential role as a stable democracy and competitive economy. On one hand, liberalization and privatization has unleashed new entrepreneurial energy, created new markets and consumer interest and introduced new cultural practices, as witnessed in KBC. On the other hand, there is increasing wealth inequity, hunger and social-cultural deprivation (Global Hunger Index, 2006). The emerging television experience in India, as "techno-social spaces" (Rajagopal, 2001) where audiences negotiate social change, is therefore characterized by differences in material and socio-cultural power. To the extent that the right answer can only become possible when we pose the right question, as the KBC promo film teaches us, it is debatable if the right question for national development is "Who wants to be a millionaire?" However, in the meantime, such questions continue to frame the narratives of cultural and national identity.

References

Abu-Lughod, L. 2005. *Dramas of Nationhood: The Politics of Television in Egypt.* Chicago and London: Chicago University Press.

Aiyar, V.S. and Chopra, A. 2000. "The Great Gamble." *India Today.* New Delhi. July 17. 48–54.

Appadurai, A. 1990. "Disjuncture and Difference in the Global Cultural Economy." *Public Culture*, 2: 1-24.

Barman, A. 2001. "Unshackling the Locked Gates." *Outlook India.* New Delhi. June 4.

Basu, S. 2008. Personal Interview. February 15, 2008.

Bourdieu, P. 1973. "Cultural Reproduction and Social Reproduction." In *Knowledge, Education and Cultural Change*, Ed. R. Brown. 71–112. London: Tavistock.

—— 1990. *The Logic of Practice.* Stanford, CA: Stanford University Press.

—— 1998. "Neo-liberalism, the Utopia (Becoming a Reality) of Unlimited Exploitation." In *Acts of Resistance: Against the Tyranny of the Market.* 94–105. New York: The New Press.

Business Today. 2006. "Hot Seat Just Got Hotter: Can KBC III Rake in the Ratings Like Before?" December 31. 74.

Busselle, R. W. and Greenberg, B. S. 2000. "The Nature of Television Realism Judgments: A Reevaluation of their Conceptualization and Measurement." *Mass Communication and Society*, 3(2&3): 249–268.

Cardoso, F. H. 1973. "Associated Dependent Development: Theoretical and Practical Implications." In *Authoritarian Brazil*, Ed. A. Stephan. 142–178. New Haven, CT: Yale University Press.

Chopra, R. 2003. "Neoliberalism as Doxa: Bourdieu's Theory of the State and the Contemporary Indian Discourse on Globalization and Liberalization." *Cultural Studies*, 17(3/4): 419–444.

Derne, S. 2005. "The (Limited) Effect of Cultural Globalization in India: Implications for Culture Theory." *Poetics*, 33: 33–47.

Dutta, A. 2002. "Spark off a Revolution." Times Education Supplement. *Times of India.* New Delhi. June 24.

Evans, P. 1979. *Dependent Development: The Alliance of Multinational, State and Local Capital in Brazil.* Princeton, NJ: Princeton University Press.

Fairclough, N. 1992. *Discourse and Social Change.* Cambridge, U.K.: Polity.

—— 1995. *Critical Discourse Analysis.* London: Longman.

Garcia-Canclini, N. 2001. *Consumers and Citizens: Globalization and Multicultural Conflicts.* Minneapolis and London: University of Minnesota Press

Garnham, N. 1977. "Towards a Political Economy of Culture." *New Universities Quarterly*, 31(3): 340–357.

Geertz, C. 1973. *The Interpretation of Culture*. New York: Basic Books.

Global Hunger Index: A Basis for Cross Country Comparison. Report published by International Food Policy Research Institute and German Agro Action, 2006.

Golding, P. 1977. "Media Professionalism in the Third World: The Transfer of an Ideology." In *Mass Communication and Society*, Ed. J. Curran, M. Gurevitch and J. Woollacott. 291–308. London: Edward Arnold.

Gramsci, A. 1971. *Prison Notebooks: Selections*. London: Lawrence and Wishart.

Gupta, A. and Ferguson, J. 1992. "Beyond Culture: Space, Identity and the Politics of Difference." *Cultural Anthropology*, 7 (1): 6–23.

Hall, S. 1980. "Encoding/Decoding." In *Culture, Media, Language: Working Papers in Cultural Studies, 1972–79*, Ed. S. Hall, D. Hobson, A. Lowe, and P. Willis. 128–38. London: Hutchinson.

Hindu Business Line. 2005. "KBC 2 Boosts Star Ratings." Accessed on 11/30/06. Available online: www.blonnet.com/2005/08/13/stories/2005081302530800.htm

Hindustan Times. 2007. "Future's Digital." New Delhi. December 20. 1.

Hobson, D. 1982. "Housewives and the Mass Media." In *Culture, Media, Language*, Ed. S. Hall, D. Hobson, A. Lowe, and P. Willis. 105–14. London: Hutchinson.

India Today. 2000. "Question and Answer with R. K. Singh." New Delhi. November 6. 59.

India TV News. 2006. "Big B's Bye, Bye to KBC." January 26. Accessed on 12/06/2006. Available online: www.indiatvnews.com/common/main.php?id=40&tid=4

Kang, B. 2002. "Labouring Under a Misconception." *Outlook India*. May 29.

Kaushik, Meena. 2007. "Ruler and Lover: Hero's Choice Lies in Mass Appeal." *The Economic Times*. New Delhi. January 30. 4.

Kraidy, M. M. 2005. *Hybridity or the Cultural Logic of Globalization*. Philadelphia, PA: Temple University Press.

Krishna, S. 2007. "Star Power: King Khan gives KBC III a Fair Start." *The Economic Times*. New Delhi. January 24. 4.

Malik, A., Dhawan, H. and Ram, A. 2000. "Enter the Clonepati." *India Today*. New Delhi. November 6. 54–59.

McCarthy, A. 2004. "Stanley Miligram, Allen Funt, and Me: Postwar Social Science and the 'First Wave' of Reality TV." In *Reality TV: Remaking Television Culture*, Ed. S. Murray and L. Ouellette. 19–39. New York and London: New York University Press.

Morley, D. 1980. *The* Nationwide *Audiences: Structure and Decoding*. London: British Film Institute. TV Mono. 11.

—— 1981. "*Nationwide*: A Critical Postscript." *Screen Education*, no. 39(Summer): 11.

—— 1995. "Active Audience Theory: Pendulums and pitfalls." *Journal of Communication*, 43(4): 255–261.

Mowlana, H. 1986. *Global Information and World Communication: New Frontiers in International Relations*. White Plains, NY: Longman.

Mulvey, L. 1975. "Visual Pleasure and Narrative Cinema." *Screen*. 16(3): 6–18.

Murdock, G. 1977. "Capitalism, Communication and Class Relations." In *Mass Communication and Society*, Ed. J. Curran, M. Gurevitch and J. Woollacott. 12–43. London: Edward Arnold.

Murray, S. and Ouellette, L. 2004. *Reality TV: Remaking Television Culture*. New York and London: New York University Press.

Nair, S. 2008. Personal Interview. February 12, 2008.

Radway, J. 1984. *Reading the Romance: Feminism and the Representation of Women in Popular Culture.* Chapel Hill: University of North Carolina Press.

Rajagopal, A. 2001. *Politics After Television: Religious Nationalism and the Reshaping of the Indian Public.* Cambridge: Cambridge University Press.

Ray, S. G. 2000. "The Bettor Nationality: Quizzes, Scratch-Card Freebies and Online Punting Whet India's Hunger for More." *Outlook India.* New Delhi. December 11. 38–40.

Scannell, P. 1992. *Culture and Power: A Media, Culture and Society Reader*, Ed. P. Schlesinger and C. Sparks. London, Newbury Park, CA and New Delhi: Sage.

Schiller, H. I. 1971. *Mass Communication and the American Empire.* Boston: Beacon Press.

Singhal, A and Rogers, E. M. 2001. *India's Communication Revolution: From Bullock Carts to Cybermarts.* New Delhi and Newbury Park, CA: Sage.

Sinha, S. 2000. "The Great KBC Effect." *India Today.* New Delhi. November 6. 56.

Star TV. 2006. "Three Letters That Spell Magic." Press Release. November 26. Accessed on 12/07/06. Available online: www.startv.com/pressroom/pressrelease.jsp?seq=3061

Straubhaar, J. 1991. "Beyond Media Imperialism: Asymmetrical Interdependence and Cultural Proximity." *Critical Studies in Mass Communication*, 8(1): 29–38.

Thompson, J. 1990. *Ideology and Modern Culture: Critical Social Theory in the Era of Mass Communication.* Stanford, CA: Stanford University Press.

Times of India. 2007. "Interview with Amitabh Bachchan on Times Nation." New Delhi. January 29. 14.

Williams, Raymond. 1974. *Television: Technology and Cultural Form.* London: Fontana Collins.

17

GLOBAL FRANCHISING, GENDER, AND GENRE

The Case of Domestic Reality Television

Sharon Sharp

In the *Chappelle's Show* parody of the domestic reality television *Wife Swap* format, comedian Dave Chappelle sends up the reality format's emphasis on housekeeping and social difference. Playing both the black and white husbands as the fictionalized show "goes interracial" for the first time, Chappelle comically points to some typical elements of the format: racial, gender, and class conflict played out around the domestic routines of housekeeping. In observational documentary mode, Chappelle's working-class black husband Leonard orders his new wife around and refuses to do any housework. Chappelle's middle-class white husband Todd makes unappreciated gourmet dinners and sends his new son to take a time out. Later, in the "diary cam" sequence as each relates what they learned from the experience, Leonard expresses his disgust at the hygiene of his new family while Todd talks about his first foray into interracial sex. While the skit, which swaps husbands rather than wives, pokes fun at the exploitive and trashy dimensions of the format, it also highlights the format's basic element of dramatizing social difference through housekeeping and its twin imperatives to "educate and entertain" which results in contradictory texts. The format's emphasis on difference and housekeeping has traveled across the globe as the *Wife Swap* format has been adapted in over 20 countries in both licensed and unlicensed forms, making it a global phenomenon.

The cultural work of the British and American versions of the program has occupied both academics and popular critics (Brancato, 2007; Fairclough, 2004; Matheson, 2007; Piper, 2004). However, the global circulation of this series, which has received comparatively little sustained attention, deserves examination, particularly in terms of the relationship between global franchising and the format's thematic preoccupations with social difference and housekeeping. The global reach of this format has significant implications for understanding the industrial and cultural circulation of meanings about gender, nation, race, class, and genre. In addition, as Susan Murray and Laurie Ouellette (2004: 9) have suggested, "as media conglomerates become international entities, and as television formats are exchanged and revamped across national contexts, we need to revise our political economic frameworks and ways to understand how meaning can be culturally specific and globally relevant". What, then, about this format enables it to be adapted in so many distinct national contexts? How does it articulate ideas about home, gender, race and class in relation to its diverse cultural contexts? This essay seeks to answer these questions by comparing the articulation of difference through the emphasis on home and housekeeping in the British, American and Chilean iterations of this globally franchised domestic reality television format.

Domestic Reality Television and Global Franchising

The *Wife Swap* format in all its global iterations belongs to the domestic reality television genre as it dramatizes conflicted housewifery when two women from radically different social backgrounds swap households. Domestic reality television, one of the most prominent globally franchised genres, combines domestic settings with observational documentary aesthetics, the lifestyle and gameshow genres, and the "life experiment" program format, which involves "ordinary people experimenting with their lives in various different ways" (Hill 2005: 36). Part of the appeal of the genre is that it promises that the normally private interior space of the home will be exposed to public visibility, revealing the dirty laundry and other aspects of its inhabitants. Domestic reality TV shows are about surveillance, but they are also about transformation, as they incorporate life experiment aspects and participants try out different lifestyles, values, domestic and work arrangements and are often changed in the process (Hill 2005: 37). Domestic reality TV, which combines elements from existing genres, is produced and circulated to account for changing historical conditions and for previously unexpressed industrial and cultural needs within various national contexts.

The industrial impetus for the global franchising of this genre is multifold. As many academics have detailed, reality television series are considerably less expensive to produce than fictional programming. Reality television is premised on the idea of "providing viewers with an unmediated, voyeuristic, yet often playful look into what might be called the 'entertaining' real" (Murray and Ouellette 2004: 4). The domestic reality television genre's emphasis on capturing the "entertaining real" of families in their homes means that this genre is much less costly to produce in terms of labor than scripted fictional genres. Domestic reality television's casting of non-actors rather than professional actors and the production of narrative content by producers and editors instead of unionized writers offers cost savings. In addition, the documentary look of the genre, which features location shooting and does not require standing sets, elaborate lighting set-ups, costumes, make-up, or props offers comparatively low production costs. As Chad Raphael has observed, the low production costs of the reality television genre provide considerable savings compared to fictional programming; reality television can cost up to 50 percent less than fictional television (Raphael 2004: 127).

In addition, as Silvio Waisboard has detailed, perhaps even more so than fictional television, reality television offers an easily replicated narrative formula or recipe that can easily flow across borders. Domestic reality television producers can take the structure of a format that is not particularly tied to a national context—trading domestic or work arrangements, inviting a nanny to transform children and parents or inviting a housekeeping goddess to inspect the cleanliness of one's home—and customize it to a national context through the insertion of local flavor by casting national "types" as the requisite characters. In this way, the domestic reality television format, like other reality television formats, can be customized to different domestic contexts and adapted to the tastes of national audiences (Waisboard 2004: 368). The domestic reality television genre is particularly suitable to transborder flows because it depends on social difference and requires the participation of people from regions across the national landscape to produce the desired narrative conflict. So rather than fictional genres like the *telenovela*, which reflects the urbanity of the urban settings in which it is produced, domestic reality television usually features participants from across the nation selected for their contrasting lifestyles, which offers more diversity to appeal to local tastes within the nation.

The domestic reality television genre has also figured heavily in terms of filling programming needs for the multiplication of commercial channels with the privatization of public service television and the expansion of satellite and cable throughout the world beginning in the 1980s. The growth of new commercial channels created a demand for new programming to appeal to audiences in a newly competitive market (Raphael 2004: 131). Domestic reality series, like other forms of reality television, were a cheap and relatively flexible form of programming to appeal to audiences who preferred to see themselves and their nation rather than imports from other countries. Likewise, international media conglomerates as well as independent production companies were increasingly financially invested in producing the next global franchise rather than individual shows, and were eager to license and co-produce domestic reality television series in multiple national contexts. As Newscorp's former Fox Television president Angela Shapiro, who oversaw Fox World's global franchises, explained in 2005, "I look at our business as one that is responsible for creating franchises and not just shows . . . As the world gets smaller, my goal is to create franchises that are global at their core" (Carugati 2007). Domestic reality television, like other forms of reality television, is therefore appealing to both international media conglomerates and national television producers alike because it carries a proven track record of success with multiple audiences in different national iterations, minimizing financial risk for television producers and networks (Waisboard 2004: 368).

In addition to the industrial reasons for the proliferation of the global franchising of the domestic reality television genre, there are cultural factors at work as well. Domestic reality television, with its explicit emphasis on home, family, nation, and everyday life is uniquely positioned to speak to national identity. As Joseph Straubhaar has argued, "cultural producers use forms and genres that have spread globally to express ideas of what home is like" (2002: 191). Domestic reality television is uniquely suited to express ideas of home as its focus is explicitly the home and housekeeping. Moreover, the genre's focus on everyday life and people in which national audiences might recognize themselves provides an opportunity for a sense of national identity to be articulated. Waisboard has suggested that reality television formats help to "organize experiences of the national":

> Format television shows then, organize experiences of the national. Even "reality" shows, which unlike "period" or "contemporary" fiction are not ostensibly designed to articulate national narratives, provide spaces for the representation of national cultures . . . . reality shows also offer opportunities for audiences to recognize themselves as members of national communities. The question of how the national is expressed and recreated in these genres, however has not received sufficient attention. . . . More than in specific moments when programming appeals to nationalistic discourses, television has the power of naturalizing cultural connections in everyday viewing.
>
> (2004: 372)

If the global format of the domestic reality television genre can provide opportunities for audiences to recognize themselves and articulate national identities and narratives, what kinds of narratives does the *Wife Swap* format articulate in terms of gender, class and race?

The *Wife Swap* Format, Housekeeping, and the Circulation of Social Difference

The *Wife Swap* format was first produced in Great Britain by independent production company RDF Media Group and began airing on Channel 4 in 2003. Even before *Wife Swap* aired and became an immediate hit with British audiences, the format was licensed to TVNZ in New Zealand, Network 9 in Australia, Holland Media group, C4 in Finland and TV Norge in Norway ("Wife Swapping Travels"). Later the format was licensed to M6 in France, RTL in Germany, TV3 in Denmark, ABC in the United States, the Viasat network in Estonia, TV Markiza in Slovakia, the TNT Channel in Russia, Keshet TV in Israel, TV3 in Lithuania and a factual channel in Spain ("Wife Swap in Further Deals," Grant 2004, Racas 2005, Hazen 2005: 24). Several unlicensed versions were adapted, including Fox's *Trading Spouses* in the U.S.A., Channel 13's *¿Quién Cambia a Quién? Intercambio de Esposas* in Chile, RTL2's *Frauentausch* in Germany, ATV-Plus's *Family Swap* in Austria and RTLKlub's *Family Swap* in Hungary (Cozens).

The basic elements of the format are premised on social difference, as Sarah Matheson has noted in relation to the American version, in order to instigate the narrative conflict central to the domestic reality television genre. The premise is simple; two women from radically different social backgrounds switch places for two weeks. For the first week, the wives live by the rules of their counterparts. For the second week, the wives institute their own rules.[1] Usually, only wives with partners and children who live at home are eligible for swapping.[2] What better way to ensure conflict than to pit a housewife on the dole with eight children living in public housing with a British yuppie, or a white liberal lesbian working mother with an affluent African American Republican fundamentalist Christian stay-at-home mother, or a Chilean gypsy with a middle-class Chilean woman of Italian descent with a gypsy phobia? The juxtaposing of clear opposites in terms of class, race, sexuality, ethnicity, and political and religious worldviews produces a more heterogeneous image of family and home in relation to their national contexts. In this way the format offers an opportunity to explore questions of social difference from a distinctly feminine perspective that is not usually seen in primetime programming, as many critics have noted. However, even as the format offers a somewhat diverse representation of the family and home, the premise of the show is structured around conventional notions of gender as it relies on the assumption that domesticity is strictly a female-oriented sphere as it is the wives, not husbands who are swapped for dramatic conflict and only wives who are mothers are suitable for swapping. In this way the format's premise reinforces the "mutual identification of the woman, the mother, and the home" (Morley 2000: 63). It is based on the idea that through the swap, the couples, but more specifically the wives, gain insight about their marriages and families.

The narrative formula of the format labors to highlight the social differences between wives and their new families through the representation of housekeeping. Each episode begins with an introduction of the opposing families. An exterior shot of their homes is featured as the voiced-over narrator boils down the identifying features of each family to the city in which they live, their occupations, their parenting and housekeeping styles and other lifestyle markers. The conflict that will follow is set up by positioning the families' class status, race, religion, and housekeeping styles through the voyeuristic survey of their homes and behavior and by the voiceover narration which draws together the difference between the families for the viewer. Next, each wife is shown packing, saying goodbye to her family and traveling to her new home, during which time she muses on her expectations for the swap. Many wives say that they want to learn something about their lives through the experiment, although particularly in the American version, the wives tell the camera that they want to teach the other family their values.

Soon after, the wives arrive at the empty homes that they inspect; pointing out housekeeping errors or gawking at the Zen-like order of the household and judging the taste and implicit social position of the other mother. Like the popular

British programs Morley analyzes, there is "a collapsing of the image of the wife/mother into the image of the home itself" and "the woman and the home seem to become each other's attributes" (2000: 65). The voyeuristic impulse of the format, like all reality TV, invites women participants, and the audience at home, to inspect the homes of other women and to diagnose problems that can be resolved by each participant educating the other. The problems diagnosed are either explicitly or implicitly blamed on the wives, embedding the idea that women, by decorating and maintaining the cleanliness of the home, maintain their family's social normativity and their own normative femininity. In case the viewer missed anything in this critical inspection or fails to blame the housewife for the problems, each swapped wife reads a house manual prepared by the other which outlines the quotidian routines of the family as well as the worldview of each wife and family. In order to stage the ensuing conflicts of the episode, each wife reads the manual and openly mocks or disapproves of the lifestyle of the other, while plotting her makeover. The narrative then proceeds to each wife living uncomfortably in the other's shoes for one week, which usually includes conflicts over quotidian but gendered domestic chores, work outside the home, parenting and lifestyle choices. Cooking, which as Morley argues "retains a central symbolic significance in the culture of domesticity" (2000: 71) is often a site of conflict and is staged as an artificial platform for articulating problems of difference. A rule setting ceremony follows, in which each wife sets out to make over the family and more conflict ensues. After the week is over, the couples meet at the "final table meeting" and emotionally reflect on what transpired during the swap and sometimes vow to change their lives after the experience or confirm their existing values and lifestyles.[3]

The style of the format cuts between voiceover narration which frames the narrative, observational sequences in which contestants perform for the camera, and first person address by the contestants to the camera in "diary cam" sequences. The format's style explicitly foregrounds "citizen as subject" which amplifies the possibilities for articulating national and gendered experiences in the domestic sphere. As James Walters (2006: 63) has detailed in relation to the British iteration, the emphasis on the "diary cam," the extensive use of close-ups to register emotion, and the privileging of the participants' words over that of a controlling narrator or outside experts "aims to give exclusive attention to the citizens it represents" and forges an intimate bond between viewers at home and the participants on screen. In addition, although the format proposes that it is capturing social difference that exists in real life as it mimics the conventions of observational documentary, it is a highly constructed and artificial format. As John Corner has observed about the format, "the status of the visual depictions in *Wife Swap* have the character of display rather than observation" (Corner 2006: 72). Indeed, many of the eruptions of angry behavior give the perception of performance rather than spontaneous behavior given the artificial nature of the circumstances. Social difference is also staged in the preproduction process, as producers craft episodes around preconceived social types, such as "rocket scientist," "tattoo artist" and "midwife," that they hope to match with actual families, and episodes involve months of research in terms of ferreting out difference (Steinberg 2005: E1). Moreover, as many participants have noted, the format relies on scripted material and editing practices that transform hundreds of hours of footage into 43 minutes and which narrates behavior in line with how the producers wish to present the story that shapes the "reality" captured.

The rigid standardization of narrative structure of the format ensures that conflict will be generated around social difference but that the conflict, although predictably around housekeeping, will vary with the pairing of the participants. To varying degrees the elements of the structure emphasize housekeeping as it is tied to notions of gendered and national experience articulated around the notion of home. Home as it is represented in the *Wife Swap* format is close to Karen Fog-Olwig's (1998: 226) observation that home "is a contested domain, an arena where differing interests struggle to define their own spaces within which to localize and cultivate identity". In the *Wife Swap* format, the idea of home as a contested domain is played out in conflicts over gendered and other social differences through the conflicts around housekeeping. This emphasis serves to not only produce notions about gendered identity, but normative ideas about nation: who does and does not belong to the national imaginary is articulated through the circulation of housekeeping. In the case studies that follow, I compare how housekeeping (which includes cleaning, cooking, home decorating, child rearing and domestic consumptive practices) articulates notions of gender and nation in each iteration. I argue that in the adaptation of the format, social differences, and conflicts particular to each location are played out through housekeeping in the contested domain of the home, which in effect "localizes" each adaptation for their respective national audiences.

Wife Swap Britain

RDF Media's *Wife Swap* emerged out of a long tradition of social documentaries broadcast on British screens, as well as a general move away from the more serious aspects of documentaries and current affairs programming and towards "factual entertainment," a category that comprises hybrid forms such as docu-soaps, and lifestyle and makeover programs (Brunsdon et al. 2001: 29). As the Midlands TV Research Group has documented, the increase in factual programming such as *Wife Swap* involves "the interplay of supranational factors, such as the expansion of satellite broadcasting, and national factors, such as the requirement in the 1992 Broadcasting Act that 25 percent of programmes should be produced by independents" (Brunsdon et al. 2001: 31). Both factors demand more programming to appeal to an audience defecting from broadcast stations to satellite and cable services. The factual programming trend also constitutes a "feminization" of primetime television in the focus on lifestyle programming resulting from an increase in home ownership, the continuing expansion of women entering the workforce, the privatization of leisure and the postponement of childrearing until later years (Brunsdon 2004: 78).

The original British version of the *Wife Swap* format established the format's emphasis on the articulation of social difference, gender and nation through the observation and performance of housekeeping. These themes were established in the context of changing gender roles and state of the family in Great Britain. Like other Western countries, in the later years of the twentieth century the U.K. experienced a rise in divorce rates, a decline in marriage, an increase in having children out of wedlock and more women entering the workforce (Crompton 2006: 6). In addition, sociological studies have also documented the increase in male housekeeping duties and a slow move toward equality in the domestic sphere (Sullivan 2000). In its surveillance of housekeeping across the United Kingdom, *Wife Swap U.K.* works through changing concepts of gender, family and nation and articulates and manages conflicts around these issues.

Gendered labor is of particular interest to the series as it interrogates the gendered division of domestic routines through the household manual, the camera's surveillance of housekeeping chores, and the wives' authority to evaluate housekeeping and set new rules for each family. Although the series often acknowledges that the women perform an unequal burden of housekeeping, the series also labors to offer a more complex array of differently gendered house-keeping. In particular, the British version focuses on the sharing of domestic labor between couples by consistently revisiting the representation of masculinity and fatherhood through the figure of the "new father." The new father is exemplary of "masculine caring behavior" and the "uncoupling of domestic labor from women's work" (Sullivan 2004: 214). In *Wife Swap,* usually the new father is pared with a more "traditional" wife who is solely responsible for housekeeping in her own home. The "Nicola/Jayne" (1/7/2003) episode provides an interesting example for analysis in this regard. Middle-class Welsh housewife and part-time interior decorator Nicola is paired with her working-class estranged brother-in-law Dave from Newcastle. The episode presents contrasting views of both husbands and wives. Nicola's husband Jason, shown playing a slot machine in his private game room, is introduced as a financial investor who "plays as hard as he works, spending an average of four hours a night at home in his games room," while Nicola shows off her interior decorating and is shown performing housekeeping chores. The couple is established as traditional, with Jason as the breadwinner who is divorced from housekeeping labor, while Nicola is responsible for domestic labor and making consumption choices. This vision of the traditional family is immediately contrasted to Jayne and Dave, who live in decidedly downmarket surroundings. The family is shown together at the kitchen table playing a game. The narrator introduces Dave as "the very model of a new man" who "works, takes care of the kids, cooks the meals, and even washes up," as he is shown performing housekeeping chores. Judgment and shame is circulated in relation to the housekeeping chores performed by the spouses in each household. Nicola rifles through the kitchen and chastises Dave for its lack of amenities and tells him she is uncomfortable with him doing everything. Jason complains about Jayne's ineptitude with cooking, cleaning and ironing, while she chastises him for his laziness and lack of involvement with the children.

Some critics have critiqued the cultural politics of the show as conservative and "vicious" because it is "staged so that the women are positioned against each other from the outset and naturally the situation is exacerbated to make 'good TV'" (Fairclough 2004: 345). However, in this episode, as in many others, the representation of the "new father" is clearly privileged. While Nicola initially criticizes Jayne for Dave's unequal share of housekeeping, she eventually begins to compare her own situation to Dave's and begins to doubt her future with her husband:

> Seeing all that he does, I don't want to go home. I look at him and I see me, and I'm not happy doing it. I'm not a slave and if I wanted to be a cleaner and a cook and a mother and a nurse and all that I could get paid for it.

Dave, forced to be a new father by Jayne, at first fails but then sees the benefits of more equal housekeeping. Resolution is achieved at the end of the episode as Jayne promises to express her appreciation for Dave and cook meals, while Jason, at risk of losing his family, vows to be a new father. In a sense then the different gendering of housekeeping and the representation of the British "new father" in which men participate to greater degrees in caring for their children becomes normalized and is represented as part of everyday national life. This episode is instructive because, although it unmoors housekeeping from femininity in the privileging of the "new father" archetype, it is achieved through the recognition of women's authority in the domestic sphere to evaluate, judge, and advise through the format's emphasis on the wives setting rules.

Domestic consumption related to women's authority in the home also figures prominently in the British series and is figured as a way in which to articulate and manage social difference. Normative ideas about proper Britishness and the imbrication of race with national identity are articulated by the wives evaluating, judging, and setting new rules in relation to the domestic consumptive practices of each family. The "Dee/Sonia" episode is informative in this regard. Sonia, who is black and working-class and living with a sexist black man, is swapped with Dee, a working-class racist white woman who is overly permissive with her daughters. Dee's racist ideas about what constitutes proper Britishness are articulated and challenged in her views about Sonia's home. When Dee inspects Sonia's kitchen and finds various ethnic food, for example, she informs the camera that the home's occupants are "not English." However, by the episode's end, Dee's experience with Sonia's son somewhat softens her racist views. Similarly,

Dee's family's racist attitudes are exposed and somewhat transformed throughout the course of the episode through housekeeping. Sonia's attempts to reform the family's dysfunction by removing the family's obsessive collection of bric-a-brac from the living room and daughters' bedroom result in an outburst from one of the daughters who calls Sonia a "black bitch." Her tantrum in relation to Sonia's streamlining of the home exposes not only her racism, but also the father, Dave's inability to be a proper parent as he is forced by Sonia to discipline her. By the conclusion of the episode, Dave concedes that Sonia's domestic authority enabled him to be a better father and the problems of racial difference that the episode foregrounds are partially ameliorated. The performance of housekeeping by the wives in these episodes and many others are a way in which the series exposes and shames racist attitudes in relation to who is considered properly British. Moreover, the diversity of families represented in the series, that the "Dee/Sonia" episode illustrates, unmoors the national family from whiteness and works to represent a more multifaceted image of Britishness. Throughout, the series stages and resolves conflicts around housekeeping in which national and gendered experiences are fought over and managed through women's advice and domestic authority. These are the basic elements that the other iterations adapt and transform to their national contexts.

Wife Swap/Trading Spouses U.S.A.

A licensed adaptation of the British *Wife Swap* format appeared on the ABC network in the United States during the fall of 2004, and an unlicensed version called *Trading Spouses* was broadcast on the Fox Network in the summer of the same year. ABC's *Wife Swap* and Fox's *Trading Spouses* belong to the phenomenon of U.S. adaptations of British content that began in the late 1960s with Normal Lear's adaptations of British sitcoms *Steptoe and Son* and *Till Death Us Do Part* (Miller 2000: 139–168). Increased competition for dwindling audiences that can choose between various media platforms led U.S. broadcast stations to purchase reality formats such as *Wife Swap* with proven track records. Produced by RDF USA, *Wife Swap* exhibits the British format's elements whole cloth, except for an added closing segment which revisits the contestants weeks after the swap in order to explore how much each family has changed. (The British format adopted the revisiting segment thereafter). The unlicensed Fox version, *Trading Spouses*, shifts the format elements and slightly sensationalizes them to fit with the Fox brand image of brash, over-the-top content directed toward a youthful demographic. In *Trading Spouses* the swap is condensed to one week, the wives meet the extended family and friends of their new families, and a $50,000 prize allotted by each wife is added to up the dramatic ante. Although both American versions feature the similar casting of opposites in terms of social difference, the Fox version tends to cast more outré contestants, such as self-proclaimed "god warrior" Marguerite Perrin, who gained national notoriety for her "televised tantrum" about living with non-Christians (Fernandez 2005). Moreover, although the Fox version is more exploitive, both American adaptations of the format depart from the more sober social documentary tone of the British original in its first few seasons, using music and editing to underscore the differences and moments of conflict and comedy, and choosing more hyperbolic pairings in terms of lifestyle (midget performers v. body builders, animal activists v. crocodile hunters, beauty queen moms v. radical feminists, and the like). Both versions are explicitly positioned as articulating the national through the representation of the American family, which is represented as a site of conflict between different sexual, racial, ethnic, gender, and religious identities brought about through debates about gay marriage, the move toward fundamentalism, and changing gender roles in relation to the growth of women in the work force, and non-nuclear family arrangements in America.

Like the British original, both American formats articulate and manage problems of social difference through the performance of housekeeping. However, the American versions tend to display a more normalizing process of transformation through the circulation of shame and evocation of cultural stereotypes of gender and race. The "Flumerfelt/Bray" episode (2/23/2005), which foregrounds racial and gender difference as well as domestic consumption through the performance of housekeeping, highlights the differences involved in the translation of the British format. In the Flumerfelt family, African American working mother Doreen is depicted in terms of the lazy black woman stereotype: she eats dinner alone in bed every night while her two African American sons from previous marriages and white husband Guy wait on her hand and foot. Moreover, domestic consumption is represented as leading to family dysfunction as everyone has their own electronic device "so we don't have to do anything together," as Doreen explains. The central problems of social difference the episode seeks to manage are announced when Doreen explains that she doesn't have a maternal bone in her body and that she thinks black men make terrible husbands. In the Bray family, white housewife Michelle explains that she prefers black men because they know how to be "real men." Michelle does all of the housework and home schools their five children while her African American husband Eric tells the camera that "cooking, doing the laundry, that's what women do." Like the British version, the format's emphasis on housekeeping works to dramatize these problems of social difference. In the rule setting segment, Doreen forces Eric to do all the housekeeping, and his experiences cleaning, cooking, and caring for the children transform his views about gendered domesticity. At the conclusion of the experience he tells the camera that he has "definitely assessed what a man's role and what a woman's role is and have come to believe that men can do what are traditionally considered women's roles." Meanwhile, Doreen, after spending time with the Bray children, rediscovers her maternal feelings and refines her views on race, telling the camera that "Eric is a good man, whether he be black, or white, or whatever. He's a good man, and that's all that matters." In the Flumerfelt household Michelle uses her more normative femininity to enforce family togetherness by forbidding the use of the electronic devices that fragment the family and requiring that they play board games together. At the conclusion of the episode, Doreen is sufficiently disciplined by her experience and she is shown out of bed and playing board games with her family and confessing that her family is the most important thing in the world. In this episode and others, housekeeping serves to both articulate and manage social difference. Through the practice of performing housekeeping under the direction of women's authority in the home, dysfunctional families are disciplined and transformed into more normative ones, and problems of racial intolerance are ameliorated in a manner similar to the British version. Like the original British version, the American *Wife Swap* diversifies the image of the American family that had been tightly tied to the white nuclear family in primetime television programming (with notable exceptions) since its inception. Yet, as the "Flumerfelt/Bray" episode demonstrates, the American version often circulates pernicious stereotypes about race, unlike the original British version. While the national American family is diversified in relation to race and ethnicity in the series, racial others are somewhat pathologized under the normalizing gaze of this iteration.

Problems of social difference are staged around housekeeping as well in Fox's unlicensed version of the format, *Trading Spouses*; however, the $50,000 prize that Fox includes adds a material dimension to the investigation of social difference, particularly in terms of class conflict. While there are many episodes dealing with this conflict, the "Biggins/Nakamura" (7/20/2004) episode provides an interesting example for analysis in relation to the American translation of this format. In the episode, the working-class African American Biggins family is paired with the upper-class Nakamura family. Tammy Nakamura, who is represented as a lazy, pampered white woman, attempts to reform the class-based eating and housekeeping practices of the Biggins family, while Mela Biggins attempts to adjust to her new family's higher socio-economic status. Class conflict is staged through the representation of domestic routines. Tammy's paternalistic counseling of her new black family about stereotypically African American problems such as teenage pregnancy and poor eating habits is contrasted with Mela's inability to meet the health-based cooking requirements of her new family with a higher socio-economic status. However, these class and racial differences are partially resolved in this episode by the distribution of the money, which Tammy allocates to paying off bills and a down payment for a new and better house for the Biggins family. In this way, *Trading Spouses* attempts to dramatize and ameliorate problems of social difference in a problematic way through women's domestic authority as well as with money. While *Trading Spouses* is slightly different as it foregrounds the game show element of the format with the addition of the prize money, both iterations adapt the *Wife Swap* format to dramatize and manage particularly American social rifts around race, class, religion and gender in order to appeal to American audiences.

¿Quién Cambia a Quién? Intercambio de Esposas Chile

The *Wife Swap* format traveled to Chile vis-à-vis a licensed adaptation of Fox World Television's *Trading Spouses*, (which was an unlicensed adaptation of RDF's *Wife Swap* Format). Co-produced with Chile's Channel 13 ¿*Quién Cambia a Quién? Intercambio de Esposas*, which aired in 2007, is part of the trend of reality television programming, which is second only to the *telenovela* in Chile (Sutter 2001: M20). Reality television has become increasingly important to Chilean broadcast stations like the Catholic University's Canal 13, which are competing with cable and satellite stations that are free from the censorship regulations imposed on broadcast stations so there is "pressure to produce local content" which "may provide product that occasionally lures viewers back from cable" (Franklin 2000: 52). However, local programs are so expensive to produce that many broadcast networks are partnering up with international media conglomerates like Foxworld to produce content.

Because *Intercambio de Esposas* follows the *Trading Spouses* format rather than the original British *Wife Swap* format, it shares some of the same modifications to the original: the swap lasts for just one week rather than two, and a monetary prize is included. However, the Chilean iteration of the format includes some additional changes, which affect its articulation of home, gender, and the "symbolic family" of the nation. One of the most striking changes to the format is the addition of a Chilean host to introduce the families in place of the off-screen anonymous narrator used in the British and U.S. versions. Cecilia Bolocco —former Miss Universe, wife of former president of Argentina Carlos Menem, and television star—introduces and concludes each episode of the series. The addition of Bolocco works to localize the format; her star image is embedded with associations of Chilean broadcasting as she has appeared as a talk show host for the popular Chilean programs *Porque hoy es sábado*, *Martes 13*, *Viva el lunes*, *La noche de Cecilia* and the Mexican telenovela *Morelia*, which was syndicated in Chile, not to mention her televised appearances as Miss Chile and later the first Chilean Miss Universe. Bolocco, who is strongly associated with Chilean television and someone who has stood as a symbol for the nation itself as Miss Chile/Universe, works to translate the format to local audiences, connecting the codes of the variety, talk and *telenovela* formats with which she is tied to the *Intercambio de Esposas* series. Bolocco also figures prominently in the promotion of the show as a national text that explores the nature of the Chilean nation. In one promo, she tells the audience that the strength of the show is that it chose the most representative families out of thousands who "portray the Chilean family."

Like the British and American versions, *Intercambio de Esposas* attempts to portray the diversity of the Chilean family, pairing hippies with conservatives, intellectuals with working-class fairground workers, Gypsies with middle-class families, and recent African immigrants with Chileans of Italian descent. In addition, the show is positioned as explicitly taking up the national experiences as articulated through the home and family. The series was promoted as an "X-ray of the Chilean family: how we live, what we like to do. Are we classists, tolerant, xenophobic or infidels?" (http://enescena.canal13.cl). Perhaps owing to the influence of the Catholic Church and because the series appears on the Catholic University's Channel 13, the diversity represented is decidedly more restrained than the British and American versions: there are no homosexual couples, interracial marriages, or unmarried mothers. However, similar to the British and American versions, the Chilean iteration is clearly preoccupied with social difference and represents the home as a conflicted terrain. The localized conflicts of *Intercambio de Esposas* are about class, race and gender relationships as in the other case studies, but the specificities of the conflict are particularly Chilean, which is highlighted by changes to the format.

Similar to its British and American counterparts, the Chilean iteration of the *Wife Swap* format is staged around conflicts related to the gendering of house-keeping. In *Intercambio de Esposas*, however, there is more emphasis on the equation of woman with home and less exploration of the unmooring of the gendering of housekeeping from femininity as in the British and American versions. In most episodes, it is the wives of each household who are responsible for the house-keeping chores. Many husbands proclaim that they never do anything around the house because it is a woman's duty to be the housekeeper. Sometimes the *machista* (sexist) attitudes of the men are represented hyperbolically, as when con-testant Tito Urzua in Episode 3 (5/4/2007), was shown lounging in bed in his underwear drinking coffee, bragging that he doesn't do any housework. There are no explorations of the "new father" that the British and American versions dwell upon here. That the series details the domestic labor of the wives and the *machista* attitudes of the husbands warrants exploration in relation to social conditions in the local context of the series. In Chile, gender relations are changing, but perhaps more slowly than in Great Britain and the United States. Chile has been by and large a distinctly patriarchal society, where *machismo* has been the norm. Until 2004, Chile was one of only three countries where divorce was illegal, which left many women vulnerable to their husbands. Although women are entering the workforce in larger numbers and are taking up positions of power, such as Michelle Bachelet, the country's first female president, women are often still expected to be solely responsible for housekeeping and men are often expected to be the authority of the household.

The Chilean format's elimination of the requirement that each family live under the rules of the visiting wife is striking in this regard, perhaps reflecting *machista* attitudes about male authority in the home. The elimination of this element— essential to providing narrative conflict—means that the women contestants exercise much less authority in the home. Rather than focusing on the families' experience of living under a different set of domestic arrangements, the Chilean version focuses on the wives' perspective of living in another woman's shoes much more explicitly than in the British and American versions. Moreover, the lack of any rules element means there is less focus on the evangelical mission of making over another family through housekeeping, but rather the emphasis is on the household patriarch judging the housekeeping of his new wife. Often this aspect is played out in the performance of cooking, which usually only the wives are seen engaging in. Sometimes the wives complain about the unequal burden of household labor that they are forced to carry. In Episode 11 (5/21/2007), for example, Fedora Bustamante, a *Pinochetista* housewife, is paired with farmer Pepe Arab. Several conflicts are staged around housekeeping that showcase Pepe's *machista* attitudes: Pepe demands that Fedora clean the toilet, do everything that he says, and yells at her when she gives him housekeeping advice. Fedora refuses to comply with his demands, saying she "is not a maid." Because the adaptation has eliminated the rule change, Fedora never gains the opportunity to use her authority to change the domestic arrangement, and Pepe is never encouraged to evaluate his *machista* attitudes about gendered housekeeping. In effect, the elimination of the rules, in this episode and many others, reinforces the patriarchal authority in the home.

Patriarchal authority and class conflict are also emphasized in the Chilean adaptation's emphasis on the 4 million pesos prize to be allocated. While *Trading Spouses* adapted the format to include a cash prize of $50,000 to be allocated by the swapped wives for each family, it is not the focus of the show. In the Chilean iteration however, the cash prize is the biggest dramatic element of the format and the episodes are built around the dramatic tension of how each wife will allocate the money for the other family. In one promotion for the show, for example, a white middle-class family is interrupted at their genteel dinner table when the new wife, figured as a rock star with tattoos and sexy attire, arrives. She is shown disrupting their middle-class lifestyle by playing the electric guitar in the living room, but her most potentially disruptive behavior is announced by the voiceover narration which explains the show's premise: "When a wife from another family can spend it all." The anxiety around women usurping patriarchal authority by spending household money is emphasized in the way in which the prize money is foregrounded, unlike the American version.

In addition, the foregrounding of the 4 million pesos prize emphasizes the class conflict embedded in the series. Throughout, the series emphasizes providing the families with domestic consumer goods that promote social status, which has everything to do with the class-consciousness "which pervades every corner of Chilean social life" within the domestic sphere (Van Bavel and Dell-Yrujillo 2003: 355). Class-consciousness is foregrounded in the representation of domestic consumption in relation to the consumerism associated with Chile's neoliberal makeover during the Pinochet regime. As René Van Bavel and Lucía Dell-Yrujillo (2003: 344) have noted, in Chile, "sustained levels of economic growth over the past 20 years have gone hand-in-hand with a rise in consumerism". Moreover, consumption is strongly tied to notions of class-consciousness in Chilean society as "people indulge in conspicuous consumption in order to earn respect and to cultivate a sense of identity and self-esteem" (356). With the elimination of the rules-change element of the format, the series emphasizes making over each family with the prize money in a more focused way than the American version. Often, the wives award children of their adopted families electronics and other social status items as well as money for the wives to upgrade their kitchens with domestic consumer goods.

In addition to the prize money, the series explores class conflict in other ways as well, often offering resolution narratives in which attitudes about class are explored and at times transformed. Middle-class contestants are paired with working-class contestants in several episodes which explicitly examine class-consciousness, particularly by naming the distinctly class based locations of the family residences in various suburban Santiago regions. Episode 5 (4/19/2007), which pairs the Vicencios, a family of liberal hippies who live without electricity and running water in Laguna Verde, with the conservative, middle-class Giagnoni family who live in the Santiago suburb of Las Condes, exemplifies this tendency. The episode foregrounds class tensions as middle-class Mirella Giagaoni is paired with hippie Gerardo Vicencios. Mirella expresses her disgust with Gerardo, who constantly talks about money and their economic differences and bathes naked in a nearby creek. Gilda Vicencios is represented as uncomfortable around Luis Giagaoni's upper-class friends while Luis tries to make amends by providing Gilda with the luxuries she doesn't have. Unlike the British and American versions where shame is often circulated to articulate class conflict, here affect is circulated instead in order to resolve the differences. Gerardo teaches Mirella how to make jewelry and she grows to appreciate his talents, while Gilda teaches Luis to be more involved with his family. When Gilda leaves the family, they assure her that though "she doesn't have material things, she has much love to give." The allocation of the prize money solidifies the remediation of class conflict. The Vicencios are given money for social mobility: their son receives money to attend veterinary school, Gilda gets a kitchen remodel and Gerardo a metal cutter, along with a trip to Brazil. The Vicencios weep with the prospects of seeing their friends again but also for the social mobility the money has given them. Meanwhile, the Giagaoni's receive money for household expenses but are grateful for the change in their father. This episode, like many others that feature class conflict, offers closure and resolution of problems related to social difference through domestic consumption.

While the British and American versions consistently address race in relation to national identity, in addition to gender and class, race is not as foregrounded in the Chilean version. Most episodes feature participants from the *mestizo* majority and only one episode takes up race directly. In Episode 2 (2/22/2007), the Bikaka family, recent immigrants from the Congo, are paired with the Cerda family of Italian descent, which produces racial conflict within the home. Conflicts are mainly played out around ideas of parenting, as former Congo minister of defense Godelive Bikaka's conservative views about teenage girls dating clash with the Cerda's patriarch, while Isabel Cerda tries to take on the Bikaka's unruly son Julio, whose behavior is the result of discrimination. Moreover, the episode explicitly figures problems of racial difference as Julio is figured as a victim of a racially motivated assault that takes place in the course of the episode. The racial conflicts are resolved with affect and consumption as Godelive and Isabel bond with their respective families. At the conclusion of the episode, Julio proclaims that love has no color boundaries, and Godelive says she learned a lot about the goodness of Chileans through the program. In addition to the emotional bonds of the families symbolically resolving the racial differences of the nation, the distribution of the prize money helps to solve the remaining problems. The Cerdo's are awarded money for a computer to increase their social status, but also money to repay their debt and stave off losing their home, while the Bikaka family is allotted money for clothes and a heart transplant for Godelive. In this episode and others, housekeeping and domestic consumption work to dramatize and ameliorate problems of social difference in contradictory ways.

Conclusion

The British, American, and Chilean iterations of the *Wife Swap* format demonstrate how formats are like genres, which as Patrick Sharp argues, are circulated to account for changing historical conditions and for previously unexpressed industrial and cultural needs within local contexts (53–54). The differences and the similarities between each iteration are equally important in understanding the transformation of gender and genre in global franchising. The rigid standardization of the format and its emphasis on housekeeping allows for the dramatization of changes related to gender, class, race, and nation in each context. As decidedly national characteristics are worked through in each iteration to make it appeal to national audiences, the format has provided a remarkably flexible way in which to address the problems of social difference in each context. Each series explores the gendered relationships to the material spaces and objects within the home in specifically local ways, relating to national normative ideas about class, race, consumption, and nation. Home and housekeeping function as a microcosm of larger problems of social difference that the format attempts to resolve through affect, feminine intervention, and in the case of *Trading Spouses* and *Intercambio de Esposas*, material goods. However, the format's emphasis on housekeeping simultaneously manages and reaffirms social inequity by proposing that arranging housekeeping practices differently can solve social problems. Although the format is highly standardized and rigid, particularly in its artificial domestic arrangements, notions of race and gender are transformed in the transborder flows of the format, working through the specificities of race and gender in relation to home and nation. While the British and American versions foreground the unmooring of housekeeping from femininity and the image of the new father in contradictory ways, gender is much more fixed in the Chilean iteration, which the changes to the format work to reinforce. Moreover, while the British and American versions articulate a much more racially diverse national family in problematic ways, the Chilean version constructs the national family mainly in terms of its *mestizo* majority.

However, what is not transformed in the global franchising of the series is equally enlightening. As these three series attest, family is represented in the format with a controlled sense of diversity. Family structures and domestic arrangements remain decidedly nuclear, even in Britain and the United States, which have had legalized divorce for a much longer period as well as diverse domestic and family arrangements. Although working-class families are represented in all three instances of the format, families living in real poverty are absent, as are instances of real deviance or pathologies. Particularly when more families in Britain, America and Chile have suffered from social and economic disenfranchisement due to the effects of the neoliberal economic policies that each country has adopted, such an exclusion speaks to the conservative nature of the normalizing process that the format demands.

Notes

1   Fox's *Trading Spouses* and *¿Quién Cambia a Quién? Intercambio de Esposas* boiled the format down to a one-week exchange and instituted a monetary prize of $50,000 and 4 million pesos respectively to ratchet up the conflict.
2   Some iterations have swapped husbands as one-off episodes and have occasionally featured single mothers as well as featured wives from different countries.
3   In the unlicensed Fox versions, only the wives meet. Then they read out to their families how the money is to be distributed as decided by the other wife.

References

Brancato, Jim. "Domesticating Politics: The Representation of Wives and Mothers in American Reality Television." *Film and History* 37.2 (2007): 49–56.

Brunsdon, Charlotte. "Lifestyling Britain: The 8–9 Slot in British Television." *Television AfterTV: Essays on a Medium in Transition*. Lynn Spigel and Jan Olsson, eds. Durham, NC and London: Duke University Press, 2004. 75–92.

Brunsdon, Charlotte, Johnson, Catherine, Mosely, Rachel and Wheatley, Helen. "Factual Entertainment on British Television: The Midlands Television Research Group's '8–9 Project.'" *European Journal of Cultural Studies* 4.1 (2001): 29–62.

Carugati, Anna. "Fox's Shapiro." *WorldScreen.com*. www.worldscreen.com/interviews archive.php?filename=ShapiroFMT_2005.htm. Accessed 5 January 2007.

Corner, John. "Studying Factual Television." *Tele-Visions: An Introduction to Studying Television*. Glen Creeber, ed. London: BFI Publishing, 2006. 60–73.

Cozens, Claire. " Wife Swap Accuses 'Rip-off' Rivals'." *MediaGuardian,* 23 February 2004. www.guardian.co.uk. Accessed 3 January 2008.

Crompton, Rosemary. *Employment and the Family: The Reconfiguration of Work and Family Life in Contemporary Societies*. Cambridge: Cambridge University Press, 2006.

Esposito, Maria. "Endemol Appoints Head of New Chilean Arm." *Channel 21*. 9 June 2004. www.c21media.net. Accessed 8 January 2008.

—— "The Future of Factual." *Channel 21*. 26 January 2004. www.c21media.net. Accessed 26 January 2007.

Fairclough, Kristy. "Women's Work? *Wife Swap* and the Reality Problem." *Feminist Media Studies* 4.3 (2004): 344–347.

Fernandez, Maria Elena. "Swapped Spouse Gains National Notoriety: Marguerite Perrin's Outburst Has Made Her Reality TV's Latest Star. Bobblehead, Anyone?" *Los Angeles Times*, 18 November 2005: E1.

Fog-Olwig, Karen. "Contested Homes: Home-making and the Making of Anthropology." *Migrants of Identity: Perceptions of "Home" in a World of Movement*. Nigel Rapport and Andre Dawson, eds. Oxford: Berg Publishers, 1998. 225–236.

Franklin, Jonathan. "Television/International: Chile: Cablers, Satcasters Luring Viewers, but Local Fare King." *Variety* 380.6 (25 September 2000–1 October 2000): 52.

Gibson, Owen. "Media: Making it, Not Faking it: RDF Broke the Mould with Shows Such as Wife Swap and Supernanny." *Guardian*, 23 October 2006. Media pages 6.

Grant, Jules. "Sheiking it in the Middle East." *Channel 21*, 20 October 2004. www.c21media.net. Accessed 3 January 2008.

Hazen, Jenny. "Who's Your Mommy?" *The Jerusalem Post*. 24 November 2005: Arts 24.

Hill, Annette. *Reality TV: Audiences and Factual Television*. London and New York: Routledge, 2005.

Matheson, Sarah. "The Cultural Politics of *Wife Swap*: Taste, Lifestyle Media, and the American Family." *Film & History* 37.2 (2007): 33–47.

Miller, Jeffrey. *Something Completely Different: British Television and American Culture*. Minneapolis: University of Minnesota Press, 2000.

Morley, David. *Home Territories: Media, Mobility, and Identity*. London: Routlege, 2000.

Murray, Susan and Oulette, Laurie, eds. *Reality TV : Remaking Television Culture*. New York : New York University Press, 2004.

Piper, Helen. "Reality TV, Wife Swap and the Drama of Banality." *Screen* 45.4 (2004): 273–286.

¿Quién Cambia a Quién? Intercambio de Esposas website. http://enescena.canal13.cl/espectaculos/enescena/html/Television/Especiales/Intercambio_De_Es posas/index.html

Racas, Arturo. "Lithuanian 'Wife Swap' TV Reality Show Sparks Row Over Family Values." Agence France Presse, 25 March 2005. Lexis Nexis Academic Database. California State University–Los Angeles Library. Accessed 11 February 2007.

Raphael, Chad. "The Political Economic Origins of Reali-TV." *Reality TV : Remaking Television Culture*. Susan Murray and Laurie Oullette, eds. New York : New York University Press, 2004. 119–136.

Sharp, Patrick. "Introduction: Reading and Writing SF." *Practicing Science Fiction: Critical Essays on Writing, Reading, and Teaching Genre*. Eds. Karen Helleckson, Craig B. Jacobsen, Patrick B. Sharp, and Lisa Yaszek. Jefferson, NC and London: McFarland, 2010. 53–73.

Steinberg, Jacques. "One Show's Unexpected Lessons in Reality." *New York Times*, 16 March 2005: E1.

Straubaar, Joseph. "(Re)asserting National Television and National Identity." *In Search of Boundaries: Communication, Nation States and Cultural Identities*. Joseph Chan and Bryce McIntyre, eds. Westport, CT and London: Ablex Publishing, 2002. 181–205.

Sullivan, Oriel. "Changing Gender Practices within the Household: A Theoretical Perspective." *Gender and Society* 18.2 (April 2004): 207–222.

—— "The Division of Domestic Labor: 20 Years of Change?" *Sociology* 34.3 (2000): 437–56.

Sutter, Mary. "Spotlight: MIP TV: Latin America: Latins Like Ultra-Reality." *Variety* 382:6 (26 March 2001–1 April 2001): M20.

Van Bavel, René and Dell-Yrujillo, Lucía. "Understandings of Consumerism in Chile." *Journal of Consumer Culture* 3.3 (2003): 343–362.

Waisboard, Silvio. "McTV: Understanding the Global Popularity of Television Formats." *Television and New Media* 5.4 (2004): 359–383.

Walters, James. "Emotional Blood on Undusted Carpets: The Citizen as Subject in *Wife Swap*." *Critical Survey* 18.3 (2006): 51–54.

"Wife Swap in Further Deals." *Broadcast*, 17 October 2003. Factiva. Dow Jones and Reuters. California State University–Dominguez Hills Library. 6 January 2008.

"Wife Swapping Travels." *Broadcast*, 18 October 2002. Factiva. Dow Jones and Reuters. California State University–Dominguez Hills Library. 6 January 2008.

18

REITERATIONAL TEXTS AND GLOBAL IMAGINATION

Television Strikes Back

Tasha Oren

Format television is so ubiquitous a presence on the contemporary broadcast grid that, even more than the multi-strands of convergence media or the proliferating arcs of revitalized dramatic series, it has come to typify what television is in our contemporary moment. Yet, serious scholarly considerations of format, as we note in our introduction, have been curiously few.

Not only an industry bonanza, the format is also a theoretical challenge. The first scholar to undertake a sustained study of format as structure and industry, Albert Moran, defined, explained and explored the form as an international phenomenon, and his work remains foundational for format-scholarship. However, with his definition, Moran may have also pre-empted thinking of the format in terms of traditional television studies since he so definitively characterized it as a textual no-thing. Formats, as Moran explained, have no core essence and are not a tangible commodity: "The term has meaning not so much because of what it is but because of what it permits or facilitates."[1] Format is a business relationship, an industrial condition, a legal arrangement, a set of rules for sale; look too closely at it *qua* program, however, and content generalities diffuse and float away.

Yet Moran also takes care to call formats a mobile technology. This, in light of the format's fundamental global appeal, is especially important as I try in what follows to offer some closing thoughts and opening initial suggestions for further study of formats as televisual texts.

Following Moran's field-forming definition, it has been easier for scholars (as we review in the introduction) to think about formats specifically, in terms of their generic affiliations, subject matter, representational strategies, etc. Such specificity is, of course, far from a disadvantage. However, a big picture perspective remains wanting. In an effort to argue for format as a particularly important aspect of the contemporary development of global television and for an understanding of what television is at a moment when its demise is discussed as often as its output, a consideration of alternative theoretical thinking about format is worth trying out. Note, too, that in the statement above I linked television's global inter-connection with a suspiciously breezy characterization of its essence. As scores of scholars have argued (myself included), the history of television is replete with the medium's specific, explicit (and often aggressive) articulation as, first and mainly, a national medium. In fact, institutional histories of television are told primarily and necessarily as narratives of location, national ideology, and—if only perceived or hoped-for—expressions of collective culture and identity. To this extent, early histories of television are by definition histories of national aspiration and distinction. However, contemporary television development, along with a broadening of the media field to include satellite, Web-based media, and other global content flows, presents challenging new opportunities to reconceive tele-vision's place in the global media field. This "field" is not only a content exchange and commercial marketplace but also a larger cultural frame of reference that shapes our collective sense of the global.

Understanding television as one exemplary aspect of cultural production and reception where global and local are experienced in terms of one another is a major assumption in what follows (and indeed, in practically all considerations of specific format programming). However, I will also attempt to suggest addi-tional and complementary ways of thinking about contemporary format television beyond and along this (spatially and temporally bound) framework.

In what follows, I'd like to take up formats not as a global tidal wave but as pseudo-organic formations, constructed yet now-naturalized televisual protocols that do not only shape the global industry and the television text but also serve as useful models for understanding, indeed defining, current and future television in the global context.

The Structure of Format—Reverse Engineering

To begin thinking of format as a worthy unit of theoretical inquiry, it may be helpful to examine it in terms of other reiterational texts. Linda Hutcheon defines adaptation as just such an entity: a "form of repetition without replication."[2] While this definition serves her purpose of redirecting critical weight and regard from the "prior" or original work and disdain for the adaptation as secondary (the source of adaptation, as she notes, is still critically regarded as "better" because it is original), this definition is also extremely useful in thinking about format as a textual particularity. To go further, the notion of an original at all, in the case of format, is flimsy; although a production reel/book is often sold to format licensors (and "borrowed" without formal agreement), formats can be, and are resold before production. Moreover, the classic industry notion of a format is a text *made* for maximum reproduction.[3] As Keane and Moran observe, format distribution also differs from the structure of finished (or "canned") programs by the importance of each format's production history.[4] With every iteration, the format gains in complexity, cultural richness, and industrial value.

In thinking further about the notion of medium-specificity, Hutcheon's definition can also help us by deduction, as the classic notion of adaptation (a cross-platform move of content from one media form to another) does not sit well with format either. Formats differ from narrative adaptations in that they are not "repurposed" from another medium or recycled (made into an other) but are, paradoxically, essential duplicates. What's more, they are largely media specific. Imagine a film/play/comic book adaptation of *Big Brother*, *Top Chef* or *So You Think You Can Dance*? An actual format adaptation is hardly conceivable but their use as procedural settings for a narrative overlay is not only possible but has already occurred in *American Dreamz* (Paul Weitz, 2006) and more famously in *Slumdog Millionaire* (Danny Boyle, 2008).[5]

As several authors in this collection point out, format is an umbrella term used across program types; so-called "reality TV" is often used interchangeably with format yet the latter's scope is broader. For the sake of easy classification, let us name formats that transfer narrative or character-specific adaptations *narrative-based formats* and formats of quiz, make-over, or contest structures as *procedure-based formats*. The latter category is dominated by—and recognizable as—game-formats in as much as each program and season-arc most commonly feature the emergence of a "winner" through an elimination process.

However, when moving beyond the market base definition of format as *sold* property to a focus on format as a widely-adapted set of form/content televisual conventions, a vast, third category of formats opens up in non-fiction, "real world" events programs such as news or sports shows. As we have argued in the introduction—and Tony Schirato develops in his essay for this volume—these programs too have a televisual format logic but, unlike the other two, can be thought of as *indexical formats* as they present events accessible outside televisual creation.[6] My interest, for the rest of the chapter, is in theorizing the most readily identified of the format categories, the procedure-based format. What I also want to suggest, and what these three categories already illustrate, is that the procedural format is uniquely *hyper-televisual*. Unlike story, event, character or theme—the transferable elements of the narrative and indexical categories—what is transferred (or "formatted") about the programs within the procedural category is precisely their television-essence: their look (set design, logos, placement), their sound (theme, musical and audio cues), and their programmability (rules, structure, sequence, and overall meaning).

Structures (Narratives and Stylistic Grammar)

Repetition and reconfiguration are the lifeblood of television. Indeed, television revels in ritualized predictability. This understanding is mythically synonymous with television's coming of age in the U.S. context, ushering out early experimentation and its theater affinity and shepherding in the grid-based program types and the demise of the so-called first golden age. As countless television scholars point out, duplication and recombination are much more stable components of television than novelty, not only for the sheer imperatives of continuous demands for content but also in the domestic, repetitive, and scheduled nature of its consumption and the conditions of its sustained production. Innovation within conventions is thus the primary logic of television itself.

The appreciation for variation within the constraint, the give and take between the syntagmatic and paradigmatic elements within, and the pleasures of familiarity and repetition for an engaged audience, have been some of the first hard-won battles for television scholarship. As Reeves and later Sconce emphasize, that very tension between constraint and freedom, the formulaic and the original, the new and the repetitive, are essential to televisual textuality (and its audience's knowing complicity in its repetitive formulation) and constitute the inherent aspect of their production, readability and enjoyment.[7]

Classic formats are not only repetitive across programs—in terms of their conceptual foundation and set of rule-bound actions and outcomes—but also internally (each program performs a repetitive set of action-events in tight, regulated recurrence). Here, the notion that this structure is itself, in Moran's term, "generative" is essential: Formats are not only codification of serial program production but also, both paradoxically and importantly, a creative concept.[8] It is precisely from the rules (and limitations) of format law that various permutations emerge. Such injunction is also coded into many of format's most successful iterations' DNA: the time constraint, the narrow and arbitrary task, the resulting emotional duress, etc., are all crucial for the production of, and variations on, action and audience interest.

Indeed, formats are the quintessential marriage of restrictive rules and pithy pitch; they are nothing if not conceptual. Format creators, known as devisors, look to generate such rules, more commonly known as "engines"—a set of visual, formal or structural elements that would characterize a format pitch. In a now classic example, Mike Briggs, the U.K. talk show host who co-devised *Who Wants To Be A Millionaire?*, pitched the engines as: the major prize, "giving contestants a set of possible answers, offering a series of lifelines, using a host with a supercilious manner, and soundtrack, lighting and dark wardrobe to dramatic effect."[9] Julie Christie of Touchstone Production also stressed the importance of brevity for initial format engine description: "If you cannot say it in a paragraph, you cannot say it at all."[10] As Christie explained, a format is all about the rules you put on an idea. Christie's definition is simple, elegant and right on the money: Format is a protocol. As some ludologists suggest about chess, the rules make the game; the engine makes the format go.

The television industry's use of the term "engine" recalls another's: that of the computer game industry. This association may be ontologically accidental, but it is rich in relevance as game engines refer to base game software components (for example, the "skeleton" structure of a first-person shooter game) that are licensed by subsequent game developers and built on for content. A sparse and flexible base-software configuration, the game engine is designed as reusable foundation for various reversionings. Similarly, the format engine is thought of primarily as a mobile set of rules and procedures designed to be both flexible and generative. We can think of the game engine then as having significant (albeit distant) family resemblance to the format engine, that bundle of protocol and base components at the heart of the television format.

Games, and computer games in particular, are a unique form of reiterational text, and as such can lend insight and dimension to our understanding of format. David Marshall and John Dovey have recently suggested game models, playfulness, and video game influence as central for thinking about contemporary media modes. Marshall charts the development of a "paedocratic regime" of play aesthetic and game-like structure from its child-targeted origins to current mainstream media texts and practices. As he argues, game culture and the rise of a play aesthetic have not only emerged as an organizing experience in media culture but are central to an industry-wide reconfiguration towards interactivity and intertextual associations across media products.[11]

Dovey regards the elimination-contest formats like *Big Brother* as simulations— behavior-models set loose within dynamic rule-based systems—and indicative of the emergence of an alternative, ludic order of representation. This logic of the playful and gamelike, he argues, has replaced empiricism as the dominant mode of contemporary public culture. Although televisual, game format television, he maintains, is a "new media" product, best considered through the interdisciplinary understanding of media that includes software studies, human–computer interaction and cyberculture studies. By this logic, formats are "text machines" of identity simulation, populated by character algorithms set within a ludic zone.[12]

While diverging in focus, both authors see the emergence of games (and computer games in particular) as constitutive in a major turn for both media culture and media studies. In this sense, video games loom large in the *feel* of culture, even for those who have never played them.

In an effort to carve out more space within television studies for format theory, I take these forays into alternative systems of cultural analysis as more useful here than the traditional regard for formats as generic categories. This is not to say that genre is unsuitable or useless for format application. As some contributions in this volume demonstrate, genre analysis is the one graspable textual instrument we have to begin considering format television as a serious and varied aspect within the televisual expressive field.[13] However, such conventional genre approaches can also limit the types of questions we can ask, get mired in sub-categorical tangents, and cannot adequately account for the particular relationship between form and content that procedural format TV relies on. Moreover, formats appear as near-inversions of genre: textual patterns where the "seams" of rules and cross-textual conventions are not only visible but highlighted. Genre theory may help us classify the varieties within format programming but can tell us little about why and how such classifications of nakedly-repetitive patterns matter or mean.

Alternatively, a terminology—and its accompanying vantage point and emphasis —loosely borrowed from gaming offers a productive consideration of code-based structures, affective repetition, modular development, elaborations on convention and rule-motivated content. It may also be helpful in figuring out just what's going on: How are format-based narration strategies different from other television conventions? What does the growing popularity of playful and game-like structures mean for audience engagement? Are there broader cultural implications for the changing shapes of digital media and their global exchange?

It is also important, in any invocation of gaming in a discussion of television, to distinguish between the use of game as a helpful—if imprecise—structuring conceptual framework and the notion of play as a primary, experiential base for gaming studies. As gaming scholars insist, games fundamentally differ from media texts in that they are most decidedly *not* "read" but played.[14] And while it is tempting, for the sake of symmetry, to argue that much of format programming also comprises games and competitions "played" by the contestants, this formulation is myopic at best: Games are made for the people who play them, TV game formats are made for the people who *watch* the game. Functionally, the concepts are fundamentally and operationally dissimilar, and practically, no easy alignment of gaming and television is possible or advisable. However, both digital games and format television share a culturally identifiable playful structure, procedural logic, and iterational legibility. In this sense, I propose the context of an increasingly familiar gaming culture an important, sympathetic component of media and digital culture, and contemporary comfort with modularity, configuration, and an algorithmic structure in which rules are both foregrounded and constitutive. Thus I am not claiming paternity but rather a larger cultural common denominator from which both contemporary televisual and digital games products draw cultural legibility. In this, the pleasure of format also involves the self-conscious and referential aspect of programmer's configuration and the audience's appreciation of the back-of-the-camera rules, design, and the more contemporary pleasures of customization.[15] The codification of format is thus a fundamental part of its enjoyment, along with the audience's absolute complicity in, and understanding of, the highly artificial order that other television tools (such as editing or casting) bestow and impose on the already determined raw material in this procedural, modular text.

In his work on the culture of television production, John Caldwell has argued persuasively that television's survival in the so-called convergence era has depended not on radical transformations but rather on tweaked or re-emphasized industry strategies that have characterized the business and creative structures of television from the very start. Two of the tendencies he analyzes are migratory and ritualized textualities (or syndication and pitch). While Caldwell only touches on format—and views the ubiquity of format as a cannibalized and hybridized form that has evolved through the "pitch" culture of creative textual mutation—both modes of televisual textual organization are crucial to understanding the current development and proliferation of the format as culturally contemporary but essentially televisual.

So far, I have suggested the format as located in the cross-current of two seemingly contradictory temporal flows: The current success of format television is associated with larger contemporary techno-cultural forces and shifts, yet its basic structure and logic is fundamentally linked to television's intrinsic tendency towards formulaic regularity. As Caldwell argues, to understand this mode and practice of textual production in its current stage is to understand the basic workings of television.

I now turn to another Janus-faced quality of the format structure: its function as a localized product of a global formula.

What's Global in Global Format?

To invoke global television in the convergence age and to suggest a synergetic relationship between contemporary television and a framework drawn from digital game scholarship brings up yet another in a series of current "crises" for contemporary television studies. Graeme Turner has identified a tendency within television studies towards "techno-political hierarchy" that views the emerging interactive and Web-based media in opposition to traditional television.[16] This formulation perceives television as a dying technology, wedded to outmoded nationalism, top-down distribution of power and ideological closure, just as digital media are celebrated as democratizing, user-oriented, progressive and global: "The closer to the global consumer we come . . . the further we are from the nation state . . . the technology liberates the consumer from political and regulatory containment."[17] Here Turner further notes the exuberant enthusiasm of television scholars—following other social and cultural theory—to endorse and embrace a model of post-national, globally-felt television consumption (mostly via the Internet) as both progressive and widespread, a much-overstated notion on both fronts.

The argument that fuses the dilution of television as a site- (and technology-) specific medium with cosmopolitan identity appears to contradict recent program-specific scholarship (like many chapters in this collection), that argues for a particular national and cultural identity that is both reproduced and affirmed in local production—particularly of format television. Indeed, satellite television, Web-based programming, mobile media, convergence technology, and the growing popularity and accessibility of regional and transborder television—in addition to the robust trade in "finished programs"—demand that traditional television scholarship take account of a growing transnational media presence. As Jean Chalaby observes, "International TV channels are not simply deterritorializing but deterritorialized cultural artifacts themselves. Many of their features, including coverage, schedule and patterns of production tear apart the relation between place and television."[18]

Moreover, other scholars have urged television studies to move away from the nation-centered stance that insists and affirms the resiliency of nation in the face of globalizing media—a perspective sociologist Ulrich Beck influentially dubbed "methodological nationalism." As Kevin Robins and Asu Aksoy have recently insisted, such models fall short of accounting for the contemporary globality and mobility of media texts. In their London study of Turkish-speaking communities, Robins and Aksoy argue for a cosmopolitan, transnational perspective that accounts for a dialogic imagination of co-existing ways of life and experience, rich and complex beyond the grasp of monologic, national-centric approaches.[19] Drawing heavily on Beck's argument and his evocative description of the nation-based analysis as a "zombie category," they go on to accuse such studies of a lack of imagination and mechanized thinking at best, or characterize their authors as cheerleading stakeholders in the nation-state's power at worst. As they argue, television scholars who have recently articulated the centrality of nation in their discussions of global television and media culture "mobilize the rhetoric of political pragmatism and realism, intending to convey the idea that the old national model still 'works'—and aiming to rule out possibilities that there could be any meaningful potential in new transnational or global media developments."[20]

Arguments like these are valuable in their insistence on alternative identity formations through media and their caution against academic automation. And while in Robins and Aksoy's hands "The Nation" looms as a stifling and homogenizing soul-prison, their argument also resonates with a kind of fatigue for the standardized essay that keeps restaging, ad infinitum, a celebrated nation-local's triumph over global-Western groupthink. Yet, at its weakest, the argument falls into the same dialectic system it aims to reject when it casts the national as a thin, ideologically-pungent broth, set against the rich, fragrant stew of multi-locational, multi-cultural, post-national complexity. The possibilities of alternative, transnational models of media do not preclude, nor describe in toto, the current experience of intimate, domestic, and more often than not, nationally-based programming. Such programs often anchor a sense of collective recognition to mundane details of social interaction, habits, routines, and shared practical knowledge, as well frustrations, divisions, and acknowledged tensions within these structures of experience—particularly so when we move away from U.S./U.K.-based studies. As Minna Aslama and Mervi Pantti observe in their study of Finnish reality television formats, the sense of belonging is not by any means bound to authoritative, official version of culture and identity.[21]

That television's relationship to space can no longer be taken for granted is indisputable. However, the current explosion of format television appears to disturb traditional theoretical approaches preoccupied with media's relationship with cultural articulation on both "sides" of the nation-centric debate. No doubt the current success of global formats is intimately tied to a particular logic of global-ization—both capital and popular. It is also, as many scholars argue in these pages, an especially good example of how contemporary global cultural exchange differs from older models of influence and imperialism while simultaneously unseating cherished characterizations of local culture as resistance to the crushing span and ubiquity of global/Western media products. Arguments that insist on a break or opposition between national experience and global or transnational consciousness conflate the former with state-powered nationalism from above, and sweepingly ascribe chauvinistic and insular disposition to various articulations of national linkages that may operate quite differently, ignoring currently occurring multiplicities that *necessarily* make up the national experience of viewing. More importantly, they cut off the possibility of national address as itself part of the meaning viewers make of transnational media texts. Here I suggest the international format as one such textual category where the national frame comes into view precisely *because and within* the understanding of such programming as multi-national reiterations.

Before addressing viewers' experiences, it is important to step back and consider how and why the base "software" of formats is enjoying so much current global success. While the phenomenon of formats is easily dismissed as mere industry clamoring to repeat a proven money-maker, Silvio Waisbord argues that they are better understood as revealing important developments in the globally interconnected television industries and institutions on the one hand, and the efforts of transnational producers to deal with the resilience of national cultures on the other.[22] The simple economic advantages of formats over original pro-ductions and "canned" imports are surely an important factor, as are the local development of commercial television, and the internationalization of the television marketplace.[23] Another important factor, however, as Timothy Haven points out, is the rapidly changing and standardizing television profession itself.[24] As a generation of professionals worldwide begins to think about TV in similar ways, they likewise define the imaginary connections that bind together different segments of the public both within and beyond the nation-state. These forms of standardization are, Havens argues, far more powerful (and, for Havens, pernicious) than the representational strategies of television texts, the meanings that viewers make from television or global patterns of media ownership. Waisbord makes a similar point while making a counter-argument: "Structural regulations and institutional expectations limited programming choices, for programming trends to become truly globalized, television systems needed to be patterned along the same principle."[25]

In light of such stylistic and economic centralization, the future, as Graeme Turner suggests, is in indigenizing: "(T)he way to examine the local within the global is through mapping processes of appropriation and adaptation rather than proposition of any thoroughgoing specificity or uniqueness."[26]

Global standardization of the institutional shape of television here actually facilitates (indeed, demands) a shift in the logic of programming. I want to think of this shift not as a radical departure (or reconfiguration) but rather as a counter-move deeper into the primary, modular logic of television—just as various non-format texts break it apart. In this global logic, content is local but systemic conventions of the apparatus are both deterritorialized and naturalized. The news show, the interview program, the sitcom, the soap and the variety show are all base-formats that have specific, recognizable and classifiable codes. These soft protocols of content organization emerged—through particular processes of exchange–within various television systems and quickly solidified with the naturalization of a televisual space in each context. Such a codification of protocols cannot be separated, as Havens, Wasibord and others observe,[27] from the growth of a cosmopolitan industry elite whose shared business sensibilities and homo-genizing tastes make up a large part of the explanation for format growth. As such, these sensibilities' Western (and particularly U.S./U.K.) roots can hardly be denied, but neither should their industrial and stylistic provenance—in all their historically imbued signifiers of global power and ideology—be read as forever fixed and loaded. This origins-based approach is further bolstered by many theorists' tendency to call local reiterations of global formats "hybrids." The term may be generically useful but also insists on parity and equivalence between structure and content, fixing both as specific, similarly meaningful cultural entities, and rendering their encounter a "cultural mix" of ontological equals. This understanding permanently fuses television's cultural allegiance to its site of invention. We may, to better understand format's operational logic in the present, think (strategically) beyond the hybrid (what, after all, is not?) and towards the modular and peripatetic. Further, if globally-coalescing centripetal forces produce the format to transmit and infuse cultural value, the value transmitted here is that of televisuality itself—as a particular, formal, globally shared and modular experience.

So What's Local?

At the same time, a central tenet of this homogenized understanding of the format's appeal—right along with its globally-shared formal conventions—is its essential, ever present, particularity. As Waisbord insists, "formats are culturally specific but nationally neutral . . . because formats explicitly empty-out signs of the national, they can become nationalized."[28] The Israeli iteration of *So You Think You Can Dance* ("Nolad Lirkod"), for example, was heavily promoted as an international format sensation and compared (even within the text of the show itself) to the *Idol* format—also a hit in Israel. However, its first episode (the obligatory pre-season audition segment with its ritualized, heavily edited clips of triumph and ridicule) began with historic 1948 footage following the declaration of Israel's formation as a state, when hundreds of Israelis broke into spontaneous celebratory dancing in the city streets. The segment continued with contemporary footage from various locations in Israel, where groups gather to dance in styles ranging from folk to the cha-cha, krumping and ballet. Layered over clips of spinning toddlers, hip-hopping youth, and swinging elderly couples, the host's voiceover confirmed Israel's special affinity to the show's subject (with more than a hint of comic flare): "Israelis were born to dance . . . we're a nation of dancers. The English celebrate with a drink in the pub, the French luxuriate with a nice fois gras . . . and Israelis, we dance!" This effort to locate the dance format in such over-the-top nationalist context is amusing precisely in light of the show's formal allegiance to the SYTYCD format—whose U.S. version is familiar to the Israeli audience. The format's essential playfulness and global reproducibility thus anchors its audience in watching, reading and experiencing this and other format texts as having deep local resonance, nested within a larger format logic that is fundamentally televisual and globally connected. This mix is further enforced in the show's opening credits where the globally reproduced theme song and credit sequence also includes a snippet of Israeli folk dance and song, in between the segments of Broadway, ballet and Bollywood styles (see Dana Heller's essay, Chapter 2 in this volume, for her analysis of this Israeli format version).

As this example illustrates, an important aspect of the format as a modular unit of television programming is that it often travels, and announces itself, *as* an iteration.

While the practice of format adaptation existed throughout television history, the procedure has largely gone unacknowledged outside the television industry itself.[29] For example, hit U.S. shows of the late 1980s and early 1990s, *America's Funniest Videos* and *America's Most Wanted*, appeared as distinct and original texts without any revelation of their origins as a popular Japanese program or German and British formats. By contrast, *Big brother, Survivor, Idol,* and *So You Think You Can Dance,* as well as *Ugly Betty*—all massive international hits that ushered in the format era—are read, and often promoted, in terms of their proliferation, popularity and global presence. Thus, the format's recent large-scale standardization has also produced a meaningful shift in its mode of self-representation as a text—a newly found reflexive self-consciousness in light of its acquired visibility.

Reading the Japanese iterations of *Who Wants to Be a Millionaire?* and *Survivor,* Koichi Iwabuchi notes that the shows make wide reference to their constitution as local versions of global formats that are popular all over the world. Iwabuchi concludes:

> The format business has given audiences a pleasure in sharing the common frameworks and the irreducibly different appearances that manifest in local consumption. Put differently, what is being promoted is not simply global localization that aims to adopt the common to the difference but also local globalization that makes audiences feel glocal, that is, a sense of participation

in a global society through the reciprocated enjoyable recognition of local (in most cases synonymous with national) specificities articulated through the shared formats. The western gaze of modernity thus melts into a global modernity.[30]

As Iwabuchi suggests, the sense of (and pleasure in) "global modernity" is fundamentally dependent on the presence of a recognizable, irreducible difference that comfortably and assertively sits within the shared format engine. The complex web of global and domestic linkages which television systems (and audiences) find within the format exchange were similarly—if less buoyantly—described by one Australian format producer as "parochial internationalism."[31]

I would further suggest that formats, in their very existence and acknowledged structure of local repetition within a multi-national framework, can do more than just express national identity in content: they often cement the national quality of television.

Format Diplomacy

As a final, extended example, I offer the curious case of the Israeli reality contest format, *The Ambassador* ("Ha'shagrir").[32] A loose adaptation of *The Apprentice*,[33] the show employs the same formal and stylistic elements as its unofficial progenerator: A group of young and ambitious men and women, divided into initial teams by gender, compete in each episode by performing difficult and stressful missions. Each week, the losing team is summoned to a solemn board-room to face an imposing expert panel, after each of the weakest performers argues their case (and blames fellow contestants), judgment is rendered and one contestant is selected for elimination. As in *The Apprentice*, the loser is dispatched with a catch phrase intoned by the head judge: "Take back your portfolio and go home."

The portfolio in question, however, is a political reference. Despite its immed-iately recognizable format conventions (the histrionic segment-theme music, the rapid tension-seeking narrative editing, the indication-heavy soundtrack, the confessionals, the contestant's own retelling of events, the set piece sections in each episode, etc.), *The Ambassador* differs dramatically from the Mark Burnett version in a major engine detail; in this show, contestants compete to become a spokesperson for Israeli policy around the world, charged with representing the Israeli point view to often hostile audiences. The show follows a long-held belief in Israel that much of the animosity felt towards it throughout the world is the result of Israel's failure in the arena of public relations—of *hasbara* (literally, explanation). The show seeks confrontational situations in international settings (on university campuses, encounters with a skeptical foreign press, sales-pitches to international businesses, meetings with foreign leaders, etc.) and every such encounter enacts the same tension: contestants face negative attitudes about Israel, attempt to address questions of politics and policy, and try mightily to change hearts and minds. The show's central preoccupation is, of course, self-representation.

Despite its generic, play-by-numbers formula that makes the show's look, sound, structure and narrative-making strategies a classic and instantly familiar format, *The Ambassador* fits perfectly into Israel's particular media past and the preoccupation of "self to the world." As I've written elsewhere, Israel's television origins are sourced in the image of broadcasting as a kind of border-crossing electronic visiting card. The notion that broadcasting can help Israel's self-representation and "speak to" Israel's enemies (and Palestinian residents) was widely regarded as even more important for its founding than what television programs could say to Israeli citizens. The idea of harnessing television in the service of *hasbara* was a primary motivator for the establishment of state television in 1968, the year that followed Israel's occupation of East Jerusalem, Gaza, the West Bank, the Sinai and Golan Heights in the Six-Day War.

Yet, for all of its heightened, ultra-nationalist concept, the political priorities of articulating the nation are repeatedly, and studiously challenged in practically every episode of this hugely popular program. In various settings around the world, the contestants are addressed by challenging, often hostile, interlocutors who question Israel's basic moral position, invoke the abuse and humiliation of Palestinians, decry its refusal to consider the right of return or condemn its settlement building activity. In these confrontations, contestants are rarely in control and are often caught at a loss for words, or worse, as they misspeak. In a famous incident in the first season, a contestant was unceremoniously and uniformly dumped from the show after she defensively asserted, during a visit to Oxford's campus, that "Israel has never taken anything from anyone." This, the august panel (made up of a foreign affairs journalist, an ex-Hasbarah spokesperson and corporate advisor, and the former head of Israel's security agency, Shabak[34]) concluded, was simply the wrong answer. Far from smoothing out ideological challenges, the show seems to relish moments in which the contestants falter in the face of such challenges. Their awkward equivocations are highlighted and mercilessly repeated within the show, online, and in future programs. And, in telling repetition, the winning contestants are those who prevail through charm, personality, and an affable skill to circumvent specific policy discussions in favor of communicating Israelis' love of peace and hopeful vision for a better future. While it unquestionably supports and celebrates national identity and the underlying myth of Israel's poor PR, the show far from assumes such identity and nationalist pride as unproblematic, and instead gives voice and moral credence to a range of political realities and non-Israeli perspectives, undermining the show's premise as easy explanation for Israel's status. It is this very tension that animates the space between the format's global game-like protocol and its local content and meaning.

The Ambassador elevates such tension to thematic heights by positioning a local iteration of a global format within the context of national soul-searching and global performance. Said differently, the program enacts a nation's deepest anxiety over global scrutiny through self-representation.[35]

Since global formats, as I've argued above, are most influential in their capacity to carry and disseminate the value of playful, standardized modular televisuality —and transnational imagination—this quality is also essential to how meaning is made (and solutions are posed) in *The Ambassador*. It is here that the natural-ized televisual logic of format and its restrictive expressive palette meets and profoundly shapes local expressions of particularity, as Israel's self-conscious preoccupation is processed *through* the circumscribed soft protocol of reiterational televisual style.

As offered here, the case of *The Ambassador* is (instructively) extreme in its explicitness, and fits the Israeli fixation and hyper-awareness of national identity and action under global scrutiny. Further, both Israeli examples I relied on here (*Nolad Lirkod* and *Hashagrir*) appropriate the global format code to articulate specific and explicit national identities for their audiences. However, I do not argue that such negotiation of local formats in a globalizing television environment functions in this way in every case. Rather, I want to stress that *when* such national expressions or invocations appear, they do so in the context of international presence and participation. Such global acknowledgement is not just about references to one national identity in comparison to others, but also in full textual acknowledgment of the format qua format, as a local version of a globally traveling formula.

As Linda Hutcheon reminds us, there is no such thing as an autonomous text.[36] Textual dependencies are not only inevitable but also vital to the legibility of each text in turn. The format's ubiquity, its global recurrence, formulaic structure and intertextual dependence are all essential to how this televisual text is made meaningful and pleasurable in each reiteration. Through its particular ability to invoke a local specificity within global textual exchange, the contem-porary format provides us with a clear-cut example of television's specific cultural work in an expanding media environment. As I've argued above, both sides of the nation-centric debate can contribute to our understanding of the format phe-nomenon, but only when coupled with a consideration of its industrial development, the globally-linked standardization of the television industry—with its expressive costs and benefits—and the format's assimilation into, and legibility within, a wider digital and modular mediascape.[37] Neither polarity on the nation-centric debate accounts fully for how formats work, since formats are most useful in helping us understand how television can consistently oscillate between— and hold in mutual dependence—a domestic, communal, national, regional, transnational and global address. In terms of its functionality and the dynamic feedback loop it generates between convention and innovation, locality and the (mediated) world, the global TV format is now television in its purest form.

Notes

1 Moran, A., "Television Formats in the World/The World of Television Formats," in *Television Across Asia: Television Industries, Programme Formats and Globalization*, Moran, A. and Keane, M., eds., Abingdon: RoutledgeCurzon, 2004, p. 6.
2 Hutcheon, Linda, *A Theory of Adaptation*. Abingdon: Routledge, 2006, p. xvi.
3 This definition also distinguishes programs made *as* formats from those which become format adaptations "after the fact" (telenovelas such as *Ugly Betty* are the most common examples). More complicated still are translations-turned-format adaptations like the slow evolution of the Israeli *Betippul*, its "straight up" translation to HBO's *In Treatment* and now "formatization" in several other national versions that jettisoned its narrative and kept only its structural rules. Whether fiction programs narrowly qualify as formats is less interesting here than what categories one applies to make such distinctions.
4 Keane, M. and Moran, A., "Television's New Engine," *Television and New Media* 9(2) (2008): pp. 155–169.
5 A fictionalized *American Idol* film is rumored to be in early pre-production at the time of writing this article (spring 2009).
6 This reduction can also be, at least philosophically, disputed as many sports events, and increasingly news events are both staged and performed for television. This category, then, does not refer to the anatomy of programming but rather to a more basic notion of "real world access" to events, even if they are, finally, performed for TV consumption.
7 Reeves, J., "Rewriting Culture: A Dialogic View of Television Authorship," in *Making Television: Authorship and the Production Process*, Thompson, R. and Burns, G., eds., Westport, CT: Praeger, 1990. Sconce J., "What If?: Charting Television's New Textual Boundaries," in *Television After TV: Essays on a Medium in Transition*, Spigel, L. and Olsson, J., eds., Durham, NC: Duke University Press, 2004.
8 Moran A. "Television Formats in the World/The Work of Television Formats," in *Television Across Asia*, Moran, A. and Keane, M., eds., Abingdon: RoutledgeCurzon, 2004.
9 Moran A. and Malbon J., *Understanding the Global TV Format*, Portland, OR: Intellect Press, 2006, p. 38.
10 Ibid., p. 39.
11 Marshall, P. David, "The New Intertextual Commodity," in *The New Media Book*, D. Harris, ed., London: BFI, 2002.
12 Dovey, Jon, "It's Only a Game Show: Big Brother and the Theater of Spontaneity," in *Big Brother International*, Mathigs, E. and Jones, J., eds., Brighton, U.K.: Wallflower Press, 2004.
13 Further, format heavily relies on structures of narration and signification in ways that certainly lend themselves to productive textual analyses.
14 See *First Person: New Media as Story, Performance and Game*, Wardip-Fruin, N. and Harrigan, P., eds., Cambridge, MA: MIT Press, 2004, for an extended multi-author debate about the specificity of game theory—especially in regards to narrativity and textual approaches.
15 Jason Mittell has developed a similar mode of audience pleasure for complex television narratives. See Mittell, J., "Narrative Complexity in Contemporary American Television," *The Velvet Light Trap*, no. 58, Austin: University of Texas Press, 2006.
16 Turner, G., "Television and the Nation," in *Television Studies After Television*, Turner, G. and Tay, J., eds., London: Routledge, 2009.
17 Turner, G., ibid., p. 57.
18 Chalaby, J. *Transnational Television Worldwide: Towards a New Media Order*, Jean Chalaby, ed., London: I. B. Tauris, 2005, p. 8.

19 Robins, R. and Aksoy, A., "Whoever Looks Always Finds: Transnational Viewing and Knowledge Experience," in *Transnational Television Worldwide: Towards a New Media Order*, Jean Chalaby, ed., London: I. B. Tauris, 2005.

20 Robins, R. and Aksoy, A., "Whoever Looks Always Finds," p.18.

21 Aslama, M. and Pantti, M., "Flagging Finnishness: Reproducing national Identity in Reality TV," *Television and New Media* 8(1) (2007): pp. 49–67.

22 Waisbord, S. "McTV: Understanding the Global Popularity of Television Formats," *Television and New Media* 5(4): pp. 359–383.

23 See Moran, A. and Keane, M., "Cultural Power in International TV Format Markets," *Continuum: Journal of Media and Cultural Studies* 20(1) (2006): pp. 71–86.

24 Havens, T. *Global Television Marketplace*, Basingstoke: Palgrave Macmillan, 2008.

25 Waisbord, "McTV," p. 363.

26 Turner, G., "Cultural Identity, Soap Narrative, and Reality TV," *Television and New Media* 6(4) (2005): pp. 415–422.

27 See also Toby Miller's discussion of the planet Hollywood phenomena and the international division of cultural labor, in Miller, T. (with Nitlin Govil, John McMurria and Richard Maxwell), *Global Hollywood*, London: BFI, 2001.

28 Waisbord, "McTV," p. 368.

29 Moran, Albert, *Copycat TV: Globalization, Program Formats and Cultural Identity*, Luton, U.K.: University of Luton Press, 1998.

30 Iwabuchi, K. "Feeling Glocal; Japan in the Global Television Format Business," in *Television Across Asia*, Moran, A. and Keane, M., eds., London: RoutledgeCurzon, 2004, p. 34.

31 Moran, A., "Distantly European? Australia in the Global Television Business," in *Television Across Asia*, Moran, A. and Keane, M., eds., London: RoutledgeCurzon, 2004, p.170.

32 The Keshet Network, 2004–2006.

33 The show was not an officially purchased format although its structure and style is clearly drawn from the Fermantle format. In fact, Mark Burnett's production company began lawsuit proceedings against the Keshet network.

34 Rina Matzliach, Nachman Shai, and Ya'akov Perry made up the first season's judging panel. Former Shabak head Perry was replaced in the second season by an ex-fighter pilot, Gil Segev, a military hero turned industrialist. Perry returned as a special guest judge in the semi-finals.

35 *Ha'shagrir* perfectly typifies and encapsulates Israeli political anxiety, internal conflict and Israel's own acute self-consciousness at the feel of global scrutiny. It is then significant that its first season, in the fall of 2004, appeared less than a year after then-prime minister Ariel Sharon's historic reference to Israeli policies as "occupation." The show's airing corresponded with a fierce internal Israeli debate over dismantling settlements in Gaza and the media spectacle of violent clashes between Israeli soldiers and evacuated settlers in the summer of 2005, just weeks after the first season's finale.

36 Hutcheon, Linda, *A Theory of Adaptation*, London: Routledge, 2006, p. 111.

37 Importantly, the format's fit within the broad scope of digital media is at once structural and cultural, and involves industry and television audiences as much as a digitally-sympathetic modular structure.

INDEX

Page numbers in *italics* denotes an illustration/figure/table.

Master P 47
Matamat with Kabir Suman 203–4
Matheson, Sarah 350
Mazziotti, Nora 153
MBC (Middle East Broadcasting Center)
  288, 289
Mda, Thobeka 247, 252
media ecology 9, 72, 77, 81
media imperialism thesis 76–8
Meet the Press 124
Meizel, Katherine 264–5, 266
Melakar, Sanjaya 13
melodrama 148, 153–4; and telenovela
  genre 153–4
Mernissi, Fatima 295
methodological nationalism 373
Mexican telenovelas 157, 171, 172
Mi espose favorito ("My Favourite
  Husband") 95
Miceli, S. 164–5
Middle East Broadcasting Center *see* MBC
Milanesi, L.A. 158
mimetic isomorphism 307
Ministry of Information and Broadcasting
  204
Mittell, Jason 92, 151
mobile phones: and Saudi Arabia 293
Moran, Albert 2, 3, 6, 24, 26–7, 34, 41,
  56, 74, 75, 91, 131, 149, 150, 155,
  186, 195, 226, 245, 255, 308, 366,
  367–8
Murray, Susan 329, 347
Mussolini, Benito 135
MyTVAfrica 244

Nair, Meera 214
Nair, Sameer 327, 328, 334, 335, 338,
  341
Nanjing Television 315–16
Nanny, The 189
narrative-based formats 368
Naspers 244, 245
National Bandstand 41
national-popular 132
nationalization: and globalization 125
NBC 193, 194
neoliberalism 332
neorealism 128
New TV 297
New Zealand 14; ethnic diversity of 224
New Zealand television 223–5 *see also* NZ
  Idol
News Corporation 327

news format 65, 124
NFL 62, 63–4, 67
Nilsen, Kurt 271
19 Entertainment 226
Nolad Lirkod 8, 44, 48–50, 375–6
NZ Idol 14, 223–40; adaptation of *Idol*
  format 227–30; biographical vignettes
  233–9, 240; cultural appropriation and
  the Maori 237; and cultural diversity
  230–4; and nation building agenda 223,
  239; representation of ethnic and
  cultural diversity 223, 239–40; success
  of 223, 239
NZ On Air 224, 225, 239

O'Connor, Briar 237
O'Donnell, H. 73, 84
Office, The 193
Olson, J. 60
One1000 Dance Stars 40
Opoku-Mensah, Aida 244
Oren, Tasha 27
Ouellette, Laurie 347

Pantti, Mervi 373
Pardon the Interruption 66
Parks, Lisa 261
Paul, Amit 212
Pedroso, Bráulio 164
performance: format adaptation as 7,
  23–36
pleasures, formatted 8, 71–87
poker 67
Polish Idol 268, 273
political economy, and formatted pleasures
  8–9, 71–87
Pop Idol see *Idol* format
Pop Stars 122, 149
Portas da Esperança ("Gates of Hope") 32
Pradel, Jacques 119
Price is Right, The 117–18
privatization 10, 17
procedure-based formats 368
public service broadcasting (PSB) 10, 74,
  113–14, 117

Qué pasa U.S.A.? 9, 90–106; addressing
  difficulties of assimilation 98;
  bilingualism in 103–4; creation of
  atypical image of Cuban community
  98; critics applause for 103–4;
  educational objective 96, 97; ending of
  production 104; expertise in casting